AMBULATORY HEALTH SERVICES IN AMERICA
Past, Present, and Future

Milton I. Roemer, M.D.

Professor of Health Services
School of Public Health
University of California, Los Angeles

AN ASPEN PUBLICATION®
Aspen Systems Corporation
Rockville, Maryland
London
1981

Library of Congress Cataloging in Publication Data

Roemer, Milton Irwin.
Ambulatory health services in America.

Includes index.
1. Ambulatory medical care—United States.
I. Title.
RA395.A3R625   362.1'2   81-3554
ISBN: 0-89443-388-1   AACR2

Library of Congress Catalog Card Number: 81-3554
ISBN: 0-89443-388-1

Printed in the United States of America

1 2 3 4 5

Table of Contents

Preface

The ambulatory services are, in a sense, the most critical components in the overall spectrum of personal health services. Usually constituting the initial point of contact of a patient with the health care system, they have great impact on the procurement of and expenditures for other health services. This is especially true of hospitalization, the most expensive element in health care, but it is also true of the use of pharmaceutical products, various diagnostic (laboratory and x-ray) procedures, rehabilitation modalities, and to some extent, dental and visual refraction services. There is much reason to believe that the method by which ambulatory medical services are rendered is a major determinant of the type and volume of these other health services utilized. Therefore, an understanding of ambulatory health service dynamics has implications for the entire range of personal health services.

These words were written in August 1971, as part of the application for a federal grant to support the research on which this book is based. In this application I continued:

Yet, compared with the other principal sectors of health service—the environmental and the institutional—the ambulatory health services are least organized or structured and least subject to reasonable social controls. The environmental and the institutional (hospitals, sanatoria, etc.) services, by their very nature, have long demanded mobilization of manpower and materiel through various systematic processes. The ambulatory health services, on the other hand, have traditionally been provided mainly on the basis of a one-to-one relationship between patient and healer. They have been characterized by a low order of organization both intrinsically and in their articulation with other health care elements.

This weak organization of ambulatory health service, however, is only relative to the other health service components. In fact, as noted later, a great many sectors of ambulatory care have been subjected to organization through various social pressures. The organization has occurred along many, often overlapping, paths. Certain such services have been primarily for preventive purposes, such as the establishment of programs for immunizations or early disease screening. Organization has also been applied to the therapy of certain diseases, like tuberculosis or alcoholism, or for an array of services (both preventive and therapeutic) to certain classes of persons, such as the school child, the industrial worker, the indigent family, or the military veteran.

Because of the separate social and technological inducements of these organized ambulatory care programs, historically, the current picture is very confused. Their very complexity and pluralism in the United States—not to mention other components of health service—impede an understanding of their dynamics, necessary for reasonable planning. Community health planners—both professionals and citizen advisers—are frequently lost among the trees and do not see the forest in which they are wandering. The forest is all the harder to comprehend because it is continually changing its configuration.

Study of the structure and function of organized ambulatory health services, in fact, began some time before these words were written. In January 1969, with support from the California Center on Health Services Research, work began on a study of organized ambulatory services in Los Angeles County. During these dozen intervening years, the configuration of ambulatory services has obviously changed further both in California and the nation, but the trend of affairs has not altered. In each of the pathways defining the various types of ambulatory care, the extent of organized activity has heightened.

Precise trend data on the growth of clinics and their utilization in the United States are not available, except for selected categories in quite recent years. In Chapter 13 of this book, we estimate that by the mid-1970s at least half of the ambulatory medical services in the United States were being provided in organized settings. For 1900, one cannot offer a corresponding proportion, but for that year it was estimated that in the entire country there were about 100 dispensaries or clinics. In 1923, the U.S. Bureau of the Census reported the existence of 2,526 clinics, of which 42 percent were under governmental auspices. In 1926, the number of clinics (each of which, of course, provided many services), was estimated as follows:[1]

Type of Clinic	Number
Outpatient departments of general and special hospitals	1,790
Unattached condition-specific units (mental, tuberculosis, children, etc.) both public and voluntary	2,793
Clinics for special groups (federal beneficiaries and industrial workers)	923
Private group practices	220
Total	5,726

Source: Harry H. Moore, *American Medicine and the People's Health* (New York: Appleton and Co., 1927), p. 30.

The very crudeness of these categories for 1926, compared with the analyses that can be made today, reflects the meager American development of the clinic concept only a half-century ago. A corresponding aggregate number of clinics cannot be offered for 1976, for reasons that will be evident throughout this book, but one may simply note a few selected categories on which figures are readily available:

Category	Number
Hospital emergency units	5,136
Private group practices	8,461
Freestanding community health centers	937
Public health clinics (assuming only five per unit)	6,500
College health services	1,200
American Indian clinics	400
Freestanding psychiatric clinics	1,164
Partial total	23,798

Thus, even a very partial total of about 23,800 clinics in the nation around the mid-1970s—the categories being chosen because they constitute an unduplicated count—comes to four times the number estimated in 1926. If one were to overlook the problem of double counting, an additional 4,660 clinics for family planning and some 2,500 organized home health programs might be noted. Based on selected types of clinics, such as those in hospital outpatient departments, on which utilization data have been available for some time, it is evident that the rate of increase of clinic *services* has probably been much greater than the growth of clinic facilities.

The growth of clinics has been under several types of *sponsorship,* which this study classifies broadly as follow:

1. hospitals (outpatient departments)
2. public health agencies
3. schools and colleges

4. industrial enterprises
5. private physicians (group practices)
6. special government agencies
7. special voluntary agencies
8. insurance plans (health maintenance organizations)

Within each of these main sponsorships there are numerous subcategories of clinics. The same universe of clinics may be classified according to their *purposes*—for special persons, special health problems, or special technical services—as illustrated in Chapter 11. One might also classify clinics as public or private, as freestanding or attached to a larger entity (hospital, school, factory, etc.), or by other criteria—size, source of financing, or personnel staffing. Whatever axis of classification is used, certain problems of overlap are faced.

Perhaps it is this very complexity and heterogeneity of organized ambulatory health services that have retarded the development of a defined professional discipline in the field of clinic administration. Such identity—expressed in professional associations, in journals, in academic training programs, etc.—is observable in many other sectors of the health services. There is widespread recognition of fields such as public health, hospital administration, or occupational medicine. Within the bailiwick of clinics, there is the Medical Group Management Association (composed of group medical practice managers) or the new National Association of Neighborhood Health Centers. But regarding the full range of clinics reviewed in this book, there is not any overall organization, nor any recognized academic or professional discipline. Only recently has a relevant periodical been launched: the *Journal of Ambulatory Care Management*. One can understand the reasons for separate affiliation of clinic administrators with their several sponsoring entities. But there still are enough common problems for analysis, research, exchange of ideas, and dissemination of knowledge to suggest the value of formulating a broad new professional field in ambulatory health services. The issues in the field as a whole are becoming increasingly recognized.[2,3] Perhaps this book may help to define the boundaries of such a professional field of endeavor.

Great appreciation must be expressed to many agencies and persons for making possible the preparation of this book. Most important, I wish to express my appreciation to the National Center for Health Services Research of the U.S. Public Health Service for its grant support during the period June 30, 1972 to May 31, 1977 for research on "Ambulatory Health Services: Organization, Problems, and Future Models" (HS 00874). Other obligations delayed completion of the writing during that period, but I am very grateful to the Commonwealth Fund for its Book Program Award to support essential secretarial services during the period July 1, 1978 to June 30, 1980. I must also record my gratitude to the School of Public Health of the University of California, Los Angeles

(UCLA), as well as to the UCLA Biomedical and Research Libraries, for providing me the conditions and assistance that made this work possible.

The individuals to whom I am indebted for direct research assistance in conducting this study are many. As indicated on the title page, my debt is greatest to John Newport for his unflagging assistance during a four-year period in collecting information on the landscape of clinics, both in Los Angeles County and throughout the nation. In the early stages of the research, the assistance of Elizabeth A. (Jackie) Hefferin was also invaluable. To Karen Horak, these colleagues and I are deeply grateful for highly competent secretarial services.

For work on specific sections of this study, the helpful collaboration of several other persons must be gratefully acknowledged. Information on hospital outpatient services was collected by Charlene Spellman and Lawrence Krain. The complicated field of emergency services was analyzed nationally by Martita Roberts. Joanna Haas did a major literature review on industrial health services, and data on the Los Angeles County scene in this field were gathered by James Lubitz, Richard Froh, and Mary Ann Nadler. A special survey of group medical practices in that county was conducted by Jorge Mera.

The agencies and organizations that provided relevant information about various types of clinics are too numerous to recite; among the references at the end of each chapter their names will be found. Special appreciation for direct personal assistance, however, must be extended to the U.S. Public Health Service; within this agency, the National Center for Health Statistics and the Bureau of Community Health Services kindly furnished many hours of personnel time to answer questions—including the provision of unpublished tabulations. Such special unpublished data were also kindly furnished by other branches of the U.S. Public Health Service, including the Alcohol, Drug Abuse, and Mental Health Administration and the Office of Health Maintenance Organizations. Special reports or preliminary documents were provided by the American Hospital Association, the National Industrial Conference Board, the American College Health Association, and the American Medical Association. Numerous voluntary health agencies, both at the national level and in Los Angeles County, responded kindly to requests for information. The Los Angeles County Department of Health Services and the California State Department of Health Service were similarly very helpful in furnishing unpublished tabulations. Finally, I am grateful for the assistance at UCLA of the Survey Research Center and for the kind cooperation of my faculty colleague, William Shonick, in providing a special statistical computation of data from his study of local public health agencies.

The completion of this study obviously has been dependent on the kind cooperation of many persons and agencies. It also has taxed the tolerant understanding of several colleagues and friends, but none more fully than my remarkable legal consultant and wife, Ruth Roemer.

Study of even one component of the nation's health care system, such as this, reveals a panorama of very wide scope. In my attempt to sketch the details of this landscape, I shall be happy if errors of omission or commission or fallacies of interpretation are not too numerous. To any readers who detect such errors or fallacies, I shall be very grateful for your advice.

MILTON I. ROEMER
Los Angeles
September 1, 1980

NOTES

1. Moore, Harry H., *American Medicine and the People's Health* (New York: D. Appleton and Co., 1927), pp. 30–32.

2. Bodenheimer, Thomas S., "Patterns of American Ambulatory Care," *Inquiry,* Septmber 1970, pp. 26–37.

3. Blendon, Robert J., "The Reform of Ambulatory Care: A Financial Paradox," *Medical Care,* 14 (June 1976): 526–534.

Chapter 1

Ambulatory Medical Care: The Traditional Pattern

The ambulatory patient encounter with a physician, as it is now the fashion to call it, is the oldest method of provision of health service. Long before social actions were taken to establish hospitals or develop environmental programs to prevent disease, ailing men or women sought help from persons considered skilled in healing.[1]

The ancient and traditional relationship of patient to healer was a one-to-one affair. In the several other strategies for coping with disease that evolved later, social or group processes were involved. Hospitals necessarily demanded organization—accumulating money for construction and operation, mobilization of nurses and other health workers for care of the sick in bed, and so on. Environmental protection, and eventually broader public health programs, demanded social action; laws had to be enacted and implemented to influence the behavior of people so as to reduce the spread of infectious disease.[2]

By contrast, the ambulatory health services, until quite recent times, have been individualistic and nonorganized. A vast tradition has evolved in most countries, especially the wealthier industrialized ones, about the privacy, even the sanctity, of the personal patient-physician relationship. When organized systems for financing these ambulatory services evolved in nineteenth century Europe—first voluntarily and then mandatorily (Germany in 1883)—the social insurance financing was used, in the main, to support the costs of the private patient-doctor contact. Only decades later was any value seen in organizing the provision, or the "delivery" of socially insured ambulatory services in some sort of organized framework.[3]

In spite of this predominantly individualistic character of the ambulatory health services historically, in recent times they, like the institutional and environmental services, have gradually become more organized. The motivations have been diverse and the modes of organization have been highly varied, but in all parts of the world—perhaps more elsewhere than in the United States—

the health services to the ambulatory person, for both therapeutic and preventive objectives, have been provided along increasingly systematized lines.

The principal purpose of this book is to examine the attributes of this organizational process and where it appears to be heading. As will be seen, it has occurred along several distinct paths, definable according to sponsoring agencies, special population groups, certain disorders, or in other ways. The evolution has had a complex dynamics and, as in biological evolution, when new forms of organized ambulatory health service (OAHS) take shape, the older ones do not necessarily die out; the old and new forms continue to function side by side.

Before tracing this historical process of OAHS development, it may be helpful first to review the prevailing patterns of private or nonorganized ambulatory health services in modern America and how they developed. Then, in the next chapter, the early origins of organized ambulatory services can be considered. This, perhaps provides better perspective for examining in more detail each of the main types of OAHS found in America today—their structures, functions, problems, and trends.

HISTORICAL BACKGROUND OF THE INDIVIDUAL DOCTOR

In spite of great ferment and change, the most prevalent pattern by which personal ambulatory health services are currently provided in the United States is still through contact between the individual patient and the private doctor. The United States National Health Survey, for example, reports for 1977 that the average American had about 4.8 contacts with a doctor per year.[4] The frequency of these contacts has long been greater among women than among men, and tends to increase with age level.

Information from the same national survey for 1974, analyzed according to the *usual* setting where the ambulatory medical care was obtained, shows the following distribution:[5]

Usual Source of Ambulatory Care	Percent
Private doctor's office	62.8
Group practice clinic	27.2
Hospital outpatient department	5.3
Industrial clinic	0.3
Patient's home	0.2
Other or unknown	4.2

Source: U.S. National Center for Health Statistics, "Access to Ambulatory Health Care: United States, 1974," Advancedata, no. 17 (February 1978), p. 4.

Thus, the "usual place" for obtaining medical care is the private doctor's office among nearly 63 percent of those surveyed. The remaining 37 percent "usually" obtain care in other settings and, as will be seen, the proportion of *medical visits* in diverse organized settings is doubtless higher than this, but the major source of all ambulatory care provided is still perhaps the individual physician in private practice. This remains true whether the service is paid for directly by the individual or purchased indirectly through a third party (voluntary insurance, social insurance, public revenue or other collectivized method) mechanism.

In primitive societies, almost the totality of health services was represented by the ministrations of the medicine man or shaman. Relying on religious or magical precepts, and to some extent practical experience, the healer invoked supernatural forces or applied physical or medicinal treatments to cope with disease. In the rural areas of developing countries today, there still is a variety of indigenous healers, offering magical procedures or empirical remedies to treat the sick.[6] While modern physicians are backed up by a complex array of equipment, assistants, institutions, and agencies, and constrained by much law and regulation, their relationship to the average patient is still mainly on the one-to-one basis originating in primitive times.

As society became more complex, acceptable practices for medical care became formulated in law and collective actions were taken to enforce them. In ancient Babylonia, for example, most healers were priests, and their incantations or interpretations of omens followed theological principles. At the same time, there were surgeons, and at about 2000 BC the Code of Hammurabi formulated a tariff for various surgical procedures. It also specified punishments to the surgeon if the outcome of his acts was unfavorable, with the severity of punishment, incidentally, depending on the social class of the patient.[7] In ancient Greece most physicians were craftsmen who, through natural observation (rather than supernatural processes), developed techniques of diagnosis and therapy attributed to the teachings of Hippocrates. These doctors traveled from town to town, setting up shop in the market places. In classical Rome the first physicians were slaves, brought from Greece and attached to the large agricultural estates. Later, free Greek physicians were attracted to Rome with offers of citizenship and tax exemptions if they would settle in the towns.[8]

With the growth of Christianity, Greek and Roman doctors came to be looked on as practitioners of a pagan art, and most new physicians were monks. This meant that their practices became governed by an increasingly organized church. By the 12th century, however, a reaction set in against the preoccupation of monks or priests with so worldly a matter as treatment of the patient's body. Surgery was particularly unsuitable for them; therefore, laymen became involved in medicine and surgery. The first medical school for laymen was founded at Salerno, Italy, in the 10th century and it flourished for several hundred years. In the 13th century, the Emperor Frederick II issued public decrees requiring passage of examinations to authorize a person to practice medicine in the towns.

These were the first medical licensure laws.[9] In the 12th and 13th centuries, universities were established throughout Europe, educating physicians among others.

As urbanization developed, after the Renaissance, doctors educated in the universities settled in the towns as private practitioners. A coveted goal, however, was to be appointed to a royal court or to a feudal estate as a salaried body physician to the lord and his family as well as caretaker of the vassals and serfs and their families. At the same time, in the towns a lower class of artisan offered, for a fee, special skills such as setting bones or extracting teeth. The barbers did bloodletting and evolved into barber-surgeons. Another occupational group, not initially trained by the universities, were the apothecaries, who set up shops with all sorts of drugs from animal, vegetable, or mineral sources. In the later Middle Ages, these occupational groups formed guilds to protect their trade interests and established standards for admission to the guild.[10]

With the growth of cities and the rise of industrialization in the 18th and 19th centuries, hospitals, which had been established earlier by the church as shelters for the indigent aged and the seriously sick, were expanded in the main urban centers.[11] Gradually they derived financial support from local governments. By the latter half of the 19th century, hospitals became places for the treatment not only of the sick poor but also occasionally of the well-to-do, in private sections. They also sometimes became centers of medical education, associated with universities. Only the better educated and usually upper-class physicians in Europe, however, were appointed to treat patients in the hospitals; some of these specialized in certain medical or surgical procedures or in conditions of women or of children. Thus, by the early 20th century, two classes of physicians had developed—those attached to hospitals, a sort of elite with special qualifications, and those practicing entirely out in the community as "family doctors."

With the settlement of North America in the 17th century by Europeans, the whole medical evolution of Europe was replicated on the new continent, but in a much shorter time. The early doctors came from Europe, as the first Roman doctors had come from Greece, and others were trained by apprenticeships. With few feudal estates, however, virtually all doctors set up shop as small tradesmen in the villages and towns. With the rapid growth of population after the American Revolution—through heavy immigration from Europe, and the less sharp class lines, in most cities small hospitals were built to which nearly all local doctors had access. The sharp distinction between hospital and town doctors that characterized Europe, therefore, did not develop. To train more doctors, medical schools multiplied, and by the end of the 19th century there were 160 of them—most unassociated with any university.[12]

Thus, by 1900 there was a large supply of doctors in the United States—about one to 700 population—which was more than in any European country at the time. Their qualifications, of course, were quite uneven. The states had passed medical licensure laws after the Civil War, but they were relatively lax.[13] A movement by the medical associations and some philanthropic foundations set in, culminating in the epochal Flexner Report on medical education in 1910. This led to the grading of medical schools, the eventual closure of the poor ones, and a sharp reduction in the output of physicians.[14] Meanwhile, training of other types of health personnel such as nurses, pharmacists, technicians, and optometrists, was accelerated so they could perform tasks previously done by doctors.

After the ''germ theory of disease'' had become generally accepted and antisepsis and aseptic techniques were widely applied, hospitals grew rapidly. Specialization also increased in America after 1900, but was not so closely linked to hospitals as in Europe. While some doctors and other health personnel served in salaried positions (in mental and tuberculosis institutions, the military services, public health agencies, etc.), the overwhelming majority were engaged in private practice. With World War I (1914–18) and the Great Depression of 1929, a series of social forces was set in motion that led eventually to the organization of personal health services—therapeutic, and preventive—at a much more rapid rate.[14]

PRIVATE MEDICAL PRACTICE IN THE UNITED STATES

In the free enterprise economy of the United States today, it is only to be expected that the predominant pattern for providing physicians' care of the sick should be through private medical practice. In the main, whether buffered by insurance or by revenue support or not, ambulatory doctors' care is a service bought and sold in an open market.[15] Both general practitioners and specialists offer their services principally from private premises. Except in some small towns, however, doctors' offices are seldom located now in their own homes. The ''medical arts building'' in the business sections of cities is increasingly the locale of doctors in various specialties, as well as dentists, private laboratories, optometrists, pharmacists, and other health care providers. The doctor is usually assisted by an office nurse (who may or may not be qualified by R.N. training), and sometimes there is a receptionist who also handles the business side of the practice.[16] As third party payment programs, both governmental and voluntary, have grown, these business affairs have become more complicated; in addition to maintenance of clinical records on each patient, an American medical practice must now cope with a variety of bureaucratic forms to collect charges for the services rendered.

Most of this business paperwork of private medical practice is due to the prevailing system of fee-for-service remuneration. For each medical act such as an injection, a complete physical examination, the lancing of an abscess, or countless other ambulatory care procedures, a specific fee is charged. Custom in a community usually influences the amount of this fee, and under certain third party payment programs it may be specified in a "fee schedule." Individual doctors, however, often vary their fees from the prevailing levels, especially in relation to the income of the patient. This has been called the "sliding scale of fees" and is defended as a method by which the individual doctor spreads the financial burden of medical costs, so that the rich help to pay for the care of the poor. Economists, however, have criticized it as the application in medicine of the well-known commercial principle of charging what the traffic will bear.[17] In any event, the sliding scale of fees has become less important as organized programs of medical care have assured payment for services provided even to the poorest patient.

Not all American physicians, however, earn their living under fee-for-service arrangements. As will be seen, an increasing proportion are engaged in institutions or in organized ambulatory care programs on salaries, full-time or part-time. In the 1970s, nevertheless, the fee system was still the predominant one.

Much emphasis is placed today on free choice of doctor. The patient, it is argued, should be free to select the particular doctor who most appeals to him or her; this freedom is said to be important for the development of an understanding and therapeutically effective physician-patient relationship. Moreover, the resultant competition among doctors is said to induce all of them to do their best work.[18]

There is obviously some validity to this concept, but its weaknesses also must be appreciated. For one thing, patients seldom are qualified to judge medical competence; they can be influenced unduly by personality traits or bedside manner that may bear little relationship to technical capabilities. For another, the major influence in the choice of a doctor may simply be location—that is, being close to where the patient lives. In a rural district, only one doctor may be accessible. Still another problem concerns the great extent of specialization; more than four-fifths of physicians are now in one specialty or another whether or not they are certified by the appropriate specialty board.[19] It may be desirable for patients to choose their general practitioner or family doctor, but how well can they choose the proper specialist for their cases? Indeed, primary practitioners theoretically refer their patients to the appropriate specialist. In practice, patients often go directly to specialists, without such referrals, a process that may lead to much waste and inefficiency.

The complexity of medical specialization and subspecialization (in surgery, for example, there are about ten subspecialties for different organs or organ systems) makes the delivery of integrated medical care to a patient very difficult. With some 25 principal specialties (not to mention the subspecialties) certified by the American specialty boards, as well as such other health care providers such as optometrists, podiatrists, dentists, pharmacists, or physiotherapists available, the patient is often bewildered. The generalist or family doctor has been decreasingly available, especially in the larger cities, to oversee the whole medical care process.

Fortunately, in the late 1960s a reaction set in and new recognition was given to *general* medicine. After many years of effort by the American Academy of General Practice, a new specialty in "family practice" was established in 1969, requiring residencies and other qualifications for certification. With this greater prestige and earning potential for general medical practice, the pendulum of excessive specialization began to swing back.[20]

Parallel with the long-term decline of general practice in America, the rate of demand for medical care has been rising steadily. This has come from the extended life expectancy, with higher proportions of aged persons (in whom more chronic illness naturally occurs), as well as from better transportation, higher educational levels, and the greater potential of and popular expectations from medical science.[21] Specialists in internal medicine and pediatrics to some degree have replaced general practitioners, although they have clearly not been able to meet the demands for primary care. To save precious time, moreover, most doctors have reduced home calls sharply. A better examination admittedly can be done in a properly equipped medical office, but a degree of understanding is doubtless lost when the physician never sees patients in their homes.

Still another problem arises from the set of incentives induced by competitive fee-for-service remuneration. As noted earlier, a separate fee for each medical act may induce a doctor to work hard, but it may also lead, overtly or subconsciously, to multiplication of services in order to maximize earnings. It must be realized that, after the initial encounter, nearly all medical and related services are decided upon by the doctor rather than the patient. This applies to hospitalization (the costliest component of medical care), laboratory or x-ray examinations, prescribed drugs, rehabilitative therapy, and so on. In hospitals or in organized ambulatory care settings, group discipline can be applied to minimize unjustified services, but in private individual medical practice, this is very difficult. Under third party payment programs, moreover, the dangers (or wastage) of excessive services are aggravated because the patient is spared from feeling any direct economic pinch and, except for the impact of a cost-sharing requirement, only an impersonal agency or company is called upon to pay the bill.[22] This problem has generated many claims review procedures to detect such abuses in socially financed programs, whether governmental or voluntary.[23]

The prevailing fee-for-service pattern of private medical practice also may discourage needed referrals of patients to another doctor. Referral of a case may mean not only loss of a fee but also loss of a patient. On the other hand, a primary physician may refer a patient to a particular surgeon on the understanding that the latter remit a portion of the surgical fee. This practice of "fee-splitting" has been condemned repeatedly by medical societies and hospital staffs, but the widespread prohibitions may reflect the prevalence of the problem.

Opposition to fee-splitting is only one of several provisions in the codes of medical ethics that have evolved over the years to discipline the behavior of doctors working in a competitive marketplace.[24] Another prohibition is against advertising, so widely accepted in other competitive enterprises. Yet judicial decisions in the 1970s challenged this ethical policy as illegal restraint against free competition in the medical marketplace.[25] The most fundamental ethical precept is that the physician's goal must always be to help the patient and, above all, to do no harm, as declared in the traditional Hippocratic Oath.

Medical societies—local, state, and national (the American Medical Association)—are generally the formal guardians of medical ethics.[26] They constitute, theoretically, an organized mechanism to hear complaints or charges about individual doctors and to strengthen the collective conscience of the medical profession in order to affect the behavior of each practitioner. Unfortunately, all too often medical societies have confused their proper concern for the ethical behavior of doctors with their role as spokesmen for "small medical tradesmen" who fear innovations in the economic or structural arrangements for medical care. Thus, over the past 50 years American medical societies have opposed payment of physicians by salary as "unethical," condemning it with the epithet "contract practice." They have opposed group medical clinics with charges that they constitute "advertising" and obstruction of free choice of doctor. Medical societies have been particularly hostile to organized measures—whether in the private or governmental sphere—that would modify the basic patterns of private practice or impose any form of social regulation on what they regard as the "freedom" of the doctor.[27]

Nevertheless, long-term trends in American medical practice have been toward numerous forms of organizational and disciplinary control. Much of this has occurred in hospitals, where pressures from within—the hospital board, conscientious physicians, and alert administrators—combined with influences from without—hospital licensure authorities, the Joint Commission on Accreditation of Hospitals, and various professional bodies—have led to increasing controls on physician performance, usually mediated through the medical staff organization. With rising standards for hospital appointment and staff surveillance (tissue committees, infection committees, drug and therapeutics committees, etc.), and more rigorous demands for consultation on cases and attendance at staff meetings, the behavior of private doctors in the hospital is obviously being subjected to increasing discipline. Inevitably this influence spills over to affect the work done by doctors in their private ambulatory practices.[28]

Besides the medical society and the hospital, there are numerous other influences exerted on the performance of the once ruggedly independent medical practitioner.[29] Under state licensure laws, the state boards of medical examiners, facing public pressure for greater quality controls, have become somewhat more rigorous in detecting serious deviance or deterioration of medical performance.

The various specialty boards, mentioned earlier, have come to assure reasonable standards for training and examination. Judicial decisions in malpractice suits, sometimes overdone by zealous lawyers, have put doctors on their toes to keep apprised of scientific developments and the demands of good medical care. Continuing education programs have expanded steadily to keep physicians abreast of advancing scientific knowledge. Several proposals have been made for periodic relicensure of physicians to assure continuing competence, and a few states have acted to require participation in postgraduate training that meets minimum criteria.

Perhaps the greatest impact on medical performance has come from the requirements of governmental programs, using public monies to pay for the care of certain beneficiaries. Older federal programs, such as those for crippled children, vocational rehabilitation, and some of the state worker's compensation laws, have long demanded minimum qualifications of the participating physician. The Medicare law of 1965 (social insurance for hospital and medical care of the aged) exerts most of its effects through the "conditions for participation" of institutions. Indirectly, however, the doctor's behavior is affected by "utilization review" procedures in hospitals or the surveillance, limited though it has been, over charges for and the "medical necessity" of services paid for by fiscal intermediaries (on behalf of the government).[30] The 1972 Amendments to Medicare and Medicaid, establishing Professional Standard Review Organizations (PSRO) throughout the country, increased the monitoring of medical performance in hospitals.[31] They may also be a harbinger of still greater surveillance to be applied over the behavior of individual doctors in their private practices.

Somewhat comparable features characterize the social setting of other individual practitioners of the healing arts—the dentist, the optometrist, the podiatrist, the private psychologist—that need not be reviewed. Similar measures of social control are increasing in these fields.[32]

THE EXTENT OF INDIVIDUAL MEDICAL PRACTICE

Private medical practice in America is obviously in ferment as various social forces impose greater regulation upon it. The sheer numbers of personnel in the expanding health industry increasingly place doctors in a position where they must function as members—usually "captains"—of a multidisciplinary team of health workers. Thus in 1900, when the United States had 120,000 physicians, the aggregate of all other professional health personnel (registered nurses, dentists, technologists, etc.) amounted to only about 70,000. By 1950, when there were 200,000 physicians, the associated health personnel had spiralled to 670,000 a ratio of 3.65 such personnel for each doctor. By 1973, when the nation had 340,000 doctors, there were 4,060,000 other health workers, a ratio of about 12 to 1.[33] The lion's share of these allied health personnel are employed in hospitals, but hundreds of thousands are in other health care settings.

There is little doubt that the rising rates of utilization of health services in America have been accommodated mainly because of this vast expansion of the health workforce, outside the ranks of the traditional medical profession. After the Flexner Report on medical education in 1910, and the closure of dozens of medical schools, the supply of doctors, in relation to the U.S. population, actually declined. In 1900 there were 158 physicians per 100,000 U.S. population; this ratio declined to about 138 per 100,000 in 1920, and decreased to 126 per 100,000 in 1931.[34] After this there was a slight rise in the national ratio, but it remained at a level of about 130 or 135 physicians per 100,000 population until the mid-1950s.

In the years after World War II, with the rapid rise of purchasing power for medical care, the viewpoint grew that the United States was facing a serious shortage of physicians.[35] As a result, in 1963 the federal government, under the Health Professions Educational Assistance Act, began to subsidize the education of doctors and other health personnel. In addition, with postwar elimination of many of the previous restrictions on immigration, thousands of graduates of foreign medical schools came to the United States and remained.[36] As a result, since the 1960s, the national supply of doctors has steadily increased, reaching 393,792, or about 183 per 100,000 people, by 1975. With expectation of a ratio of 200 physicians per 100,000, or one doctor to 500 people, by 1990, voices were being raised in the late 1970s that the United States was facing a surplus of doctors.

The 394,000 physicians recorded for 1975 should not, of course, suggest that this number represents the complement of doctors available exclusively for the care of patients. Still less should it be interpreted to reflect the count of doctors in individual medical practice. Tabulations of the American Medical Association (AMA), based on questionnaires sent to every physician licensed by any state in the nation, clarify the mode of practice of U.S. medical manpower. The percentage distribution of these physicians is shown in Table 1-1.[37]

In interpreting Table 1-1, it is important to realize that it refers to all licensed physicians in the nation in 1975, including those in federal employment. About 28,000 physicians in that year were in federal government posts, principally in the Veterans Administration and the military departments. Most of these are "hospital-based" physicians who are, of course, providing patient care. Some tabulations omit these and apply only to "nonfederal" physicians, which tends to give an incomplete picture.

The figure of 66,842 physicians in "group medical practice" is based on another AMA source.[38] In some tabulations, these doctors are aggregated with those in individual practice to show a total of 215,429 "office-based physi-

Table 1-1 Mode of Practice: U.S. Licensed Physicians, 1975

Mode of Practice	Number	Percent
Office-based individual practice[a]	148,587	37.7
Group medical practice[b]	66,842	17.0
Hospital-based, in training[c]	57,802	14.7
Hospital-based, full-time staff	38,706	9.8
Medical teaching or research	14,439	3.7
Administration	11,161	2.8
Other	2,793	0.7
Inactive or unknown status[d]	53,462	13.6
	393,792	100.0

[a] Many of these physicians may be in combinations of two but would not qualify as a medical group.

[b] Groups of three or more physicians practicing together and sharing income. See Chapter 8 for detailed definition.

[c] These include interns and residents, all of whom are licensed physicians.

[d] This total includes 21,449 inactive physicians, 26,145 of whom are active but not classified as to mode of practice, and 5,868 of whom have unknown address.

Source: L. J. Goodman and A. R. Mason, Physician Distribution and Licensure in the United States (Chicago, Ill: American Medical Association, 1978).

cians.'' In Table 1-1 this figure has been disaggregated to clarify the proportion of all physicians who are in the more organized settings of group practice clinics. As we will see in Chapter 8, the majority of these physicians are in larger medical groups with many more than three doctors.

Table 1-1 also includes the 57,802 predominantly young physicians in hospital work as interns and residents. Even though these physicians are still in training, it is important to realize that they are licensed and providing care to patients. If they were not working in hospitals, it would doubtless be necessary to have other physicians to do the work. Thus, they should properly be counted as part of the nation's medical manpower, even though some tabulations may omit them. The composition of the 53,462 physicians who are inactive or of unknown status is indicated in the footnotes to Table 1-1.

Thus, from the 1975 universe of 393,792 licensed physicians in the nation, 148,587, or less than 38 percent, could by clearly identified as being engaged mainly in nonorganized work settings. We know that many of these individual doctors, moreover, have part-time positions in various types of clinics. There can be little doubt that a similar calculation 50 years ago, if the data were available, would have shown a much higher proportion of doctors in private, independent medical practice. In other words, the trend toward organized settings for provision of medical care has clearly been upward. These settings, as we shall see, constitute a great variety of types—differing in their sponsorships, their purposes, their mode of economic support, and in other ways. The 148,587 private office-based and essentially individual medical practitioners, therefore, still constitute the most common pattern of health care delivery in the United States. It is a pattern, however, that is gradually losing the preeminent position that it has traditionally occupied in American health care.

Within private medical practice, moreover, many new patterns of professional work are being developed. A study published in 1973 examined a national sample of 863 medical practices, and found their character to be undergoing numerous changes.[39] Within the previous five years, 43.5 percent of doctors had modified their setting by joining up with one or more other physicians by sharing certain facilities with other doctors or in other ways. Much greater use is being made of nursing or other allied personnel to increase practice efficiency. More equipment is being used to aid in diagnosis—laboratory devices, electro-cardiographs, x-ray machines, and so on. Medical record systems are becoming more sophisticated, including the use of self-administered patient history forms. The business aspects of medical practice are also changing. Many individual practitioners are becoming incorporated to achieve certain financial advantages. The billing of patients or third party agencies is becoming automated. In a sense, this increased organization of individual medical practice constitutes a further movement in the direction of generally organized ambulatory care delivery, which the following chapters will discuss.

NOTES

1. Castiglioni, Arturo, *A History of Medicine* (New York: Alfred A. Knopf, 1941), pp. 19–26.

2. Winslow, C. E. A., *The Conquest of Epidemic Disease* (Princeton, N.J.: Princeton University Press), 1944.

3. Roemer, Milton I., *The Organization of Medical Care under Social Security* (Geneva, Switzerland: International Labour Office, 1969).

4. U.S. National Health Survey, *Current Estimates from the Health Interview Survey, United States - 1977* (Washington: National Center for Health Statistics, Series 10, No. 126, September 1978).

5. U.S. National Center for Health Statistics, "Access to Ambulatory Health Care: United States, 1974," *Advancedata*, No. 17, February 23, 1978, p. 4.

6. Bryant, John, *Health and the Developing World*, (Ithaca, N.Y.: Cornell University Press, 1969).

7. Sigerist, Henry E., *A History of Medicine: I: Primitive and Archaic Medicine*, (New York: Oxford University Press, 1951).

8. Sigerist, Henry E., "The Physician's Profession through the Ages," in *Sigerist on the History of Medicine* (Felix Marti-Ibanez, editor) (New York: MD Publications, 1960), pp. 3–15.

9. Sigerist, Henry E., "The History of Medical Licensure," *Journal of the American Medical Association*, 104 (1935): 1056–1060.

10. Sigerist, Henry E., *Medicine and Human Welfare* (New Haven: Yale University Press, 1941), pp. 105–145.

11. Sand, René, *The Advance to Social Medicine* (London: Staples Press, 1952), pp. 65–106.

12. Sigerist, Henry E., *American Medicine* (New York: W. W. Norton & Co., 1934).

13. Shryock, Richard H., *Medical Licensing in America, 1650–1965* (Baltimore: Johns Hopkins Press, 1967).

14. Berliner, Howard S., "A Larger Perspective on the Flexner Report," *International Journal of Health Services,* 5 (1975): 573–592.

15. Freymann, John Gordon, *The American Health Care System: Its Genesis and Trajectory* (Baltimore: Williams and Wilkins, 1974).

16. Wolf, George B., *The Physician's Business* (New York: Lippincott, 1949).

17. Kessel, Reuben, "Price Discrimination in Medicine," *Journal of Law and Economics,* 1 (1958): 20–53.

18. Roemer, Milton I., "On Paying the Doctor and the Implications of Different Methods," *Journal of Health and Human Behavior,* 3 (1962): 4–14.

19. Stevens, Rosemary, *American Medicine and the Public Interest* (New Haven: Yale University Press, 1971), pp. 175–266.

20. Somers, Anne R., *Health Care in Transition: Directions for the Future* (Chicago: Hospital Research and Educational Trust, 1971).

21. Roemer, Milton I., "Changing Patterns of Health Service: Their Dependence on a Changing World," *The Annals of the American Academy of Political and Social Science,* 346 (1963): 44–56.

22. Hall, Charles P., "Deductibles in Health Insurance" *Journal of Risk and Insurance,* 23 (1966): 253.

23. Institute of Medicine (National Academy of Sciences), *Advancing the Quality of Health Care,* (Washington: 1974).

24. Bloom, S., *The Doctor and His Patient* (New York: Free Press, 1965).

25. Havighurst, Clark, "Health Care Cost-Containment Regulation: Prospects and an Alternative," *American Journal of Law and Medicine,* 3 (1977): 309–322.

26. Garceau, Oliver, *The Political Life of the American Medical Association* (Cambridge, Mass.: Harvard University Press, 1941).

27. Cray, Ed, *In Failing Health: The Medical Crisis and the A.M.A.* (Indianapolis: Bobbs-Merrill Co., 1970).

28. Roemer, Milton I. and Jay W. Friedman, *Doctors in Hospitals: Medical Staff Organization and Hospital Performance* (Baltimore: Johns Hopkins Press, 1971).

29. Roemer, Milton I., "Controlling and Promoting Quality of Medical Care," *Law and Contemporary Problems,* 35 (1970): 284–304.

30. Myers, Robert J., *Medicare* (Homewood, Ill.: Richard D. Irwin, 1970).

31. Welch, C. W., "PSROs—Pros and Cons," *New England Journal of Medicine* 290 (1974): 1319.

32. Institute of Medicine, *Controls on Health Care* (Washington, D.C.: National Academy of Sciences, 1975).

33. Axelrod, S. J.; A. Donabedian; and D. W. Gentry, *Medical Care Chart Book,* 6th ed. (Ann Arbor, Mich.: University of Michigan, School of Public Health, 1976), p. 141.

34. U.S. Public Health Service, *Physicians for a Growing America* (Report of the Surgeon General's Consultant Group on Medical Education) (Washington D.C., 1959), p. 83.

35. Fein, Rashi, *The Doctor Shortage: An Economic Diagnosis* (Washington D.C.: The Brookings Institution, 1967).

36. U.S. Public Health Service, *Foreign Medical Graduates and Physician Manpower in the United States* (Washington D.C.: 1974).

37. Goodman, L. J. and A. R. Mason, *Physician Distribution and Licensure in the United States* (Chicago: American Medical Association, 1976).

38. American Medical Association, *Register of Group Practice 1975*, (Chicago, 1976).

39. Lewis, Charles E. and Rosalyn A. Deigh, *An Annotated Inventory of Innovative Changes in Health Care in the United States 1971–1973* (Los Angeles: University of California School of Public Health, 1973).

Chapter 2

Origins of Organized Ambulatory Health Care

The rise of organized arrangements for provision of ambulatory health service, compared to the social actions generating hospitals and community preventive services, is a relatively recent phenomenon. Just as the needs of the poor stimulated the founding of hospitals in the early Middle Ages, medical service to the poor stimulated the efforts to provide ambulatory care outside the premises of the individual physician or apothecary.

THE EARLY DISPENSARIES IN EUROPE

Hospitals of a sort had provided bed care for wounded soldiers and sick slaves in ancient Rome, but the precursors of the modern hospital are usually considered the charitable institutions for the poor in European cities of the eleventh and twelfth centuries A.D.[1] These early hospitals of the Christian church saw their mission as succor to the impoverished person who was seriously sick and needed shelter, a bed, food, and care. "Care" called for ministrations to the patient's soul as well as to his or her body. It was several centuries, however, before these hospitals considered it appropriate to give attention to outpatients not requiring bed care as well as to inpatients.[2]

The earliest systematic effort to provide medical attention to the ambulatory sick poor has been attributed by René Sand, the Belgian scholar, to a Protestant French doctor, Théophraste Renaudot, who founded a free consultation service in Paris in 1630.[3] Renaudot was wealthy and, not being with the Catholic majority that controlled the hospitals, he established his service in a separate building that he either owned or rented. He assembled 20 doctors to give out-of-hospital consultation to the sick poor, either directly or by correspondence. As so often applies to social innovators, Renaudot was from an ethnic minority, the French Huguenots (Protestants), who suffered many discriminations for their faith. Not surprisingly, therefore, his actions were opposed by the leading doctors of the day, including the Faculty of Medicine of the University of Paris.

Many poor people in Paris used this free consultation service, and it became increasingly popular and attracted donations from other philanthropists. (The doctors were not paid, but funds were nonetheless needed to purchase medications for the poor.) The opposition to Renaudot's service was ineffective, and goaded by its success, the Faculty of Medicine organized its own ambulatory consultation service for the poor in the late 1630s.

The French Medical Faculty service was offered two mornings a week, preceded by a Catholic mass. In 1641, the dispensing of drugs was added—hence, the name "dispensary." In 1644, with the death of many of the patrons of the original Renaudot dispensary, the French Parliament ordered this pioneer unit to be closed. By then, however, the idea had become established, and it was adopted in other cities of France. By 1707, King Louis XIV (not renowned for his generosity to the poor), ordered that a free ambulatory care dispensary be established at every French medical school. The prestigious medical faculty physicians received no pay for this work, since their earnings came from charges to their upper class patients, who were usually treated in their private homes. The ambulatory sick poor, moreover, served as useful teaching cases for medical students, just as they do today.

In England a similar development occurred somewhat later. England was not Catholic, but other social forces seem to have been at play. The sick poor would go directly to apothecaries for care, without benefit of medical advice, even as today the corner drugstore serves often as the poor person's doctor. Hospitals, as on the Continent, only gave treatment to poor patients sick in bed, within their walls. In 1675, in the Royal College of Physicians of London, a plan was proposed to provide a free consultation service to the poor.[4] The College asked the Society of Apothecaries to cooperate by providing drugs at low prices that the poor could afford, but agreement could not be reached. In 1687, the Royal College of Physicians resolved that all members should give free advice to the poor within London and for seven miles around, but no provisions were made for drugs nor for definite times and places for the service. It was not until 1696 that the Royal College, in response to a plea from the Common Council of the City of London, decided to provide at its own expense (each doctor contributing ten pounds to start the scheme) a repository of drugs. These would be dispensed free to the poor at the headquarters of the College itself.

Opposition continued, however, not only from the apothecaries but also from some physicians, who objected to losing any patronage, even that of the poor. In 1725, therefore, the Royal College Dispensary was terminated. It was not until 1770 that the dispensary idea gained support again. After 1775, dispensaries grew rapidly in London and the English countryside, still separate from hospitals. Each dispensary had a board of governors composed of wealthy persons who financed the charity. For entitlement to care, poor patients were often expected to produce an introductory letter from one of the governors. By the late 18th century, however, doctors were busier with private patients, and it became necessary to pay them salaries (50 pounds per year in 1783, and 100 pounds in 1786) to attract them to dispensary work. After 1800, many of the London dispensaries offered smallpox vaccinations to supplement ambulatory services.

EARLY DISPENSARIES IN THE UNITED STATES

The idea of the dispensary as a freestanding place for treatment of the ambulatory poor spread to the New World soon after the American Revolution. The first dispensary was established in 1786 in Philadelphia, the same city where the first American hospital had been founded in 1751.[5] The two institutions, however, were not related. A dispensary was set up in New York City in 1791, in Boston in 1796, and in Baltimore in 1800.

Dispensaries grew slowly at first, with no additional ones until 1816, when managers of the Philadelphia Dispensary set up two satellite units as the city spread north and south. Between 1827 and 1852, four new dispensaries were set up in New York. By 1874, there were 29 dispensaries in New York, and by 1877 there were 33 in Philadelphia. Dispensary use also increased; records in New York show a total of 134,000 patients served in 1860, and the number rose to 876,000 by 1900.

These early American dispensaries had certain features in common. All of them were intended to serve the urban poor who did not require inpatient hospital care. All had a central building, with the exception of the Boston Dispensary, which had none until the 1850s. There was usually one full-time person in charge, an apothecary or a physician, who performed minor surgery, gave smallpox vaccinations, extracted teeth, and prescribed medications. By the mid-nineteenth century, the larger dispensaries had both a physician and a pharmacist. Young physicians were appointed to visit sick patients at home; such "district visiting," was in fact the principal function of the Philadelphia Dispensary when it was started in 1786, and it remained the sole activity of the famous Boston Dispensary until 1856. After they were well-established, the dispensaries appointed community practitioners as attending staff for certain scheduled times.

Financial support of the early dispensaries was meager. They were dependent mainly on private donations, which were principally used for the purchase of drugs. Physicians ordinarily volunteered their services without compensation. The dispensaries in New York were an exception; they received subsidies from the city and state governments. The Boston and the Philadelphia Dispensaries gradually accumulated some endowment funds. Often earnings would be derived by renting space in the dispensary building to commercial tenants.

Most cases reported in early dispensary records were relatively minor—colds, bronchitis, dyspepsia, lacerations, and so on. As one still finds in clinics for the poor, women patients outnumbered men. Not until the end of the nineteenth century did some dispensaries stay open in the evenings for the convenience of workers, who were predominantly male. Smallpox vaccinations were provided free to the poor not only in the dispensary quarters, but also through door-to-door home visits. In periods of threatened smallpox epidemics, dispensaries even provided vaccine to private physicians.

The most frequent activity of dispensaries, however, was dispensing drugs, as might be expected under crowded conditions where the doctor could spend only a few minutes with each patient. In private practice, physicians could calmly advise their middle- or upper-class patients to vary their diets, visit the seaside, take up horseback riding, or make other changes in (as we would now say) life style. But how could such advice be given to the poor? A quick prescription was the practical solution, as is still all too often the case in medical practice today in urban slums.

Dispensaries naturally became linked with urban charities, both voluntary and official, such as the Association for Improving the Conditions of the Poor in New York or the Board of Guardians for the Poor in Philadelphia. Conscientious physicians would serve, in effect, as social workers, sending notes to these agencies, for example, to request a ration of coal for a poor family in the winter. In the later nineteenth century, when visiting nurse services were established, dispensary doctors would ask them to visit the homes of the poor to offer advice on hygiene and diet. Kitchens were organized in association with dispensaries in New York and Boston to prepare meals to the malnourished poor.

Specialization became more common in dispensaries toward the second half of the nineteenth century. Sessions were scheduled for women and children, for conditions of the heart and lungs, for eye and ear problems, for nervous and genitourinary diseases, and so on. By 1905, the outstanding Boston Dispensary took pride in having ten types of specialized clinic sessions. Some late nineteenth century dispensaries specialized exclusively in treating particular ailments.

Although humanitarian benevolence was evidently the major motivation of the founders of the early dispensaries both in America and in Europe, the task of raising funds to support their growth invoked other considerations. In appeals for philanthropic funds, dispensary leaders would maintain that the early ambulatory treatment of the poor would save tax dollars needed for the care of the chronically sick poor in hospitals or almshouses. The dispensary, it was claimed, was also a first-line defense against epidemic disease that could spread from the poor to the comfortable classes. Finally, dispensaries had little difficulty in attracting the volunteer services of physicians, because they offered clinical education along with an opportunity to demonstrate conspicuously the benevolence of the medical profession. In fact, as Charles Rosenberg has pointed out, "mid-century medical schools vied actively in establishing dispensaries for the benefit of (teaching) their students."[6] Moreover, dispensary posts were stepping stones in the careers of young physicians, who would not only gain experience but also acquire a community reputation and become acquainted with the prestigious physicians who usually directed the dispensary programs.

American dispensaries in the first decades of the nineteenth century followed a practice used previously in England. To assure that patients were poor, but "worthy" and not undeserving, referrals were required from one of the contributors to the dispensary's financial support. Indeed, the number of referrals acceptable from a particular donor was roughly proportional to the size of his or her donation; an annual donation (or subscription) of $5, for example, would entitle the patron to refer two patients during the year, while a $50 donation would permit an unlimited number of referrals. Underlying this practice was the concept, according to Rosenberg, that the voluntary charity represented by the dispensary was intended for the diligent and virtuous poor, while the hospital, typically supported by government had responsibility for the prostitute, the drunkard, the lunatic, and so on. Later in the nineteenth century, the requirement of referrals, along with the concepts supporting them, died out.

The moralistic ideology underlying the sponsorship of the early dispensaries, with their definite differentiation from the hospitals, was made explicit in such rules as were applied in the early years of the Boston Dispensary. The rule was that "persons suffering from venereal disease or from the effects of alcohol should not be treated by the dispensary, as being the victims of their own sensual indulgence."[7] On the other hand, for the "worthy poor," the dispensary, particularly insofar as its physicians visited patients in their homes, had such advantages as these:

> The sick, without being pained by a separation from their families, may be attended and relieved in their own houses. The sick can, in this way, be assisted at less expense to the public than in the hospital. Those who have seen better days may be comforted without being humiliated; and all the poor receive the benefits of a charity, the more refined as it is the more secret.[8]

According to Michael Davis and Andrew Warner, freestanding dispensaries in the United States grew from 3 in 1800 to about 100 by 1900.[9] Toward the end of the nineteenth century, however, new forms of health service provision were arising that would lead to the decline and eventual disappearance of the independent dispensary. Most important among these were the hospital, the public health movement, and the private medical practitioner. These health care developments were occurring within a rapidly expanding population that resulted not only from a high birth rate but also from massive immigration from Europe.

After the Civil War, with the rapid growth of the population, the movement of the frontier to the west, and the great progress in medical science—such as aseptic techniques, anesthesia, and surgical advances due to organ pathology—hospitals multiplied at an amazing pace. In 1873, there were 149 hospitals and allied facilities for bed care in the United States, with about 35,500 beds. By 1909, when the American Medical Association (AMA) reported its first census of hospitals, the number had spiralled to 3,600 hospitals, with about 150,000 beds.[10] At first, hospitals served only inpatients, but toward the end of the nineteenth century they began to develop outpatient departments. By 1916, when the Committee on Dispensary Work of the American Hospital Association (AHA) conducted a survey, it reported 255 independent dispensaries and 645 outpatient departments (OPD) connected with hospitals.[11] In spite of the numerical growth of separate dispensaries, their attendance was declining as the more technically advanced equipment attracted poor patients to hospital OPDs and a growing number of physicians transferred their interests to hospital work. Because of the fees received from private patients for inpatient care, moreover, the financial support of hospital OPDs became much firmer than that of dispensaries.

The AHA was founded in 1899. Significantly, however, it had been preceded by a national meeting held in Chicago in 1893, described as the first "Congress of Hospitals and Dispensaries."[12] The two types of facility were then considered quite different, yet only six years later, dispensaries, which for a while were simply equated with outpatient departments, became merely the province of a committee of the AHA.

The public health movement in the nineteenth century had been concentrated on environmental sanitation, on isolation and quarantine of patients with communicable diseases, and, to some extent, on giving vaccinations and immunizations.[13] Organized clinics, however, were rare. In 1904, according to the AHA, there were only 20 public health dispensaries in the nation, all of which were devoted to tuberculosis. By 1916, this number had risen up to 1300—about 500 for tuberculosis, 400 for baby hygiene, 250 for school children, and 150 for other purposes. These clinics were all preventive in orientation, and their clientele were virtually limited to low-income groups. Being supported by tax funds, they had a stronger financial base than the dispensaries which were dependent on charitable donations. Thus, further inroads were made on the functions previously performed by the dispensaries.

Finally, the rapid growth of private medical practice, particularly between 1880 and 1910, produced a flood of practitioners who gradually came to look upon dispensaries as competitive. Increasingly, the average doctor spoke of "abuse of the dispensary" by patients who could properly afford private medical care.[14] It became increasingly difficult to attract physicians to do dispensary work. Similar charges were made of "abuse" of hospital OPDs by affluent patients, but the general hospital had no difficulty in staffing its outpatient clinics, insofar as such service could be expected from staff physicians, particularly the younger ones, in return for the privilege of admitting private patients for inpatient care.

After World War I, all three of these movements—hospitals, public health agencies, and private medical practice—continued to expand and flourish, spelling the steady decline of the separate charitable dispensary. By 1969, only one facility in the inventory of the AHA still carried the old name: the Hartford Dispensary.[15]

From the ashes of the early dispensary, there arose not only the hospital OPD, but also, somewhat later, another type of facility linked mainly to local government and the public health movement. This was the "health center," which warrants separate consideration.

THE HEALTH CENTER IN EUROPE

Although the outpatient department within the general hospital and the specialized clinic session (for tuberculosis, for infants, etc.) within the public health agency gradually replaced the independent charitable dispensary, another type of facility for organized provision of general health services arose in the early twentieth century. This came to be known as the health center, and several social currents contributed to its development.

The first official formulation of the health center concept came from Great Britain in 1920. In that year, the Consultative Council on Medical and Allied Services, set up as a link between the ministry of health and the private medical profession, issued its historic *Interim Report on Future Provision of Medical and Allied Services*.[16] This called for provision of primary health care by teams of physicians and allied personnel based in "primary health centers." It proposed that a network of such facilities should cover the entire nation and serve the whole population, not just the poor. In the language of what is better known as the "Dawson Report" (from the name of the council's chairman), the health center would be "an institution equipped for services of curative and preventive medicine to be conducted by the general practitioners of that district, in conjunction with an efficient nursing service and with the aid of visiting consultants and specialists."[16]

The physicians would remain in private practice, but the close association with government nurses and other allied personnel would presumably strengthen the quality and effectiveness of their services.

As Vicente Navarro has pointed out, the Consultative Council was established soon after World War I as a response of the relatively conservative British government to the demands of the British Labour Party for a new social order."[17]

This was just after the success of the Bolshevik Revolution in Russia, and a State Medical Services Association, on behalf of the Labour Party was demanding that all health facilities be nationalized and all medical personnel become salaried civil servants. As so often happens in the history of social movements, the Dawson Report recommendations were a relatively moderate response to these demands. The State Medical Services Association later became the Socialist Medical Association, which still exists in Great Britain.

Nevertheless, even the relatively moderate Dawson Report proposals were too radical for implementation by the government in face of the opposition of private physicians and with the declining militancy of the Labour Party. It was not until the Labour Party proposals after World War II, which resulted in the British National Health Service in 1948, that the issue of health centers as the customary locale for primary care, was revived. Once again, the government, even though under Labour Party control, did not press the idea too vigorously. Viscount Dawson himself, writing in 1942, stated that a trend:

> . . . more and more apparent during the last 25 years, is the need for greater institutional provision. The increase of knowledge, and with that the development of teamwork, has made this inevitable. The doctor works best where equipment and ancillary services are available, and side by side with his fellows. Further, such institutional provision is economical of both time and cost and makes a health service available for all citizens. In short, the tendency is for the centre of gravity of practice to shift away from the (patient's) home to organized surgeries, clinics, health centres, and hospitals, and these would . . . constitute a coordinated scheme of service . . . [18]

Finally, in the 1960s the health center idea took on new life in Great Britain; hundreds were built throughout England and Scotland, and private general practitioners located their "surgeries" in them, side by side with government visiting nurses, social workers, technicians, and other allied personnel.[19] Concepts of regionalized hierarchies of primary, secondary, and tertiary services, also proposed in the Dawson Report, were embodied in the National Health Service from its onset in 1948.

While it took more than 40 years for the health center idea to be implemented in Great Britain, a modified version of it was introduced in 1926 in Ceylon (now Sri Lanka), a British colony at the time.[20] The crucial modification, however, was the major focus on preventive services. Patients needing treatment were referred to a hospital outpatient department. This pattern of health centers, as facilities limited to preventive services (though a broad range of them) was promoted throughout the developing countries by the Rockefeller Foundation in the 1930s and 1940s. There were valid reasons for this stress on prevention in a period when the treatment of diseases—which were indeed preventable—absorbed most of the efforts in developing countries. By the 1950s, however, the value of combining prevention with primary treatment of the sick became recognized almost everywhere.[21]

On an international level, the first effective implementation of the health center as a facility for providing integrated curative and preventive services for a total population in its area, was in the Soviet Union. Soon after the Russian Revolution of 1917, health services were converted from a private entrepreneurial enterprise into a governmental function. Physicians and all other health personnel became public employees, facilities for both ambulatory and inpatient care became governmental, and the whole system of health care delivery was supported by public funds.[22] This pattern was adopted by the several other countries having socialist revolutions following World War II. Even in the non-socialist or free enterprise countries, moreover, it has been adapted very widely for some segments of the population, in the developing world and to an increasing extent in the industrialized world.[23]

EARLY HEALTH CENTERS IN AMERICA

Reflecting some of the commonalities in the worldwide development of health services, it is noteworthy that in 1920, the year of the Dawson Report, the New York State Commissioner of Health, Herman Biggs, proposed a network on health centers to serve the rural population (not solely the poor) with both preventive and curative services. While the emphasis was to be on health promotion and prevention, the scope of the Biggs ambulatory care facilities was to be explicitly comprehensive.[24] In the atmosphere of post-World War I conservatism, the idea was vigorously opposed by the private medical profession and was not implemented. A similar proposal with deliberate restriction to serving the poor was made in 1919 by the health officer of Los Angeles County, California, J. L. Pomeroy. It, too, failed to be implemented.[25] In place of the comprehensive primary care facilities originally advocated by Pomeroy, district health centers were developed for basic preventive services. Patients needing medical treatment were referred to private physicians.

If we think of health centers as ambulatory care facilities limited to the provision of a full range of preventive services, their origins in America can be traced to an earlier period. Such facilities were offshoots, in a sense, of settlement houses for service to the poor, originating in large city slum districts in the 1890s.[26] These facilities attempted to bring together various educational, social work, and recreational services that would be helpful to largely immigrant low-income families. In the same sense, around 1910 and after, a movement developed to integrate various organized ambulatory health services—for child health, for tuberculosis, for immunizations, for feeding the poor—that had begun to spring up under both public and private services at separate locations.

Key figures in this early movement were Wilbur C. Phillips and his wife, Elsie.[27] Phillips had served as secretary of the New York Milk Committee, which was established in 1907 by the Association for Improving the Condition of the Poor. In 1911 he moved to Milwaukee, Wisconsin where he persuaded the local health department to set up a health station in a depressed district that would serve the babies and mothers in a 33-block area with a population of 16,000. Phillips was a Socialist, and Milwaukee was the first large American city to elect a Socialist municipal administration. Great emphasis was put on the organization of "block committees" to encourage mothers to bring in their babies for preventive attention. By 1912, however, the Milwaukee government changed, and the demonstration project terminated.

The time was obviously ripe, nevertheless, for implementation of the health center idea in other cities. Phillips returned to New York, where in 1916 he founded the National Social Unit Organization, to promote democratic citizen participation in the organization and operation of "social units" for health and welfare services. In 1917, such a unit was organized in Cincinnati to serve a poor neighborhood of 15,000 citizens. The Anti-Tuberculosis League, along with the Associated Charities, the Better Housing League, and other voluntary agencies, participated in the work of the social unit, which also enlisted the help of neighborhood block workers. Health activities included maternal and child health preventive services, dental examinations of school children, visiting nurse service, and even some medical care during the influenza epidemic of 1918, as well as antituberculosis work. But, as in Milwaukee, political changes intervened, and a newly elected mayor, along with the local medical society and the director of public welfare, branded the social unit a "Red plot." In the highly patriotic atmosphere at the end of the World War I, this was a fatal charge, and in 1920 the project was killed.

Meanwhile, under less controversial auspices, health centers for coordinated provision of a variety of social and preventive services, but not for treatment of the sick, were organized in other major cities. In Boston, Charles Wilinsky, a practicing physician who later became the city health officer, founded the Blossom Street Health Center in 1912. This facility included offices for the "Consumptive Hospital Department, Instructive District Nursing Association, Milk and Baby Hygiene Association, Visiting Physician of the Boston Dispensary, and Hebrew Federated Charities."[28] Later district health centers became the framework for provision of services by Boston's Department of Public Health. In New York City, an experimental district health center was established in 1915 on the lower east side of Manhattan (a poverty area of mostly European Jewish immigrants) by S. S. Goldwater, the city's health commissioner. Such district facilities were extended to other parts of the city by Health Commissioner

Haven Emerson in 1916 and 1917. Beginning with one experimental health center in 1914, the Department of Health in Buffalo, New York established a network of seven centers by 1920.[29]

The spread of health centers as facilities for coordinated delivery of several types of health services was doubtless linked to the "efficiency movement" that pervaded American industry in the first two decades of the twentieth century. The concept was that combining several specialized functions under one roof would permit greater productivity per dollar spent. The American Red Cross, searching for a new purpose at the end of World War I, decided to promote the health center movement. A survey by this agency reported that in January 1920 there were 72 health centers in 49 communities, and that 33 more centers were being planned in 28 other places.[30] Considering both existing and proposed units, 33 were entirely governmental, 27 were private, and 16 were under combined public and private control. According to the Red Cross analysis, in the 72 health centers actually in operation, the functions performed were as follows:

Service	Number of Centers Providing Service
Visiting nurse services	34
Child welfare	29
Antituberculosis work	27
Venereal disease clinics	22
Dental clinics	14
Eye, ear, nose, and throat clinics	11
Laboratories	10
Milk stations	9

Source: James A. Tobey, "The Health Center Movement in the United States," *Modern Hospital* 14 (1920): 212–214.

The notable characteristic of all these functions was their essentially preventive nature—except perhaps for the "eye, ear, nose, and throat clinics;" the latter may well have prescribed corrective eyeglasses (probably for children) or referred children for tonsillectomies.

The predominant feature of the health centers that survived into the 1930s and grew was their dedication to prevention and their deliberate policy of leaving treatment to the province of the private medical practitioner or the hospital outpatient department. As Michael Davis pointed out, health centers were devoted to serve the population of a particular district and to coordinate specified health services within this district.[31] Although this was not necessarily explicit policy, the people served by health centers were expected to be poor, if only by reason of the neighborhoods in which the centers were located.

As often happens in a movement that becomes fashionable, a wide diversity of programs adopted the popular label. We cannot be certain, therefore, of the meaning of data collected for the 1930 White House Conference on Child Health and Protection. This study reported 1,511 "major and minor health centers" operating throughout the nation, about half under governmental and half under private auspices. Eighty percent of these had been established since 1910.[32]

By the Great Depression of the 1930s, the concept of the health center as a locale for coordinating numerous different public and private agencies in an area had begun to wane. Agencies depending on charitable donations lost their philanthropic patrons. The medical profession, also hit hard by loss of many of its private paying patients, became increasingly suspicious of any organized community facility that might deliberately or surreptitiously become competitive. The immigrant population, which had provided a natural neighborhood grouping for the charitable services of multiple agencies, was no longer so geographically concentrated.

As a result, like the dispensary movement in an earlier period, the health center movement lost its missionary zeal. Structures known as health centers continued to be built in the United States, but they became essentially facilities for housing official public health agencies, i.e., branches of the health department in large metropolitan cities or the central headquarters of health departments in rural counties.[33] Except for venereal disease and tuberculosis clinic sessions, at which treatment was necessary to prevent contagion, any vestige of medical care, even for the poor, was eliminated. Treatment was appropriate only in the outpatient department of hospitals, where an admission clerk or social worker had to make certain of the patient's indigence; for those who could afford to pay, a private physician was the only acceptable resource.

For 30 years, well into the 1960s, this strictly preventive and public health agency definition of the health center prevailed. Not until the urban riots of the ethnic minorities in large city slums during the mid-1960s, was the comprehensive, i.e., preventive and curative, "neighborhood health center" revived. With the rediscovery of poverty, in the midst of urban affluence, structures for organized provision of general ambulatory health care again became an accepted concept in America.[34]

There is much more to be said about the history of organized ambulatory health services in America. The dispensary and the health center represent *generalized* models of the idea. The other streams of development constitute forms of organized ambulatory care characterized by much more *specialized* objectives with respect to certain population types, certain disease categories, or other characteristics.

The backgrounds of each of these *special* forms of clinic will be reviewed in the later chapters, which will explore each of these forms as they now are found in the United States. It will first be helpful to take a bird's eye view of the general panorama of clinics operating in America today. This is the objective of Chapter 3.

NOTES

1. Sigerist, Henry E., "An Outline on the Development of the Hospital," *Bulletin of the Institute of the History of Medicine,* 4 (1936): 573–581.

2. Risley, Mary, *House of Healing* (Garden City, N.Y.: Doubleday & Co., 1961).

3. Sand, René, *The Advance to Social Medicine* (London: Staples Press, 1952), pp. 80–82.

4. Hartston, William, "Medical Dispensaries in Eighteenth Century London," *Proceedings of the Royal Society of London,* 56 (1963): 753–758.

5. Rosenberg, Charles E. "Social Class and Medical Care in Nineteenth Century America: The Rise and Fall of the Dispensary," *Journal of the History of Medicine and Allied Sciences,* 29 (1974): 32–54.

6. Ibid. p. 40.

7. Davis, Michael M. and Andrew R. Warner, *Dispensaries–Their Management and Development* (New York: Macmillan Co., 1918), p. 6.

8. Ibid., p. 5.

9. Ibid., p. 10.

10. Davis, Michael M., "The Hospital's Position in Society," in *Modern Concepts of Hospital Administration* (J. K, Owen, Editor) (Philadelphia: W. B. Saunders Co., 1962), pp. 7–8.

11. Davis and Warner, *Dispensaries,* p. 36.

12. MacEachern, M. T., *Hospital Organization and Management* (Berwyn, Ill.: Physician's Record Co., 1962), pp. 1–28.

13. Smillie, Wilson G., *Public Health Administration in the United States,* (New York: Macmillan Co., 1940), pp. 11–21.

14. Rosenberg, *"Social Class,"* pp. 51–52.

15. American Hospital Association, *Hospitals* (Guide Issue), Part Two, August 1969, p. 291.

16. England and Wales, Ministry of Health, Consultative Council on Medical and Allied Services, *Interim Report on the Future of Medical and Allied Services* (London: H. M. Stationery Office, 1920).

17. Navarro, Vicente, *Class Struggle, the State, and Medicine: An Historical and Contemporary Analysis of the Medical Sector in Great Britain* (New York: Prodist, 1978), pp. 14–24.

18. Dawson, Viscount of Penn, "Medicine and the Public Welfare," *Medical Care* 2 (1942): 322–336.

19. Curwen, M. and B. Brookes, "Health Centres: Facts and Figures," *Lancet* 2 (1969): 945–948.

20. Chellappah, S. F. and W. P. Jacocks, *A Guide to Health Unit Procedure in Ceylon* (2nd ed.) (Colombo: Ceylon Government Printing Office, 1949).

21. Roemer, Milton I., *Evaluation of Community Health Centres,* (Geneva: World Health Organization [Public Health Papers 48], 1972), pp. 12–20.

22. Field, Mark G., *Soviet Socialized Medicine* (New York: Free Press, 1967).

23. Roemer, Milton I., "Organized Ambulatory Health Service in International Perspective," *International Journal of Health Services* 1 (1971): 18–27. Number 1, 1971.

24. Terris, Milton, "Herman Biggs' Contribution to the Modern Concept of Health Centers," *Bulletin of the History of Medicine* 20 (1946): 387–412.

25. Pomeroy, J. L., "Health Center Development in Los Angeles County," *Journal of the American Medical Association* 93 (1929): 1546–1550.

26. Addams, Jane, et al., *Philanthropy and Social Progress: Seven Essays,* (New York, 1893).

27. Rosen, George, "The First Neighborhood Health Center Movement—Its Rise and Fall," *American Journal of Public Health* 61 (1971): 1620–1637.

28. Stoeckle, John D. and Lacy M. Candib, "The Neighborhood Health Center—Reform Ideas of Yesterday and Today," *New England Journal of Medicine,* 280 (1969): 1385–1391.

29. Rosen, George, "The First Neighborhood Health Center Movement." *op. cit.*

30. Tobey, James A., "The Health Center Movement in the United States, " *Modern Hospital* 14 (1920): 212–214.

31. Davis, Michael M., "Goal-Post and Yardsticks in Health Center Work," *American Journal of Public Health,* 17 (1927): 433–440.

32. Rosen, George, "The First Neighborhood Health Center Movement." *op. cit.*

33. Handley, Harry E., *Health Center Buildings* (New York: Commonwealth Fund, 1948).

34. Bamberger, Lisbeth, "Health Care and Poverty: What Are the Dimensions of the Problem from the Community Point of View?" *Bulletin of the New York Academy of Medicine* 42 (1966): 1140 ff.

Chapter 3

The Panorama of Clinics in America Today

With its free-wheeling, pluralistic culture, it is only to be expected that organized ambulatory health services (OAHS) in the United States today present an enormous diversity of forms. Each has arisen from specific social needs and is associated with diverse types of organizational sponsors or with varying objectives.

INTRODUCTION

In this chapter, we offer an overview of the panorama of OAHS programs in America. For convenience, we will refer to varied organized activities as "clinics," the commonly used American term. Readers from other countries should be reminded that "clinic" in the United States has a narrower connotation than in Europe or elsewhere. It typically means a setting where health service is given to outpatients, or ambulatory patients, as distinguished from inpatients. The meaning elsewhere is more akin to the American usage of the adjective "clinical" and refers to the signs and symptoms of patients that lead to a specific diagnosis and treatment, whether the patient is ambulatory or bedridden. Thus, a French study entitled *The Birth of the Clinic* explores not the same subject as this book, but rather the development of knowledge in "clinical medicine," particularly the achievement of linkage between the basic sciences and the symptomatology of patients observed on hospital wards.[1] A clinic or a "polyclinic" in many countries, accordingly, often means a teaching hospital. In America, the clinic is so clearly identified with ambulatory care that when a hospital serves outpatients, this is said to be done in the "clinic."

Just as for many social phenomena, the multitude of types of clinic may be classified along several axes of analysis. They may be categorized according to the several forms of organization—governmental, voluntary nonprofit, or proprietary—that sponsor and control them. The same universe of clinics may be classified according to the types of persons they serve: the poor, the military veteran, the rural person, the child, and so on. Thirdly, clinics may be ordered according to the disease entities or, indeed, health-oriented objective with which they are concerned. Clinics might also be classified by their physical settings— whether they are part of a larger establishment (such as a hospital, a school, a factory, a prison, or such) as distinguished from having a separate and free-standing location; the latter setting might be further subdivided into urban and rural. There are doubtless still other approaches to clinic classification.

Different schemes of classification may be appropriate for differing purposes. In this study our principal approach is to classify and analyze clinics according to their sponsorship. The choice of this axis of classification has been dictated only partially by the fact that data are most readily available on this basis; that is, hospitals report on hospital clinics, schools report on school health units, and so on. More important, the social structure of the nation's health care system is largely determined by organized entities.[2] Authority is exercised and decisions are made by organizations of various sorts. To some extent organizations may, indeed, be devoted to particular types of disease; more often they may take shape to serve particular types of persons. Yet most organizations in the health arena address many types of disease and diverse demographic groups. If we wish to modify the structure and functioning of the health care system, we must deal with organizations and agencies that sponsor various health programs.

Taking an overview of clinics in contemporary America, one soon finds several major types of sponsorship. Oldest and perhaps most important in their broad availability to the population are clinics sponsored by hospitals. Public health agencies, usually known as health departments, sponsor a variety of clinics, usually with preventive objectives. Schools and colleges sponsor clinics or some type of organized ambulatory health service for their students; industrial enterprises may do likewise for their employees. Physicians, as private medical practitioners, may join together and establish group practice clinics.

These are the five principal types of clinic sponsorship in the United States, but there are numerous other types of smaller proportions; they depend upon a multitude of sponsorships, both governmental and voluntary. Many are sponsored by private bodies although financially supported mainly by government. Some may be transitory or unstable, arising suddenly to meet a perceived need and then declining. To make the analysis manageable, these heterogeneous units will be clustered together under the rubric of "specially sponsored clinics."

This study devotes one chapter to each of the types of clinics mentioned above. Theoretically, one could also examine the same universe of clinics according to the other possible axes of classification noted earlier. This would be rather tedious, but one chapter (Chapter 11) has been prepared to demonstrate the feasibility of such alternative approaches; in it, clinics are analyzed by objective. Within this concept, examples are selected to illustrate analyses of clinics categorized by the type of person served, the type of disease treated, or the type of technical service offered.

Finally there are certain clinics with a significance that comes not so much from their sponsorship or their objective, but rather from their linkage with a certain form of financing—namely, the insurance mechanism. These are clinics of "health maintenance organizations" (HMOs), to which Chapter 12 is devoted. To offer some perspective on this panorama of clinics in America, a few salient highlights will now be offered on each type of clinic.

CLINICS SPONSORED BY HOSPITALS

As reviewed in Chapter 2, the earliest form of OAHS, the dispensary, evolved by the late nineteenth and early twentieth centuries into outpatient departments of hospitals, predominantly general hospitals for relatively short-term illness (customarily defined as facilities where the average stay is less than 30 days). Hospitals, in turn, may be under several types of sponsorship or control, the principal types being: (a) governmental (federal, state, or local); (b) voluntary nonprofit (sometimes subdivided into church-related and nonsectarian); and (c) proprietary (i.e., operated for profit).

It would be unduly complicated to review hospital outpatient departments (OPD) or clinics separately for each of these basic types of sponsorship. We will instead simply speak of sponsorship of clinics by hospitals. The overwhelming majority of such clinics are in the hospital facility itself or perhaps a separate structure adjacent to the main hospital building; however, some hospital-controlled clinics are located at a certain distance from the central facility and function as satellites to it.

In terms of their meaning to the population of the United States, the hospital OPD is probably the most important type of clinic in the nation. In 1977 there were 7,300 hospitals of all types in the United States, including about 200 that were not registered with the American Hospital Association (AHA) (and do not, therefore, enter into the statistics to be reviewed later).[3] From the viewpoint of accessibility, the community hospital is most important. The AHA defines these as "short-term general and other special (but not including mental or tuberculosis institutions) hospitals of any sponsorship except the U.S. federal government, and excluding hospital units of special institutions (such as factories or prisons)."[3] These community hospitals numbered 5,881 in 1977.

Scheduled clinics, as of 1977, were provided in 30.1 percent of all hospitals, or 1,955 facilities. In community hospitals available to the total population the proportion was slightly less: 26.8 percent, or 1,452 facilities. Many hospitals, however, which do not operate scheduled clinics (for medical cases, surgical cases, obstetrical care, etc.) provide emergency care to outpatients at various hours of the day or night. This was done by 79.1 percent of all hospitals (5,136 facilities) and 89.8 percent of community hospitals (4,860 such facilities) in 1977.

The detailed aspects of hospital outpatient services—their utilization rates, their variations by main hospital sponsorship-type and by hospital size, their staffing, the sorts of patients served, their financing, and other administrative features will be the subject of Chapter 4.

PUBLIC HEALTH CLINICS

The movement for health centers, as noted in Chapter 2, evolved into little more than provision of a certain type of physical facility for official public health agencies, known usually as health departments. The evolution of health departments in the United States and their range of functions, including the operation of a variety of specialized clinics, will be considered in Chapter 5. Here we may take note of only a few general features of these agencies, insofar as they sponsor clinics.

All 50 states, as well as the several U.S. territories have a general public health authority, although an increasing trend has been to merge these agencies with other branches of state government into a combined "health and welfare" or other composite agency. The great majority of clinics, however, are operated by *local* health departments, and in all but three of these, funds were granted from the state government to the local entities.[4]

Local health departments are of several main governmental types. A study in 1977 identified 1,929 local public health units throughout the United States, and 31.5 percent of these covered two or more jurisdictions (cities, counties or both). The percentage distribution of these units, along with the populations they served, was as follows:[5]

Types of Health Departments

	Percent of Units	Percent of Population
County	49.3	48.5
City	19.1	23.2
Local health district	17.6	12.2
City/county	10.3	12.7
State health district	3.0	2.5
Other	0.6	0.8
All types:	100.0	100.0

Source: William Shonick and Walter Price, "Organizational Milieus of Local Public Health Units: Analysis and Response to Questionnaire," *Public Health Reports* 93 (1978): 648 ff.

Of the above distribution, 83 percent represented separate health departments and 17 percent constituted public health agencies that were subdivisions of some larger branch of each type of local government. All of the 1,929 agencies were considered "full-time public health units" in the sense that each had at least one full-time employee, with an address separate from that of a private physician's office. Yet, as the authors of the above study point out, there has been a trend toward sharing of top leadership of many public health agencies of the several types: in 1977, as many as 25 percent of the jurisdictions were led by an official who headed also one, two, or even more other jurisdictions.

The clinics conducted by these local public health agencies have a wide variety of functions, although their main orientation is disease prevention. The proportions of each type of clinic, along with various administrative characteristics will be reviewed in Chapter 5. Here we may simply note that the trend over the last 50 years has been toward a wider range of clinic functions. Of special significance in recent years has been the tendency of public health clinics to serve ambulatory patients with diverse health problems, in contrast to the specialized focus (such as tuberculosis, venereal disease, or infant health) of the past. The social forces responsible for this rise of general ambulatory care clinics under health department auspices will also be explored in Chapter 5. This is one visible symptom of the tendency of public health agencies to be concerned about treatment of the sick, as well as health promotion and prevention.

SCHOOL AND COLLEGE HEALTH SERVICES

Originating out of concern for communicable diseases in school children, various forms of personal health services have been developed in the nation's approximately 90,000 elementary schools and 32,000 secondary schools. Although schoolteachers are often expected to identify health problems, acute illness as well as obvious physical or mental defects, in their pupils, the operation of a school clinic is typically the responsibility of a school nurse. These nursing personnel may be either full-time in one large school or part-time in several smaller schools. In either case, there are typically clinic quarters where the nurse is located and sees pupils. Physicians, usually part-time, may also render services in these school clinics.

Personal health services constitute only one part of a general school health program. The other two parts are customarily health education and maintenance of a safe and hygienic school environment. Our focus in this study, however, is only on the personal health service aspect, insofar as it includes OAHS. This latter aspect, in the great majority of schools, is administratively controlled by educational authorities in local governments. (The other two aspects are universally under these authorities.) In about 20 percent of cities surveyed in 1966 and in a larger, (though undetermined) proportion of rural communities, however, the responsibility for personal health services in schools has been delegated to the responsibility of public health agencies.[6] Our discussion of this category of clinic in Chapter 6, nevertheless, will treat the sponsorship of these services as being by schools, whether or not educational authorities carry direct responsibility for them.

In large part, the functions of school clinics are somewhat intermediary in the medical care process. That is, children are examined by a physician or other type of personnel (nurse, audiologist, psychologist, etc.) but are referred elsewhere for treatment of any identified problem. First aid is usually given by the school nurse to the child who is injured or suddenly sick, but for treatment the child is sent back to the family or sometimes directly to a physician. Likewise, for nonurgent health problems school children who come to the school nurse or doctor for advice are rarely given definitive help, but rather are counseled where to seek help. Despite this modest role, school clinics play a part in the nation's health care system which is important and may sometimes be crucial.

In the colleges and universities, the scope of OAHS activities is generally much broader. There were 2,900 traditional institutions of higher (post secondary) education in the United States, in the early 1970s.[7] Typically these institutions award academic degrees; their enrollment in the same period was about 9,300,000 students. In addition, there were some 7,000 smaller technical schools with some 1,600,000 students learning various trades or vocations. The U.S. government reports also some 3,500 schools of nonspecified character beyond secondary school level, over and above those already noted.

The vast majority of college students in the nation are at campuses that operate health service programs, primarily for ambulatory care. Since in virtually all these institutions, a fraction of the students are living away from their homes, there is a special need for providing health care that might otherwise be a responsibility of the student's family. Particular needs arise in college athletics from which many injuries occur. The characteristics of these organized health programs are presented in Chapter 6.

INDUSTRIAL HEALTH UNITS

The social forces that have stimulated the organization of clinics to serve the employees of various industrial or related enterprises will be explored in Chapter 7. The range of ambulatory health services at workplaces is very wide, varying mainly with the number of employees in the establishment. Strange as it may seem, there appears to be little relationship between the degree of hazard in a work setting and the likelihood of in-plant medical services; other factors, such as the company's personnel policy or its size, would appear to be greater determinants.

Although the exact number of industrial or other firms operating clinics for their employees is not known, a survey of the U.S. Department of Labor in 1972 yielded relevant information.[8] The employment of nurses by a firm may be taken as a rough indicator of in-plant clinic availability. In 1972 there were about 60 million nonfarm workers employed at about 5 million workplaces. Of these, 21 percent (12,139,500 workers) were at establishments where the services of 56,300 industrial nurses were available, 80 percent of whom were registered nurses (R.N.) and 20 percent of whom were licensed practical nurses (L.P.N).

The tendency of various types of industry to have nursing services, and accordingly some type of clinic, is reflected by the following tabulation:

Type of Industry	Percent of Workers	Percent of Industrial Nurses
Manufacturing	32.50	32.7
Wholesale and retail trade	26.92	14.2
Services	21.07	36.8
Finance, insurance, real estate	6.74	4.8
Transport and public utilities	6.73	9.2
Contract construction	6.04	2.3
All industries	100.00	100.0

Source: U.S. Dept. of Labor, Occupational Injuries and Illnesses by Industry, 1972, Bulletin no. 1830 (Washington: Bureau of Labor Statistics, 1974), pp. 6–8.

Thus it is evident that manufacturing firms have the same share of the total number of industrial nurses as their proportion of the total workforce. For service industries and for transportation and public utilities, the provision of nursing service is more than might be expected from their share of the national nonagricultural labor force. In wholesale and retail trade; finance insurance and real estate; and in contract construction, the availability of nursing service is less than might be expected. This may be quite appropriate in wholesale and retail trade, where working conditions are not very hazardous; in contract construction, however, working hazards are great, so that the undersupply of nursing services is cause for concern.

The characteristics of the various types of clinics in American industrial firms involve many features beyond their nursing personnel. Many establishments without in-plant nursing service have arrangements for emergency medical care with physicians who are on call and not located regularly at the industrial workplace. Some facilities for ambulatory care of industrial workers, moreover, are sponsored by labor unions and are quite deliberately separate from any particular plant. These matters will be explored in Chapter 7.

PRIVATE MEDICAL GROUP PRACTICES

An increasingly important type of OAHS in America has long been sponsored by private physicians themselves. Many doctors may work together in coordinated teams under the sponsorship of hospitals, public health agencies, industries, and other bodies, but in this category we are referring to groups of physicians who join together on their own initiative to provide ambulatory care. The most widely accepted definition of this pattern is that offered by the American Medical Association (AMA): three or more physicians practicing together in a formally organized arrangement and sharing their income according to some specified plan.

The historic development of private medical group practice, which will be reviewed in Chapter 8, has been closely related to trends in the specialization of medicine and the need for coordination among the diverse specialties. In spite of this original motivation, during the last two or three decades an increasing share of private group practice has involved physicians of a single specialty. Thus, tabulations of group practice now customarily distinguish "multispecialty" and "single specialty" groups. In 1969 about half of the group practices in the United States were of the single specialty groups; however, these included about one-third of the group practice physicians, while two-thirds were in multispecialty groups.[9]

In 1975, there were reported to be 8,461 group practices in the United States, containing 66,712 physicians.[10] This constitutes 23.7 percent of all active physicians (excluding those in federal government employment, as well as all interns or residents in training), in the country. If we consider only doctors in office-based medical practice (numbering 218,527 in 1975), the share in group practice comes to 30.5 percent. Since this proportion has been steadily rising, one may safely state that, as of 1980, about one-third of American physicians engaged in clinical practice outside a hospital setting were working in groups. From the viewpoint of both medical manpower and patients served, group practice clinics may well constitute the most significant pattern of OAHS in the country. The group medical practice clinic constitutes, in a sense, the ambulatory care equivalent of the systematic organization of personnel and equipment applied for centuries in hospitals for the care of inpatients. Legal status and organizational arrangements vary greatly among group practices; these and other attributes will be discussed in Chapter 8.

SPECIALLY-SPONSORED CLINICS

Beyond the five main types of clinics reviewed above, there are large numbers of clinics of other sponsorships that have been developed out of special historical circumstances. The populations reached by these are not very large, but for those served the clinics may have great importance. Their very heterogeneity is a central characteristic of the U.S. health care system. The sponsorships may be governmental or private.

One category of these clinics is sponsored by agencies of the federal government for selected beneficiaries. In virtually all nations there is a special medical care system for military personnel, and in the United States such programs operate for each of the main military branches—the Army, the Navy, the Air Force, and the Marine Corps. Within these programs, clinics serve eligible persons in time of war or peace. Family dependents may also be served, if they live near the military post.

Military veterans are another important population for which the federal government makes special health care provisions. As of 1970, 28 million American veterans were entitled to services, under specified conditions, at a network of hospitals and clinics throughout the nation. Perhaps because the United States is one of the few industrialized nations without a general national health insurance system, the Veterans Administration (VA) provides veterans a great deal of care for conditions not necessarily connected with military duty. In fact, the lion's share of VA medical services relates to physical or mental illness unconnected to the veteran's period of military service.

Other special beneficiaries for whom the federal government operates clinics, hospitals, and related facilities are American Indians and merchant seamen. Both of these programs have deep historical roots. The services to more than 800,000 Indians, living on or near reservations, grew out of the provision of treaties concluded with various tribes in the 19th century. Services for thousands of merchant seamen originated with legislation in 1798 that set up a network of marine hospitals at the young nation's major ports. This program evolved into the U.S. Public Health Service, which currently administers the services for both seamen and Indians.

Of great interest in recent years has been a variety of freestanding health centers for general ambulatory health care financed by the federal government, through grants, but sponsored and operated by various local organizations, some public but most being voluntary. These started in the early 1960s, with the launching of a national "war on poverty," spearheaded by a new federal agency: the Office of Economic Opportunity (OEO). Among many other activities, the OEO launched nearly 100 neighborhood health centers in "pockets of poverty" around the nation.[11] The same concept was soon implemented also by the U.S. Public Health Service, through several of its divisions. The concept of general treatment and preventive services for the poor, at facilities close to where they lived, aroused widespread interest; every year or two Congress appropriated special funds for support of these units under some new theme: "community health centers," "family health centers," "rural health initiative," "migrant health clinics," and so on. The administrative situation became very complicated, since many facilities acquired funds from several sources. Some coordination was achieved by eventually channeling most of the funding through the Bureau of Community Health Services.[12] By 1979, close to 1,000 of these general ambulatory care centers were being supported from diverse legislative sources throughout the country.

Still another category of specially sponsored clinics is the type operated by agencies of state and local government other than the general public health and the school authorities. These include clinics for mental problems under special mental health agencies; important among these has been a growing network of community mental health centers, that may in fact be sponsored by many types of agencies.[13] There are separate and specialized clinics for coping with problems of alcoholism and drug abuse, and still other state and local agencies may be concerned with rehabilitation of the handicapped on an ambulatory basis.[14] The clinics attached to hundreds of state prisons and local jails must also not be overlooked, in spite of the many deficiencies of these units.

Finally there is a vast number of voluntary health agencies in the United States, some national with local chapters, others entirely local. The great majority of these are focused on specific diseases such as cancer, heart disease, or cerebral palsy, and most of the funds they raise through campaigns go to support medical research and professional education.[15] Several voluntary agencies, nevertheless, operate clinics, such as those for crippled children. A relatively recent innovation in voluntary health activity has been the "free clinic" started usually by young people with an antiestablishment ideology. These clinics, which tackle a broad scope of health problems, depend a great deal on the volunteer services of physicians and others, and are unstructured in their mode of operation.[16] Finally, general social organizations, such as churches or business clubs, sponsor clinics for defined conditions.

CLINICS OF HEALTH MAINTENANCE ORGANIZATIONS

One type of clinic requires separate analysis in the current U.S. health care scene, not because of a unique form of sponsorship, but because of a significant relationship to a special form of financing, that is, insurance from a defined population. For many years, this clinic pattern was known as "prepaid group practice," but in the early 1970s it came to be known as the "health maintenance organization," or HMO.

HMOs may be sponsored by many different types of entities: groups of physicians, hospitals, consumer associations, industries, insurance companies, and others. Moreover, not all HMOs utilize clinics, although most of them do.[17] Because of their special form of combination of insurance for comprehensive health benefits and their pattern of health care delivery, HMOs usually provide health care for their members at lower costs than those that prevail in the conventional medical market. Largely for this reason, HMOs have been stimulated by federal government subsidies since legislation enacted in 1973.[18] As a result, in the late 1970s, the number of HMOs in the nation grew rather rapidly, and their enrollment expanded. By mid-1979 there were 215 HMOs or HMO-type organizations in the United States, with more than eight million members, the great majority of whom are of the clinic type. The detailed characteristics and trends of HMOs will be analyzed in Chapter 12, along with evaluation of the quality of health care they render in the light of their manifest economies. Since the rising expenditures in the U.S. health sector have become a major social and political issue in recent years, HMOs and their clinics have come to occupy a special place in national debates about the country's health care system.

CLINICS ACCORDING TO PURPOSE

As noted earlier, the universe of clinics in the United States, under diverse forms of sponsorship, may also be analyzed along other dimensions. To persons concerned about the welfare of the poor, for example, the salient task would be to learn about all clinics serving the poor, regardless of their sponsorship. Similarly, advocates of improved mental health are naturally concerned about the whole array of psychiatric and related clinics under diverse types of public and private agencies and programs.

As an illustration of the feasibility of analyzing clinics in these ways, Chapter 11 offers a few selected examples of clinics according to dimensions other than their sponsorship. Three major *purposes* are considered: (a) to serve the needs of certain types of persons, (b) to tackle certain types of diseases in any person, and (c) to provide for any person with any disorder requiring certain types of technical services. A few words may be said about each of these three approaches.

Clinics for Certain Types of Persons

The oldest type of clinic, as shown in Chapter 2, was developed to serve the needs of certain types of people, namely the poor. Levels of poverty, of course, may be variously defined, but in the health sector poverty most commonly refers to an individual's inability to afford to secure needed health service in the private medical market.

In recognition of the social costs of untreated disease or the failure to avert preventable disease, clinics under many types of sponsorship have been organized mainly for rendering service to *the poor*. The social objective of charitable care of the poor was the major impetus to their origin; although inpatient care in hospitals has long ago evolved away from this limiting objective, it still applies in large part to many hospital outpatient services. Eligibility to use many other types of clinics may also formally or informally be limited to the poor, particularly when these facilities are operated or financed by government agencies. On the other hand, some clinics, such as private group practices or clinics linked to HMOs, may serve patients of all income levels, including the poor, because many public and charitable programs deliberately intend to finance care in "mainstream" health facilities. Since poverty has long been recognized as a major social problem with facets in many sectors (health, employment, housing, education, etc.), arrangements for ambulatory care of the poor constitute a special challenge in the health care system of all modern nations.[19]

The child is another type of person for whom specially organized programs, including clinics, have long been offered. Assigning high priority to child health care satisfies various social objectives, humanitarian as well as pragmatic.[20] As a result, there are many clinics under diverse sponsorships specifically for children. Among the clinics operated by health departments, those for the health promotion of children are very prominent. In schools, of course, the personal health care programs are solely concerned with the health of the children. In many clinics with broader objectives, however, children may also be served. They constitute a substantial share of the patients treated, for example, in hospital emergency departments. Even in clinics at military posts, the dependent children of uniformed personnel are often served.

Still another type of person for whom special clinics have been organized is the *country-dweller*. The many handicaps of rural life, with respect to health care, have long generated compensatory programs of rural health service.[21] As in the other programs above, rural clinics may be launched under special legislative authorization, like that for primary care centers under the recent federal "Rural Health Initiative" legislation, or they may simply be part of the program of health departments or school systems serving both rural and urban people. For certain reasons, to be explored in Chapter 8, group practice clinics have developed to a relatively greater degree in rural than in urban regions.

Clinics for the above three types of persons—the poor, children, and rural people—under the sponsorship of diverse organizations or agencies, are explored in Chapter 11. One could also analyze variously sponsored clinics that serve industrial workers, women, the aged, or even certain ethnic or racial populations. In each instance, the clinic may be oriented specifically toward such persons or it may serve them among others. For someone interested in the gerontology movement, for example, it would not be difficult to identify many OAHS programs that serve the aged.

Clinics for Certain Types of Health Problems

Much of the most dedicated social effort in the health sector is focused on the conquest of certain diseases or health problems. An inventory of the disease entities against which special programs have been launched by government or voluntary agencies would resemble the table of contents of a medical textbook, and the list grows longer every year. Most, if not all, of these programs include the operation of special clinics under diverse sponsorships. In Chapter 11, clinics for three such types of diseases or health problems have been chosen for illustrative purposes.

Mental illness encompasses a broad category of diseases, including scores of diagnoses, that has engendered the organization of special clinics under many types of auspices. Because of the mysterious character of many mental disorders, society has long shown different attitudes toward them than toward most somatic disease. Within the last century, however, the recognition of mental disturbance as sickness, rather than immorality, has led to a wholly different approach to treatment both in hospitals and in ambulatory care settings.[22]

Especially since about 1950, clinics have offered a variety of approaches to the ambulatory diagnosis and treatment of mental illness. One of the strongest movements has been the establishment of a federally supported program for blanketing the nation with community mental health centers (CMHC), which offer a broad range of ambulatory and inpatient services for the mentally ill. CMHCs now exceed 700 in the nation, and they are sponsored by local government agencies, hospitals, medical schools, voluntary health agencies, and other entities.[23] In addition, there are hundreds of freestanding psychiatric clinics of other types, also under diverse sponsorships, in addition to psychiatric sessions in general hospital OPDs, in university health services, and even in prison health programs. Still other specialized clinics are operated by both voluntary and governmental agencies to cope with the problems of alcoholism and drug abuse. Although patients with these addictions may be served in general psychiatric clinics, more often they are treated in clinics focused on these specific disorders.

Another grouping of disorders that has summoned special social action may be designated as *crippling conditions*. In a sense, almost any chronic disease might be described as crippling, but the private and public agencies that sponsor special clinics for crippled children or adults usually employ the term in a more restricted sense, applying to disorders of the limbs. Following World War I and World War II, when many disabled soldiers returned home and received care from the VA, a serious national consciousness arose about the great numbers of disabled civilians. From this there evolved the movement for rehabilitation of the handicapped, which led to the organization of many facilities for outpatient or ambulatory rehabilitative services.[24] Rehabilitation facilities are sponsored by government and voluntary agencies, hospitals, and universities. The same applies to clinics for crippled children, which have been subsidized by special federal grants under the Social Security Act of 1935.

Family planning illustrates another health problem that has been the subject of attention of special clinics under many sponsorships. Because of worldwide recognition of problems associated with population growth, especially among the poor—even in affluent nations like the United States—agencies of several types have begun to operate family planning (FP) clinics. Special subsidies for FP programs have been awarded by the U.S. government since 1967, enabling scores of organizations to operate FP clinics. The National Center for Health Statistics conducts periodic surveys to keep Congress and the whole nation informed. The survey in 1975 identified nearly 5,000 FP clinic sites, where contraceptive services were offered by a wide variety of agencies in local and state governments and in the private sector.[25]

There is hardly a disease category for which one would not find specialized clinics throughout the United States under more than one type of sponsorship. Venereal disease (VD) clinics, for example, are sponsored predominantly by public health agencies; in addition, however, there are VD clinics in the military medical services, in many hospital outpatient departments, in community health centers, and under voluntary agency auspices (the branches of the once-large American Social Health Association, founded in 1912).

Tuberculosis clinics are also predominantly under health department sponsorship, but some are conducted in hospitals, while others are operated by the American Lung Association (successor to the National Tuberculosis Association). Likewise, cancer detection clinics have been operated by the American Cancer Society, as well as by numerous public health agencies and hospitals. The American Diabetes Association provides clinic services in its field, as do hundreds of large hospitals. For a rare disease, such as hemophilia, the National Hemophilia Foundation is probably the major sponsoring agency, outside of a few large teaching hospitals. Cerebral palsy, epilepsy, deafness and speech disorders are other disease categories for which clinics are conducted under multiple sponsorships. Clinics for treating dental disease are operated by several public and voluntary agencies.

Illustrative of the American tendency to organize various programs, including clinics, focused on special disease categories, were the findings of a survey in Los Angeles County conducted in 1972. At that time, organized programs of ambulatory care for 47 distinct disease categories were identified in Los Angeles County alone.[26] To give an idea of the extent of these health problems or disease entities, concerning which diverse agencies operated clinics, those listed under just three letters of the alphabet (A, M, and S) were:

Abortion	Malnutrition	Sexual problems
Adjustment problems	Mental retardation	Sickle cell anemia
Aphasia	Multiple sclerosis	Sterility
Arthritis	Muscular dystrophy	Stroke
Asthma	Myasthenia gravis	Suicide
Autism		

One must realize, furthermore, that in addition to the specialized clinics for each of these diagnostic categories, most of these conditions—e.g., arthritis, multiple sclerosis, sterility, etc.—also may be treated in general clinics of hospitals, group practices, community health centers, and so on.

Clinics Providing Certain Types of Technical Services

Still another dimension along which clinics may be categorized and studied is according to certain technical types of health services that they provide— usually for all or many types of persons and for many categories of disease. Thus, clinics might be classified by their provision of surgical services, of health care employing drugs, of services requiring nursing skills, and so on, but there would be little practical value in preparing such a list. Regarding certain technical modalities, however, there are social reasons for identifying the relevant clinics, and a few examples of these are explored in Chapter 11.

The part played by clinics in providing *emergency medical care* is crucial. For many types of trauma or disease, the provision of skillful services rapidly and efficiently can make the difference between life and death. In addition to clinics, communications and ambulance transport are important. It is easy to understand, therefore, why comprehensive systems on emergency medical care have been mobilized by social efforts throughout the United States and in most industrialized countries.[27]

Emergency clinics in hospitals are regrettably used for many purposes beyond the treatment of conditions requiring urgent attention, but this is due to problems in the nation as a whole. With inadequate resources for general primary care in most communities, patients turn to the hospital OPD even for simple ailments. Many other clinics such as industrial health units and school clinics may also provide emergency services just because of their physical convenience. Likewise, community health centers may provide much emergency care, particularly because rates of trauma are especially high in poverty areas where most of them are located. Some private group practices are under contract to staff the emergency sections of one or more hospitals or to provide emergency care for nearby industrial firms.

Another special type of service organized for patients outside of hospitals is given in *home care programs*. Although these are not clinics in the usual sense, they ordinarily require the coordination of personnel with diverse skills and the sponsorship of some agency. As the extent of chronic disease has risen in the U.S. population, the value of systematic health care outside institutions and in the patient's home, if appropriate, has become increasingly appreciated.[28] In their comprehensive form, organized home care programs were sponsored initially by hospitals, to free beds for acute care, but they are now sponsored mainly by local health departments, voluntary visiting nurse associations, and even agencies (both nonprofit and proprietary) devoted entirely to this type of service. Provisions of the Medicare law of 1965 gave a strong boost to these programs through financial support of services from "home health agencies," illustrating clearly the interdependence of financing and delivery of health services.

Other organized out-of-hospital programs serving many types of persons and diseases, with respect to special technical services, may simply be mentioned: independent clinical laboratories, dental clinics, and "surgicenters." Holistic health centers should probably also fit under this rubric. As the complexities of modern health service increase, the merits of organization become more appreciated, and new clinics to provide special combinations of skills arise every year.

This completes our overview of the various types of organized ambulatory health services in contemporary America. It is evident that the clinic in the United States has many meanings. More careful probing of these diverse forms of clinic—their structures, functions, numbers, problems, and other features— in subsequent chapters will deepen our insights into the dynamics of the American health care system.

NOTES

1. Foucalt, Michel, *The Birth of the Clinic: An Archeology of Medical Perception*, translated from the French, (New York: Pantheon Books, 1973).

2. Etzioni, Amitai, *Modern Organizations* (Englewood Cliffs, N.J.: Prentice-Hall, 1964).

3. American Hospital Association, *Hospital Statistics—1978 Edition* (Chicago: American Hospital Association, 1978), p. vii.

4. Association of State and Territorial Health Officials, *Programs and Expenditures of State and Territorial Health Officers, Fiscal Year 1974* (Washington: 1975), p. 11.

5. Shonick, William, and Walter Price, "Organizational Milieus of Local Public Health Units: Analysis and Response to Questionnaire," *Public Health Reports* 93 (1978): 648–665.

6. Wolf, J. M. and H. C. Pritham, "Administrative Patterns of School Health Services," *Journal of the American Medical Association* 193 (1966): 195–199.

7. National Commission on the Financing of Post-Secondary Education, *Financing Post-Secondary Education in the United States* (Washington: Government Printing Office, 1973).

8. U.S. Department of Labor, *Occupational Injuries and Illnesses by Industry, 1972,* (Washington: Bureau of Labor Statistics, Bulletin 1830, 1974), pp. 6–8.

9. Todd, C. and M. E. McNamara, *Medical Groups in the U.S. 1969* (Chicago: American Medical Association, 1971).

10. U.S. National Center for Health Statistics, *Health—United States 1978* (Washington: Department of Health, Education, and Welfare, 1978), p. 343.

11. Zwick, Daniel I., "Some Accomplishments and Findings of Neighborhood Health Centers," *Milbank Memorial Fund Quarterly* 50 (1972): 387–420.

12. Bureau of Community Health Services U.S. Public Health Service "Grants and Contracts, Program Support and Position History Table," Washington, processed report, 1977.

13. U.S. National Center for Health Statistics, *Health Resources Statistics: Health Manpower and Health Facilities, 1976–77* (Washington: 1979), p. 365.

14. Ibid., p. 439.

15. Hamlin, Robert H., *Voluntary Health and Welfare Agencies in the United States,* (New York: The Schoolmaster's Press, 1961), p. 1.

16. Williams, Frank G., *An Exploratory Descriptive Study of Free Medical Clinics* (Iowa City: University of Iowa, 1972).

17. Coleman, John R., and F. C. Kaminsky, *Ambulatory Care Systems: Vol. IV Designing Medical Services for Health Maintenance Organizations* (Lexington, Mass.: Lexington Books, 1977).

18. Strumpf, George B.; F. H. Seubold; and M. B. Arrill, "Health Maintenance Organizations, 1971–1977: Issues and Answers," *Journal of Community Health* 4 (1978): 33–54.

19. Lave, Judith R. and Samuel Leinhardt, "The Delivery of Ambulatory Care to the Poor: A Literature Review," *Management Science,* 19 (1972): P-78-P-99.

20. Silver, George A., *Child Health—America's Future* (Germantown, Md.: Aspen Systems Corp., 1978).

21. Ahearn, Mary C., *Health Care in Rural America* (Washington: U.S. Department of Agriculture, Information Bulletin No. 428, July 1979).

22. Joint Commission on Mental Illness and Health, *Action for Mental Health* (New York: Basic Books, 1961).

23. Rumer, Richard, "Community Mental Health Centers: Politics and Therapy," *Journal of Health Politics, Policy, and Law,* 2, no. 4 (Winter 1978): 531–559.

24. Kessler, Henry H., *Rehabilitation of the Physically Handicapped* (New York: Columbia University Press, 1947).

25. U.S. National Center for Health Statistics, *The National Inventory of Family Planning Services: 1975 Survey Results* (Washington: DHEW, Pub. No. (PHS) 78–1814, 1978).

26. Cauffman, Joy, *Inventory of Health Services (Los Angeles County)* (Los Angeles, Calif.: University of Southern California, 1972), pp. 38–43.

27. Hanlon, John J., "Emergency Medical Care as a Comprehensive System," *Health Services Reports* 88 (1973): 579–587.

28. Stewart, Jane, *Home Health Care* (St. Louis, Mo.: Mosby Co., 1979).

Chapter 4

Hospital Outpatient Departments

As noted in Chapter 2, freestanding dispensaries for ambulatory treatment of the sick poor were developed centuries before hospitals provided services for outpatients as well as inpatients. Being in large part custodial shelters for the seriously sick who were destitute and homeless, it did not seem appropriate in the beginning to offer services to those who did not need shelter with food and bed care. Only after the separately sponsored and operated dispensaries had demonstrated the value of the idea did hospitals recognize the importance of departments for outpatients, particularly when it became evident that such early attention might avert the need for bed care later.

HISTORICAL BACKGROUND

Aside from the early concept of the hospital's role, there were other reasons for the relatively late development of hospital outpatient departments (OPD) in the late nineteenth century. One must recall that ambulatory care of the poor, in contrast to inpatient care, was the traditional responsibility of the individual doctor or apothecary; the doctor's sliding scale of fees would enable him to treat the poor at very low or no charges, essentially at the expense of the practitioner's affluent patients. It was not only the demonstrated popularity of the independent dispensaries that led hospitals to broaden their role to include outpatient care. It was also the demands of medical education, which was closely linked to large hospitals. Thus, OPD clinics could enable the faculty, who were also the hospital physicians, to show students examples of disease at an earlier stage, before hospitalization had become necessary.[1]

Another factor retarding the organization of OPDs, at least in those hospitals not linked to a medical school, was the active opposition of their medical staffs. In American hospitals, more so than in Europe, these staffs were composed of physicians in private medical practice; the hospital OPD, therefore, was regarded as competitive. Medical journals in the late nineteenth and early twentieth centuries had frequent articles about OPD "abuse" by patients who could afford to pay for private care.[2] Thus, a major function of medical social workers in American hospitals was doing "means tests" on patients, to make certain that they were poor enough to qualify for charitable service.[3]

After 1910, when the population rose rapidly as the result of massive immigration from Europe and the number of medical school graduates was reduced (following the Flexner Report), the situation changed. By 1914, there were an estimated 250 OPDs attached to hospitals in the United States; in 1926, there were about 1,790 OPDs.[4] The American Medical Association (AMA) estimated in 1922 that almost 8 million (out of a national population of about 107 million) persons were being served by hospital clinics. In a 1919 study in Chicago, it was reported that, from a sample of families that excluded any who had applied for "general charity," 18 percent had received some form of hospital clinic service in the past year.

As we will see in this chapter, the number, scope, and complexity of hospital OPDs have expanded steadily since the 1920s. In the depression years of the 1930s, the growth was understandably rapid. Although programs of voluntary health insurance to support private medical and hospital care have grown since the 1930s, their benefits have been largely confined to inpatient hospital and medical service. As a result, the costs of ambulatory care have remained predominantly a personal responsibility, and accordingly increasing numbers of low- or even middle-income families have continued to seek care at hospital OPDs.

In spite of the obstructive or lukewarm attitude of most doctors to hospital OPDs in the early part of this century and to some extent up to the present, it has not been too difficult to staff these clinics with young physicians. For one thing, this was a way to build up a practice, i.e., getting known to clinic families, some of whose members would eventually see the doctor in his or her private office. For another, nonremunerated service in the hospital OPD was a price the young physician would pay to earn admitting privileges to a hospital for private patients. Both of these factors still facilitate the staffing of hospital OPDs. In addition, they offer an opportunity for the young doctor to learn a great deal from diagnosis and treatment of the ambulatory sick.

Today, therefore, the hospital OPD, a much more complex system than in 1910, is probably the most accessible setting for delivery of organized ambulatory health services (OAHS) in the United States. The nearly 264 million patient visits made to American OPDs in 1977 is the largest volume of OAHS encounters in any clinic setting, with the exception of private group practices.[5] In this chapter, we will examine the structure and function of hospital OPDs, the trends in use of various types of OPD services, the persistent problems they face, and various innovative approaches to the provision of ambulatory care by hospitals.

GENERAL OVERVIEW

The rapid expansion of hospital OPD services since 1900 is only one aspect of the growth of hospitals as a whole. With their enlarging numbers, both absolute and relative to population, there has occurred a steady expansion of hospital functions. From their early role as places of shelter for the impoverished sick and the destitute, they have evolved into facilities for the most advanced diagnosis and treatment of the seriously sick of all socioeconomic levels, for medical, nursing, and allied health personnel education, for biomedical research, for services to outpatients, and even to some extent for prevention and for home care of patients.[6] While not every hospital performs all these functions, the scope usually being wider in larger institutions, the overwhelming majority of the nation's 7,300 hospitals offer some ambulatory care, if only for emergency cases.

Trends

The rate of growth of hospital OPD utilization in America, particularly since the end of World War II, has been phenomenal, far greater than the growth rate of the U.S. population or even the trend of admissions of persons for inpatient care. Since 1965, the AHA has been collecting data on utilization of OPD services from all hospitals in the nation. The trends of both inpatient admissions and outpatient visits and their ratios from 1965 to 1977 are revealing; they have been as follows:[7]

Year	Inpatient Admissions (a)	Outpatient Visits (b)	Ratio b:a
1965	28,812,000	125,793,000	4.37
1967	29,361,000	148,229,000	5.05
1969	30,729,000	163,248,000	5.31
1971	32,664,000	199,725,000	6.11
1973	34,352,000	233,555,000	6.80
1975	36,157,000	254,844,000	7.05
1977	37,060,000	263,775,000	7.12

Source: American Hospital Association, *Hospital Statistics,* 1978 edition (Chicago: AHA, 1978), p. 12.

Thus, in spite of the steady increase in the number of inpatient admissions, much of which is associated with the benefits of voluntary insurance, as well as the publicly financed Medicare and Medicaid programs, the rise in utilization of OPD services has been greater. Roughly speaking, OPD utilization has risen at a rate of about 10–15 percent a year since 1965, and inpatient admissions have risen at about 5 percent a year, while the U.S. population has grown at a rate of about 1 percent a year. Thus, in spite of the great national concern about the rising rate of use of hospital beds and evidence of overutilization, the relative escalation of OPD services has been much greater.

The many reasons for this increasing use of OPD services will be explored later. The reasons, in fact, differ for the several types of outpatient services and also for the provision of any OPD service by various categories of hospitals. Before proceeding, therefore, we should take note of these different categories of OPD service as well as different types of hospitals and offer some definitions of them.

Types of OPD Services (Definitions)

The oldest type of hospital OPD service was that which evolved from the early freestanding dispensary, i.e., scheduled sessions for treating the sick who came at an appointed day and hour. In time, other types of services came to be rendered, so that it is now customary to classify OPD services into three types: (1) general, (2) emergency, and (3) referred. The U.S. Public Health Service has offered definitions of these as follows:

> General: Diagnostic or treatment services given to an outpatient, who has not been referred for such services by a private physician, for a condition of non-emergency nature.
>
> Emergency: Health services given for a condition which the patient (or his agent) considers urgently in need of care.
>
> Referred: Services to a patient referred by a private physician and expected to return to that physician for subsequent care.[8]

These definitions were published in 1964, and since then the differentiation among these types of services has become sharper, particularly in the ways that they are organized in hospitals. Many patients coming for emergency care, for example, are not in need of urgent attention, but they seek care in an emergency room because it is available on short notice at any hour of the day or night. General services, on the other hand, are typically offered at scheduled hours. Since hospitals report the volume of the several types of services mainly on the basis of the departments or sections of the institution providing them, we shall identify and define these types of OPD services somewhat differently.

General services will be considered the services of *organized clinics*. These are sessions scheduled at specific times of the week that are staffed by appropriate medical or surgical specialists. Patients come to them either on their own decision or on the recommendation of a physician, but in either case they come for definitive care without expecting to return to a referring physician. Their predominant characteristics, in practice, is their scheduled times, and their categorization by specific medical specialties.

Emergency services will be identified by the same term, *emergency services,* but with a modified definition. They will be considered to be services to any type of patient (i.e., with an urgent or nonurgent condition) rendered by a hospital's emergency personnel at any time of the day or night. It is the provision of these services at any hour and on short notice, as distinguished from services in a systematically scheduled time and place, that is their most significant characteristic. As we shall see, the physician providing these services is not necessarily qualified or specialized in treatment of the condition presented by the patient, but is expected to be capable of coping with a wide variety of diseases or traumas on very short notice, even if only to provide simple first aid.

Referred services will be designated the same way—*referred services*—and defined in the same manner as above. Their predominant characteristic is that they require special personnel or equipment found in the hospital (but seldom in the private doctor's office) that is needed for the diagnosis or treatment of a patient under the regular care of an outside physician. This physician may or may not be a member of the medical staff of the hospital. Referred services may be provided at one of the scheduled sessions of an organized clinic or at some other time.

These three types of OPD services may be given in the same quarters of the hospital or in different quarters. The personnel providing the service are ordinarily different, but at certain times of the day the same personnel may render services of two, or even three types.

As mentioned, several different types of *hospitals* provide these three categories of service. Hospitals may be classified according to the types of patients they receive or by the type of social entity that sponsors or owns them. With respect to the patients they serve, hospitals are customarily classified as: (1) general short-term, (2) general long-term, (3) psychiatric, (4) tuberculosis (TB), and (5) other special. Most numerous, both in number of facilities and aggregate number of beds, are general short-term hospitals, which serve the great majority of all hospital patients with a wide range of medical or surgical conditions, as well as maternity cases. These patients typically occupy beds for short periods (under 10 days) and the average length of stay is under 30 days. General long-term hospitals serve patients with a wide variety of chronic conditions. The average stay is over 30 days and, in certain cases, may be for months or years.

Although the average length of stay at psychiatric and tuberculosis hospitals is also typically long-term, it is the diagnostic category that distinguishes them from "general long-term" hospitals. In recent years, the duration of stay has been shortening in both of these types of hospitals. Moreover, with the great reduction in prevalence of TB, the numbers of sanatoria have been declining and may soon cease to be specially identified. Psychiatric patients are also being admitted more frequently to general hospitals, usually in designated wards or wings of the facility. Other special hospitals include institutions with a wide variety of purposes, such as treating disorders of the eye, orthopedic conditions, or leprosy, or for taking care of maternity cases or sick children.

With respect to sponsorship or ownership (sometimes designated as "type of control"), hospitals are customarily classified as: (1) governmental, (2) voluntary nonprofit, and (3) proprietary. Governmental hospitals, in turn, may be owned and operated by federal, state, or local (county or city) public authorities. Voluntary nonprofit hospitals are the most numerous type in the United States, both in facilities and in aggregate beds; they are sometimes further delineated as being under religious or nonsectarian sponsorship. Proprietary hospitals are institutions, typically of small bed capacity, owned by private individuals and operated for profit. They are the least numerous type in the United States, in terms of aggregate beds, although in certain localities (Los Angeles County, for example) they may be quite common.

Combining these two dimensions of classification, we derive a simple matrix, as follows:

	Type of Patient				
Sponsorship	General short-term	General long-term	Psychiatric	Tuberculosis	Other special
Federal government	1	2	3	4	5
State government	6	7	8	9	10
Local government	11	12	13	14	15
Voluntary nonprofit	16	17	18	19	20
Proprietary	21	22	23	24	25

Some hospitals in America are found in each of these 25 cells and, among these, outpatient departments may exist in a subgroup. The numbers of hospitals in the different cells vary greatly. In cell number 16, for example, (general short-term hospitals under voluntary nonprofit sponsorship) the number is very large. To simplify statistical presentations, the AHA usually aggregates the count of "short-term general" with that of "other special" (a relatively small number), so that the sum of cells 16 and 20 is identified as "nonprofit voluntary short-term general and other special" hospitals, and in 1977 there were 3,371 such institutions with 680,000 beds. This is nearly half the hospitals with nearly half the beds of the total in all 25 cells of the matrix.

Similarly, the greatest number of hospital beds limited to psychiatric patients are in facilities sponsored by state governments, hence, in cell number 8. State mental hospitals tend to have large capacities, so that the number of facilities is not very high, although the aggregate beds total several hundred thousands.

Proprietary hospitals are mainly for general short-term illness, so that the number of these facilities in cell 21 which in 1977 was 751, is larger than that in any of the other cells on this row (numbers 22, 23, 24, and 25).

Even these 25 categories are not sufficient to clarify the significant variations in types of hospitals, and correspondingly in their characteristics with respect to OPD services. Thus, in cell 11, for example, there are about 1,800 government-owned hospitals, but they fall into two very different subgroups. About 100 of them are relatively large public general hospitals in major cities and are devoted specifically to serving the poor; they tend to have large, complex, and active outpatient departments. The balance of some 1,700 hospitals are relatively small facilities predominantly in smaller towns or rural counties, owned and operated by local units of government, but serving all types of patient, rich and poor.[9]

For statistical reporting purposes, there is a tendency to aggregate the hospitals. Thus, the general short-term hospitals in cells 11, 16, and 21 are sometimes lumped together under the term "community hospitals." In certain contexts, only cells 16 and 21, or cell 16 alone, may be described as community hospitals. Also some references to "governmental" hospitals apply only to facilities of the federal government, and not to state and local facilities. One must be cautious about terminology in discussing hospital affairs, therefore, to avoid misunderstanding, and this applies to hospital OPD services as well.

Finally, it is noteworthy that outpatient hospital services as a whole are decidedly stronger in large cities than in small towns or rural districts. This should not be surprising from the history of the early dispensaries (Chapter 2), responding to the needs of immigrant populations which clustered in big city slums. Hospital OPDs, in a word, replaced the services previously offered by the dispensaries. Thus, in the nation's 50 largest cities, containing 20 percent of the nation's population, Piore and her colleagues found in 1969 that about 40 percent of all OPD services were being provided.[10]

Moreover, in these cities there is a certain equilibrium between OPD services provided in organized clinics and those provided in emergency units. Relating total OPD visits to urban populations, the highest rate in 1969 was 2,795 per 1,000 population in Oakland, California, and the lowest rate was 181 visits per 1,000 in Fort Worth, Texas. In Oakland, only 12 percent of the high volume of OPD services were in emergency units; the balance being organized clinic or referred services. In Fort Worth, at the other extreme, 70 percent of the relatively low volume of OPD care were emergency services.[10]

Types and Distribution of OPD Services

For perspective on hospital OPD services, we may consider some overall distributions of the three main types. The numbers and trends of the different categories of outpatient service, as well as their breakdowns by type of hospitals, show great variations.

In the approximately 7,100 U.S. hospitals (in AHA tabulations) in 1977, "organized clinics" were operated in 30.1 percent. Separately defined "emergency services" were provided in 79.1 percent of institutions. Considering only short-term general hospitals of any type of sponsorship, the corresponding proportions were 27.5 and 89.4 percent. A separate tabulation for the provision of referred outpatient services is not available, but it may be considered close to 100 percent; that is, nearly every hospital and certainly nearly every general hospital (short-term or long-term) performs certain diagnostic or treatment procedures for private patients sent by their doctors to the institution for ambulatory services only.

The trends of the three types of OPD services are significant in their changing proportions over time. For community hospitals (defined as short-term general institutions under any nonfederal sponsorship) data are available going back to 1954.[11] Between 1954 and 1977, the trends of OPD visits of the different types were as follows:

Type of OPD Visit	Number		Percent	
	1954	1977	1954	1977
Organized clinic	26,405,000	55,227,000	56.6	27.0
Emergency	9,419,000	72,956,000	20.2	35.7
Referred	10,851,000	76,055,000	23.2	37.2
All OPD visits	46,675,000	204,238,000	100.0	100.0

Source: American Hospital Association, *Hospital Statistics 1977: Annual Survey* (Chicago: AHA, 1978).

It is apparent from the above figures that the volume of all three types of OPD services (as measured in patient visits per year) has markedly increased over these years, but at different rates. For organized clinic visits, the number has doubled; for referred visits, it has increased exactly seven fold; and for emergency visits, it had increased by nearly eight times. The proportions have changed markedly as well. In 1954 organized clinic visits were 56.6 percent of the total, and emergency visits only 20.2 percent; by 1977 organized clinic visits (while still twice as many as in 1954) had declined to 27.0 percent of the total, and emergency visits had risen to 35.7 percent of the total. Referred visits increased in both number and percentage, constituting the largest share in 1977. Thus, the largest number of outpatients are those referred to the hospital for some service that was evidently not available elsewhere. If the same trends continue, however, emergency visits will eventually constitute the lion's share of all OPD visits.

The size of hospital has a marked effect on a hospital's tendency to offer outpatient services. For emergency services, in short-term general hospitals of all sponsorships, facilities were available as of 1977 in 70.9 percent of hospitals with under 25 beds, this proportion rising to 98.0 percent of such hospitals with 500 beds or more. For organized clinics, the gradient is sharper; they were provided in only 23.8 percent of short-term general hospitals with fewer than 25 beds in 1977, rising steadily to 81.3 percent of such hospitals with over 500 beds.

Correspondingly, the volume of OPD services in relation to the number of inpatient admissions varies with hospital size, but the relationships differ for different categories of service. If we relate *emergency visits* to inpatient admissions in hospitals of differing bed-size the following relationships are found as of 1977:

Hospital Size (beds)	Admissions (A)	Emergency Visits (E)	Ratio E:A
25–49	1,505,426	3,217,850	2.14
200–299	6,759,854	15,218,601	2.25
500 and over	8,163,975	15,244,857	1.87

Source: AHA, *Hospital Statistics 1977* (Chicago: AHA, 1978).

In a word, the ratio of emergency visits to inpatient admissions is roughly the same, around 2:1, in hospitals of different sizes.

If we examine the ratio of *organized clinic visits* to admissions, however, for the same year, the findings are quite different:

Hospital Size (beds)	Admissions (A)	Organized Clinic Visits (C)	Ratio C:A
25–49	1,505,426	7,679,699	5.1
200–299	6,759,854	13,667,940	2.0
500 and over	8,163,975	38,250,939	4.7

Source: AHA, *Hospital Statistics 1977* (Chicago: AHA, 1978).

In other words, there is a U-shaped curve reflecting greater activity in providing organized clinic services in the smallest and the largest hospitals, with the least activity in hospitals of middle size.

With respect to hospital sponsorship, the relationships of OPD activity are most clearly seen by focusing on short-term general hospitals of varying sponsorship types. For *emergency visits* in such nonfederal hospitals of three sponsorships, as of 1977, we find:

Hospital Sponsorship	Admissions (A)	Emergency Visits (E)	Ratio E:A
State & local government	7,220,000	19,042,901	2.6
Voluntary nonprofit	24,284,417	49,660,412	2.0
Proprietary	2,848,799	4,252,506	1.5

Source: AHA, *Hospital Statistics 1977* (Chicago: AHA, 1978).

Thus, the emergency service ratios show a definite but small gradient in relation to what one might call the social character of a hospital's sponsorship, being strongest in governmental facilities, next strongest in voluntary nonprofit ones, and weakest in proprietary units.

With respect to *organized clinic visits,* the corresponding figures for 1977 were as follows:

Hospital Sponsorship	Admissions (A)	Organized Clinic Visits (C)	Ratio C:A
State & local government	7,220,000	25,098,602	3.5
Voluntary nonprofit	24,284,417	28,886,202	1.2
Proprietary	2,848,799	1,242,399	0.4

Source: AHA, *Hospital Statistics 1977* (Chicago: AHA, 1978).

Clearly the gradient for organized clinic visits is much steeper in relation to a hospital's social character. Thus, comparing governmental with voluntary nonprofit hospitals, the ratio of organized clinic visits to admissions is three times greater in public institutions, but, compared with proprietary hospitals, the ratio is nearly nine times greater.

These quantitative data give a general picture of hospital OPD services of the different types, their trends over the years, and their variations by hospital size and sponsorship. Finally, a few more observations about overall trends are in order.

Growing Importance of OPD Services

The growing importance of the hospital in the overall provision of health services has been evident throughout the world and especially in the United States. As reflected in U.S. personal consumer expenditures, hospitalization cost 27 cents of each "medical care dollar" in 1960, and this share rose to 32 cents by 1975.[12] Considering total national expenditures, private and governmental, the hospital sector absorbed 31 cents of the medical care dollar in 1950, 33 cents in 1960, and nearly 40 cents in 1974.[13]

Many factors contribute to this trend, including advances in medical technology, the growing prevalence of serious chronic disease requiring hospital care associated with greater longevity of the population, the extent of insurance and general revenue support for hospitalization, the widening scope of hospital functions, and so on. In any event, a reaction to this heavy emphasis on inpatient hospital care has been setting in for several years. One important expression of this reaction has been to call for greater attention to systematic ambulatory services that would prevent serious illness or treat it promptly, thereby reducing the need for costly hospitalization.

Accordingly, hospitals themselves have put increasing emphasis on outpatient services. As noted earlier, the rate of growth of OPD services has exceeded that of hospital admissions for all three outpatient categories, though to varying extents. Likewise, the population has looked increasingly to hospitals for meeting primary care needs, in the face of the diminishing supply of private general medical practitioners. Of all clinically active physicians in the United States in 1973, those devoted to general practice constituted less than 15 percent, a decline from 83 percent in 1931.[14] Combined with this have been the generally escalating costs of medical care and relatively weak coverage for office and home visits of physicians under voluntary health insurance programs; only 59 percent of the population had such protection in 1974, and most of this involved some degree of personal cost-sharing by the patient.[15] Low-income patients, therefore, seek care at a hospital OPD, where they expect to pay little or nothing, even though significant charges are often made.

For obtaining care from a private physician, whether generalist or specialist, an appointment is ordinarily required; to obtain an appointment, the patient may have to wait for days or weeks, while the hospital OPD is regarded as a source of immediate attention. In addition, the hospital is regarded as the center of advanced medical technology, where patients have confidence that they will get whatever services are needed more rapidly and conveniently than in a private medical office. Finally, there is the widespread availability of rapid transportation in America so that a hospital can be reached easily, even though it may require a longer trip than going to a private doctor's office.

In response to these rising demands for ambulatory service, hospitals have enlarged their physical facilities for outpatient care. Financial assistance for this was provided by Amendments to the national Hospital Survey and Construction (Hill-Burton) Act in 1970.[16] Additional staffing for the outpatient department has been provided in a variety of ways, as discussed later. Many voluntary health insurance policies, limited initially to paying solely for inpatient care, have been broadened to cover the costs of hospital OPD services, particularly for cases of trauma. The resources of other federal programs, such as the Regional Medical Program for Heart Disease, Cancer and Stroke (RMP) in the

1960s and the National Health Planning and Resources Development Act in the 1970s, have been used to strengthen certain aspects of hospital OPD services.

There are other indications of the growing importance of hospital outpatient departments, to be discussed later, but we should now proceed to examine more closely the characteristics of OPD delivery for the three principal categories of these ambulatory services.

ORGANIZED OUTPATIENT CLINICS

The pattern of organization of scheduled clinics, in the 2,137 hospitals having them in 1977, reflects the growing specialization of medicine, a trend that is more pronounced in America than in other countries.[15] Various scheduled clinic sessions have generally become more finely specialized than the structure of hospital inpatient wards. While a small general hospital might divide its clinic sessions simply among the major specialties (internal medicine, surgery, obstetrics, and pediatrics) most hospitals with organized clinics are larger facilities where specialty sessions would be much more elaborately subdivided.

For example, a general hospital of 300 beds would have clinic sessions scheduled at certain times each week in such fields as: allergy, arthritis, cardiovascular disorders, chest diseases, dermatology, endocrinology, gynecology, maternity, orthopedics, pediatrics, tumors, venereal disease, and more, in addition to "general medicine" and "general surgery." The latter two fields would commonly hold sessions daily, and serve in part as entry points from which patients would be referred to other subspecialty clinics. The former might hold sessions only once or twice a week.

In very large hospitals, particularly those affiliated with medical schools, clinics may be even more specialized, such as for diabetes, headaches, cerebral palsy, psoriasis, and so on. Cutting across specialties, but responding to changing perceptions of health needs in the population, clinic sessions might also be scheduled in geriatrics and, most recently, in family medicine. The latter comprehensive type of clinic has been multiplying as a locale for training young doctors in the newly defined specialty of family practice.[17] Sometimes, to stress the nonspecialized or holistic approach of these clinics, they are physically separated from the other clinics and located in a small structure adjacent to the hospital.

As shown earlier, organized clinics are more frequently found in hospitals under the sponsorship of state and local governments, as well as in hospitals of larger size. In a national study of 51 large public hospitals oriented mainly to serve the poor, the average number of specialty clinics regularly scheduled was

58; one large hospital in New York City operated 127 different specialized clinics.[18]

Clinic Staffing

The patterns of staffing organized OPD clinics vary greatly with hospital sponsorship and size.[19] The most effective staffing with physicians is found in large hospitals that are under either governmental or voluntary nonprofit sponsorship and affiliated with medical schools. In these hospitals, there is most likely to be an adequate complement of house staff (doctors in training). Residencies approved by the AMA, however, were maintained in only 17 percent of all the nation's hospitals, as of 1977. The doctors in training who staff the organized clinics in these hospitals are theoretically supervised by the senior staff physicians, who often hold teaching positions in the medical school, although amidst the many demands on professional time the supervision may be slight.

In the hospitals with organized clinics but lacking house staff, the clinics are usually staffed, on some rotation basis, by practicing physicians on the active medical staff. These tend to be the younger doctors who are usually not paid but donate their services in order to earn the privilege of admitting private patients to hospital beds. As public funds have become available from Medicare, Medicaid, and other statutory programs to pay for clinic services to low-income patients, sessional stipends are sometimes paid to these physicians. Such payments have been found to improve the regularity of attendance by doctors, whose principal devotion is typically to their private practices.

Along with the clinic doctors, there are nurses, receptionists, clerks, and other personnel on the OPD staff. Often an experienced nurse serves as supervisor of the whole outpatient service and has the responsibility of assuring the attendance of physicians at the scheduled times or finding replacements. In large hospitals with active teaching programs, whether affiliated with medical schools or not, there may be a physician on salary, part-time or full-time, in charge of the scheduled clinics and other ambulatory services.[20]

To adapt to the frequent shortage of physicians in OPD clinics, increasing use is being made of specially trained "nurse practitioners." These extended-role nurses may screen out patients with minor ailments, even giving them primary care (under a physician's authorization); they may also monitor the progress of chronic disease patients with established diagnoses.[21] A seasoned nurse may sometimes perform a triage function in larger OPDs, referring the new patients to the appropriate specialty clinic or sending them directly to the emergency service.[22]

To staff some scheduled clinics in hospitals lacking a house staff, residents from other nearby hospitals may be borrowed and paid for the work. This pattern is more frequent for the staffing of emergency services, and will be discussed.

Patients Served

Organized OPD clinics, unlike the other two categories of hospital OPD services, are meant to be limited to the poor. While the historic orientation to the poor of hospital inpatient care has entirely changed, eligibility to use hospital clinics remains like that of its earliest forms—places for ambulatory treatment of those who cannot afford private care. Many private physicians on hospital staffs still regard scheduled clinics as competitive and discourage their organization or development.

To assure that patients are poor enough to qualify for care at a clinic, some sort of financial screening is ordinarily performed. Although "means testing" was the earliest function of social workers in hospitals, it is now typically done by clerical personnel. If a patient is found to be above the financial level for eligibility, he or she is referred to a private physician. Borderline patients may be allowed to use the clinic on a "part pay" basis.

Since 1966, many clinic patients have become beneficiaries of the Medicaid program, which pays for the OPD services. The hospital simply bills the public agency or its intermediary. The same applies to aged persons covered by Medicare, even though this social insurance program is not limited to the poor. For a few years after 1966 when both these programs were started, organized clinic attendance slowed down, since the patient could then seek care from private physicians at public agency expense. Then, as private physicians became busy with other patients and found the fees payable by Medicaid too low (as well as objecting to certain bureaucratic aspects of this program), clinic attendance resumed its previous rate of growth.[23]

A high proportion of clinic visits are by poor persons not eligible for support from any public program and yet not able to pay for care. These "medically indigent" cases must be financed from other sources, such as a local government welfare source (not Medicaid), voluntary philanthropy (such as the Community Chest), a hospital endowment, or by the earnings of the hospital from private patients. It is easy to understand why many hospitals look upon clinics as a burdensome financial drain and are not eager to invest in improving them.

This "charitable" aspect of organized clinics explains a good deal about their physical facilities and atmosphere. The dimly lit clinic waiting room, with long wooden benches where patients may wait for hours before seeing the doctor, is a sordid picture familiar to many.[24] These conditions are worst in the older public hospitals; in newer voluntary or public hospitals, or even in some old ones with energetic and sensitive leadership, clinic quarters may be designed or renovated to be spacious and attractive.[25] Patients may be encouraged to come by appointment so that waiting times are shorter and the entire atmosphere is brighter.

Administrative Aspects

The management of large OPD clinics presents many problems, especially in hospitals affiliated with medical schools. The physicians staffing each of the specialty clinics are members of clinical departments concerned predominantly with inpatients. They regard their particular specialty clinic simply as an appendage of the inpatient ward. Yet, if the overall outpatient department is to function efficiently, it requires coordination among the several specialties and unified leadership. Administrative conflicts are common between the general director of the clinics (if there is one) and the heads of the hospital's various specialty departments. Typical difficulties concern the assignment of house staff physicians and other personnel to clinic work, and use of the hospital's many ancillary services for clinic patients.[26]

The main rationale for locating organized clinics within hospitals, rather than in separate structures, is the availability at the hospital of so many resources in skilled staff and equipment. The hospital x-ray department, its laboratory, its equipment for electrocardiographs and many other procedures, can be available for service to clinic patients, although these are typically regarded as second in priority to inpatients. To avoid bottlenecks, sometimes a small laboratory or other resource may be maintained solely for clinic patients. Record systems present a special problem, and most hospitals maintain a separate set of records for clinic patients—even separate sets for patients attending each of the specialty clinics. This fragmentation of information obviously obstructs attainment of an integrated understanding of the patient as a whole.[27]

In spite of the several negative aspects of organized OPD clinics, their use continues to increase because they meet a manifest need. Clinics in hospitals linked to medical schools may offer excellent service on a technical level, even if it is deficient humanistically. It is noteworthy that while only 8 percent of nonfederal general hospitals had medical school links as of 1972, these 467 institutions provided 53.4 percent of the hospital clinic visits. Many patients, particularly the aged with chronic disorders, appreciate the wide range of diagnostic and treatment procedures that can done at one place. Even if, as beneficiaries of Medicare or Medicaid, these patients could seek care from a private doctor, they continue to use the hospital clinic with which they are familiar and satisfied. If they are treated with reasonable humaneness and dignity, chronically ill patients seldom object to serve as teaching cases for medical students.

EMERGENCY SERVICES

Hospital emergency services are quite different from organized clinics in structure and function. As noted earlier, they are offered in hospitals much more frequently than in clinics, but they are not subdivided among specialties. They are typically open for service at all hours of the day and night. They are staffed by emergency physicians and allied personnel, with a wide range of capabilities for quick management of trauma or disease. Their services are by no means limited to the poor; everyone coming to the emergency room (ER) is served to some extent.[28]

Levels of Service

The extraordinarily rapid increase in demands for immediate medical help in hospital OPDs has generated a variety of responses. In order to plan effectively for regional or metropolitan emergency systems, several schemes of categorization have been developed, so that everyone may know the level of service available at each hospital.

The AMA has proposed classifying emergency units into four types.[29] Starting with the least developed, they would be staffed as follows:

- Basic Emergency Service. A designated physician is "on call" from either inside or outside the hospital for 24 hours a day. A registered nurse or a licensed vocational nurse is also on call at all times, along with other allied personnel as may be necessary.

- General Emergency Service. A physician within the hospital is on call 24 hours a day, along with a registered nurse. Allied health personnel with special training in emergency lifesaving procedures are also available in the hospital at all times.

- Major Emergency Service. A physician with special training in emergency services is in the emergency quarters of the hospital at all times, along with specially trained registered nurses and allied personnel.

- Comprehensive Emergency Service. A full-time physician is responsible for direction of emergency services, and the emergency quarters are staffed by specially trained physicians, registered nurses, and other allied personnel at all times.

With each of these four levels of emergency service resources, there would be appropriate equipment, drugs, and supplies for rapid lifesaving procedures. Also, x-ray, laboratory, blood bank, operating room, and other services would be available within the hospital for use at all times. There are still further requirements specified in this AMA scheme of categorization; the essential concept is that each hospital's capability to respond to emergencies should be clearly indicated, with certain minimum standards for each level.

In 1973, the federal government enacted the Emergency Medical Services Systems Act that provides grants to communities and states to enable them to develop improved systems of emergency care.[30] As a condition for receiving such grants, a state system for planned and organized response to emergencies must be developed. Progress is occurring rapidly in this field. Even before the federal Act, some states, such as Illinois, had developed a statewide emergency system requiring minimum standards for every hospital. Three levels were specified, in accordance with the position of each hospital in the regional or statewide network.[31] In 1973, the AHA called for somewhat greater flexibility than was implied in the AMA categorization, and urged that the general population be advised only whether a hospital had: (a) "basic emergency services," or (b) more than these. It would be left to each hospital to refer the patient to another facility with the appropriate resources, if this were necessary.[32] Other aspects of emergency systems, such as communication arrangements, ambulance transportation, and so on, will be discussed later.

Staffing

Hospitals have responded to the increasing demands for emergency services with varied staffing arrangements. In earlier years, when only an occasional patient, usually an accident case, came for help, the OPD nurse would simply make contact with the nearest doctor on the medical staff. But as the demands have increased and requirements have become formalized in state regulations, a variety of strategies have been developed.

For the 80 percent of hospitals that lack house staff (interns or residents), one approach has been to organize a rotation for ER duty among members of the hospital's regular medical staff. If the staff is large enough, it may mean night-time or weekend duty only occasionally. If the "stand-by" arrangement (that is, one or more physician's being "on call" at all times) is adequate, a similar rotation may be arranged for the doctors to be reachable by telephone or by some other communication system. Sometimes the hospital may contract with a private medical group practice nearby to assure coverage for ER services at all times.[33]

As private physicians have become busier, however, or as high earnings have led many practitioners to shorten their workweeks, another arrangement for ER coverage has been growing. It has become commonplace for the many hospitals lacking their own house staffs to employ young doctors from the 20 percent of hospitals with them. Such supplemental work is done, of course, when the intern or resident is finished with his or her regular duties, principally in the evenings and on weekends. This "moonlighting" is generally lucrative for the young doctor, who is usually paid on an hourly basis. It is also stressful and tiring, however, and some large teaching hospitals prohibit their interns or residents from undertaking such supplementary work.

The distribution of these varying models for emergency program staffing is obviously changing rapidly, especially because of the steadily increasing demands. In 1970, the AHA included in its "Annual Survey of Hospitals" a question on the pattern of staffing emergency services. Since respondents could indicate one or more methods among seven listed, the resultant numbers are not mutually exclusive. Findings were as follows:[34]

Type of Emergency Medical Staffing	Percent of Hospitals
Rotation of attending medical staff	64.6
Salaried physicians, part-time	18.9
House staff (interns and residents)	15.7
Salaried physicians, full-time	15.4
Rotation of a panel of staff doctors	12.4
Contract with a group practice	11.6
Other arrangements	6.4

Source: AHA, Annual Survey of Hospitals for 1970 (Chicago: AHA, 1971). Analysis based on AHA computer tapes.

Since these percentages add to over 100 percent, it is evident that many hospitals use two or more methods, but the most common is clearly rotation of attending medical staff. It was evident from other data reported in this 1970 survey, that the rotational method was used predominantly by small hospitals, which serve much less than 65 percent of the total emergency cases. On the other hand, the various methods involving salaried physicians or house staff were used mainly in large urban hospitals, which serve much higher proportions of emergency cases.

Type of Patient

Since OPD emergency services are available to virtually anyone who comes to the hospital, the patient composition is very different from that of organized OPD clinics. Numerous studies have shown that patients seeking OPD emergency services display a relatively wide range of income groups. Low-income families do take recourse to ER services more frequently, but the distribution still includes persons of moderate or even high income. A study in 1967 on families coming for emergency care to a children's hospital, for example, found the greatest utilization by families with annual incomes of $3,000 to $6,000; at the time this was moderate income, and certainly well above the poverty level.[35] Some 6 percent of ER families earned more than $7,500 a year, which, at the time, was relatively high income

Nevertheless, low-income families use the OPD emergency services more frequently and repeatedly than higher income families. This is because they are less likely to have a well-established relationship with a private doctor. Under such circumstances, low-income families seek ER service even for minor nonurgent conditions. Higher income families tend to use it more selectively for truly urgent conditions.[36] Since the majority of families in any urban population are of low income, it is no surprise that a high proportion of patients seen in hospital emergency rooms have nonurgent conditions, this proportion being variously estimated as between 60 and 75 percent.

The proportion of urgent and nonurgent conditions served in emergency units varies also with the location of the hospital. A study of patients coming for emergency care to four institutions of the New York metropolitan area found very different mixes in relation to hospital location.[37] Thus, in a suburban hospital located near middle-class homes, only 32 percent of the cases were disorders appearing nonurgent; 68 percent were cases of trauma, reasonably requiring immediate attention. By contrast, in a city hospital near a slum area, only 8 percent of the cases were traumas, and nearly all the remaining 92 percent were medical conditions seldom requiring urgent attention. The reasons would seem to be obvious. Not only are low-income families less likely to have a regular private doctor, they are also less able to pay for private attention and regard the hospital as a place for free care, even though they may actually be charged for the service.

Another study in Boston showed the bewildering mixture of patterns for ambulatory care as a whole among families coming to an OPD emergency service.[38] In an urban hospital, as many as 14 percent of individuals coming to the ER unit regarded it as their most important and regular source of medical care, and another 15 percent regarded it as being midway in importance, along with a private doctor. Perhaps the best overall interpretation of emergency services users has been offered in a study reported in 1978 that showed that low-income inner city residents tend to use hospital ER services as a substitute for the family doctor, while others use them when their family doctor is not available.[39] Both groups use ER services for trauma, but since middle-income families use them less routinely, their trauma cases are a higher proportion of their total utilization. It is evident that the OPD emergency unit serves many purposes, for different types of persons and various types of conditions. The steadily rising rate of ER unit use makes clear, nevertheless, that in relation to other sources of medical care it is becoming a source of enlarging importance.

Administration and Financing

In the administrative structure of hospitals, the emergency services may be under separate direction or under an overall hospital department for ambulatory care. Physicians who work on ER services tend to press for separate administrative status on the ground that the problems involved are very different from those in organized clinics; they include, in effect, conditions relevant to a wide range of medical and surgical specialties. Even so, there has emerged a new specialty of emergency medicine, and some medical schools have established departments or divisions in this field.[40] An American College of Emergency Physicians has been formed and by 1979 it had more than 9,000 members.[41]

The emergency quarters are nearly always located on the ground floor of the hospital, easily accessible to an outdoor ramp where ambulances may come. Even though the majority of patients do not come by ambulance, this location simplifies the traffic of emergency cases at busy hours. Also, even though only a minority of all ER patients are urgent cases of trauma, cardiovascular crisis or the like, equipment for handling such conditions is usually on hand.

The financial support of emergency services is quite different from that for organized clinics. These are not regarded as charitable or welfare activities, but rather as services that must be reimbursed in some manner. For Medicare and Medicaid beneficiaries, of course, these agencies are billed for the services. Many self-supporting persons are covered by health insurance policies that pay for hospital emergency care, even when ambulatory services from private physicians are not included in the benefits. Some low-income patients, who are "medically indigent" and not protected by any third party agency, are simply asked to pay for the services at reduced rates.

Hospitals typically charge ER patients separately for the hospital services and the physician services. The latter collections are either simply passed along to the doctors or are used for paying them a flat hourly fee. Even though some ER patients may pay nothing, the emergency service (unlike the scheduled clinics) is ordinarily self-supporting and may even earn extra revenue for the hospital. A small proportion of emergency patients require hospitalization which may yield substantial earnings for the institution. One can appreciate why so many general hospitals that have not considered it necessary to respond to social needs for organized clinics for the poor, do not hesitate to establish emergency units.

REFERRED OPD SERVICES

The third component of hospital OPD activities consists of referred services, namely, services rendered to private patients referred by an outside physician (usually on the hospital's medical staff). Typically a specific diagnostic or therapeutic procedure is requested, and on completion a report is sent to the referring physician, who continues to serve the patient. The AHA definition states: "A referred outpatient is one who utilizes only the special diagnostic or therapeutic facilities and services of the hospital upon referral of a physician."[41] In responding to the AHA survey collecting these data, however, it is possible that some hospitals may have interpreted "referred" visits to include patients simply referred from one hospital specialized clinic to another, making these data less reliable than those on the other two types of OPD services.

With hospitals obviously becoming the centers for more and more types of advanced medical technology that cannot feasibly be maintained in most individual medical offices, it is easy to understand why referred services have increased so rapidly. Thus, the use of outpatient departments for referred services would be expected to be highest in those hospitals that are well-equipped and also have large numbers of private physicians on their staffs, namely voluntary nonprofit institutions. An analysis of 1968 data by Nora Piore and colleagues confirms this: of all referred OPD visits that year, 85.7 percent occurred in voluntary hospitals (containing about 50 percent of the nonfederal beds), compared with only 12.6 percent in state and local government hospitals and 1.7 percent in proprietary hospitals.[42] This high proportion of referred visits in voluntary hospitals may also be compared with the 67.1 percent of emergency visits and 54.1 percent of organized clinic visits made to those hospitals.

Similar dynamics are evident in the less urbanized areas, where physicians' offices would be less well equipped than in metropolitan centers, so that more technical assistance would be sought from hospitals. Thus, analysis of AHA survey data for 1972 shows that in nonmetropolitan area hospitals, referred OPD visits were 42.1 percent of the total, compared with 30.6 percent of total OPD visits in metropolitan hospitals.

The patients who receive OPD services on referral from private physicians are in general relatively affluent or adequately covered by health insurance. From the hospital's viewpoint, therefore, they are desirable as sources of revenue, and one can understand why the rate of increase of these services has been about as rapid as that of emergency services. This naturally motivates hospitals to purchase elaborate equipment, such as computerized tomography (CT) scanners, cobalt therapy equipment, or renal dialysis machines, that may serve both inpatients and outpatients. Rehabilitation therapy departments also have special relevance, since they can devote a great part of their time to ambulatory outpatients.

SOME PERSISTENT PROBLEMS

Even though hospitals in America have been providing outpatient services for more than a century, this part of their work remains beset with problems. The function of providing service to outside patients seems often to be accepted reluctantly, as though the institution were being distracted from its primary function of serving seriously sick inpatients. Particularly in a free enterprise setting, where private physicians are regarded as the normal source for ambulatory care, demands for outpatient services often tend to be resisted by both the hospital's private attending physicians and its administration.

It is small wonder, therefore, that the outpatient department is often regarded as the "stepchild" of hospital administration. Its space allotment is rarely adequate and its equipment is seldom as well-maintained as that on the inpatient wards. Hospital personnel tend to look upon assignment to the OPD as unattractive or even demeaning.

The historical tradition of dispensaries and hospital OPDs as places for the poor, while most inpatient beds have come to serve the affluent or at least the self-supporting, doubtless contributes to these attitudes. In American society, where class lines are allegedly disappearing, hospital organization keeps them sharply defined.[43] Both organized clinics and emergency services, with their steadily rising rates of use, serve to remind everyone of the inadequacies of our predominantly private system of physicians' care and its dependence on personal purchasing power.

It is this image of the hospital OPD that has caused the skewed distribution of outpatient services among hospitals of different sponsorship and function. In large urban public hospitals organized specifically to serve the poor, one can naturally expect a proportionately greater development of OPD services. In the 51 largest public general hospitals for the poor, as of 1969, there were 14.1 outpatient visits (of all types) per inpatient admission, compared with 4.7 such visits per admission in all nonfederal short-term general hospitals at that time.[44]

In the large organized clinics and the emergency services units, conditions are typically crowded and impersonal. Patients may wait hours to see the doctor, since all are usually asked to come at the opening hour and then are seen sequentially. To reach public hospitals with fully developed clinics and lenient means testing, the low-income patient may have to take a long trip by public transportation. When the doctor is finally seen, examinations are often perfunctory because of time pressures. With interns and residents intent on their own education, cases are often discussed aloud without sensitivity to the patient's feelings.[45]

In cities with large public general hospitals, another special problem has developed. Voluntary or proprietary hospitals in those cities are under less pressure than elsewhere to provide adequate OPD services, and they regard the large public hospital as the principal place for serving the poor. Therefore, when indigent patients come to a nonpublic hospital emergency unit, if they are not covered by Medicaid or Medicare, they are often simply sent to the public hospital—which may be some distance away. This "patient dumping" has led to tragedies, with critically sick patients dying before they reached the public OPD. A 1969 study of 33 counties, with both large public hospitals and several voluntary ones, demonstrated that the OPD caseload in the public facility, in terms of annual visits per 1,000 county population, was inversely related to the services rendered by the local voluntary hospitals.[46] In other words, the fewer OPD services that voluntary hospitals gave, the more public hospitals were required to give. Moreover, the overall volume of OPD services in the county depended on how great a share of the burden was carried by the nonpublic hospitals.

Much of the high quality performance in hospital inpatient care has been due to the pressure of external monitoring agencies, such as the Joint Commission on Accreditation of Hospitals (JCAH) and prior to 1952, by the American College of Surgeons. The JCAH standards on recordkeeping, infections, drug therapy, surgical procedures, and so on have done much to upgrade the quality of inpatient hospital care. It is noteworthy, however, that not until 1973 did the JCAH broaden its reviewing standards and processes to encompass hospital outpatient services.[47] This was surely in response to widespread concern about the mounting costs of inpatient care and recognition of the need for greater attention to ambulatory health services, if only because of their potential for prevention and avoidance of hospitalization.

It is encouraging that several hospitals have undertaken innovative programs to correct the widely recognized problems of hospital OPDs. Usually these efforts have been supported by demonstration grants or particularly generous third-party reimbursement. It has been in teaching hospitals with academic affiliations that most new approaches to serving OPD patients have been explored.

A review of innovative programs of ambulatory care in eight leading hospitals throughout the nation was published in 1974.[48] In all instances a new administrative unit to operate the OPD had been established. Likewise, in all cases, the pattern was shifted from a mixture of specialty services to a model of integrated ambulatory health care for patients. Appointment systems were set up, both for administrative efficiency and for protection of the patient's dignity. Thus, the traditional distinction between the handling of private patients (with appointments) and indigent patients (without appointments) was broken down: "one class care" became the rule. Triage systems were set up to channel the flow of patients in accordance with the severity or urgency of their conditions. New types of health personnel, working in teams with doctors and nurses, were usually involved. Evaluation of these eight programs by outside expert observers found them all to yield increased medical care productivity per hour; with this, the overall volume of ambulatory services provided also increased. The attitudes of both attending and house staff physicians toward OPD work noticeably improved. Although the eight hospitals in this study were by no means typical institutions, the experience clearly demonstrated that improvement is possible.

In response to the escalation of OPD utilization and importance, attention has come from many quarters. The AHA has called for "reshaping ambulatory care programs" in hospitals.[49] In New York City, a special program of state and local grants was launched around 1970 to strengthen the OPD services of this city's many voluntary hospitals. Known colloquially as the "ghetto medicine" program, supervision was by the New York City Health Department. The standards for grant entitlement included, for example, that organized hospital clinics be comprehensive and "family-oriented," that each hospital have a director of ambulatory care with specific qualifications, that an appointment system for patients be organized, that all necessary equipment be procured by the hospital, and so on.[50] In a word, the pressures of social need have stimulated many actions to improve the quality of organized ambulatory health services in hospitals.

OTHER HOSPITAL OUTREACH PROGRAMS

In several other ways, community health needs have stimulated special actions by American hospitals to extend care to ambulatory patients. Although far from universally adopted, these several innovative programs may be early indicators of major future hospital developments.

Organized Home Care

An important innovation launched soon after World War II was the organization by Montefiore Hospital in New York City of a systematic program for providing medical services to patients in their own homes.[51] Home care, of course, was as old as medicine, but the new feature was its management and supervision by a general hospital with all the technical resources at its command.[52] The idea started with transfer to their homes of terminal cancer patients to release hospital beds for more acute cases, and it was soon extended to other types of patients. The home patient, who was still regarded as a responsibility of the hospital, received services at home from dietitians, social workers, physical therapists, laboratory technicians, visiting nurses, hospital-based physicians, and other personnel. If necessary, readmission to a hospital bed was assured.

It soon became evident that this modality of care for chronic and convalescent patients was not only more economical, but also more appropriate medically, if home conditions were suitable.[53] To operate effectively, however, the hospital had to organize a special staff and a separate administrative unit to carry responsibility for the home service. Providing organized home care to the patients of private doctors sometimes presented problems in maintaining agreeable relationships.[54] Gradually the idea spread to hospitals throughout the country, though mainly to large institutions with public ward facilities. In 1977, home care programs were conducted in 456, or 7.0 percent of the nation's hospitals; this varied from only 1.8 percent of hospitals with 6-24 bed capacity to 18.2

percent of hospitals with 500 beds or more. A total of 2,572,000 home visits were provided in 1977 to patients under these programs.

The organized home care concept was subsequently adopted by other agencies, especially by visiting nurse associations (VNA), which had been providing home nursing services for decades. The VNA traditionally served patients from many hospitals and contracted with each to obtain the other ancillary services required.[55] When the Medicare law for health insurance of the aged was enacted in 1965, statutory benefits included the services of "home health agencies" as a lower cost replacement for long-term institutional care, and hundreds of additional community programs were launched under a variety of auspices.

Satellite Ambulatory Care Units

Since the mid-1960s, and the initiative of the U.S. Office of Economic Opportunity (as noted in Chapter 3), a variety of ambulatory care facilities for either comprehensive care or for services focused on special populations (mainly children and mothers) have been established in low-income areas.[56] The sponsorships of these free standing units are diverse, but some of them are sponsored and operated directly by hospitals. In its 1969 *Annual Survey of Hospitals,* the AHA asked if the hospital was "actively involved in providing patient care through a neighborhood health center or clinic." Out of 5,442 nonfederal short-term general hospitals, 429 or 7.9 percent answered affirmatively, with the rate rising in larger hospitals.[57] This involvement might have many meanings and often may simply refer to provision by the hospital of certain backup diagnostic or treatment services for the ambulatory unit.

For a portion of the separate organized ambulatory care facilities, a hospital has indeed been the sponsoring body. Even though special federal government grants have usually supported these initiatives, administrative management rests with the hospital. The operation by the Denver General Hospital (a public institution oriented to the poor) of several neighborhood health centers, staffed by hospital-based doctors and other personnel, provides one outstanding example.[58] In New York City, the operation of a separate major polyclinic by the Beth Israel Hospital is another illustration.[59] A 1974 survey of community hospitals (i.e., nonfederal short-term general or other special institutions, but not psychiatric or TB hospitals) by Columbia University focused on 913 such facilities with OPDs containing both organized clinics and emergency services. Ten percent of these hospitals reported that they were in the process of developing satellite clinics, and another 27 percent were discussing the idea.[60]

Some of the satellite units are devoted to general ambulatory care for low-income pregnant women, children, and youth; they are supported by special federal grants administered by the hospitals. The majority of these facilities, however, are under other sponsorships, and will be discussed later.

Hospital-based Group Practices

For many years, general hospitals have encouraged or taken responsibility for structures to house private medical offices adjacent to the hospital.[61] This physical proximity provides obvious advantages for both the hospital and the doctors, even though the two are administratively independent.

Much more integrated, however, are the situations in which a group medical practice is located within or closely adjacent to a hospital, and the two entities share x-ray, laboratory, or other hospital services in the management of ambulatory patients. There are several types of such relationships. In one, the medical group is closely affiliated with a hospital, to which all its patients requiring hospitalization are admitted. The hospital, however, is independent of the group clinic and also serves the patients of other doctors. This arrangement is illustrated by the hospitals linked to the Summit Medical Group in New Jersey, the Lahey Clinic in Massachusetts, the Hertzler Clinic in Kansas, or the Lovelace Clinic in New Mexico.[62]

In another type of relationship, the group practice is completely united with the hospital, and serves as its "closed" medical staff, excluding the patients of other doctors. This pattern is illustrated by several prestigious institutions, such as the Henry Ford Hospital in Detroit, Michigan, the Mary Imogene Bassett Hospital at Cooperstown, N.Y., and the Mary Hitchcock Memorial Hospital in Hanover, New Hampshire, all of which have been established through special philanthropic grants. The same sort of relationship may prevail in hospitals which are, in effect, the offshoots of a private group practice, such as the Robert Packer Hospital in Pennsylvania, staffed by the Guthrie Clinic; the Cleveland Clinic Hospital in Ohio, staffed by the Crile Clinic; or the Ochsner Foundation Hospital in New Orleans, Louisiana, staffed by the Ochsner Clinic.[63]

Thirdly, there has developed in the 1970s a tendency for hospitals to take the initiative in promoting the organization of new group practice clinics nearby.[64] This has often been done in response to the high demands being made on hospital OPDs; it has also been a strategy to attract new physicians and their patients to an area where inpatient occupancy has been declining. Whatever the objective may be, the movement is one more reflection of the broadening scope of hospital functions.

Physicians in private group practices ordinarily admit their patients to community hospitals in the same way as do physicians in solo practice. The special significance of the group practice clinics discussed here is their *affiliation* (often with legal contracts) with hospitals. The most profound form of such affiliation is seen in health insurance programs linked to group practice clinics and controlling their own hospitals, such as the Kaiser-Permanente Medical Care Program. These will be discussed in Chapter 12.

Mental Health Outpatient Units

With the extension of ambulatory services for the mentally ill, many hospitals have come to play a role in this field. The federal Community Mental Health Centers Act of 1963 provided grants to local organizations offering a minimum of five types of services, including both inpatient and outpatient care. These several types of care need not necessarily be at the same location, but in fact many of the mental health centers have been established by and in hospitals.[65] Out of the 541 approved mental health centers in the nation as of 1973, the majority had an association with hospitals and some were being hospital-sponsored.[66]

Beyond these comprehensive mental health programs, of course, many hospitals operate psychiatric clinics as part of their organized clinic programs. In 1977, there were 1,231 such hospitals, or 19.0 percent of the total. Among purely psychiatric hospitals of any nonfederal sponsorship it is not surprising that 43.9 percent should be operating such mental clinics, but it is noteworthy that among nonfederal short-term general hospitals, the proportion was 13.6 percent. Sometimes the responsibility for conducting these clinics is carried by a mental health agency, public or voluntary, that is legally independent of the hospital but uses its OPD quarters.

Outpatient Surgery

With the spiralling costs of hospitalization, ways are naturally being sought to economize. One approach has been the performance of certain surgical procedures on an outpatient basis. These may include such relatively simple operations as vasectomies, tonsillectomies, breast biopsies, or abortions.

Many such "surgicenters" are established by surgeons entirely independent of hospitals, while others are set up as part of the outpatient department.[67] When this is done, the patient typically obtains the necessary laboratory or other examinations on a previous day, comes in for the surgery the next morning, and returns home later in the day. The general development of surgicenters under diverse sponsorships will be discussed later.

Preventive Services

As hospitals have become more conscious of their general community role, some have made deliberate efforts to offer preventive services. These may include health education activities, such as diet lectures for patients with diabetes or general obesity, classes for expectant mothers, group discussions to help individuals break the habit of cigarette smoking, and so on. Specific services to counsel patients on genetic risks were reported to be offered by 4.4 percent of all hospitals in 1977. Of course, educational posters on nutrition, mental health, and so on, often adorn OPD walls, and health educational pamphlets are commonly distributed.

Systematic provision of screening tests for early detection of chronic diseases, especially cancer, are being offered in some hospital OPDs. The initiative for these programs may be taken by voluntary agencies, such as those concerned with cancer or heart disease, but the hospital provides the setting for conducting the examinations. The AHA has encouraged hospital OPDs to offer a "full spectrum of services, including health education and maintenance, prevention of disease, early diagnosis" as well as "treatment and rehabilitation."[68]

COMMENTARY

These are only some of the highlights of special outreach activities of hospitals for ambulatory patients. Hardly a development occurs in American health service that is not in some way expressed in the world of hospitals. The pendulum swing against specialization and toward family medicine is expressed by a mushrooming of generalized OPD clinics in this field.[69] Multiphasic screening is done in hospitals, as in other settings.[70] As U.S. legislation and practice on abortions have changed, these relatively simple surgical procedures are done increasingly in hospital OPDs; in 1974, they were performed in 7.5 percent of all hospital OPDs, and this rose to 9.3 percent by 1977. After the treatment of terminal kidney disease was made a Medicare benefit, renal dialysis became available in the OPDs of 685, or 10.5 percent of the nation's hospitals (as of 1977). As consumerism has gained strength in American health care, the hospitals have formulated a "Patient's Bill of Rights" for both inpatients and outpatients.[71]

The hospital OPD articulates with two other major movements in the American health scene. One is the nationwide drive to promote HMOs. This strategy for modifying the basic pattern of medical care financing and delivery in the nation is discussed in Chapter 12, but here we may note that in a 1975 census of HMOs in the nation, out of 178 identified, 31 (17 percent) were sponsored by hospitals, alone or in combination with other entities.[72]

The other national movement concerns legislation for statutory national health insurance (NHI). It is noteworthy that the AHA has sponsored a bill in Congress that would blanket the nation with "health care corporations," presumably sponsored by hospitals. Through these entities, into which any insured person could enroll, comprehensive ambulatory and inpatient services would be provided. In 1975, this NHI bill was known as the "National Health Care Services Reorganization and Financing Act.''[73] If it should be enacted in whole or in part, the organized ambulatory care functions of hospitals would expand enormously.

HOSPITAL OPD SERVICES IN LOS ANGELES COUNTY

To offer a microcosm of the diversity of hospital OPD services in one metropolitan county of about 7,300,000 population, data were gathered as of 1971. Of the 172 short-term general (nonfederal) hospitals then in Los Angeles County, the AHA survey received responses from 129, and these provided 7,005,000 outpatient visits that year.[74] Even with this underreporting, the rate of hospital OPD visits amounted to about 1.0 per person per year, or around 20 percent of the national average of 5.0 ambulatory care encounters per capita. The percentage distributions of these services in Los Angeles County, by type of OPD visit and hospital sponsorship, were as follows:

Type of OPD Visit
(in percent)

Hospital Sponsorship	Organized Clinics	Emergency	Referred
State & local government	24	23	2
Voluntary nonprofit	73	62	88
Proprietary	3	16	10
All types	100	100	100

Source: AHA, *Annual Survey of Hospitals for 1971,* unpublished data.

The very high proportion of all three types of OPD services occurring in voluntary nonprofit hospitals is exceptional. It is probably due to the inclusion, in this category, of the ambulatory services provided through the Kaiser Health Plan and other HMOs that have large local memberships. While exceptional, this suggests a trend that may develop elsewhere if the substantial development of HMOs occurring in Los Angeles County were to characterize the whole nation. Another artifact of the data is the nonreporting of emergency services by two of the four large Los Angeles County public general hospitals in 1971.

The Los Angeles County Comprehensive Health Planning Council also surveyed a sample of local hospital OPD services in 1974.[75] This survey included eight hospitals under county government sponsorship at the time, four being short-term and four being long-term. The demographic composition of the patients visiting the county government hospitals, in comparison with those visiting a sample of 20 nonpublic hospitals (16 voluntary and 4 proprietary), is of interest. By ethnic background, the distribution of these patient visits was as follows:

Ethnic Background	Total County Population	County Government Hospital Visits	Nonpublic Hospital Visits
Caucasian	67.1	34.2	40.4
Black	10.8	42.6	17.9
Hispanic	18.3	21.3	35.9
Other	3.8	1.9	5.8
All backgrounds	100.0	100.0	100.0

Source: Comprehensive Health Planning Council of Los Angeles, *1975 Health Systems Plan: Los Angeles County* (Los Angeles, Calif., 1974).

It is apparent that outpatient services are utilized at higher rates by minority ethnic groups, who are predominantly of lower income levels. Greater use of public hospitals, however, is made by Blacks and greater use of nonpublic hospitals is made by persons of Hispanic background.

With respect to sources of payment for OPD services, information was reported by the two types of hospitals in percentage distributions, as follows:

Source of Payment for OPD Services	County Government Hospitals	Nonpublic Hospitals
Self-pay (whole or part)	30.4	29.5
Medicaid	32.9	20.3
Voluntary insurance	14.6	21.9
Medicare	9.1	9.7
Other sources	0.5	5.1
No payment	12.5	13.5
All sources	100.0	100.0

Source: Comprehensive Health Planning Council of Los Angeles, *1975 Health Systems Plan: Los Angeles County* (Los Angeles, Calif.: 1974).

It is noteworthy that almost one-third of the visits in both types of hospitals are paid for, at least in part, by the patient, and that complete nonpayment applies to only about one-eighth of the visits. More than half the visits in both types of hospitals are financed by various social support programs.

Another noteworthy finding of this Los Angeles County study was the greater use of auxiliary personnel in county hospital OPDs. For each outpatient physician in such facilities, there were 2.3 auxiliary health workers, compared with 1.8 in the nonpublic OPDs. The patterns of physician remuneration were also substantially different in the two types of hospitals. In the government OPDs, 99 percent of the physicians were paid on a salary basis. In the voluntary facilities, only 49.3 percent of OPD physicians were paid salaries: 7.3 percent received fees for each patient served, and 43.4 percent gave services without payment.

Los Angeles County is particularly active with respect to the organization of emergency services in hospitals. For some years a County Coordinating Council on Emergency Medical Services has been functioning. This council categorizes hospital emergency resources somewhat differently from the nationally recommended classification, as follows:[76]

1. First Aid and Referral. A registered nurse available for minor care and referral.
2. Emergency Standby. A registered nurse present at all times and a physician on call within 15 minutes.
3. Basic 24-hour Service. A physician and nurse present in the emergency unit at all times, with ancillary x-ray and laboratory services on call.

On the basis of this classification, a 1973 survey of all hospitals in the county identified a total of 190 institutions that provided 2,429,225 emergency visits. The percentage distribution of these, by type of emergency service offered, was as follows:

Type of Emergency Service	Hospital Emergency Resources (percent)	Emergency Visits (percent)
First Aid and Referral	38	0.4
Emergency Standby	8	2.6
Basic 24-hour Service	54	97.0
All types	100.0	100.0

The skewed distribution in this table gives a rather impressive indication of rational behavior by the county population, and reflects the use of good judgment concerning where to seek emergency help. Thus, in the 54 percent of hospitals with well developed emergency care resources, 97 percent of the services are provided; in the 38 percent of facilities with minimal resources, only a fraction of 1 percent of the emergency services is provided.

A further analysis of the 97 percent of services (2,351,000 visits) provided in the best-developed emergency facilities gives further insights. These 54 percent of facilities in the county include 102 hospitals. Among these, 70 have contractual relationships with the Los Angeles County Department of Health Services, which guarantees payment for all "truly urgent" cases served under its "Emergency Aid Program" (EAP) initiated in 1947, so long as the above-stated standards are maintained. These 70 hospitals provide the lion's share of the services offered by the basic 24-hour service emergency units. County government hospitals, and the facilities of the Kaiser Health Insurance Plan also meet the required standards. Thus, within the basic 24-hour service emergency programs, the percentage distribution of patient visits was as follows:

Type of Facility	Number of Hospitals with Basic 24-hour Emergency Service	Patient Visits (percentage)
With EAP contract (nonpublic)	70	48.9
County government	4	22.6
Kaiser HMO hospitals	5	15.9
All other hospitals	23	12.6
Total	102	100.0

This distribution again suggests that people are, in the main, obtaining emergency services at OPD facilities that are well suited for the purpose. Nevertheless, this does not justify complacence, since many patients seen at the 23 "other hospitals" must doubtless be referred elsewhere for care. Furthermore, many of the patients seen at EAP hospitals are probably not truly urgent cases warranting reimbursement by the county government; these cases also may be sent elsewhere for service.

Other Hospitals Offering OPD Services in Los Angeles County

Throughout this chapter, principal attention has been directed to outpatient departments in nonfederal short-term general facilites, (or community hospitals). In Los Angeles County, as in most major metropolitan areas, there are several other types of hospital offering OPD services.

The federal Veterans Administration (VA) operates five hospitals in the county: two short-term general, two neuropsychiatric, and one long-term general. Each of these has an OPD, but data on their volume of services were available only for the three largest. In 1974, these reported 535,000 visits by military veterans. In addition, there is a freestanding VA outpatient clinic that antedates all of the five hospitals and this accommodates approximately 125,000 outpatient visits per year.

The U.S. Navy maintains a large hospital, the Navy Regional Medical Center, in Los Angeles County, reporting 256,500 visits in the 1974–75 fiscal year. As satellites to this large regional facility there are seven freestanding navy dispensaries, to which 217,800 visits were made in the same year. The U.S. Army, Air Force, and Public Health Service operate other small separate clinics that are backed up by the Navy Medical Center.

The OPDs of public hospitals operated by Los Angeles County for general short-term care have been included in the discussion above. In addition, there are four other county public hospitals providing long-term care for general chronic illness, as well as TB and mental disorders. In 1974 ambulatory care provided by these long-term institutions amounted to 1,157,000 visits over and above the 1,548,000 OPD visits in the short-term general county public hospitals.[75]

The two major state mental hospitals serving residents of Los Angeles County are in a neighboring county. These institutions do not provide outpatient mental health services. Ambulatory mental health services are furnished as part of the general outpatient organized clinics of other hospitals already discussed, not to mention the numerous separate public and private mental health clinics, which will be reviewed later.

Thus, analysis of hospital outpatient services in one county can shed further light on the many characteristics of clinics sponsored by hospitals throughout the United States.

NOTES

1. Davis, Michael M. and Andrew R. Warner, *Dispensaries—Their Management and Development* (New York: Macmillan Co., 1918), pp. 8–11.

2. Rosen, George, "The Impact of the Hospital on the Physician, the Patient and the Community," *Hospital Administration* 9 (1964): 15–33.

3. Cannon, I. M., *On the Social Frontiers of Medicine* (Cambridge, Mass.: Harvard University Press, 1952).

4. Moore, Harry H., *American Medicine and the People's Health* (New York: D. Appleton & Co., 1927), p. 30.

5. American Hospital Association, *Hospital Statistics: 1978 Edition* (Chicago: AHA, 1978), p. 12.

6. Owen, Joseph K., *Modern Concepts of Hospital Administration* (Philadelphia: W. B. Saunders, 1962).

7. American Hospital Association, *Hospital Statistics: 1978 Edition*, p. 4.

8. U.S. Public Health Service, *Facts and Trends in Hospital Out-patient Services* (Washington: Division of Hospital and Medical Facilities, June 1964), p. 3.

9. Hospital Research and Educational Trust, *The Future of the Public General Hospital: An Agenda for Transition* (Chicago: 1978).

10. Piore, Nora; D. Lewis; and J. Seliger, *A Statistical Profile of Hospital Outpatient Services in the United States: Present Scope and Potential Role* (New York: Association for the Aid of Crippled Children, 1971), pp. 177–178.

11. American Hospital Association, *Hospital Statistics 1972 (Annual Survey)* (Chicago: AHA, 1973). Also, same report for 1978.

12. Mueller, M. S. and R. M. Gibson, "National Health Expenditures, Fiscal Year 1975," *Social Security Bulletin,* February 1976, p. 7.

13. Cambridge Research Institute, *Trends Affecting the U.S. Health Care System* (Washington: Government Printing Office, 1976), p. 155.

14. Silver, George A., *A Spy in the House of Medicine* (Germantown, Md: Aspen Systems Corp., 1976), p. 93.

15. Mueller, M. S. and P. A. Piro, "Private Health Insurance in 1974," *Social Security Bulletin,* March 1976, pp. 3–18.

16. Roemer, M. I. and Ruth Roemer, *Health Manpower Policies under Five National Health Care Systems* (Washington: U.S. Health Resources Administration, 1978), pp. 3–4.

17. Center for Community Health Systems, *Community Hospitals and the Challenge of Primary Care* (New York: Columbia University, 1975), pp. 145–164.

18. UCLA School of Public Health, *Large Urban Public Hospitals* (Washington: National Technical Information Service (PB 264 167), 1976), p. 817.

19. Rosenfeld, Leonard S., *Ambulatory Care: Planning and Organization* (Washington: National Technical Information Service (PB 204 925), 1971).

20. American Hospital Association, *Outpatient Health Care* (Chicago: AHA, 1969).

21. Lewis, Charles E. et al., "Activities, Events, and Outcomes in Ambulatory Patient Care," *New England Journal of Medicine* 280 (1969): 645–649.

22. Weinerman, E. R., and H. R. Edwards, "'Triage' System Shows Promise in Management of Emergency Department Load," *Hospitals, JAHA,* November 16, 1964, p. 55.

23. Kisch, Arnold and F. Gartside, "Use of a County Hospital Outpatient Department by Medi-Cal Recipients," *Medical Care* 6 (1968): 517.

24. DeHartog, Jan, *The Hospital* (New York: Atheneum, 1964).

25. Shortridge, M. H., "Quality of Medical Care in an Outpatient Setting," *Medical Care* 12 (1974): 283–300.

26. Jonas, Steven, *Quality Control of Ambulatory Care—A Task for Health Departments* (New York: Springer Publishing Co., 1977), pp. 8–23.

27. Murnaghan, Jane (editor), "Record Format Study," in *Report of the Proceedings of the Conference on Ambulatory Medical Records* (Chicago: U.S. National Committee on Vital and Health Statistics, 1972).

28. Noble, John H. Jr., et al., *Emergency Medical Services: Behavioral and Planning Aspects* (New York: Behavioral Publications, 1973).

29. American Medical Association, *Categorization of Hospital Emergency Capabilities* (Chicago: AMA, 1971).

30. Public Law 93-154, Title XII, *Emergency Medical Services Systems,* 1973.

31. Boyd, David R. and W. A. Pizzano, "Illinois Medical Service System, Status Report II," *Illinois Medical Journal,* September 1973.

32. American Hospital Association, *Categorization of Hospital Emergency Services: Report of a Conference* (Chicago: AHA, 1973).

33. Krembs, G. A., et al., "Contracting with a Physicians' Group for Emergency Room Coverage," *Hospital Progress,* January 1970, pp. 51–53.

34. American Hospital Association, *Annual Survey of Hospitals for 1970.* Analysis made from computer data tapes furnished by the AHA.

35. Alpert, Joel J., et al., "The Types of Families that Use an Emergency Clinic," *Medical Care* 7 (1969): 55–61.

36. Lavenbar, Marvin A., et al., "Social Class and Medical Care: Indices of Non-urgency in Use of Emergency Services," *Medical Care* 6 (1968): 368–380.

37. Torrens, Paul R. and Donna G. Yedvab, "Variations Among Emergency Room Populations," *Medical Care* 8 (1970): 60–75.

38. Solon, Jerry A., and Ruth D. Rigg, "Patterns of Medical Care Among Users of Hospital Emergency Units," *Medical Care* 10 (1972): 60–72.

39. Davidson, Stephen M., "Understanding the Growth of Emergency Department Utilization," *Medical Care* 16 (1978): 122–132.

40. "Birth Pangs of a Specialty: Emergency Physicians," *Medical World News,* November 6, 1970, p. 20.

41. American College of Emergency Physicians, unpublished membership report, April 1979.

42. Piore, Nora, et al., *A Statistical Profile of Hospital Outpatient Services in the United States: Present Scope and Potential Role,* p. 120.

43. Yerby, Alonzo S. "The Hospital Outpatient Department as a Source of Medical Care," *Medical Care,* July–September 1964, pp. 225–227.

44. UCLA School of Public Health, *Large Urban Public Hospitals,* p. 669.

45. de Vise, Pierre, "Persistence of Chicago's Dual Health System," *Regional Hospital Study* (Chicago (Paper IV 14): March 1970).

46. Roemer, Milton I., and Jorge Mera, " 'Patient-dumping' and Other Voluntary Agency Contributions to Public Agency Problems," *Medical Care* 11 (1973): 30–39.

47. Joint Commission on Accreditation of Hospitals, *Accreditation Manual for Hospitals 1970, Updated 1973* (Chicago: 1973), pp. 123–124.

48. Pincus, Steven B., et al., *A Study of Selected Innovative Hospital Programs in Ambulatory Care* (Burlington, Mass.: Bio-Dynamics, Inc., May 1974).

49. American Hospital Association, *Reshaping Ambulatory Care Programs,* Report and Recommendations of a Conference on Ambulatory Care (Chicago: AHA, 1973).

50. McLaughlin, M. C., et al., "Ghetto Medicine: Program in New York City," *New York State Journal of Medicine,* October 1, 1971, p. 2321 ff.

51. U.S. Public Health Service, *Coordinated Home Care Programs, 1964 Survey* (Washington: Division of Medical Care Administration, PHS Pub. No. 1479, 1967).

52. Bluestone, E. M., "The Principles and Practices of Home Care," *Journal of the American Medical Association,* 155 (1954): 1379 ff.

53. Littauer, David; I. J. Flance; and A. Wessen, *Home Care* (Chicago: American Hospital Association, Monograph Series No. 9, 1961).

54. Richter, Lorraine, and Alice Gonnerman, "Home Health Services and Hospitals," *Hospitals JAHA,* May 16, 1974.

55. Davidson, Robert C., "The Future of Home Health Agencies," *Journal of Community Health* 4 (1978): 55–66.

56. Schorr, Lisbeth B., and J. T. English, "Background, Context, and Significant Issues in Neighborhood Health Center Programs," *Milbank Memorial Fund Quarterly* 46 (1968): 289–296.

57. American Hospital Association, *Annual Survey of Hospitals, 1969,* unpublished data.

58. Denver Department of Health and Hospitals, *A Study of Patient Satisfaction with Outpatient Services—Denver General Hospital and the Denver Neighborhood Health Programs* (Denver, October 1970).

59. Brown, H. J., and R. S. Alexander, "The Gouverneur Ambulatory Care Unit: A New Approach to Ambulatory Care," *American Journal of Public Health,* 54 (1964): 1661.

60. Olendzki, Margaret C., "Evolving Forms of Hospital-Related Ambulatory Care" in *Community Hospitals and the Challenge of Primary Care* (New York: Columbia University, 1975), pp. 69–79.

61. Rorem, C. Rufus, *Physician's Private Offices at Hospitals* (Philadelphia: Hospital Council of Philadelphia, 1958).

62. American Association on Medical Clinics, "Clinic-Hospital Relationships," *Group Practice,* March 1960.

63. Roemer, Milton I., "The Hospital's Relation to Prepaid Group Practice: Review and Analysis," in *Proceedings of the Tenth Annual Group Health Institute* (Chicago: Group Health Association of

America, 1961), pp. 108–117.

64. Williams, Stephen J., et al., "Hospital-Sponsored Primary Care Group Practices: A Developing Modality of Care," *Health & Medical Care Services Review,* September–December 1978, pp. 1–13.

65. Feldman, S., and H. H. Goldstein, "Community Mental Health Centers in the USA: An Overview," *International Journal of Nursing Studies,* 8 (1971): 247–257.

66. National Institute of Mental Health, *The Community Mental Health Center Program: Special Report* (Washington: U.S. Public Health Service), December 1973.

67. O'Donovan, Thomas R. (editor), *Ambulatory Surgical Centers: Development and Management* (Germantown, Md.: Aspen Systems Corp., 1976).

68. American Hospital Association, *Outpatient Health Care—The Role of Hospitals,* (Chicago: AHA, 1969), p. 10.

69. Berarducci, A., et al., "The Teaching Hospital and Primary Care," *New England Journal of Medicine,* 292: (1975): 615–620.

70. Montgomery, R. L. and D. Singman, "Hospital-based Mass Health Screening Services at an Automated Clinic: Berkeley, California," *Hospitals, JAHA,* March 16, 1970, pp. 71–74.

71. "Hospitals Must Adopt Patient's Bill of Rights or Courts Will Tell Them What It Means, Lawyer Warns," *Modern Hospital,* June 1973, p. 33.

72. Wetherville, Rhonah and J. M. Nordby, *A Census of HMOs* (Minneapolis: Interstudy, July 1975).

73. U.S. Congress, House Committee on Way and Means, Subcommittee on Health, *National Health Insurance Resource Book* (Washington: Government Printing Office, August 30, 1976), pp. 457–464.

74. American Hospital Association, *Annual Survey of Hospitals, 1971,* unpublished data.

75. Comprehensive Health Planning Council of Los Angeles County, *1975 Health Systems Plan: Los Angeles County* (Los Angeles, Calif., 1974).

76. Los Angeles County Council on Emergency Medical Services, *Draft Recommendations and Issues regarding an Emergency Medical Services System for Los Angeles County,* (Los Angeles, Calif.: June 11, 1975).

Chapter 5

Public Health Clinics

Another role in the movement toward provision of organized ambulatory health services (OAHS) is played by public health agencies. The earliest tasks of such agencies were the various actions considered necessary to prevent the spread of communicable disease, principally by the promotion of a sanitary environment, the isolation of patients with contagious disease, and the quarantine of their contacts. Long before pathogenic microorganisms were discovered, epidemics in the cities of Europe led to the establishment of "boards of health" to attempt to halt the spread of disease (plague, cholera, typhus, etc.). After an epidemic passed, the boards were usually disbanded. Permanent boards of health were established in the main European cities only in the early nineteenth century and in America in the last years of that century.[1] The first state department of health in the United States was set up in Massachusetts in 1869.[2]

THE RISE OF HEALTH DEPARTMENTS AND PREVENTIVE CLINICS

It was decades after the organization of public health agencies, with their central focus on the prevention of communicable disease, that deliberate social action was taken to operate clinics for personal health service with similar preventive objectives. The initiative, moreover, was taken not by the official public health agencies, but by private individuals or groups. Thus, in 1887 Dr. Robert Philip, a private physician in Edinburgh, Scotland, founded the Victoria Dispensary for Consumption (tuberculosis) in that city.[3] This was only five years after Robert Koch had announced discovery of the tubercle bacillus, and the dispensary was the first such unit to be focused on one specific disease. The objectives were to diagnose tuberculosis (TB), educate patients about the danger of spreading it, and give whatever advice was possible about treatment.

The idea of such clinics soon spread throughout Europe, with the initiatve taken everywhere by private citizens, usually physicians who would muster support from other people. Various associations and leagues against tuberculosis were organized in country after country. To finance the work, private donations had to be attracted; soon after 1900 a Danish postal clerk, Einar Holboell, had thought of the idea of selling "Christmas seals" as a technique for fund raising—an idea employed throughout the world to the present day. In these years, the official public health agencies in Europe limited their role to requiring the reporting of tuberculosis cases and educating the general population about the contagiousness of the disease. It was some decades before these governmental agencies took responsibility for the operation of TB clinics.

In the United States the sequence of events was similar. The pioneer action was taken in 1892 by a Philadelphia physician, Dr. Lawrence F. Flick, who, with both medical and lay associates, organized the Pennsylvania Society for Prevention of Tuberculosis. By 1904, some 23 state and local TB associations had been formed, leading that year to the founding of the National Association for the Study and Prevention of Tuberculosis (later the National Tuberculosis Association). It was not until the 1930s, however, with the severe decline of private financial donations, that the operation of TB clinics in America became a customary function of governmental public health agencies.

Public health agency initiative in the operation of clinics in America, however, was shown earlier in another aspect of prevention. The objective was to reduce infant mortality, and again the first initiative had been shown in Europe. "Milk stations," where mothers who could not breast-feed their babies might obtain clean cow's milk, had been set up in Paris by two pediatricians, Drs. J. Comby and G. Variot during 1890 to 1892. In 1893, the American philanthropist Nathan Strauss began a network of similar milk stations in New York City.[4]

In 1897, the Health Department of Rochester, N.Y. sponsored two milk stations, and broadened their functions to include advice to mothers on the care and feeding of infants. In 1908, the New York City Health Department organized a Bureau of Child Hygiene, the first such unit in the world in a public health agency. The bureau had nurses who visited the mothers of newborn babies in the tenements, supervised midwives, inspected schoolrooms, etc., and also conducted general child health clinics.[5] Voluntary agencies continued to play an important role, with the National Association for Study and Prevention of Infant Mortality forming in 1909. By 1910, about 100 infant welfare stations had been set up in the United States; these expanded rapidly to 538 child health clinics in 141 American cities, under both health department and voluntary agency auspices, by 1915.

By 1910, most American cities had a board of health, with an official "health officer," even though he might, in smaller towns, be a private physician who was assigned the legal responsibility.[6] In the coming decade the operation of clinics gave a meaning to public health agencies that was somewhat more personal and humanistic than the purely regulatory functions associated with environmental sanitation. It was around 1910 that the idea of public health agency protection was extended to rural populations, with the founding of the first *county* health departments—in Jefferson County, Kentucky (1908), Guilford County, North Carolina (1911), and Yakima County, Washington (1911).[7]

A third type of preventive clinic—the venereal disease (VD) diagnostic and treatment station—also arose from the initiative of voluntary agencies. In 1905, the Society for Social and Moral Prophylaxis was founded, and most of its efforts were devoted to attempting to persuade public health agencies to establish clinics for syphilis and gonorrhea. Only a few courageous city health officers, however, responded. Then, with the U.S. entry into World War I, a powerful new stimulus arose that would strengthen public health agencies greatly: the federal grant-in-aid to states. In 1919 the Chamberlain-Kahn Act was passed, providing federal grants to the states for VD control, especially around military camps. These programs included VD clinics for indigent patients.[8] Although the grants continued only until 1925, they established the operation of VD clinics as a health department function.

Federal grants-in-aid had a more powerful impact in the maternal and child health (MCH) field. Two years after the Chamberlain-Kahn Act, in 1921, the Sheppard-Towner Act was passed for federal grants to the states for development of preventive health services for mothers and children.[9] By 1921 there were already about 1,000 "well baby clinics," as they came to be called, throughout the nation under both public health and private auspices. The federal grants stimulated the organization of hundreds more of these clinics, particularly under local public health agency auspices. They also led to the establishment of MCH divisions in virtually all state health departments. In the 1920s, however, a conservative antigovernment wave swept over the country; the American Medical Association (AMA) attacked the Sheppard-Towner MCH grants as an "imported socialistic scheme."[10] As a result, in 1929 the U.S. Congress terminated this program, and it was reactivated only at the depths of the Great Depression in Title V of the Social Security Act of 1935.

Mental health was another field in which voluntary initiative paved the way to action by government agencies, including health departments. A National Association for the Protection of the Insane and the Prevention of Insanity had been founded in 1880, as an offshoot of the National Conference of Social Work.[11] Its principal purpose was to promote improvement of conditions in mental institutions. Although this organization survived only four years, the same idea was reborn a quarter-century later, when Clifford Beers organized the Connecticut Society for Mental Hygiene in 1908. The idea spread to other states and soon the National Committee for Mental Hygiene was formed. By this time, the goals of the movement included *prevention* of mental disorder through psychiatric clinics for children and youth.

In the decade between 1910 and 1920, child guidance clinics were established in the schools, clinics for juvenile delinquency in the prisons, and eventually general mental health clinics in communities under the auspices of both mental health associations and health departments. The assumption of these clinics was that the early treatment of mental and emotional problems would prevent the later development of serious psychoses requiring institutionalization.

Thus, from the late nineteenth century until about 1910, public health agencies in America were devoted almost exclusively to environmental sanitation and collection of statistics on communicable diseases. The development of clinics, first for tuberculosis, then for child health, VD, and mental hygiene grew primarily from the initiative of voluntary organizations. Between 1910 and 1920, public health agencies gradually began to operate clinics in these four fields, responding to the stimulus and demonstration of the voluntary agencies. In the 1920s, federal grants to the states gave a strong impetus to extension of health department clinics in the fields of VD control and MCH. The principle behind these clinics was the same as that in back of environmental sanitation: disease prevention. Treatment of TB or VD was offered only insofar as this was necessary to prevent the spread of infection to others.

Up to 1930, public health activities were largely a big city phenomenon. In 1927, out of 2,850 counties in the United States, only 337 (less than 12 percent) had full-time health officers, and most of these had very small staffs.[12] The major turning point in the public health movement came in 1935, with enactment of the Social Security Act. National insurance for medical care had been considered for inclusion in the act, but was rejected. Instead provisions were included for relatively large federal grants to the states for development of public health programs. As a component of most of these programs, there were developed an increasing number of organized clinics in an expanding variety of special fields.[13]

PUBLIC HEALTH CLINICS AFTER 1935

The combination of massive poverty following the economic crisis of 1929 and the stimulating effect of federal grants beginning in 1935 led to a surge of strength and spirit in the American public health movement. Initially health departments at the state level were strengthened. In almost all state public health agencies there came to be a "division of local health administration" or its equivalent, whose objective was to build up local public health agencies.

In 1935, 762 counties out of about 3,100 in the nation had health departments with full-time health officers. By 1942, after the stimulus of the Social Security Act grants, this number leaped to 1,828 counties.[14] One of the difficulties in making public health services accessible was the small population in hundreds of rural counties—too few people to support an adequate public health program. If cities would combine with county governments to form city-county health units, and if several adjacent rural counties would coalesce into "districts," the resultant populations could afford a reasonable level of public health protection. Just such a policy was urged by the American Public Health Association (APHA) in 1945.[15] By such cooperative action, it was argued that about 1250 "local health units" could blanket the nation.

Of the 3,071 counties in the United States, 2,347 were served by Health Departments by 1966, although 520 of these had part-time health officers or vacancies in these positions. Many of these were, indeed, multicounty units, as recommended by the APHA report. Within the covered counties, moreover, there were an additional 362 separate city health departments.[16] Altogether 1,710 local health units of either a single or multijurisdictional nature were functioning in 1966.

We have noted in Chapter 3 that a study of 1977 identified 1,929 local units in the nation and that 31.5 percent of these covered combinations of two or more jurisdictions. There appears to have been further consolidation of rural counties into districts along the lines of the 1945 APHA policy recommendation. While exact data on the population covered by public health agencies are not available, it appears that only very thinly settled rural counties are completely noncovered, so that it is safe to say that as of 1979 some 85 to 90 percent of the U.S. population was served by official local health departments.

Not all health department heads are physicians, but almost every multijurisdictional unit has a medical director. Of the single jurisdictional agencies, about one-third were headed by nonmedical administrators in 1966.[17] The unavailability of physicians, with or without public health training, for many posts is not too surprising in the light of the comparatively low salaries they offer.[18] Another unfortunate reality, in the setting of U.S. free private enterprise, is the relatively low prestige of public health and preventive medicine as a specialty.[19] With these handicaps, it is all the more remarkable that public health programs have made the progress they have. Some of the features of public health clinics that have evolved, despite such difficulties, will now be considered.

We have observed the historical priority, in terms of organized ambulatory services, for tackling TB, VD, and infant mortality. In a study reported in 1968, Beverlee Myers and her colleagues examined the kinds of personal health service programs, which virtually always involved the operation of clinics, and were conducted by local health departments throughout the nation.[20] Responses to a mailed questionnaire were received from 1,323 agencies (78.1 percent) of 1,703 local health units surveyed. Of these responses, the ten most frequently provided types of personal health service program, in rank order, were as follows:

Personal Health Programs	Number of Local Units	Percent of Units
Tuberculosis	1278	97
Venereal disease	1124	85
Child health	1060	84
Crippled children	950	72
Dental health	869	66
Prenatal service	822	62
Heart disease control	759	57
Mental hygiene	730	55
Adult health	694	52
Cancer control	561	42

Source: Beverlee Myers, et al., "The Medical Care Activities of Local Health Units," Public Health Reports 83 (1968): 757–769.

Compared with the findings of a somewhat similar study done in 1947 (with 690 full-time local public health units reporting), there had been a rise in the proportion of health departments offering all these personal health services, with the exception of venereal disease work, which showed a slight decline. The latter was doubtlessly associated with the introduction of penicillin during the intervening decades for treatment of syphilis and gonorrhea; with this therapy, which was much simpler than former methods, VD cases could be easily treated in private physicians' offices.

In 1974, a further nationwide survey of local health department activities was conducted by Arden Miller and colleagues.[21] Through state health departments, 2,093 addresses of local public health units were collected, but many of these (predominantly in towns of 10,000 population or less) yielded no response. Out of 1,355 responses, 10 were from units without a single full-time employee, leaving 1.345 health departments meeting the minimal criterion of having at least one full-time health worker. (This figure was remarkably close to the 1,323 agencies analyzed in the 1968 survey by Myers.) Public health functions were classified somewhat differently in the Miller study, but regarding activities that involved organized ambulatory service of some type, the findings are reported in Table 5-1.

Especially noteworthy in this 1974 survey is the finding that the local Health Department was the sole source for immunizations, tuberculosis control, and venereal disease control services in more than half the jurisdictions nationally. With respect to organized MCH services, doubtless involving clinics, the health department was the sole source in nearly half the jurisdictions. It is also note-worthy that a large proportion of health departments carry out activities concerning chronic diseases, mental health, and general ambulatory care.

Table 5-1 Personal Health Service Functions of Local Health Departments: Percent of 1,345 Units Providing Specified Services, United States, 1974.

Service	Percent of Units with Service	Percent of Units as Sole Source in Area
Immunizations	96.3	62.3
Tuberculosis control	93.9	63.3
Maternal and child health	89.4	48.5
School health	89.2	38.5
Venereal disease control	88.0	57.7
Chronic disease programs	84.3	25.7
Family planning	63.3	38.0
General ambulatory care	50.3	7.6
Mental health	47.4	5.4

Source: C. Arden Miller, et al., "A Survey of Local Health Departments and Their Direction," American Journal of Public Health 67 (1977): 931–937.

The 1974 Miller survey found that aggregate annual expenditures by the reporting local health departments was $1.8 billion, averaging $760,000 per unit per year. The sources of these funds were distributed as follows:

Source	Percent
Local government	59.8
State government	21.6
Federal government	8.6
Patient fees	5.3
Other and unknown	4.7
All sources	100.0

Source: C. Arden Miller, et al.: "A Survey of Local Public Health Departments and Their Direction," American Journal of Public Health 67 (1977): 931–937.

In the above percentage figures, the federal contribution is probably understated, since some of the state government funds undoubtedly come from federal grants. Patient fees, although constituting only 5.3 percent of total funds, were collected to some extent by 57 percent of the units.

The average local health department in 1974 employed 34 persons. Only one in 30 was a physician; the balance was divided equally among administrators, nurses, and sanitarians or others. The average local health officer was 50 years old. Thirty-five percent of these top officials were not physicians and in only 60 percent of units was the director full-time. The widely espoused ideal of having a physician with a Master of Public Health (M.P.H.) degree as the local health officer was realized in only 23 percent of the units. This is not surprising, since the average annual salary of local health department directors was only $20,096.

Neither the survey by Myers and colleagues in 1968, nor that of Miller and colleagues in 1974, provides data on the number of clinics operated under each of the personal health care programs reported. From other sources, however, we may gather further information about the principal clinics under health department auspices. These will be considered below under five main categories: communicable disease control, MCH, chronic diseases, other specialized purposes, and general ambulatory care.

COMMUNICABLE DISEASE CONTROL

With sharp decline in both mortality and morbidity from *tuberculosis* over the last century, it may seem surprising that in 1966 and 1974, TB control activities were as frequent in health department programs as indicated above. The explanation seems to be that with the decline in the disease and with the availability of new forms of effective therapy (streptomycin, isoniazide, etc.), ambulatory management has become feasible for many cases. Thus, patients who in former years would have been isolated and treated in tuberculosis sanatoria are now allowed to remain at home and receive chemotherapy and surveillance. Of the 1,278 public health units active in this field in 1966, almost 1,100 were providing drugs to ambulatory cases, and 816 furnished physicians' services. TB clinics also offer diagnostic services on contacts of TB patients and do screening procedures (chest x-rays or tuberculin skin tests) on population groups: 1,245 of the 1,278 public health units carried out such work in 1966.

We noted earlier that the initiative in developing organized clinic services for TB was taken first by voluntary health agencies, and only after several decades did health departments perform such services. By 1960, 68.6 pecent of the 1,176 TB clinics in the United States identified in a national survey had come under public health agency sponsorship.[22] Of the remainder, 17.6 percent were part of a TB hospital, 5.6 percent were in the outpatient department of a general hospital, 4.5 percent were operated by branches of the National Tuberculosis Association, and 3.7 percent were under other auspices.

The importance of ambulatory management of TB patients was reflected by a survey of the U.S. Public Health Service in late 1969. There were 12,451 cases identified in 82 local programs, and 52.4 percent of these were under ambulatory management outside of sanatoria or hospitals. Of these noninstitutionalized patients, 64 percent were being served in health department clinics, 20 percent were under the care of private physicians, and the remaining 16 percent were under other types of care or unknown status.[23]

Regarding the function of TB clinics in examination of patient contacts, a 1970 study in New York State is of interest. Of all such persons examined, 75.4 percent were found to be free of any chest disease. Of the balance, 12 percent showed some evidence of TB, but the condition was usually inactive; by coincidence, other chest disorders were found in 13 percent of the examinations.[24]

The trend toward ambulatory management of TB patients is clearly continuing. As of 1974, the U.S. Public Health Service reported 29,000 active cases on TB registers throughout the United States.[25] Of these, only 19 percent were hospitalized, and 81 percent were being supervised on an ambulatory basis, predominantly through health departments. If we assume only four visits per TB patient per year to each health department clinic, this would mean approximately 60,000 clinic visits in the United States annually.

The trends in *venereal disease* and clinics to treat patients with such conditions have been different from those for TB. Federal subsidies for VD control were particularly strong after 1935. In 1940 there were 2,405 separate VD clinic locations in the United States, with a great diversity of scheduled sessions; some clinics were open to patients only one morning, afternoon, or evening per week, with gradations up to a full 40- or 48-hour workweek.[26] The functions of VD clinics include not only diagnosis and treatment, but also examination of contacts and general health education. In addition, health departments also conduct and encourage mass screening programs through serological tests for syphilis.

Until about 1945, the regimes of therapy for both syphilis and gonorrhea were relatively complex. Patients might require periodic treatments for months or years. A great deal of effort was necessary to encourage attendance by patients for these long periods, especially after the acute symptoms of the disease had passed. Public health nurses and sometimes special VD investigators would often follow up recalcitrant patients with home visits, as well as attempting to seek out patients' sexual contacts for examination.

With the advent of penicillin in 1945 for treatment of both syphilis and gonorrhea, the cure of these diseases became both simpler and more effective. The rates of new cases declined steadily through the 1950s. The energies put into VD control programs declined. In the 1960s, however, the incidence of new cases of gonorrhea rose again; certain strains of gonococcus had become resistant to penicillin, and sexual activity in the youth population was increasing.[27] Accordingly in the mid-1960s, health departments reactivated their VD programs, while other organized clinics—the neighborhood health centers, the free clinics, and special children and youth clinic programs—also gave attention to patients with venereal infections.

In 1974, VD clinics were operated in 2,014 communities in all 50 states. In large cities they were often available at several different locations.[28] California had the largest number of VD clinics (207), New York had 147, Florida had 127, and North Carolina had 110. The majority of these clinics are sponsored by health departments, although some are still sponsored by voluntary groups, universities (as part of student health services), or hospitals. In 1972, about 10 percent of the VD clinics were located in hospital outpatient departments, even though many of these were operated by public health agencies.[29] The majority of physicians staffing VD clinics are private practitioners who do this work part-time.[30] For many years, the Center for Disease Control of the U.S. Public Health Service, in Atlanta, Georgia, has offered technical consultation in this field, and has assigned trained personnel to state and local health departments for VD activities.[31]

The great preponderance of VD clinic patients have gonorrhea. The volume of a clinic's attendance is highly variable. In New Haven, Connecticut, for example, clinic visits in 1971 were reported to average 450 per month, or about 5,400 visits per year.[32] For New Haven's population of 348,000, this would amount to 15.0 visits per 1,000 population per year. In Los Angeles County, the VD clinic attendance in 1970 was 16.6 visits per 1,000 population per year. These two communities probably have VD control programs under public health agency sponsorship more active than the national average, so that a realistic estimate for the nation as a whole might be 13.0 VD clinic visits per 1,000 per year. On this assumption, the visits to VD clinics in the United States in the early 1970s could be estimated at about 2,600,000 per year.

Nevertheless, the relative simplicity and speed of venereal disease therapy with antibiotic drugs has meant that today the great majority of VD patients probably seek care in private medical offices. The National Commission on Venereal Disease in 1972 estimated this proportion to be 80 percent.[33] The 20 percent of cases seen in VD clinics, however, are probably from a low-income sector of the population, where the danger of nontreatment could be especially great. Moreover, the very existence of VD clinic services in a community, which include doing contact tracing, screening tests, and health education, undoubtedly leads to uncovering of many cases that end up in private medical offices for care.

Clinics for the management of both VD and TB are probably the clearest demonstrations of a pattern of organized ambulatory health care that can prevent the spread of disease and the later need for costly hospitalization. Early treatment of pulmonary TB has long been shown to retard advancement of the disease. Untreated early syphilis soon becomes quiescent, but later the disease process can cause severe disorders of the heart, central nervous system, or other organs. Gonorrhea, especially in women, can lead to serious pelvic disease and also sterility, not to mention infectiousness for others (even after acute symptoms have subsided). Ambulatory care early in the course of these chronic infectious diseases, therefore, is not only important in preventing contagion, but also in preventing serious complications in the primary patient.

Organized ambulatory services for other communicable diseases are essentially concerned with mass immunization campaigns. When poliomyelitis vaccines were developed by Dr. Jonas Salk in the mid-1950s and later by Dr. Albert Sabin, public health agencies set up clinics in the schools and elsewhere for rapid immunization of large populations. The same was done in the 1970s with vaccines against swine influenza, particularly for the older age groups that were most vulnerable. The most widely applied immunizations, however—against diphtheria, pertussis (whooping cough), tetanus, and more recently measles— are typically given to infants as part of the services of well baby clinics.

MATERNAL AND CHILD HEALTH CLINICS

Although both the 1966 and 1974 surveys reviewed earlier found a somewhat smaller proportion of local health departments to be offering organized child health services than communicable disease control programs, the number of clinics in this field and the frequency of their regular sessions are probably greater. With the continuing flow of federal subsidies for MCH services under Title V of the Social Security Act since 1935, clinics for both babies and pregnant mothers have come to occupy a major place in the programs of most local health departments. MCH clinics are theoretically open to families of any income, although in practice their services are largely concentrated on low-income families. Families of moderate or higher incomes are typically referred to private physicians. Nevertheless, well baby clinics probably make more families aware of their local health department than any other official activity.

In 1970, about 1.5 million children were served by child health clinics or "well-child conferences," as they are often termed, to emphasize their purely preventive and educational purpose throughout the United States.[34] About 42 percent of these (630,000) were under one year of age and were brought back to the clinic every month or two. Since there were about 3,500,000 births in the nation that year, this meant that about 18 percent of newborns were seen, at least once, in these public health clinics; the balance were presumably examined by private physicians or perhaps not at all.

The regularity with which an infant or child is brought to a clinic for periodic examinations is highly variable. If we assume an average of about five visits per infant during the first year of life, this would amount to about 3,150,000 infant visits. Children 1–4 years of age visiting these clinics in 1970 numbered 583,000, and 5–17 years of age, 268,000. These older children, however, made only one or a few visits each. One may roughly estimate the grand total of these clinic visits by infants and children in 1970 to have been about 5,000,000.

The birth rate obviously influences the volume of services provided by MCH clinics. Between July 1, 1970 and June 30, 1971, the U.S. birth rate declined; accordingly, the infants visiting clinics fell from 623,000 to 552,000. At the same time, children in the 1–4 year age bracket rose in attendance from 583,000 to 701,000, and those 5–17 years of age rose from 268,000 to 293,000. In spite of the decline in birth rate, women receiving services at public health maternity (prenatal and postpartum) clinics increased between 1970 and 1971 from 331,000 to 352,000.[35]

The preventive orientation of MCH clinics is shown in their functions: examination of the child or mother to detect any abnormality, counseling of mothers on infant feeding and childrearing practices, immunizations of infants and children, and so on. If any abnormality is detected, the patient is referred elsewhere for treatment. Sometimes very minor illness, such as a common cold or a minor skin rash, will be treated in the MCH clinic, but nothing that would require continuing medical care. This strictly preventive emphasis was not modified to include comprehensive health care (that is, both treatment and prevention) until the Social Security Act Amendments in the 1960s authorized special grants for "maternal and infant care" (MIC) clinics and "children and youth" (C & Y) clinics. These services, which are mainly sponsored by agencies other than the health department, will be discussed in a later chapter.

Although, as noted earlier, only 18 percent of U.S. newborns were served in MCH clinics in 1970, this was still an increase over 1957, when only 13 percent of newborns were seen. The proportion of older children 1–4 years of age seen in 1970 was about 4 percent and in the 5–17 year age group only about 0.5 percent, reflecting very little change from the level in 1957. The best developed MCH clinics are in urban centers; about 25 percent of the children served are from nonmetropolitan counties, where 35 percent of the national population (and doubtless a higher share of the children, since rural families tend to be larger) reside. Urban MCH clinics tend to be staffed with pediatricians rather than general practitioners. Much of the examination of children and the counseling of mothers in all child health clinics, however, is done by public health nurses.

A related type of health department clinic exists for the diagnosis and surveillance of crippled children, although in a few states this federally subsidized program is operated by a welfare department or other agency. In 1970, there were 6.1 children under 21 years of age per 1,000 in the nation receiving such services. This amounted to about 490,000 children, of whom 72 percent, or 353,000, were served in organized clinics. With 2.2 clinic visits per child during the year, this amounted to 770,000 clinic visits for a variety of handicaps. In 1950, crippled children's programs had reached only 4.0 children per 1,000 child population; thus, the 1970 rate constitutes a 50 percent increase over this 20-year period.[36]

Crippled children's clinics are generally well staffed with medical specialists in orthopedics or physical medicine, nurses, psychologists, physiotherapists, social workers, and others. Among many programs supported by federal grants to the states, this one has put a special emphasis on high technical standards.[37] When a child is found to need surgery or other inpatient therapy, he or she is typically referred to a private physician (on an approved list) who treats the patient in a community hospital and is paid according to a fee schedule. Eligibility for services under this program ordinarily requires a definite "means test" to determine if the family income is low enough to qualify.

Organized clinics under health department auspices for pregnant women are devoted typically to prenatal and postpartum care, while nearly all births occur in hospitals. The 331,000 mothers served in these clinics in 1970 constituted about 9 percent of the live births that year, an increase from 5.5 percent in 1957. If we assume an average of three or four visits per pregnant woman (although nine or ten visits are recommended), this would amount to about 1,000,000 such visits. Of these clinic services, 52.5 percent occurred in nonmetropolitan counties, a higher share than that found for child health services. This may be due to the limited supply of obstetricians in rural county practice, so that public health clinics in this field have a larger role. While the objective of these maternity clinics is preventive, i.e., to attempt to assure a safe and normal delivery, minor illnesses.in the pregnant woman are usually treated.

Another related service of health departments given through organized clinics is *family planning* (FP). Some FP services are provided through maternity clinics, usually in the postpartum phase, while others are offered through clinics exclusively for this purpose.[38] In addition, a great variety of other organizations sponsor FP programs. Thus, in 1975 more than 5,100,000 women made 8,282,000 visits to FP clinics in the United States. These services were provided at more than 5,600 sites.[39] The precise sponsorships of these clinics are not clear, but the sites at which they were held suggests that about 41 percent were operated by health departments. The distribution of clinic sites in 1975, according to a survey of the National Center for Health Statistics, was as follows:

Clinic Site	Percent
State or local health department	41.4
Hospital	14.2
School or community building	12.0
Physician's office	3.7
Church	2.6
Store	1.2
Welfare department	1.0
Other	24.1
All sites	100.0

Source: U.S. Center for Health Statistics, *The National Inventory of Family Planning Services: 1975 Survey Results,* Washington: Series 14, No. 19, April 1978.

Certain health department clinics may be located in hospitals, schools, or elsewhere so that this form of sponsorship may exceed 41.4 percent. Insofar as this type of clinic service is sponsored by many types of organizations, it will be discussed further in a later chapter.

A final type of child health clinic service operated by health departments is the school health clinic for examination of school children to detect any correctable disorders. Some school clinics, staffed by public health nurses, provide first aid services to children injured or struck with acute illness while at school. The great majority of school clinics, however, are sponsored by educational, rather than public health, authorities, and they will be discussed in Chapter 6.

CHRONIC DISEASE AND OTHER SPECIAL CLINICS

Various organized ambulatory programs concerned with chronic (noncommunicable) diseases represent a newer development in health department services. Perhaps the prototype of such activities has been the cancer detection clinic.

Many diverse efforts of public health agencies, of course, are directed toward prevention of chronic diseases. Since cigarette smoking, for example, has been shown to contribute significantly to both lung cancer and arteriosclerotic heart disease, much health education is devoted to discouraging people, particularly youth, from smoking. Antismoking educational clinics have even been organized. The value of exercise is broadcast as a preventive of heart disease, and there are many educational programs on avoiding obesity. The importance of detecting hypertension and receiving antihypertensive drugs is emphasized. Occupational health programs are concerned about identification and elimination of carcinogenic substances in industry.

Our focus here is on personal health services offered in organized clinics for ambulatory service. In a 1955–56 survey of 271 full-time local health departments, the APHA found "only meager assumption of responsibility for control of chronic disease and disability."[40] Ten years later in a study by Beverlee Myers and colleagues, "heart disease control" activities and "cancer control" were reported by 57 and 42 percent of local public health units respectively. These programs included several components, but "screening or diagnosis or both" was the most prominent activity. Thus, of 759 local health units with heart disease control functions, 581, or 77 percent, did screening or diagnostic work. Of 561 units doing cancer control, 497, or 89 percent, did screening or diagnosis.[41] We cannot be sure how much of this activity was carried out in clinics exclusively focused on early detection of these diseases, as against being incidental to other purposes, such as Pap smears for cervical cancer detection that are done on women attending prenatal clinics. Similarly, health examinations of school children or food handlers might turn up signs of heart disease. The 1974 survey by Miller and colleagues, furthermore, reported "chronic disease programs" in 84 percent of local health departments.

In the decade after World War II, special interest developed in establishing cancer detection centers, where medical examinations with laboratory tests and x-rays were performed in order to detect early cancers. Largely stimulated by local branches of the American Cancer Society, more than 250 such clinics were organized in this period.[42] Some of these were operated entirely by health departments or jointly by these agencies with the local Cancer Society branch.

Around 1960, the strategy of the American Cancer Society changed from promoting organized cancer detection clinics to encouraging medical examinations for the same purpose by all private physicians. Accordingly, the funding for many of these clinics ended and they closed. Meanwhile a variation on the same theme developed, with a movement to offer a wide battery of screening tests for early detection of many different chronic diseases. Periodic medical examinations of adults had been promoted by life insurance companies for many years.[43] The idea of selecting special laboratory or x-ray procedures (not requiring a physician to perform) for different age and sex groups and scheduled at varying intervals was proposed in 1945.[44] The special feature of the activity promoted after World War II was the provision of multiple screening tests in an organized clinic setting, with subsidies from the federal government. The U.S. Public Health Service encouraged such "multiphasic screening" programs under the auspices of local health departments.[45]

As so often happens in innovative public health programs, state and local medical societies initially were resistant to the multiphasic screening idea as an invasion of the private doctor's prerogative. To overcome this opposition, health departments often collaborated with voluntary groups in offering screening services. It was eventually recognized that the effect of these programs was to identify patients who might have an unrecognized disease and would be referred to a private physician for definitive diagnosis and care. In 1955, the AMA reviewed 33 multiphasic screening surveys conducted between 1948 and 1954, testing 2,500,000 persons in 14 states. The surveys varied from one examining 572 employees of one firm in California to a statewide program in Georgia examining 1,376,000 people. In 23 of these 33 programs, a local or state health department was the sponsoring agency, usually in cooperation with other organized bodies.[46] While the initial enthusiasm for multiphasic screening surveys as a health department activity has somewhat waned, the idea has been taken up by labor unions, by hospitals, by HMOs (health maintenance organizations), and other entities.[47]

Controversies exist, especially between American and British investigators, on the ultimate benefits derived from presymptomatic detection of various disorders. British epidemiologists are skeptical about the evidence that early detection of most diseases leads to greater longevity.[48] American investigators argue that for certain groups of people, and for selected diagnoses (e.g., hypertension or cervical cancer) the evidence points to extension of life at relatively low costs.[49] It is argued, furthermore, that the very performance of a series of screening tests has value in promoting general health consciousness and a more prudent life style in any individual.[50] In 1970, the U.S. Public Health Service issued *Provisional Guidelines* on the planning, organization, and operation of multiphasic health testing programs.''[51] While the number of systematic multiphasic screening programs under the auspices of health departments and other agencies is not known, the general movement has undoubtedly heightened awareness of early detection in many settings. Pap smears for detecting cervical cancer in women, mammography in middle-aged or older women, hypertension readings in all persons over 40 years of age, glucose tolerance tests for detection of incipient diabetes, and other procedures are being routinely performed in hospitals, private medical offices, public health clinics, industrial health units, and elsewhere.

Clinics for diagnosis and treatment of emotional and mental disorders are another activity of some state and local health departments. The first national Mental Health Act of 1946 offered grants to state agencies for organization of such clinics, and we have noted earlier that 55 percent of local public health units have done so. The great majority of mental health clinics are sponsored by mental hospitals, special public mental health agencies, and voluntary associations, but health departments also operate them. Thus, out of 138 mental health clinics functioning in California in 1963, 12 were under local health department sponsorship. The overall picture of mental health clinics under diverse forms of sponsorship will be considered in Chapter 11.

Closely related to mental health clinics are organized ambulatory services for coping with drug abuse and alcoholism. Occasionally health departments offer such services, usually in cooperation with other agencies.

For certain types of persons, as distinguished from categories of disease, health departments offer other clinic services. Migratory agricultural families, for example, were served by a special health program of the U.S. Department of Agriculture in the 1930s and 1940s; some 250 "migrant labor clinics" were operated by the federal government in that period.[53] After World War II, this federal program was terminated, and in its place after 1962 the U.S. Public Health Service gave grants to state and local agencies for operation of family health service clinics to serve migrant families. Most of the agencies managing these clinics are local health departments, often in cooperation with medical societies, religious missions, or other groups. In 1970 there were about 200 of these clinics supported throughout the country for service to an estimated 420,000 migrant persons.[54] The Migrant Health Act of 1962 was amended in 1975 to define more accurately the local conditions warranting a federal grant for a "migrant health center." In 1978 there were 112 such clinics serving nearly 600,000 migrant and seasonal farm workers.[55]

In small jurisdictions, where correctional authorities are weak, clinics in local jails may sometimes be conducted by the health department. Examination of food handlers for possible nonsymptomatic communicable disease has been another purpose for public health clinics. American Indians are entitled to health care from a special federal program, but in certain areas with a small Indian population the local health department may serve these persons under contract. In response to the free clinic movement, mentioned in Chapter 3 and explored more fully in Chapter 10, some health departments have sponsored youth clinics held in the evening hours with an informal atmosphere and providing a variety of services. At the other end of the age spectrum, a few health departments conduct geriatric clinics.

To highlight the extent of public health agency involvement in personal medical care outside hospitals, the U.S. Public Health Service made a special study of 13 selected local health departments in 1966–67.[56] These units were chosen, not as stellar examples of highly energetic health departments, but rather as a sample representative of units of different sizes and character in various regions of the United States. Not surprisingly, the most frequent medical care activity identified was "direct provision of health services to individuals . . . through health department clinics." Some of the units took responsibility for meeting the general medical needs of the poor or medically indigent. Special clinics were sometimes held for examining applicants for employment and for general checkups on aged persons. Other clinics were held for dental care and for immunizations.

Obviously, there are great variations in the degree to which a particular health department develops any personal health service program. In 1966, Robert Mytinger studied the program content of the 58 county health departments in California, scoring them according to their extent of innovativeness, i.e., their inclusion of new types of health services.[57] He found greater degrees of innovation to be associated with health departments serving large cities, where the health officer was courageous and inventive, where the public health staff as a whole was younger, where the local ratio of private doctors to population was relatively lower, and where new external funds (typically from state or national governments) for a defined purpose were available.

GENERALIZED AMBULATORY CARE CLINICS

In long-term perspective, perhaps the most important recent development in health department clinics has been the rebirth of the comprehensive service for primary care or general ambulatory health care. We have reviewed the attempts of imaginative public health leaders to launch this idea in the 1920s, only to be obstructed by the political opposition of the private medical profession. Then, after 50 years of highly categorical OAHS programs, in the mid-1960s there was a rediscovery of poverty in America and with it the rise of the generalized neighborhood health center, followed by other forms of community health centers under diverse sponsorships. Long-established health departments were inevitably influenced also by this movement: many widened their horizons and extended the scope of their clinics from purely preventive functions, directed to specific diseases or population groups, to provision of general ambulatory care.

This broadened viewpoint was demonstrated particularly in large cities, where several district health centers (with conventional clinics) had operated for years. Adding a primary care or family health clinic to the roster of scheduled sessions in these existing facilities would not appear too sensational. Moreover, this was visibly justified by the mounting pressure on the outpatient departments of hospitals, especially governmental general hospitals for the poor, as reviewed in Chapter 4. In a period when accessibility to general primary care was becoming increasingly difficult, the rationale for a response by public health agencies was obvious.

In 1969, a survey of "comprehensive health centers" under health department auspices was made in the 25 largest U.S. cities.[58] In four of those cities—Denver, Washington, D.C., New York, and Philadelphia—the health departments reported that they were operating or planning clinics for general medical care to all persons who came on a citywide basis. Nine other cities were operating or planning such clinic services in selected, usually low-income, districts. Thus, half the nation's largest cities were moving in the direction advocated by Herman Biggs and others a half-century before. This does not include the generalized public health clinics for children and youth authorized in the 1965 Amendments to the Social Security Act.

The extent of this broadened scope of public health clinics has manifestly increased since the 1969 study. The various forms of general clinics are located predominantly in low-income neighborhoods, but the prevailing policy is to turn no one away on grounds of ability to afford private care. Patients with problems too complex to handle in these ambulatory care centers are typically referred to a hospital OPD. The most complete data on this matter were collected from a nationwide survey in 1975 by William Shonick and Walter Price.[59] These investigators sent questionnaires to the universe of 1,929 local public health units identified in the United States and received responses from 784, which served 62 percent of the national population. Among many questions posed, one inquired: "Does your health department operate any programs to deliver comprehensive ambulatory health care?" Of the 784 respondents, 193, or 24 percent, stated that they operated such comprehensive care clinics. Out of these 193, moreover, 112 operated clinics intended to serve persons of all age-sex groups who came. Among the 112 agencies with truly comprehensive clinics, 84 made care available to persons of any socioeconomic level, rather than being limited to indigent or medically needy persons. (The above information was based on separate computer runs of the data, kindly provided by Professor Shonick).

Judging by the earlier studies of comprehensive health centers in the nation's largest cities, the launching of such clinics is being done largely in metropolitan communities. This action, in turn, would seem to be closely linked to a recent movement in urban centers to merge local government departments responsible for public health with those responsible for public hospitals. The very exercise of authority over hospitals naturally broadens the concern of such merged departments with curative as well as preventive services. Surely, it is no accident that in all four cities noted above, where citywide networks of general ambulatory care are being organized, there has also been a consolidation of previously separate departments of health and departments of hospitals.

In Denver, such a consolidation took place in 1912. Although only one large general hospital, oriented to the poor, is operated, since 1966 some 28 ambulatory care facilities offering "family-centered health care" have been organized.[60] These neighborhood clinics are directed mainly to low-income families, but no one is turned away. The clinics vary in their staffing, equipment, and hours of service, but all offer general ambulatory medical care. Funding comes from several federal, state, and local government sources, yet the demands for service have generally exceeded the resources.

In New York City, a network of district health centers for the traditional public health (preventive) programs was launched in the 1930s. In 1966, with the wave of interest in better general health care for the poor, eight of the old centers were renovated and eight new ones were contructed.[61] In the consolidated New York City Department of Health Services Administration, which in 1966 had absorbed the Department of Health and Hospitals, the Department of Community Mental Health, and the Office of the Chief Medical Examiner, responsibility for the new comprehensive ambulatory services was assigned to the unit derived from the previous Department of Public Health. Before 1966, the latter department had operated 28 district health centers, 100 well baby stations at other places, and the school health services. Altogether these clinics had accommodated 1.8 million visits per year, nearly all of which were preventive.[62]

Under the consolidated agency in New York City, the medical staffs of the 19 public hospitals in the municipal system were assigned to work in the ambulatory care health centers, as well as in the hospitals. Another interesting reflection of the broadened scope of New York City's consolidated Department of Health Services Administration was the establishment in 1969 of an Office of Group Practice Development. This was done with the support of a special federal grant to assist private physicians and voluntary hospitals to form group practice clinics, particularly for service to low-income patients.

Baltimore, Maryland, illustrates another way in which health departments have been broadening the scope of their traditional services to include general primary medical care. Since 1944, Maryland had been one of only a few states in which the administration of medical care of recipients of public assistance had been assigned to the State Health Department, despite the financial aspects of public assistance remaining a responsibility of the Department of Social Welfare.[63] The state, in turn, had largely delegated this responsibility to the Baltimore City Health Department. These services were rendered in the main, however, by private doctors or other practitioners and by existing hospitals (for both inpatient and outpatient care), the health department essentially paying fee-for-service claims.[64]

In the 1970s, the Baltimore City Health Department extended its horizons further by stimulating the organization of health insurance plans that would render services both through fee payments to individual doctors and through health centers in low-income neighborhoods; these plans involved new consortia between the health department and private agencies.[65] Furthermore, the traditional MCH program, which had long operated well baby clinics at 33 locations for 28,000 preschool children in Baltimore, is gradually expanding into operation of general primary care clinics for children and then "hopefully adult health care" for other members of the family.[66] In a promotional, rather than actual service delivery role, the Baltimore City Health Department has also recently played a key part in coordinating and systematizing the provision of general emergency medical services by 20 hospitals in that city.[67]

Other examples might be cited, but this may be enough to illustrate the broadening involvement of health departments, or larger health agencies into which they are merged, in the provision of general OAHS. While this broadened OAHS role has been assumed mainly in larger cities, and has been stimulated by the widely recognized needs of the poor, it was notable from the national survey by Shonick and Price that most of the local health departments do not confine services to low-income persons.[68] As a practical matter, few people of moderate or high income would tend to use these clinics, but no one is turned away. Perhaps the major impact of general OAHS clinics under health department auspices is to reduce pressures on hospital outpatient departments. Nevertheless, because of their geographic dispersion in large cities, these newer forms of public health clinics undoubtedly add to the total volume of organized ambulatory health care in the nation.

Evaluation of public health clinics as a whole defies any generalization. The variations are tremendous between the structure, function, and style of units in one health department compared with another, and even within the same department, there may be great differences in the diligence and quality of service between one special clinic and another. The dedication of the leadership in child health services, for example, may set standards of performance not seen in the VD clinics, or vice versa. Part-time young physicians staffing clinics may use the opportunity only as a way station, until they can build up a private practice and therefore put only perfunctory efforts into the work. On the other hand, some public health programs attract idealistic and socially oriented persons at all levels. The patient with an infectious disease serves as the signal for epidemiological follow up of family and other contacts. If poor home conditions are suspected, a public health nurse is alerted for a field visit that could yield improvements. While prevention is usually the central purpose of the public health clinic, referrals can be conscientiously made to other resources for treatment or rehabilitation. Without vested interest in personal gain, the major motivations of the health department physician and staff are most likely to be advancement of community welfare.

PUBLIC HEALTH CLINICS IN LOS ANGELES COUNTY

In this metropolitan county, we were able to examine more closely the operation of OAHS provided by a department of health. As everywhere in the world, the earliest public health actions were taken in the urban settlements, with Los Angeles City ordinances on garbage disposal enacted as early as 1833.[69] After several epidemics, the Los Angeles City Council appointed a city health officer to supervise sanitary conditions and handle smallpox (through isolation and quarantine) in 1868. A permanent Los Angeles City Board of Health was created in 1873. In 1889, Los Angeles claims to have been the first American city to hire its own visiting nurse, and in 1904 an official public health nurse. A public health laboratory for communicable disease tests was opened in 1903.

The County of Los Angeles appointed a health officer for duties outside the city limits in 1910. A permanent county health department was not established however, until 1913. In the period 1915–19, plans were formulated for consolidation into the county health department of the public health activities of 36 smaller incorporated cities (not counting Los Angeles City) in this large county area. To be feasible, this meant decentralization of the work through districts. The first of many such district facilities was opened in 1919 at a private brickyard, financed partially by the Simon's Brick Company and the Montebello Women's Club. A more well developed "district health center," with a full-time deputy health officer, was opened a little later that year in Pomona, after a contract was made with that separate incorporated city. By 1924, some 19 separate cities had entered into similar contracts with the county government, and by 1936 there were 38 such cities. It was not until 1964, however, that the large Los Angeles City Health Department, operating separately since 1873, combined with the county unit.

To carry out effectively the decentralization strategy and to provide proper quarters for public health clinics, Dr. John L. Pomeroy, the full-time county health officer since 1915, mapped out a network of district health centers to cover the county; the first of these, built specifically for the purpose, was erected in the town of San Fernando in 1926. It is noteworthy that this first health center was designed to house not only the preventive clinics, but also contained emergency beds, treatment facilities, and was equipped for performing minor surgery for lacerations or even tonsillectomies for indigent patients.

At the instigation of local doctors, who looked upon the health center as competitive with private practice, the legality of the emergency beds and the operation of clinics for noncommunicable disease was challenged in 1932. This was the depth of the Great Depression, and many doctors were barely making a living. The legal challenge combined with the political pressures prevailed, and in 1933 the health centers discontinued all curative work. Instead, the "San Fernando Plan" provided for treatment of the indigent sick in the offices of private doctors, who were paid fees by the Los Angeles County Department of Charities; social workers of the department were stationed at the health centers to apply a means test to anyone seeking medical care. This "outdoor medical relief" (OMR) program operated into the 1970s for a small number of noncategorical poor people (i.e., persons not fitting into one of the four federally assisted public aid categories) in Los Angeles County. Meanwhile, district health centers for purely preventive services continued to be built, and by the time of the public health consolidation between Los Angeles County and City in 1964, there were 23 health districts, each served by a health center. As the population grew, subcenters were built in almost all the districts, until there were 30 of these in 1970, or a total of 53 facilities for ambulatory service as well as other public health functions. Beyond these were about 75 other clinic quarters (usually rented), used for well baby sessions in the main, to bring these services closer to the people in need.

In 1972, a further chapter was written when the Los Angeles County Department of Health, along with the Department of Hospitals, the Department of Mental Health, and the county veterinarian were unified into a single entity called the County Department of Health Services. This followed several years of study on how to achieve greater economy and efficiency, as well as better coordination of health services for the population.[70] With respect to the latter goal, as the first director of the new enlarged department wrote in September 1972: "our immediate emphasis will be upon ambulatory care which is comprehensive in nature, accessible, and which encourages and teaches the patient to keep himself in good health and provides him with the means of doing so."[71] One of the first administrative acts of the new superdepartment was to establish a middle echelon of five "health service regions" encompassing the 23 health districts of the county, plus the two still independent city health departments of Long Beach and Pasadena. Through this additional level of decentralization, it was hoped to achieve better integration of ambulatory services rendered by the district health centers and the hospitals under both county government and voluntary auspices, the latter by way of contracts.

Data on OAHS activities were collected for the period prior to the 1972 consolidation of numerous county programs to keep our analysis confined to clinics under classical health department sponsorship. Accordingly, Table 5-2 presents figures on nine categorical types of clinic conducted by the Los Angeles County Health Department in 1970.[72] It is noteworthy that, in terms of both absolute volume and rate of services per 1,000 population, "health officer" clinics had the largest attendance. This clinic session, originally designed for special immunizations, food handler examinations, etc., has evolved into one which sees patients for miscellaneous minor ailments; it is essentially for primary health care. Significantly, it was after the 1972 merger of several departments that Los Angeles County, like other urban centers discussed earlier, developed explicit primary medical care clinics at several of its district centers, without the diplomatic shield of an obscure label.

The data in Table 5-2 describe only the most important types of health department clinics—those held in virtually all 23 districts in the county. Omitted are figures on clinics held only in certain districts, such as sessions for cancer detection, alcoholism, vision testing, or the treatment of common ailments in adolescents. The latter, known as youth clinics, were started only in 1969, as a local governmental response to the free clinic movement promoted by counterculture young people.[73]

Despite the generally decentralized policy of the Los Angeles County Health Department, a central headquarters provides overall direction and technical consultation to the districts. Thus, there are specialists in maternal and child health, communicable disease control, environmental sanitation, and other fields. At the head of the entire public health program is the county health officer who, until 1970, reported to the County Board of Supervisors, but since the 1972 integration reports to the administrator of the unified Department of Health Services. In order to reduce the inevitable tensions that develop between peripheral units and headquarters, there are three deputy county health officers— for technical problems, for district relations, and for administrative matters.

Each of the 23 districts is under the direction of a district health officer, who heads a staff of public health nurses, sanitarians, social workers, health educators, nutritionists, laboratory technicians, communicable disease investigators, clerks, and others. All personnel are paid by salary and hired by the headquarters office on the basis of county civil service qualifications. Although general program policies are established at headquarters, a certain amount of variation or innovation is permitted in the districts.

Financial support for the operation of all county public health clinics is derived almost entirely from general government revenue. These emanate, however, from several political levels—local, state, and federal. Thus, the overall 1969–70 budget of the Los Angeles County Health Department, whose population exceeds 7 million, was about $26,000,000, or $3.50 per capita. Some 75 percent of these funds came from local sources, about 10 percent from state sources, and 14 percent from the federal government; a trivial balance comes from licensing fees or patient charges for certain services (e.g. immunizations for international travelers).

The overall volume of public health clinic services for Los Angeles County is indicated in Table 5-2, but it may be of interest to note the services furnished in one of the 23 districts. The Harbor District, as of 1968, had a population of 159,200 people living in 44.7 square miles (a density of 3,560 persons per square mile). The organized ambulatory health services provided in this district during 1968 are presented in Table 5-3. The total of 19,421 patient visits, for a district population of 159,200, means about 0.12 clinic visits per person per year. The 1,245 clinic sessions held on the 261 weekdays of the year amount to 4.8 sessions per day, with about 15.6 patients per session. The great majority of patients were seen by a physician, but 24 percent were seen by such other personnel as nurses, dental hygienists, or family planning assistants.

The personnel available to operate these clinics (and to perform other public health functions), in the Harbor District, as of 1968, were as follows:

Public health nurses	16.3
Clerical personnel	9.0
Social workers	6.7
Sanitarians	6.0
Public health physicians	4.0
Communicable disease investigators	3.5
Health educators	1.5
Laboratory technicians	1.5
Dental personnel	0.6
Nutritionists	0.1
All personnel	49.2

For the total district population, these personnel amount to a ratio of about 1:3,200. They are backed up by specialists at the headquarters level. Since, in reality, services are largely focused on persons of low income, perhaps 25 or 30 percent of the district population, the effective ratio would be stronger than this. The quality of performance of all these health personnel is subject to surveillance by the usual pyramidal structure of organizational work. Periodic reports are submitted to the county health department headquarters by each district.

Reviewing the ambulatory services of the Los Angeles County Health Department as a whole, it is evident that their impact is not massive, but their content is changing. The range of services is continually widening. General primary care (family health service, comprehensive ambulatory care, primary medical care, etc.), mental illness screening and referrals, abortion counselling, cancer or glaucoma screening, cardiac evaluation, diverse health services for youth, smoking withdrawal programs, drug abuse clinics—these and other spe-

Table 5-2 Public Health Clinics in Los Angeles County, by Number of Sessions, Persons Attending, Average Attendance per Session, and Average Cost per Person Visit, 1970.

Type of Clinic	Persons Attending	Number of Sessions	Persons Per Session	Attendance Per 1,000	Cost Per Visit
"Health officer"	338,245	9,891	34.2	48.1	$ 3.12
Child health	166,190	9,305	17.9	23.6	8.48
Venereal disease	116,499	5,317	21.9	16.6	11.07
Prenatal	86,573	7,301	11.9	12.3	18.19
Dental	67,359	8,071	8.3	9.6	—
Tuberculosis	58,655	3,240	18.1	8.3	13.42
Family planning	40,327	1,940	20.8	5.7	17.50
Drug control	31,505	1,195	26.4	4.5	—
Mantoux test	25,552	778	32.8	3.6	—

Source: U.S. Bureau of the Census, *Social & Health Indicators System, Los Angeles* (Washington, D.C.: 1973).

cial services are steadily being added. While the number of programs is not great, they are innovative in design.

Certain new ambulatory service programs in Los Angeles County have been conducted jointly with other agencies. Mental health services were offered, in many instances, jointly with the Department of Mental Health (this was before amalgamation under the Health Services Administration). A large C & Y project was conducted in East Los Angeles jointly with the department of hospitals.

Table 5-3 Health Department Clinics in Harbor District of Los Angeles County, by Type, Number of Sessions, Attendance, and Care Provider Seen, 1968

Type of Clinic	Attendance	Number of Sessions	Served by Physician	Served by Other Personnel
"Health officer"	5,664	272	2,909	2,755
Prenatal	3,010	241	2,485	525
Child health	2,739	194	2,627	112
Tuberculosis	2,049	100	1,596	453
Primary care	1,976	30	1,416	566
Venereal disease	1,621	151	1,569	52
Dental	1,558	202	1,337	221
Family planning	525	39	92	333
Mantoux test	238	4	150	88
Alcoholic rehabilitation	41	12	25	16
Total	19,421	1,245	14,600	4,821

Source: Los Angeles County Health Department, unpublished data, 1969.

Along with the Economic and Youth Opportunity Administration (EYOA), the health department provided services to preschool children registered with the federally funded "Headstart" program. There are two special MIC projects, under the health department, giving comprehensive preventive and treatment services to pregnant women and infants in selected poverty neighborhoods. Along with the growing number of district health centers offering general primary care at specified hours, there are some making plans to offer 24-hour emergency services.

No two local public health programs providing clinic services are exactly alike. This overview of one metropolitan county, however, may give an impression—both in strengths and weaknesses—of the contribution of the health department to the organization of ambulatory health services in the nation.

NOTES

1. Rosen, George, *A History of Public Health* (New York: MD Publications, 1958), p. 71.

2. Shattuck, Lemuel, *Report of the Sanitary Commission of Massachusetts 1850* (Cambridge, Mass.: Harvard University Press, 1948).

3. Rosen, *A History of Public Health,* p. 385.

4. Ibid., pp. 353–355.

5. Schmidt, William M., "The Development of Health Services for Mothers and Children in the United States," *American Journal of Public Health,* 63 (1973): 419–427.

6. Mustard, Harry S., *Government in Public Health* (New York: Commonwealth Fund, 1945).

7. Smillie, Wilson G., *Public Health Administration in the United States,* 2nd ed. (New York: Macmillan Co., 1940), p. 371.

8. Mustard, Harry S., *Government in Public Health,* pp. 160–161.

9. Schmidt, "Development of Health Services."

10. Ibid., p. 421.

11. Deutsch, Albert, *The Mentally Ill in America: A History of Their Care and Treatment from Colonial Times* (Garden City, N.Y.: Doubleday, Doran, & Co., 1938), p. 458.

12. Moore, Harry H., *American Medicine and the People's Health* (New York: D. Appleton & Co., 1927), p. 73.

13. Roemer, Milton I. and Barbara Faulkner, "The Development of Public Health Services in a Rural County: 1838–1949," *Journal of the History of Medicine and Allied Sciences* 1 (1951): 22–43.

14. Kratz, F. W., "Status of Full-time Local Health Organization at the End of the Fiscal Year 1941–42," *Public Health Reports* 58 (1943): 345–351.

15. Emerson, Haven and Martha Luginbuhl, *Local Health Units for the Nation,* American Public Health Association (New York: Commonwealth Fund, 1945).

16. U.S. Public Health Service, *Directory of Local Health Units, 1966* (Washington: PHS Pub. No. 118, 1966).

17. U.S. Public Health Service, *Local Health Officers: Statistics and Characteristics* (Washington: PHS Pub. No. 1636, April 1967).

18. Druzina, George B. and Earl E. Phillips, "Salary Trends for State and City Health Officers, 1935–1965," *American Journal of Public Health* 56 (1966): 905–911.

19. McConnell, Frances S., et al., "The Selection of the Field of Public Health by Workers in Local Public Health Departments," *American Journal of Public Health* 56 (1966): 764–775.

20. Myers, Beverlee A. et al., "The Medical Care Activities of Local Health Units," *Public Health Reports*, 83 (1968): 757–769.

21. Miller, C. Arden, et al., "A Survey of Local Public Health Departments and Their Direction," *American Journal of Public Health* 67 (1977): 931–937.

22. American Public Health Association, *Tuberculosis* (Cambridge, Mass.: Harvard University Press, 1969), p. 36.

23. U.S. Public Health Service, *Tuberculosis Program Reports* (Atlanta: Center for Disease Control, 1970), p. 57.

24. New York State Department of Health, *Tuberculosis Control 1970* (Albany, N.Y.: 1971), p. 72.

25. U.S. Public Health Service, *Tuberculosis in the World* (Atlanta: Center for Disease Control, 1976), p. 103.

26. Anderson, Odin W., *Syphilis and Society—Problems of Control in the United States 1912–64* (Chicago: Center for Health Administration Studies, Research Series 22, 1965), p. 10.

27. U.S. Center for Disease Control, *Report of the National Commission on Venereal Disease* (Washington: DHEW Pub. No. HSM 72-8125, 1972), p. 42.

28. U.S. Public Health Service, *Directory of Venereal Disease Clinics* (Atlanta: Center for Disease Control, September 1974).

29. American Social Health Association, *Today's VD Control Problem 1974* (New York: 1974).

30. Pan American Health Organization, *Report of the International Travelling Seminar on Venereal Disease in the United States of America* (Washington: PAHO Pub. No. 280, 1974), p. 15.

31. Pariser, Harry, "Organizational and Clinic Facilities," *Journal of the American Venereal Disease Association* 1 (1974): 63–66.

32. Atwater, John B., "Adapting the Venereal Disease Clinic to Today's Problem," *American Journal of Public Health* 64 (1974): 433–437.

33. U.S. Center for Disease Control, *Report of the National Commission on Venereal Disease*, p. V.

34. U.S. Public Health Service, Maternal and Child Health Service, *Maternal and Child Health Services of State and Local Health Departments, Fiscal Year 1970* (Washington: 1971).

35. U.S. Public Health Service, Maternal and Child Health Service, *Promoting the Health of Mothers and Children Fiscal Year 1972* (Washington: 1973), p. 27.

36. U.S. Public Health Service, Maternal and Child Health Service, *Children Who Received Physicians' Services under the Crippled Children's Program Fiscal Year 1970* (Washington: 1971).

37. Lee, Evelyn (editor), *Administration in Crippled Children's Services* (Berkeley, Calif.: University of California, School of Public Health, 1962).

38. Wallace, Helen M. et al., "Administrative Relationships between Maternal and Child Health Programs and Family Planning Programs in Health Departments," (Berkeley: University of California, School of Public Health, processed, 1973).

39. U.S. National Center for Health Statistics, *The National Inventory of Family Planning Services: 1975 Survey Results*, (Washington: Series 14, No. 19, April 1978).

40. American Public Health Association, *Chronic Disease and Rehabilitation* (New York: 1960), p. 22.

41. Myers, Beverlee et al., "The Medical Care Activities," p. 761.

42. International Union Against Cancer, *Cancer Detection* (New York: Springer-Verlag, 1967), pp. 63–64.

43. Metropolitan Life Insurance Company, "The Value of Periodic Medical Examinations," *Statistical Bulletin* 2, no. 11 (November 1921).

44. Roemer, Milton I., "A Program of Preventive Medicine for the Individual," *Milbank Memorial Fund Quarterly* 23, no. 3 (1945).

45. Chapman, A. L., "The Concept of Multiphasic Screening," *Public Health Reports,* 64 (1949): 1311–1313.

46. American Medical Association, Council on Medical Service, *A Study of Multiple Screening* (Chicago: 1955).

47. Gelman, Anna C., *Multiphasic Health Testing Systems: Reviews and Annotations* (Washington: National Center for Health Services Research and Development, March 1971).

48. McKeown, Thomas, et al., *Screening in Medical Care: Reviewing the Evidence* (London: Oxford University Press, 1968).

49. Dales, L. G.; G. D. Friedman; and M. F. Collen, "Evaluation of a Periodic Multiphasic Health Check-up," *Methods of Information Medicine* 13 (1974): 140–146.

50. Cutler, John C., et al., "Multiphasic Checkup Evaluation Study," *Preventive Medicine* 2 (1973): 197–206.

51. Advisory Committee to the National Center for Health Services Research and Development, *Provisional Guidelines for Automated Multiphasic Health Testing and Services* (Washington: U.S. Public Health Service, 1970).

52. U.S. National Institutes of Health, *Directory of Outpatient Psychiatric Clinics, Psychiatric Day-Night Services and Other Mental Health Resources in the United States and Territories* (Washington: 1964), pp. 7–23.

53. Mott, F. D., and M. I. Roemer, *Rural Health and Medical Care* (New York: McGraw-Hill, 1948), pp. 422–431.

54. U.S. Department of Health, Education, and Welfare, *1970 Annual Report* (Washington: 1971), p. 158.

55. Rural America, *National Rural Health Council—Rural Health Update,* (Washington, D.C., August–September 1979), p. 7.

56. U.S. Public Health Service, *What Thirteen Local Health Departments are Doing in Medical Care* (Washington: PHS Pub. No. 1664, June 1967).

57. Mytinger, Robert E., *Innovation in Local Health Units* (Washington: U.S. Public Health Service, Pub. No. 1664-2, February 1968).

58. Renthal, Gerald A., "Comprehensive Health Centers in Large U.S. Cities," *American Journal of Public Health* 61 (1971): 324–336.

59. Shonick, William and Walter Price, "Recent Changes in and Current Organizational Status of Local Public Health Units" (Los Angeles: University of California, School of Public Health, 1975), unpublished data.

60. Cowen, David L. and John A. Sbarbaro, "Family-centered Health Care—A Viable Reality? The Denver Experience," *Medical Care* 10 (1972): 164–172.

61. McLaughlin, Mary C., "Issues and Problems Associated with the Initiation of the Large-scale Ambulatory Care Program in New York City," *American Journal of Public Health* 58 (1968): 1181–1187.

62. Brown, Howard T., "Planning for Rational Organization of Urban Health Services—The Health Services Administration of New York City," *Medical Care* 5 (1967): 169–173.

63. Terris, Milton and N. A. Kramer, *General Medical Care Programs in Local Health Departments* (New York: American Public Health Association, 1951).

64. "Guarding the Health of Baltimore—1973," *Baltimore Health News* 51 (1974): 116.

65. De Hoff, John B., "Health Care Consortiums—New Roles for Local Health Departments," *American Journal of Public Health* 63 (1973): 672–674.

66. Rhyne, Jimmie L.; Albert Chang; and Robert E. Farber, "Transition from Traditional Public Health to a System of Primary Medical Care in Maternal and Child Health of the Baltimore City Health Department," Baltimore City Health Department, unpublished report, 1973.

67. De Hoff, John B., "Involvement of an Urban Health Department in Emergency Medical Systems," Baltimore City Health Department, unpublished report, 1973.

68. Shonick and Price, Recent Changes.

69. County of Los Angeles Health Department, *History and Functions of the County of Los Angeles Health Department* (Los Angeles, Calif.: 1970).

70. American Public Health Association (Malcolm H. Merrill, Director of Study), *Future Direction for Health Services—County of Los Angeles 1970* (Los Angeles, Calif.: 1970).

71. Witherill, L. A., Memorandum to All Personnel, Department of Health Services, Los Angeles County, unpublished document, September 1972.

72. U.S. Department of Commerce, *Social and Health Indicator System, 1973, Los Angeles* (Washington: Bureau of the Census 1973).

73. Minkowski, William L.; R. C. Weiss; and G. A. Heidbreder, "The County of Los Angeles Health Department Youth Clinics," *American Journal of Public Health* 61 (1971): 757–762.

Chapter 6

School and College Health Services

As places where the vast majority of children over five years of age gather together nearly every day, the schools of the United States—primary, secondary, and higher levels—provide a natural institutional sponsorship for organized ambulatory health services (OAHS). As noted in Chapter 5 some health services in elementary and secondary schools are sponsored by public health agencies, but the great majority are under the responsibility of educational authorities.

HISTORICAL BACKGROUND

Because children are especially susceptible to communicable diseases and to other hazards from the environment, the importance of some medical surveillance was appreciated soon after primary education was made compulsory and publicly financed in Europe. In 1842, the French government required that every school in Paris be visited periodically by a physician who should inspect the environment and observe the general health of the children.[1] In 1874, Brussels appointed doctors to visit the schools three times a month. The idea of such periodic inspections spread gradually throughout Europe. The policy in Germany, starting at Wiesbaden in 1896, was especially comprehensive. England passed a national "School Medical Inspection Act" in 1908.[2]

In 1840 in the United States, William Alcott, a distinguished educator, called for periodic visits to the schools by physicians, who would see children referred by teachers. In 1872, Elmira, New York appointed a "sanitary superintendent" to cope with an alarming outbreak of smallpox in school children. It was not until 1892, however, that New York City appointed the nation's first permanent school medical officer. Two years later Boston appointed 50 "medical visitors" to go to schools throughout the city and examine children identified as sick by the teachers. Other large cities soon followed this pattern, emphasizing the identification and removal from school of children with contagious diseases.

113

Connecticut in 1899 took the first statewide legal action on a noncommunicable disease, requiring that all public school children be examined for visual defects. In 1903, New Jersey authorized all local boards of education to employ school doctors, and in 1904 Vermont required "annual examinations of the eyes, ears, and throats of school children." Massachusetts passed similar legislation in 1906.

Nursing services were first brought into the schools in New York City in 1902, when, at the initiative of the voluntary Henry Street Visiting Nurse Association, it was demonstrated that children with scabies and other minor skin diseases could be cured if nurses could offer instruction to the parents. This pattern also spread, and by 1923 among 86 cities surveyed all but two had school nursing services. Some form of physical examination of school children by doctors was also being carried out in all 86 cities.

Gradually the scope of functions of school doctors and nurses broadened.[3] Dental services were also added, the first school dentist having been appointed in Reading, Pennsylvania in 1903. The tuberculosis problem, which became prominently recognized around 1905, led to greater attention to the general nutrition of children and later to tuberculosis testing and chest x-rays. Attention was gradually given to the general growth and development of children, as knowledge in this field expanded. High rates of rejection of military draftees in World War I focused national attention on the neglect of physical defects, that might have been detected in school children and corrected before they reached military age.[4] The same sequence occurred 20 years later in World War II. Meanwhile, the leadership of the National Education Association (NEA), the American Public Health Association (APHA), and other bodies promoted support for and further broadening of the scope of personal health services in schools.

STUDENTS AND SCHOOLS IN AMERICA

In the fall of 1976, out of a population of 215 million, there were about 60 million students enrolled in schools, constituting some 28 percent of the American people.[5] Their distribution at different levels of education was as follows:

Type of School	Number of Students
Elementary school (kindergarten–grade 8)	34,172,000
Secondary school (grades 9–12)	15,821,000
Universities and colleges	10,105,000

Source: Grant W. Vance and C. George Lind, *Digest of Education Statistics, 1976 Edition,* (Washington: U.S. National Center for Education Statistics, 1977).

The majority of these students are entitled to receive some sort of ambulatory health care under the auspices of an organized system, although the content of these services is highly variable.

More than 87 percent of the students are enrolled in public (governmental) schools. At the elementary and secondary school levels, this proportion is about 90 percent, with only 10 percent of students attending private or parochial schools. As many as 76 percent of the students enrolled in higher education are in public colleges and universities.

Elementary and secondary schools under public auspices are organized in systems generally congruent with local units of government. Since 1940, however, there has been a marked tendency for small school systems (of towns or even counties) to consolidate in order to achieve the economies and greater capabilities of larger scale. In 1940, there were 101,000 more or less self-governing local public school systems and, although total enrollments have almost steadily risen, by 1976 the number of systems had declined to 16,300. This greater strength per school system has, among other things, enabled the school authorities to support better developed programs of school health services.

Health programs in public elementary and secondary schools are typically administered at the headquarters of the school system, but the services are ordinarily delivered within each school. The great majority of school structures are solely for elementary education of young children. In 1974–75, the overall distribution of all levels of schools, both public and private, was as follows:

Level of School	Public	Private	Total
Elementary	61,759	14,372	76,131
Secondary	23,837	3,770	27,607
Combined and special*	3,099	—	3,099
Universities and colleges	1,214	1,533	2,747
All levels	89,909	19,675	109,584

*Special schools are principally for the handicapped or retarded.
Source: Grant W. Vance and George C. Lind, *Digest of Education Statistics, 1976 Edition* (Washington: U.S. National Center for Education Statistics, 1977).

The scope, staffing, and other characteristics of OAHS in these nearly 110,000 American schools vary greatly among communities of different socioeconomic levels, since local property taxes are the major source of financial support of schools below the college level. The content of ambulatory services also varies greatly between the educational levels, since health needs change rapidly in the childhood, adolescent, and young adult years. Personal health services offered at each of these levels may be reviewed, within the limitations of the data available.

ELEMENTARY SCHOOL HEALTH SERVICES

We have noted that health services in elementary schools grew out of concern for limiting the spread of childhood communicable diseases. Although vigilance continues for control of such diseases and certain immunizations are required, the trend has clearly been toward broader concern for the health of the child.[6] In its most basic formulation, the ideal school health program has come to encompass three components: (a) health education of the child, (b) maintenance of a safe and healthful school environment, and (c) personal health services.

Within the third component—personal health services—activities may be of differing scopes. In various combinations they include mainly the following:

- health status appraisal (examinations)
- first aid to cases of trauma
- referral for needed care (medical or psychological)
- immunizations
- dental service

Beside immunizations, other preventive activites in the school setting are embodied in classroom health education, school lunch programs, safety measures to reduce accidents, and so on. But, insofar as we are concerned with ambulatory personal health services, the range rarely goes beyond the five types of services listed above. Moreover, in most of the nation's 76,000 elementary schools, the scope of personal health services would seldom be so comprehensive as to include all five of these activities.

The content of ambulatory health services in United States elementary schools can be given only in rough approximations. The first nationwide survey of such services was made in 1946 by the American Academy of Pediatrics, in cooperation with the U.S. Public Health Service and the U.S. Children's Bureau.[7] At this time, it was observed that, with respect to "early detection of disease or impairment of growth" in school children, the most common pattern was "examination by a physician and follow-up by a nurse to facilitate corrections." Therapeutic correction of defects or disorders detected was (and still is) dependent on referral of the child to a personal physician outside the school system.[8]

This survey simply identified the presence or absence of school medical examinations of the above type in the 3,076 counties of the nation. It was found that 1,545 counties (or about half) had no schools providing medical services along the lines defined above. These were mainly rural counties with small populations. They enrolled about five million children, or some 22 percent of the children 5–14 years of age at the time. Viewed positively, 78 percent of the nation's children of elementary school age lived in counties where schools did offer some medical examination services. Moreover, in 967 (or 63 percent) of the counties with no medical services, the schools did have nursing services, and these counties had 11 percent of all school-age children. Thus 89 percent (78 plus 11) of the nation's children in 1946 lived in counties where the schools were served by medical or nursing personnel or both.

Administration of these school health services in 1946, as now, was divided among education authorities, public health authorities, or combinations thereof. In general, school health programs in the urban districts, where most of the children lived, were controlled by education authorities, while in the more rural districts with fewer children, public health agencies were more often responsible. The frequency of medical examinations was greater in school health systems under education authorities. In some school systems, policy called for examination of all children annually; in others, only the children in certain grades were examined annually; in still others, there was no regular pattern, and only children with some possible disorder, identified by the teacher or school nurse, were referred for medical examinations. The percentage distribution of these three patterns in 1946 was as follows:

Frequency of Medical Examinations	Education Agencies	Public Health Agencies
All pupils annually	64	10
Certain grades annually	26	53
Referral of pupils only	10	37
All frequencies	100	100

Source: American Academy of Pediatrics, *Child Health Services and Pediatric Education* (New York: Commonwealth Fund, 1949).

Since the enrollment of the schools (predominantly urban) where health services were controlled by education agencies was much greater, one may infer that most children in 1946 were getting school health examinations annually.

In 1946, about 8,000 physicians were estimated to be participating in this school health work. The vast majority were private practitioners who did school work part-time, and only 4 percent of them were pediatricians. About 20 percent of these doctors were public health officials and school activities also occupied only a fraction of their time.

During 1946, there were 15,720 nurses in the United States involved in school health services. Thirty-eight percent, or 4,440, were full-time in school health work, and the balance were part-time. In addition, certain relatively simple tests for vision and hearing—obviously important for the child's classroom performance—were given by teachers or by special technicians. In 14.2 percent of the school health systems teachers did all the vision testing, and in another 28.7 percent they were assisted in this task by other personnel. Hearing tests were done by teachers in 4.9 percent of the school health systems, and in another 13.6 percent these tests were done by teachers along with technicians. Whenever defects of vision or hearing were detected, a communication was sent to the parents advising them to have the child's condition diagnosed and corrected.

The next major nationwide study of health services in elementary schools was conducted by the U.S. Office of Education in 1950.[9] Questionnaires were sent to 3,186 U.S. cities of 2,500 population or more, and responses came from 2,886, or 91 percent. Nearly all of the nonrespondents were small towns of under 10,000 population. This study found that 63 percent of the city school systems employed physicians or "medical advisers," and 85 percent employed school nurses. In 17 percent of the schools, from 8 to 14 medical examinations were performed on the children during the eight elementary school years; in 83 percent of the schools at least one medical examination was performed during these years. In 40 percent of the school systems, dental examinations were also done, and 16 percent employed dental hygienists.

Sixty percent of the school health programs (with a larger percentage of the children) were controlled by education authorities, 11 percent by health departments, and 23 percent by a combination of the two. In general, it was clear that the comprehensiveness of school health services was directly proportional to the size of city.

A study in New York City during 1952 showed that the initial health examinations of about 50 percent of entering school children were performed by family physicians, and they yielded about 8,000 recommendations for some corrective medical measures.[10] The other 50 percent of such examinations, performed by appointed physicians on the school premises yielded nearly 30,000 recommendations for follow-up studies. One may infer that the examinations in organized school settings, done by physicians experienced in this type of work, are more productive than those done in private medical offices. As corroboration of this inference, in another special series of 14,132 children examined by New York City school physicians during a ten-day period, 9,003 health problems were identified and referred to family doctors for follow-up and care.

As one might expect, the school health services of New York City, the nation's largest metropolis, have been well developed.[11] Although differing from the practice in other large cities by being under the department of health (rather than education), that agency's bureau of school health in 1953 employed a staff of 250 part-time physicians, working in the schools under the direction of four full-time pediatricians. The health department's bureau of nursing allotted 47 percent of its nursing personnel time—the equivalent of 375 full-time nurses—for work in the schools. Medical examinations were required for all children entering school, for sixth graders, and for children finishing the eighth grade.

In addition, as necessary, children were referred by teachers or nurses to the school physician for special examinations; the school doctors sometimes conferred with the parents, home visits were made by the school nurse or doctor, and school nurses often conferred with the child's family physician.

The American Association for Health, Physical Education, and Recreation undertook a national survey of school health practices in 1961.[12] Data were gathered on the several components of school health programs through questionnaires addressed to state departments of education. The responses were unfortunately not tabulated, but with respect to personal health services, such summary statements were made as the following:

> Many school boards employ nurses, while some school boards in the larger metropolitan areas employ their own school physicians. . . . The school health service program in the United States is predicated on the principle that the family has primary responsibility for the health of the school child. In general, then, medical treatment is not provided by local schools except in the case of emergencies. . . .[12]

In the responses to this 1961 survey from certain states, somewhat more specific answers are furnished. New Jersey, for example, stated:

> Each school district must employ a school health physician . . . and may employ other health personnel. In New Jersey, over 1,000 school nurses are employed; about 90 percent of this number are employed directly by individual Boards of Education, the remainder being employed by contract between Boards of Education and either official or non-official agencies. . . . The school nurse works cooperatively with parents and teachers, informing them of the scope and function of the health service program, alerting them to defects discovered, and, when necessary, assisting parents to find ways of having defects corrected.[12]

New York State reported that:

> The (health service) personnel are employed by local Boards of Education, except in the cities of New York City, Buffalo, and Rochester, where health services are provided through the Public Health Department. . . . All children attending public schools (outside the three cities noted) have an annual medical examination, including tests for vision and hearing. . . . We recommend the employment of the school nurse-teacher for every 1,000 students in an urban area, or 500 in a rural area. . . . School nurse-teachers . . . spend approximately 50 percent of their time outside of school, following through with parents and community organizations on the defects found . . .[13]

The State of Wisconsin reported that:

> A great difference exists (among) many of the 2700 school districts. Some employ medical, dental, psychological, nursing, social work, and other specialized personnel. Some districts employ few such personnel, many districts employ no health service personnel.[14]

In 1964, the School Health Section in the U.S. Public Health Service (PHS) solicited information about school health programs from a stratified national sample of 118 local school systems. Responses were received from 83 systems in 40 states and the District of Columbia.[15] Administrative sponsorships and the systems having physicians as directors were as follows:

Sponsorship	Number	Physician Directors
Board of Education	51	25
Health Department	12	6
Combinations of above	20	5
Total	83	36

Source: U.S. Public Health Service, School Health Section, *A Survey of School Health Services in 83 School Systems* (Washington: 1964).

Of 62 community school systems reporting on the kinds of health personnel employed, the distribution was as follows:

Type of Health Personnel	Percent of 62 School Systems
Nurses (full-time)	100
Physicians (full-time)	50
Physicians (part-time)	32
Dentists (full-time or part-time)	32
Dental hygienists	31

Source: USPHS, School Health Section, *A Survey of School Health Services in 83 School Systems* (Washington: 1964).

The most nearly universal component of school health service programs in the 83-system sample was "health appraisals." Some procedure was carried out in all 83 school systems, but not all of them did complete physical examinations of the child. The frequency with which different types of examinations were routinely performed was as follows:

Type of Health Examination	Percent of 83 Systems
Vision screening	89
Hearing test	88
General physical examination	71
Weight and height	46
Tuberculin skin test	45
Dental inspection	37
Dental examination	17

Source: USPHS, School Health Section, *A Survey of School Health Services in 83 School Systems* (Washington: 1964).

The frequency of these examinations was highly variable. Thus, only 3 of the 83 districts performed general physical examinations annually, while 54 percent of them examined the children four times or less between kindergarten and secondary school graduation. On the other hand, simple recording of weight and height, if done at all, was done annually in most of the districts. Of the 71 percent (59 districts) of school systems performing routine physical examinations, 31 estimated the number of children examined, which aggregated to 1,250,000 in 1962. In six districts giving statistics on hearing tests, 356,000 pupils were tested, among whom 12,600 cases of impaired hearing were detected. In 6 of the 83 school districts, special cardiology clinics were conducted for diagnosis of heart conditions in any child in whom a murmur was found in the general physical examination.

General diagnostic and treatment clinics may be conducted in some school systems for the follow-up of defects found in children from needy families. Out of the 83-system sample in the U.S. Public Health Service study, 11 (13 percent) operated such clinics regularly. In addition, another 25 percent of school districts made arrangements with a nearby hospital or medical school to examine needy children with defects. First aid and emergency care were a definite function of the school nurse (or sometimes of the teacher under the nurse's instruction) in 53 of the 83 districts, or 64 percent. There were three cities (Los Angeles, California; Cleveland, Ohio; and Seattle, Washington) reporting figures on first aid services. The total school population was 789,000 in these cities in 1962; that year 627,400 visits were made to school nurses for first aid service. If this rate of about 0.8 visits per year per child is applied to the U.S. national population of 50,000,000 elementary and secondary school children as of 1976, it yields an estimate of 40,000,000 such first aid visits. This does not include other minor health problems that were handled by schoolteachers.

The latitude for service by the school nurse was highly variable. In some districts, for everything except "the most minor scratch," the child would be sent to his home or, if no parent was there, to a hospital. In other districts, the nurse was authorized to treat all but the most serious injuries. One school district, in Cleveland, Ohio, gave a tabulation of first aid services in 1962, which was as follows:

First Aid Service	Number	Percent
Minor dressings for injuries	21,088	44.2
Initial diagnosis, with referral	20,783	43.5
Serious emergencies, with referral	3,905	8.2
Treatment of minor skin disorders	1,021	2.1
Treatment of conjunctivitis	956	2.0
All services	47,753	100.0

Source: USPHS, School Health Section, *A Survey of School Health Services in 83 School Systems* (Washington: 1964).

Thus, altogether the school nurse in Cleveland gave total care to about 48 percent of the children coming to her, and she referred 52 percent of cases to a physician.

Special mental health services were provided for children identified with such problems in 19 of the 83 school systems. In only 2 of these, however, did the school authorities operate this clinic, while in 17 the child was referred to a mental health clinic sponsored by another local agency. Regarding immunizations, school cooperation with health departments is particularly great. Although only 12 or 14 percent of the school health services in the 83 systems sampled were under health department supervision, in 62 (75 percent) of them the local health department participated in mass immunization programs.

In 1966, a survey of 230 cities throughout the United States found health services still administered predominantly by boards of education in 80 percent of the school systems.[16] Perhaps it is this supervision by school authorities—to whom health care is naturally secondary to education—that explains why personal health services in the school setting rarely move beyond the traditional sphere of prevention and detection. While many public health clinic services, as we have observed, have evolved into comprehensive programs, including treatment, school health policies seem to change relatively little. These programs have cautiously avoided infringing on the jurisdiction of private medicine, even when this has meant inadequate followup of disorders detected in children.[17] When therapeutic services in organized settings have been provided for school children of low-income families, it has usually been through resources, such as "neighborhood health centers," sponsored by agencies other than the schools. Sometimes there is systematic liaison between such centers and the schools. Insofar as overall school health programs have been innovative in the 1960s and 1970s, it has usually been through enriched content of health education in the classroom, through improved nutrition in school lunches, or safety in the design of school playgrounds, rather than in the content of ambulatory health services.

A somewhat more recent survey of school health services was made in 1970 in California. Out of 793 reporting school districts, 71 percent of health programs were directed by school administrators, and another 26 percent by nurses employed within the school system. Only 3 percent of programs were directed by a health department physician,[18] yet 2,700 nurses and 576 physicians gave full-time or part-time service in these 793 school districts.

The time trend reflected in these several surveys suggests that over the years health departments have played a declining role in provision of health services to school children, and departments or boards of education have assumed increasing responsibility. A U.S. government report indicates that in 1970, health department physicians did physical examinations of only 2.9 percent of school-age (5–17 years) children, which was a decline from 5.4 percent of such children in 1957.[19] Dental screening examinations of school children also declined from 6.4 to 4.6 percent over this period. There was an upward trend only for perception tests by health department technicians: from 10 to 17 percent of school children being screened for vision (between 1957 and 1970), and from 7 to 11 percent for hearing.

In most states, legal responsibility for school health services is delegated by the state government to local governments, which in turn implement programs along the lines described. As physicians have become less readily available for school health examinations, a growing emphasis has been put on alerting school teachers to detect signs of illness or defects in their pupils and to refer them to the school nurse for followup.[20] Sometimes voluntary Parent Teacher Associations (PTA) put special efforts into strengthening school health services. Perhaps the most disturbing problem, however, is the failure or inability of many parents, especially those of low income, to follow up on recommendations for correction or treatment of disorders detected in school medical examinations.[21]

Our interest in this review of school health services and their associated clinics, is their actual status, rather than theoretical requirements. A 1977 study of state legislation, however, gives some reflection of the official priorities that have reached the stage of being written into law.[22] This study was done by a legal research center on the basis of a nationwide questionnaire, followed up by various other communications. A summary of the basic legal statutes for the 50 states of the United States is shown in Table 6-1.

In amplification of the simple figures in Table 6-1, it may be noted that "immunizations" vary in the types required; most often these are limited to smallpox, diphtheria, tetanus, and whooping cough. The only states without any mandatory immunizations of school children are Montana and Wyoming. Many states also require poliomyelitis immunization, and some require measles inoculation. Ordinarily the requirement applies to the child at entry to elementary school. In most states, it is expected that the child will have been immunized by a private physician or a public health agency before entry, not at the school.

In 14 states, however, the law specifies that the school should provide the mandated immunization for indigent children.

The specifications on screening for vision and hearing usually indicate that these procedures should be conductd in the school setting. The same applies to dental examination and treatment, scoliosis screening, tests for sickle cell traits, and measurement of height and weight. The provisions for school health records are typically very general.

Regarding general medical examinations, the laws do not necessarily demand that they be done by school health personnel. In fact, the most common policy implemented is to encourage these being done by the family doctor before the child enters school. Some states, however, call for periodic reexaminations, which explains the practice of having these services provided by a school physician in the school premises. Two states (New Jersey and Alaska) specifically authorize a school nurse to perform general physical examinations. It must be realized that for general examinations, and, indeed for all other procedures the *local* school boards may mandate a frequency greater than that specified by state law; likewise, in states where a procedure is optional or completely absent in the state law, local school boards may still require its performance.

Regarding the "special need examination," the intent is to identify children having special educational needs because of physical or mental handicaps. The 15 states requiring or recommending such examinations have probably been stimulated by a 1975 federal law (Education of the Handicapped Act) that pro-

Table 6-1 Legislation in 50 States on School Child Health Appraisals, United States, 1977

	States in which Procedure is:		
Health Procedure	*Mandatory*	*Recommended or Optional*	*No Legislation*
Immunizations	48	2	0
Vision screening	26	14	10
Hearing test	26	14	10
General medical examination	16	15	19
Health record	15	10	25
Special need examination	12	3	35
Dental examination	10	19	21
Dental treatment	0	12	38
Sickle cell test	6	1	43
Scoliosis screening	3	10	37
Height and weight	3	7	40

Source: Margaret A. Kohn, *A State Survey of School Health Laws and Regulations and Health Service Requirements in Day Care Centers—Minimum Licensing Standards* (Washington: Center for Law and Social Policy, 1978).

vides federal financial aid for programs specially designed to help the handicapped and requires, among other things, that such screening examinations be done in the schools.

Aside from the immunizations for indigent children, only two states (Indiana and New York) mandate that schools must provide general medical *treatment* for indigent children. In a few states treatment is authorized for indigent children with specific disorders—such as vision or hearing defects—but not mandated, and in a few other states it is authorized for any medical condition in an indigent child. First aid or emergency services in the schools are required by most states, and these are usually provided by school nurses.

The most common uncorrected physical defect found in elementary school children is dental disease, which probably explains why the schools have taken greater initiative in establishing clinics for treating dental disorders than any other type.[23] Ordinarily these clinics are available only to children from low-income families. Less frequently, and usually in larger cities, clinics are operated for low-income children with hearing or visual defects. Voluntary agencies, such as Lions Clubs, often contribute funds for providing corrective eyeglasses to poor children needing them. The initiative and energy of school nurses are crucial in arranging for the correction of defects or disorders found in school children, but family concern and economic capabilities are doubtless decisive in the end.

A study of Los Angeles school children in whom physical defects had been identified, found several factors to influence the likelihood of corrective measures being taken. Family income and the educational status of the parents were most influential.[24] But beyond these influences, family coverage by insurance for medical care also played a part; in low-income families, health insurance coverage often seemed to determine whether or not a child's defects were corrected.[25]

One of the few longitudinal studies of the nurse staffing of elementary school health services was made in Eugene, Oregon. Here it was found that the complement of school nurses did not keep up with the increasing enrollment of children in the 1950s and 1960s. In 1957 the student to nurse ratio was 1,373 to 1, and this increased to 1,527 to 1 by 1963.[26] In this community, as in many others, voluntary organizations, business person's clubs, and even the local medical and dental societies came forward to fortify the weakening position of school nursing services.

It generally has been found that the adequacy of staffing and functions of school health services increases with the size of school. A study of the achievement of standards in health appraisals, dental examinations, communicable disease control, emergency care, etc. in the secondary schools of Indiana showed a direct linear relationship.[27] Thus, in schools with under 200 students enrolled, ideal standards were met or approached (according to a scoring system) by 23.5

percent. This rose to 29.8 percent in schools of 200 to 499 students, and to 50.0 percent in schools with 500 students or more. The highest level of achievement in schools of all sizes was for communicable disease control; for this, the gradient of achievement rose from 44.7 percent in the smallest schools to 65.9 percent in the largest.

Expenditures for personal ambulatory health services in the schools are not reported separately, but the overall expenditures for health care are available. In 1956, data from 40 states showed an annual expenditure of about $2.70 per pupil per year for public schools at both primary and secondary levels. The per student expenditures were estimated at $3 per year in elementary schools and $2.50 in secondary schools.[28] These outlays have risen considerably, even though health services in 1973–74 constituted hardly 1 percent of total expenditures of school systems.[29] In 1970–71, the per student health expenditure was up to $8.21, and it had risen to $10.36 by the 1973–74 school year. By 1979, in fact, the Robert Wood Johnson Foundation estimated that in elementary schools alone (with 43,700,000 children), expenditures on health activities amounted to one billion dollars.[30] If so, this would mean an outlay of nearly $23 per child per year in the elementary schools.

Of these expenditures, the largest share goes for school health personnel, principally nurses. It has been estimated that, in full-time equivalents, about 25,000 health personnel work in American public school systems, of whom 17,000 are school nurses.[31] The nurse to pupil ratio largely determines the per pupil expenditures. These ratios vary from 1:912 in New Hampshire, 1:1,035 in Pennsylvania or 1:1,377 in Wyoming to ratios such as 1:5,556 in Arkansas, 1:8,350 in Kentucky, or 1:9,502 in Tennessee. If the estimate above on 17,000 school nurses (full-time equivalents) is approximately correct, for the 50 million primary and secondary school children in the United States the overall ratio would be one nurse for each 2,940 schoolchildren.

Financial support of school health services is predominantly from local taxes. In 1973–74, the financing of local public school systems in the United States came 54 percent from local revenues (city and/or county), 39 percent from state revenues, and 7 percent from federal grants.[32] The general trend toward increasing federal financing of health services in America has evidently not applied to those rendered in the schools. Yet school systems have legal responsibility for the welfare and health of millions of children during many hours almost every day. The hazards of contagious disease, which stimulated the earliest attention of school authorities to health matters, are no longer very great in the United States. But new problems have taken their place, including serious accidental injuries (that are now the leading cause of death in the school-age years). To cope with these hazards, aside from providing the first aid services of school nurses, many school systems purchase insurance policies to cover the costs of medical treatment of children injured on the school premises.

SECONDARY SCHOOL HEALTH SERVICES

The adolescent years of children in American secondary schools yield a rather different pattern of health services than that of the primary schools. The nation's 28,000 secondary schools—86 percent public and 14 percent private—are, in a sense, tumultuous places where 16 million young people are passing through the turbulent years of puberty.[33] Sexuality develops rapidly, and it is inevitable that problems of venereal disease and premarital pregnancy should become prominent. Young people, eager to grow up, adopt many habits—such as cigarette smoking, alcohol consumption, experimenting with various mood-modifying drugs, etc.—that may become firmly ingrained and affect their health for the rest of their lives. These are the years of vigorous athletics, legal authorization to drive automobiles, and also the formation of strong emotions, all of which lead to a high rate of trauma and sometimes violence.

These characteristics of high school students obviously influence the content of ambulatory health service programs. The detection of physical defects through medical examinations and the control of communicable diseases no longer hold the priority that they had in primary schools. Great attention tends to be given to the health education of youth on the process of sexual maturation, the hazards of unwanted pregnancies and venereal disease, and the risks of drug abuse, excessive alcohol consumption, and tobacco. Because of the special hazards from careless use of automobiles, many high schools have introduced courses in driver training; this instruction is mandated by law in numerous states.

Because of the great interest of teenagers in athletics, secondary school departments of physical education are often combined with health education and even sometimes with health services. School nurses are quite well distributed in the nation's secondary schools (which are on the average much larger than elementary schools) but their roles are different. While they give first-aid emergency services, as required, referring serious trauma cases to the nearest medical office or hospital, they spend most of their time in counseling individual students with personal health problems.

Pregnancy in teenage secondary school girls has been typical of a problem increasing in recent years due to changing social norms among young people. In 1968, there were in the United States 165,700 live births to young women under 20 years of age, compared with 42,600 in 1940.[34] These births are not only usually out of wedlock, presenting great social difficulties, but they are also biologically high-risk for both mother and infant. Obviously such pregnancies in secondary schools present serious challenges to their health programs.

A survey of school superintendents and health officers of the nation's 150 cities of 100,000 population or more in 1971 yielded 130 responses.[35] Of these, 85 percent reported on special programs for the pregnant girls, most frequently including counseling, social service, special education, health classes, and instruction in family life. Less frequently, the health program in the secondary school offered arrangements for pregnancy testing, maternity home care, day care for infants, and abortions. Contraceptive advice was offered to sexually active adolescents in 65 of the 130 cities; medical care was provided in 68 cities, but mainly through referral to public health agencies, hospitals, or private physicians. In general, the scope of services was greater in the larger cities.

The growing problem of alcohol consumption and drug abuse among secondary school youth is tackled principally through health education. Use of marijuana is particularly widespread, and has been the subject of much debate on the soundest method of control. The substance is widely available and its biological effects are still not entirely clear. In New York, a special school for young narcotic addicts was established as long ago as 1952, to accommodate 250 youths.[36]

The conscientious nurse in a secondary school often assumes the role of confidential adviser to high school youths who are reluctant to take up health problems, physical or emotional, with their own parents. The nurse may play a crucial part in giving hygienic advice to adolescent youth or in referring them to other resources for needed health services.

COLLEGE AND UNIVERSITY HEALTH SERVICES

Since a large proportion of students attending colleges or universities are away from their family homes, the importance of some provision for general medical care—not merely the health appraisal and first aid services conventional in elementary and secondary schools—has long been appreciated. In the 1860s, Amherst College, in Massachusetts, was the first American institution of higher education to provide health services, although it was oriented largely to promotion of physical fitness and treatment of athletic injuries.[37] In the 1890s, the larger and more affluent colleges engaged "medical visitors"—local physicians who would visit the campus periodically. In 1906, the University of California at Berkeley organized a general medical service, probably the first in the United States offering comprehensive care.

By 1917, there were enough physicians serving college students to form the organization that later became the American College Health Association (ACHA). By 1924 there were 131 colleges with organized health programs, supported often by an annual student fee but sometimes by the general tuition or state government funds.[38] Around 1930, the important national Committee on the Costs of Medical Care included a study of "university student health services" in its series of investigations; out of 539 colleges and universities in the United States at the time, special health care programs were organized in 153 of them.[39]

As noted earlier, in 1976 there were more than ten million students enrolled in nearly 2,800 colleges and universities throughout the United States. The majority of these young adults are in schools that make some organized arrangements for health services, including the treatment of sickness as well as disease prevention and health promotion. Generally, the scope of services is broader in the larger institutions, whether private or public. In colleges with a high proportion of students living away from home, provision is frequently made for "infirmary" care, i.e., inpatient care of acute illness (that would simply confine the patient to bed in his or her own home) as well as for organized ambulatory health services.

In 1953, a major survey was made of the health services offered at all colleges and universities listed in the federal government's *Education Directory of Higher Education*. Out of 1,887 institutions then listed, responses were received from 1,573, but satisfactory information was obtained from only 1,157. The following findings are based on this 61 percent sample of the universe.[40]

Nine hundred fifty-seven institutions, or 83 percent, had some type of organized health service. Those without any such program were concentrated among two-year colleges, schools with a specialized training program, and small colleges (with enrollment under 500). Of the 957 institutions reporting some health service, 90 percent required a medical examination of the student on entry; about half of these examinations were done by college health service physicians, the other half were done by outside physicians. About half the colleges also required further periodic medical examinations on all students. Chest x-rays were required in about 60 percent of the colleges, and other special procedures (such as visual examinations and psychological tests) in lesser percentages. Immunizations of various types were also required in varying proportions of colleges.

About three-quarters of the student health services maintained cumulative individual records on all students or on those who made some use of the treatment aspects of the program. Of the 957 institutions with health programs, 80 percent offered medical care for illness or injuries. About half of these, however, limited their concern to minor disorders. It is especially noteworthy that nearly half the 957 colleges provided clinical services for faculty and staff also, and 10 percent provided services to the spouses and children of students.

Student health directors in 70 percent on the institutions estimated that the majority of students made use of the clinical services. Only one-fourth, however, maintained records that permitted calculation of utilization rates by different students. Total clinic visits were, nevertheless, tabulated by two-thirds of the programs and indicated a nationwide average of 3,170 visits per 1,000 enrolled students per academic year. If this rate of about three clinic visits per student per school year in 1953 were applied to the approximately 10 million students currently enrolled in American colleges and universities, it would yield a theoretical volume of 30 million ambulatory care encounters.

About 80 percent of student health programs in 1953 furnished prescription drugs, and some 60 percent performed diagnostic x-ray and laboratory procedures. Of the 80 percent of programs offering medical care, three-fourths operated some type of infirmary or hospital. These inpatient facilities, however, were ordinarily only for minor disorders, and only one in ten admitted patients for major surgery. Three-quarters of these facilities were small, with less than 20 beds. Health education was a component of the great majority of college health programs, as were surveillance of environmental sanitation and special care for athletic injuries.

In about 40 percent of the college health programs, the director was a physician, usually full-time. The remainder were directed by nurses or staff in the field of physical education. Altogether in 1953, there were 465 full-time physicians and 1,530 part-time physicians engaged in this work. Estimating the aggregate physician time in college health work yielded a figure of 28 medical hours per week for every 1,000 enrolled students. Full-time nurses numbered 1,610. The median cost for all student health services in 1953 was $7.25 per student per school year. Special prepaid health fees were imposed in 30 percent of the programs to cover these costs, but in most the costs were derived from general tuition and other school income. In general, the expenditures for and resources of college and university health programs, on a per student basis, increased with the size of the institution.

Since this national survey of college and university health programs in 1953, the evidence suggests that organized ambulatory services to college student populations in the United States have been strengthened. An especially well-developed program at Yale University, for example, covered 9,000 students plus 6,000 college staff and their dependents in 1975.[41] For these 15,000 persons, there were 17.8 full-time equivalent physicians and a utilization rate of 5.37 encounters per eligible person per school year. At the University of California at Los Angeles (UCLA) in the 1976–77 academic year, student clinic visits were as follows:[42]

Primary and general clinics	37,406
Laboratory and radiological visits	30,508
Specialty clinic visits	29,179
Total	97,093

Source: UCLA, "Report of the UCLA Student Health Service, Fiscal Year 1976–77," Los Angeles, Calif., 1977, unpublished report.

For about 31,000 enrolled students, this meant 3.1 clinic visits per student per school year. The lesser rate at UCLA than at Yale may be explained by the high proportion of UCLA students living at home (and obtaining needed medical care through family resources), and by the noncoverage of university personnel (of older age levels) at UCLA.

The nature of health problems presented to college health service programs in recent years has changed. Problems relating to sexuality, drug dependence, contraception, alcoholism, and neuroses—as well as the perennial common cold—are increasingly common. Serious disorders include viral hepatitis, streptococcal pharyngitis, infectious mononucleosis, gonorrhea, and pregnancy.[43]

The ACHA undertook a survey of student health service programs throughout the nation in 1977. Questionnaires were sent to all member institutions in the Association (about 400), plus a sample of other colleges to yield a mailing of 728.[44] Returns were received from only 225 colleges and universities, which doubtless constituted a sampling of the institutions (among more than 2,700 in the nation) with more highly developed student health service programs. Nevertheless, some conclusions may be drawn from this survey.

In general, the larger and older universities, offering at least four-year academic degrees, tend to have more well developed ambulatory care systems. Smaller four-year colleges or junior colleges offering less than full degree programs (typically for two years) often provide health services only from a nurse, with one or more physicians being on call. In recent years the problem of costs has become a serious obstacle to health program development. With pressures felt by college administrations in meeting the costs of their regular academic program, health services tend to receive lower priority.

The ACHA survey yielded clear evidence of economies of scale. Thus, institutions with enrollment of 15,000 to 20,000 students, and with full-time physicians in their student health services, incurred costs in 1977 of $60.45 per student per year. The comparable per student annual cost of health services in larger universities of greater than 20,000 enrollment was $49.32. The rate of ambulatory service utilization in both these sets of institutions was equal, about 2.5 encounters per student per year.

Because of financial pressures, college health programs have tended to reduce their provision of inpatient care. Compared with the 75 percent of these programs offering bed facilities in the 1953 survey, the 1977 survey found that in even the larger universities only about 57 percent provided hospital or infirmary care. Moreover, about 30 percent of these programs intended to reduce their complement of beds. The annual health program cost per student was strikingly higher in those institutions maintaining bed facilities.

Although one must realize the bias of the ACHA sample, the medical staffing in the 225 responding colleges and universities aggregated to 574 full-time equivalent physicians, or 2.6 physicians per institution. Unfortunately the overall student enrollment was not reported, so that the ratio of students per doctor cannot be calculated. College health service leaders, however, sometimes advocate a ratio of one doctor to 2,000 students as optimal. It was noteworthy that of the 574 physicians (in full-time equivalents) reported in the 1977 survey, 16 percent were psychiatrists.

To cope with financial constraints, it has been customary for four-year colleges to charge a student health fee, over and above the regular tuition. Where such fees are required, they usually cover the great majority of health service costs, but often they must be supplemented by funds from other sources. Perhaps the major response to cost pressures in recent years has been the use of health insurance plans. Students are encouraged, or even required to enroll in an established insurance program that will pay for all or part of medical and hospital costs provided in the local community. Of the 225 responding institutions in the ACHA survey, 211 offered students some type of health insurance coverage. Sometimes this cost protection was intended mainly for graduate students or foreign students, but usually it was for undergraduates as well. Of 203 institutions with health insurance plans for undergraduates, enrollment was mandatory in 22 percent. The parallelism of this trend to health insurance programs for industrial workers is noteworthy.

Based partly on the 1977 survey and partly on other sources, the executive director of ACHA estimated in November 1979 that in about 1,200 of the nation's nearly 2,800 colleges there was some type of organized student health service. This constituted 44 percent of the institutions, but, being the larger ones, they had about nine million, or 82 percent of the eleven million students. Although we know that the scope of these services is highly variable, college health programs clearly constitute a significant source of organized ambulatory care for young adults in America.

LOS ANGELES COUNTY SCHOOL HEALTH SERVICES

In Los Angeles County, personal ambulatory health services in the public schools began in the 1890s, with the initial emphasis, as elsewhere, on communicable disease control. Teachers inspected the pupils daily for signs of such infections. As early as 1880, the Los Angeles Board of Education directed its school personnel to be concerned about proper classroom temperatures and ventilation.[45] Soon after 1900, nurses were engaged to conduct periodic screening of elementary school children for defects of vision and hearing as well as dental disease. After World War I, with its revelation of a high rate of physical defects in military draftees—defects which might have been corrected in the school-age years—impetus was given to regular medical appraisals by physicians.

Initially nursing services in the schools were provided by public health nurses from the Los Angeles County Health Department, but gradually after about 1920 (in accordance with California State law) nurses came to be employed directly by the school system. The health department has retained responsibility for services in the nonpublic (i.e., private) schools and occasionally on contract with some of the smaller local school systems in the county. Health services in the 657 Los Angeles City schools, the largest school system in the county, are completely under the direction of the city school district. A series of evaluative studies in the late 1950s led to expansion of nursing and medical services throughout the Los Angeles City school system.[46]

In 1971, when we surveyed a small sample of local school health programs, there were 2,350 elementary and secondary schools (both public and private) in Los Angeles County, with about 1 million students enrolled. The 1,750 public schools among these were aggregated into 82 school districts, which are the framework for providing health services. Many of these school districts are assisted by school health advisory councils that attempt to mobilize services from other local health agencies and to attract part-time services from private physicians and dentists.

California state law requires that vision testing be performd on all school children in kindergarten, first, third, and seventh grades; hearing tests by audiometer must be done in the first grade. No routine screening tests are done in the secondary school years. Children with possible vision or hearing defects are referred for medical attention through a note sent to their parents. In private schools, where student family income levels tend to be higher, policies often impose on the families responsibility for all screening or medical examinations.

In a sample of 38 public and private schools of Los Angeles County visited in 1971, wide variations were found in the physical facilities for personal health care and in the diligence with which services were provided. Generally, both of these characteristics were stronger in schools located in more affluent neighborhoods, and also in schools with personnel who showed deep commitment. It is noteworthy, however, that out of 15 public schools visited, all but one had a room designatd specifically for ambulatory health services or emergencies; out of 18 private schools visited, such resources were lacking in 5.

As customary throughout the nation, screening or full medical examinations in the Los Angeles County schools were intended solely to identify defects in the child. Correction was regarded as a family responsibility. Increasingly, there appears to be reliance on the classroom teacher to identify signs of possible disease in a child and to refer him or her to the school nurse. Another growing policy has been appointment of some teacher or administrator on the school staff to serve as health coordinator. This person is expected to promote implementation of the various phases of the school health program—environmental and educational programs, as well as personal health services in their preventive, emergency, and referral aspects. The quality of services is influenced by the California state requirement that nursing personnel have credentials in public health nursing or school nursing, as well as being fully registered with the state (that is, having R.N. certification).

A unique feature of the school health service in the City of Los Angeles is the sponsorship of six special clinics for diagnosis, and some treatment of school children by the local PTAs.[47] Low-income children from several schools are referred to these clinics for diagnostic examinations by part-time salaried physicians. Eyeglasses may be prescribed for children needing them; and dental care may also be provided. A means test determines whether or not a fee is payable, scaled according to family income. For more serious conditions, the child is referred to an outside physician. The PTA clinics are staffed by school district health personnel, but about half the costs are met by funds from the PTA.

California state law mandates that children entering school shall have been immunized against important childhood infections, such as diphtheria, pertussis, smallpox, measles, and poliomyelitis. Ordinarily this is determined by the school nurse, through reports from the parent or guardian at the child's initial entry. In recent years, some Los Angeles County schools were found to be lax in enforcement of these public health requirements, and renewed attention has been directed to their implementation.

There are several universities and colleges, both public and private, in Los Angeles County. The two largest are UCLA, a state government institution with 31,000 students, and the University of Southern California, a private institution, with 24,000 students. Both have well-developed health care systems providing a wide range of ambulatory services to their students. In addition there are four campuses of the state university system (Los Angeles, Northridge, Long Beach, and Dominguez Hills) that likewise operate student health service programs. There are 20 junior or community colleges operated by cities in the county with some 100,000 students enrolled. Finally, there are numerous private and relatively small colleges, most of which provide some ambulatory care to their students. The numerous other technical or trade schools in Los Angeles County, as in most metropolitan centers, do not ordinarily operate organized health programs.

Thus, at every level of schooling—elementary, secondary, and university—organized ambulatory health services are provided. For this age level in the United States—roughly ages 5 to 21 years—health problems are, on the whole, relatively minor. Accidental injuries are the major cause of mortality in these age groups, and minor respiratory tract infections the major cause of morbidity. At all three levels, much emphasis is put on prevention and health promotion. At adolescence, problems relating to sexuality and mental and emotional difficulties assume greater importance, stimulating health services in these fields. Insofar as more than 60 million young people, some 28 percent of the U.S. population, are enrolled for most of the year in some form of school, the organized health services provided by schools make a substantial contribution to ambulatory medical care in the nation.

NOTES

1. Gulick, Luther S. and Leonard P. Ayres, *Medical Inspection of Schools* (New York: Russell Sage Foundation, 1908).

2. Wilson, Charles C. (editor), *School Health Services,* 2nd ed. (Washington: National Education Association, 1964), pp. 361–387.

3. Veselak, K. E., "Historical Steps in the Development of the Modern School Health Program," *Journal of School Health,* 29 (1959): 262–269.

4. Patty, W. W., "Trends in the School Health Program," *Journal of Health and Physical Education,* 16 (1945): 183–185; 223–225.

5. Grant, W. Vance, and C. George Lind, *Digest of Education Statistics, 1976 Edition* (Washington: U.S. National Center for Education Statistics, 1977).

6. Wilson, *School Health Services.*

7. American Academy of Pediatrics, *Child Health Services and Pediatric Education* (New York: Commonwealth Fund, 1949).

8. Ibid., pp. 114–115.

9. Kilander, H. F., *Health Services in City Schools* (Washington: U.S. Office of Education, Bull. No. 20, 1952).

10. Jacobziner, Harold, and R. W. Culbert, "The Role and Function of the Private Physician in the School Health Service Program," *New York State Journal of Medicine* 53 (1953): 51–56.

11. Culbert, Robert W., and H. Jacobziner, "Health Services to School Children in New York City," *New York State Journal of Medicine,* 53 (1953): 47–50.

12. American Association for Health, Physical Education, and Recreation, *School Health Practices in the United States* (Washington: 1961).

13. Ibid., p. 151.

14. Ibid., p. 232.

15. U.S. Public Health Service, School Health Section, *A Survey of School Health Services in 83 School Systems* (Washington: processed, c. 1964).

16. Wolf, J. M., and H. C. Pritham, "Administrative Patterns of School Health Services," *Journal of the American Medical Association,* 193 (1966): 195–199.

17. Eisner, Victor, and L. B. Callan, *Dimensions of School Health* (Springfield, Ill.: Charles C. Thomas, 1974), pp. 5–8.

18. California State Department of Public Health, *A Report to the 1970 Legislature on Reimbursement of Public School Health Services in California* (Sacramento, Calif.: Human Relations Agency, 1970).

19. U.S. Department of Health, Education, and Welfare, Maternal and Child Health Service, *Children Who Received Physicians' Services under the Crippled Children's Program, Fiscal Year 1970,* (Washington, D.C.: 1971).

20. Yankauer, Alfred, "A Further Evaluation of the Astoria Plan of School Medical Services in New York City Elementary Schools," *American Journal of Public Health* 41 (1951): 383–387.

21. National Education Association, "United States of America," in *Child Health and the School* (Washington: World Confederation of Organizations of the Teaching Profession, 1960), p. B–31.

22. Kohn, Margaret A., *A State Survey of School Health Laws and Regulations and Health Service Requirements in Day Care Centers—Minimum Licensing Standards* (Washington: Center for Law and Social Policy, processed, September 1978).

23. Mayshark, Cyrus, and Donald D. Shaw, *Administration of School Health Programs: Its Theory and Practice* (St. Louis, Mo.: Mosby Co., 1967), pp. 194–198.

24. Cauffman, J. G.; E. L. Peterson; and J. A. Emrick, "Medical Care of School Children: Factors Influencing Outcome of Referral from a School Health Program," *American Journal of Public Health* 57 (1967): 60–73.

25. Cauffman, J. G.; M. I. Roemer; and C. S. Shultz, "The Impact of Health Insurance Coverage on Health Care of School Children," *Public Health Reports* 82 (1967): 323–328.

26. Mayshark, C., and R. L. Covey, *School Health Administration—A Case Study,* (Corvallis, Oreg.: Oregon State University, 1963).

27. Ludwig, D. J., "Evaluation of School Health Programs in Selected Indiana Public Schools," read before American School Health Association, (Chicago, Ill.: October 17, 1965).

28. Schloss, Samuel, and Carol J. Hobson, *Statistics of State School Systems: Organization, Staff, Pupils, and Finances, 1953–54* (Washington: U.S. Office of Education, 1956).

29. Kahn, G., *Statistics of Local Public School System, Finance 1973–74* (Washington: U.S. National Center for Education Statistics, DHEW, July 1975).

30. Robert Wood Johnson Foundation, "New Approaches to Child Care Services Focus Attention on the Nation's Schools, " *Special Report,* Number One, 1979, p. 5.

31. Nader, Philip (editor), *Options for School Health* (Germantown, Md: Aspen Systems, 1978), p. 108.

32. Ibid., p. 117.

33. Josselyn, Irene M., "Psychological Problems of the Adolescent," *Social Casework,* 32 (1951): 183–190.

34. Wallace, Helen M. et al., "A Study of Services and Needs of Teenage Pregnant Girls in the Large Cities of the United States," *American Journal of Public Health* 63 (1973): 5–16.

35. Ibid.

36. *New York Times,* May 17, 1952, p. 19.

37. Dalrymple, Willard, and Elizabeth F. Purcell, *Campus Health Programs* (New York: Josiah Macy, Jr. Foundation), 1976.

38. Mock, H. E., et al., "Report of the Committee on Student Health Maintenance," *Interfraternity Annual Minutes,* 1924, pp. 111–131.

39. Falk, I. S.; C. Rufus Rorem; and Martha D. Ring, *The Costs of Medical Care,* Committee on the Costs of Medical Care, Pub. No. 27 (Chicago: University of Chicago Press, 1933), pp. 464–465.

40. Moore, Norman S., and John Summerskill, *Health Services in American Colleges and Universities 1953* (Ithaca, N.Y.: Cornell University, 1954).

41. Rowe, Daniel S., "Community Health Service Programs for Faculty and Students," in *Campus Health Programs* (New York: Josiah Macy, Jr. Foundation), pp. 121–133.

42. UCLA, "Report of the UCLA Student Health Service, Fiscal Year 1976–77" (Los Angeles, Calif.: University of California, June, 1977), unpublished report.

43. Klotz, Addie L., "The Goals of Student Health Services: Who Can Meet Them?" in *Campus Health Programs* (New York: Josiah Macy, Jr. Foundation), pp. 61–70.

44. American College Health Association, "Survey of College and University Health Programs" (Washington: October 1979), unpublished data.

45. Veselak, K. E., "Historical Steps in the Development of the Modern School Health Program," *Journal of School Health* 29 (1959): 262–269.

46. Los Angeles City Schools, *Evaluation of the Health Program in the Los Angeles City Schools 1954–1961* (Los Angeles, Calif.: 1962).

47. Los Angeles City School Districts, Health Services Branch, *Annual Report 1964–65* (Los Angeles, Calif.: 1965).

Chapter 7

Industrial Health Units

Most adults in America work, and their places of work provide a natural setting for certain organized ambulatory health services (OAHS). Many types of work, furthermore, are hazardous, and this has long stimulated special social measures—organized efforts to prevent or to take care of injuries or diseases associated with work. In this chapter we will examine the extent and characteristics of OAHS activities at workplaces. We cannot explore all aspects of occupational health or industrial medicine—a specialized discipline of very great proportions[1]—but an appreciation of modern industrial clinics requires first a glimpse of history.

HISTORICAL BACKGROUND OF OCCUPATIONAL HEALTH SERVICES

Recognition of the special health hazards of work can be traced to ancient Egypt and to classical Greece and Rome.[2] The importance of understanding a patient's occupation and working conditions for good medical practice, however, was first emphasized by Bernardo Ramazzini, an Italian physician who published a comprehensive account of "occupational diseases" in 1700.[3] This led to development of a defined specialty of "occupational medicine"—a discipline concerned largely with the diagnosis, treatment, and prevention of such disorders as lead poisoning, silicosis, blood dyscrasias from exposure to diverse chemicals, and so on. As this specialty has matured, however, it has broadened its view to consider all the circumstances affecting the health of workers.

Our interest is on the organized actions taken in industry—typically by the management of enterprises—to cope with work-connected injuries and diseases. These activities, in the form of safety, health, and medical programs, did not come rapidly, but rather built up slowly over the course of industrialization throughout the nineteenth century in response to social and governmental pressures. As mechanization rapidly spread, and increasing numbers of workers were killed or crippled by industrial accidents, legal actions were taken in the courts. With the growing political strength of European workers, laws were passed in the mid-nineteenth century establishing "employer's liability" for work injuries.[4] But even under these laws, the employer had many defenses— the worker's "assumption of risk," the "fellow-servant doctrine" (negligence of another worker, rather than the employer, being responsible), etc.—against the claims on behalf of a disabled or killed worker. This led to the Industrial Accident Insurance Bill in Germany (1884) and then to the more far-reaching "Workmen's Compensation Law" of England in 1897. The latter established a principle that had been slowly forming in English common law; namely, the basic responsibility of employers for work accidents, regardless of negligence or fault of the worker.[5]

Employers could assume this responsibility with least risk by obtaining insurance. Commercial companies soon sold policies to furnish compensation both for loss of wages (typically a certain percentage of the worker's usual wage) and for the costs of necessary medical care. Since the premiums payable by employers for this insurance varied with the accident record of each firm, the employer had every incentive to introduce safety measures to keep the accident rate as low as possible. The principle of varying insurance costs with accident experience, or "experience rating," became a crucial feature of industrial injury compensation all over the world.[6] Experience rating, or "merit rating," would not only create incentives for reducing the frequency of accidents, but also for furnishing prompt first aid, so that the effect of any trauma could be minimized. These legislative dynamics have doubtless played a crucial role in the organization of in-plant medical services in Europe, America, and elsewhere.

In the United States, the first workmen's compensation act was passed by New York State in 1910. On the grounds of the Fourteenth Amendment of the U.S. Constitution, related to the banning of slavery after the Civil War, (i.e., no deprivation of a person's life, liberty, or property "without due process of law"), this act was declared unconstitutional because it deprived employers of property "without due process." In a few years, after countless further on-the-job deaths of workers, the courts decided otherwise, and by 1949 all states had enacted workmen's compensation laws. The provisions of the state laws show enormous variations, but their general tendency has been toward broadening of both the types of work covered and the benefits provided for both accidents and work-connected disease.[7]

Even before the stimulation of the workmen's compensation laws, state governments in America, as European countries had done before, had enacted "factory inspection" laws to require safeguards of machinery, proper ventilation, and so on. Massachusetts had passed the first such state law in 1867, and by 1908 factory inspection legislation existed in 17 states. The staffs to carry out these inspections and enforce the laws, however, were typically small and inadequate. In effect, these resources were so weak that inspections and positive corrective actions would tend to be taken only in response to specific complaints initiated by employees.[8] The impact of the workmen's compensation legislation, with its positive financial inducements, was therefore much greater.

Thus, it was not until after 1910 that the organization of clinics within factories and other workplaces became a significant practice. Reflecting the development of this type of service was the founding in 1915 of the American Association of Industrial Physicians and Surgeons.[9] This was a period also of struggles for the unionization of workers, for the eight-hour workday, for banning child labor, for higher wages, and for better working conditions. Provision of health services in the workplace, therefore, would not only yield possible savings in workmen's compensation insurance, but also would constitute a humane personnel policy that could discourage unionization. It coincided also with the concepts of the industrial efficiency movement (that is, a healthy worker would be more productive), which was strong at the time. The whole reasoning in support of health services in industry was concisely summarized in a 1921 report of the National Industrial Conference Board (NICB), (an association of large enterprises), which stated:

> The value of medical service in industry became emphasized when workmen's compensation laws were enacted and the burden of the expense of injuries to workmen was placed largely on the employer. It became necessary for the employer to provide medical and surgical treatment for workers injured while in his employ and, in addition, to prevent injuries so far as lay within his power. Preventive medical work in industry proved itself of the greatest importance and demonstrated that early attention to trivial accidents and injuries reduced the amount of compensation to be paid by the employer and the amount of time lost by the employee. Moreover, experience showed that the best working conditions produced the least sickness among employees and the smallest loss of working time due to accidents, and that conditions inimical to the health of the workers could be removed with positive assurance that the general physical and mental health would be benefited thereby, resulting, in turn, in increased production and lessened labor turnover. In other words, it has been found that proper health supervision of workers pays in terms of the return upon the investment, besides fulfilling broad humanitarian considerations.[10]

The NICB conducted a study of medical services in firms in 1919 and 1920. Two hundred seven replies were received from companies having some type of medical service. Of these, only 9 had maintained such services before 1900, 24 had developed services between 1900 and 1910, and 164 started these programs between 1910 and 1920.[11] The impact of the compensation laws would seem to be obvious. Even so, the great majority of these firms were quite large, 92 percent having 500 employees or more.

The staffing pattern in this period, like today, consisted of physicians—full-time, part-time, and on call—plus industrial nurses. Of the 207 firms in the 1921 study, 38 percent had full-time doctors; 40 percent had part-time physicians, 19 percent had a doctor on call. Some 3 percent depended only on a nurse.[12] There were a total of 502 physicians (48 percent of them full-time) in all 207 plants. The number of nurses in these plants is not reported, but in another study of 90 plants, a total of 204 industrial nurses were evidently full-time.

Except for the smallest firms, the per worker expenditures for industrial health services in 1920 showed economies of scale, as follows:[13]

Size (employees) of Firm	Number of Firms	Annual Cost per Worker
Under 500	17	$5.94
500–1,000	35	6.18
1,000–2,000	54	6.06
2,000–5,000	59	5.41
5,000–10,000	23	4.10
10,000 and over	19	3.49
All sizes	207	$4.43

Source: NICB, Cost of Health Service in Industry, Research Rep. No. 37 (New York: 1921).

A field study by the NICB in 1920, with visits to 90 plants, showed medical records to be rather casual, except for serious accidents having legal implications under workmen's compensation. Administratively, the industrial physician reported directly to the top plant executive in 45 percent of cases, and to the personnel director or some other middle level manager in 55 percent. X-ray equipment was available in only 14 percent of the plants.

The predominant function found in the study was the prompt treatment of accident cases, but even in 1920 some additional services were performed. Thus, various plants reported that they offered health education on personal and home sanitation. They reported cases of communicable disease to public health authorities (particularly tuberculosis and venereal infection), and gave prenatal advice to pregnant workers. Of the 90 plants visited, preemployment examinations were performed in 25. In another study done in 1920, there were 56 responses to a mail survey of 100 "representative industrial establishments." Of the 56, preemployment examinations were done by 30, and by 4 additional firms after employment. These examinations were done, however, with varying degrees of thoroughness.[14] Only a few firms did periodic reexaminations.

As American industry moved into the expansive postwar 1920s, and then entered the Depression years of the 1930s, further changes occurred in health services at the workplace. With industrial growth in the 1920s, particularly in large enterprises, in-plant medical services increased. In 1928 there were 1,500 physicians employed full-time in industrial medical posts.[15] The grave economic Depression starting in 1929 caused an inevitable setback in management-sponsored industrial medical services, but another form of medical care for industrial workers rose to greater importance. This was the comprehensive health care model, which had been first launched in isolated industries—mining, lumbering, and railroad construction—in the early years of the century.[16] Instead of being financed by management, these general medical care programs (not limited to work-connected injury or illness) were supported mainly by wage deductions— essentially a form of health insurance. By 1930, an estimated 540,000 workers in isolated industries were covered by such programs. There was also the occasional firm, such as the Endicott-Johnson Shoe Company near Binghamton, New York or the Hershey Chocolate Company at Hershey, Pennsylvania, that financed general medical care for workers and also their families, as a kind of paternalistic personnel policy (intended, according to one viewpoint, mainly to discourage unionization).

In 1942, there were reported to be 2,300 full-time industrial physicians, of whom about 500 were in the comprehensive type of industrial health insurance program. Over the course of the 1930s, the general movement for health insurance in the United States gained momentum—especially with the rise of Blue Cross insurance for hospitalization.[17] This was bound to have an impact on industrial workers, as the insurance movement grew to massive proportions during the World War II years. A major source of members for Blue Cross plans, and later Blue Shield plans and commercial insurance programs, was workers who could be enrolled in large employment groups.[18] During the war years also, there arose the pace-setting general medical care program in the west coast Kaiser shipyards, financed jointly by wage deductions and employer contributions.[19] The relatively broad scope of health insurance benefits, compared with the typical in-plant medical service, was bound to have an impact on industrial health services, widening their concern beyond the traditional sphere of work-connected problems.

A federal government survey in 1943 identified 113 prepaid industrial programs providing general medical care to workers, and 42 of these also served the worker's family. Although the Kaiser Health Plan was the largest, there were programs in 33 states.[20] In addition to the 500 full-time physicians noted earlier, there were as many as 5,900 other doctors working part-time in these comprehensive health care programs, financed by the workers, the employers, or both.

Another form of medical care program for workers, broader in scope than traditional in-plant services, was developed by labor unions after 1940. The oldest such program, the Union Health Center, originated in 1913, and was founded by the International Ladies Garment Workers Union in New York City.[21] It grew out of an industrial dispute and was intended to provide ambulatory care and preventive and diagnostic services to union members. The idea was not replicated, however, until the 1940s, when the United Automobile Workers, the Amalgamated Clothing Workers, Retail Food Employees, and other unions established somewhat similar "labor health centers."[22] The principal focus of these centers was on diagnostic examinations and some general ambulatory medical care. They reflected, in a sense, a certain distrust of company doctors by union workers.

One more ingredient in development of industrial health services was an outgrowth of the public health movement. Under the Social Security Act grants to the states for "general public health purposes," funds were alloted for establishing "industrial hygiene branches" in state departments of health. Unlike the factory inspection programs in departments of labor, these units were not concerned with general enforcement of safety and sanitary standards, but rather with studies of selected occupational health hazards and with general promotion of in-plant medical services.[23] The factory was looked upon as a setting for general health promotion through nutrition, health education, venereal disease detection, etc., as well as for general counseling on medical care. Since the principal deficiencies of in-plant medical services were found in small plants, the industrial hygiene branches in many state health departments devoted special efforts to encouraging establishment of programs in such plants. One of the important strategies was to organize "cooperative" small plant industrial health programs among groups of small firms in one urban area; in this pattern, one physician with a few nurses, would provide services to several firms in the locality.[24]

As general health insurance programs expanded their enrollments and their range of benefits in the 1950s and 1960s, the labor health centers, along with the comprehensive industry-based prepaid health care programs, declined in importance. The objective both of organized labor, and of personnel policy in most industrial firms, became contracting for fringe benefits (that is, payment by the employer) that would purchase health insurance protection from existing large carriers.[25] Meanwhile, the concern of in-plant industrial medical services broadened in other ways, primarily to include general health promotion and prevention, beyond the specific hazards of occupational disease. The scope of current industrial health clinics varies in relation to the size of the firm, the type of industry, and other factors. Before examining this, we should take note briefly of the composition of the American working population.

AMERICAN INDUSTRY AND WORKERS

Of the 1974 United States population of 210,000,000 persons, 91,785,000 were in the civilian labor force, that is, they were either employed or seeking employment.[26] The balance were children under 16 years of age, adults not seeking employment, or persons retired or institutionalized. Of the civilian labor force, 85,732,000 were employed and 6,053,000 were seeking and able to work but unemployed in June 1974. By broad categories of work, the employed workers were classifiable as follows:

Occupational Class	Percent
White-collar workers (professional, managerial, sales, clerical, etc.)	48.6
Blue-collar workers (operatives, craftsmen, laborers, etc.)	34.7
Service workers	13.2
Farm workers	3.5
All types	100.0

Source: U.S. Bureau of Labor Statistics, *Labor Force Development, First Quarter 1975: News* (Washington: April 14, 1975) p. 7.

Analyzing the approximately 86 million employed workers by sex and by broad categories of industry in 1974, the distribution was as follows:

Industry	Male Workers (percent)	Female Workers (percent)
Manufacturing	25.5	13.9
Service	21.3	35.2
Wholesale and retail trade	16.8	17.2
Professional and related services	9.7	23.0
Construction	8.8	0.7
Transport, communication, and utilities	7.8	2.8
Agriculture, forestry, and fishing	5.1	1.4
Finance, insurance, and real estate	3.9	5.6
Mining	1.0	0.1
All industries	100.0	100.0

Source: U.S. Bureau of Labor Statistics, *Labor Force Development, First Quarter 1975: News* (Washington: April 14, 1975), p. 7.

Of the total 1974 population 16 years and over, 81.3 percent of the men and 45.9 percent of the women were in the labor force (i.e., working or seeking employment). This amounted to a working population composed of about 62 percent men and 38 percent women.

As noted in Chapter 3, the size of a firm, in terms of its number of employees, is the major determinant of its health service arrangements. In general, the larger the establishment, the more likely it is to have an organized health program. The distribution of the nation's workforce according to the size of plant was roughly estimated by Lorin Kerr in 1973 to be: 25 percent of the workers were employed in the 1 percent of plants that had more than 500 employees each; while 75 percent of the workers were employed in the 99 percent of plants that had less than 500 employees. Somewhat outdated but more precise relationships may be reported for the total workforce of the United States, as of 1948.[28] These distributions were as follows:

Size of Firm (number of employees)	Percent of Firms	Percent of Workers
1–49	96.48	39.71
50–499	3.25	30.96
500–999	0.16	8.41
1,000 and over	0.11	20.95

Source: Margaret C. Klem, M. F. McKiever, and W. J. Lear, Industrial Health and Medical Programs (Washington: Public Health Service, September 1950), p. 38.

Thus, in 1948 over 99 percent of workplaces, with less than 500 employees each, had over 70 percent of the workers; while fewer than 1 percent of firms, with 500 employees or more, had about 30 percent of the workers.

More recent data on the distribution of workers are available for manufacturing industry, which employed about one-third of the nation's workers in 1972. These data apply to 1967:[29]

Size of Manufacturing Plant (number of employees)	Percent of Plants	Percent of Workers
Less than 20	65.0	5.6
20–99	24.2	17.7
100–249	6.5	16.6
250–999	3.6	27.3
1,000 and over	0.7	32.8

Source: U.S. Bureau of the Census, Statistical Abstract of the U.S., 1972 (Washington: 1972), p. 716.

Thus, for manufacturing industry, there has been a greater proportion of workers in the relatively few large plants; the 4.3 percent of plants with 250 workers or more in 1967 had 60.1 percent of the workforce. This helps to explain the relationship to nursing personnel reported in Chapter 3; namely, 32.7 percent of the industrial nurses being engaged in manufacturing firms that employed, as of 1972, 32.5 percent of the workers.

More recent data are available for distribution of workers by plant size in selected localities. In 1970 in the Chicago area, for example, the relationships were as follows:[30]

Size of Plant (number of employees)	Percent of Plants	Percent of Workers
8–19	20.8	2.6
20–49	42.8	13.0
50–99	17.6	12.1
100–249	11.8	17.9
250–499	4.2	14.1
500 & over	2.8	40.4
All sizes	100.0	100.0

Source: U.S. Public Health Service (PHS), Occupational Health Survey of the Chicago Metropolitan Area (Cincinnati, Oh.: Bureau of Occupational Safety and Health, 1970).

Thus, in a metropolitan center such as Chicago the 2.8 percent of plants with 500 workers or more have more than 40 percent of the workers, a distribution that should be advantageous for the provision of health services.

In addition to plant size, the nature of an industry has an influence on the likelihood of its having health services. It has been noted previously that service industries have a disproportionately high share of the industrial nurses. Such industries employ 21 percent of male workers (second only to manufacturing) and 35 percent of female workers (the highest category of industry for women). On the other hand, the disproportionately low share of nurses in the construction industry indicated in Chapter 3 is unfortunate in the light of the high accident risk in this type of work.

Industries may be classified by their extent of hazard. As of 1973, the U.S. Bureau of Labor Statistics ranks industries according to the incidence of work-connected injuries and occupational illnesses as follows:[31]

Type of Industry	Injuries & Illnesses per 100 Full-time Workers per Year
Contract construction	19.8
Manufacturing	15.3
Mining	12.5
Agriculture, forest and fishing	11.6
Transport and utilities	10.3
Wholesale and retail trade	8.6
Services	6.2
Finance, insurance, and real estate	2.4
All industries	11.0

Source: American Public Health Association (APHA), *Health and Work in America—A Chart Book* (Washington: 1975), p. 52.

Unfortunately, this crucial aspect of a work setting appears to have little influence on the likelihood of provision of in-plant health services.

EXTENT OF INDUSTRIAL HEALTH SERVICES

Studies of the provision of OAHS at the workplace have been made since about 1920, but as we have noted above these early studies do not give a clear indication of the *total* industrial health situation; they report on only those particular firms that offered such services. Accounts of the extent of physicians and nurses serving in the totality of firms, according to various characteristics, have become available only since the late 1940s.

In 1946, the American College of Surgeons (ACS) reported on surveys of selected companies made between 1929 and 1940.[32] The samples of establishment surveyed reflect an obvious bias toward firms of larger size; since the data report only the presence of an "approved medical service," moreover, their meaning is subject to various interpretations. (To meet ACS standards, an industrial medical service must, for example, have "competent medical staff," "complete records," etc., which could have diverse meanings.) In any event, the ACS survey of industries over the years 1929 to 1940 showed the following:

Size of Firm (number of employees)	Number of Firms	Percent with ACS-approved Service
1–249	98	18.4
250–499	224	38.8
500–999	396	49.0
1,000 and over	879	69.7

Source: G. R. Hess and M. N. Newquist, *Medical Service in Industry and Workmen's Compensation Laws* (Chicago: ACS, 1946).

The aggregate percentage of firms with approved services for this sample of 1,597 firms is 57.1 percent, but this figure is meaningless due to the distorted composition of the sample. Nevertheless, the relationship of approved medical services to plant size is evident in the 1929–40 period.

The first nationwide study of health services in a reasonably representative sample of firms was made by the National Association of Manufacturers (NAM) in 1950.[33] This survey covered 3,589 NAM member companies, ranging from 53 percent in firms with less than 251 workers to 5.6 percent in firms with 2,501 workers or more—a good reflection of the totality of firms. In this large sample, the availability of health personnel was as follows:

Type of Health Personnel	Number of Firms	Percent of All Firms
Physicians: full-time	172	4.8
Physicians: part-time	613	17.1
Physicians on call	1,725	48.1
Registered nurses	1,023	28.5
First aid attendants	1,615	45.0

Source: George W. Bachman, et al., *Health Resources in the U.S.: Availability of Personnel, Facilities, and Services* (Washington: Brookings Inst., 1952).

The relationship of staffing to plant size for employed physicians and nurses was as follows:

Plant Size (number of employees)	Percent with		
	Physicians (full-time)	Physicians (part-time)	Registered Nurses
Less than 251	0.5	3.6	3.3
251–500	2.1	15.2	33.1
501–1,000	5.2	29.0	60.0
1,001–2,500	8.7	52.1	81.4
2,501 and over	45.5	61.9	88.6

Source: George W. Bachman, et al., *Health Resources in the U.S.: Availability of Personnel Facilities, and Services* (Washington: Brookings Inst., 1952).

The expected relationship of health personnel is shown again. The relatively good supply of industrial nurses, however, in plants down to the 251–500 worker size class is noteworthy. Also notable is the weak supply of full-time physicians in plants with fewer than 2,500 workers.

A survey of firms in New York State for 1950 shows slightly better staffing with health personnel, particularly in manufacturing industry.[34] In the following tabulation, "any health personnel" means physicians, nurses or both:

Plant-size (Number of Workers)	Percent with Any Health Personnel	
	Manufacturing	Other Industry
100–199	6	2
200–499	25	15
500–999	69	45
1,000–1,999	92	66
2,000–4,999	90	84
5,000 and over	100	92
All sizes	24	17

Source: N.Y. State Dept. of Labor, *Medical Personnel and Employee Feeding Facilities in N.Y. State Establishments Employing 100 or More Workers* (New York: 1952), pp. 7–10.

Studies in this period in Pennsylvania, Illinois, and New Jersey reported essentially similar findings. The technical content of industrial health programs is indicated in a Chicago survey of 1946. Limited to firms of 100 workers or more with some organized in-plant industrial health program, this survey showed the following frequency of various types of services:[35]

Type of Health Service	Percent of Employees Eligible
Treatment of job injuries	81.7
Treatment of minor illness	80.6
Placement of handicapped workers	74.9
Preemployment physical examinations	58.1
Examination after an illness	57.9
Health education program	47.1
Periodic physical examinations	46.9
Blood tests for syphilis	37.2
Chest x-ray examinations	37.0
Special eye examinations	31.5
General medical care	16.4
Dental examinations and advice	14.7
Medical care of employees' families	2.0

Source: Robert H. Flinn, Chicago—Cook County Health Survey (New York: Columbia Univ. Press, 1949), pp. 49–53.

With respect to preemployment examinations, the NAM survey of 1950 found these to be done in less than one-third of companies with 250 or fewer employees, and in 95 percent of companies with over 2,500 employees.

One of the few studies reporting the extent of utilization of clinic services was done during 1945–47, based on a survey of 278 establishments in 33 states.[36] The sample was skewed toward plants of large size, so that the overall figure is not reliable, but the average number of visits to the plant clinic per day is reported by size of the firm. Since the numbers of firms and their total numbers of workers in each size group are also reported, it has been possible to calculate the rates per 1,000 workers as well. These data were as follows:

Firm Size (Number of workers)	Average In-plant Clinic Visits per Day	Daily Clinic Visits per 1,000 Workers
Under 500	18	48.5
500–999	25	25.8
1,000–1,499	39	21.8
1,500–1,999	51	22.8
2,000–3,999	114	51.5
4,000–9,999	233	43.3
10,000 and over	772	39.4

Source: C. O. Sappington, *Industrial Health Department Functions and Relationships,* Medical Series Bull. No. 8 (Pittsburgh: Industrial Hygiene Fdn., 1948), p. 34.

There is no basis for calculating a valid average rate of clinic visits in plants of all sizes, but (recognizing that most plants in the nation are small and yet employ most of the workers) the above data suggest that a rough average would be about 40 visits to industrial clinics per 1,000 workers per day. Since there are approximately 240 working days per year (subtracting for weekends and holidays), this would yield an estimated 9,600 in-plant clinic visits per 1,000 workers per year. This estimate of nearly ten clinic visits per person per year, as of 1945–47, is higher than one might expect.

A survey of plants in Maryland in 1950 furnished information on the presence of "plant dispensaries" or clinics, both by size of firm and by type of industry.[37] The study sent questionnaires to all firms with 25 or more workers in the counties of Maryland, and to firms with 50 or more workers in the city of Baltimore. The overall response rate was 37.1 percent, being higher for the larger plants. Keeping this bias in mind, one may observe the striking relationships between in-plant dispensaries to size of firm, which were as follows:

	Percent of Firms with:	
Firm-size (Number of Workers)	In-plant Dispensary	First Aid Only
Under 100	0.9	84.6
100–499	16.6	74.4
500–999	60.7	35.7
1,000–4,999	85.2	14.8
5,000 and over	100.0	0

Source: Md. State Planning Commission, *A Survey of Industrial Medical Care in the State of Maryland* (Baltimore: 1950).

Classifying the same Maryland plants, according to type of industry, showed the following:

	Percent of Firms with:	
Type of Industry	In-plant Dispensary	First aid Only
Nonspecified	55.6	33.3
Manufacturing	20.9	72.4
Finance	7.4	42.6
Transportation	6.1	87.8
Trade	4.1	85.2
Service	3.3	86.7
Construction	0	100.0
Mining and agriculture	0	100.0

Source: Md. State Planning Commission, *A Survey of Industrial Medical Care in the State of Maryland* (Baltimore: 1950).

It is unfortunate that construction and mining, with the hazardous working conditions typical of these industries, had no regular dispensary or clinic facilities.

A national study in 1957 by the Research Council on Economic Security suggests an improvement in the use of full-time physicians, compared with the findings of the national NAM study of 1950, discussed earlier. Although the sample size is not reported, the findings were as follows:[38]

| | | Percent with | |
Size of Firm (number of workers)	Physicians (full-time)	Physicians (part-time)	Nurses (full-time)
Under 500	2.9	13.2	17.6
500–999	13.0	30.4	69.6
1,000–2,499	23.3	46.7	93.3
2,500 and over	37.5	37.5	83.3

Source: Research Council on Economic Security, *Prolonged Illness—Absenteeism* (Chicago: 1957), p. 131.

More recently, a 1970 study surveyed 803 establishments with 260,000 employees in the Chicago area; this sample was chosen from a total of 120,000 workplaces with 2,250,000 employees—with the selection emphasizing plants having potential occupational health hazards.[39] The findings on various types of medical personnel, according to plant size were as follows:

Plant Size (number of workers)	Percent of Firms with Physicians		
	Full-time	Part-time	On call
8–19	0	0	0
20–49	2.3	0	82.0
50–99	2.7	0.7	90.6
100–249	3.2	2.1	88.0
250–499	4.8	3.3	89.6
500 and over	18.9	17.3	63.0
All sizes	3.0	0.9	84.3

Source: USPHS, Occupational Health *Survey of the Chicago-Metropolitan Area* (Cincinnati, Ohio: Bureau of Occupational Safety and Health, 1970).

Analyzing the same sample of Chicago plants, according to the percentage of workers served by physicians in each category showed:

Plant Size (number of workers)	Percent of Workers Served by Physicians		
	Full-time	Part-time	On call
8–19	0	0	0
20–49	1.3	0	88.5

Plant size	Percent of Workers Served by Physicians		
(number of workers)	Full time	Part-time	On call
50–99	12.9	0.8	79.3
100–249	2.9	6.9	84.3
250–499	4.5	11.0	82.4
500 and over	46.3	12.0	41.5
All sizes	20.0	7.1	68.4

Source: USPHS, *Occupational Survey of the Chicago Metropolitan Area* (Cincinnati, Oh., 1970).

Thus, assuming the sample to be representative, 27.1 percent of workers in the Chicago area were served by full-time or part-time industrial physicians. Of the remaining workers, 68.4 percent had physicians on call and only 4.5 percent worked in plants with no prearranged physician services whatsoever.

In New York State, an industrial health survey was reported in 1972, as a followup of the 1950 survey discussed earlier.[40] The study, conducted in 1969, did not report manufacturing and other industries separately, but for all types of industry with 100 employees or more, the findings were as follows:

Plant Size (number of workers)	Percent with Any Health Personnel
100–249	5.8
250–499	18.8
500–999	53.4
1,000–1,499	80.0
1,500–2,499	83.5
2,500–4,999	91.2
5,000–9,999	93.3
10,000 and over	100.0
All sizes	16.3

Source: M. Kleinfeld, et al., "Occupational Health and Safety Services in New York State," *Journal of Occupational Medicine* 14 (1972): 693–699.

Somewhat surprising is the aggregate finding of 16.3 percent of plants in New York State with any health personnel, compared with 24 and 17 percent (and a weighted average of 19.2 percent) in 1950. This apparent decline in industrial health coverage is probably misleading, however, since it applies to "plants" rather than "workers." We know that the proportion of workers employed in large firms (with greater likelihood of in-plant programs) has increased over the years, so that the percentage of *workers* served by industrial health services in New York State may well have increased.

Another type of information reported in the 1969 New York State survey has special relevance for organized industrial clinics. Categorized by the type of clinic or "aid station" maintained, the findings were as follows:

Type of Clinic or Aid Station	Percent of Firms
In plant	24.1
At another branch of firm	3.0
Maintained by group of firms	1.3
None	71.6
All types	100.0

Source: M. Kleinfeld, et al., "Occupational Health and Safety Services in New York State," *Journal of Occupational Medicine* 14 (1972): 693–699.

Thus, in New York State, as of 1969, workers in 28.4 percent of plants were served by some type of clinic or aid station.

Data on the proportion of workers served by such clinics are found in studies conducted in the 1970s. In 1972, the U.S. Department of Labor surveyed a representative sample of all U.S. nonfarm industry—some 5 million workplaces, with about 60 million workers. The sample contained 600,000 establishments.[41] As noted in Chapter 3, considering the services of industrial nurses as an index of in-plant health care, 21.1 percent of workers were at workplaces with such nursing service. The likelihood of a worker's access to these services, however, varied greatly among different types of industry. For the 12,139,500 workers in establishments with in-plant nursing service, the frequency by type of industry in 1972 was as follows:

Type of Industry	Percent of Employees Served by Industrial Nurses
Manufacturing	69.0
Services (excluding health facilities)	15.1
Wholesale and retail trade	7.9
Transport and public utilities	5.8
Finance, insurance, and real estate	5.6
Contract construction	1.5
All industries	21.1

Source: U.S. Dept. of Labor, *Occupational Injuries and Illnesses by Industry, 1972* (Washington: Bureau of Labor Statistics, Bull. No. 1830, 1974), pp. 6–8.

The nurses serving the above 12,139,500 workers numbered 56,300, or about 4.6 nurses per 1,000 workers. The coverage of manufacturing industry is much stronger than any other type, including construction, in which the accident hazards are especially great. If the available 56,300 nurses are related to the total "nonfarm private" industrial sector population of 58,519,200 in 1972, the ratio becomes nearly 1.0 nurse per 1,000 workers.

Whether or not there is an in-plant nursing service, many firms have made some formal arrangements for physician's care for the workers. Among the 58,519,200 workers in private nonfarm employment in 1972, 35,193,800, or 60 percent, were in establishments with such medical care. Only about one-quarter of these workers had access to in-plant medical services, however, and three-quarters were served by outside doctors having special relationships with the firm. The distribution of these various medical arrangements, by type of industry were as follows:

			Physician Service		
Type of Industry	**Full-time**	**Part-time**	**On call**	**Outside Clinics**	**All Types**
Transport and utilities	21.6	5.3	45.6	27.5	100.0
Manufacturing	19.7	16.3	34.5	29.6	100.0
Finance, insurance, etc.	17.7	7.6	45.7	29.0	100.0
Services	14.3	8.6	39.1	38.1	100.0
Wholesale and retail trade	5.7	5.1	41.2	48.0	100.0
Construction	5.5	2.2	40.1	52.1	100.0
All industries	15.2	10.7	38.3	35.8	100.0

Source: U.S. Dept. of Labor, *Occupational Injuries and Illnesses by Industry, 1972* (Washington: Bureau of Labor Statistics, Bull. No. 1830, 1974), pp. 6–8.

It must be realized that the above figures apply to firms that have *some* formal arrangements for physician's care, that is, up to 60 percent of the nonfarm workers. If we calculate the percentages of the *total* workforce with each of the above types of medical services, the results are as follows:

Type of Medical Service	**Percent of Nonfarm Workers**
Full-time doctor	9.1
Part-time doctor	6.4
Doctor on call	23.0
Outside clinic	21.5
None	40.0
All types	100.0

Source: U.S. Dept. of Labor, *Occupational Injuries and Illnesses by Industry, 1972* (Washington: Bureau of Labor Statistics, Bull. No. 1830, 1974), pp. 6–8.

Thus, of the total nonfarm private workers, 15.5 percent have access to full-time or part-time doctors in the plant, mostly full-time. This may be compared with the 21.1 percent of workers served by in-plant nurses, as noted above. When physicians serve in a plant, there is virtually always a nurse present as well. Thus, one may infer that 5.6 percent of workers are at workplaces served only by in-plant nurses.

The most recent survey of industrial health services was reported by the NICB in 1974.[42] The data of this survey, however, apply to 1971, and they concern only firms with 500 or more employees. Questionnaires were sent to a probability sample of 2,240 firms; after a follow-up questionnaire, a total of 858 responses, or 38 percent of the original sample, was received. Expenditures of these relatively large firms for in-plant health services ranged around a median of $10.81 per worker per year.

Based on this sample, the NICB survey estimates that about 12 percent of all firms in the nation with 500 employees or more (a total of 7,600) engaged one or more full-time physicians. This amounts to 3,200 industrial physicians, or approximately 1 percent of the nation's doctors in active practice. In addition, there are 10,600 physicians engaged part-time in companies with 500 workers or more. Altogether about 30 percent of these large firms have full-time or part-time physicians, or both, and these firms employ about 20,000,000 workers. Over the past decade, the full-time physicians engaged in large firms increased by 20 percent and the part-time physicians by 16 percent, but the number of workers employed rose by 38 percent.

By type of industry, the health personnel staffing of large firms in the NICB survey was as follows:

Type of Industry	Physicians (full-and/or part-time)	Nurses only	No health personnel	Total firms
Manufacturing	38	33	29	100
Financial	37	25	38	100
Transport and utilities	21	13	66	100
Wholesale and retail	8	11	81	100
All others	24	10	66	100

Source: Seymour Lusterman, *Industry Roles in Health Care* (New York: NICB, 1974).

Large manufacturing firms clearly are best served with medical and nursing personnel, while wholesale and retail trade, where work hazards are undoubtedly few, are least well served.

A significant issue over the years has been the place occupied by in-plant physicians in the company structure. Traditionally industrial physicians have wanted to report to the top management, in order to have an influence on production processes affecting the health of workers. The trend, however, has been to link medical services with the general personnel management section of a firm; the NICB survey found at least 75 percent of medical directors with such channels, and only 11 percent reporting to a "top corporate level."

Regarding the content of industrial health services, the NICB survey reports an increase in the extent and thoroughness of preemployment examinations. Of all firms responding, 32 percent reported performance of additional screening procedures in these examinations, such as for drug use, hearing defects, back problems, emotional difficulties, alcoholism, and so on. Some companies reported that they were more selective in their medical standards for hiring, while others stated they were willing to hire persons with defects that were correctable or could be acceptable by placing the worker in a selected type of job. Because of the rising cost of physician services, on the other hand, many firms are using nurses or paramedical personnel for examining low risk workers, and greater use is also being made of questionnaires on health status, filled out by the job applicant.

Periodic reexaminations of workers are also being done more frequently in large firms. The examinations are also usually more thorough, including such procedures as electrocardiograms, proctoscopies, etc. Of the NICB respondent firms, 57 percent were doing such checkups on all or some of their workers. This was the policy in nearly all companies with full-time physicians, in about three-quarters of those with part-time physicians, and in about half of the companies with no physicians. In the latter group, the examinations were typically done by outside physicians, and sometimes this was the arrangement in the other companies as well. In the NICB survey ten years earlier, periodic health examinations were done by only 39 percent of firms, so that this practice is evidently on the increase. Within firms, furthermore, the scope of employees on whom periodic examinations are performed has widened; most frequently it is the top executive category in which the examinations are periodically done. There has been controversy about the ultimate value of periodic health examinations, and whether the early detection of presymptomatic disease yields clear benefits.[43] The predominant opinion, however, tends to favor such practices in industry, if only for their educational value on the individual's risk factors and life style. Everything depends, of course, on appropriate follow-up of any problems detected in examinations.[44] Such follow-up medical service, if required, usually is obtained outside the industrial setting.

The essential findings of all the above studies on the extent of industrial health services are relatively simple. In terms of the numbers and proportions of workers accessible to these organized ambulatory care programs, their number has been increasing, even though coverage is far from universal. In-plant service is clearly better developed in larger firms, and the increasing concentration of American industry in large corporations has the effect of extending overall coverage. The scope of industrial health service is also broadening from its early focus on work-related injuries (to reduce workmen's compensation insurance costs) to concern about the worker's general health, a factor obviously affecting his or her productivity. National legislation in 1970 gave a major boost to industrial health services. This subject will be considered in the next section.

CURRENT FEATURES OF IN-PLANT HEALTH SERVICES

In 1970, the U.S. federal government, after years of debate, passed the Occupational Safety and Health Act (OSHA).[45] This important legislation establishes for the first time federal (as distinguished from state) government standards for safe and healthful working conditions in every business affecting commerce in the nation. A system of workplace inspections, administered through a network of 60 regional and local federal offices, is responsible for enforcement of the standards. Only if a state government establishes standards and a procedure for enforcement equivalent to or exceeding those in the federal law and regulations, does the federal program withdraw from that state. As of late 1979, 23 states had taken such state legislative action.[46]

The major purpose of the OSHA legislation is preventive, and in this sense it is probably the major milestone in health protection of American workers since the enactment of state workmen's compensation laws in the early 20th century. The provisions of the act, however, with respect to in-plant medical services are rather weak. Under the authority for promulgation of "occupational safety and health standards," it has been mandated that every employer "shall insure the ready availability of medical personnel for advice and consultation on matters of plant health."[45] Regulations provide further that "in the absence of medical services" in the plant or nearby, some person in the establishment "shall be adequately trained in first-aid." There are no provisions for a specified ratio of physician and/or nursing services per 1,000 workers such as one finds in the labor legislation of France and other countries.

Nevertheless, the general social influence of the OSHA program has been to heighten awareness of the importance of providing healthful working conditions. The law stimulated, for example, a major study, supported by the Ford Foundation, on health hazards throughout American industry, and these were found to be very great.[47] Among the findings of this study were: (a) a 29 percent increase in the rate of reported injuries in American industry between 1961 and 1970; (b) a probable but uncertain increase in hazards of occupational disease (due to use of many new chemicals), estimated to amount to 390,000 new cases per year; (c) the multiplication of new and uncertain hazards—associated with heat, vibration, noise, etc.—due to the changes in industrial technology; (d) rising concern for general environmental pollution by industrial wastes; and (e) increased demands for healthful working conditions by workers, associated with their higher educational levels and greater general sophistication.

For political and social reasons, the implementation of the OSHA program has been much less effective than many had expected. American organized labor has pointed out the deficiencies in industrial inspections, the weak enforcement activities, and even the inadequacy of many of the official standards.[48] In spite of this, the OSHA program has made the whole matter of industrial health services more politically visible, and it has become a more salient issue in the concerns of both labor and management at the bargaining table. The definition of desirable occupational health standards, therefore, is of increasing concern, even on subjects such as in-plant medical services, which are only marginally treated in OSHA regulations.

As early as 1955, the USPHS defined minimum requirements for an "employee health service," excluding, for example, the provision of first aid by someone other than a physician or nurse.[49] In retrospect, it seems likely that the movement after World War II to expand insurance for medical care among industrial workers gave a substantial boost to the development of in-plant medical services. Being concerned with prompt treatment of injuries, as well as periodic and preemployment medical examinations, health education, advice on obtaining care for non-job-related illness, and so on, such services are inherently preventive in orientation. As the NICB said in 1959:

> Unions have pressed managements to include benefit insurance provisions covering the medical needs of workers in collective bargaining agreements. This situation is causing some managements to decide that it is smarter to have preventive health services that detect trouble in its early stages than to pay the heavy insurance costs that result from more extensive remedial care later on.[50]

In fact, in the NICB survey of 242 firms in 1959, a question was posed on whether in-plant medical services tended to lower insurance rates for sickness benefits. Thirty-six companies responded to this question, and 81 percent of these expressed the belief that insurance costs were lower because of an effective medical service. This was often attributed to the decline in short sickness absences of one or two days associated with in-plant health care programs.

The correlations of in-plant medical services with the size of the firm and the type of industry have already been discussed. There are other relationships to be noted. The 1969 NICB survey showed that firms with higher average earnings per employee were more likely to have full-time physicians and in-plant health personnel. Perhaps related to this is another finding that might at first seem paradoxical; namely, that firms with a higher proportion of women workers are *less* likely to have strong in-plant health services. The commonly held notion of labor legislation being designed to protect working women might suggest an opposite relationship, but this is evidently more than outweighed by other factors, such as the heavy employment of women in nonmanufacturing industry (e.g., wholesale and retail trade, finance, and insurance), and in clerical positions, which are also relatively low-paid. Plant location is evidently another factor influencing health service programs: the NICB study found a lesser development in cities than in suburbs. This would seem to reflect the easy availability of nearby private doctors and hospitals in urban centers, while in the suburbs management initiative to assure accessible medical care in case of urgent need is more important.

The 1972 study of the U.S. Department of Labor reported that a high proportion of medical services for industrial workers are rendered by physicians outside the plant. Considering both doctors on call and those in special outside clinics, 44.5 percent of all workers came under such arrangements, compared with 15.5 percent of workers served by doctors in the plant, full-time or part-time. The NICB study also noted that although in-plant industrial physicians had increased in the 1960s, their growth did not keep up with the expansion of the labor force; in other words, the *ratio* of in-plant physicians to workers has actually declined. Linking together these two findings suggests that, as the general demands for medical care have increased in the United States (because of health insurance, government programs like Medicare and Medicaid, the changed age composition of the population, etc.), fewer doctors have been available for in-plant positions. Instead, there seems to be a shift to the use by industry of outside private doctors or group practice clinics, with whom some type of formal agreement is concluded.

The content and range of industrial health services may be conceived as a continuum ranging from a minimally trained first aid attendant up to a comprehensive occupational health program staffed with a variety of full-time medical, nursing, and other personnel. Theoretically it should be possible to assign a "score" to each firm's program, based on where it falls on such a continuum.[51] Even without such quantified measurements, however, it is evident from the data reported above that health services in most companies in the United States fall toward the weak end of this continuum. In 1955, the University of Michigan Institute of Social Research suggested classification of occupational health services according to four levels: (a) first aid; (b) job-related care (treatment of on-the-job minor illness and preemployment examinations); (c) primary health care (the above plus immunizations, health education, follow-up of simple chronic illness, etc.); and (d) comprehensive care (diagnosis and treatment of all illness, as well as prevention).[52] This simple schema has not, however, been applied.

Nevertheless, as noted earlier, the trend is toward increasing coverage of workers by some organized health care arrangements, either in the plant or outside it. This is suggested by several factors. One is the general tendency of American industry to become deployed in firms of large size, where medical services are more likely to be developed. Another is the continuing economic impact of workmen's compensation programs, in which insurance premiums are gradually rising. Third is the general impact of the OSHA legislation, in spite of various forms of resistance from industry, on company practices; while the costly process of changing production methods to reduce occupational disease hazards may be delayed, arrangements for organized ambulatory health care for industrial workers (in-plant or outside) can be made relatively quickly and at low cost.[53] No studies of industrial medical services reported are recent enough to reflect the impact of OSHA. Fourth, organized labor is clearly becoming more concerned about health services as well as healthful working conditions in the plant. The former movement for separate "labor health centers" has lost its force, and there are now doubtless fewer than the 101 such centers (serving 1.6 million union members) estimated by the U.S. Social Security Administration in 1969.[54] Yet American workers have lost none of their suspicion of company doctors, and unions still want convenient clinics at their place of work.

As for trends in the scope of industrial health services, the tendency of established clinics has clearly been to broaden their functions. In the industrial health care continuum referred to above, a comprehensive program would include not only periodic health examinations, health education, rehabilitation of disabilities through reasonable job placements, counseling on personal medical care needs, preparation for retirement, and other services related to occupation. It would also move on along a path of service for nonoccupational health care. In the 1955 study of the University of Michigan Institute of Social Research alluded to above, it is noteworthy that in 262 establishments studied, the treatment of nonoccupational illness (colds, headaches, etc.) on the job was the second most frequent activity reported by in-plant doctors and nurses, following treatment of minor injuries. In fact, as industrial health services broaden to concern for the total health of the worker, they border increasingly on programs of general medical care. In this sense, the movement for health insurance fringe benefits discussed earlier may be viewed as an extension of the industrial health program to its ultimate degree.

Perhaps more closely akin to the in-plant health service in the general health care arena is the movement slowly emerging in some sectors of American industry toward initiation of health maintenance organizations (HMOs).[55] The mounting interest of large corporations in exploring the HMO idea, if only to economize on fringe benefit costs, has been sufficient to induce the Kaiser Medical Care Program, the nation's largest HMO, to establish a consulting office to advise other interested companies. In 1978, the U.S. Secretary of Health, Education, and Welfare sponsored a national conference of the *"Fortune 500"* (the 500 largest corporations in the U.S.) to discuss the HMO concept. The initiative of the R. J. Reynolds Tobacco Company in developing an HMO for its employees at Durham, North Carolina has attracted interest from many other companies, particularly in relatively small towns.[56] The most recent NICB survey of industrial health services reported that 18 percent of companies questioned were already involved in or considering involvement in HMO development.[57] Whether this ultimate extension of the in-plant health service will spread widely remains to be seen. The significance of HMOs extends beyond the industrial health field, as will be discussed in Chapter 12.

INDUSTRIAL HEALTH SERVICES IN LOS ANGELES COUNTY

To identify the characteristics of industrial clinics in one metropolitan area, a survey was conducted in Los Angeles County in 1972–73. As of 1970, there were about 2.9 million working people in Los Angeles County, employed in 130,300 establishments. Classified by number of employees per firm, the distribution of firms was as follows:

Size of Firm (number of workers)	Number
1–7	86,331
8–19	26,547
20–49	10,368
50–99	3,865
100–249	2,108
250–499	622
500 and over	461
All sizes	130,302

Source: U.S. Department of Commerce, unpublished data from the Bureau of the Census, 1970.

In 1970, there were 285 industrial nurses employed in these firms. Their distribution was concentrated in the companies of larger size. Classified by type of industry, the distribution of nurses was as follows:

Type of Industry	Number of Nurses
Manufacturing	218
Services and public utilities	43
Finance, insurance, and real estate	15
Wholesale and retail trade	9
All industries	285

Source: Industrial Nurse Association of Los Angeles County, unpublished data, 1974.

According to the Industrial Nurse Association of Los Angeles County, these 285 nurses were employed in 115 establishments, of which 94 were in manufacturing. The brief survey we conducted was based on interviews in 41 of these establishments, distributed among three groups: (a) three firms with under 250 workers; (b) thirteen firms with 250 to 499 workers; and (c) twenty-five firms with 500 workers or more. This rather skewed distribution reflects, of course, the concentration of industrial nurses in the larger firms.

Of firms known to have in-plant health units, two-thirds had established those units since 1950. Interviews were held principally with the industrial nurses, and in about half the companies they reported that the initial objective of the health units was to provide first aid to injured workers, presumably linked to workmen's compensation liability. Beyond this, several respondents spoke of the importance of healthy workers for maintaining industrial productivity. Screening examinations of new employees was the third most frequently stated purpose of industrial health units. (In 1979, a County public health official estimated that 500 industrial nurses were working in 350 local firms, so that in-plant nursing services have apparently been expanding.)

Limited data were obtained on the types of services rendered by industrial nurses. In spite of the occupational safety and health purposes of the programs, it was noteworthy that in all but a few workplaces the predominant share of services was rendered for health complaints unrelated to work. For example, in one establishment with 400 employees, the industrial nurse had kept records of visits to her clinic over the past ten months; these amounted to 5,330 employee visits. Of these, only 7 percent were for clearly work-related conditions, while 93 percent were for other illnesses or symptoms. In another plant with 325 employees, the nurse had seen 142 patients in the month before the survey; of these, 27 percent were for occupational conditions and 73 percent for nonoccupational reasons. The proportion of nonoccupational complaints appeared to be greater in establishments with mainly white-collar workers than in plants with predominantly manual workers. In factories with assembly line production it was estimated that about half of the employees coming to the industrial clinic came for work-related conditions, whereas in workplaces involving skilled workers engaged in light industry or nonhazardous occupations, a common estimate was that 75 percent of clinic visits were for reasons not related to work. One large department store nurse estimated that 90 percent of the workers coming to her clinic came for nonoccupational causes.

These findings would seem to be one more reflection of the general need for primary health care in the U.S. population. With difficulty in obtaining such care in the community, it is small wonder that persons employed in companies staffed with industrial nurses would tend to seek ordinary primary care for diverse symptoms at in-plant clinics. One need not accept unquestioningly the nurse's judgment about a condition being occupational in origin or not so; nonetheless, it is certain that a substantial share of on-the-job illness is not related specifically to the work situation.

In nearly all Los Angeles county plants investigated, the policy was for the nurse to give some sort of counsel or treatment (for example, aspirin or advice on diet) to the patient making an initial visit for an apparently nonoccupational condition. Second visits for such complaints, however, were discouraged, and the patient was referred to an outside physician or a hospital outpatient department.

For work-related conditions, predominantly injuries, the industrial nurse virtually always gives first aid if a physician is not present. If the condition is minor, the nurse asks the patient to return when the plant physician is expected. If the condition is serious, the nurse arranges for the patient to be sent to a nearby hospital or private clinic with which the firm has established a general relationship.

Preemployment examinations were conducted in all but two or three of the 41 plants with nurses surveyed in the county. Sometimes, however, these were performed by an outside medical group under contract with the firm. Annual examinations were done only in about half the firms, and then usually on a voluntary basis. In plants with specific hazards, selective examinations were often done annually; for example, hearing tests of workers in plants with a high level of noise. For personnel requiring great visual acuity, such as inspectors of product quality, annual vision tests were often done.

The nurse in one large insurance company, with 950 predominantly white-collar employees, kept records for the previous year, which had about 250 working days. There were a total of 5,981 patient services provided by the nurse during the year, which amounts to about six services per employee per year. The distribution of these services was roughly as follows:

Minor nonoccupational medical cases	3,600
Preemployment examinations	620
Referrals for outside care	470
First aid for minor injuries	400
Examinations after sickness absence	360
Periodic reexaminations	300
Nurse visits to patient at home or hospital	160
Immunizations (influenza)	71
All services	5,981

By contrast, in one large aircraft company with 60,000 employees, there were an estimated 200,000 visits to the clinic per year or 3.3 per person. Approximately 50 percent of the visits were for work-related conditions, 35 percent were for nonoccupational conditions, 10 percent were reexaminations after sickness absence, and 5 percent were preemployment examinations.

In six or eight of the 41 plants surveyed, special screening surveys, such as blood glucose tests for diabetes, "breathmobile" tests for lung disorders, blood pressure readings, chest x-rays, or visual examinations, had been recently conducted. Health education through posters and pamphlets was done in most of the plants. In several establishments, dietary advice was given to workers with an obesity problem.

Beyond the sample of 41 in-plant health care programs in Los Angeles County described above, a few special work-related ambulatory care activities warrant special comment. The county government operates an occupational health service for its 73,000 public employees.[58] There are 2,200 separate work classifications in which these civil servants were employed. Most in need of occupational health service were employees in such work as road maintenance, the county sheriff department, public hospitals, or solid waste disposal. Preemployment examinations were done on an average of 100 job applicants per day; since about one-third of these were from disadvantaged minority groups, a relatively high number of physical defects were found. Special services that developed in response to recognized problems have included a group psychological counseling program for persons with emotional difficulties, and other group counseling sessions for persons with obesity, and for problem drinkers or alcoholics. A general physical fitness educational program has been developed as an approach to preventing heart disease in middle-age employees.

Another unusual work-related health program in Los Angeles County is a large dental clinic operated for hotel and restaurant workers and their dependents. It is sponsored by a labor-management trust fund, the Los Angeles Hotel-Restaurant Employer-Union Welfare Fund.[59] About 37,000 persons are eligible for nearly complete dental care at this freestanding facility: 42 percent of these persons were workers, and the remainder were their dependents. Providing the dental care were qualified dentists full-time or part-time, amounting to 24 full-time equivalents. In addition there were a total of 104 dental hygienists, dental assistants, dental technicians, and clerks. The services encompass all types of dental care except orthodontia; in 1967, services were provided at the rate of 2.3 dental visits per eligible person per year. Because of the relatively extensive auxiliary staff (2.5 personnel per dentist) and generally efficient organization of services, this dental clinic was judged to be 30 to 60 percent more productive (that is, output per dentist per day) than that of the average private dental practitioner; the quality of care was also judged to be good.

Also sponsored by a labor-management trust fund, associated with the Retail Clerks Union in Los Angeles County, is a rather unusual predictive medicine program. This is essentially a multiphasic screening program, for detecting subclinical disease through a battery of laboratory, x-ray, and other tests. In 1973 about 42,000 persons (18,000 workers and 24,000 dependents) were eligible for the examination procedure, and about 5,000 of them used it in the course of a year.

A third labor-management health facility was started in Los Angeles County in 1951 and functioned until the early 1970s—a "union health center," sponsored by the International Ladies Garment Workers Union and garment industry employers.[60] In 1971 it offered diagnostic examinations, immunizations, and general care of minor illness to approximately 5,000 union members (this was a decline from 9,000 members in 1951). There were 15 part-time physicians and 5 full-time allied health personnel. As the union membership declined and as health insurance protection was extended through collective bargaining for fringe benefits, the attendance at this facility gradually declined, and by 1973 it had closed.

Finally, we should take note of certain programs linked to employment, that have provided general medical care in Los Angeles County for many years. Three of these are for railroad workers, and one is for public utility workers. The railroad program is sponsored by the Union Pacific Railroad Employees Association. It was started by the railroad operators in 1906, but was transferred to a joint union-management board of directors many years ago.[61] As of 1973, about 2,400 workers were eligible for general medical care, although dependents were not covered. The association ceased to operate its own hospital soon after World War II, but made contractual arrangements for care of its members in one selected voluntary general hospital. A clinic for general ambulatory service, however, was still functioning in 1979, staffed by two part-time physicians; attached to the clinic is a laboratory and a pharmacy, with full-time personnel. About 40 specialists serve as consultants to whom patients are referred.

The other such comprehensive medical care system serves 14,000 employees (including retired workers) of a public utility, the Southern California Edison Company. This program started in 1900, and is sponsored entirely by the company management, which also supports 80 percent of its costs (the balance coming from wage deductions). All specialty services are offered except obstetrics, pediatrics, and psychiatry; dependents do not use the clinic, but are covered by a commercial health insurance policy. The medical staff includes 13 full-time physicians and 3 part-time on salaries, in addition to some 300 private specialists to whom patients are referred (paid by fees). The clinic facility is located at the business headquarters of the company, and is well-equipped. One of the program's three pharmacists serves also as its administrator.

Thus in Los Angeles County, as in most metropolitan areas, one finds a wide range of ambulatory health care programs organized in connection with employment. Although the great majority of in-plant clinics are intended mainly to provide services for job-connected injuries or illness and to do certain general medical examinations, most of them also provide a modest level of primary care for nonoccupational health problems. A few programs, with special historical roots, provide general medical services to employees.

NOTES

1. International Labor Office, *Encyclopedia of Occupational Health and Safety* (New York: McGraw-Hill, 1972).

2. Teleky, L., *History of Factory and Mine Hygiene* (New York: Columbia University Press, 1948).

3. Stern, Bernhard J., *Medicine in Industry* (New York: Commonwealth Fund, 1946), pp. 4–6.

4. Millis, Harry A., and Royal E. Montgomery, *Labor's Risks and Social Insurance* (New York: McGraw-Hill, 1938), pp. 187–234.

5. Stern, *Medicine in Industry,* pp. 21–23.

6. Somers, Herman M. and Anne R. Somers, *Workmen's Compensation: Prevention, Insurance, and Rehabilitation of Occupational Disability* (New York: Wiley, 1954).

7. Price, Daniel L., "Workers' Compensation in the 1970's," *Social Security Bulletin* 42 (1979): pp. 3–24.

8. Stern, *Medicine in Industry,* pp. 27–28.

9. National Industrial Conference Board, *Health Service in Industry,* Research Report No. 34 (January 1921).

10. Ibid.

11. Ibid.

12. National Industrial Conference Board, *Cost of Health Service in Industry,* Research Report No. 37 (New York: May 1921).

13. Ibid.

14. Rector, F. L., "Physical Examination of Industrial Workers—Results of an Investigation by the Conference Board on Physicians in Industry," *Journal of the American Medical Association* 75 (1920): 1739–1741.

15. Stern, *Medicine in Industry,* p. 160.

16. Williams, Pierce, *The Purchase of Medical Care Through Fixed Periodic Payment* (New York: National Bureau of Economic Research, 1932).

17. Reed, Louis, *Blue Cross and Medical Service Plans* (Washington: U.S. Public Health Service, processed, October 1947).

18. Somers, Herman and Anne R. Somers, *Doctors, Patients, and Health Insurance* (Washington: Brookings Institution, 1961).

19. de Kruif, Paul, *Kaiser Wakes the Doctors* (New York: Harcourt Brace & Co., 1943).

20. U.S. Social Security Administration, Bureau of Research and Statistics, *Prepayment Medical Care Organizations,* Bureau Memorandum No. 55, 2nd edition, (Washington: 1944).

21. Price, Leo, "Health Program of International Ladies Garment Workers' Union," *Monthly Labor Review* 49 (1939): 811–829.

22. Turner, Boyd W., "The Doctor's Stake in Union-Sponsored Health Plans," *Medical Economics,* October 1943, pp. 75–79.

23. Gafafer, William M. (editor), *Manual of Industrial Hygiene and Medical Service in War Industries* (Philadelphia: W. B. Saunders Co., 1943).

24. Klem, Margaret C., and Margaret F. McKiever, *Small Plant Health and Medical Programs,* (Washington: U.S. Public Health Service, Division of Occupational Health, May 1952).

25. Munts, Raymond, *Bargaining for Health: Labor Unions, Health Insurance, and Medical Care* (Madison, Wis.: University of Wisconsin Press, 1967).

26. U.S. Bureau of Labor Statistics, *Labor Force Development, First Quarter 1975: News* (Washington: April 14, 1975), p. 7.

27. Kerr, Lorin, "Occupational Health—A Discipline in Search of a Mission," *American Journal of Public Health,* 63 (1975): 381–385.

28. Klem, Margaret C.; M. F. McKiever; and W. J. Lear, *Industrial Health and Medical Programs* (Washington: Public Health Service, September 1950), p. 38, from unpublished data from U.S. Social Security Administration, 1948.

29. U.S. Bureau of the Census, *Statistical Abstract of the United States 1972* (Washington: 1972), p. 716.

30. U.S. Public Health Service, *Occupational Health Survey of the Chicago Metropolitan Area* (Cincinnati: Bureau of Occupational Safety and Health, 1970).

31. American Public Health Association, *Health and Work in America—A Chart Book* (Washington: November 1975), p. 52, from unpublished data from the U.S. Bureau of Labor Statistics, 1973.

32. Hess, G. R. and M. N. Newquist, *Medical Service in Industry and Workmen's Compensation Laws* (Chicago: American College of Surgeons, 1946).

33. Bachman, George W., et al., *Health Resources in the United States: Availability of Personnel, Facilities, and Services* (Washington: Brookings Institution, 1952).

34. State of New York, Department of Labor, *Medical Personnel and Employee Feeding Facilities in New York State Establishments Employing 100 or More Workers* (New York City: 1952), pp. 7–10.

35. Flinn, Robert H., *Chicago-Cook County Health Survey* (New York: Columbia University Press, 1949), pp. 659–663.

36. Sappington, C. O., *Industrial Health Department Functions and Relationships* (Pittsburgh: Industrial Hygiene Foundation, (Medical Series Bulletin No. 8, 1948), p. 34.

37. Maryland State Planning Commission, *A Survey of Industrial Medical Care in the State of Maryland* (Baltimore: 1950).

38. Research Council on Economic Security, *Prolonged Illness-Absenteeism* (Chicago: 1957), p. 131.

39. U.S. Public Health Service, *Occupational Health Survey of the Chicago Metropolitan Area.*

40. Kleinfeld, M., et al., "Occupational Health and Safety Services in New York State," *Journal of Occupational Medicine,* 14 (1977): 693–699.

41. U.S. Department of Labor, *Occupational Injuries and Illnesses by Industry, 1972* (Washington: Bureau of Labor Statistics, Bulletin 1830, 1974), pp. 6–8.

42. Lusterman, Seymour, *Industry Roles in Health Care* (New York: National Industrial Conference Board, 1974).

43. Siegel, Gordon M., "An American Dilemma—The Periodic Health Examination," *Archives of Environmental Health,* September 1966.

44. Collings, G. H., et al., "Follow-up of MHS (multiphasic health screening)," *Journal of Occupational Medicine,* June 1972.

45. U.S. Department of Labor and U.S. Department of Health, Education and Welfare, *The President's Report on Occupational Safety and Health* (Washington: December 1973).

46. Tibbetts, B. L., Administrator in Federal Occupational Safety and Health Office, at Long Beach, California, personal communication, September 1979.

47. Ashford, Nicholas A., *Crisis in the Workplace: Occupational Disease and Injury* (Cambridge, Mass.: M.I.T. Press, 1976).

48. Bargmann, Russ, "OSHA: The Urgency of Revival," *The AFL-CIO American Federationist,* June 1977, pp. 19–23.

49. University of Michigan, Institute for Social Research, *Employee Health Services: A Study of Managerial Attitudes and Evaluation* (Ann Arbor, Mich.: 1955).

50. National Industrial Conference Board, *Company Medical and Health Programs* (New York: 1959).

51. Webb, Samuel B., "Objective Criteria for Evaluating Occupational Health Programs," *American Journal of Public Health* 65 (1975): 31–37.

52. University of Michigan, Institute for Social Research.

53. Benedict, Karl T., "Corporate Reaction to the Occupational Safety and Health Act of 1970," in Richard H. Egdahl (editor), *Background Papers on Industry's Changing Role in Health Care Delivery* (New York: Springer-Verlag, 1977), pp. 145–151.

54. Herriman, Thomas, "Union Health Clinics" in Richard H. Egdahl (editor), *Background Papers on Industry's Changing Role in Health Care Delivery*, pp. 40–47.

55. Dolinsky, Edward M., "Health Maintenance Organizations and Occupational Medicine," *Bulletin of the New York Academy of Medicine* 50 (1974): 1122–1137.

56. Goldbeck, Willis B., *A Business Perspective on Industry and Health Care* (New York: Springer-Verlag, 1978), pp. 51–53.

57. Lusterman, *Industry Roles in Health Care*, p. 65.

58. Felton, Jean S., "Occupational Health: Government Program for County Employees," *Journal of the American Medical Association* 217 (1971): 56–60.

59. Friedman, Jay W., *The Dental Care Program of the Los Angeles Hotel-Restaurant Employer-Union Welfare Fund* (Los Angeles Calif.: University of California, School of Public Health, 1970).

60. Igloe, M. C., *L.A. Union Health Center—I.L.G.W.U.* (Los Angeles, Calif.: processed, 31 December 1958).

61. Union Pacific Railroad Employees Hospital Association, *Regulations* (Los Angeles, Calif.: 1967).

Chapter 8

Private Group Medical Practice

Previous chapters have reviewed organized ambulatory health service (OAHS) programs or clinics sponsored by several major types of social institutions: hospitals, public health agencies, schools, and industrial firms. Another major source of clinic sponsorship is the private medical profession itself. For many reasons, linked to the particular features of American medical practice, private physicians have joined together in medical groups to form group practice clinics. Unlike the other major types of clinic sponsorship, this concept had its origins in America rather than Europe; only in relatively recent years has the idea spread to Europe and elsewhere.

HISTORICAL BACKGROUND OF GROUP PRACTICE

With its expanding economy and free enterprise policies America witnessed a rapid development of medical technology and specialization after 1900. Moreover, unlike the pattern in Europe, specialization was not confined to doctors working in hospitals. The vast majority of physicians at the turn of the 20th century were general practitioners, but they—along with the relatively few specialists—were free to treat patients in hospitals.[1] Thus, with rare exceptions in a few large cities, the hospital did not provide a setting reserved for specialists as it did in Europe, while generalists practiced outside in the "community." This was particularly true in small towns, where hospitals were most permissive in opening their doors for use by all physicians.

The origins of group medical practice have customarily been traced to the initiative of Dr. William W. Mayo who, with his two sons, formed a partnership in the small town of Rochester, Minnesota in 1887.[2] This practice, which was limited to surgery, soon won a reputation for excellence that attracted patients from many miles around. Patients were hospitalized in St. Mary's Hospital, built by a Catholic order of nuns in 1889. After 1900, as the reputation of the

Mayo group grew, specialists in other nonsurgical fields began to be added. Soon, the group's renown expanded from surgery to general skill in diagnosis of all types of illness. By 1914 it was necessary to open a special building, not connected with the hospital and devoted mainly to diagnostic service.[3] Soon this facility also proved inadequate in size, and another larger building had to be constructed—still only for ambulatory service. By 1929, the group had assembled 386 physicians of all specialties. These physicians were salaried, even though the clinic got its earnings from individual patient fees, set on a sliding scale in relation to family income. Private physicians from miles around would refer patients to the "Mayo Clinic" for diagnostic work-ups, and when the disorder had been diagnosed the patient would be sent back to the original doctor for appropriate therapy.

The Mayo Clinic idea spread to other trade centers of large rural regions in the American midwest. In this newly settled frontier, where relatively few doctors were located, this innovative pattern of medical practice grew with little restraint. In the older states and cities of the East, solo practitioners, who were in plentiful supply, looked on the idea with hostility and regarded private clinics as a form of unfair competition. Thus, when the distinguished Committee on the Costs of Medical Care (CCMC) set out to study private group clinics in 1930, data were gathered from 55 clinics,[4] and not a single one was located in a large eastern city (such as New York, Boston, or Philadelphia). The majority were west of the Mississippi River. Only three of the clinics were in eastern states (two in Massachusetts and one in Pennsylvania), but each of these was in a small town.

After World War I, when doctors returned home from military service where they had experienced working in medical team settings, there was a slight acceleration in the establishment of private group clinics. By 1930, the CCMC estimated that about 150 such clinics existed in the United States, with some 1,800 physicians.[5] There were approximately two other health personnel per physician, and every clinic had a business manager of some type. The majority of these clinics hospitalized their patients in regular community hospitals, but about ten percent owned their own hospitals, and a few medical groups served as "closed" medical staffs of certain hospitals.

Following World War II, as part of the mounting American interest in national health insurance and the development of more efficient patterns for provision of medical care, new attention was directed to the concept of group medical practice. In 1946, the U.S. Public Health Service undertook its first nationwide survey of the extent and characteristics of medical group practice in the United States. For the purpose of this survey a group was defined as:

> a formal association of three or more physicians providing services in
> more than one field or specialty, with income from medical practice

pooled and redistributed to the members according to some prear-ranged plan.[6]

It should be noted that this definition called for collaboration of physicians of more than one specialty, a fact that was understandable in the light of the development of the essential concept. In subsequent years, parallel studies included groups of physicians within a single specialty, as well as multispecialty groups, so that the data available on trends are somewhat distorted.

Nevertheless, by piecing together data derived from several different sources, it is possible to conclude that—after a slow beginning prior to 1930—the number of group practice clinics and, more important, the proportion of all active U.S. physicians engaged in group practice has increased steadily. In Table 8–1, these data from several sources are presented.

The growth of group practice clinics reflected in Table 8–1 did not occur without conflict. In the first two decades of the 20th century, the organization of group practice clinics was uncommon, being concentrated largely in rural midwest areas where local individual practitioners were so few that resistance to the idea was slight. After 1920, however, and especially after the onset of the Great Depression in the 1930s, local medical associations (representing essentially solo private practitioners) became increasingly hostile to the idea.[7] They objected not only to the prominence and visibility of clinics as unfair competition, and even as "advertising," but also opposed the basic idea of physicians being paid by salary.[8] As late as 1947 even the *Code of Ethics* of the American Medical

Table 8–1 Private Group Practice Clinic Trends: Number of Group Practices, Physicians in Them, and Proportions of Total Active Physicians, United States, 1932–1975.

Year	Number of Groups	Physicians in Group Practice	Percentage of All Active Physicians
1932	239	1,466	0.9
1940	335	2,093	1.2
1946	368	3,084	2.6
1950	500	—	—
1959	1,546	12,009	5.2
1965	4,289	28,381	10.2
1969	6,162	38,834	12.8
1975	7,733	59,809	17.1

Sources: University of Michigan, School of Public Health, *Medical Care Chart Book,* 2nd and 5th eds. (Ann Arbor, Mich.: 1964, 1972); and American Medical Association, Center for Health Statistics, *Socio-Economic Issues of Health 1975–76* (Chicago: 1976), p. 8.

Association (AMA) issued a sort of subtle warning to physicians contemplating entry into a medical group by stating:

> The ethical principles actuating and governing a group or clinic are exactly the same as those applicable to the individual doctors, each of whom, whether employer, employee, or partner, is subject to the principles of ethics herein elaborated. The uniting into a business or professional organization does not relieve them, either individually or as a group, from the obligation they assume when they enter the profession.[9]

Because of this hostility from their peers, and also because of internal tensions that frequently developed among individualistic doctors, several medical groups that formed eventually disbanded. A survey in 1950 examined the status of 441 medical groups existing in 1940; during that decade 81, or 18.6 percent, had "discontinued."[10] This figure, however, included 15 groups that had reorganized in some way, and if these are eliminated from the "discontinued" number, the percentage of group clinic terminations was only 15 percent. Perhaps it is more noteworthy that 85 percent of group practices survived in a hostile environment than that 15 percent failed.

Professional opposition to group practice was particularly strong in those situations where the group practice clinic was associated with a health insurance or cooperative program.[11] Several litigations in the courts were generated by this opposition, and medical societies in various parts of the nation were found guilty of "restraint of trade" because of their discrimination against group practice doctors. (This issue will be discussed in Chapter 12.) Less than 10 percent of group practice clinics, however, have ever been associated with insurance or prepayment programs.

In addition, the slow growth of group practice clinics in their first decades was also doubtless related to the second-class, "charity medicine" image of clinics in general. For a century or more, the word "clinic" connoted service to the poor—perfunctory and insensitive. For some, the advanced technology and numerous allied health personnel found in clinics created an impression of bureaucracy and mechanization of a service that was expected to be humanistic and personal. If a patient's dignity were to be respected, it was assumed that medical care had to be provided in a private physician's office.[12] Not until after World War II, with the general increase in bureaucratization and organization of American society, did these views change, and private group practice clinics began to increase at a faster rate.

Another change in the evolution of group practice clinics occurred in the 1950s. The trend to specialization in medicine coupled with the desire of many physicians to have less arduous working lives, gave rise to the idea to form groups of specialists in a single field, such as a pediatric group, a radiological group, or a surgical group. Within these specialties, there might sometimes be physicians in certain subspecialties; thus a surgical group might include a thoracic surgeon, an orthopedic surgeon, a urological surgeon, and a general surgeon. The number of physicians in the single specialty groups tended to be smaller than that in the multispecialty groups, but by 1970 about one-third of the physicians engaged in group practice were in single specialty clinics. More will be said later about the characteristics of each of these types of clinic.

In a sense, 1967 marked a turning point in the evolution of private group practice. In that year the concept had matured to a stage that led the U.S. Department of Health, Education, and Welfare (HEW) to sponsor a national conference with the frank objective of "promoting the group practice of medicine."[13] Much earlier, in 1926, the National Association of Clinic Managers had been formed, but this was a small group of administrators of 14 clinics who wished to discuss their common management problems.[14] In 1949, the American Association of Medical Clinics (AAMC) was formed by the physicians in 112 clinics (with at least seven full-time physicians) to "elevate standards of practice" and "have interchange of ideas."[15] Both these organizations, however, were intended to help their member clinics, rather than to promote extension of the idea. The 1967 conference signalled a national government policy to encourage expansion of private group medical practice, to control the rising costs of medical care, and to improve the quality of health service.

PRIVATE GROUP PRACTICE IN THE 1970s

Given this background, it is easy to understand why private group medical practice in the United States of the 1970s should have characteristics that are traceable to circumstances that existed nearly a century before. Largely because of controversies such as those described above, most groups today still avoid use of the term "clinic" in their names. In Arizona, for example, a 1967 directory lists 48 medical group units, of which only 14 have "clinic" in their titles; the list of 73 medical groups in New Jersey that year includes only 3 designated as "clinics."[15]

The tendency of physicians, even those in private practice, to group together in face of the mounting complexities of medicine, may be seen in patterns that do not precisely fit the widely accepted definition of group practice quoted above. In a sense, grouping may be regarded as a matter of degree, so that varying extents of it can be conceived as a spectrum.[16] Insofar as individual practitioners refer patients to one another, collaboration is being demonstrated. Grouping of specialists in the same field creates advantages in the working pattern of the doctor. It may, e.g., assure 24-hour service for the patient, which is difficult for the solo practitioner to give. The rental of space by many different physicians and allied health personnel in a large medical arts building is convenient for both patient and physician: laboratory tests, pharmaceutical products, physical therapy, optometric refractions, as well as referrals to other specialists can all be close at hand.

On the average hospital staff, where many physicians get to know each other and seek consultations among colleagues, still another degree of grouping is expressed—one that may apply to outpatients as well as inpatients. The small private group of three or four doctors, truly working together as an entity, is the threshold at which formal group practice is thought to begin. The multispecialty group practice, with a full range of medical and surgical disciplines and allied health services, demonstrates a greater degree of grouping. Finally, the large multispecialty group, linked to a prepayment plan for a defined population, involves still greater cohesiveness and joint assumption of responsibility for the care of patients. (This will be discussed in Chapter 12.)

Even if attention is limited to the "three or more physicians formally organized" definition noted above, group practice clinics of many different compositions, sizes, legal forms, and administrative structures operate throughout the United States. According to a tabulation by the American Medical Association (done somewhat differently than that included in Table 8–1), there were 8,483 group medical practices in the United States in 1975, including 66,842 physicians.[17] If this number is related, not to *all* active physicians (as in Table 8–1), but to active physicians in *office-based* medical practice (215,429 in 1975) the proportion is 31 percent. The vast majority of these physicians (89 percent) were engaged in group practice full-time, while the remainder were part-time, that is, having other work settings as well.

As noted earlier, a pattern of medical grouping by several physicians in the same specialty arose in the 1950s. This pattern grew so rapidly that by 1975 a majority of the group practice clinics were of the single specialty type. Since the average number of physicians in such groups, however, was 5.1, compared with 13.0 in the multispecialty clinics, the aggregate number of doctors in the latter clinics was greater. A small proportion of clinics and group physicians, furthermore, were limited to general or family practice by 1975. Thus, the 66,842 physicians in 8,483 group clinics, as of 1975, were distributed as follows:[18]

| | Percentage of | |
Type of Group Practice	Group Clinics	Physicians
Multispecialty	35.1	58.8
Family practice	10.7	5.9
Single specialty	54.2	35.3
All types	100.0	100.0

Source: L. J. Goodman, T. H. Bennett, and R. J. Oden, *Group Medical Practice in the United States, 1975* (Chicago: AMA, 1976), p. 10–14.

The family practice group, it may be noted, is capable of providing a more comprehensive range of services to patients than the single specialty clinic; in this sense it is more like the multispecialty clinic. If these groups and physicians are combined with the multispecialty units, we can say that 45.8 percent of the group practice clinics with 64.7 percent of the doctors are in the sort of organized ambulatory care setting that generated the group practice movement initially, that is, an arrangement for relatively comprehensive ambulatory care by a team of private physicians and allied health personnel.

Most group practices are relatively small, as measured by the number of physicians in each. Classified into four size categories, the percentage distribution of *clinics* in 1975 was as follows:

	Size (number of physicians)			
Type of Group Practice	**3–5**	**6–15**	**16–49**	**50 & over**
	(percent)			
Multispecialty	41.8	39.8	15.3	3.1
Family practice	86.0	13.1	0.9	0.0
Single specialty	75.5	23.1	1.1	0.2

Source: L. J. Goodman, T. H. Bennett, and R. J. Oden, *Group Medical Practice in the United States 1975* (Chicago: AMA, 1976), pp. 10–14.

For obvious reasons, the percentage distribution of *physicians* in these clinics as of 1975, however, is different:

	Size (number of physicians)			
Type of Group Practice	**3–5**	**6–15**	**16–49**	**50 & Over**
	(percent)			
Multispecialty	11.7	26.3	29.5	32.3
Family practice	72.7	22.0	5.4	0.0
Single specialty	55.5	35.5	4.3	4.6

Source: L. J. Goodman, T. H. Bennett, R. J. Oden, *Group Medical Practice in the United States, 1975* (Chicago: AMA, 1976), pp. 10–14.

Thus, relating these two sets of percentage distributions, the multispecialty type of clinic of 15 or fewer doctors comprise 81.6 percent of such clinics with 38.0 percent of the doctors; multispecialty clinics with more than 15 doctors comprise 18.4 percent of such clinics, with 61.8 percent of the doctors. On the other hand, the single specialty clinics of 15 or fewer doctors comprise 98.6 percent of all such clinics and 91.0 percent of the doctors. It is evident, therefore, that in multispecialty group practices the larger clinics of 15 or more doctors have a substantial majority of the medical manpower.

From the viewpoint of the patient, the size of a group practice clinic is bound to influence its atmosphere. Impersonality is likely to be associated with larger organizations.[19] Group practices with large numbers of physicians, such as the Mayo Clinic or the Permanent Medical Groups linked to the Kaiser Health Plan, make adjustments to this problem. The physical facilities for patient care are typically divided into specialty units with only a small number of physicians in each. Thus, the patient scheduled to visit a pediatrician or a gynecologist would be seen in a suite of offices accommodating only a few (perhaps three to five) physicians. In effect, modern group practices have demonstrated that clinics need not offend patient's dignity: they can offer an atmosphere as comfortable as that of the most warm-hearted solo physician.

The legal and organizational status of groups differs also. Of all medical groups in 1975, 61 percent were organized as "professional corporations."[20] This status endows the individual physicians with limited liability, so that any legal actions (such as malpractice suits) can only be taken against the whole entity. Such a structure permits easier development of retirement systems for the members, and has several other advantages from a business viewpoint. Another 27.2 percent of groups were partnerships that may grant varying shares of the earnings to different partners. The remainder were distributed among associations, sole proprietorships, foundations, and other forms.

With any of these legal forms, there may be many physicians in the group practice who are, in fact, employees; they attain full membership in the corporation, partnership, or other entity only after a trial period. A new group practice is usually a delicate structure, held together only by good will and cooperative attitudes: we have noted how many group practice organizations failed to survive in the 1940s.[21] With the less hostile environment of the 1970s, group clinics are undoubtedly more stable but the entry of a new physician always involves some uncertainty. A probationary period before full membership status, therefore, is now general policy in virtually all of the larger clinics.

The geographic distribution of group practice clinics throughout the United States still reflects their early origins and the type of social environment that encourages their growth. With the pioneering role played by the Mayo Clinic in Minnesota, there has been a heavier concentration of groups formed in the midwestern states. Thus, the census division of west north central states, with 8 percent of the national population, had 11 percent of the medical groups in 1975, while the middle Atlantic states, with 19 percent of the population, had 12.5 percent of the groups.

The proportion of all active nonfederal physicians in each state, who were engaged in group practice in 1969 ranged from 50.1 percent in North Dakota down to 4.6 percent in Maryland.[22] A number of socioenvironmental factors correlated with these proportions; in general, the newer the state (according to the year in which it became part of the United States) and the more rural it was, the more likely it was to have a greater proportion of nonfederal physicians. Simple correlations were also strong with a low overall ratio of physicians to population and a low proportion of physicians in full-time hospital-based practice. Group practice would seem to grow most rapidly in newly settled regions of low population density where hospitals or medical centers are relatively weak. In a word, this suggests a social and professional environment where innovation is probably less obstructed by tradition.

Other studies have explored the distribution of group practices on the county level. As of 1959, in metropolitan counties, the percentage of private physicians in group practice was 4.6 percent, compared with 8.0 percent in adjacent counties, and 12.6 percent in isolated nonbordering counties.[23] From the viewpoint of the population, it would seem that group practice meets a need for specialty care in small towns that serve as the trade centers of rural regions. As individual practitioners, specialists would not settle in such localities, but grouped with other specialists they attract an adequate market of patients.

FUNCTIONING OF GROUP PRACTICE CLINICS

Group practice clinics generally attempt to emulate the patterns of service to which patients are accustomed in private practice. If a patient is new and not acquainted with any of the doctors, he or she is usually sent first to a primary care physician—an internist, pediatrician, general practitioner, or sometimes an obstetrician-gynecologist. This physician then refers the patient to other specialists, as necessary. In other group practices, the patient goes directly to whichever doctor he or she chooses, and may remain with that physician alone or be referred to a colleague. Ideally the group physicians should hold periodic clinical conferences to discuss difficult cases; however, sometimes this is only done informally.

Every medical group contains numerous allied health personnel—nurses, technicians, physical therapists, record librarians, clerks, and others. In 1975, there were on the average 2.53 such personnel for every group physician. There were somewhat more in the multispecialty groups (2.63 in formal multispecialty groups and 2.87 in groups of general practitioners) and fewer (2.30 per doctor) in single specialty groups.[24] Since a laboratory technician or record librarian, for example, serves several physicians, her or his time can be utilized maximally to raise productivity; whereas an individual practitioner might also have two office assistants, but they would not have the range of special skills possessed by 10 allied health personnel, for example, associated with a group of 5 doctors.

Of the 2.53 allied health personnel per group practice doctor, the most numerous are clerical workers, followed by nurses (of different levels), and technicians. The percentage distribution of all classes of allied health personnel in the two main types of group practice clinic, as of 1975, was:

Personnel	Multispecialty Clinics	Single specialty Clinics	All Group Practice
Clerical	40.3	47.4	42.7
Nursing	28.5	20.0	26.5
Technical	18.3	24.8	20.2
Other	12.9	7.8	10.7
All types	100.0	100.0	100.0

Source: L. J. Goodman, T. H. Bennett, and R. J. Oden, *Group Medical Practice in the United States, 1975* (Chicago: AMA, 1976), pp. 44–46.

With staffs of such variety and size, as well as the many tasks to be carried out in financing—collections, disbursements, and so on—the majority of group practice clinics have full-time managers beyond the level of a clerk or secretary. Such managers serve in approximately 56 percent of all group practices, ranging from 37 percent in groups of 3 physicians to 95 percent in groups of 50 to 99 physicians. It is noteworthy that only 88 percent of the largest group practices of 100 or more physicians have managers; this is probably due to a policy of having full-time medical directors who oversee financial matters. The functions of a group clinic manager have become sufficiently specialized to lead the Medical Group Management Association (successor to the National Association of Clinic Managers) to issue manuals on medical group administration, to promote training courses, and so on.[25]

Policy matters in small group practice clinics are usually decided by discussions among all the medical members. In larger groups, there is likely to be a board of directors or executive committee. In 36 percent of medical groups, one of the physicians is chosen (usually by election) as the medical director, but this is typically a part-time responsibility. Approximately 50 percent of clinics with 100 or more physicians have full-time medical directors.

The financial mechanisms in private group practice clinics are highly varied. The overwhelming source of income is payment for services to patients on a fee-for-service basis—fees being paid by the patient or by a third party (insurance plan, public agency, or other entity) on his or her behalf. In 1975, only 8.4 percent of medical groups received any income through a prepaid global amount for care to members of a health maintenance organization (HMO); group practices earning half or more of their income from HMO sources numbered only 142, or 1.7 percent of the total. The distribution of income among physicians in the group is based on a variety of mechanisms.[26]

As of 1975, about 40 percent of medical groups applied a formula that specified certain amounts payable to physicians as salaries, varying with the individual's background, seniority, and other factors. On top of these salaries an additional payment was based on the individual doctor's ''productivity''—this being measured by the clinic income his or her service generated, hours of work, the number of patients seen, and similar factors. Fixed salaries unrelated to physician productivity were used in only 20 percent of the groups; however, these salaries virtually always varied with specialty training, seniority, responsibility, professional reputation, etc. Simple distribution of income equally among all physicians was the policy in about 30 percent of the groups. The remaining 10 percent might be described as most individualistic, that is, distributing earnings solely on the basis of the clinic income generated by each physician.[27]

These distributions, of course, are made from the clinics *net* income, after paying salaries to nonphysician staff, rent, and other overhead expenses. It is virtually unknown for group practices to share earnings in a flexible way with nonmedical staff members, although a profitable clinic may be able to attract the best qualified allied personnel by offering higher salaries. For reasons explored below, the net earnings of physicians in group practice have tended to be greater than those of solo practitioners of comparable age and qualifications.[28]

As for physical facilities, group practice clinics are usually located in separate buildings and are therefore readily identifiable to the population. This very visibility, it will be recalled, led in past years to the charge of "unethical advertising." Since the group practice movement has accelerated so much in recent years, these freestanding structures are predominantly new and well-designed. Attractive reception and waiting areas, functional examining rooms, laboratories, and x-ray departments, tastefully decorated medical consultation offices, and so on are usually impressive demonstrations that an organized clinic need not have the sordid atmosphere of many hospital outpatient departments or the early dispensaries for the poor. There are often special playrooms for children, and soft music may be heard in the background.

In 1975, nearly half (47.8 percent) of group practice facilities were owned by the medical group as a whole or by certain physicians within the group. Facilities were not owned, but presumably rented, by 41.6 percent of the medical groups, and a variety of other arrangements characterized the remaining 10.6 percent.[29] Nearly one-fourth (24.2 percent) of group practices were located adjacent to a hospital and another 13.6 percent were actually within a hospital structure. In fact, 555 private groups, or 7.7 percent of all respondents in the 1975 survey, owned or operated their own hospitals. Patients of the majority of group practice clinics, however, are treated in regular community hospitals. Often there is a preference for use of one hospital, so that in-hospital consultation by clinic colleagues can be readily arranged.

Of special interest, in connection with future planning of organized ambulatory care facilities, is that in 1975 as many as 19 percent of group practice clinics operated satellite facilities. This pattern varied with group size, ranging from 13 percent in the smallest size groupings (three physicians) to 75 percent in clinics with 100 or more doctors. Operation of such satellite units, often limited to primary care, helps to overcome the transportation problem faced by patients when several doctors join together at one location.

Beyond the direct services of physicians, private group practice clinics are capable of providing various ancillary services. Most frequently these are clinical laboratory tests and x-ray examinations. The percentages of medical groups offering diverse services in 1975 were as follows:[31]

Service	Percent of Group Clinics
Laboratory tests	65.7
X-ray examinations	56.1
Health education	10.4
Dietetic counseling	9.3
Psychological service	5.1
Drug counseling	5.1
Social work	4.2
Dental care	2.7
Podiatry	1.9
Other	6.8

Source: L. J. Goodman, T. H. Bennett, and R. J. Oden, *Group Medical Practice in the United States, 1975* (Chicago: AMA, 1976), pp. 70–72.

The range of services is much greater in larger multispecialty clinics.

EVALUATION OF GROUP PRACTICE CLINICS

The effects of providing ambulatory medical care through private group practice clinics, in contrast to the traditional pattern of individual medical offices, have been a subject of interest in the American health care scene for many years. Perhaps because of its controversial beginnings and also because of its divergence from the mainstream of the private medical profession itself, numerous efforts have been made to evaluate the performance of group practice clinics. Evaluations have been made or attempted on the quality of medical service provided, on its cost effectiveness, on the reactions of patients, on the attitudes of participating doctors, and on other aspects of this growing pattern of organized ambulatory care delivery.

Much of the assessment of group practice in America has been on purely theoretical grounds, rather than empirical evidence. On this basis, it is claimed that the provision of medical care through teams of physicians and allied personnel has to have distinct advantages as well as disadvantages for both patient and doctor.[32]

With respect to the patient, the advantages apply essentially to the multispecialty clinic, where patients may expect to obtain a wide range of specialized services conveniently in one place. They are spared the difficulty of travel to several locations for laboratory or x-ray examinations, for various specialty services, and sometimes even for a second opinion on a health problem. In the multispecialty group practice clinics of more than six physicians, which constitute 58 percent of the total, all such services are usually available. Since several doctors are helping each other, moreover, patients can usually feel confident that they are receiving high quality care. If the medical group is large enough, arrangements may be made for 24-hour coverage, which can be valuable and reassuring for the patient.

On the other hand, patients often feel that group practices as settings have the same impersonal atmosphere as clinics have had traditionally. If the clinic is large and the patient is not personally acquainted with one of its physicians, he or she may feel deprived of "free choice" of the doctor. These attitudes, however, were more common in previous decades.[33] Older persons, remembering the past, are understandably more skeptical about a group practice clinic than the young.[34] Even so, some patients may regard a certain amount of impersonality as a reasonable trade-off for getting service of high quality.

From the physician's viewpoint, group practice has many theoretical advantages.[35] The young physician, in particular, is in a position to earn a good living immediately, without the years of time and effort normally required to build up a reputation in individual private practice. He or she need not go promptly into debt to equip a new medical office. With colleagues around, the physician does not feel isolated and has the benefit of convenient consultation on difficult medical problems that may arise. Working time also is more regularly arranged, and the physician feels free for personal and family life when not on duty or on call. With colleagues to care for patients for him, he can more readily take time off for holidays or postgraduate studies. The availability of more auxiliary personnel than feasible in solo practice spares the doctor from minor clerical and administrative chores.

In return for these benefits, the physician in group practice must sacrifice some independence. While other forms of constraint (particularly in hospitals) influencé all physicians, the necessity of working closely with a number of medical colleagues and allied health personnel is stressful for many physicians.[36] In spite of the higher *average* incomes of group practice physicians at equivalent levels, an energetic doctor may feel blocked from extremely high earnings and may not enjoy sharing income with others.

These theoretical advantages and disadvantages to group practice have been discussed many times, but the more important question is the results of empirical studies. Many of these have concerned the issues of productivity or work output of the group practice doctor, compared with the solo practitioner. Most economists have demonstrated higher output per doctor in group practice, due mainly to their lower capital investment and greater use of auxiliary personnel per doctor. J. A. Boan, a Canadian economist, concludes his studies of actual group practice clinics in operation with the statement:

> . . . There is little room for doubt that productivity is higher in the group setting than in solo practice . . . Where productivity is up, costs must be down, the quality of service must be higher, or some combination of these must be the result.[37]

Using other research methods, Donald Yett concludes from various multiple regression analyses that on both statistical and theoretical grounds, "there is strong evidence to support the intuitive belief that physicians' expenses are subject to economies of scale" (that is, lower costs per unit of medical output in larger systems).[38] Seymour Harris, the distinguished senior economist, also concludes that group practice involves a lower cost of production per unit of service provided.[39]

On the other hand, based on empirical study of single specialty groups of specialists in internal medicine in one city, Richard Bailey found no increase in output of physician services with increasing size of groups.[40] These conclusions have been criticized, however, for failing to take account of the varying quality of medical service furnished.[41] Furthermore, they say nothing about the output in group practice of more ancillary services, which in many ways can replace the time and effort of physicians. Herbert Klarman also points out that economists or others must not overlook the capability of the group practice model to attract clusters of physicians to urban slum areas (or to rural regions) that otherwise would have very few physicians.[42]

Whether or not there are strict economies of scale in group practice may be debatable, but there is little evidence that, in an open market, fee-for-service setting, any reduced costs of production of medical service are passed on to consumers in lower fees. Instead, the same (or even higher) fees tend to be charged to patients, so that the economies result in higher physician earnings, a shorter workweek, or both. Only when consumer bargaining power is strengthened, through cooperation of many people in a prepayment population, are the economies of group practice translated into lower charges for service.[43]

Students of group practice in diverse settings, like Richard Weinerman, have pointed out that much of the theoretical collaboration expected among professional colleagues does not often occur.[44] There is doubtless a range of degrees of teamwork in various medical groups, depending on leadership and the characteristics of their members. Freidson and Mann have described a typology of medical groups ranging from highly cooperative teams of doctors, to groups dominated by bureaucratic and hierarchical attitudes, to still others consisting of a loose aggregate of individualists.[45]

Whatever the realities of group practice performance, there can be little doubt of the potential benefits of teamwork between physicians and allied personnel.

By being spared from many simple procedural tasks—injections, taking blood specimens, much recording of patient information, and so on—physicians can spend more time on the professional functions for which they were trained. Physician time can also be conserved by the multiple rooms in a group practice clinic, allowing one patient to be examined while another is disrobing. Effective administration should yield efficiencies that ought to be translated into financial savings.

There is one other important economic consequence of group practice, only recently recognized, even if the clinic is not linked with a health insurance plan such as an HMO. It is that patients served regularly by group practice clinics are hospitalized less frequently than those served by individual practitioners.[46] Based on experience in Hawaii, where group medical practice is very highly developed, researchers have found that many diagnostic and some treatment procedures, for which the individual practitioner would hospitalize a patient, may be done on an ambulatory basis in a well developed group practice clinic.[47] The clinic, under fee-for-service remuneration, therefore becomes competitive with the hospital to some extent. The result is less use of hospitals, greater use of ambulatory group practice clinics, and probable net savings in overall medical care expenditures.

The accelerating rate of group practice growth, in terms of the proportion of active physicians engaged in this pattern of practice (Table 8–1), suggests that the idea has become increasingly attractive to young physicians. Even in 1935–45, studies demonstrated that an increasing percentage of medical school graduates ultimately joined medical groups or partnerships.[48] With respect to three graduating classes of all medical schools in the United States in that period, the following data, gathered in 1950, are revealing:

Type of Medical Activity	Percentage from Class of:		
	1935	1940	1945
Individual practice	74.0	66.4	47.3
Group practice or partnership	9.7	12.8	27.1
Salaried Position	14.8	19.4	23.9
Other or unknown	1.5	1.4	1.7
All activities	100.0	100.0	100.0

Source: H. G. Weiskoten and Marian Altenderfer, "Trends in Medical Practice," *Journal of Medical Education* 31(1956): 70.

Succeeding medical school graduating classes (at least five years after completing school) were obviously entering partnerships, group practice, or some other type of organized medical work in rising proportions. Although similar data are not available for recent medical graduates, it is apparent that the trend has probably continued.

The general acceptance of the group practice clinic mode is reflected by the volume of patients coming for service to such clinics, even though they must ordinarily pay as much for such care as for seeing a private doctor. The AMA study of 1975 found that the average group practice doctor saw 130 patients a week, compared with 120 patients seen by solo practitioners.[49] Group practice doctors reported an average of 51 hours of professional work per week, compared with about 49 hours by individual practitioners, and both types worked about 47 weeks per year. Variations, of course, occurred among different sizes of medical groups, physicians of different ages, and so on.

Accordingly, one may infer that the average full-time group practice physician in 1975 had 6,110 patient encounters during the year. It will be recalled that 66,842 physicians were in group practice that year, counting part-time group doctors. If the part-time physicians (about 12 percent) are assumed to work an average of 33 percent of full-time, the number of full-time equivalent physicians in group practice would be 61,495. This yields an estimate of 375,734,000 patient visits to private group practice doctors per year.

Both on theoretical and empirical grounds, one may expect ambulatory services from group medical practice clinics, whether private or linked to some insurance program or other organization, to increase as a proportion of all ambulatory service in the United States each year. Even with the rise of family practice as a specialty (a reaction, in a sense, against conventional specialization), group practice growth does not seem to be affected. Family medicine specialists are becoming incorporated into group practice clinics where they provide primary care but do not perform surgery like the traditional general practitioner. The family medicine specialist serves as general overseer of the patients' health, including its psychosomatic aspects.[50]

Between 1965 and 1975, the proportion of doctors in group practice (as a share of total active physicians) rose by about 7 percent per year. The more common that this pattern becomes in the average community, the more may one expect to see newly trained physicians engaging in it. If the recent growth rate continues, one may expect that well before the year 2000, nearly all American private physicians will be working in multispecialty or single specialty groups, if they are not in hospital-based or some other form of organized medical work.

In a sense, group practice clinics apply to private ambulatory medical care the teamwork concept incorporated long before in the organization of personnel in hospitals. Perhaps this is another reason why group practice clinics arose first in rural regions of America where hospitals were few and far between.[51] As medical science has become more complex, even within a single specialty, the conscientious physician is bound to feel greater need for consultation with colleagues for reaching sound decisions on diagnosis or treatment.

When the CCMC recommended in 1932 that personal medical care should be provided by group practice clinics—preferably associated with hospitals—the idea seemed startling.[52] The AMA greeted it, along with other CCMC recommendations as "communistic and socialistic."[53] It is small wonder that the AAMC did little to promote new clinics; it did not wish to fan the flames of suspicion and hostility that already existed in the many communities where group practice clinics were in operation. It took a more crusading organization, the Group Health Association of America (founded in 1959 as an outgrowth of the earlier Bureau of Cooperative Medicine), to promote group practice, combined with health insurance or prepayment.[54] By 1970, however, the AMA was joining with the AAMC and the Medical Group Management Association in issuing guidelines on how a group practice clinic could be efficiently organized.[55]

By the 1970s, the momentum for organization of private group practices was accelerated by pressures from throughout the American health care system. Chapter 4 has noted how group practices have become a natural and convenient source of emergency medical services for several hospitals. Likewise, as discussed in Chapter 7, the solution to the occupational health needs of many firms is being found in obtaining services from an appropriately located group practice clinic. The federally financed movement for HMOs, as will be seen in Chapter 12, is providing further impetus for the establishment of new group practice clinics. Small consulting firms have been formed whose principal purpose is to advise physicians on organizing a group practice clinic.[56]

As one of the last states to be settled, California has been a very fertile environment for the growth of group practice clinics and the exploration of diverse schemes for organizing them. In this type of OAHS, perhaps more than any other reviewed in this volume, the findings in Los Angeles County should have special significance.

GROUP PRACTICE IN LOS ANGELES COUNTY

A modest field survey of group practice clinics operating in Los Angeles County was made in 1971. In 1969, when the national average proportion of active physicians in medical groups was 12.8 percent, the equivalent figure for California was 17.8 percent.[57] In Los Angeles County, where immigration of families has been especially great and ties to a particular physician therefore relatively weak, the growth of private group practices has been particularly rapid. While precise definitions of medical groups have not been uniform over the years, the count in 1950 was 18 group practices; in 1964 it was 183; and in 1970 it was 330.[58] This rate of increase in Los Angeles County between 1950 and 1970 was about 50 percent greater than the national rate, as one would expect in an area of high population mobility and relatively weak social and professional constraints of tradition.

Data on specialty composition and size of group practices in Los Angeles County for 1967 showed the following:[59]

Type of Group Practice	Number of Physicians in Groups			
	5 & Under	6–19	20 & Over	Total
Multispecialty	47	35	4	86
Single specialty	117	15	0	132
Both	164	50	4	218

Source: AMA, Chicago, 1967, unpublished data.

Among these 218 medical groups, a stratified sample of 14 were selected for study; these included 3 single specialty groups (ophthalmology, otosurgery, and urology) and 11 multispecialty groups (7 large and 4 small). Interviews with clinic managers in all 14 clinics were held in May 1971. The major characteristics of these 14 private group practices were as follows:

Basic Settings

All but one of the 14 group practices had been in operation ten years or more, and 6 were over twenty years old. The multispecialty groups had all grown in size since their origin. The doctors who had entered group practice claimed it was because of a personal preference for this type of professional work setting. Twelve of the 14 groups had experienced steady growth in their patient population over the years; in only one group was there any prospect of future termination (when two senior partners retired).

Of the 14 groups, 6 were incorporated, another 6 were partnerships, and 2 were sole proprietorships. (Because of a recent change in California law, however, most of the nonincorporated groups were contemplating incorporation.)

The formality of organizational structure increased with group size. In the smaller groups (five or fewer doctors), all policy matters were decided by group discussion. For groups of moderate size (6 to 19 doctors), daily decisions were usually delegated to one member, while for large groups (20 doctors and over) a committee typically handled routine administrative decisions. Medical and administrative problems tended to be sharply divided; all matters relating to nonphysician personnel, collection of charges, purchase of supplies, housekeeping, etc., were handled by the clinic manager. Engagement of hospital residents to cover nighttime hours, however, was done by the physicians. Only one of the 14 groups used a formal organization chart.

It is noteworthy that one of the sets of partners owned and operated two separate clinics, each of which was a distinct legal entity. Two of the larger multispecialty clinics each operated a branch office, staffed on a part-time basis by a primary physician from the main clinic.

Services Provided

As private group practices (not basically affiliated with a prepayment plan), all 14 medical groups accommodated patients coming mainly on a fee-for-service basis. Six of the 14 groups, however, rejected Medicaid patients because of alleged delays in governmental reimbursement and excessive paperwork.

Most patients of the multispecialty clinics lived nearby. One group referred patients coming from beyond the neighborhood elsewhere because the doctors did not want to expand the size of their practice. About 50 percent of group practice patients looked to one of the clinic's physicians as their personal doctor over the years. Single-specialty clinics tended to attract and accept patients from greater distances—often for one-time-only episodic service.

Patients came to the clinics primarily through word-of-mouth referral by friends or relatives, or spontaneously from the neighborhood. No clinic required referral from another physician, although 20 to 40 percent of the single-specialty group patients came, in fact, from physician referrals.

Ten of the 14 group practices reported that at least 80 percent of their patients came by appointment with individual physicians. The other four practices, in which walk-in patients were more frequent, attributed this to their arrangements for providing service to employees of certain industrial firms, or to subpopulations under prepayment contracts.

All 14 groups were open for service at least 8 hours each weekday, and most of the multispecialty (but not the single-specialty) groups were open also Saturday mornings. In addition, all 14 groups had arrangements for a doctor being on call at any hour of the day or night; in 3 of the practices (all large, multispecialty clinics) special emergency units, staffed by moonlighting hospital residents, were maintained after regular clinic hours.

Unlike hospital outpatient departments, the group practices did not schedule specialty clinic sessions. Patients arranged to see the various specialists by appointment. All 11 multispecialty groups had general practitioners or general internists who served as primary care doctors. The most common other specialties included general surgeons (in all multispecialty groups but one), obstetrician-gynecologists, and orthopedists. All but 2 of the 11 multispecialty groups (small ones) had clinical laboratories in their facilities, and all had x-ray equipment. The third most frequent ancillary service was physical therapy.

Dental and pharmaceutical services were not well-developed in the sample of group practices studied in Los Angeles County. In 3 of the 11 multispecialty clinics, dentists leased space on the premises but were not included as members of the group; similar arrangements applied to pharmacies on the premises of 3 groups. A pharmacy was included as an integral ancillary service in only one clinic.

Hospitalization for the patients of the 14 group practices was provided in one of the nearby hospitals. There were no formal contractual links, however, between any of the medical groups and any hospital.

Financing

Reliable financial data were difficult to obtain. Only a few general features are reportable.

To bill patients, all 14 group clinics used the California Relative Value Schedule (RVS), which establishes ratios of value for a long list of medical services and procedures; the exact charge depends on the dollar amount assigned to one "RVS unit" at a given time and place. Most of the groups applied the same unit value (or "conversion factor") for the services of all their medical members; in two, however, each doctor was permitted to apply his or her own conversion factor, and in a few clinics surgeons were allowed, in special cases, to apply higher than standard conversion factors.

Three of the multispecialty group practices had prepaid medical care arrangements with a fraction of their patients. In only one of these three, however, did prepaid patients entail as much as 50 percent of the work; this was a small clinic. Six of the multispecialty groups had contracts with local firms for industrial medicine service to employees.

In spite of this relatively small role played by contractual prepayment arrangements, traditional voluntary health insurance was estimated as the source of 50 percent or more of the group's income in 6 of the 14 clinics. In two of the groups, payment from governmental sources accounted for an estimated 60 percent of the total income. (One of these was located in a low-income neighborhood, with many Medicaid patients; another was located in a section with many Medicare patients.) It is noteworthy, however, that none on the 14 groups estimated personal out-of-pocket payments by patients to contribute as much as 50 percent of total income; the average share of personal payments was about 24 percent. All these figures, however, apply to group practice income from in-hospital as well as ambulatory service. (For ambulatory care alone, the third party payment sources would undoubtedly be lower, and personal sources higher.)

Operational expenditures differed somewhat for the two types of group practice. In the 11 multispecialty groups, payments to the physicians absorbed about 50 percent of the total revenue, while in the 3 single specialty groups, these payments averaged 32 percent of revenues. Salaries to ancillary personnel varied from an average of 24 percent in the large multispecialty group practices to 28 percent in the single specialty units. "Other expenses" ranged between an average of 40 percent in the single specialty groups to 23 percent in the small multispecialty units.

In all 14 group practice clinics, all personnel except physicians (not including part-time hospital residents) were paid flat salaries. For the physician members, there were varying sorts of remuneration. Only 2 of the 14 units (both multispecialty) shared all income equally among the physicians. In five clinics, the doctors were paid mainly by prearranged salary (varying with specialty and seniority). An additional 10–20 percent of their earnings was dependent on the collections for the individual doctor's services. Physicians in the remaining seven clinics shared none of the earnings equally, but rather divided them entirely on the basis of collections derived from each doctor's services. Junior physicians joining a group, however, typically received a flat monthly salary for the first year or two, until they became full partners or owners of the medical corporation.

Resources

All 14 group practices were housed in separate buildings, the majority of which were owned by the group. In contrast to most other types of organized clinics reviewed in this book, the furnishings and atmospheres were, with one exception, bright and attractive. Medical and laboratory equipment all appeared to be well-maintained, and supplies were plentiful. In general, the quantity of physical resources increased with the number of doctors in the group practice.

Part-time physicians—either as consultants or hospital residents to cover emergency care hours—were associated with two of the seven large multispecialty groups, with two of the four small multispecialty groups, but with none on the three single specialty groups. One of the small multispecialty groups with three full-time physicians had ten part-time consultants, who visited the clinic about once a week. While these relationships were obviously tenuous, in time some of the visiting specialists may have been expected to affiliate full-time with the group practice.

Recruitment of new medical members in small groups tended to be through personal contacts. Large groups often advertised in medical journals, and some medical applicants came on their own initiative. Regarding specialty qualifications, all but two of the group practices accepted either full certification by a specialty board or eligibility for the board examinations. The two requiring full board certification were both single specialty groups.

In all 14 clinics surveyed, there was little physician turnover. After full membership in the group practice was achieved, none reported any withdrawals within the previous year. Most of the multispecialty groups were seeking additional doctors to cope with their expanding utilization.

Ratios of nurses and allied personnel to physicians were highly variable among the 14 group practices. Consistent with national findings, the Los Angeles County survey found slightly higher ratios in the larger practices than in the smaller practices. There were exceptions, however, that could be explained only by special local circumstances, such as a ratio of 7.4 nonmedical personnel per doctor in one small (four physicians) single specialty group. Regarding allied personnel qualifications, only state licensure was required for those disciplines regulated by such laws (nurses, technicians, physical therapists, etc.); clinic managers frequently expressed preference for allied personnel without previous experience, so that they could be more readily oriented to follow each clinic's mode of practice. There were no detectable differences in the duties assigned to registered nurses and those assigned to licensed vocational nurses.

Quality and Cost Controls

In none of the 14 Los Angeles County medical groups surveyed were any formalized quality control procedures identified. In response to questions on this, reference was made to membership in the AAMC, which has "criteria" for membership, and to the careful process of doctor selection. Informal discussions about cases were frequently reported as a method of maintaining quality, with discussions and indirect surveillance occurring somewhat more frequently between the senior physicians and their new medical colleagues.

The time scheduled per patient visit was typically 15 minutes, but this was seldom enforced rigidly. Some patients, usually new ones, were allotted more time, while others received less. Medical records were kept on all patients; they tended to be most complete with respect to medical procedures performed, since these are the basis for determining charges.

Grievances from either patients or employees were reported to be rare. Patient complaints were directed to the physician involved, and no clinic indicated any process of appeal to the medical director. Employee grievances were typically directed to the clinic manager.

Regarding continuing education, only 2 of the 14 groups (both large multispecialty units) had systematic conferences to discuss cases. The most frequent type of formal continuing education was attendance at meetings of professional societies, for which leaves of absence were usually granted. A specific research project conducted at the clinic was reported by only one unit, a single specialty group.

All 14 group practices appeared to be managed in an efficient, businesslike manner. The complexity of administrative procedures increased with group size, but there was no evidence that financial considerations took precedence over quality of care. Aside from the normal process of fee billings, distribution of earnings, payment of salaries, and procurement of supplies, the only special fiscal procedures related to making contracts with industrial firms or prepaid programs. The larger multispecialty clinics with such contracts tended to be those engaging part-time hospital residents for 24-hour service coverage.

Thus, a survey of the organizational and operational details of a small sample of private group practices in one metropolitan county underscores the variations found in this type of ambulatory service clinic. While our study did not examine patient attitudes toward the care they received, it was quite evident from the generally large volume of patients coming to these clinics, and their trend of steady growth, that many people were satisfied.

Various studies have suggested a kind of equilibrium or trade-off in the attitudes of people toward private group practice clinics, compared with private solo practitioners. Whatever may be felt lacking in "personalized care" at the group practice is more or less compensated by the clinic's higher "technical standards."[60] The findings of population surveys in three midwestern cities, reported in 1972, indicate that a majority of persons express a preference for group over solo practice, even if they have had little experience with it.[61] The somewhat greater rate of preference for group practice patterns found among persons of higher education and middle income level forecasts a further increase of such preference in the future.

NOTES

1. Roemer, Milton I., and J. W. Friedman, *Doctors in Hospitals: Medical Staff Organization and Hospital Performance* (Baltimore: Johns Hopkins Press, 1971), pp. 29–48.

2. Clapesattle, Helen, *The Doctors Mayo* (Minneapolis, Minn.: University of Minnesota Press, 1963).

3. Sigerist, Henry E., *American Medicine* (New York: W. W. Norton, 1934), pp. 178–180.

4. Rorem, C. Rufus, *Private Group Clinics,* Committee on the Costs of Medical Care Pub. No. 8, (Chicago: University of Chicago Press, 1931).

5. Ibid., p. ix.

6. Hunt, G. Halsey, and M. S. Goldstein, *Medical Group Practice in the United States* (Washington: Public Health Pub. No. 77, 1951), p. 5.

7. Cabot, Hugh, *The Patient's Dilemma—The Quest for Medical Security in America* (New York: Reynal & Hitchcock, 1940), pp. 143–150.

8. Leland, R. G., "Group Practice," *Journal of the American Medical Association* 100 (1933): 1605–1608; 1693–1699; and 1773–1778.

9. American Medical Association, *Principles of Medical Ethics* (Chicago: AMA, 1947).

10. Dickinson, Frank G., and Charles Bradley, *Discontinuance of Medical Groups, 1940–1949* (Chicago: American Medical Association, Research Bull. No. 90, 1952).

11. Hansen, Horace, *Legal Rights of Group Health Plans* (Washington: Group Health Association of America, May 1964).

12. Freidson, Eliot, *Patients' Views of Medical Practice* (New York: Russell Sage Foundation, 1961).

13. U.S. Public Health Service, *Promoting the Group Practice of Medicine* (Washington: Public Health Service Pub. No. 1750, 1967).

14. Jordan, E. P. (editor), *The Physician and Group Practice* (Chicago: Year Book Publishers, 1958), pp. 196–206.

15. American Medical Association, *Listing of Group Practices in the United States,* 2nd edition, (Chicago: AMA, 1967).

16. Roemer, Milton I., "Group Practice: A Medical Care Spectrum," *Journal of Medical Education,* 40 (1965): 1154–1158.

17. Goodman, L. J.; T. H. Bennett; and R. J. Oden, *Group Medical Practice in the United States, 1975* (Chicago: AMA 1976), p. 10.

18. Ibid., pp. 10–14.

19. Freidson, Eliot, and J. H. Mann, "Organizational Dimensions of Large Scale Group Medical Practice," *American Journal of Public Health* 61 (1971): 786–795.

20. Goodman, L. J.; T. H. Bennett; and R. J. Oden, "Current Status of Group Medical Practice in the United States," *Public Health Reports* 92 (1977): 430–443.

21. Du Bois, Donald M., "Organizational Viability of Group Practice: I. Organizational Objectives," *Group Practice* 16 (1967): 261–270.

22. Roemer, Milton I.; Jorge Mera; and William Shonick, "The Ecology of Group Medical Practice in the United States," *Medical Care* 12 (1974): 627–637.

23. U.S. Public Health Service, *Medical Groups in the United States, 1959* (Washington: PHS Pub. No. 1063, July 1963), p. 25.

24. Goodman, et al., *Group Medical Practice in the United States, 1975,* pp. 44–46.

25. Medical Group Management Association, Accounting Committee, *Report on Cost Survey for Calendar Year 1969* (Denver: 1970).

26. Jordan, *The Physician and Group Practice,* pp. 113–126.

27. Goodman, et al., *Group Medical Practice in the United States, 1975,* pp. 63–66.

28. Owens, A., "Doctors' Economic Health Never Better," *Medical Economics,* 44 (1967): 63–67.

29. Goodman et al., *Group Medical Practice in the United States,* pp. 67–69.

30. Ibid., pp. 70–72.

31. Ibid., pp. 82–87.

32. Medical Group Management Association, *The Organization and Development of a Medical Group Practice* (Washington: Capitol Publications, 1976).

33. Goldmann, Franz, "Potentialities of Group Practice Medicine," *Connecticut State Medical Journal* 10 (1946): 289–294.

34. Metzner, Charles A., et al., "Differential Public Acceptance of Group Medical Practice," *Medical Care,* 10 (1972): 279–287.

35. MacColl, William A., *Group Practice and Prepayment of Medical Care* (Washington: Public Affairs Press, 1966).

36. Freidson, Eliot, "The Organization of Medical Practice" in H. Freeman, S. Levine, and L. Reeder (editors), *Handbook of Medical Sociology* (Englewood Cliffs, N.J.: Prentice-Hall, 1972), p. 355.

37. Boan, T. A., *Group Practice* (Ottawa, Canada: Queen's Printer, 1966), p. 31.

38. Yett, Donald E., "An Evaluation of Alternative Methods of Estimating Physicians' Expenses Relative to Output," *Inquiry* 4 (1967): 3–27.

39. Harris, Seymour E., *The Economics of American Medicine* (New York: MacMillan, 1964), pp. 140–141.

40. Bailey, Richard M., "A Comparison of Internists in Solo and Fee-for-Service Group Practice in the San Francisco Bay Area," *Bulletin of the New York Academy of Medicine* 44 (1968): 1293–1303.

41. Reder, Melvin W., "Comment on Richard M. Bailey's 'Economies of Scale in Medical Practice,'" in Herbert E. Klarman (editor), *Empirical Studies in Health Economics* (Baltimore: Johns Hopkins Press, 1970), pp. 274–278.

42. Klarman, Herbert E., "Economic Research in Group Medicine," in *New Horizons in Health Care*, Proceedings of the First International Congress of Group Medicine (Winnipeg, Manitoba; 1970), pp. 178–193.

43. Roemer, Milton I., and Donald M. DuBois, "Medical Costs in Relation to the Organization of Ambulatory Care," *New England Journal of Medicine* 280 (1969): 988–993.

44. Weinerman, E. Richard, "Problems and Perspectives of Group Practice," *Bulletin of the New York Academy of Medicine* 44 (1968): 1423–1434.

45. Freidson, Eliot, and J. N. Mann, "Organizational Dimensions of Large Scale Group Medical Practice."

46. Kralewski, John E., and Roice D. Luke, *Group Practice: Review and Recommendations for Planning and Research* (Chicago: Blue Cross and Blue Shield Association, 1979), pp. 22–25.

47. van Steenwyk, John, *Evaluation of Impact of Hawaii's Mandatory Health Insurance Law* (New York: Martin E. Segal Co., October 1978), unpublished report.

48. Weiskoten, H. G., and Marian Altenderfer, "Trends in Medical Practice," *Journal of Medical Education* 31, no. 7 (1956): 70.

49. American Medical Association, *Profile of Medical Practice 1977* (Chicago: AMA, 1977), pp. 31–55.

50. Medalie, Jack H., *Family Medicine: Principles and Applications* (Baltimore: Williams and Wilkins, 1978).

51. Silver, George, "Group Practice—What It Is," *Medical Care* 1 (1963): 94–102.

52. Committee on the Costs of Medical Care, *Medical Care for the American People* (Chicago: University of Chicago Press, 1932), pp. 114–118.

53. Cray, Ed, *In Failing Health: The Medical Crisis and the AMA* (Indianapolis: Bobbs-Merrill Co., 1970), p. 65.

54. Weinerman, E. R., "As Others See Us: The Patient's Viewpoint," in *Proceedings, 13th Annual Group Health Institute, Detroit, Michigan, May 1963* (Washington: Group Health Association of America, 1964), pp. 5–14.

55. American Medical Association, American Association of Medical Clinics, and Medical Group Management Association, *Group Practice: Guidelines to Joining or Forming a Medical Group* (Chicago: 1970).

56. Wasserman, Fred W., and Michael C. Miller, *Building a Group Practice* (Springfield, Ill.: Charles C. Thomas, 1973).

57. Roemer, Mera, & Shonick, "The Ecology of Group Medical Practice."

58. For 1950: Weinerman, E. R., "Medical Group Practice in California," *California Medicine*, 76 (1952): 383–388; for 1964: DuBois, D. M., *Group Medical Practices: Determinants of Success and Failure* (University of California, Dr.P.H. dissertation, 1966); for 1970: AMA, unpublished data, Chicago, 1970.

59. AMA, unpublished data, Chicago, 1967.

60. Weinerman, E. Richard, "Research into the Organization of Medical Practice," *Milbank Memorial Fund Quarterly* 44, no. 4 (1966): 104–145.

61. Metzner, Charles A.; R. L. Bashshur; and G. W. Shannon, "Differential Public Acceptance of Group Medical Practice," *Medical Care* 10 (1972): 279–287.

Chapter 9

Special Governmentally Financed Clinics

Previous chapters have reviewed clinics in America under five principal types of sponsorship: hospitals, public health agencies, schools, industries, and practicing physicians. Beyond these types of clinic sponsorship, there are many other organizations and agencies, public and private, that sponsor organized ambulatory health services (OAHS). Several of these categories have become extensively developed and conceptually important in recent years. Analysis is complicated by the fact that some of these clinics or health centers are financed wholly or almost wholly by government agencies, but sponsored by nongovernmental bodies. This chapter concerns clinics *financed* essentially with government funds, whether or not they are operated by government agencies. Chapter 10 will examine clinics (not previously considered) that are both financed and sponsored by voluntary agencies. As an introduction to both sorts of special clinic, a few words are in order about the incremental approach to health program development in the United States, and the resulting pluralism of the entire health sector.

PLURALISM IN THE AMERICAN HEALTH CARE SYSTEM

The pluralistic character of the American health care system is strikingly illustrated in the multiplicity of agencies that sponsor and/or operate clinics for selected persons or certain health problems. Agencies of government—other than public health, hospital, or education authorities already discussed—at the federal, state, or local level may be responsible, as well as nongovernmental or voluntary agencies of many types. Especially important since the mid-1960s has been a type of quasi-governmental and usually freestanding ambulatory care center, constituting a partnership between government and private bodies. Such centers are typically initiated and financed by government, but operated by local nongovernmental organizations.

Basic health needs usually explain the historical origin of each of the specially sponsored types of clinic. For example, the government faced obvious problems involving the health care of military veterans and of prisons' inmates. In addition, the general health needs of the poor in cities or rural areas generated governmental actions for many social and political reasons. The tragic consequences of certain diseases have stimulated countless efforts by private citizens to tackle those problems systematically. Larger social movements have played a part, such as the concerns of socially alienated youth, women's liberation, and organized labor. Special clinics have emerged from each of these interest groups.

The special needs and the considerable social drive often associated with each type of historical origin have given strength to these various clinics. There is often a certain missionary zeal that induces hard work and effective mobilization of money and resources to build these clinics. The same zeal and energy, however, often motivate the sponsors of these clinics to guard their independence jealously. When economies and efficiencies might be promoted by coordinated action, a proud sense of autonomy may stand in the way. Society as a whole may pay a high price for the complex multiplicity of administrative processes involved in the management of so many different types of clinics in a community. Once an organized entity takes shape in America, it seldom dies out. As needs change, special clinics may change their character, but in some form or other they usually live on. (Possible paths to greater clinic coordination will be considered in a later chapter.)

Our review of special clinics financed by government will start with those operated by agencies of the federal government for selected beneficiaries. The oldest of these are for military personnel, but there are many other eligible groups. Next we shall consider clinics or health centers stimulated and financed by several federal agencies, but operated by local nongovernmental bodies. Third, we shall examine clinics sponsored and operated by certain agencies of state and local government.

CLINICS FOR FEDERAL BENEFICIARIES

Comprehensive health care programs are financed and operated by various federal government agencies for selected beneficiaries. Special hospitals are an important feature of most of these programs. The outpatient departments (OPD) of these institutions have already been considered in the general discussion of hospital OPDs in Chapter 4. Here we will examine the organized ambulatory units for these federal beneficiaries that function apart from hospitals.

Military Personnel

Since the United States became a nation, the military forces have been served by an organized medical care program.[1] The U.S. Department of Defense—including the Army, Navy, Marine Corps, and Air Force—operates a worldwide system of general health services that are staffed with salaried military medical and allied personnel. The scope of services, both preventive and therapeutic, is remarkably comprehensive and it includes all types of ambulatory care furnished through highly organized patterns of delivery.

In times of peace, most military personnel spend their period of service stationed at military installations in the continental United States. Nevertheless, most enlisted men and women (i.e., personnel who are not officers) live in military barracks quite apart from a normal family life. As a result, their medical needs are relatively great, even for ailments that could otherwise be easily handled by the family. With no relatives to provide bed care, they may be hospitalized for minor illnesses, and ambulatory medical care may be sought for minor complaints.

In 1975 (a time of general peace) there were more than nine million eligible beneficiaries in the military services.[2] This included uniformed personnel on active duty (about one-fourth of the total), and their dependents; retired military members and their dependents; and survivors of both active duty and retired personnel. For military dependents there is a program that finances health services from private medical care providers, the Civilian Health and Medical Program of the Uniformed Services (CHAMPUS); however the majority of the care for active duty personnel is provided at organized military facilities. In 1975 there were about 190 hospitals and 120 freestanding clinics throughout the world where such care was furnished.

Judging by the deployment of physicians, about two-thirds of these facilities are located in the continental United States. Thus, in 1975 there were nearly 11,700 physicians on active military duty in the U.S. forces throughout the world, and slightly over 8,000 of these were in the continental U.S.[3] The detailed organizational features of the military health services need not be analyzed, except to note that in the United States each of the three medical departments—the Army, Navy (handling medical services for the Marine Corps), and Air Force—is highly regionalized. Primary care is provided in clinics or hospital OPDs, secondary care is provided in general hospitals, and tertiary care is provided in highly specialized medical centers.

In 1975, ambulatory care visits to organized facilities by all beneficiaries in the continental U.S. numbered 35,625,290; these included visits to both freestanding clinics and hospital OPDs.[4] Analyzed as rates of ambulatory encounters (for 1974 data), active duty military personnel had many more visits per person per year than the general U.S. civilian population. In the Army, there were 10.1 visits per person per year; in the Navy there were 8.8 such visits, and in the Air Force 8.5 visits. These rates compare with about 4.8 ambulatory medical encounters per person per year in the general U.S. population. The composition of these ambulatory services by active duty military personnel is also doubtless different from that in the general population. For 1974, the percentage distribution of ambulatory visits was as follows:[5]

Purpose	Percent
Disease	48.2
Injury	17.0
Screening examination	14.7
Complete physical examination	5.8
Immunization	5.2
Counseling	4.0
Flight physical exam	1.6
Pre- and postnatal exam	0.7
Evaluation	0.6
Unknown purpose	2.2
All purposes	100.0

Source: U.S. Dept. of Defense; U.S. Dept. of Health, Education and Welfare; and Office of Management and Budget, *Report of the Military Health Care Study* (Washington, D.C., 1975), p. 3

An analysis of ambulatory services classified by medical specialty can be made from data reported in the U.S. Army surgeon general's *Annual Report* for 1954. In that year, outpatient services in all army medical facilities worldwide numbered 19,237,000 visits. The percentage distribution of specialty services was:[6]

Specialty	Percent
General medicine	49.5
General surgery	14.0
Pediatrics	7.4
Otolaryngology	5.7
Ophthalmology	5.7
Physiotherapy	5.4
Dermatology	4.4
Obstetrics	4.3
Gynecology	1.8
Other specialties	1.8
All specialties	100.0

Source: Surgeon General, U.S. Army, *Annual Report: Medical Statistics of the U.S. Army, Calendar Year 1954* (Washington, D.C., 1956), p. 12.

The Army surgeon general's *Annual Report* for 1973 indicates the proportions of ambulatory care services provided to active duty military personnel in relation to dependents and others. In 1973, all army medical facilities worldwide had 19,269,000 visits; these were distributed among various types of beneficiaries as follows:[7]

Beneficiary	Percent
Active duty military personnel	39.6
Military personnel dependents	47.9
Other beneficiaries	12.5
Total	100.0

Source: Surgeon General, U.S. Army, *Annual Report: Fiscal Year 1973* (Washington, D.C., 1976), p. 13.

Considering the distribution of ambulatory visits among different types of facility, some data are reported for the U.S. naval medical facilities for 1961 in Congressional hearings held in 1964. These show the following distribution:[8]

Type of Facility	Percent
U.S. naval hospitals	34.0
Station hospitals	14.0
Dispensaries with beds	27.6
Dispensaries without beds	24.4
All facilities	100.0

Source: U.S. Congress, House of Representatives, Committee on Armed Services, Hearings before the Special Subcommittee on Construction of Military Health Facilities, Cong., 1964, p. 10047.

Thus, if the experience in the Navy reflects that in all military branches, about half of the ambulatory services are provided in dispensaries (or clinics), separate from hospitals. Accordingly, of the total 35,625,290 ambulatory visits to all types of facility of the three main military branches in the continental United States in 1975 reported above, one may estimate that about 18 million took place at clinics outside of hospitals. This volume of services would be over and above those included in the hospital OPD services reviewed in Chapter 4. It excludes also the services rendered to dependents of military personnel in private medical settings under the CHAMPUS program.

Military medical services have traditionally had a reputation of limited quality—an alleged mediocrity stemming from their being under the control of a large, rigid bureaucracy. Whether or not this was ever true, there is little to support this viewpoint in recent years. The very comprehensiveness of health services, and the organizational discipline in their day-to-day operations, would

mean that more effective health care is probably available to military beneficiaries than to the average citizen. Moreover, in order to attract competent
physicians and other health personnel into a nonconscripted military establishment, opportunities are provided for continuing education, for contacts with
major medical centers in the civilian world, and for periodic medical staff conferences within the regular program. There are constant efforts to upgrade the
quality of services, through self-analysis and efforts to correct any recognized
problems. In 1971, for example, a national conference was held to discuss
methods of improving ambulatory services in army facilities.[9]

Veterans

The nationwide system of hospitals established and operated by the federal
government for the care of military veterans has been noted in Chapter 4. Under
the law, the approximately 28 million American veterans (as of 1970) are entitled
to complete medical care, both inpatient and ambulatory, for any condition
incurred while in military service. For disorders not connected to their service,
they are entitled to hospitalization without charge, if obtaining such care privately would mean a financial hardship and if a bed is available. As a result,
the majority of patients in Veterans Administration (VA) hospitals are being
treated for nonservice-connected disorders.[10]

In addition to some 85,000 beds in 172 hospitals or medical centers, virtually
all of which have outpatient clinics, there are a number of freestanding VA
clinics. Although the veteran with a nonservice-connected condition is entitled
only to hospital care, ambulatory care clinics are regarded as an "extension"
of the hospital, where preliminary or posthospital medical service may shorten
the number of days of hospitalization required or obviate the need for hospitalization. Under this rationale, ambulatory services have been provided to all
veterans regardless of whether their disorder is service-related, since a legislative
amendment in 1973.

In 1976, there were 47 freestanding VA clinics, including 37 that functioned
as satellites of general hospitals, 7 totally independent clinics, and 3 regional
office clinics.[11] The volume of ambulatory services to veterans has been increasing rapidly, from a national total of 5,774,000 visits in 1969 to 15,053,000
in 1979.[12] These data unfortunately do not disaggregate the services given at
the nonhospital clinics, but one may estimate these to be about 20 percent of
the total, or three million visits, as of 1979.

A 1976 study of 1,800 veterans who had received ambulatory care at a VA
clinic found that 64 percent lived more than a half-hour's travel time from the
unit, suggesting that most veterans using this care are willing to spend a good
deal of time to get to it.[13] All VA clinics are open for service during all regular
working hours of the week. They are staffed with separate physicians and allied

personnel, amounting to a total of 24,100 in 1976. Professional direction of each specialty clinic service in the 37 units that are satellites of VA hospitals is usually given by the corresponding hospital specialty department.

Among the 1,800 VA outpatients interviewed in the 1976 survey, 67 percent considered the VA clinic their "usual source" of ambulatory medical care. Only 17 percent claimed to have a regular private physician, although a survey of a random sample of the general population of veterans found 74 percent to have such a regular private doctor. The veterans using VA clinics, like those using VA hospitals, tend to be past middle age; more than 40 percent were 55 years of age or more. Thus, although only a small fraction of all veterans make use of the VA network of clinics, the majority of those who do regard these clinics as their primary source of ambulatory care.

American Indians

In the early nineteenth century, treaties were concluded with most American Indian tribes, providing among other things that the U.S. government would furnish the Indians certain medical and hospital services.[14] Although most of the approximately 24 treaties specified that medical services would be offered for not more than 20 years, the government decided to continue and expand these programs, and they still operate to the present day.

As of 1970, there were 827,000 American Indians (including Alaska natives), most of whom lived on federal Indian reservations located in 24 states. Before 1955, organized health services were provided to Indians living on or near the reservations by the U.S. Department of Interior, Bureau of Indian Affairs; since 1955, responsibility for Indian health services was transferred to the Public Health Service (PHS) in the U.S. Department of Health, Education, and Welfare (HEW). The PHS administers a comprehensive scope of health services through eight area offices, mostly in the western states.[15]

The PHS operates 51 hospitals (from 5 to 183 beds) specifically for Indians; each has an outpatient department providing ambulatory services which are included in the data presented in Chapter 4. In addition, ambulatory care is provided by 99 separate health centers with full-time salaried staffs, plus about 300 small field health stations (open at scheduled sessions each week). In 1978, it was estimated that about 700,000 Indians used these health services.

In the years since the Indian health program has been under PHS supervision, the volume of organized ambulatory services has been greatly expanded. Counting visits to both the outpatient departments of hospitals and to the freestanding health centers and field stations, these rose from 455,000 in 1955 to 3,220,000 in 1978.[16] The latter does not count 1,038,000 dental care visits in 1978, nor does it count services rendered by private physicians under contract with the government. In 1971, there were 2,370,640 ambulatory services given, divided among the three types of sources as follows:

	Percent
Hospital outpatient departments	50.7
Health centers and field stations	41.9
Contract physicians	7.4

Source: USPHS, Indian Health Program, 1955–1978 (Washington: 1978).

If we apply these 1971 proportions to the data for 1978, it may be inferred that in this year ambulatory health services provided to Indians in organized settings, outside of hospitals numbered about 1,352,000 visits.

Since 1975, federal policy has stressed increasing the involvement of the Indians themselves in the operation and administration of the health services. Thus, more than 6,100 Indians have been trained as nurses and allied health personnel to serve in the program. Many Indian health advisory boards have been established, and in several localities the full management of local health services has been turned over to tribal authorities. The ultimate goal is to modify the Indian Health Service into a full partnership, under which funding would come from the federal government, while management would be by the Indians themselves.

Merchant Seamen

The PHS had its beginnings in 1798 in a program to support a network of hospitals to serve merchant seamen at the young nation's major ports.[17] Designated originally as the Marine Hospital Service, this activity was gradually expanded to include foreign and interstate quarantine services, a national "hygienic laboratory," and eventually a broad range of activities in prevention, medical research, hospital planning, and many other fields. The agency's name was changed to the United States Public Health Service in 1912. The original network of hospitals, and later clinics, for merchant seamen is still in operation. The special beneficiaries of these federal facilities have been extended to include members of the U.S. Coast Guard and other designated groups.

As general health insurance programs have grown in recent decades, seamen have become covered for the costs of health care under contracts negotiated between seamen's unions and shipowners. For various legal reasons, moreover, American merchant ships are often registered under the flags of other nations. As a result, the population served by this special federal health care system has actually declined, and accordingly PHS hospitals have declined in number and in the volume of patients served. Thus, in 1947 there were 24 marine hospitals, which admitted 79,320 cases that year,[18] but there were only 9 hospitals and 31,351 admissions during 1976.[19]

On the other hand, organized ambulatory services for these federal beneficiaries have increased. In 1947 there were 18 separate dispensaries, in addition to the outpatient departments of each of the 24 hospitals, plus 96 "medical relief stations" on the premises of private physicians under contract. Ambulatory care visits at all sites in 1947 numbered 1,608,303. By 1976, the separate outpatient clinics had increased to 29 and the "contract physician care locations" had risen to 268, although the hospital OPDs were down to 9. The aggregate volume of ambulatory services in 1976 had risen slightly to 1,811,512. Of the latter, the visits to the 29 freestanding PHS clinics numbered 791,405. For the 29 clinics, this amounts to an average of 27,290 visits to each per year, or 109 visits per workday. These clinic services are rendered by full-time salaried physicians and other health personnel of the Public Health Service.

The discrepancy between the trend for ambulatory and inpatient hospital services is probably explained by changes in eligibility for care. Since the 1950s, military personnel from all branches of the Department of Defense have been free to use the facilities of other branches (Army, Navy, etc.), including PHS facilities. Such cross-overs in site of care are relatively infrequent for hospitalization, but for ambulatory care they are common. Thus, out of the 1,811,512 ambulatory visits to PHS clinics in 1976, over 600,000 were services rendered to beneficiaries of the military branches; such personnel did not use PHS clinics in 1947. If these services are subtracted from the 1976 data, we find that the net volume of PHS clinic utilization in recent years has actually declined since 1947, in somewhat the same manner as the trend for hospital utilization. Nevertheless, the overall utilization of PHS clinics, by all types of federal beneficiaries has been rising and—for facilities independent of hospitals—now totals around 800,000 visits per year.

Other Federal Beneficiaries

There are several other departments in the federal government with varied health functions, among which are health care programs for special populations. A complete account of these would require a comprehensive study in itself, but some of the main activities may be noted.

The U.S. Department of Justice operates a system of federal prisons or penitentiaries through its Federal Bureau of Prisons. In 1970, there were 30 federal prisons, with some 23,000 inmates.[20] The capacity of federal prisons is highly variable, ranging from 200 to 2,200. Linked to this system are 28 hospitals, and each of the prisons has a clinic for ambulatory care. Considering the nature of prison life, it is not surprising that these clinics should have a high rate of utilization. In 1972, for example, when the average total federal inmate population was 21,860, there were an average of 1,946 clinic visits by prisoners per day, for a total of more than 700,000 annual clinic visits in federal prisons. The larger federal prison clinics are staffed by full-time salaried medical officers of the PHS; the smaller ones are staffed by part-time private physicians under contract. Compared with state and local prisons, the federal institutions provide services of relatively high quality.

Nearly all civilian federal government employees obtain medical care in the general community where they live, rather than through special governmental facilities. Since 1959, however, federal agencies (as employers) have offered to share the costs of private health insurance for their employees and dependents through the Federal Employees Health Benefit Program, administered by the U.S. Civil Service Commission.[21] Employees are allowed to select one of several health insurance carriers operating in the region where they work, but with the exception of on-the-job first aid care, no general ambulatory care is provided in special government clinics.

An exception to this rule applies to major federal construction projects in isolated places. Thus, at the site of construction of large dams for water supply or hydroelectric power generation, where hundreds of workers (some with families) congregate, the federal government may provide direct general medical services through special clinics. Since about 1900, the U.S. Department of Interior has constructed 153 major dams throughout the nation.[22] After the project is completed and in operation, the only special health care provided is in the sphere of occupational health service, as discussed in Chapter 7.

One federal public utility project has been of such magnitude that it has been the responsibility of an independent federal agency, the Tennessee Valley Authority (TVA). At the peak of the construction of numerous projects on the Tennessee River and its branches in the 1940s, there were 10 medical centers providing ambulatory and also bed care.[23] Since then, permanent medical centers have been maintained at three sites (Knoxville, Chattanooga, and at the Wilson Dam) to serve employees from any TVA installation.[24] Of special interest is the extension of influence of the TVA health program in recent years beyond service to federal employees. Among the 201 counties reached by electrical power of the TVA system, 169 have been designated as medically "underserved." TVA medical personnel have given advice to local communities on methods of attracting doctors and surplus mobile homes have been provided for use as temporary clinic facilities.

While they are mainly of historical interest, note should be taken of a special medical care program for migratory agricultural workers and their families operated by the U.S. Department of Agriculture. Starting under the Farm Security Administration in the 1930s, this program grew during World War II to include clinics or health centers at 250 areas of seasonable labor concentration throughout the country.[25] These units were typically staffed by a full-time nurse, with panels of local physicians engaged for several sessions each week. About 150,000 persons were served by these clinics each year in the 1940s, at an estimated rate of 4.2 services per person—a total of 630,000 visits. Although this was terminated as a federal government program after World War II, it was revived in another form under the Migrant Health Act of 1962 (to be discussed below).

In addition to operating clinics for special beneficiaries, the federal government has played another role in recent years. It entails granting funds to a variety of local entities for the establishment and/or operation of facilities for ambulatory care to designated populations. Although these clinics are sponsored predominantly by local voluntary groups, their origins have been mainly stimulated by and dependent upon federal grants. They are most widely known as "community health centers" and will be discussed in the next section.

FEDERALLY FINANCED AND LOCALLY SPONSORED HEALTH CENTERS

The health center movement, as a strategy for coordinating various ambulatory care programs in the early years of the twentieth century, has been discussed in Chapter 2. After some 30 years of development predominantly as facilities for furnishing preventive services, the community health center came to be seen as a means of providing comprehensive ambulatory care once again in the 1960s. As in earlier decades, this was an organized response to the health problems of the poor.

Neighborhood Health Centers

The 1960s was a period of social and political turbulence in the United States. In 1961, American military advisers were sent to Vietnam, initiating a chain of events involving deep U.S. commitment to a war in southeast Asia. Unlike World War II, this conflict was not supported by large sections of the population, particularly the youth and families with children of draft age. In the second term of President Lyndon B. Johnson, 1964–68, the escalation of the Vietnam War and U.S. involvement in it were especially intense. Public demonstrations, student riots, and political rallies against the war occurred throughout the nation.[26]

During the early 1960s, after the quiescent postwar decade of the 1950s, national consciousness became focused on the social problems acquiring increasing visibility in the large cities. In 1962, on the basis of demographic data coming from the 1960 census, Michael Harrington's book, *The Other America*, was published.[27] The census statistics showed clearly that a large portion of the

U.S. population, perhaps 30 or 40 percent, was living at a very low standard. Malnutrition, miserable housing, broken families, crime, and squalor characterized the lives of millions, particularly in slum sections of the larger cities. In a word, there emerged a rediscovery of poverty in America—in the nation envisaged by most of the world as the land of comfort and affluence.

The combination of a politically divided nation due to the Vietnam War and the rediscovery of poverty stimulated an obvious response from the federal government: "Let us wage a war on poverty."[28] To implement this benificent "war," Congress enacted the Economic Opportunity Act of 1964, which established the U.S. Office of Economic Opportunity (OEO). This was a new agency, independent of any established federal department, which reported directly to the president. The principal OEO efforts were concerned with vocational training and employment, but under the agency's Community Action Program there were a variety of social welfare activities. Prominent among these was an approach to improving health services for the poor, not simply by purchasing medical care in the private market, but by providing ambulatory care directly, in the heart of poverty districts, through neighborhood health centers (NHC).[29]

The first NHC was the Gouverneur Health Center at the lower tip of Manhattan Island. This facility had existed as a public hospital (the Gouverneur Hospital) serving the poor of New York's lower east side for many decades. As the demographic composition of the district changed, the use of the hospital declined and the physical structure deteriorated. Rather than closing it completely, however, the old building was remodeled by the City of New York and converted into an ambulatory care center in 1961. Later, in accordance with a general city policy of forging links between municipal facilities and voluntary hospitals, management was turned over to the Beth Israel Hospital, a nearby voluntary general hospital.[30] When the OEO program of federal grants for neighborhood health centers started in 1965, a substantial grant was given to Gouverneur Health Center, permitting expansion of its services to 24 hours a day.[31] Financial support became 50 percent federal and 50 percent municipal, with any deficit to be absorbed by the Beth Israel Hospital.

Another early project that contributed to NHC policy formulation was at a low-income housing project located in the Columbia Point section of Boston, Massachusetts. The initiative here came from faculty members (Drs. Count D. Gibson and H. Jack Geiger) at the Tufts University Medical School in Boston. Their idea was that to teach medical students in preventive and community medicine—as well as to influence faculty concerning the importance of primary care—a "clinical teaching service" involving general ambulatory care for a defined population was needed.[32] The residents of this housing project provided the appropriate basis for such a teaching program. At the same time, the value of consumer participation in administration of a medical care program could be demonstrated through formation of a local health association, serving in an advisory capacity to the medical school. To support the project, Tufts Medical School received a substantial NHC grant from the U.S. OEO in 1965.[33]

A third trailblazer in the NHC movement of the 1960s was the Mile Square Health Center in Chicago, sponsored by the Presbyterian-St. Luke's Medical Center, affiliated with the Rush Medical School.[34] Initiative here was taken by the teaching hospital, where the outpatient department was greatly overcrowded. To reduce this pressure, the hospital's department of medicine established a section on community medicine, which would operate the satellite facility. In July 1966 an OEO grant was received for this purpose. Residents (doctors in training) from the hospital rotated through the ambulatory care center, and difficult cases were referred to the hospital's regular outpatient department.

Several other local projects undoubtedly contributed to the concepts that eventually shaped OEO policies on neighborhood health centers. It is noteworthy, in retrospect, that the principal pioneering was done by established organizations: a city government, a medical school, and a teaching hospital. In the mid-1960s, however, another important social influence emerged—demands by poor people to participate actively in the management of services intended for them. Consumerism, as it came to be called, had many roots, including the anger of ethnic minorities (predominantly black people) at their general lack of power in society. In several cities, violent race riots erupted, one of the first and most dramatic occurring in the Watts district of Los Angeles, California, in the summer of 1965. Searching for causes of the riots (in which more than a hundred people were killed), investigators cited deficient health resources in the "riot area."[35] Among the many corrective responses was the establishment of the Watts Health Center from an OEO grant in 1967.

The course of events at the Watts NHC was typical of the history of the establishment of many neighborhood health centers in this period. The initial OEO grant was given to the University of Southern California (USC) Medical School, an institution not far from Watts that played a constructive role in community health affairs.[36] This private medical school was also responsible for medical services in the Los Angeles County General Hospital, a large public facility that had long provided ambulatory and inpatient services to residents of the Watts area. A Community Health Council, composed of local area residents, was established to advise USC authorities. Conflicts soon developed on numerous aspects of the program, including the staffing of the facility and the pattern of service to be provided. These problems were not solved until the community health council was converted into the responsible body, controlling both policy and funds of the Watts Health Center. Experiences of this type throughout the nation made the issue of consumer control a top priority consideration in the NHC movement.[37]

As national OEO policy on support of neighborhood health centers crystallized, the basic features came to be formulated as follows:[38] (1) focus on needs of the poor; (2) an integrated facility, convenient to the homes of the poor, in which virtually all ambulatory health services were provided; (3) intensive involvement of the population served, both in policymaking and as employees; (4) full linkage with other sources of services and funds; (5) qualified professional personnel who could assure personalized, high quality care; (6) close coordination with other community resources; and (7) sponsorship by a variety of public and private entities.

By mid-1966, 8 NHC projects had been funded; and by mid-1967, an additional 33. By mid-1968, there were 30 neighborhood health centers in operation, and 44 others had been approved for development. Seldom has an innovation in health care organization generated such nationwide interest, analysis, and evaluation. Studies were conducted on every aspect of NHC operations. Strategies for successful partnerships between consumers and health care providers were a subject of special interest.[39-43] This aspect of governance of clinics was perhaps a greater departure from past custom than any other in the NHC movement—hence, its great attraction of analyses. Not surprisingly, many difficulties were encountered in achieving compatible relationships between consumer representatives and professional personnel. Countless administrative problems had to be solved to achieve efficient management of finances, personnel, and day-to-day controls.[44]

Evaluations of NHCs were made on several levels. Based on "medical audits" of records, and comparisons of performance with that of teaching hospital (i.e., those affiliated with medical schools) outpatient departments and other organized clinics, it was concluded that "the neighborhood health center program performance is generally equal to and in some instances superior to that of other established providers of health care."[45] A study of the population served by the early NHC at Columbia Point, Boston showed a reduced rate of hospital admissions, which was attributed to the effectiveness of the convenient ambulatory care.[46] In terms of consumer satisfaction, evaluations were favorable, as reflected by rates of NHC utilization by the population in the nearby catchment areas.[47,48]

Probably the most controversial aspect of NHC evaluation was their cost per ambulatory visit, compared with other patterns, including private medical practice. Financial studies suggested relatively high NHC per unit costs, but it was generally argued that the comprehensive content and the high accessibility of the service to the poor justified the differential.[49,50] It was also argued that the economic value of neighborhood health centers located in urban ghettoes should take account of the jobs created and their sociopsychological benefits for distressed populations, quite aside from measurable health benefits.[51] One of the few health outcome studies on neighborhood health centers was done in Denver, Colorado, where a reduction in infant mortality was attributed to NHC services.[52]

Much more could be written about the performance, characteristics, and impact of the OEO-supported neighborhood health centers in the late 1960s and early 1970s. One may speculate that the remarkably dynamic growth of this pattern was due not only to its effectiveness in meeting health needs of the poor, but also to the relatively calm acceptance of (or at least the weak resistance to) the idea by the private medical profession. This was a time when physicians were very busy, earning high incomes, and being well paid for services to the poor and the aged by Medicaid and Medicare. There was little reason to look upon NHC facilities as a source of competition. Moreover, many physicians, full-time or part-time, were paid relatively high salaries for clinical NHC services.

Due to the overall success of this OEO program, the PHS began to give grants to very similar projects for ambulatory medical care in low-income areas in the late 1960s. This was done under certain general authorities in the PHS, starting with grants of about $7 million in 1968 and reaching $64 million by 1971.[53] Between 1965 and 1971 about 100 neighborhood health centers were initiated with the assistance of OEO grants. In addition, approximately 50 ambulatory care health centers, very much like NHCs, were started on the basis of grants from the PHS.[54] This does not include another 120 health centers giving comprehensive ambulatory care to children and youth (C&Y) and for maternity and infant care (MIC) in low-income areas (to be discussed below).

The rise of consumerism in the governance of neighborhood health centers is reflected in the percentage distribution of OEO grants to various types of local sponsoring bodies between 1966 and 1971.[55] Without respect to the numbers of NHCs started, which tended to increase each year over this five-year span, the nature of the local grant recipients was as follows:

	Percentage	
NHC Grant Recipient	**1966**	**1971**
Hospitals	50	10
Medical schools	37	7
Health departments	13	—
Private group practices	—	3
New organizations	—	59
Other	—	21
All sponsors:	100	100

Source: Daniel I. Zwick, "Some Accomplishments and Findings of Neighborhood Health Centers," *Milbank Memorial Fund Quarterly* 50 (1972): 387–420.

The "new organizations" and "other" categories were essentially consumer-controlled organizations. Moreover, as noted above with respect to the Watts Health Center, in many cases initial sponsorship by a medical school or other long-established agency was transferred to sponsorship by a new community organization over this span of years.

Beginning about 1970 some of the OEO-financed neighborhood health centers were transferred to the federal surveillance and financing of the Public Health Service. In 1973 the entire NHC program under OEO was terminated and all facilities were transferred, for purposes of funding and federal administration, to the Public Health Service.[56] Soon after, to avoid confusion in terminology, the freestanding facilities for general ambulatory care initiated by either OEO or PHS came to be designated as "community health centers."

Community Health Centers

The transfer of all OEO neighborhood health centers to supervision and funding by the PHS, completed in 1973, meant the start of a new phase in the national development of general ambulatory care facilities for the poor. Beyond the new term, "community health centers," several new legislative authorizations and the appropriation of additional federal funds ushered in a movement that may well have significance beyond programs for serving the poor. The several steps along the way from 1973 to 1980 are worth summarizing.

The importance attached to further development of community health centers was reflected in establishment of a new Bureau of Community Health Services in the Health Services Administration of the PHS in July 1973.[57] In 1974, Congress passed the "Community Health Center Act," which added a new Section 330 to the PHS Act. This provided, among other things, for a defined scope of services that must be offered by community health centers to warrant receipt of federal grants. In connection with appropriations in subsequent years, the definitions of mandated services were modified, and criteria were also stipulated through which to determine underserved localities entitled to the subsidized construction or establishment of a health center. Without cataloging the step-by-step formulation of these definitions, as of 1978, the services mandated for provision in all federally supported community health centers, under the amended PHS Act (Section 330) were as follows:

1. diagnostic, treatment, consultative, referral, and other services rendered by a physician or a "physician extender" (nurse practitioner or physician assistant)
2. diagnostic laboratory and x-ray services
3. preventive health services, including nutritional assessment, medical-social services, well child care, immunizations, etc.
4. emergency medical services
5. transportation, as required for patient care
6. preventive dental services
7. pharmaceutical services (drugs)

In addition, certain further types of services had to be funded by the PHS, unless the local body or the PHS could demonstrate that they were not needed. These were described as "high priority supplemental services" and were the following:

8. home health services
9. dental services
10. health education
11. bilingual and outreach services.[58]

For defining underserved areas warranting establishment of such health centers, the legislation specified four general criteria that were to be quantified by HEW regulation:[59]

1. poverty level, defined by local per capita incomes,
2. an excessive infant mortality rate,
3. a shortage of primary care physicians (including general practitioners, pediatricians, internists, and family practice specialists),
4. a certain proportion of people over 65 years of age.

Quantified measures of these four features of an area yielded a formula that, under regulations, indicated whether a locality was entitled to federal subsidy for a community health center.

Family Health Centers and Networks

With competition for restricted federal funds during the 1970s, various strategies were developed, both through legislation and HEW regulation, to yield money to keep the older community health centers (including some units still labeled as neighborhood health centers) viable and to establish new ones. One strategy, developed in the early 1970s, was to strengthen financial support through a prepayment or insurance mechanism. Thus, Medicaid recipients were invited to "enroll" for the services of a health center, so that monthly premiums could be collected from the state Medicaid program. Similar enrollment was theoretically open to other low-income families, although few responded. Facilities using this prepayment device were called "family health centers." By 1976 there were 39 such facilities; however, the insured population numbered only 35,000 persons nationally, making it evident that this source of funding was not great. In subsequent years, the family health center term was dropped, although support from Medicaid sources through fee-for-service payments gradually increased.

Another strategy in the early 1970s was applied in certain metropolitan areas, where several organized ambulatory care facilities might receive consolidated grant support as a "health network." As of 1976, there were ten of these nationally, and they provided services to only 25,000 persons in all. By 1980, this term was no longer in use, except in one city (Rochester, New York), where several thousand Medicaid recipients were enrolled as prepaid members in a network of three health centers in poverty areas.

Rural and Urban Health Initiatives

In 1975, still another approach emerged. By then, community health centers of both OEO and HEW origin had acquired the reputation of providing relatively comprehensive services and had gained a somewhat imposing character. To expand greatly the number of ambulatory care centers, but to keep them more modest in design and scope, the Bureau of Community Health Services (BCHS) took administrative action (under existing legislative authority) identified as the Rural Health Initiative (RHI).[60] Under this, relatively small grants were given to local nonprofit organizations to strengthen and widen the scope of existing health facilities in underserved rural areas. The local facility might have originally been limited to maternal and child health services, or to care for migratory agricultural families, or the like; with an RHI grant, it could provide primary care to all nearby low-income people. By late 1977, the RHI program was supporting 350 local projects that served 667,000 people.

Two years later in 1979, the same concept was applied to poverty sections of cities, through funding labeled as the Urban Health Initiative (UHI). Applying the criteria of local need listed earlier, some 111 high priority urban areas were identified, containing some eight million people. In its first year the BCHS awarded UHI grants to 35 such local urban projects. Both the RHI- and UHI-funded facilities grew more rapidly than the first wave of community health centers, because they seldom involved new construction and they encouraged the active efforts or initiative of local people.

Other Health Center Support

Still other governmental agencies and legislative programs contributed to the movement for development of freestanding community health centers that eventually came under the supervision of the BCHS. In the late 1960s, the U.S. Department of Housing and Urban Development (HUD) administered and funded a program to rehabilitate urban slum areas with construction of new housing and community facilities. These urban renewal activities were identified as the "model cities" program, and often included funds for strengthening local health services, through grants to enlarge established clinics for children, drug abusers, or others. Some HUD grants also strengthened community health centers and UHI facilities. Thus, in 1977, HUD reported that it had granted to local public housing agencies some $36 million used for providing social services (including health care) to the tenants in its housing projects.[61]

Another source leading to the strengthening of health centers for general ambulatory care in rural areas arose through a special provision in the Medicaid program (Social Security Act, Title 19), launched in 1974. In accordance with the authority under Medicaid for "research and demonstration" projects, the Social Security Administration in HEW (later the Health Care Financing Administration or HCFA) set out to integrate various resources in rural areas to improve the delivery of services to Medicaid recipients. Identified as the Health Underserved Rural Area (HURA) research and demonstration projects, there were by 1979 some 41 rural health centers demonstrating some special form of service, e.g., transportation methods, use of nurse practitioners, or integrating services from diverse health programs. After 1979, Congress barred further use of Medicaid funds for these projects, and the HURA program was absorbed into the regular activities of the BCHS.

Appalachian Regional Commission

In the mid-1960s, linked to the general war on poverty strategy of the Johnson administration, there was started the Appalachian Regional Commission (ARC).[62] Its concern was for general economic and social development of the rural regions of Kentucky, West Virginia, Tennessee, and other Appalachian states. Included in this program was assistance to local communities in organizing small clinics for providing general primary health care. Some of these ARC units were no more than private physician offices, but others were small organized facilities using physician assistants and nurse practitioners who worked under the supervision of a physician in a nearby city. The *Annual Report* of the ARC for 1978 reported that in the past year 41 new clinics for primary medical and dental care had been started; added to 60 such clinics previously established, this meant 101 rural clinics sponsored by the ARC in the Appalachian region.[63] In the 1978 fiscal year, the ARC granted more than $10.1 million for the support of these clinics.

Some of the ARC units were situated within existing local hospitals or health departments. About 80, however, were freestanding facilities that qualified also for financial support from the BCHS. These were estimated to be serving about 150,000 persons per year, and providing about two visits per person; thus, there were about 4,000 patient visits at each clinic per year.

Migrant Health Clinics

Earlier in this chapter, reference was made to the clinics for migratory agricultural workers organized by the Department of Agriculture in the 1930s and

1940s. After World War II, that program was terminated, and only a few of these clinics survived under the sponsorship of local health departments or local charitable agencies. Then, in 1962 along with the rediscovery of poverty in America there was a new recognition of the miserable living conditions of agricultural migrants. In response, Congress passed the Migrant Health Act of 1962, providing special federal funds for grants to states and localities to establish ''family health clinics'' for migrant agricultural workers and their dependents.[64] Conditions for these grants were periodically revised by legislation, and in 1975 extensive legal revisions were made, placing the program under the supervision of the BCHS.[65]

Migrant health clinics operate according to a variety of schedules. An unpublished document of the BCHS classifies them as: (a) full-time comprehensive, (b) intermittently scheduled comprehensive, (c) scheduled medical, (d) scheduled categorical (for example, venereal disease or child health); (e) nonscheduled health services (referring patients to private doctors); and (f) administrative-consultative. In 1979, BCHS grants were made to 112 clinics serving an estimated 557,000 migrants in 35 states. Based on roughly two visits per patient per year, this meant some 1.1 million migrant visits—supported by federal grants of $34,500,000. The variety of sponsorships of these clinics serving migrant families is illustrated by a listing of the names and locations of nine clinics partially funded by this program in California in 1975. These were:[66]

1. San Joaquin County Medical Society Clinic (Stockton)
2. Stanislaus County Medical Society Clinic (Modesto)
3. Clinica de los Campesinos (Lamont)
4. Orange Cove Family Health Campesinos
5. Clinica de Salubridad de Campesinos (Brawley)
6. Merced Family Health Center
7. San Luis Obispo County Health Department Clinic
8. Northern Sacramento Valley Rural Health Project (Yuba City)
9. Regional Rural Health Program (Dixon)

Because of the multiple sources granting funds to particular facilities, in order to avoid double counting, the BCHS estimated that in 1979 of the 112 migrant health grants, 73 went to health centers linked to other programs (such as the RHI): thus, there were 39 migrant health facilities in the nation not identified in another way.

In December 1977, Congress passed the Rural Health Clinic Services Act, which needs special explanation.[67] For some time, as we have noted, rural clinics of various types had been staffed by physician extenders (physician assistants and nurse practitioners). If a patient covered by Medicare or Medicaid was served by a physician extender in such a clinic, the clinic could not be reimbursed by either of these federal programs unless a physician was present at the time. The 1977 Act changed this policy to authorize use of Medicare and Medicaid funds to pay rural clinics even though a physician was not permanently on hand. To qualify for such payment, however, the clinic had to meet six conditions: (1) be located in a rural area (as defined by the Bureau of the Census); (2) be in an area designated by HEW as having a shortage of personal health services or of primary care physicians; (3) be engaged essentially in providing ambulatory primary health care; (4) employ at least one physician extender legally approved by the state; (5) comply with all applicable federal, state, and local requirements; and (6) meet health and safety regulations of the Medicare and Medicaid programs.

National Health Service Corps

Relevant to clinic staffing, still another federal program has acquired increasing importance since the enactment of the federal Emergency Health Personnel Act in 1970.[68] After starting slowly in 1972, to furnish doctors and other health personnel to localities of critical health manpower shortage, the program grew from support of 20 health professionals sent to 16 sites throughout the nation to 1,725 health professionals sent to 800 sites in July 1979. About 750 of these health personnel were doctors of medicine or osteopathy, and the balance were dentists, nurses, or other types of health personnel. In order to attract physicians and dentists to this program, it was named the National Health Service Corps (NHSC), and some enrollees were allowed to substitute Corps service for military duty. Moreover, a provision of other federal legislation, the Health Professions Educational Assistance Act of 1976, which gave loans to medical and other students, allowed "forgiveness" of these loans in return for work in the NHSC. In 1979, out of a total of 1,824 personnel in the NHSC, 38 percent were serving in order to earn forgiveness for educational scholarship loans, and 62 percent were volunteers.

NHSC personnel may serve at a variety of sites, but in every instance a local organization or community group must request the assignment. About one-third of these health professionals are located in individual offices, although fees collected for their services go to the government rather than to the practitioner, who is salaried by the federal government. Two-thirds of NHSC personnel are assigned to work in one of the many types of community health centers or clinics reviewed above.

There is more to be said about the general significance of the diverse health centers developed in the United States during the 1960s and 1970s, but before doing so, we must take note of still another type of organized ambulatory facility—clinics for specific demographic groups: mothers, infants, and children.

Maternal and Child Comprehensive Care Clinics

In Chapter 5, the preventively oriented maternal and child health clinics of health departments were discussed, and brief note was made of authorization in Social Security Act Amendments of the 1960s for comprehensive services to mothers and children. There were, in fact, two separate amendments to Title V of the Social Security Act (SSA), the basic legislation authorizing grants to the states for "maternal and child health and crippled children's services."[69]

The White House Conference on Mental Retardation in 1962 highlighted the relationship of mentally retarded infants and complications occurring during the mother's pregnancy. Acting upon this finding, in 1963 Congress amended SSA Title V to authorize federal grants to the states for "necessary health care" to prospective mothers having a high risk of giving birth to infants with physical or mental defects. Grants could also be used for "necessary health care to infants during their first year of life who have any condition or are in circumstances which increase the hazards to their health." The crucial phrase in this amendment was "necessary health care," in contrast to the original 1935 authorization of grants for "promoting the health of mothers and children" through provision of "maternal and child health services." Whatever may be the precise legal meaning of this language, until 1963 "maternal and child health services" (MCH services) were ordinarily restricted by state and local health departments to preventive and counseling services to expectant mothers and their infants and did not include medical treatment.

With the 1963 amendment, grants were given to state health departments for establishing special clinics for comprehensive maternity and infant care (MIC) in selected geographic areas of high risk. These areas were usually poverty districts in large cities. Thus, in 1971 there were 56 MIC projects nationally in 35 states, located in cities or counties having much higher infant and maternal mortality rates than the nation as a whole. In that year 141,000 new mothers and their infants were served by clinic physicians and allied staff who furnished comprehensive obstetric and pediatric care.[70] By 1979, the MIC special clinics had been increased to 88, serving 741,000 mothers and infants.

The sponsorships of MIC clinics are varied. While the basic grant goes to the state health department, the local clinics may be operated by medical schools, hospitals, voluntary agencies, or local health departments. The care is ambulatory for both mother and infant; thus, it includes the mother's care during both the prenatal and postpartum periods, but the obstetrical delivery is ordinarily done in a hospital by other physicians (usually a public hospital under municipal or county government). Similarly, the infant's ambulatory care is comprehensive, but it does not include hospitalization.

Various studies have attempted to evaluate the achievements of MIC clinic projects in terms of changes in maternal and infant mortality rates. Reductions in these rates have indeed been reported with respect to populations served by MIC clinics.[71,72] On the other hand, these studies have lacked control or comparison groups. One careful study in Los Angeles County, California, completed in 1975, examined perinatal outcomes of samples of mothers served by two MIC clinics (one serving predominantly black women and the other serving women of predominantly Hispanic background), and compared them with matched samples of mothers served by traditional health department prenatal clinics, which had a more narrowly preventive orientation.[73] Both groups of women gave birth in the same public general hospital. The perinatal outcomes, by several indicators, were essentially the same for the two populations. One might infer that in low-income populations living in poor environments, the additional medical services in a comprehensive MIC clinic, compared with those offered by conventional public health agency prenatal clinics, have no significant impact; the general influences of socioeconomic circumstances overshadows the influence of a broader scope of medical care.

Authorization of federal grants to the states to support comprehensive medical care for advancing the health of "school and pre-school children" was included in the 1965 Amendments to the Social Security Act—the same legislation that established the Medicare and Medicaid programs. The program started in 1966 and by 1972 there were 59 special children and youth (C and Y) clinics throughout the nation.[74] Like the special MIC clinics, all of these were located in poverty areas, mainly in inner city slums and some rural areas. Of the initial 59 projects, 34 percent were sponsored and operated by medical schools, 24 percent by hospitals, and 42 percent by state or local health departments. Many of the clinics under public health agency sponsorship, however, were located in general hospitals where the staff and equipment of the facility could be used in patient care.

A 1971 study comparing the operation of C and Y clinics under these three forms of sponsorship found that those under medical schools and hospitals draw a high proportion of their young patients from emergency sections of outpatient departments, and hence the children were often seriously ill at the time of entry.[75] Clinics sponsored by health departments, on the other hand, reflected greater outreach into the community, and the children served were less likely to be sick on entry to the program.

The C and Y program steadily expanded, and by 1979 there were 98 such special clinics, serving 579,000 children. Since 1975, the federal grants for operation of these clinics have been included with the traditional MCH service grants going to each of the states. The patients attending C and Y clinics are different from those attending traditional MCH clinics. In the C and Y clinics, e.g., some 25 percent of patients are adolescents—with problems like drug addiction, obesity, unwanted pregnancy, etc. They present problems that are almost never encountered in the typical health department MCH clinic.[76]

Government Funded Comprehensive Health Centers: Comment

The above overview of comprehensive health centers, typically freestanding and financed through special federal grants, may serve to show the great complexity of these resources for providing organized ambulatory health care that have been developed since the 1960s. It is hardly possible to indicate in one statistical table the changes in terminology, sponsorship, and function that have characterized these clinics over the years, but the main features of the situation as of 1979 are shown in Table 9–1. Thus, it may be noted that the several types of health center listed in Table 9–1 do not include neighborhood health centers, family health centers, health networks, HUD facilities, National Health Service Corps sites, or other categories discussed in the preceeding pages. As explained partially in the footnotes to Table 9–1, the terms given are those currently in use and include facilities previously identified in other ways. Most important, one must realize that the 937 comprehensive health centers described in Table 9–1 are an unduplicated count only of those ambulatory care facilities receiving

Table 9–1 Comprehensive Health Centers Supported by Federal Grants: Unduplicated Count, 1979

Type of Health Center	Number
Community Health Center[a]	158
Rural Health Initiative Clinic (RHI)	356
Health Underserved Rural Area Clinic[b]	41
Migrant Health Clinic[c] .	39
Urban Health Initiative Clinic	77
Appalachian Health Clinic[d]	80
Maternity and Infant Care (MIC) Clinic	88
Children and Youth (C & Y) Clinic	98
All health centers[e]	937

Notes:

[a] These include the original neighborhood health centers of the OEO, plus the equivalent health centers initiated by the HEW. They also include health centers partially supported by prepayment, formerly termed "family health centers" or "health networks."

[b] These HURA clinics were originally funded by the SSA Medicaid program, but later transferred to the BCHS of the PHS, where they now are regarded as equivalent to RHI clinics.

[c] Beyond these 39 migrant health clinics, there are an additional 73 projects receiving migrant health project grants, thus totalling 112 clinics serving migrants. These 73 are, however, included in other categories (such as RHI clinics), and therefore excluded here to avoid double counting.

[d] These 80 clinics are the facilities, among the 101 mentioned in the text, that meet qualifications entitling them to grants from the BCHS.

[e] See the accompanying text for explanation of the probable understatement of this total.

grants from the BCHS in the PHS. This undoubtedly understates the true number of comprehensive health centers in the nation under special sponsorship (that is, excluding the five types of agencies discussed in Chapters 4 through 8) for at least three reasons: (1) it omits facilities not receiving BCHS grants (for example, 21 of the ARC clinics, as of 1978); (2) several of the projects receiving one federal grant (for example, the community health centers) may have clinics at more than one site; and (3) it omits comprehensive health centers with no links whatever to government, such as the free clinics discussed in the next chapter

Furthermore, the data in Table 9–1 can also be considered only an approximation of the numbers of comprehensive health centers under special forms of sponsorship (i.e., other than hospitals, health departments, schools, industries, or private physicians) because of possible fallacies in the quantitative data available. The situation in the pluralistic American health care system has become so complicated that the responsible government agencies themselves are apparently unable to produce internally consistent figures. Thus the BCHS, from which the data in Table 9–1 have been compiled, issued a *Directory of Community Health Centers*, with mutually exclusive names and addresses, in January 1978.[77] Analysis of the 192 entities listed in this directory reflects the recording problems.

One may note the discrepancy between these 192 listings and the 158 community health centers recorded in Table 9–1. Fortunately the initial source of funding or organizational category of each of the 192 community health centers is shown in the *Directory*. Tabulation of these origins shows the following:

Funding Source or Initial Type of Organization	Number	
Neighborhood Health Centers (OEO)	96	
Community Health Centers (HEW)	34	
Family Health Centers (prepayment)	13	
Health Networks	5	
Subtotal		(148)
Urban Health Initiative	35	
Group Practice Buy-ins	8	
Health Maintenance Organizations	1	
Subtotal		(44)
All Community Health Centers	192	(192)

Source: U.S. Bureau of Community Health Services, *Directory of Community Health Centers*, (Washington: January 1978), unpublished report.

If the same 192 listings of community health centers are classified by the type of sponsoring body that may be inferred from the unit's name, one finds the following:

Sponsoring Body	Number
Hospital	11
University	8
Local health department	9
Other local government agency	9
All other sponsorships	155
All types of sponsorship	192

Source: U.S. Bureau of Community Health Services, *Directory of Community Health Centers*, (Washington: January 1978), unpublished report.

Thus, of the 192 community health centers, 155 (81 percent) are sponsored by agencies *other* than well-established entities, such as hospitals, universities, health departments, or other local government agencies. Indeed, only 9 (4.2 percent) of these health centers are operated by health departments (of which there is more to be said later). The sponsoring bodies for 81 percent of the health centers consist of a variety of autonomous consumer groups, formed often for the sole purpose of operating the health center.

Further illustration of the complexities is reflected in the "President's Budget for Fiscal Year 1981," submitted to the U.S. Congress in January 1980. This important document, intended to summarize all federal activities in health and every other field, states that: "A proposed $54 million increase in 1981 budget authority above the 1980 level of $320 million would support 886 community health centers serving over 5 million people."[78] Reference to "886 community health centers" obviously uses the term in the broad sense applied to comprehensive health centers in Table 9–1. Yet in that table, for an *earlier* period the total of these facilities amounts to 937, with the latter figure also being drawn from official sources.

Still another federal source, published in 1979 by the National Center of Health Statistics, includes a section on "neighborhood health centers." Here we read:

The first *neighborhood health centers,* also known as *community health centers* [italics in the original], in the United States were developed in the early 1900s . . . There exists very little information on the number and scope of neighborhood health centers in operation in the United States. It is estimated that in 1973 there were approximately 300 to 500 neighborhood health centers in the Nation. Data are available nationally only on federally funded community health centers. As of June 1976, 160 such centers were in operation in 42 States, the District of Columbia, and Puerto Rico.[79]

The 160 community health centers reported for 1976 may be compared with the 158 reported in Table 9–1 for 1979, in spite of *both* figures being derived from the BCHS, and in spite of the clear evidence of expansion of these facilities across the 1976–79 period. All these discrepancies are cited not to "fault" the federal government for inconsistent recordkeeping; the changes in definition have been so frequent and bewildering that one can marvel that the statistical discrepancies are not even greater. These problems are reported mainly to demonstrate the difficulties in even the collection of information, let alone in program management, regarding the incredibly complex system of organized ambulatory health resources in the pluralistic American health care system.

Much more important than difficulties in recordkeeping are the problems created by the great multiplicity of sponsorships of these community health centers. As we have noted, the current era of multipurpose health centers began in the 1960s, with the war against poverty. A crucial feature of the strategy evolving was the participation of citizens in the management of health programs serving them.[80] The political rationale of this emphasis was clear enough, but there is another side of the picture that is too often overlooked.

In brief, the dispersal of authorities controlling important resources for the delivery of ambulatory care further aggravates the fragmentation in a health care system that is already incredibly complex. Lack of coordination means not only waste in administrative efforts and higher costs, but also countless problems for people seeking care. Duplications and even rivalries may characterize one district of a city or county, while gaps persist elsewhere. Meanwhile, legally and historically important public health agencies—being repeatedly bypassed—assume a relatively weaker position in community health affairs.

It has become commonplace for one local health center to be sponsored by several different federal programs, as well as by various state and local agencies. Obtaining grant support from the appropriate source has come to demand a level of sophistication quite lacking in many communities. A locality with someone skilled in grantsmanship may draw support from numerous sources, while another needier place may not know where to turn for help. To acquaint consumers and new health personnel with the intricacies of the process of funding and organization, a National Association of Community Health Centers, with an office in the nation's capital, has been established.[81]

Regarding the internal operations of many community health centers, it is not surprising that personnel problems, inefficiencies, and even scandals are relatively common. In 1974, the U.S. General Accounting Office (GAO) reviewed 12 health centers—4 funded by OEO and 8 by HEW. The findings of a detailed GAO analysis were summarized as follows:

(1) Health center physicians treated two patients an hour on the average. Most health care officials said they should be able to treat between three and four an hour. (2) Dentists averaged one patient an hour. Most health care officials said they should be able to treat two an hour. (3) Of the 12 health centers, 11 were overstaffed with phy-

sicians. The average overstaffing at the centers was 69 percent. A total of 70.3 full-time equivalent physicians were on staff at the 12 centers when 41.5 were required. (4) All 10 centers with dental staffs were overstaffed with dentists. The average overstaffing at the centers was 86 percent. A total of 27.6 full-time equivalent dentists were on staff at the 10 centers when 14.8 were required. (5) On the basis of the average annual salaries of the full-time physicians and dentists at the 12 centers, annual costs of the overstaffing in these centers exceeded $1 million. (6) Only five of the 12 centers reviewed had received site visits by OEO or HEW within the two-year period ended March 1973. Two centers had never received a site assessment visit. (7) Data on professional staff use was generally inaccurate and/or inadequate for making internal management decisions or external evaluations.[82]

In late 1979, internal conflicts in the management of a community health center in San Francisco, California became intense enough to lead to a bitter lawsuit.[83] Regarding a rural health center in California, an official HEW program review in July 1979 concluded, among other things, as follows:[84]

On the basis of lengthy findings concerning financial administration, the review team found deficiencies in the accounting system, the financial management procedures manual, the annual audit, the development of the budget, the handling of contractual arrangements, the documentation of travel procedures, and the use of credit cards. . . . The review team also made findings with respect to community relationships and program linkages, e.g., on lack of contractual relationships between (the health center) and other agencies resulting in few referrals. . . . [84]

Perhaps in time, as consumer groups acquire more experience, these deficiencies will be corrected, but one can hardly expect a coordinated system of ambulatory care to emerge from so diverse a medley of autonomous nongovernmental bodies sponsoring community health centers throughout the country. Yet, the federally financed facilities discussed here, as we have seen, are only one of many types of clinics serving the poor or other classes of persons or diseases in the American health scene.

In addition to these federally financed community health centers, as we will see in Chapter 10, there are numerous community clinics supported wholly from local resources. If this whole array of freestanding ambulatory care facilities constitutes a movement, it is not easy to generalize about it. Perhaps the only uniform feature is their policy control by groups of local residents; yet even this feature must be qualified, insofar as certain standards are set by the outside funding sources. Otherwise, the range of services may vary from primary care to a wide spectrum of general and specialist services, with laboratory, x-ray, and other backup procedures. As suggested by the GAO review above, the use of personnel resources may be seriously inefficient. Being substantially autonomous, each health center or clinic tends to become preoccupied with its own survival, rather than with meeting community needs most effectively. One may hope that, in time, the inherent assets of conveniently located primary care facilities can be retained, while ultimately these units are integrated into functional networks for good ambulatory care of the total population in each area.

CLINICS OF OTHER STATE AND LOCAL GOVERNMENT AGENCIES

There are various agencies of state and local government—aside from health departments, school systems, and public hospitals—that sponsor and operate clinics for special diseases, persons, or services. Among these are agencies for persons with mental health problems or disease or with physical handicaps, for family planning, for prisoners, or for other special purposes.

Mental Health Clinics

Probably the most numerous type of clinic under this category relates to mental health or disease. In Chapter 5, we have noted that 55 percent of local health departments in 1968 conducted mental health programs; in a California survey, however, it was found in 1963 that out of 163 mental health clinics in the state, only 12, or 7.4 percent, were under health department auspices. Thus, even in a state with particularly strong public health services, mental health clinics were sponsored predominantly by other types of entities in government.

Ambulatory care facilities for mental health service are particularly difficult to classify by sponsorship without double counting, since so many units are related to mental hospitals or general hospitals whose outpatient departments have already been analyzed in Chapter 4. There is, however, a type of psychiatric clinic, described by the National Institute of Mental Health (NIMH) as "freestanding." In January 1978, there were 1,164 of such clinics in the United States, of which 401 (34 percent) were under the auspices of governmental bodies of some type.[85] The level of government responsible for these clinics was as follows:

Government Level	Percent
County	43.6
County and state	26.9
State	20.9
City-county	3.7
City	3.5
Federal (VA)	1.2

Source: NIMH, Division of Biometry and Epidemiology, Washington, D.C., 1980, unpublished data.

Thus, 99 percent of these freestanding mental health clinics are sponsored by units of state and/or local government, and the great majority of these are special mental health agencies other than health departments. It is possible that some of these clinics operate as satellites to state mental hospitals—particularly the 47.8 percent (20.9 plus 26.9) under state or county and state auspices, but they are, in any event, separate from the hospital structure. (The 66 percent of freestanding mental health clinics under nongovernmental auspices will be considered in Chapter 10.)

The services provided by ambulatory care clinics for psychiatric disorders are varied. Some are devoted mainly or entirely to children with emotional difficulties, designated often as "child guidance" clinics or centers. Some are intended mainly for adults with diverse psychoneurotic problems (depression, anxiety, personality disorders, or even psychoses), as well as alcoholism and drug dependence.[86] The latter two problems, however, have increasingly become the concern of other specialized clinics, discussed below. In recent years, special clinics have been devoted to suicide prevention and crisis intervention; these are places to which persons in great distress may come at almost any time, without an appointment, to get immediate assistance of some type—if only a referral elsewhere.

The staffing of these clinics is typically by combinations of psychiatrists (usually part-time), clinical psychologists, social workers, clerks, psychiatric nurses and others. Most of these clinics are open for service to patients during normal working hours and sometimes in the evenings. Some have only a few sessions per week. The NIMH maintains records on services rendered by psychiatric clinics, in terms of "episodes," measuring the number of different patients seen at clinics (each patient typically being seen numerous times) during a year. In 1971 there were 2,317,000 such "outpatient episodes," of which about three-quarters took place at freestanding psychiatric clinics and at community mental health centers (to be discussed below). The remaining one-fourth of episodes were at hospital OPDs.[87]

Since federal legislation of 1963, the United States has become rather widely covered with a special type of psychiatric facility known as community mental health centers (CMHC). These are structures at which five basic types of mental health services were originally required: (1) outpatient services, (2) emergency services, (3) inpatient care, (4) partial hospitalization, and (5) consultation and education.[88] In subsequent years, other services became mandated, such as alcohol and drug abuse services, and followup care for discharged mental hospital patients.

With the years, CMHCs have acquired increasing importance in the provision of ambulatory mental health services. In 1976 there were 548 fully operational, although about another 100 had received federal grants but were not yet in operation. The majority of these had some connection with a general or mental hospital, but 68 of the 548 were freestanding, i.e., separate from any previously existing hospital, although containing some beds. The percentage distribution of CMHC settings in 1976 was:[89]

Type of CMHC	Percent
General hospital-affiliated	64.1
General hospital-based	18.8
Freestanding	12.4
State mental hospital-affiliated	2.7
Private hospital-based	2.0

Source: NIMH, Division of Biometry and Epidemiology, Washington, D.C., 1980, unpublished data.

Although the sponsorship of CMHCs may be either governmental or voluntary, it is evident that all of them have been started with government grants, and they continue to receive federal grants for many aspects of their operations. In 1975 there were 1,619,000 patients under care at the CMHCs (a much larger number of visits, of course), more than four times the number served in 1969. The CMHC is intended to serve patients with mental health problems in the surrounding geographic area (ranging usually from 75,000 to 200,000 population), regardless of their economic status. In other words, unlike the typical disease-specific organized clinic in general hospitals, they are not restricted to low-income persons.

Suicide prevention centers, noted earlier, have evolved into another specialized form of program, equivalent to a "clinic," although much of the service is given by telephone "hot lines" accessible 24 hours a day. In 1977, there were 189 such units in the United States, the largest number (32) being in California.[90]

Clinics for Alcoholism and Drug Abuse

Problems of chronic alcoholism and drug abuse have become increasingly prevalent in the United States in recent years. It is difficult, however, to identify the clinics specifically devoted to these problems, as distinguished from general or mental health clinics that serve substance abuse patients as well as those with other mental disorders. The importance of alcoholism and drug abuse in the United States is reflected by the establishment in the early 1970s in the U.S. PHS of a separate National Institute on Alcohol Abuse and Alcoholism (NIAAA) as well as a National Institute on Drug Abuse (NIDA). Then in the late 1970s, these were combined with the older National Institute of Mental Health (NIMH) into a major new agency: the Alcohol, Drug Abuse, and Mental Health Administration (ADAMHA).

The Office of Program Planning and Coordination of ADAMHA has compiled data on facilities for treating disorders with which each of its three component institutes is concerned.[91] Thus, facilities with alcoholism treatment programs were reported in 1979 to number 5,570 in the nation. The great majority of these were associated with general hospitals, mental hospitals, CMHCs, or other institutions providing inpatient care. A category labelled simply as "other," however, appears to apply mainly to outpatient facilities and social agencies, and it includes 1,224 units. (This does not count a much larger number of non-governmental self-help groups, such as Alcoholics Anonymous, which will be considered later.)

Regarding drug abuse, an equivalent tabulation shows 3,215 treatment facilities, of which 1,996 in 1978 were not part of hospitals. The breakdown of the latter was:

Drug Abuse Clinics	Percent
Freestanding drug abuse treatment centers	69
Various outpatient clinics	13
Social service agencies	9
Schools and miscellaneous	9

Source: ADAMHA, Office of Program Planning and Coordination The Alcohol, Drug Abuse, and Mental Health Data Book (Washington: 1979).

These figures for ambulatory care clinics for alcoholism and for drug abuse cannot simply be added to the freestanding mental health clinics discussed above, since there is much overlapping. It is also not clear how many of the substance abuse clinics are governmentally sponsored, but it is likely that most of them are. Whether governmental or not, moreover, a large proportion of both types of unit receive financial assistance from the federal government.

Utilization data for nonhospital facilities treating substance abuse patients are also very difficult to gather. In 1977, ADAMHA estimated that 2,383,000 persons received treatment for alcoholism, but the great majority of these were in Alcoholics Anonymous, in hospitals, in private medical offices, etc. With regard to facilities given financial assistance by the NIAAA (predominantly ambulatory care clinics), the number was 260,000. Likewise, with respect to federally assisted drug abuse treatment programs, the number of patients estimated for 1977 was 204,000. Although some of these substance abuse patients are, as noted, treated in general mental health clinics, the great majority are served in facilities specializing in alcoholism or drug abuse problems.[92]

Rehabilitation Facilities

Special facilities for rehabilitation of crippled children or adults, both on an outpatient and inpatient basis, can be traced back at least to 1889, when the Cleveland Rehabilitation Center was started.[93] A national movement to construct specialized facilities for multidisciplinary service (physical therapy, occupational therapy, speech therapy, psychological counselling, education, job training and placement, etc.) to the physically disabled developed as a sequel to World War II.[94] As general hospitals came to organize rehabilitation (mainly physical therapy) services for both inpatients and outpatients, however, the enthusiasm for specialized and separate rehabilitation centers seemed to decline.

In 1971, it was estimated that in the United States, there were more than 1,700 rehabilitation facilities. Excluding "sheltered workshops," about 400 of these were freestanding.[95] From another source, one finds that 29 percent of total rehabilitation facilities in 1968 were governmental in sponsorship, nearly all the rest being under voluntary nonprofit sponsorship.[96] Unfortunately, a percentage figure on sponsorship is not available for the freestanding (that is, those facilities that are not part of hospitals or other general institutions), but if this proportion is applied to the 400 free-standing facilities, there would be 116 rehabilitation units under government sponsorship. Many of these operate in association with state government programs for serving crippled children or for vocational rehabilitation of adults; most of the latter and some of the former are in state agencies other than the state health department.

We do not know how many ambulatory visits were made to government-sponsored and free-standing rehabilitation facilities. In 1972, however, the federal Rehabilitation Services Administration reported that there were 199,000 clients of state vocational rehabilitation agencies who were served in various types of rehabilitation facilities (including sheltered workshops).[97] As for crippled children, virtually every state government agency administering services to these children operates clinics for diagnostic evaluation and treatment planning, even though most of the final treatment is given by private physicians and in regular community hospitals. In 1971, 498,000 children received physician services under these state programs.[98] It seems likely that all or nearly all of these would have been seen at least once during that year in an organized clinic for crippled children. Although the great majority of state crippled children's programs are under the jurisdiction of public health agencies, some are administered by welfare departments or by other agencies.

Some state agencies for rehabilitation of crippled children or adults operate special clinics for persons with problems of speech or hearing, but data on their numbers or the volume of services given are not available.

Another type of state government agency is concerned with workers disabled due to some injury or disorder connected with their employment: the state Workmen's Compensation agencies. The treatment of injured or disabled workers in the United States is done ordinarily by private physicians, using community hospitals, but the monetary compensation for any residual disability is typically determined by a governmental administrative agency. Sometimes there are serious disagreements on the degree of disability determined by a physician representing the worker, compared to that determined by a physician representing the employer (or the general insurance company, by which the employer is insured). In some states the worker may appeal the decision on degree of disability by the administrative agency, since the amount of his monetary compensation depends on this. The "appeals board" in these states, such as New York or California, maintain special disability evaluation clinics, staffed by officially employed physicians.[99] Although the volume of services, essentially diagnostic, provided by these units is not very large, they still constitute a separate category of state government clinic.

State and Local Prison Clinics

Organized health services in federal prisons were discussed earlier, but there also are a great many more penal institutions at the state and local levels. In 1974, under state governments there were 671 prisons for adults and 427 correctional institutions for youthful offenders.[100] As of 1970, the state prisons for adults had 176,000 inmates, or an average of about 412 prisoners each.[101] In virtually all of these, there were arrangements for some type of ambulatory medical care, although its content was highly variable. Studies of state prison health services have typically found serious inadequacies. A 1973 study of Pennsylvania state prisons, for example, pointed out that entering prisoners received only cursory medical examinations and access to "sick call" at the clinic was often obstructed by guards.[102] Nevertheless, prisoners—so often from poor and distressed sections of the population—may receive more medical care while incarcerated than when they are out in the community.

Health services in local jails are clearly much less adequate. In 1970 there were 4,037 jails, predominantly operated by county governments, throughout the nation. They had 161,000 inmates, or an average of only 40 each. Since the sentences in local jails are typically rather short and budgets for their maintenance are meager, it is not surprising that in most jails regular medical services are very deficient or totally absent. A survey of local jail medical care resources, made by the AMA in 1972, found—among 1,159 responses to a questionnaire—

the following distribution of arrangements:[103] in 66 percent of the jails there were provisions for first aid only; 17 percent of the jails had no formal arrangement for medical care whatever; and in the remaining 17 percent there were small examining rooms, drug dispensaries, or other arrangements for ambulatory care. It would probably not be justified to consider these resources as clinics.

Other Government Clinics

Almost all other types of governmental clinic at state or local levels have already been discussed in connection with public hospitals (in Chapter 4), public health agencies (in Chapter 5), and public schools and colleges (in Chapter 6). A few other sponsorships of governmental clinics may be noted.

In the family planning field, it may be recalled from Chapter 5 that in 1975 about 1.0 percent of the clinics were located in state or local welfare department buildings.[104] It is likely that these units were sponsored by departments of social welfare or public assistance—amounting to about 50 such clinics in the nation. In many local law enforcement agencies there are special clinics for examination and ambulatory treatment of members of the police department; similar arrangements apply to fire fighters in the fire departments of larger cities or counties. Fire departments sometimes operate ambulance services for prompt response to emergencies in large cities. Also in those local governments operating public utility systems, such as agencies for water or electricity, there are often health services of wider scope than the typical occupational health program.

This completes a national overview of special clinics sponsored or substantially financed by the federal government or by state and local public agencies, other than those reviewed in previous chapters. In the next chapter, we turn to clinics that are wholly nongovernmental, both in their sponsorship and their predominant source of financing.

NOTES

1. Engelman, Rose C., and Robert J. T. Joy, *Two Hundred Years of Military Medicine* (Fort Detrick, Md.: U.S. Army Medical Department, 1975).

2. U.S. Department of Defense; Department of Health, Education, and Welfare; and Office of Management and Budget, *Report of the Military Health Care Study* (Washington: December 1975), p. 3.

3. Ibid., p. 28.

4. Ibid., p. 191.

5. Ibid., pp. 599–601.

6. U.S. Army Surgeon General, *Annual Report: Medical Statistics of the U.S. Army, Calendar Year 1954* (Washington: 1956), p. 12.

7. U.S. Army Surgeon General, *Annual Report, Fiscal Year 1973* (Washington: 1976), p. 13.

8. U.S. Congress, House, Committee on Armed Services, Special Subcommittee on Construction of Military Hospital Facilities, *Hearings*, 1964, p. 10047.

9. Stuart, Richard B. et al., *Proceedings of the Seminar on Ambulatory Health Services Held at Brooke Army Medical Center*. Sponsored by the Surgeon General, Department of the Army (Washington: National Technical Information Service, November 8–12, 1971).

10. National Academy of Sciences and National Research Council, *Study of Health Care for American Veterans* (Washington: U.S. Senate Committee on Veterans' Affairs, 1977).

11. U.S. Veterans Administration, *Veterans Administration Facilities Number and Type* (Washington: March 31, 1979).

12. U.S. Veterans Administration, *Veterans Administration Summary of Medical Programs* (Washington: September 1979), p. 15.

13. National Academy of Sciences and National Research Council, pp. 113–120.

14. U.S. Public Health Service, *Health Services for American Indians* (Washington: PHS Pub. No. 531, 1957), pp. 86–97.

15. U.S. Public Health Service, *The Indian Health Program* (Washington: Government Printing Office, 1972).

16. U.S. Public Health Service, *Indian Health Program 1955–1978* (Washington: 1978).

17. Straus, Robert, *Medical Care for Seamen: The Origin of Public Medical Service in the United States* (New Haven: Yale University Press, 1950).

18. Mountin, Joseph W., "Direct Medical Services Provided by the Federal Government" in Haven Emerson (editor), *Adminstrative Medicine* (Baltimore: Williams and Wilkins Co., 1952), pp. 185–207.

19. U.S. Bureau of Medical Services, *Annual Statistical Summary Fiscal Year 1976 on PHS Hospitals and Clinics* (Washington: Public Health Service, 1978).

20. U.S. Bureau of Prisons, Health Services Division, *Federal Prison Medical Program* (Washington: Government Printing Office, January 1973).

21. Ruddock, A. E.; H. B. Henderson; and G. S. Perrott, "Federal Employees Health Benefits Program," *American Journal of Public Health,* January 1966, pp. 352–366.

22. U.S. Department of Interior, Bureau of Reclamation, *Statistical Report of the Commissioner* (Washington: 1972).

23. Bishop, Eugene L., and H. L. Case, "Medical Care at a TVA Project," *Medical Care,* 2 (1942): 247–253.

24. Tennessee Valley Authority, *Annual Report 1978* (Knoxville, Tenn.: 1979).

25. Mott, F. D., and M. I. Roemer, *Rural Health and Medical Care* (New York: McGraw-Hill, 1948), pp. 422–431.

26. Ruskin, M. G., and B. B. Fall, *The Viet-Nam Reader: Articles and Documents on American Foreign Policy and the Viet-Nam Crisis* (New York: Random House, 1965).

27. Harrington, Michael, *The Other America* (New York: Macmillan Co., 1962).

28. Alinsky, Saul D., "The War on Poverty: Political Pornography," *Journal of Social Issues,* January 1965, pp. 41–47.

29. Schorr, Lisbeth B., and J. T. English, "Background, Context, and Significant Issues in Neighborhood Health Center Programs," *Milbank Memorial Fund Quarterly* 46 (1968): 289–296.

30. Light, H. L., and H. J. Brown, "The Gouverneur Health Services Program: An Historical View," *Milbank Memorial Fund Quarterly* 45 (1967): 375–390.

31. Battistoni, K. J., et al., "Neighborhood Health Centers: A Preliminary Analysis," *Working Papers in Comprehensive Health Planning* (Ithaca, N.Y.: Cornell University Center for Housing and Environmental Studies, May 1968), pp. 21–25.

32. Geiger, H. J., "The Neighborhood Health Center: Education of the Faculty in Preventive Medicine," *Archives of Environmental Health* 14 (1967): 912.

33. Schwartz, Jerome L., "Early Histories of Selected Neighborhood Health Centers," *Inquiry* 7, no. 4 (December 1970).

34. Lashof, Joyce, "The Health Care Team in the Mile Square Area in Chicago," *Bulletin of the New York Academy of Medicine* 44 (1968): 1363.

35. Roemer, Milton I., "Health Resources and Services in the Watts Area of Los Angeles," *California's Health,* February–March 1966, pp. 123–143.

36. Davis, M. S., and R. E. Tranquada, "A Sociological Evaluation of the Watts Neighborhood Health Center," *Medical Care,* 7 (1979): 105–117.

37. Banta, H. David, and R. C. Fox, "Role Strains of a Health Care Team in a Poverty Community: The Columbia Point Experience," *Social Science and Medicine* (England) 6 (1972): 697–722.

38. Schorr, L. B., and J. T. English, "Background, Context, and Significant Issues," p. 291.

39. Salber, Eva J., "Community Participation in Neighborhood Health Centers," *New England Journal of Medicine,* 283 (1970): 515–518.

40. Sparer, G.; G. B. Dines; and D. Smith, "Consumer Participation in OEO-Assisted Neighborhood Health Centers," *American Journal of Public Health* 60 (1970): 1091–1101.

41. Cambel, J., "Working Relationships Between Providers and Consumers in a Neighborhood Health Center," *American Journal of Public Health* 61 (1971): 97–103. January 1971.

42. Abrams, H. K., and R. A. Snyder, "Health Center Seeks to Bridge the Gap Between Hospital and Neighborhood," *Modern Hospital,* May 1968, pp. 96–101.

43. Brieland, Donald, "Community Advisory Boards and Maximum Feasible Participation," *American Journal of Public Health* 61 (1971): 292–296.

44. Torrens, Paul R., "Administrative Problems of Neighborhood Health Centers," *Medical Care* 9 (1971): 487–497.

45. Morehead, Mildred A.; R. S. Donaldson; and M. R. Seravalli, "Comparisons Between OEO Neighborhood Health Centers and Other Health Care Providers of Ratings of the Quality of Health Care," *American Journal of Public Health* 61 (1971): 1294–1306.

46. Bellin, S. S.; H. J. Geiger; and C. D. Gibson, "Impact of Ambulatory-Health-Care Services on the Demand for Hospital Beds," *New England Journal of Medicine,* 280 (1969): 808–812.

47. Bellin, S. S., and H. J. Geiger, "Actual Public Acceptance of the Neighborhood Health Center by the Urban Poor," *Journal of the American Medical Association* 214 (1970): 2147–2153.

48. Salber, E. J. et al., "Utilization of Services at a Neighborhood Health Center," *Pediatrics* 42 (1971): 415–423.

49. Sparer, G., and A. H. Anderson, *A Comparative Cost Data Analysis for Providers of Ambulatory Health Services* (Washington: HEW, 1970).

50. Sparer, G., and J. Johnson, "Evaluation of OEO Neighborhood Health Centers," *American Journal of Public Health* 61 (1971): 931–942.

51. Elinson, J., and C. E. A. Herr, "A Socio-Medical View of Neighborhood Health Centers," *Medical Care* 8 (1970): 97–103.

52. Chabot, A., "Improved Infant Mortality Rates in a Population Served by a Comprehensive Neighborhood Health Program," *Pediatrics* 47 (1971): 989–994.

53. Zwick, Daniel I., "Some Accomplishments and Findings of Neighborhood Health Centers," *Milbank Memorial Fund Quarterly* 50 (1972): 387–420.

54. Ibid., p. 390.

55. Ibid., p. 399.

56. U.S. Public Health Service, Bureau of Community Health Services, "The Community Health Center Program," preliminary processed report, 1979.

57. U.S. Public Health Service, *Bureau of Community Health Services Programs,* (Washington: 1978).

58. USPHS, Bureau of Community Health Services, "The Community Health Center Program" (processed).

59. This and much subsequent information was provided in a personal interview with Edward Martin, M.D., Director of the USPHS Bureau of Community Health Services, February 1980.

60. Much information on the grant programs of the Bureau of Community Health Services has been provided by BCHS staff members, including J. White, M. Samuels, R. Schaeffer, M. Gooch, and A. Jordan, at a meeting held in Washington, February 5, 1980.

61. U.S. Department of Housing and Urban Development, *1977 Annual Report,* (Washington: 1978), p. 55.

62. Appalachian Regional Commission, *1976 Annual Report* (Washington: 1977).

63. Appalachian Regional Commission, *1978 Annual Report* (Washington; 1979).

64. Johnston, Helen L., and J. Robert Lindsay, "Meeting the Health Needs of the Migrant Workers," *Hospitals, JAHA,* July 16, 1965, pp. 78–82.

65. U.S. Public Health Service, Bureau of Community Health Services, *The Migrant Health Program* (Washington; 1976).

66. U.S. Bureau of Community Health Services, *Migrant Health Projects, Fourth Quarter 1975: Summary of Project Data* (Washington; 1976) (processed).

67. U.S. Health Care Financing Administration, *Rural Health Clinic Services* (Washington: (HCFA-02109), 1979).

68. Mullən, Fitzhugh S. M., "The National Health Service Corps," *Public Health Reports* July–August 1979 (suppl.), pp. 1–6.

69. U.S. Public Health Service, *Legislative Base for Maternal and Child Health Programs (includes 1976 Supplement)* (Washington: DHEW Pub. HSA 78-5221, 1978).

70. U.S. Public Health Service, *Promoting the Health of Mothers and Children Fiscal Year 1971* (Washington: 1971), p. 17.

71. Hunt, E., "Infant Mortality Trends and Maternal and Infant Care," *Children* 17 (1970): 88–90.

72. Kessner, D. M., *Infant Death: An Analysis of Maternal Risk and Health Care* (Washington: National Academy of Sciences, Institute of Medicine, 1973).

73. Johnson, Dorothy K., *Perinatal Outcomes of Patients with Selected High-Risk Characteristics Who Enter Two Different Modes of Prenatal Care,* unpublished doctoral dissertation (Los Angeles: University of California, 1975).

74. U.S. Health Services and Mental Health Administration, *The Children and Youth Projects: Comprehensive Health Care in Low-income Areas* (Washington: July 1972).

75. De Geyndt, W., and L. M. Sprague, "Differential Patterns in Comprehensive Health Care Delivery for Children and Youth," *American Journal of Public Health* 60 (1970): 1402–1420.

76. Ross Laboratories, "C & Y Projects: A Chance for Children—What Are Children and Youth Projects?" *Public Health Currents* 12, no. 2 (1972).

77. U.S. Bureau of Community Health Services, *Directory of Community Health Centers,* (Washington: January 1978) (processed).

78. President of the United States, *The Budget for Fiscal Year 1981,* (Washington; 1980), p. 252.

79. U.S. National Center for Health Statistics, *Health Resource Statistics, 1976–77 Edition* (Washington: DHEW Pub. No. PHS 79-1509, 1979), p. 366.

80. Feingold, Eugene, "A Political Scientist's View of the Neighborhood Health Center as a Social Institution" *Medical Care* 8 (1970): 108–115.

81. National Association of Community Health Centers, *Legislative Status Report* 5, no. 3, October 1979.

82. Group Health Association of America, "GAO Report Urges HEW to Establish Effective Guidelines for Better Use of Physicians and Dentists in Health Centers," *Group Health and Welfare News,* 15 (1974): 2.

83. Wright, Guy, "Health Center Future," *San Francisco Examiner,* November 22, 1979.

84. U.S. Public Health Service, Region IX, unpublished "Program Review," San Francisco, Calif., July 1979.

85. U.S. National Institute of Mental Health, Division of Biometry and Epidemiology, Washington, D.C., unpublished data furnished in January 1980.

86. Lemkau, Paul V., "Mental Health Services" in Maxcy-Rosenau, *Preventive Medicine and Public Health* (10th edition), Philip E. Sartwell (editor) 1973), pp. 547–590.

87. Taube, Carl A., *Utilization of Mental Health Facilities 1971* (Washington: National Institute of Mental Health, 1973), p. 15.

88. U.S. National Institute of Mental Health, *1977 Directory-Federally Funded Community Mental Health Centers* (Washington: DHEW Pub. No. (ADM) 77-258, 1978).

89. U.S. National Institute of Mental Health, Division of Biometry and Epidemiology, Washington, D.C., unpublished data furnished in January 1980.

90. U.S. National Center for Health Statistics, *Health Resources Statistics 1976–77 Edition* (Washington: 1979), pp. 441–442.

91. Alcohol, Drug Abuse, and Mental Health Administration, Office of Program Planning and Coordination, *The Alcohol, Drug Abuse, and Mental Health National Data Book* (Washington: processed, December 1979).

92. Thomas Plout, Director of the Office of Prevention, National Institute of Mental Health, personal communication, February 1980.

93. U.S. Office of Vocational Rehabilitation, *The Planning of Rehabilitation Centers* (Washington: HEW, 1957).

94. U.S. Public Health Service, Division of Hospital and Medical Facilities, *Hill-Burton State Plan Data: A National Survey as of 1 January 1967,* (Washington: PHS Pub. No. 930-F2, 1968).

95. U.S. National Center for Health Statistics, *Health Resources Statistics 1975,* pp. 515–516.

96. Association of Rehabilitation Centers, *1968 Directory of Rehabilitation Facilities* (Washington: 1968), p. 81.

97. U.S. Rehabilitation Services Administration, *State Rehabilitation Facilities Specialist Exchange* (Washington: September–October, 1973), p. 1.

98. U.S. Maternal and Child Health Service, *Promoting the Health of Mothers and Children Fiscal Year 1972* (Washington: HEW, 1972), p. 29.

99. U.S. National Commission on State Workmen's Compensation Laws, Compendium on Workmen's Compensation (Washington: 1973), pp. 233–234.

100. American Correctional Association, *Directory-Juvenile and Adult Correctional Institutions of the United States and Canada, 1974–75* (College Park, Md.,: 1975).

101. U.S. Department of Justice, *National Prisoner Statistics: Prisoners in State and Federal Institutions for Adult Felons 1968, 1969, 1970* (Washington: Bureau of Prisons NPS Bull. No. 47,

April 1972).

102. Newport, John, "Review of Health Services in Correctional Facilities in the United States," *Public Health Reports* 92 (1977): 564–569.

103. American Medical Association, *Medical Care in U.S. Jails* (Chicago: AMA, 1973).

104. U.S. National Center of Health Statistics, *The National Inventory of Family Planning Services: 1975 Survey Results* (Washington: Public Health Service Pub. No. (PHS) 78-1814, April 1978), p. 2.

Chapter 10

Special Voluntary Agency Clinics

Beyond the many forms of special clinic or health center under voluntary agency sponsorship, but financed substantially by government funds, discussed in Chapter 9, there are other voluntary agency clinics that are both financed and operated by nongovernmental bodies. A fraction of their support may, indeed, come also from governmental sources, but these entities do not depend on public funds for their survival.

In contrast to the quasi-voluntary ambulatory care units discussed in Chapter 9, the clinics to be considered here have arisen entirely from private initiative. Most numerous and diverse among these are clinics focused on specific diseases or health problems. Other voluntary agencies sponsor clinics for certain populations. Still other clinics are offshoots of organizations with other principal purposes, such as labor unions or farmers' associations. Each of these types of clinics will be examined. Finally, we will offer a view of the whole spectrum of special clinics, both public and voluntary, in one metropolitan county.

VOLUNTARY HEALTH AGENCIES

The pluralism of the American health care system is nowhere more evident than in the enormous number and variety of voluntary or nongovernmental health agencies, devoted most frequently to tackling specific disease problems. In earlier chapters we have seen how many programs of public health work were started as an outgrowth of initiative by voluntary citizen groups—in tuberculosis control, in venereal disease control, in preventive maternal and child health services, and so on. Most of the pioneering was in the establishment of specialized clinics—usually serving the poor. After the soundness of an idea was demonstrated and public interest was aroused, government agencies would develop it further. With the more firm support of tax funds, various disease control or health promotional programs could usually be more extensively developed.[1]

Yet after governmental services in specific fields became firmly grounded and the goal of the voluntary agency was essentially achieved, the private organization seldom disbanded. Usually it focused its efforts on some other aspect of the same health field or on a closely related field. As a result, the number of voluntary health agencies has increased steadily. A survey in 1961 estimated that—counting national, regional, and local voluntary bodies—the health and welfare field in the United States absorbed the attention of more than 100,000 organizations.[2]

Most numerous among the voluntary health agencies are still the earliest types—those tackling specific diseases. Secondly, there are agencies or groups with broader health functions that are devoted to providing personal services (rather than research, for example, or education); a noteworthy type of the second category in recent years are the "free clinics." Thirdly, there are many general civic and social organizations that, among many functions, include certain health activities. Insofar as all three of these classes of voluntary agency provide organized ambulatory health services (OAHS), we will discuss each in turn.

Voluntary Disease-Specific Agencies

As noted, many of the disease-specific agencies originated decades ago, although their functions have changed. The National Tuberculosis Association was founded in 1904, after action at the local level in several communities, the earliest being at Philadelphia in 1892. As tuberculosis declined, the association's focus changed to "chest diseases," and it became the American Lung Association. The National Society for the Prevention of Blindness was founded in 1908 and is still active in the same field, although with different approaches. Other organizations have started since World War II, such as the National Foundation for Neuromuscular Diseases or the National Association for Retarded Children (later Retarded Citizens), both founded in 1953.[3] In 1974, considering only the disease-specific voluntary health agencies with donations in that year exceeding $10 million, the list was as follows:[4]

Voluntary Health Agency	Donations (1974) (millions of dollars)
American Cancer Society	$97.5
American Heart Association	58.9
The National Foundation (formerly National Foundation on Poliomyelitis)	48.7
American Lung (formerly Tuberculosis) Association	40.2
National Society for Crippled Children and Adults	37.8

Voluntary Health Agency	Donations (1974) (millions of dollars)
Muscular Dystrophy Association of America	27.1
National Association for Retarded Citizens	24.0
Planned Parenthood Federation of America	20.0
United Cerebral Palsy Association	19.7
National Association for Mental Health	14.8
National Multiple Sclerosis Society	13.7
The Arthritis Foundation	10.8

Source: D. L. Wilner, R. P. Walkley, and E. J. O'Neill, *Introduction to Public Health*, 7th ed. (New York: Macmillan Co., 1978), p. 57.

The funds collected by these organizations to support their programs are raised through voluntary donations, large and small. Typically, funds are raised through campaigns conducted in a community by the local chapter of the national body; a percentage of the collections is sent to the national headquarters and the balance is retained for local programs. The national office is ordinarily located in a large city and is linked through a network of regional and state offices to the local chapters. General policies, literature, and supplies for program activities are usually produced by the central office and distributed nationally.

In contrast to policies in the early twentieth century, the major emphasis and greatest expenditures of most voluntary health agencies have shifted from direct personal health service to support of medical research and education—both of the health professions and the general population. A portion of expenditures, however, continue to be devoted to health services, including the operation of various clinics. Thus, for the 1978–79 fiscal year, the American Cancer Society (ACS) had available nearly $150 million; this was planned for activities according to the following distribution:[5]

Purpose	Percent
Cancer research	32.4
Public education	16.7
Professional education	9.7
Patient services	11.7
Community services	7.7
Fund-raising	12.1
Management and general purposes	9.7
All purposes	100.0

Source: American Cancer Society, *Annual Report 1978* (New York: 1978), p. 20.

In previous years, "community services" included the operation of cancer detection clinics, where anyone could come for a medical examination along with certain x-ray and laboratory procedures. The ACS approach is now reflected in the slogan: "every doctor's office is a cancer detection center," but clinics are still supported for other purposes. In 1978, e.g., in cooperation with the American Hospital Association (AHA), a network of "Quit Smoking Clinics" was started as part of the campaign against lung cancer. ACS patient services now stress assistance to postoperative patients in physical rehabilitation. In 1978, for example, 320,000 postsurgical patients were provided such services through organized programs.

To cite another example, the National Multiple Sclerosis Society had income of $25.2 million in 1978. These funds were spent for the following purposes:[6]

Purpose	Percent
Medical research	18.3
Professional education	7.0
Public education	13.5
Community service	10.7
Patient service	25.7
Fund-raising	14.6
Administration	10.2
All purposes	100.0

Source: National Multiple Sclerosis Society, *Annual Report 1978* (New York: 1979), p. 16.

The relatively large fraction of this organization's expenditures for "patient service" included the support of 75 multiple sclerosis treatment centers throughout the United States; these are typically ambulatory rehabilitation facilities.

The National Easter Seal Society for Crippled Children and Adults is somewhat unusual in spending the great bulk of its funds for direct services to patients. In 1977, the society spent 73 percent of its $90 million income for direct services to handicapped persons.[7] These included such activities as physical therapy, occupational therapy, speech therapy, and audiological services—offered ordinarily at special clinics.[8] Included among patient services also are vocational training, the loan of equipment, and transportation. Altogether in the 1977–78 fiscal year such services were provided to more than 280,000 disabled persons at 728 sites.

The National Foundation March of Dimes, formerly devoted to combatting poliomyelitis and currently concerned with birth defects, in past years made the large research investment that culminated in the Salk vaccine in 1954. In 1979, however, with the new focus on birth defects, the relative support for research was much lower while support for services was much higher, as shown by the following percentage distribution of expenditures of its $68.6 million income:[9]

Purpose	Percent
Medical research	16.9
Professional education	7.1
Community health education	19.8
Community health services	17.2
Medical services	13.1
Administration and fund-raising	25.9
All purposes	100.0

Source: National Foundation March of Dimes, *Annual Report 1979* (New York), pp. 30–32.

Among the National Foundation's "medical services" has been establishment of prenatal clinics (to prevent birth defects) in areas of acute need, often as rural satellites of large medical centers. Among "community health service" programs, educational and clinical service units are being established to reach pregnant adolescent girls ". . . at the highest risk, either because of minority status or poverty or both."

The American Heart Association has long spent the greatest share of its funds on supporting research and professional education, mostly through distribution of grants from its national office.[10] At the same time, local chapters are encouraged to support patient services, such as special clinics to screen for risk factors in coronary heart disease, hypertension screening clinics, nutrition counseling service, and programs on vocational readjustment for cardiac patients.

These accounts of some of the major disease-specific voluntary health agencies may be enough to clarify their general character, and to show the degree to which most of them still provide some direct personal health services through clinics or other forms of organized activity. There are two other types of voluntary health agencies that are not oriented to specific diseases, but are similar in that they focus on special health problems. These are organizations concerned with family planning and with mental health. Both of these fields are the subject also of major governmental programs supporting specialized clinics, but here we may take note of voluntary agency efforts.

In the field of birth control or *family planning* (FP), the pioneering efforts were made by private citizens for years before government agencies entered this controversial arena. Margaret Sanger, a visiting nurse in New York, organized a "birth control clinic" in 1916 to advise low-income women on how they might limit the size of their families.[11] Yet after government agencies—predominantly health departments—began to offer FP services in the 1940s and after, voluntary agencies lost none of their momentum.

Even though thousands of private physicians—gynecologists as well as general practitioners—offer FP services to their private patients, the numbers and utilization of FP clinics under voluntary, as well as governmental auspices have steadily expanded. Major impetus to the growth of both types of FP agencies and clinics came with the beginning of substantial federal subsidies to both types of program in 1968.[12] Thus, in 1969 there were 1,983 agencies in the United States offering FP services, the majority of which were health departments and hospitals; of these, 146 were voluntary organizations affiliated with the Planned Parenthood Federation of America.[13] By 1976, the total agencies had grown to 2,523, of which 180 were Planned Parenthood affiliates. In addition, aside from hospitals and health departments, other agencies discussed elsewhere in this volume (community health centers, free clinics, etc.) sponsored many FP clinics.

The patients served by each voluntary FP clinic, however, are more numerous than those served by other agencies. In 1976 there were some 4,083,000 persons served by all FP clinics in the nation, of whom 1,108,000 were in the voluntary FP facilities. This amounted to 6,158 patients per voluntary FP clinic per year, compared with an annual average of 1,618 patients for all types of FP clinic combined. By far the most common birth control method used by women served in all types of FP clinic was the oral contraceptive pill (67 percent of patients in 1976).

In the field of *mental health service,* we have discussed the variety of clinics under the sponsorship of special state and local government agencies, as well as under health departments. The 548 federally funded and fully operational community mental health centers (as of 1976) under diverse local sponsorships have also been discussed. There remain for consideration 763 freestanding psychiatric clinics in the nation under voluntary auspices, as of January 1978. These constituted 66 percent of all freestanding mental health clinics at that time; their sponsorship more precisely was as follows:[14]

Sponsorship	Percent
Nonprofit corporation	90.4
For-profit corporation	3.4
Other nonprofit organization	2.9
Church	1.8
Other for-profit entity	1.4
All voluntary sponsorships	100.0

Source: National Institute of Mental Health, Division of Biometry and Epidemiology, 1980, from unpublished data.

In 1975, all types of freestanding psychiatric clinics were estimated to have served 1,590,000 different patients.[15] Although 66 percent of the clinics were under voluntary agency sponsorship, their average attendance was generally lower than that of the governmentally sponsored clinics. Hence, a plausible estimate of the utilization of these voluntary freestanding clinics in 1975 would be about half the total patients stated above, or 795,000.

Closely related to voluntary mental health clinics are the many organized self-help groups tackling problems of *alcoholism*. In 1978, there were 25,900 such groups in the United States, the best known of which (nearly 17,000 groups) is Alcoholics Anonymous.[16] One can only guess at the number of alcoholic persons or "problem drinkers" participating in these groups, but if the average were 100 persons per group per year, it would amount to 2,590,000 patients.

The major voluntary agency in the mental health field is the Mental Health Association (until 1976 known as the National Association for Mental Health). This organization grew out of several other organizations, starting with the National Committee for Mental Hygiene, which was founded in 1909.[17] Unlike the other disease-specific voluntary health agencies discussed here, the Mental Health Association does not provide any direct health services. It serves rather as a social action body, promoting improved services for the mentally ill through governmental agencies, hospitals, and other entities.

Voluntary Agencies with General Health Functions

Less numerous than the disease-specific voluntary health agencies, but still important in the United States, are other voluntary organizations with more generalized health objectives. Among these there may be clinics or similar OAHS.

Best known perhaps is the American Red Cross, part of a worldwide network of organizations. Founded in the United States in 1881, it is concerned with relieving human distress in countless ways. In 1979 the American Red Cross had 3,108 chapters and made national expenditures of nearly $400 million.[18] More than half of the national expenditures go to support the blood service, involving collection of voluntary blood donations and distribution of the preserved blood to hospitals and other facilities. Health and related services for care of people involved in disasters (fires, floods, tornadoes, major accidents, etc.), however, absorbed 9.2 percent of the largest budget in 1979; some services were provided in more than 40,000 disaster incidents in 1979. These events affected 494,000 people, many of whom received emergency medical care.

Somewhat related is another worldwide organization, The Salvation Army, founded in London, England in 1865. Inspired by religious principles, this remarkable organization tries to help people in distress through a variety of social service programs in 83 countries.[19] In the United States the hundreds of local chapters are best known for their help with food, shelter, and efforts at rehabilitation of destitute men and women, often alcoholics and ex-convicts.

While material assistance is usually linked with attempts at religious persuasion, the service of local "Corps community centers" may also include urgently needed medical care, prenatal and childbirth service to young unwed mothers, and emergency care in disasters.

Many American religious denominations sponsor overseas church missions that include hospitals and health centers providing ambulatory care in the developing countries. Some also sponsor "home missions," offering clinic services to depressed populations in the United States—often in rural areas. Likewise, voluntary international health agencies, such as Project HOPE, operate occasional domestic programs to provide primary health care to American Indians or other low-income populations.

Social services without religious content of any sort are given by thousands of nongovernmental family service agencies throughout the United States. If one recognizes medical social work and referral for medical service as components of health care, many of these agencies have systematic arrangements for health care to some of their clients.[20]

A very different form of voluntary agency with general health care objectives has arisen in recent years. Rather than being founded by community leaders to help those in need (often in a spirit of noblesse oblige) these organized voluntary efforts have arisen with almost an opposite motivation: a sense of self-help outside the channels of the "establishment." Sparked by a certain defiance of conventional methods of providing medical care, and particularly in rejection of governmental procedures, these voluntary initiatives have concentrated on simple and direct methods of providing ambulatory health service.

Best known are the programs started by young people in California, under the name of "free clinics," but somewhat related are other self-help activities including women's clinics and holistic health projects.

FREE CLINICS AND OTHER SELF-HELP PROJECTS

The rise of consumerism in American health services during the 1960s has been discussed earlier. No innovation in ambulatory care is more dramatically representative of this than the free clinic.

Origins and Definition

In contrast to the neighborhood health centers initiated by substantial grants from the federal government, there arose in 1967 a new pattern for providing ambulatory care entirely planned and supported by consumers, usually groups of young adults. The first such facility was the Haight-Ashbury Free Medical Clinic, opened in a bohemian section of San Francisco, California in the summer of 1967.[21] Before the end of that year four other similar clinics had opened in

Cincinnati, Ohio; Detroit, Michigan; Seattle, Washington; and Vancouver, British Columbia. By the end of 1969, it was reported that 59 free clinics had started in the United States, but nine had closed down, leaving 50 in operation. As of early 1971 about 175 free clinics were believed to be active throughout the country.[22] The largest concentration (about one-third of the total) was in California.

The essential characteristic of the free clinic was linked to the motivation responsible for its origin. This was clearly a feeling of distrust and antagonism to the "establishment" in the American health care system—a disdain, especially by youth, for what was regarded as offensive bureaucracy in hospital outpatient departments, public health agency clinics, and other such facilities in the average community. Such feelings were held not only by young people of the political left, but by all sorts of socially alienated youth who were most commonly called "hippies."[23] The free clinic was an expression of these people in the health sector, equivalent to free schools, legal collectives, or communes in other sectors.

Accordingly, the free clinics, while inevitably a product of organized efforts, attempted to embody as little formal structure, rules, and regulations as possible. They were determined to avoid the categorical lines of most organized ambulatory care units reserved for special classes of people or specific types of disease. Often located in vacant stores or old houses, they were open to anyone and everyone who came. No charges were made (although voluntary donations were welcome), and an attempt was made to offer help to patients with any disease.[24] In reaction to the impersonality and indignities that low-income patients often encountered in traditional public clinics at hospitals, free clinic staff attempted to treat everyone with sympathy and respect. To create an atmosphere congenial for young people, colorful psychedelic posters often adorned the walls, and rock music came from a record player at all times.

Types of Free Clinics

In undertaking the first national survey of free clinics in early 1970, Jerome Schwartz defined them as having seven characteristics: (1) a physical facility, (2) professionally trained personnel, (3) various health personnel are volunteers, (4) direct provision of medical, dental, or psychological service (including treatment of drug abuse), (5) availability to everyone without eligibility tests, (6) specified hours of service, and (7) no set payment required (although small fees might be charged for specified services, and donations might be requested).[25]

On the basis of the first 70 clinics that had been established between June 1967 and December 1969, the free clinics could be classified into four types, according to their initial sponsorship: (1) the neighborhood clinic, started by young residents in a particular neighborhood and often based on an ethnic association (such as the Black Panthers or the Latin American Defense Organization); (2) the street clinic started by hippies who might live in many localities but tended to gather for companionship in certain districts; (3) the youth clinic, started by adults (often businessmen's clubs) concerned about drug abuse and other problems of high school youth, and (4) the sponsored clinic, started by an official health agency. The distribution of these four types in the initial survey of 70 free clinics was:[26]

Type of Clinic	Percent
Street	36
Neighborhood	34
Youth	24
Sponsored	6
All types	100

Source: Jerome L. Schwartz, "Preliminary Observations of Free Clinics," in D. E. Smith, D. J. Bentel, and J. L. Schwartz, eds. *The Free Clinic: A Community Approach to Health Care and Drug Abuse* (Beloit, Wis.: Stash Press, 1971), p. 147.

The "sponsored" type was found only in Los Angeles County, California, and one may question whether this sort of facility should properly be considered a "free clinic."

Services and Staffing

While precise data are lacking, it is obvious that all free clinics are devoted principally to the health problems of young adults, such as drug abuse, venereal disease, contraception, unwanted pregnancies, and minor respiratory or gastrointestinal disorder. There is no hesitation to refer patients beyond the capability of management by the free clinic, to established hospital OPDs. Of the four clinic types described above, only the neighborhood clinics serve any appreciable proportion of families, including mothers and small children. A careful study of one free clinic of the street type in Los Angeles found 88 percent of patients to be under age 25 years, and 56 percent to be female.[27]

To provide services for these patients, the free clinics have attracted the services (predominantly volunteer) of many physicians, nurses, and other professionals, as well as nontrained personnel. The pattern found in the 1970 Schwartz survey was an average of 17 physicians working in a clinic, typically scheduled so that each would handle only a few sessions per month. About 24 percent of the physicians were interns or residents from a nearby hospital, and the balance were predominantly young specialists (mainly in internal medicine, pediatrics, and obstetrics-gynecology). Registered nurses averaged ten per clinic, rotating also on a sessional basis.

Free clinics also attracted the part-time services of laboratory technicians, pharmacists, medical and nursing students, and numerous community aides. In about half the clinics surveyed in 1970, there were also psychological counseling programs that attracted the services of psychiatrists, psychologists, social workers, and lay counselors. While the great majority of these personnel were not paid for their services, a few administrative and clerical workers were paid modest salaries. This was found necessary to be assured of the services of these persons full-time and to maintain continuity in the whole clinic program.

Most free clinics attempted to keep a supply of medications, bandages, and similar supplies. These ordinarily had to be purchased and constituted a major expense for the free clinics.

Medical and related services of the free clinics are provided primarily at two-to-three-hour evening sessions. This scheduling accomplishes the double purpose of being feasible for attracting the volunteer services of professional personnel, and also being more appropriate for most of the patients. In the Schwartz 1970 survey, the average clinic offered medical services 14.5 hours per week.

Since free clinics deliberately avoid the formality of maintaining medical records, it is difficult to know the volume of services they provide. The pioneer Haight-Ashbury Free Clinic in San Francisco claimed in 1971 to be averaging as many as 3,000 client visits per month, with medical services provided by 30 part-time volunteer physicians and 100 other personnel (only a few being full-time).[28] In his 1970 survey, however, Schwartz obtained rough estimates of patients served per month in 56 clinics, and these estimates yielded an average of 359 patient-visits per month. If this rate is applied to a national count of 175 free clinics, we derive an estimate of about 754,000 patient visits per year. This figure applies to medical services; in addition, an indeterminate additional (but smaller) number of patients were provided psychological counseling services, dental care, and social work or even legal services.

Financial Support

In spite of their name, virtually all free clinics require some funds for operation; money may be needed to pay rent, to purchase drugs and supplies, and usually to pay salaries (even though small) to administrative and clerical personnel. At one free clinic in Baltimore, Maryland, the operating cost in 1971 was about $1,000 per month.[29] The costs have doubtless increased since then.

Funds for these expenses are derived from several sources. As noted, voluntary donations are solicited from patients, and small fees occasionally are collected for drugs. Secondly, donations are sought from ordinary families or businesses, especially when youthful members of those families or proprietors use the clinic. Thirdly, in spite of their initial aversion to government, many free clinics have applied for and accepted grants from government, typically at the local level. In 1970, the Los Angeles County Health Department allocated $60,000 to 11 local free clinics, mainly for the purchase of drugs.[30] In a study of 110 free clinics published in 1972, it was found that about one-third received funds from government sources.[31]

Lack of financial support has doubtless been the most serious stumbling block in the free clinic movement. The donated funds and volunteer services available in the early, enthusiastic years of the movement have become less assured in the later years. When free clinics close, it is usually due to financial deficiencies, and many clinics that stay open are in a continual financial crisis.

The problems of funding have led the free clinics to undertake actions contrary to their original concept of avoiding organizational structure: around 1970 they set up a National Free Clinic Council. The main purposes were to advise on methods of establishing new free clinics, to train clinic administrative personnel, and to suggest sources of financial support.

Commentary

Quantitative evaluation of the quality of health care (curative or preventive) provided at free clinics has not been made. The sparsity of records and the generally cavalier atmosphere would hardly permit a medical audit analysis, and evaluation of outcomes would be even less feasible. The remarkable growth of these clinics, nevertheless, both in number of facilities and in volume of services, surely indicates that they have met a need felt by thousands of young people. Their informality has perhaps even given signals to more conventional clinics on a style of operation that may be attractive to all types of patients, not only the young.

Free clinics have made health services available to youth and sometimes to families who, for one reason or another, did not wish to seek help at traditional facilities. For the professional and administrative personnel who staff them, they provide an opportunity for socially useful work that is both interesting and gratifying. It is important to recognize that the medical care given at free clinics is not cultist or antiscientific; chiropractors or naturopaths are not used. The tenets of scientific medicine are accepted, but stripped of the overlay of modes and manners that many people, particularly youth, find elitist and offensive. By being nonjudgmental and nonmoralistic, the free clinics attract patients with conditions that deter them from consulting either private physicians or conventional clinics. No stigma is associated with any disorder, such as venereal disease, unwanted pregnancy, drug abuse problems, and mental and emotional difficulties.[32]

It hardly need be mentioned that the free clinics are not the first clinics to offer services without payment. Yet their origin in the late 1960s, with the seemingly naive label, is doubtless not accidental: not only was this the period of widespread antiestablishment feeling among young people, but it was also the period of entry of Medicare and Medicaid on the sociomedical scene. These massively financed governmental programs supported abundant medical care for millions of people—but only those who met strict eligibility tests and were willing to be involved with various bureaucratic processes. This was (and is) a period when most physicians and hospitals expected fees for each and every service rendered. The volunteer service of young physicians and other health personnel was their way of expressing a reaction to the prevailing commercialization of conventional medical practice. The free clinic movement was a dramatic symbol of the initiative of American young people who, a few years earlier, were simply protesting angrily about the dominant culture, and then instead managed to do something about it. As Rosemary Taylor wrote in 1979, free clinics were a vivid reaction to the prevailing U.S. medical care system of the late 1960s, but they hardly provided a foundation for extensive remodeling of that system.[33]

The future of the free clinic movement, in its original form, does not seem bright. After the nationwide surveys done in the early 1970s, unfortunately no further general survey has been conducted. However, according to observers in California, where a high proportion of the original free clinics were concentrated, many have disappeared; thus, in the San Joaquin Valley, where 11 free clinics had existed in 1971, by 1975 only 3 were still in operation.[34] Piecing together information from various sources, it seems that most of the original free clinics—estimated in 1970 as numbering about 175 nationally—had died out by 1980. After the initial enthusiasm waned, and the stock of volunteer health workers—so many of whom were medical or nursing students, interns or residents in nearby hospitals—moved on, most of these self-help clinics had a hard struggle to survive.

Those that did survive became dependent on financial support from government. Thus in 1972, the National Institute on Drug Abuse (in the U.S. Public Health Service) gave a grant of $1 million to the National Free Clinic Council, which had just been organized and was located at the site of the pioneer Haight-Ashbury Free Clinic in San Francisco.[35] The council distributed these funds (averaging $20,000 each) to about 50 free clinics around the country, but this grant support was not continued. Some free clinics were subsidized by medical schools, in return for providing patients for clinical teaching. Acceptance of support from diverse public and private grant sources meant that the free clinics were departing from their original theoretical foundation.

In adjustment to this reality, most of them changed their names—usually to "community clinics." This was especially true for the clinics serving ethnic minorities. For the care of certain patients, claims were submitted to the Medicaid program and payments were accepted. In effect, many of the free clinics evolved into community health centers of the type described in Chapter 9. Perhaps a small fraction of the original free clinics were able to cling to their principles of independence and continued to operate solely on the basis of services from volunteer health personnel and a marginal budget from the voluntary donations of patients.[36] Some of the units merged into the women's clinics and the holistic health center movement, discussed below. Occasionally the clinic organizers, who had originally lacked any formal training in a health discipline, went on to professional schools. In the main, however, the price of survival of these clinics was the abandonment of the antiestablishment posture that inspired their founding, and conversion to the status of small modest primary care facilities within the heterogeneous framework of the American health care system.

Women's Clinics

A similar self-help clinic movement arose soon after the launching of the free clinic idea, as an aspect of the women's liberation movement. Originating also in California, the Feminist Women's Health Center of Los Angeles opened in 1971, and the idea soon spread. A nationwide survey in 1974 identified over 1,200 women's groups providing various sorts of health education throughout the country.[37] Most of these groups were, and are, devoted to informing women about their own anatomy and physiology, counseling on sexuality, making referrals regarding contraception or abortion, and related matters. Some, however, operated clinics providing personal health service for women on a variety of specifically female problems.

In 1976, it was estimated that about 50 feminist women's clinics were in operation throughout the United States.[38] Most of these clinics have a physician (usually female) in attendance, at least part-time, but the principal staff consists of women who have become knowledgeable about methods of contraception, self-care of minor gynecological complaints, channels for obtaining legal abortions, problems of sexuality, or preparation for childbirth and child rearing. These self-help clinics have attracted educated young women who are active in the women's liberation movement more perhaps than needy, low-income women. In 1978, in fact, there was organized a Federation of Feminist Women's Health Centers to promote the general concept. This organization estimated that in 1980 there were 75 to 100 women's self-help clinics in the country.[39] Some of these, like the free clinics, have been awarded small grants by local government agencies. In addition, there were estimated to be about 24 women-controlled abortion clinics, where unwanted pregnancies were terminated legally by licensed physicians, but where ancillary supportive services were given by the sponsoring women; the fees charged for these abortions were often not as high as those charged in private medical or hospital settings.

A related ambulatory service has developed with the movement—long existent but acquiring fresh vigor in the 1970s—to train midwives (who were not necessarily nurses) to offer "birthing service" at the mother's home. Associated with such training programs, such as one in Seattle, Washington, there may be clinics for prenatal and postpartum patients that provide care while furnishing training opportunities for the midwifery students.

Holistic Health Centers

Another form of clinic has taken shape in recent years as a reaction, not so much to formal bureaucracies in the American health care system, but rather to the highly technological character of so much of modern medical science. Such reactions had occurred in previous eras: examples are the rise of homeopathy in early nineteenth century Germany led by Hahnemann, or the rise of Christian Science in Boston under Mary Baker Eddy around 1900. These earlier movements in reaction to the dominant medical doctrines of the day were expressed, however, through individual practitioners and while these have numbered in the thousands, the healing services were not provided through organized teams of personnel.[40]

The holistic (sometimes spelled "wholistic") health movement, on the other hand, involves the provision of service quite deliberately by interdisciplinary teams in health centers. As defined in the 1970s by the Society of Wholistic Medicine, the "wholistic health center" is:

> a church-based family practice medical care facility that utilizes an interdisciplinary team of physicians, pastoral counsellors, and nurses who focus on all aspects of individuals' needs. Wholistic health care is based on the metaphysical affirmation of body, mind, and spirit integrated in a whole, independent of and greater than the sum of its parts. In practice, wholistic care means actively searching with people all dimensions of their lives . . . for causes and symptoms of disease, then creatively exploring these same aspects for treatment strategies to restore or maintain health.[41]

An inventory of holistic health centers throughout the United States in 1978 identified 49 such ambulatory care facilities.[42] In spite of the definition just quoted, the underlying principles and forms of implementation of these were variable. One classification suggested three types: (1) expanded medical practices, (2) alternative health services clinical and educational centers, and (3) professional collectives.[43] About half of the total units included qualified physicians (with MD degrees) on their staffs (along with others), and the other half were under the leadership of psychologists, chiropractors, dentists, clergymen, or others. Typically there are fees charged for treatment at holistic health centers; their appeal is evidently to middle-class people with psychic or psychosomatic complaints that have not been satisfactorily treated by conventional medical care. Whatever may be the future of holistic medicine, its provision through health centers reflects the pervasiveness of organized approaches to the current delivery of health services, whether traditional or innovative.

SOCIAL ORGANIZATIONS WITH SPECIAL HEALTH PROJECTS

Finally, brief mention should be made of the wide variety of general social organizations—with economic, professional, fraternal, or other objectives—that, among their activities, sponsor special health projects, including clinics. Our discussion must be brief, because information on this subject has not been systematically collected.

The sponsorship of "mission" clinics by some religious organizations has been noted. The very origin of hospitals, which later developed outpatient clinics, can be traced to churches—for which the health service was initially a means to a religious end. Indirectly related to religious faiths are social service societies, such as Catholic Charities, Jewish Federations, or the American Friends Service Committee, that may provide organized health services for certain disadvantaged people as part of general assistance programs.

Business clubs may support selected philanthropies in the health field. The Lions Clubs, for example, as a nationwide policy in the United States, have long supported projects of vision testing and correction for needy school children. In some communities this involves the operation of clinics at which eyeglasses are prescribed.

Fraternal lodges in earlier decades played a part in the origins of the health insurance movement. Organizations such as the Elks, the Odd Fellows and the Masons, in the early twentieth century sometimes sponsored insurance for doctors' care; most often this involved "lodge practice," for low salaries, by a few selected general practitioners, but occasionally a clinic with a few physicians in attendance might be sponsored. Other forms of health insurance have now replaced these small lodge programs. The Masonic order known as the Shriners, however, is still sponsoring a national network of hospitals for crippled children and for burn victims, and these institutions offer outpatient services.

In Chapter 7, brief reference was made to "labor health centers," i.e., ambulatory care facilities sponsored by labor unions for several purposes, most frequently for diagnosis of illnesses that might be work-related and for general ambulatory primary care. In 1954, an American Labor Health Association was organized. At that time, it was estimated that about two million workers and their dependents were served by some 150 group medical centers, meaning health centers staffed by medical care teams and financed by prepayment. Nearly 60 of these were sponsored by labor unions or by labor and management jointly.[44] Over the years, these labor health centers have risen and declined—some linked to health insurance plans, others not. As recently as 1976 a network of four primary care clinics was sponsored in California by the United Farm Workers of America (at the expense of growers) for Spanish-speaking agricultural workers.[45]

The role of labor unions in arranging health care for their members in recent years has shifted very largely to collective bargaining with management for fringe benefits to pay for health insurance protection in the open medical market.[46] A handful of local unions, however, have continued to sponsor prepaid group practice clinics. Under the 1970s definition of health maintenance organizations (HMOs), there were 213 such entities in the United States in 1975, of which 10 were sponsored by labor unions.[47] (This excludes another four union-sponsored HMOs, that did not include group practice clinics.)

The HMO movement will be discussed more fully in Chapter 12, but here it may be noted that various other types of social organizations, aside from labor unions, also serve as sponsors. Of the 213 HMOs with group practice clinics noted above, 35 were sponsored by consumer groups in 1975. Among these would be general consumer cooperatives operating stores for food or other products. One of the earliest precursors of HMOs was sponsored in Elk City, Oklahoma in the 1930s by a farmers' association, the local chapter of the National Farmers Union.[48] General commercial insurance companies may also sponsor clinic-based HMOs.

Other social organizations may play a part in the organization or operation of specialized clinics reviewed in previous chapters. Thus, associations of military veterans have long supported the extension of health services by the federal Veterans Administration. Likewise, parent teacher associations often give direct assistance in the operation or extension of clinics for school children. In a detailed investigation of all types of organizations involved in the support or provision of health services in one rural American county as far back as 1948, some 128 local civic and social associations were identified.[49] With the free-wheeling spirit of voluntary organizations in America, countless numbers of them play a part in supporting the operation of established clinics or initiating new types of clinics, when special health needs are perceived.

SPECIALLY SPONSORED CLINICS IN LOS ANGELES COUNTY

The bewildering picture of specially sponsored clinics, governmental and voluntary, observed nationally is replicated in Los Angeles County. As one would expect in a metropolitan area, there are numerous local units of organized ambulatory health care representative of each of the main special sponsorships discussed earlier in this chapter as well as in Chapter 9.

The information offered here is, in large part, a summary of the findings of two field studies made in 1972 and 1973 of operating agencies. The 1973 study examined 73 clinics operated by 130 governmental agencies; these agencies were identified from several previously published compendia and surveys.[50-52] The 1972 study was concerned with special voluntary agencies; these were much more numerous, and detailed data were gathered on a sample of 43 from a county universe of 350 such agencies. The latter agencies were identified from the same sources as those just cited, plus telephone directories and one other local survey.[53] On selected topics, more recent information also was gathered from sources indicated below. The several types of specially sponsored clinics in Los Angeles County will be discussed in the same sequence as that followed in reviewing the national scene.

Clinics for Federal Beneficiaries

As the major metropolitan area in the southwestern part of the United States, Los Angeles County is the site of several clinics intended for special beneficiaries of the federal government.

Long Beach, the second largest city in the county, served as a U.S. Navy base during World War II, and in 1967 the Long Beach Naval Hospital was opened. The hospital outpatient department provides ambulatory care for naval personnel, but there is a separate freestanding Long Beach Branch Dispensary that serves predominantly the dependents of these personnel. This is a large, well-equipped clinic, staffed with full-time salaried naval medical officers and ancillary personnel for laboratory, x-ray, and physiotherapy services. Scheduled sessions are offered in pediatrics, psychiatry, minor surgery, general adult medicine, allergy, and other special fields. The dispensary is open all regular working hours of the week and provides for emergency service at any time. In 1972 it provided 57,200 patient-visits, or about 225 per workday.

The U.S. Army also maintains in the county an Armed Forces Examining and Entry Station. This unit does not provide medical care, but medical officers in it examine candidates for any branch of the military services. About 150 men and 5 to 10 women are examined per weekday, in a somewhat assemblyline style. Thus, ancillary personnel handle vision testing, chest x-rays, blood counts, urinalyses, etc. One physician takes medical histories, a second physician does the physical examination, and a third discusses the findings with the candidate and makes the decision on medical qualification for military service. About 20 to 25 percent of persons are medically disqualified. While no followup is done on rejected candidates, this military procedure may serve as a screening program detecting unrecognized disease in young adults.

The U.S. Public Health Service (USPHS) maintains an ambulatory care clinic at San Pedro, a port town in Los Angeles County. It is located on the second floor of a local post office in somewhat modest quarters, but is well supplied with drugs and medical equipment. In addition to serving merchant seamen it serves military personnel and their dependents. In 1971 the San Pedro Clinic had 68,000 visits from 23,500 different patients. The recent trend in utilization, however, has been declining.

Also operated by the USPHS at the San Pedro port is the Los Angeles Quarantine Station. Perhaps this unit should not be considered a clinic, since its function is simply to screen ship passengers arriving from foreign countries. These checks are done by paramedical personnel trained only to identify quarantinable communicable disease. Thus, in 1972 some 650,000 arriving passengers were checked; of these, about one percent may be detained for a further screening by a physician—not a PHS officer, but a nearby private physician on contract. It is noteworthy that this quarantine unit is linked administratively to the USPHS Center for Disease Control (formerly the Communicable Disease Center) in Atlanta, Georgia.

Still another facility of this type is a freestanding clinic of the Veterans Administration. This is a relatively large clinic in downtown Los Angeles, some 15 miles from the nearest VA Hospital. It is open all working days and is staffed by full-time salaried VA physicians; as many as 28 specialty sessions are scheduled each week, including a gynecology service. In 1972, nearly 125,000 patient visits were made to this VA facility, a substantial proportion of these being low-income veterans whose ailments were not connected with military service. (It will be recalled that since 1973, VA regulations have been modified to permit ambulatory as well as hospital care to veterans with nonservice-connected conditions, on the grounds that such earlier attention might avert the need for hospital admission. This policy change, in fact, was being tested at the Los Angeles VA Outpatient Clinic in 1972 on a pilot basis.)

Other smaller clinics for federal beneficiaries in Los Angeles County include a U.S. Air Force Clinic, a U.S. Army Dental Clinic, and the clinic of the Federal Correction Institute (with 600 male and 150 female inmates) on Terminal Island, which is part of the county. This federal prison is staffed with four salaried physicians (of whom two are psychiatrists), two psychologists, two dentists, two nurses, and eight medical assistants.

The financial support of all these federal programs for ambulatory care is from national general revenues. Unlike many other types of clinics reviewed in this chapter, there are no personal payments chargeable for any service.

Federally Financed and Locally Sponsored Clinics

Since Los Angeles County was the scene of a particularly distressing urban riot in 1965, it attracted support from the federal Office of Economic Opportunity for one of the first neighborhood health centers in the nation. The South Central Multi-purpose Health Services Center (later named the Watts Health

Center), opened in 1967, was constructed and also operated with federal funds. The grants were made initially to the University of Southern California, with an advisory board composed almost entirely of residents (predominantly black) of the local area. Of some 60,000 people living in the precisely defined geographic area, an estimated 38,000 were eligible to use the Center free of charge; the balance could use it for small fees.

The scope of ambulatory services at the Watts Health Center is remarkably broad. In addition to a full array of medical specialists, full-time or part-time, the staff includes dentists, health educators, social workers, nurses, nutritionists, and neighborhood health agents; the latter are mainly young women from the local area, trained briefly to explain to families the services offered. In order to achieve good personal relationships with patients, the personnel are organized into three or four multidisciplinary teams; each new patient is assigned to one of the teams. These teams are available during regular working hours of the week, and at all times there is a walk-in basic care service for first aid.

During 1971, some 14,000 persons from the area (23 percent of the defined population) made use of the health center. A high proportion of local residents were covered by the Medicaid program, which entitled them to service from private doctors; yet in spite of the impressive range of services at this organized facility, many of these people still preferred the atmosphere of a private medical office or were loyal to their physician from past experience. The 14,000 patients had about 105,000 visits with a primary care provider (physician, dentist, or nurse) during the year, or 7.5 contacts per patient. Thus, for the minority of local persons who make use of the Watts Health Center, the rate of utilization is rather high. The federal grant to support these services in 1971 was $5.5 million, which was supplemented by fees payable for patients who were covered by the Medicare or Medicaid programs.

In later years, the Watts Health Center, faced with declining federal grant support, responded by attempting to enroll its regular users into a prepayment plan.[54] Accordingly in 1972, it changed its name once again to the Watts Health Foundation, starting enrollment of people on a prepaid basis in 1973. In so doing, persons from a wider geographic area than that served by the original neighborhood health center could enroll. For persons eligible under Medicaid who chose this pattern of health service, the state government program would pay the insurance premiums; other people, however, could also enroll by paying the premiums personally. In addition, nonenrolled low-income people were still free to use the health center; after 1977, however, they were charged small fees scaled according to their incomes. To accommodate the greater clientele, a second ambulatory care facility was constructed (with federal funds) and two additional structures were rented from branch clinics.

By 1979, the population served by the Watts Health foundation during a year was about 35,000. These consisted of the following types of persons:

Medicaid beneficiaries (prepaid)	12,000
Private enrollees (prepaid)	1,000
Medicaid beneficiaries (through fee-for-service)	4,000
Other poor persons (through sliding scale of personal payments)	18,000
All users during one year	35,000

Source: Clyde Oden, Director of the Watts Health Foundation, Los Angeles, 1979, personal communication.

The fees charged to non-Medicaid persons of low income were typically low (about $2 per visit). Altogether there were about 180,000 patient visits per year at the four sites of the Watts Health Foundation. Funds to finance all these services were derived from several sources. As noted earlier, in 1973 the federal government agency responsible for neighborhood health centers had been changed from the Office of Economic Opportunity (OEO) to the Department of Health, Education, and Welfare (HEW). Thus, the sources of financial support in 1979 were as follows:

Federal HEW Grant	$4,200,000
Prepaid Amounts from Medicaid	6,800,000
Medicaid fees	450,000
Privately paid fees	550,000
Total	$12,000,000

Source: Clyde Oden, Director of the Watts Health Foundation, Los Angeles, 1979, personal communication.

In addition to the health centers operated by the Watts Health Foundation, ambulatory care facilities now known as "community health centers," were financed substantially by federal grants to two other organizations in Los Angeles County. These were the Northeast Valley Health Corporation and the East Los Angeles Health Task Force. The latter organization served persons mainly of Hispanic background, and the former, like the Watts Foundation, had predominantly black members. Both of these programs provided general ambulatory health services to low-income people, either on a prepaid or a fee-for-service basis, and both received payments also from either the Medicaid program or from the individual. In all three programs with community health centers, the physicians were paid predominantly part-time salaries, although some were full-time.

Another activity financed by the federal OEO, with local projects in Los Angeles County, was the Headstart Program. Since its objectives were mainly educational development for preschool children (usually four years of age) from poor families, it has not usually been considered a health program, but a health component was included. Each child enrolled received a screening examination from a public health nurse on the staff of the program, and the child was referred for appropriate care to a private physician or dentist. In Los Angeles County there were 18 Headstart Program sites in the early 1970s.

At each site, there was a full-time public health nurse and also consultative relations with a private pediatrician. Enrollments of children varied among the local sites from about 150 to 600. Approximately half of the children were from Medicaid-eligible families. For them, the services of private physicians were paid for by the Medicaid program, but for other children, medical costs were met by the OEO grant; for each such child $50 per year was budgeted for medical purposes. Thus, the Headstart Program did not operate clinics in the usual sense, but it included organized arrangements leading to the provision of medical examinations and treatment.

Certain other federally financed ambulatory care centers providing fairly comprehensive services in Los Angeles County may be noted, even though the local sponsorship has been by long-established agencies. Thus, the federal Department of Housing and Urban Development (HUD) supported three "model cities" programs in the 1970s, under which new housing was constructed or old housing was improved in slum areas. In the county an Urban Affairs Department was established to receive HUD grants and supervise the program. Separate health facilities, however, were not established. Instead, the services of the existing district health centers of the Los Angeles County Health Department were strengthened; extra funds were granted to this department to support stronger programs in the model cities areas. Thus, three selected district health centers were enabled to offer: (a) general primary health care clinic sessions, (b) expanded dental care, (c) more comprehensive maternal and child health services (including treatment of sick babies), and (d) services for drug abuse patients.

Finally, the specialized federal Maternal and Infant Care (MIC) and the Children and Youth (C and Y) programs, authorized in 1963 and 1965, supported three special projects in Los Angeles County. Two comprehensive MIC clinics were established in two of the district health centers of the county health department—one in a predominantly black population area, and the other in a predominantly Hispanic population area. A C and Y clinic was established as a satellite to the Los Angeles County/University of Southern California Hospital, a large public facility under the county government.

In all these federally financed and locally sponsored programs a social function is served that may sometimes be overlooked. This is simply to provide employment for local low-income families. Many jobs in community outreach work, in clerical and maintenance services, etc. can be filled by unemployed people with limited skills. At the same time, the participation of local minority ethnic groups in the administration of these programs and on policy-making or advisory boards, heightens their general self-respect and personal dignity.

Other State and Local Government Agencies

In Los Angeles county one finds clinics of virtually all the other types of state and local public agencies observed throughout the nation—clinics for patients with mental disorders, for rehabilitation, for prisoners, and for others.

For mental conditions, the Los Angeles County Department of Mental Health was established—separate from the general County Department of Health—in 1960. In September 1972, for purposes of coordination and efficiency, these two county agencies, along with the County Department of Hospitals, were consolidated under a unified County Department of Health Services. In 1977, however, reflecting the special requirements and legal aspects of services for the mentally ill, the County Department of Mental Health was re-established as a separate agency. Perhaps contributing to this independent role of the mental health services was California state legislation of 1957 (the Short-Doyle Mental Health Services Act) providing for state grants to the counties for operation of mental health clinics and other out-of-hospital activities in this field.

Then in 1969, this state law was amended (the Lanterman-Petris-Short Act) to encourage even further development of both ambulatory and inpatient psychiatric care in the counties, with the specific objective of reducing the large census of patients in state mental hospitals.[55] The strategy was for the state to provide 90 percent financial support for a range of mental health services in the counties, but also to require the counties to reimburse the state government for 10 percent of the costs of any patients from the county who had to be admitted to and kept in state mental hospitals. Moreover, the state law required that no patient could be admitted to a state mental institution unless he or she had been previously examined in a county mental health facility. As a result of this strategy, the patients in California state mental hospitals declined from 36,000 around 1960 to 7,200 in 1972.[56]

Thanks to this generous financial support from the state government, the Los Angeles County Department of Mental Health in the early 1970s came to operate 12 "regional mental health centers (RMHC)." These are geographically distributed to be reasonably accessible to the entire population of this county of more than seven million people. Although theoretically open to everyone in their catchment areas, these clinics are intended largely for low-income patients; anyone who is able to afford private psychiatric care is seen only once and then referred to a private psychiatrist or psychologist.

Each of the county's RMHCs is staffed with one or more psychiatrists (usually part-time), psychologists, psychiatric social workers, psychiatric aides, and clerks. The services provided by each center include: (a) psychiatric emergency care, involving response by a team of personnel to episodes suggesting serious psychosis; the team is often summoned by the police, goes to see the patient, and decides whether immediate hospitalization or some other action is required; (b) crisis intervention, for any patient who comes with an acute mental problem for help; these patients may be provided psychotherapy in small groups or individually, for an average of six to eight 45-minute sessions per case; (c) followup of patients discharged from mental hospitals; periodic visits are intended to monitor and help the patient readjust to community life; and (d) medication service to patients for whom psychotropic drugs (tranquilizers, antidepressants, etc.) have been prescribed. Beyond these four basic functions, RMHC staff provide consultation to other local agencies and maintain liaison with various nongovernmental psychiatric programs with which the county agency has contracts.

The features of one RMHC may illustrate the general pattern of these clinics, although no two are exactly alike. Its staff had 16 professionally trained personnel, including special psychiatric nurses, as well as psychiatrists, psychologists, and social workers. The center is intended to serve a surrounding population of 36,000, most of whom are black, Hispanic, or disaffected youth. The average monthly caseload has been 538 patients, including 188 seen for the first time that month; about half the patients are estimated to require long-term service. Some 40 percent have been previously treated in a mental hospital. About 30 percent of new patients have posed threats of suicide, so that effective crisis intervention has high priority; drug addiction is another important problem in the population served. One may calculate a rough caseload of 34 patients per professional person in this RMHC, but this understates the work done. In addition, there is a high volume of mental health counseling by telephone. There are numerous relationships to maintain with other agencies under contract to render mental health services, and everyone has well-defined administrative responsibilities.

In 1972, the 12 RMHCs in Los Angeles County reported a total of 176,414 patient visits, and the volume was rising rapidly each year. Beyond this were another 332,792 psychiatric ambulatory patient visits provided by other agencies (including general hospital outpatient departments, voluntary psychiatric clinics, etc.) with which the county department of mental health had contracts or with which it jointly operated certain programs. In fact, the cost of the latter types of services was much greater than that of operating the 12 RMHCs. The budget of the entire county mental health program in 1973 exceeded $85 million, with a percentage distribution for various purposes as follows:

Mental Health Program	Percent
Regional mental health centers	10
Programs jointly operated with other agencies	28
Contractual services purchased	14
Hospitalization of county residents in state mental hospitals	33

Mental Health Program	Percent
Central county office administration	3
Miscellaneous and unallocated	12

Source: Los Angeles County Department of Mental Health, unpublished data, 1973.

Beyond this extensive local governmental mental health program, there are further services furnished in Los Angeles County directly by the California State Department of Mental Hygiene. In order to cope with the large number of patients being discharged from state mental hospitals or institutions for the mentally retarded in the early 1970s—some 20,000 per year with residence in Los Angeles County—the state agency has established 11 district offices in the county. These offices come under the direction of the Alternate Care Services Unit (ACSU) in the State Department of Mental Hygiene, and their major purpose is to monitor patients discharged from state institutions, so as to prevent the need for readmission. Each ACSU district office is staffed with a psychiatric social worker; some also have a public health nurse.

Many mentally ill or retarded patients discharged from state institutions cannot return to a normal home environment, and must be placed in other residential arrangements—local "board and care facilities," foster homes, or skilled nursing homes. It is estimated that about 25 percent of discharged patients still require such a protective setting. For the year 1972, the caseload of the 11 state ACSU district offices in Los Angeles County was 5,430 persons with mental illness and 2,656 mentally retarded persons. The ACSU social workers carry out their responsibilities by liaison with the county's RMHCs, as well as with other agencies that provide vocational training, sheltered workshops, public assistance, legal advice, and general medical care.

A third type of mental health facility in Los Angeles County providing ambulatory care, largely through governmental financing, are the federally funded Community Mental Health Centers (CMHC). The scope of services that must be furnished by CMHCs has been discussed in Chapter 9, and there are 11 such facilities. Of these, nine are sponsored by established hospitals or other facilities discussed elsewhere in this volume, and two are freestanding. Both of these are located in poverty districts and were initiated as a direct result of the federal grant program. One of these, the Central City CMHC serves an area with about 100,000 people, nearly all of whom are black.

Four of the five basic mandated services are furnished at the Central City CMHC, but the fifth—hospitalization—is provided through agreements with other hospitals. In addition, through support by supplementary federal grants there are: a child advocacy program, a counseling service for the mentally retarded, a program for rehabilitation of drug addicts (including special housing arrangements), assistance to ex-convicts, an alcoholism rehabilitation program, and a general community service program that includes vocational guidance, advice to the aged, and welfare counseling. During one year in the early 1970s, this CMHC had some 7,100 patient visits specifically for psychotherapy alone.

Other governmentally organized ambulatory psychiatric services in Los Angeles county may be mentioned briefly. The County Probation Department, concerned mainly with youthful offenders (juvenile delinquents), operates a special psychiatric clinic; here about 300 young people are examined each month, and those for whom psychotherapy would be considered helpful are referred elsewhere for service. There is a Narcotics Prevention Project, organized by a group of ex-addicts aided by a psychologist, but established through the support of three federal agencies—the National Institute of Mental Health, the OEO, and the model cities program of the HUD. This project was carrying an average caseload of 400 persons in the early 1970s, and its services included supportive counseling and referral to certain hospitals for medical detoxification.

Problems of alcoholism are tackled largely by nongovernmental groups (such as Alcoholics Anonymous), but the Alcoholism Counseling Project in a central-city black population area was established through a federal OEO grant in 1971. General counseling is given to alcoholics, and health education is carried out in the community. Visits are made to alcoholic patients in the hospital and in their homes. Referrals are made to psychiatric clinics and to various branches of Alcoholics Anonymous.

For rehabilitation of the physically disabled, the Los Angeles County Department of Hospitals (before its consolidation with other agencies into the County Department of Health Services) administered the Crippled Children's Service (CCS) in this county, by delegation from the state government. Any surgical correction of a child's defect under this program is done by approved private physicians in community hospitals, with payment made by the CCS authority. For initial examination and diagnosis of cases, however, and for continued physical and occupational therapy, the CCS program operates 22 clinics. Known as "medical treatment units" (MTU), these clinics are located in elementary school buildings throughout the county. Having such locations, a handicapped child can get necessary rehabilitative treatment with very little interruption of school attendance. Pediatricians and orthopedists staff these MTU clinics on a part-time sessional basis, but the physical and occupational therapists work full-time.

Another form of rehabilitation is provided at three Speech and Hearing Clinics, operated on campuses of the California State University (CSU) system in the county; these are at the CSU-Long Beach, the CSU-Northridge, and CSU-Los Angeles campuses. These serve the double function of helping in the education of speech therapists and audiologists, while also providing clinical service to patients with speech and/or hearing problems. Persons of any income level are welcome at these clinics, and charges are made on a sliding scale.

The CSU-Long Beach clinic is the largest of the three, with a caseload at any one time of 200 to 275 patients. The typical patient is seen for several weeks, coming for two half-hour sessions per week. The CSU-Long Beach program also operates an off-campus branch clinic in a rented store located in a poverty neighborhood.

Indirectly related to rehabilitation is a clinic in Los Angeles maintained by the California Department of Industrial Relations, for assessment of disability in workers injured on the job. Physicians employed by this department examine workers, about whom there are claims contested under the state workmen's compensation program; these doctors make final judgment on the degree of disability incurred, and also make recommendations on appropriate rehabilitation.

With respect to ambulatory services for prisoners, there are a variety of clinics in Los Angeles County, under state and local governments. Under state authority, there is a Parole Outpatient Clinic operated by the California Department of Corrections; this is essentially for helping parolees with mental and emotional problems. There are, in addition, 11 subclinics throughout the county and nearby, located at the offices of the state Adult Parole Authority. The staffs consist of psychologists and psychiatric social workers, and most patients are referred to the clinics by probation officers. The typical patient is seen once a week, and therapy may continue for a year or more, even after the expiration of the parole period. The California Youth Authority also provides medical clinic services for young offenders at two places in the county.

The Los Angeles County Sheriff's Department operates five prisons, with a total capacity of 9,300 inmates. At least one nurse is stationed at each prison, and there is a full-time medical director supervising the services provided by part-time visiting physicians. At the largest facility, the Men's Central Jail (3,000 inmate capacity), a general medical examination including chest x-ray and laboratory tests, is done on all new prisoners. "Daily sick call" permits the inmate to see a nurse, who decides whether the patient should be examined by the doctor. During the daytime hours several physicians are on duty, and at night one physician is also on hand. For this 3,000 inmate jail there is an infirmary with 300 beds. In 1972 the entire country prison system reported 276,000 patient visits.

The Los Angeles City Police Department maintains 13 local jails to accommodate up to about 2,000 offenders with short sentences. At the two largest jails there are medical stations staffed by full-time physicians. At the 11 smaller jails a registered nurse makes daily rounds to inquire about any ailments; occasionally physicians also make such rounds. Any prisoner with a serious medical problem is taken to a nearby contract hospital or to the large Los Angeles County General Hospital. The two city jails reported a total of 63,700 clinic visits in 1972.

Other small health-related programs, connected with the law enforcement field, include a family counseling service attached to the Superior Court of Los Angeles County. There is also a crisis intervention counselling clinic for youthful offenders in Pacoima, a low-income community. The Pacoima program is known as the Juvenile Rehabilitation Service (JRS) and is financed by a grant from the federal Department of Justice funneled through the California Council on Criminal Justice. The counseling help at the JRS is given by relatively young black people, rather than by trained psychiatric personnel.

Still other ambulatory health services sponsored by state or local governments may be identified in Los Angeles County. The Los Angeles City government had operated a "receiving hospital" for emergency accident cases since 1890. After the county public hospitals were established, with links to medical schools and much better staffing and equipment, use of the receiving hospital declined and the institution gradually deteriorated. Around 1970, all inpatient care was terminated and the facility was converted into the central receiving clinic. Although "walk in" patients are given first aid and then referred elsewhere, the clinic now serves mainly as an occupational health unit for the Los Angeles City government. New city employees are given preemployment examinations here, compensable injuries of a city employee are treated, and medical screening is done on persons arrested by the city police before they are imprisoned.

Another emergency clinic has been maintained by the city of Pasadena since 1925. At this time, emergency services were not available in local hospitals, so that the local government organized this City of Pasadena Emergency Center. Attached to it are two ambulances with suitable equipment. A full-time medical director and several part-time physicians staff the clinic, along with nurses and other personnel. As the outpatient departments of two local general hospitals have developed, the utilization rate of the emergency center has declined, but in 1972 it was still providing clinic visits or ambulance calls for 10,700 cases. The majority of these were not true emergencies, but essentially primary care for low-income people who could not afford or could not obtain the services of a private doctor. Small fees, nevertheless, are collected from patients who are willing to pay.

Family planning (FP) services are provided at many clinics, throughout Los Angeles County. In order to coordinate the allocation and use of federal grant funds in this field, the Los Angeles Regional Family Planning Council (LARFPC) was organized in 1968.[57] Since FP clinics were intended mainly for low-income persons, the U.S. OEO granted the money necessary to establish this council. In the 1970s there were 16 entities sponsoring FP clinics. All but one of these were associated with hospitals, health departments, general community health centers, or other organized units for ambulatory care, discussed elsewhere in this volume.

One FP program in the county, however, may be considered a specially sponsored governmental clinic, as defined in this chapter. The sponsoring body is a consortium of three low-income municipalities—Compton, Willowbrook, and Enterprise. These three local government units established a Community Action Agency (CAA) with the aid of a grant from the federal OEO. Among other things, this CAA conducted an Outreach Family Planning Program. The program is unusual in that it does not furnish direct FP clinical services to women or men, but devotes its main effort to sending outreach workers to the homes of poor people in order to urge them to come to the local project office, where they receive counseling on contraception as well as other matters (such as applying for public assistance or obtaining food stamps). To obtain direct FP service, the client is referred to the outpatient clinic of one of the county public hospitals or one of the health department's district health centers.

Voluntary Health Agencies

As noted earlier, the numbers and variety of voluntary health agencies in Los Angeles County are very great; detailed information was gathered in 1972 on only a sample of 43 out of 350 agencies that appeared to be providing some direct ambulatory health service. The great majority (32) of the 43 projects in the sample proved to be in the category of "disease-specific voluntary agencies," as defined earlier in this chapter.

Somewhat surprising, however, was the finding that only 6 of the 32 disease-specific agencies were local chapters of a national voluntary agency (such as the ACS or the National Society for the Prevention of Blindness). The balance were essentially autonomous local organizations that had developed to tackle specific diseases; an especially large share of these were concerned with mental disorders or related fields. Several of the latter were identified with certain localities in the county—such as the Pomona Valley Hearing Society or the Pasadena Child Guidance Center—or with individuals being memorialized— such as the John Tracy Clinic (for deaf children) or the Marianne Frostig Center (for educational therapy).

Another noteworthy feature of the sample was that the great majority of the voluntary agencies raised the funds for their operation independently; only 11 (25 percent) participated in the local community fund-raising program, the county "United Way" campaign. This coordinated effort raises money for about 265 social welfare and health agencies in Los Angeles County—classified into ten categories.[58] Of these ten, two are identified as health-related ("health and therapy services" and "mental health services"), and these include 48 agencies.

It is also worth noting that about two-thirds of the agencies received fees for health services rendered in their clinics, either from the patient directly or from government agencies (usually on behalf of indigent persons). Related to this was the finding that only 6 of the 43 agencies studied limited their clinic services to patients of low income (even though, in practice, very few higher income patients seek care at most of these clinics). Budget analyses showed that in all the local clinic projects studied, the lion's share of expenditures went to support personnel, except in the free clinics, discussed below.

Access to almost all the voluntary clinics was unrestricted, in the sense that no formal referral of the patient was required; only three of the agencies required such referral. Nevertheless, in eight of the agencies, referral to the clinic by a private physician, a school, or a social welfare authority was the usual path of entry. Nine of the 43 voluntary agencies, furthermore, facilitated access to their services by having clinics at two or more locations; the ACS chapter, in fact, had clinics at twelve locations and the Crippled Children's Society at seven.

Although most of the clinics of disease-specific voluntary agencies had physicians, usually part-time, on their staffs, the scope of services offered was seldom comprehensive. Typically services were supportive or auxiliary to the diagnosis and treatment by a physician. Thus the Crippled Children's Society, which served adults as well in 1972, offered speech evaluation and speech therapy, social work counseling, psychological testing, aid in obtaining prosthetic appliances, vocational therapy, etc. at its seven clinic locations; it is evidently assumed that basic treatment services, such as orthopedic surgery or other types of physicians' care, would be obtained through other private or public channels.

As noted above, voluntary agencies operating mental health clinics appear to be particularly well developed in Los Angeles County. A directory of ambulatory psychiatric services in Los Angeles County for 1979 lists 72 clinics under voluntary auspices (only 4 or 5 of which were in hospital outpatient departments).[59] About half of these were limited to children or adolescents; the remainder served adults exclusively or adults and children. This was outside of numerous voluntary (and governmental) clinics or clubs in the county limited to the problems of alcoholism or drug abuse.[60]

FP was the main focus of two voluntary agencies in the 1972 study, and one of these (Family Planning Centers of Los Angeles) operated seven clinics. In addition to information and devices on contraception, these clinics offered sex education and premarital and marital counseling. In the previous year these clinics had over 24,000 client visits, divided ethnically among blacks (40 percent), Hispanic (20 percent), and whites (40 percent). The other FP agency (Planned Parenthood World Population, Los Angeles) offered, in addition, referrals for abortion to women with unwanted pregnancies; its services were offered at one location, where nearly 10,000 visits were made per year. The women coming to this clinic, by contrast with those visiting the other agency's clinics, were 71 percent white.

Free clinics, it will be recalled, were first launched in California, so that it is not surprising to find many of them in Los Angeles County. In the 1972 study sample, there were eight free clinics, including both the street and the family types, as defined earlier in this chapter. All of these clinics offered, in addition to medical services, counseling on other problems, such as legal difficulties, employment, or family interpersonal problems. One of the free clinics, located in Long Beach, was unusual in maintaining statistics on medical visits; these amounted to nearly 1,200 per month or about 14,000 per year.

Although all of the free clinics reported financial difficulties in 1972, they managed to survive and even expand, at least until 1975. In that year, a published directory listed 18 free clinics in Los Angeles County. While the movement had been started by white (mostly middle-class) youth, these included in 1975 several clinics oriented mainly to Hispanic youth and families, to black youth, to American Indians, and two clinics identified as serving "gay" or homosexual patients.[61] Some indication of the viability of free clinics, at least in this region, was the formation in 1974 of the Southern California Council of Free Clinics; the council, moreover, was supported by a governmental grant from the California Regional Medical Program (RMP) for Heart Disease, Cancer, and Stroke. In emulation of the free clinics, it may also be recalled that the Los Angeles County Department of Health established a network of youth clinics with similar features.

In addition to the free clinics, there were four feminist women's clinics in Los Angeles County in 1975. All of these gave a wide variety of services including referrals for abortions, but one seemed to specialize in the outpatient performance of legal abortions; the latter were done by physicians, and fees were payable on a sliding scale.

In the discussion of voluntary health agencies on the national scene, it was observed that these agencies seldom die. Even if their functions are assumed by governmental agencies, the voluntary group usually finds another related objective to which its energies may be devoted. This observation was strikingly confirmed in Los Angeles County. Although most of the 43 agencies studied in 1972 reported financial problems, not one responded negatively to a question about its future role. Of the 43 agencies, 26 reported that their clinic caseloads were increasing, and another 12 indicated that these had stabilized because the clinic capacities had been reached. In the late 1970s, one of the nationally affiliated disease-specific voluntary agencies terminated its affiliation, but this led to no diminution of its local services; the organization and its several clinics simply continued under another name, and services may even have expanded.

Constraints on local tax collections and government expenditures created serious problems for all types of governmental medical services in California in the late 1970s.[62] In this environment, it seems likely that voluntary health agencies, offering personal health services, may be expected to play an even larger role in the future.

NOTES

1. Gunn, Selskar M., and Philip S. Platt, *Voluntary Health Agencies: An Interpretive Study* (New York: The Ronald Press Co., 1945).

2. Hamlin, Robert H., *Voluntary Health and Welfare Agencies in the United States* (New York: The Schoolmaster's Press, 1961), p. 1.

3. Ibid., pp. 84–87.

4. Wilner, Daniel L.; R. P. Walkley; and E. J. O'Neill, *Introduction to Public Health* (7th edition) (New York: Macmillan Co., 1978), p. 57.

5. American Cancer Society, *Annual Report 1978* (New York: 1978), p. 20.

6. National Multiple Sclerosis Society, *1978 Annual Report* (New York), p. 16.

7. National Easter Seal Society for Crippled Children and Adults, *1978 Annual Report* (Chicago, Ill.: 1978), p. 11.

8. National Easter Seal Society for Crippled Children and Adults, *Directory of Easter Seal Direct Services 1977–78 Edition* (Chicago, Ill.: 1978), pp. 145–146.

9. The National Foundation March of Dimes, *Annual Report 1979* (New York), pp. 30–32.

10. American Heart Association, *Annual Report 1978* (Dallas, Tex.: 1979).

11. Guttmacher, A. F., *Babies by Choice or by Chance* (Garden City, N.Y.: Doubieday, 1959).

12. U.S. Office of Economic Opportunity, *Need for Subsidized Family Planning Services: United States, Each State and County, 1968* (Washington: 1969).

13. Torres, Aida, "Organized Family Planning Services in the United States, 1968–1976," *Family Planning Perspectives* 10 (1978): 83–88.

14. National Institute of Mental Health, Division of Biometry and Epidemiology, (Washington, D.C.: January 1980), unpublished data.

15. Alcohol, Drug Abuse, and Mental Health Administration, Office of Program Planning and Coordination, *The Alcohol, Drug Abuse, and Mental Health National Data Book* (Washington: December 1979, unpublished report), p. 52.

16. Ibid., p. 23.

17. Mental Health Association, *Annual Report for the Year 1978* (Arlington, Va.: 1979), p. 5.

18. American Red Cross, *Service Modeled for the Future: Annual Report 1979* (Washington: 1979).

19. Salvation Army, *Changing the World One Life at a Time,* leaflet distributed by The Salvation Army, Los Angeles, California Chapter, 1980.

20. Hollis, Florence, *Casework: A Psychosocial Therapy* (New York: Random House, 1964).

21. Schwartz, Jerome L., "First National Survey of Free Medical Clinics 1967–69," *HSMHA Health Reports* 86 (1971): 775–787.

22. Turner, Irene R., "Free Health Centers: A New Concept?" *American Journal of Public Health* 62 (1972): 1348–1353.

23. Taylor, Rosemary C. R., "Alternative Services: The Case of Free Clinics," *International Journal of Health Services* 9 (1979): 227–253.

24. Smith, David, and D. Bentel, "A New Phenomenon has appeared on the American Health Care Scene—the free clinic, directed and operated by the people who use it, with small or no charges, no red tape, and a nonjudgmental climate," *California's Health* April 1970, pp. 1–4.

25. Schwartz, Jerome L., "Preliminary Observations of Free Clinics" in D. E. Smith, D. J. Bentel, and J. L. Schwarts, eds. *The Free Clinic: A Community Approach to Health Care and Drug Abuse* (Beloit, Wis.: Stash Press, 1971), pp. 144–206.

26. Ibid., p. 147.

27. Schatz, Bernard E., "Free Clinic Patient Characteristics," *American Journal of Public Health* 62 (1972): 1354–1363.

28. California Medical Association, "Free Clinics in California, 1971," *Socio-Economic Report,* October 1971.

29. Simborg, M. B., "Free Clinics," *New England Journal of Medicine* 284 (1971): 159.

30. Schwartz, Jerome L., "Sources of Funding for Free Clinics and Neighborhood Medical Programs," in D. E. Smith, D. J. Bentel, and J. L. Schwartz, eds., pp. 46–56.

31. Williams, Frank G., *An Exploratory Descriptive Study of Free Medical Clinics* (Iowa City, Ia.: University of Iowa, July 1972).

32. Corner, Rosemary et al., "Appraisal of Health Care Delivery in a Free Clinic," *Health Services Reports* 87 (1972): 727–733.

33. Taylor, Rosemary C. R., "Alternative Services."

34. Hayes-Bautista, David, Berkeley California: August 1980, personal communication.

35. Schwartz, Jerome, Davis, California; August 1980, personal communication.

36. Hayes-Bautista, David, "Marginal Health Care Organizations," *Proceedings of the 1978 Health Forum* (San Antonio, Tex.: Trinity University, 1979), pp. 79–98.

37. Women's Health Forum, "Women's Health Movement, Where Are We Now?" *Health Right* 1, Issue L, Fall 1974, p. 1.

38. Marieskind, Helen, *Gynaecologocal Services: Their Historical Relationship to the Women's Movement with Recent Experience of Self-Help Clinics and Other Delivery Modes* (unpublished dissertation) (Los Angeles: University of California, School of Public Health, 1976), p. 209. See also: Marieskind, Helen, "The Women's Health Movement," *International Journal of Health Services* 5 (1975): 217–223.

39. Downer, Carol, ed., *Women's Health in Women's Hands* (Los Angeles, Calif.: Federation of Feminist Women's Health Centers, 1980).

40. Reed, Louis S., *The Healing Cults: A Study of Sectarian Medical Practice: Its Extent, Causes, and Control* (Committee on the Costs of Medical Care, Publ. No. 16) (Chicago: University of Chicago Press, 1932).

41. Weeks, Lewis E., and R. A. De Vries, "Wholistic Health Centers: Where Are They Going?" *Inquiry,* 15 (1978): 3–9.

42. Kaslof, Leslie, *Wholistic Dimensions in Healing* (New York: Doubleday & Co., 1978).

43. Newport, John, "An Investigation of Organizational Characteristics and Service Orientations of Emerging Holistic Health Center Models, and Potential Ramifications Affecting Mainstream Care," (unpublished dissertation proposal) (Los Angeles: University of California School of Public Health, 1978).

44. Weinerman, E. R., "Group Practice and Union Health Centers," in *National Conference on Labor Health Services: Papers and Proceedings* (Washington: American Labor Health Association, 1958), p. 68.

45. Chamberlain, R. W., and J. F. Radebaugh, "Delivery of Primary Care—Union Style," *New England Journal of Medicine* 294 (1976): 641–645.

46. Munts, Raymond, *Bargaining for Health: Labor Unions, Health Insurance, and Medical Care* (Madison, Wis.: University of Wisconsin Press, 1967).

47. Wetherille, Rhona L., and Jean M. Nordby, *A Census of HMOs* (Minneapolis: Minn.: Inter-Study, July 1975), p. 14.

48. Shadid, Michael, *A Doctor for the People* (New York: Vanguard Press, 1939).

49. Roemer, Milton I., and E. A. Wilson, *Organized Health Services in a County of the United States,* Public Health Service Pub. No. 197 (Washington, 1952), p. 78.

50. Los Angeles County Information and Referral Service, *Directory of Health, Welfare, Vocational, and Recreation Services in Los Angeles County,* 1971.

51. Los Angeles County Mental Health Division, *Mental Health Resources in Los Angeles County* (Los Angeles: 1972).

52. American Public Health Association, *Future Directions for Health Services: County of Los Angeles/1970* (Los Angeles: Los Angeles County Health Department, 1970).

53. Cauffman, Joy G. et al., "A Survey of Health Information and Referral Services within Los Angeles County" (Los Angeles: University of Southern California, School of Medicine, 1972), (unpublished report).

54. Clyde Oden, Director of the Watts Health Foundation, (Los Angeles Calif.: 1979), personal communication.

55. California Department of Mental Hygiene, "Lanterman-Petris-Short: Ten Services," *Progress: California Mental Health* (Berkeley, Calif.: October 1968).

56. California Department of Mental Hygiene, "Local Communities Provide the Best Setting for Mental Health Services," *California's Health,* February 1973, p. 9.

57. Los Angeles Regional Family Planning Council, *Annual Report* (Los Angeles: February 1972).

58. The United Way Campaign, "Give Once and for All," leaflet distributed in Los Angeles County, 1979.

59. Information and Referral Services of Los Angeles County, *Psychiatric Outpatient Services in Los Angeles County,* Bulletin 45 (Los Angeles: 1979).

60. Information and Referral Services of Los Angeles County, *Info's Crisis Bulletin on Emergencies After-Hours,* (Volume 3) (Los Angeles: 1979).

61. Southern California Council of Free Clinics, *Directory-Free Clinics & Community Health Centers* (Los Angeles: 1975).

62. Lorimer, Ann, and Ruth Roemer, *Public Sector Health Services under Proposition 13—The First Year* (Los Angeles,: UCLA Health Services Research Center, processed, 1979).

Chapter 11

Clinics According to Purpose

The previous chapters have analyzed organized ambulatory health services (OAHS) in the United States, according to their principal sponsorships. We have examined the major sponsoring entities—hospitals, public health agencies, schools and colleges, industrial enterprises, physician groups—and also a great variety of more specialized governmental and voluntary bodies. It has been quite evident that services with similar objectives may be offered by clinics of diverse sponsorships.

In planning health services to meet selected needs, it is usually necessary to consider the overall availability of those services, regardless of the differing sources from which they emanate. In this chapter, therefore, we will examine a number of selected health problems and consider the clinics of differing sponsorships that address those problems. To do this for all health problems would be a formidable task. There may be value, however, in reviewing a few types of clinics found along each of the three major dimensions by which health problems may be defined. These are problems of (a) certain types of persons, (b) certain diseases, and (c) certain technical services.

CLINICS FOR CERTAIN TYPES OF PERSONS

The many special types of persons for which clinics have been organized have included almost every identifiable social and demographic characteristic. There are clinics for young and old, for industrial workers and farmers, for military and civilian personnel, for the poor and the affluent, for urban and rural people, for white-collar and blue-collar workers, and so on. To clarify this general dimension by which clinics may be analyzed, we shall consider three types of persons: the poor, children, and rural people.

Clinics for the Poor

The very origin of organized ambulatory service, in the early dispensaries of Europe and America, has come from the objective to serve the poor. The same objective, explicitly although sometimes implicitly, defines the role of many clinics today.

In hospital outpatient departments, we have seen in Chapter 4 that services are customarily categorized into three types: organized or scheduled clinics, emergency care, and referred services. The latter two types of OPD services are ordinarily considered available to persons of any income level, but organized clinic sessions are almost always intended for the poor. Unlike the other two forms of OPD services, the scheduled clinics reflect the historic origin of hospitals as a whole—as places of refuge for the poor and destitute.

Hospitals differ, of course, in the rigor with which they examine the income status of clinic patients. Social workers are now seldom engaged to apply "means tests," as in the early decades of this century, but it is common for an admissions clerk to determine a patient's eligibility (by reason of poverty) for OPD care. Some hospitals charge relatively low clinic fees on a sliding scale, varying with income level. If patients are Medicaid beneficiaries or eligible for third-party financing by other programs oriented to the poor, information is gathered so that the agency may be billed.

Unlike emergency services—offered by the great majority of American hospitals—organized clinics are operated only in a minority of hospitals; in 1977, such resources for the poor were provided in about 30 percent of the nation's 7,100 hospitals. The degree of specialization of clinics varies markedly with hospital size; as of 1977, they were provided in 24 percent of short-term general hospitals of under 25-bed capacity, compared with 81 percent of such hospitals with over 500 beds. This means that smaller hospitals in small towns and rural districts are less likely to have scheduled clinics. Even for the same hospital size, moreover, organized clinics are less likely to be provided in rural hospitals. Clinics are also more likely to be well developed in large, government-sponsored hospitals, contributing further to the advantages for low-income people in larger cities.

The multispecialty clinic sessions customary in large hospitals, particularly teaching institutions (for medical students, interns, and/or residents), create many difficulties in the medical care of the poor. It is common for the older, chronically ill patient to be under treatment in several different clinics at the same time; yet each clinic may maintain its own medical records, with little coordination among them. As we have noted in Chapter 4, some large hospitals are making special efforts to overcome this fragmentation by appointing OPD medical directors responsible for coordinating patient care. Family practice clinics also often serve a coordinating role. With their increasing rates of utilization and the complex problems of coordinated management, hospital outpatient departments have probably generated more efforts at improvement, in recent years, than any other hospital department.[1-3]

For many poor people, to whom hospitals without organized clinics but offering emergency services are accessible, the latter often are used as a source of general primary care.[4] Even though hospital emergency departments are open to patients of all income levels and they typically charge for the full cost of the service (that may be quite high), these services are used much more frequently by the poor, even for minor, nonurgent conditions, than by the well-to-do. In spite of the frequently changing doctors who staff OPD emergency services, low-income people from inner city slums often regard these clinics as their "family doctor."

Public health agencies operate numerous clinics, as discussed in Chapter 5, and they are theoretically open to everyone in a community. In practice, however, these clinics are largely patronized by the poor. Seldom is there any formal procedure for determining eligibility to use a health department clinic, but nurses or other personnel may make casual estimates of a person's economic status. If someone is judged to be moderately affluent, he or she would not be turned away, but is usually advised to seek private medical attention in the future. This is particularly the practice for pregnant women and children, who would be expected to make repeated visits to the clinic.

In health department clinics for tuberculosis or venereal disease (VD), restriction of eligibility to the poor is hardly ever implemented, even informally. Such clinics are, nevertheless, attended essentially by the poor for other reasons. These diseases in recent decades have been largely concentrated in low income groups. Furthermore, because of the seriousness and possible chronicity of such diseases (particularly VD), and the associated social stigma, almost anyone who could afford private medical care would typically seek it.

In public health clinics for diagnosis or treatment of crippled children, whose care may involve surgical procedures and/or rehabilitation, determination of low-income eligibility is often a formal process. Because of the high cost of treatment and rehabilitation of the child with a serious physical handicap, however, families of even moderate income levels may be eligible for crippled children's program services; thus, a crippled child whose family is not poor enough to qualify for Medicaid may still be referred to his program. In spite of declining U.S. birth rates, the numbers of cases served by crippled children's services have steadily climbed. In 1972 the number nationally was 513,000, compared with 492,000 in 1970.[5] Medicaid amendments, for which regulations were issued in 1972, provided financing for better means of identifying serious handicaps among low-income children; the EPSDT (Early and Periodic Screening, Diagnosis and Treatment) program authorized support for medical examinations of children from families not poor enough to qualify for Medicaid.[6]

Although the EPSDT program has been delayed in its implementation in many states, numerous patients with crippling disorders detected through it are referred to crippled children's clinics for further assessment and care.

Dental health programs in health departments involve many educational and preventive components but, insofar as they include clinics where restorative dental care is given, services are almost always limited to the poor. Most such dental clinics are intended for children and, in some cases, expectant mothers. Mental health clinics under health department auspices are usually set up in localities where low-income people live; private psychiatric care is so expensive that almost anyone who comes is accepted.

With respect to chronic diseases such as cancer or heart disorders public health agency clinics are almost always devoted to case detection and diagnosis, with referral elsewhere for treatment. They would ordinarily serve persons of any income level, but once again these services are used mainly by the poor. The development in recent years of general primary care clinics under health department auspices has been discussed in Chapter 5; as resources for medical treatment these clinics are typically intended for the poor, and persons of higher income would typically be referred elsewhere (except for emergencies).

Thus, the degree to which health department clinics are devoted specifically to poor people varies with the nature of the clinic, particularly whether its orientation is purely preventive or includes treatment. The avoidance of treatment for higher income patients is obviously dictated by the health department's usual concern for amicable relationships with private physicians. Still, in recent years when private physicians have generally been very busy and earned high incomes, their attitudes to public health clinics as "competitive" have softened. The policies of local public health agencies vary in different states and counties—being usually more cautious in small towns, where physician earnings are not so high and the private practitioner wants patronage even from families of modest income.

A new strategy of some health departments has been to levy charges for certain clinic services, such as prenatal care, child health services, or general primary medical care, on a sliding scale that is proportional to family income. Thus, no one is turned away as "not economically eligible," but higher income patients may be expected to pay fees similar to those charged by private doctors. Collection practices are usually lenient, but this policy may reduce demands on public health clinics, while also raising some funds for governmental agencies faced with public revenue cutbacks. Of course, whatever may be the extent of services to higher income patients, health department clinics remain a substantial resource for ambulatory services to the poor for selected health problems.

With respect to other major sponsorships of clinics—schools, industries, and physician groups—services for the poor are decidedly less important than in the clinics of hospitals and public health agencies. Perhaps school health services have special meaning for the children of poor families, insofar as these services are freely available. Families of adequate income would typically consult private physicians for their children's medical needs; even school entrance medical examinations or periodic re-examinations would be done by a personal doctor. For children of poor families, on the other hand, the health personnel in school clinics may provide services—even if only screening examinations or first aid—that might otherwise not be obtained.

Some school systems, as noted in Chapter 6, operate clinics for corrective treatment—particularly for dental conditions or for health problems relevant to learning, such as visual or hearing defects. Such clinics are nearly always limited to children from low-income families, and determination of eligibility is usually made by the school nurse. The rationale for these restrictions has long been not only to refrain from competition with private medical care providers, but also to use limited school health resources for those with greatest financial need.

Organized clinic services in industry, by definition, are limited to employed workers. One must recognize, however, that some workers get very low wages, so that by widely accepted standards they are poor—all the more so, if they have large families to support. Thus, to some extent even in-plant clinics may serve poor people; such service, of course, is of greater value if its scope extends beyond job-related disorders and first-aid.

Private group practice clinics might be regarded as the only sponsorship type of no relevance for the poor, but even this statement must be qualified. Insofar as public medical care programs pay for services in the private sector, they can enable poor people to seek care at private group practice clinics.[7] Indeed, the major policy thrust of the Medicaid program—by far the largest such public financing program in the nation—has been to provide the poor with "mainstream" medical care; thus, the great bulk of Medicaid funds goes to pay for the services of private physicians, hospitals, and other nongovernmental providers. Physicians' services, of course, include those rendered in group practice clinics. Furthermore, a large proportion of persons over 65 years of age are poor, so that additional support for care in group practice clinics comes from the Medicare program.[8]

For a small percentage of Medicaid beneficiaries, the use of group practice clinics has been made a customary policy, through their enrollment in "prepaid health plans" (PHPs). Mainly in California, but to a small extent in other states, some persons under Medicaid have chosen to be enrolled in PHPs providing care through group practice clinics.[9] The state Medicaid agency pays monthly premiums for enrollees in the PHP, instead of paying customary fees to doctors and other providers. In many of these programs, the poor were seriously underserved, and new regulatory measures were enacted by state governments to prevent such abuse. The PHP has been a type of health maintenance organization (HMO), to be discussed in Chapter 12, but here it may simply be noted that in spite of abuses and other difficulties, this mechanism has underwritten the use of group practice clinics by the poor in a systematic way. The average nonprepaid group practice clinic, furthermore, usually has a small proportion of poor patients, whether or not they are financed by Medicaid or Medicare.

In the multifaceted category of "specially sponsored clinics," discussed in Chapters 9 and 10, a wide variety of freestanding ambulatory care facilities have been established primarily to serve the poor. The initiative of the U.S. Office of Economic Opportunity (OEO) in the mid-1960s, establishing neighborhood health centers in poverty districts, served to resurrect the concept of the early nineteenth century dispensary for the poor (discussed in Chapter 2). This started a chain of legislative and administrative actions that yielded hundreds of new and variously defined ambulatory care centers throughout the United States. Mere listing of the titles of the several types of centers or the special programs that financed them reflects the diversity of the movement: community health centers, family health centers, community health networks, rural health initiative projects, urban health initiative projects, housing and urban development (HUD) projects, health underserved rural area (HURA) research and demonstration projects, Appalachian Regional Commission clinics, migrant health clinics, National Health Service Corps sites, Rural Health Clinic Services Act, maternity and infant care (MIC) clinics, children and youth (C & Y) clinics, and the original neighborhood health centers.

In aggregate, as estimated from the data in Chapter 9, there are close to 1,000 publicly financed ambulatory care centers of various types. One government budgetary document estimated that 886 federally supported community health centers were "serving over 5 million people" during the year.[10] This would amount to about 5,650 patients using the average such health center per year, and each patient might make several visits. As discussed in Chapter 9, an important aspect of the community health center movement of the 1960s and 1970s has been its involvement of low-income community people, particularly from ethnic minorities, in policy-making and management of these facilities. Although sponsorships are diverse, they are predominantly by nongovernmental bodies in which poor people themselves have a major voice. This voice has even been strengthened by establishment of a National Association of Community Health Centers, the leadership of which is drawn essentially from ethnic minorities.[11]

Finally, among the specially sponsored clinics, one must take note of certain types oriented clearly to low-income people. These include the large network of ambulatory care units for American Indians. As federal government beneficiaries, these predominantly low-income people (more than 800,000) are served by about 100 freestanding health centers and 300 small field health stations throughout the country. Low-income patients with mental or emotional problems may obtain ambulatory psychiatric service at a great variety of mental health clinics sponsored by special agencies, public or voluntary. Family planning service is the focus of still other specially sponsored clinics, whose patients are predominantly low-income women. Clinics wholly financed and operated by disease-specific voluntary health agencies, discussed in Chapter 10, seldom apply means tests, but their patients are typically of low income. This is true also of the young people coming to the free clinics, even though their families (from which they have often become separated) may be of moderate income.

Children's Clinics

Since the nineteenth century, when demands for public education of children and opposition to child labor became widespread, special protection of the child has been the subject of social movements throughout the world. Health service, of course, has been among the objectives of these movements, and has included organization of various types of special clinics.

Among the early activities of health departments, as discussed in Chapter 5, was the operation of clinics for newborn infants and small children. These evolved from "milk stations" and their orientation from the outset to the present day has been preventive. In large part, the purpose of child health, or well baby clinics, is to educate mothers about sound methods of feeding and caring for children.

The great majority of local public health agencies conduct child health clinics, and virtually every state health department offers consultant services in this field. Between 1974 and 1976, the average number of children served in these clinics throughout the United States was 1,703,000 per year.[12] Of these, 78 percent were under five years of age, and about one-third were infants (under one year). Relating the latter (about 580,000 infants) to the U.S. infant population in 1976 yields an estimate that about 18 percent of newborns are seen at least once in a health department well baby clinic. This proportion, while much smaller than in many European countries, has risen gradually from 14 percent in 1961. The total number of infant visits per year is not reported, but probably averages about 3 or 4 per newborn. Infants and small children not seen at these preventive clinics may, of course, be served by private physicians, although many babies in low-income families may not get regular preventive services at all.

Pregnant women are also served at preventively oriented maternity clinics of health departments. The underlying social purpose is doubtless to help assure healthful prenatal conditions for the future infant. The impact of these prenatal services, however, is somewhat less than direct services to infants; in 1976 there were 413,400 women served in these clinics, amounting to 14 percent of live births (approximately equal to the number of full-term pregnancies).[13] It is likely, however, that many other low-income women obtain prenatal care at the outpatient department of a hospital, where the mother expects to deliver her baby. Higher income women typically receive prenatal care from a private obstetrician.

Immunizations are provided in the child health clinics, but many health departments offer these basic preventive services in other organized settings as well. Special clinic sessions may be organized for immunizations in the schools or elsewhere. The number of children immunized by public health agencies exceeds the total number seen in child health clinics. Thus in the 1974–76 period, some 3,218,000 children got antipoliomyelitis immunizations during a year. This was almost double the number seen in the child health clinics. The children immunized against diphtheria, tetanus, and pertussis through public health auspices also exceeded the number seen at these clinics.

Clinics for diagnosis or followup care of crippled children are another activity of many state or local public health agencies, although in some states the sponsorship of such clinics is by other agencies, such as medical schools, public hospitals, or welfare departments. Crippled children's services are financed in large part by federal grants to the states from the U.S. Public Health Service (PHS); in 1973, this program served 513,130 children. Of these, 373,300 were seen in various clinics, for a total of 824,000 visits.[14] The diagnostic categories eligible for these services are defined by each state; in 1973 the most common were diseases of the nervous system and sense organs, disorders of the bones and organs of movement, and congenital malformations.

Aside from crippled children's services, treatment of other conditions in children is offered by the health departments in about one-third of the states, predominantly in the southeastern region of the nation and in U.S. territories. Such clinics served 450,400 children in 1976. Special children's clinics for dental care are more widespread, and served more than one million children in 1976.

An important recent development in health department child health clinics, occurring principally in larger cities, is the broadening of their focus from purely preventive service to general ambulatory pediatric care. Thus, since 1972 in low-income neighborhoods of New York City, 18 out of 76 traditional child health stations have been converted to "pediatric treatment centers."[15] Full-time pediatricians were appointed in these clinics, backed up by laboratory and pharmacy resources. This change led to an increase of clinic utilization by 50 percent after only about one year. Health departments in Los Angeles County and other metropolitan areas are also broadening the scope of traditional child health clinics in poverty districts. This is quite aside from the initially comprehensive scope of services offered in the specially funded Maternity and Infant Care (MIC) and Children and Youth (C & Y) clinics, under the sponsorship of diverse agencies (to be discussed later).

Hospital outpatient departments serve children as well as adults in all three of their types of clinics: scheduled, emergency, and referred. Pediatric clinic sessions are common in those hospitals that maintain scheduled outpatient services. As is the case with scheduled hospital clinics in general, those for pediatrics are restricted to children of low-income families. Infants or children seen at health department preventive clinics and found to have a disease requiring treatment are often referred to hospital pediatric clinics.

In the National Health Survey, physician visits by the U.S. population have been tabulated both by place of visit and by age level. In 1975, for example, 13 percent of all physician visits were made to a "hospital clinic or emergency room." Of these, 28.6 percent were made by children under 15 years of age.[16] This percentage may be applied to the total number of organized clinic and emergency visits made to U.S. hospitals in 1977, which was 128,183,000; by this calculation there were 36,600,000 clinic services to children in that year. This is a much greater number than the volume of child health services rendered by public health agencies.

Organized clinics in elementary schools are naturally devoted to children. As discussed in Chapter 6, the scope of services in these clinics is typically narrow, but their coverage is wide. The vast majority of some 50 million children in the nation's elementary and secondary schools are entitled to the first aid attention of school nurses and to referrals for medical care. Most school children also receive general examinations by a physician, at varying intervals, and some (typically children from low-income families) receive corrective treatment, most often for dental disease and for visual or hearing defects.

Much state legislation requires immunization of children against specified communicable diseases. In the main, these preventive services are provided by private physicians or at health department clinics; sometimes, however, school health personnel provide immunizations.

The trend of emphasis in ambulatory school-based health services has shifted from an earlier focus on communicable disease to concern for mental health problems and general psychosocial child development. This is evident at all educational levels, but is more prominent in the adolescent years of secondary school and also at the university level.

Private group practice clinics may serve children as well as adults. In the 35 percent of such clinics that have multispecialty composition, pediatricians are usually included. Child care would also, of course, be available in the 11 percent of medical groups devoted to family practice. Among the single specialty group practices, furthermore, a certain proportion consists entirely of pediatricians. Only industrial clinics, among the major sponsorship types, would not be expected to serve children.

The specially sponsored types of clinics, reviewed in Chapters 9 and 10, include many that serve children, among others, and some that are principally oriented to children. Thus, insofar as military clinics serve dependents, children are seen. The same applies to clinics for American Indians, in whose families there are typically many children.

The growing number and variety of federally financed and locally sponsored clinics, most of which are oriented to low-income persons, are likewise serving many children. This applied to the earliest neighborhood health centers, launched by the U.S. OEO, and it applies equally to the many subsequent types of community health center. The health centers receiving grants under the Migrant Health Act (numbering 112 in 1979) are particularly important for children, since migratory agricultural workers often have large families.

The MIC and the C & Y clinics also concentrate their services on the young. While sponsored by several types of agencies, the 186 clinics of both sorts in the nation are expected to give a comprehensive range of ambulatory services to young people living in poverty districts, where all these clinics are located.

Clinics sponsored by other state and local government authorities, as noted in Chapter 9, include those devoted to mental health. Special mental health agencies often conduct child guidance and other clinics intended solely for children with emotional or developmental disturbances. In addition, the variously sponsored community mental health centers or other psychiatric clinics, either freestanding or linked to a hospital, serve children as well as adults. Counting all types of mental health clinics (but excluding community mental health centers) in 1975, 25 percent of the 1,406,000 different patients served were under 18 years of age.[17]

Finally, as discussed in Chapter 10, there is an enormous variety of voluntary health agencies that sponsor disease-specific and other types of clinics. The clinics of several of these have special importance for children, such as units of the National Society for Crippled Children and Adults, the United Cerebral Palsy Association, or the National Foundation March of Dimes (concerned mainly with birth defects). Voluntary mental health agencies tend to devote their efforts to disturbed children, probably more than governmental agencies; children's problems have long attracted voluntary donations with special force. Even the free clinics launched in the 1960s by young adults now may serve the children of young parents.

Thus, when one considers the full panoply of clinics in America, services to meet various needs of children are offered by almost every type. This is not to say, of course, that all the health needs of children are being met. Far from it: the evidence of deficiencies and inequities is abundant.[18] In spite of the myriad clinics, a large share of which are oriented to children of poor families, the infant mortality rate, the prevalence of disabling disease, and other indices of unmet need are substantially higher among children of the poor and particularly among children from ethnic minority groups.

Many of the health disadvantages of poor children are related more to the general living conditions of their families than to a lack of health service as such. Low-income families tend to have greater numbers of children, which aggravates the handicaps of meager family incomes. The child rearing capabilities of an impoverished mother are compromised often not only by inadequate finances but also by the demands of a job, lack of community child care resources, a heavy burden of other social problems, and limited education. A child with sickness that could be cured or could have been prevented is usually the result of a long chain of social deficiencies that could be averted in a better organized and more humanitarian society.

Yet the health of children in America has probably been the object of more social organization than that of any other demographic group. From the legislation outlawing child labor in the nineteenth century, to the founding of the U.S. Children's Bureau in 1912, to the Sheppard-Towner Act of 1921, to the child health provisions of the Social Security Act of 1935, to the great variety of contemporary child health programs summarized in these pages, corrective social actions have been stimulated by the obvious appeal of healthy children for reasons that are pragmatic and political as well as humane.[19] Organized clinics are only part of this general social movement, which includes also many programs of public financing (such as Medicaid to poor families with dependent children) and proposals for national health insurance that would focus initially on children. Most of the clinics for children, nevertheless, are notable in their combination of mechanisms of organized financing with patterns of organized delivery of health services.

Clinics for Rural People

A third type of person for whom clinics of many sponsorships are organized is the resident of rural areas. For many reasons, the free market of medical economics, which has long characterized the American scene, has failed to satisfy the health needs of rural populations.[20] In response, numerous special clinics in rural areas have arisen.

Organized ambulatory services under hospital sponsorship are generally weaker in rural sections than in large cities. Hospitals in small towns or in non-metropolitan areas seldom offer scheduled medical, surgical, or other specialized clinics, as do the hospitals in large cities. They do, however, usually offer emergency services at day or night. Rural populations in the United States have acquired improved access to emergency services in recent decades, mainly due to federally subsidized hospital construction since the Hill-Burton Act in 1947.

Thus in 1942, before the Hospital Survey and Construction Act, the eight most rural states had 2.2 general hospital beds per 1,000 population, compared with 4.5 such beds in the six most urban states. By 1965, the planning strategies of the Hill-Burton program had been successful in achieving almost complete equalization in hospital bed supplies. Although the measurement indices were slightly different, in 1965 the ten most rural states had 3.62 general hospital beds per 1,000, compared to 3.86 such beds in the ten most urban states.[21]

These inpatient resources doubtless reflect corresponding rural-urban equalization in resources for outpatient *emergency* services, in spite of the rarity of scheduled outpatient clinics outside the large cities.

Public health clinics of health departments, on the other hand, probably play a relatively greater role in rural counties than they do in urban centers. It is not that rural counties have stronger public health agencies than highly urban counties; they generally do not. But the very weakness of hospital outpatient departments (except for emergency care) and the limited supply of private physicians—and particularly pediatricians—in rural districts leads naturally to greater reliance on public health well baby clinics. In small towns, moreover, new young mothers often tend to look upon the health department clinic as a place for periodic social exchanges with friends.

Indirect evidence of relatively greater utilization of child health clinics by rural families may be inferred from the U.S. population distribution in 1976; in that year 27 percent of the national population were in nonmetropolitan counties. Yet in spite of the weaker public health organization in those counties and the greater problems of transportation, 28 percent of the children using health department clinics (in 36 states providing rural-urban breakdowns) resided in nonmetropolitan counties.[22] With fewer private physicians around, there seems to be less tendency for rural public health agencies to restrict their clients to the very poor.

With respect to school health services, we have noted in Chapter 6 that these are best developed in the larger cities. Nevertheless, most rural schools offer some primary care services—provided most often by nurses from the local health department (rather than by education department personnel, as in the cities). One might expect that this arrangement yields closer coordination between rural school clinics and public health services than occurs in the cities, where two separate agencies are usually responsible.

Industrial health services are principally urban, insofar as factories are concentrated in the cities. Certain enterprises, such as mining and lumbering, however, tend to be isolated and rural. These, along with construction sites of dams or reservoirs, often furnish workers particularly comprehensive health services, both on and off the job, because of their isolated locations. Some of the earliest industrial medical care programs, linked to health insurance support, were organized in such isolated establishments.[23] At many coal mines, large lumber mills, hydroelectric power plants, and the like, general medical clinics (and sometimes small hospitals) have been long maintained to serve both workers and dependents.[24] Some of these programs are supported and administered solely by management; others by employer-employee boards. While the families receiving health care in these programs are not agricultural, they are still part of the rural population.

Private group medical practice clinics may be customarily regarded as city-based, but their development has actually been greatest in nonmetropolitan areas.

Although the last survey of group practice physicians, tabulated by county, was done in 1959, its findings are still probably meaningful. As a proportion of all physicians in private practice at that time, those in group practice constituted 4.6 percent in the metropolitan counties, compared with 8.0 percent in counties adjacent to the former and 12.6 percent in isolated rural counties.[25] In 1969, a study of group practice development in the 50 states tended to confirm this relationship. The percentage of nonfederal physicians in group practice in a state was correlated with low population density by a coefficient of 0.55.[26] Many factors obviously play a part in the growth of group practice patterns, but two features of generally rural regions would seem to be relevant: (a) the handicaps of isolated specialty practice in small towns, and (b) less resistance from medical societies, which are usually weak in rural counties. Group practice clinics are, therefore, more readily established and make specialized medical and surgical services available to rural people for miles around.

Among the diverse specially sponsored and publicly financed clinics analyzed in Chapter 9, several are devoted specifically to meeting rural health needs. The federal health program for American Indians serves a rural population. Even the outpatient facilities of the Veterans Administration probably have greater value for rural veterans, who have lesser access than urban veterans to other forms of ambulatory medical care. Among the federally financed and locally sponsored community health centers, the rural focus of several types is explicit.

The Rural Health Initiative (RHI) grant program, launched in 1975, contributed to the establishment of hundreds of organized primary care facilities. By 1979 there were 356 RHI clinics, serving about 700,000 rural people. Over and above these were 41 rural clinics, started with Medicaid funding under legislative authority for "research and demonstration projects in health under-served rural areas" (HURA). Although initially limited to Medicaid beneficiaries, HURA clinics were later open to other low-income rural people as well.

State governments have also sometimes launched rural primary care clinics. In Tennessee, for example, there were 52 primary care units in isolated communities in the late 1970s. These were predominantly subsidized by federal grants, but six of them were funded directly by the State Department of Public Health's Division of Primary Care.[27] The State Department of Health of North Carolina has given corresponding support to certain rural communities. In both these states, nurse practitioners furnish most of the primary medical care (including diagnosis and treatment of common ailments) with indirect supervision from private physicians. A controlling board of directors, chosen from local residents, is ordinarily appointed. Complex cases are referred to private physicians or hospital OPDs.

The 101 clinics supported by the Appalachian Regional Commission, as reported in Chapter 9, are also essentially rural facilities. Most specifically rural are doubtless the clinics for agricultural migrants, started under the U.S. Farm Security Administration in the 1930s, reactivated with the Migrant Health Act of 1962, and supervised now by the Bureau of Community Health Services of the USPHS. As noted in Chapter 9, there were 112 such clinics serving about 557,000 migrants in 1979. (Many of these clinics, one must realize, get support also from other sources beyond the Migrant Health Act allocation.) Strictly speaking, migrant families eligible to use these clinics have come to include seasonal farm workers, who may reside year-round in a locality but are typically of very low income.[28]

Finally, one must not ignore the clinics of numerous voluntary health agencies for mental health service or other disease-specific purposes discussed in Chapter 10. In the main, such activities are concentrated in large cities, although there are small towns with dynamic leadership on certain problems, such as cerebral palsy, cancer, or family planning, that attract voluntary initiative. Voluntary agency clinics are seldom categorized by urban-rural location, but in the family planning field the 1975 nationwide survey included among clinic sites a category of "mobile units." Out of 4,660 medical family planning clinics in the nation, 119 were designated as such mobile units.[29] One may reasonably infer that these were serving largely rural populations.

Indicative of the resourcefulness shown in some rural areas has been a recent program in Utah. Here, a voluntary, nonprofit corporation has been set up to provide general medical services through rural clinics. This is the Health Systems Research Institute (HSRI), headquartered in Salt Lake City.[30] In 1976, HSRI had contracts with local governments to serve residents in 14 communities. Fees are charged to those who can afford to pay, and services to others (not eligible for Medicaid or Medicare support) are financed by the local government funds.

Organized social efforts to improve rural health services have been prominent in the United States for many years. Since the Depression years of the 1930s, numerous organizations of farmers and other rural people have included among their objectives the expansion of health facilities and health personnel to serve rural populations.[31] In the current period, however, these efforts have become rather sharply focused on the establishment of special facilities for the delivery of ambulatory health care. Perhaps because the federal Hill-Burton program has succeeded in essentially equalizing the hospital bed resources (as reflected in bed-population ratios) between rural and urban states, much greater attention is now being directed to clinics for primary care.

Thus, in the early 1970s the American Rural Health Association was organized, with headquarters in Washington, D.C., where lobbying could be done in connection with federal health legislation. Since 1975, a periodical on rural health program developments has been issued by this body.[32] In 1978, there was founded the National Rural Primary Care Association, with headquarters at Waterville, Maine.[33] This organization works closely with the National Association of Community Health Centers to promote establishment of primary care facilities in as many rural localities as possible.

For many years the American Medical Association has had a Council on Rural Health. It has stimulated state and local medical societies to cooperate with medical schools and government agencies to set up special rural community clinics—for example, in California, Iowa, upstate New York, and Oklahoma.[34] Similar activities have been undertaken by the American Osteopathic Association; since 1948, this body has sponsored 11 rural clinics in rural northeast Missouri, in connection with the Kirksville College of Osteopathy and Surgery.[35] In 1979, the Health Services Research Center at the University of North Carolina (Chapel Hill) launched the publication of a six-volume *Rural Health Center Development Series*. These publications are intended to offer guidance to rural community groups on the legal, architectural, clinical, administrative, and other aspects of establishing health centers for primary care in rural localities.[36]

The multiplicity of sources for financing the establishment and operation of rural clinics is a striking illustration of the pluralisitic ideology of the U.S. health care system. In Fresno County, California, for example, there is a local organization known as the "West Side Rural Health Conference," the staff of which is subsidized through the federal Comprehensive Employment and Training Act (CETA) program. Through the efforts of this group, five rural clinics, staffed by nurses and part-time physicians, have been organized for low-income agricultural families. To achieve this, funding was obtained in the late 1970s from several sources, including: (a) a federal revenue-sharing grant to the county government, (b) the Fresno County Health Department, (c) the RHI program of the USPHS, Bureau of Community Health Services, (d) the Migrant Health program of the same federal agency, and (e) a private California philanthropic foundation. A physician was provided also by the federal National Health Service Corps. An enormous amount of the administrative sophistication is obviously required to mobilize funds and resources from this array of agencies.[37]

Similarly, in 1979, West Virginia had a network of 63 nonprofit primary care clinics serving its predominantly rural population; each clinic offered physician services for at least eight hours a week.[38] The definition of these units excluded hospital emergency rooms, public health clinics, private group practices, and clinics operated primarily for teaching purposes. To establish these clinics required resources from (a) the Health and Retirement Fund of the United Mine Workers of America, (b) the Regional Medical Program for Heart Disease, Cancer, and Stroke, (c) the Appalachian Regional Commission, (d) a private philanthropic foundation, (d) the U.S. National Health Service Corps, and (e) the Region III Office of the USPHS. The last resource, in turn, informed local community groups of funding available from the U.S. Bureau of Community Health Services, through its RHI and HURA programs.

The diversity of settings in which rural primary care clinics may be organized is no less complex. A 1976 publication of the federal Bureau of Community Health Services classifies these as (a) freestanding, community-owned primary health care centers, (b) community-based corporations operating satellite clinics,

(c) community-based centers assisted by hospitals, (d) primary health care centers developed jointly by two hospitals, (e) hospital-operated satellite health centers, (f) primary care clinics within hospitals, and (g) primary care health centers developed by conversion from small hospitals.[39] These varied models, moreover, are above and beyond the categorically sponsored rural clinics under schools, health departments, industrial enterprises, etc., discussed earlier.

This overview of clinics for rural people, like the reviews of clinics oriented to the poor and of clinics for children, is not complete. It may be sufficient, however, to indicate the diversity of sponsorships and administrative structures of facilities for organized ambulatory care of certain categories of persons.

CLINICS FOR CERTAIN HEALTH PROBLEMS

From previous chapters it is clear that clinics of many sponsorships may be focused on designated diseases or health problems in all persons, regardless of their background. There are clinics for tuberculosis, for venereal infection, for poliomyelitis or other communicable diseases. Others may focus on heart disease, arthritis, cancer, diseases of the eye, or other chronic disorders. To illustrate the variety of sponsorships and functional models along this dimension, we will consider clinics focused on three general types of health problems: mental disorder, crippling conditions, and family planning.

Clinics for Mental Disorder

Clinics under all the principal types of sponsoring agencies discussed in earlier chapters may serve patients with mental disorders, and many may be devoted entirely to such cases. Thus, hospital outpatient departments, both in scheduled clinics and in emergency services, may serve psychiatric patients. In 1977, out of the universe of 6,495 hospitals that reported to the American Hospital Association on their range of special services, 1,231, or 19 percent, operated scheduled psychiatric clinic sessions.[40] In 23.6 percent of the reporting hospitals, psychiatric patients were seen on an emergency basis.

Not surprisingly, psychiatric hospitals offered OPD psychiatric services much more frequently. In the 476 nonfederal mental institutions, outpatient psychiatric services were offered by 44 percent; in 25 federal mental facilities, OPD psychiatric services were offered by 100 percent. Among the nonfederal short-term general hospitals, psychiatric clinics were provided in 17 percent of those under voluntary nonprofit sponsorship, in 11 percent of those under state and local government, and in 3 percent of those under proprietary control. These hospital-based psychiatric clinics nearly always offer the services of psychiatrists, along with social workers and sometimes other personnel. Even in general medical and other hospital OPD clinics, however, it is common for many patients to have conditions that are basically psychogenic.

Public health agencies also offer mental hygiene services in their special clinics. In 1968, as noted in Chapter 5, this was done in 55 percent of local health departments. In the structure of local government, however, special mental health agencies have come to play a larger role than health departments in recent years. Between 1967 and 1976 freestanding mental health clinics of all types of sponsorship (governmental and voluntary) actually declined from 1,278 to 1,076.[41] Contributing largely to this was the great expansion of federally funded community mental health centers (CMHC). These grew from 125 in 1967, to 528 in 1976, and to 701 in 1979.[42] Very few CMHCs are under health department sponsorship. Pediatricians and public health nurses serving in the maternal and child health clinics of health departments, however, often point out that much of their counseling to mothers on child rearing is essentially in the sphere of developmental psychology.

Clinic services under the sponsorship of educational institutions are rarely oriented to mental health problems at the elementary school level, but with increasing frequency they do address these problems at the secondary school and university levels. In the major national study of 83 city school systems in 1964, as noted in Chapter 6, identifiable mental health services were provided in 19, but in only 2 of these did the school authorities operate a mental health clinic. (The other 17 make referrals to other agencies.) In secondary schools, the growing problems of drug abuse and alcohol consumption have focused attention on the mental health of adolescents. The major approach to this problem has been through the classroom, where students are taught about the hazards of addictive drugs and the principles of mentally healthful behavior and attitudes.

At the college or university level, systematic clinic services for mentally or emotionally disturbed students are much more highly developed.[43] Certain large and outstanding universities, such as Yale or Massachusetts Institute of Technology, maintain major divisions within their health service programs for psychiatric service. In the 1977 survey of the American College Health Association, it may be recalled that of 574 full-time physicians identified in this type of service, 16 percent were psychiatrists.

Psychiatric services are seldom offered at the workplace. By far the most common arrangement is to include limited benefits for ambulatory psychiatric care under employment-linked health insurance programs. One study of 79 large corporations reported in 1977, however, found that in 8 of them (10 percent), certain psychiatric services were offered within the in-plant clinics.[44] One can appreciate that some workers might be suspicious of psychiatrists on the company payroll.

In private group medical practice clinics, psychiatric services are exceptional. As indicated in Chapter 8, more than 80 percent of multispecialty clinics in

1975 had 15 physicians or less, and in groups of this size psychiatrists are rare. In larger medical groups, however, participation of psychiatrists or neuropsychiatrists is becoming increasingly common. The services of psychologists, full-time or part-time, were offered by 5.1 percent of group practice clinics in 1975.

Among the numerous specially sponsored and publicly financed clinics, psychiatric services are offered to varying extents. All of the nationwide programs for special federal beneficiaries include psychiatric clinics to which cases may be referred. In the nearly 1,000 federally financed and locally sponsored health centers, psychiatric services are exceptional; with the emphasis on primary care, patients needing psychiatric attention are typically referred elsewhere. Psychiatric care is not included among the services mandated by the Community Health Center Act of 1974.

On the other hand, among miscellaneous other types of agencies, public or voluntary, sponsoring clinics, agencies devoted specifically to mental health are important. As discussed in Chapter 9, in January 1978 there were 1,164 free-standing psychiatric clinics in the nation, of which 401 were under governmental sponsorship (nearly all at the state or local level)—usually within a specialized mental health agency. Many of these clinics have subspecialties in such fields as child psychiatry, crisis intervention, or group psychotherapy. Alcoholism and drug addiction have become serious enough to engender the organization of other special clinics and are no longer identified under the rubric of mental health.

Since federal mental health legislation in 1963, the most important facility for organized delivery of ambulatory psychiatric care (as well as other services) in the United States has become the CMHC. While financed by the federal government, the majority of these are sponsored locally by voluntary bodies—either general hospitals or organizations affiliated with general hospitals. The 701 CMHCs operational in 1979 were not included among the freestanding psychiatric clinics noted above.

Among national voluntary agencies with a disease-specific focus, considered in Chapter 10, there is the Mental Health Association (formerly the National Association for Mental Health), but its work is basically social and political advocacy. At the local level, however, there are hundreds of community voluntary agencies sponsoring independent psychiatric clinics—763 of them in 1978. Account must also be taken of the voluntary free clinic movement of the 1970s, discussed in Chapter 10; in most of these, limited help (often from motivated but untrained young men and women) is offered to youthful patients with emotional difficulties. Finally, there is the recent holistic health movement, with its health centers, in which a strongly psychosocial approach is taken toward all forms of sickness.

An overview of these varied resources for ambulatory psychiatric care is difficult to offer, but the USPHS, specifically the Alcohol, Drug Abuse, and

Mental Health Administration (ADAMHA) within it, has made estimates of the spectrum of total psychiatric care (inpatient and ambulatory) in the nation, as of 1975.[45] These estimates and their percentage distribution are presented in Table 11-1. To clarify the meaning of this tabulation several comments are in order.

Out of the total of 7,107,000 patients seen in all psychiatric settings, ADAMHA estimates that about 70 percent are ambulatory cases; this proportion would presumably be 100 percent at freestanding psychiatric clinics and lower than 70 percent at state and county mental hospitals. Considering all 11 types of settings in the tabulation, it is noteworthy that more than 80 percent of the cases are served in organized frameworks; only 18 percent are patients of privately practicing psychiatrists or psychologists. Thus, in contrast to service for most disease entities, treatment for psychiatric disorders is delivered overwhelmingly in clinics or other organized settings.

The estimates in Table 11-1 apply to psychiatric services for patients with mental disorders. One must realize, however, that many patients coming to other office-based physicians or various other types of clinic may have mental or emotional problems, for which they may be treated by nonpsychiatric personnel. ADAMHA estimated these patients, in fact, to number about 22 million

---

Table 11-1 Psychiatric Services Provided in Various Settings: Estimated Patients[a] Treated for Mental Disorders, by Type of Setting, United States, 1975.

Setting	Patients Seen or Treated	Percent
Community mental health centers	1,627,000	23
Freestanding psychiatric clinics	1,590,000	22
General hospital (nonfederal) psychiatric units	927,000	12
Private psychiatrists' offices	854,000	12
State and county mental hospitals	789,000	11
Private psychologists' offices	425,000	6
Veterans Administration psychiatric units	351,000	5
Multiservice clinics	173,000	2
Private mental hospitals	172,000	2
College mental health clinics	131,000	2
Other inpatient facilities	67,000	1
All settings:	7,107,000	100

[a] About 5 percent of the patients were seen at more than one setting.

Source: ADAMHA, *The Alcohol, Drug Abuse, and Mental Health National Data Book* (Washington: 1980), p. 52.

in 1975, or three times the patients seen in psychiatric settings. Those with more serious and more long-term mental disorders, one may presume, are eventually referred to a psychiatric resource for care.

Clinics for Crippling Conditions

Definitions of "crippling" are variable, but in the context of clinics we may restrict the meaning to orthopedic conditions or disorders impairing the functioning of limbs. Even in this relatively narrow sense, crippling conditions in children or adults are treated in many types of clinics.

Thus, among 6,495 hospitals reporting in 1977 on "facilities and services," 942 (14.5 percent) provided rehabilitation services in their outpatient departments.[46] In the main these services are for persons with locomotor problems due to paralysis, trauma, or other crippling conditions.

Clinics for crippled children, under federally subsidized, state-operated "crippled children's programs" (usually under public health agency administration) have been discussed earlier in this chapter. The somewhat equivalent state program for handicapped adults is the "vocational rehabilitation program," supported by the Rehabilitation Services Administration in the U.S. Department of Health and Human Services (formerly Department of Health, Education and Welfare). These programs seldom operate clinics of their own, but rather refer clients to physicians, hospitals, or rehabilitation facilities under various sponsorships.

The state agencies responsible for vocational rehabilitation programs are usually connected with departments of education, since vocational training for employment is the objective to which medical rehabilitation services are contributory. Insofar as disabled adults obtain such services in organized settings, these are not clinics in the usual sense. Rehabilitation centers or rehabilitation facilities, as distinguished from hospitals, typically offer a range of services in physical restoration (physical and occupational therapy), social adjustment, speech therapy, vocational training, sheltered employment, and so on, for disabled persons who live at home or elsewhere. In June 1977, there were 700 such facilities in the United States, approved by the Commission on Accreditation of Rehabilitation Facilities.[47] In a report for 1968, out of 484 rehabilitation facilities responding to a survey questionnaire, 69.5 percent were under voluntary sponsorship, 29.0 percent were governmental, and 1.5 percent were proprietary.[48]

The physical setting and organizational character of these facilities for serving crippled patients are quite heterogeneous. Thus, there were 46 facilities reporting from California in the 1968 survey, and these were distributed as follows:

| Sponsorship | Main Rehabilitation Emphasis | | | |
	Physical	Mental	Vocational	Total
Federal government hospitals	4			4
State government institutions		5	1	6
State university hospitals	3			3
County government hospitals	7	1		8
Voluntary hospitals	9			9
Other voluntary agencies	7	3	6	16
All sponsorships	30	9	7	46

Source: Association of Rehabilitation Centers, *1968 Directory of Rehabilitation Facilities* (Washington: 1968).

Only 16 of the 46 facilities were operated by voluntary agencies other than hospitals. The other 30 were part of the administrative structure of governmental or voluntary hospitals (although some were doubtless in separate adjacent buildings).

Returning to consideration of ambulatory care for crippling conditions, under diverse sponsorships, schools as such do not operate clinics in this field, but many school systems provide special classes, or even entire school buildings, for physically handicapped children. The general trend has been toward integrating disabled children into normal classroom settings, but in certain metropolitan areas the special school policy is still followed. With either arrangement, schools are making adjustments to the educational requirements for rehabilitation and proper development of crippled children. At the state government level, moreover, the administrative responsibilities of departments of education for most vocational rehabilitation programs has been noted above.

In industry, the major contribution of in-plant clinics to persons with crippling conditions is referral to resources for rehabilitation. Beyond this, many large enterprises have a policy of employing handicapped workers in jobs for which they are capable; thus a worker with paralyzed legs can be assigned to a sedentary task requiring functional ability only in his arms. During the World War II years of labor shortage, great attention was given to the maximum use of disabled workers through careful job placement.[49] The United States does not have legislation, as does Great Britain, requiring that in all companies with 20 or more workers, at least 5 percent must be physically handicapped (as certified by a public official). Through the influence of state rehabilitation agencies and labor unions, however, many firms have adopted somewhat equivalent policies. In 1970, of the total U.S. work force of about 90 million persons, 8.0 percent of the males and 5.1 percent of the females had a partial work disability.[50] We do not know, however, just what proportion of these have jobs that make an appropriate adjustment to their disabilities.

In group medical practices persons with crippling conditions are treated along with others. Some such clinics have physical therapists on their staffs, although these were not specifically identified in the 1975 survey discussed in Chapter 8. In single specialty clinics composed of orthopedic surgeons, treatment of patients with locomotor disabilities would naturally be frequent.

Among the specially sponsored and publicly financed clinics, some for federal beneficiaries (particularly military personnel and veterans) include physical therapy services for ambulatory patients with crippling conditions. The many and varied types of federally financed and locally sponsored health centers, however, could seldom be expected to serve crippled patients; community health centers concentrate on primary health care, and patients with significant crippling conditions would typically be referred elsewhere for treatment and rehabilitation. The review of "Clinics of Other State and Local Government Agencies" in Chapter 9 takes note of an estimated 116 freestanding rehabilitation facilities under governmental sponsorship.

Among the variety of clinics discussed in Chapter 10, those with greatest relevance to crippling conditions are under the voluntary disease-specific agencies. In previous years, the National Foundation on Poliomyelitis devoted a major part of its efforts to rehabilitation clinics for polio victims. As noted in Chapter 10, the National Easter Seal Society for Crippled Children and Adults devotes 70 percent of its substantial budget to direct services to handicapped persons; in 1977–78 these were provided at 728 sites. The United Cerebral Palsy Association is another agency sponsoring disease-specific clinics.

Like health services for children, services for treatment or rehabilitation of crippling conditions have wide social and political appeal. Both governmental and voluntary agencies have responded to this. The crippled child or adult not only arouses pity, but suffers from disorders that are ordinarily of long duration. Inevitably this means that care is expensive, furnishing a continuing stimulus for the organization of clinics supported by funds from numerous social sources.

Family Planning Clinics

Few organized ambulatory services have developed as rapidly in recent years as clinics for contraceptive or family planning (FP) purposes. In private medical practice, FP advice and procedures have been provided to women for many decades, but organized clinics, financed and sponsored by many sources and clearly visible in the community, have become common only since the mid-1960s.

A turning point occurred in 1967 when, in an amendment to the federal Economic Opportunity Act, family planning was designated for "special emphasis" in the national anti-poverty program. The Child Health Act was also amended that year to earmark for FP projects at least 6 percent of funds appropriated for maternal and child health programs, to require the states to extend FP services throughout their jurisdictions by 1975, and to mandate the availability of FP services to all appropriate public assistance recipients.[51] In 1969 organized FP programs were serving 1,094,000 women in the United States; this number spiralled to 5,113,000 by 1975.[52]

As with so many federal subsidy programs, the clinics are of several different sponsorships and attributes. Many are part of scheduled clinics in hospital outpatient departments. In 1977, FP service on an outpatient basis was offered in 419 (6.5 percent) of reporting hospitals; some of these were sponsored by other agencies that were provided clinic quarters by the hospital. Nearly 1,285,000 visits were made to these units in 1977.[53] In hospitals of 500 beds or more, the proportion with FP services rises to 19.5 percent.

Health departments, as we have noted in Chapter 5, are providing FP services, in connection with prenatal and postpartum clinics, at an increasing frequency. Between 1969 and 1976, the number of patients served at health department FP clinics increased by 325 percent, a rate more rapid than the increase of patients in clinics of any other type of sponsorship.[54] In light of the controversy in this field, it is important to understand that these services are never forced upon a woman but only offered on her request. Availability of advice on several different forms of contraception has come to be recognized as a standard component of virtually all health department maternal and child health programs in the United States.[55]

Many university health service programs offer FP services to students as a routine matter. Moral objections to such policies have been more than outweighed by realistic assessment of the risks of unwanted pregnancies in young, unmarried women. Even some secondary public schools offer such services, sometimes requiring parental consent.[56]

Industrial firms employing many women sometimes furnish FP services, but this is not frequent. Private group practices, with gynecologists or general primary care doctors on their staffs, offer FP services to their patients. Over the years, private medical practice generally has probably been the major resource for contraceptive service to American women.

Among the specially sponsored and tax-supported clinics, the federal program for American Indians, among whom the birth rate has been traditionally high, gives a great deal of attention to FP clinic services. The same is true of the multiplicity of federally financed local community health centers in both urban and rural areas. The range of preventive measures encompassed in primary health care normally includes FP service, which may be offered at specially scheduled sessions or simply in connection with routine maternal health care.

The free clinic movement (Chapter 10) counts FP service among its more important activities. The interest of young women in obtaining such services, without moralistic overtones, was among the major motivations for initiating this movement. This is even more the case in the feminist women's clinics.

Among other voluntary health agencies oriented to specific health problems, there are hundreds of local nonprofit bodies devoted to education about birth control and the operation of FP clinics. Only a minority of them are affiliated with the Planned Parenthood Federation of America, but these serve more women than the numerous independent local units.[57] As noted above, many of the clinics sponsored and staffed by voluntary FP agencies are located in hospital outpatient departments, but most such clinics are in other sites.

The National Center for Health Statistics has done repeated national surveys of FP services offered throughout the United States under diverse sponsorships. The findings of the 1975 survey, reported in 1978, show that the majority of FP clinics are sponsored by agencies of government at different levels. The percentage distribution of sponsorships of the 4,660 service units responding in 1975 was as follows:[58]

Sponsorship	Percent
County government	25.8
State government	19.6
Health district	6.0
City or metropolitan area	5.5
Indian Health Service	2.5
Other federal government	6.6
Other nonfederal government	0.3
All government	66.3
Nonprofit corporation	21.0
For-profit corporation	1.0
University	4.1
Hospital	5.4
Church	0.3
Individual or partnership	0.6
Other nongovernment body	1.4
All nongovernment	33.8
All sponsorships	100.0

Source: U.S. National Center for Health Statistics, *The National Inventory of Family Planning Services: 1975 Survey Results* (Washington: PHS Pub. No. 78–1814, April 1978), p. 3.

As noted earlier, the location of clinics under these diverse sponsorships may vary. A breakdown of these locations, according to sponsoring body is shown in Table 11-2. This table also reflects the precise meaning of certain sponsorship categories; thus, under county government more than two-thirds (855 out of 1,200) of the clinic locations are in state or local health department buildings, suggesting that these agencies are, in fact, the sponsors of the clinics. Similarly,

Table 11-2 Family Planning Services: Sponsorship of Clinics, by Location, United States, 1975.

Sponsorship	Health Dept.	Hospital	School	Welfare Dept.	Store	Doctor's Office	Church	Mobile Unit	Other	All Sites
County government	855	53	106	11	4	15	27	38	91	1,200
State government	564	59	82	18	9	17	8	2	155	914
Health district	194	5	19	3	1	12	2	30	15	281
City or metropolitan area	121	24	42	2	4	3	8	12	40	256
Indian Health Service	10	41	11	—	1	2	—	3	50	118
Other federal government	32	106	36	2	2	15	7	13	94	307
Other nonfederal government	6	3	3	—	—	—	—	—	2	14
Nonprofit corporation	109	131	138	11	2	—	52	19	461	923
For-profit corporation[a]	—	—	—	—	25	75	—	—	—	100
University	22	26	84	1	3	4	1	1	47	189
Hospital	8	202	16	—	1	4	3	1	16	251
Church	—	3	4	—	—	—	6	—	—	13
Individual or partnership	—	3	1	—	1	22	—	—	2	29
Other nongovernment	7	4	15	—	2	2	6	—	29	65
All sponsorships	1,928	660	557	48	55	171	120	119	1,002	4,660

[a] The distribution of sites has been estimated from data in the original survey.
Source: U.S. National Center for Health Statistics, *The National Inventory of Family Planning Services: 1975 Survey* (Washington: PHS Pub. No. 78–1814, April 1978), p. 3.

of the 923 clinic sites under nonprofit corporations (essentially voluntary agencies), 461 or about half are at "other" locations, as distinguished from those occupying space in health departments, hospitals, or schools.

This heterogeneity of sponsorship and physical setting of FP clinics in the nation is another striking illustration of the pluralism of American health services. The above data, moreover, are not complete, being based on 4,660 responses to questionnaires sent to 5,636 addresses where FP clinics were identified as being in operation in 1975.[59] Even so, the Alan Guttmacher Institute, the major research organization in this field, estimates that less than 60 percent of the national needs for FP service are being met.[60] This is a conservative calculation, in which women of very low or marginal income are estimated to number 9,908,000 in the nation. Of these, 36.8 percent were estimated to be receiving FP services from organized programs in 1976, and another 22.0 percent from private physicians, a total of 58.8 percent of the poor women. The degree of regularity with which these women receive services, however, is uncertain. We know that the U.S. birth rate has been declining—from about 24 per 1,000 population per year in 1960 to about 15 per 1,000 in 1974. Nevertheless, if one considers educational attainment as a rough indirect reflection of income level and social class, in the period 1966–70, the rates of unwanted births (that might have been averted by effective contraception) were as follows:[61]

Educational Attainment	Unwanted Births per 1,000 Fertile Woman-years
Less than high school	43
High school completion	34
Some college	24

Source: N. B. Ryder and C. F. Westoff, "Wanted and Unwanted Fertility in the U.S. in 1965 and 1970, in *Demographic and Social Aspects of Population Growth* (Washington: U.S. Commission on Population Growth and the American Future, 1972, vol. I, pp. 467–468.

Expressed in terms of birth control practice, the use of the contraceptive pill or intrauterine device by women in 1970, according to educational level attained, was:[62]

Educational Attainment	Percent of Women Using Contraception
Less than high school	33
High school completion	39
Some college	42

Source: N. B. Ryder, "Recent Trends and Group Differences in Fertility," in C. F. Westoff (editor), *Toward the End of Growth* (Englewood Cliffs, N.J.: Prentice-Hall, 1973).

The differentials in these rates of contraceptive practice would doubtless be greater, if not for the impact of FP clinics available to low-income women. The small charges usually collected at these clinics are intended only to cover the costs of medications and devices. Since 1970, the U.S. birth rate has continued to decline, suggesting an increasing impact of the FP clinic movement.

When contraception fails or has not been used, a last resort for coping with unwanted pregnancies is abortion. Although this was an illegal and clandestine practice in the U.S. for decades, numerous changes in state legislation in the 1960s and a landmark Supreme Court decision in 1973 changed the whole status of this medical procedure.[63] As a result, the rate of abortions of unwanted pregnancies rose rapidly, and organized programs developed to facilitate the procedure for women wanting it. These included clinics at which women could obtain advice on how to get abortions at relatively lower costs, and also clinics, about half of which were in hospital outpatient departments where safe abortions could be obtained without an inpatient admission.[64] In some feminist women's clinics legal abortions are done for the ambulatory patient, with the entire procedure requiring only a few hours.

While abortion remains a subject of legal and philosophical contention in the U.S., and there is general agreement that contraception is preferable to unwanted pregnancy, abortion must realistically be regarded as one medical option contributing to FP. On a world level, abortion—both legal and illegal, varying among countries—continues to be a major form of birth control and even population policy.[65] FP, by diverse methods, has become a worldwide movement intended to stem the growth of the earth's population. The numerous American clinics for this purpose are a response to this general concern.

This account of various clinics for family planning service, like the overviews of clinics for mental disorders and for crippling conditions, is meant mainly to illustrate heterogeneous approaches to certain health problems. Similar overviews might be taken of clinics for cancer, heart disease, malnutrition, or visual disorders.

CLINICS PROVIDING CERTAIN TYPES OF TECHNICAL SERVICES

Organized ambulatory services are also definable by still another dimension: the type of technical service rendered. By this criterion, persons of many types with health problems of many sorts may be provided a certain type of technical service. This approach might classify clinics according to services provided by: (a) physicians, and (b) other personnel; or according to (a) preventive services, and (b) therapeutic services. Such categories, however, would be too broad to be of value in clarifying understanding of the clinic movement.

We shall consider, therefore, two types of organized technical services of more restricted scope: emergency services and organized home care. Both constitute movements involving ambulatory care, but also involve other activities. Finally a few words will be offered about certain new modalities for the organized delivery of certain other technical services.

Organized Emergency Services

The clinic for any type of health service may be regarded as one place in a continuum of activities, starting with the patient (at home or elsewhere) recognizing a symptom indicating a need for care, transportation to the clinic, provision of service, possible referral for further care in a hospital or elsewhere, immediately or later, then final recovery, stabilization, or death. One usually takes this flow of activities for granted. The continuum of activities in which the *emergency care* clinic is a part, however, is of exceptional importance; it influences substantially the degree to which the clinic services are effective. For this reason, emergency services must be discussed not simply as the product of a clinic but rather as the content of a dynamic *system*.

Emergency care systems operate everywhere in the world. Focusing just on the United States, they may vary from the weak system in an impoverished rural county, where communication and transportation are deficient, where medical and other health care resources are inadequate, and where there are no personnel or equipment to cope with unusual or especially severe illness or injury, to a strong system in a large prosperous city. Here, communication by a prearranged telephone code is rapid, transportation by ambulance is fast and skillful, first aid is given by well-trained personnel, diagnostic equipment and staff are available to determine the nature of the injury, and surgical or other intervention can be promptly undertaken if necessary.

An overview of organized emergency services in the United States requires, then, consideration of communication and transportation resources—subjects not discussed in earlier chapters. A major problem in any community is to create widespread access to a channel of communication to summon immediate medical help. In Los Angeles County, for example, as of 1972 there were 54 different telephone numbers through which rapid medical assistance could be sought.[66] In January 1968, however, the American Telephone and Telegraph Company established a "universal emergency telephone number"—number 911. By 1972 this had been adopted in 230 communities, ranging from towns of a few thousand to the nation's largest metropolis, New York City.[67] Through this single number, a police dispatcher connects the caller with the nearest ambulance service appropriate for transportation of the case.

Ambulance transportation is a crucial component in any effective system of emergency services. In the United States, the concept was first developed in the military operations of the Civil War, after which ambulances began to be operated by large municipal hospitals.[68] Gradually other organizations, not linked to any one hospital, began to operate ambulances that could not only transport emergency cases to the hospital, but also could transfer patients between hospitals or from hospital to home. By 1977, there were an estimated 13,780 ambulance-operating organizations in the United States with about 27,000 vehicles.[69] In small towns, the service has often been provided by funeral directors, since their hearses are structurally appropriate for carrying patients on stretchers.

In 1968, a nationwide sample survey of entities owning ambulances was published, with findings on sponsorship as follows:[70]

Sponsorship	Percent
Funeral company	36.2
Other commercial firm	31.2
Volunteer group	31.3
Local government	26.4
Hospital	4.8
Other	0.7

Source: Dunlap and Associates, *Economics of Highway Emergency Ambulance Service: Final Report,* 2 vols. (Washington: 1968).

The above percentages, it may be noted, add to more than 100 because the investigators collected information from several sources and did not eliminate duplication in their final tabulations. If rough adjustments are made for this problem, it would appear that about half of the nation's ambulance services are operated by proprietary companies (funeral and other commercial firms) and the balance by local government and voluntary agencies. Among local government entities, fire departments are most common and police departments next; health departments are very rare.

Recognition of the many deaths due to delays in the proper treatment of emergency cases—trauma, heart attacks, etc.—mounted in the years after World War II. In 1962, the Ambulance Association of America was formed by about 100 private and public operators from around the nation, and issued a set of professional standards.[71] The National Academy of Sciences and National Research Council drew widespread attention to the needs in 1972 by issuing a survey of governmental resources and recommended standards for emergency care.[72] Substantial progress in extending minimum technical standards for ambulance staffing, equipment, and operations, however, did not come until federal enactment of the Emergency Medical Services Systems (EMSS) Act in 1973.[73] Under this law, grants are made to the states for development of "emergency medical service systems," including 15 mandatory components. Important among these are proper training of ambulance attendants in crucial first aid procedures, suitable staffing and identification of hospital emergency care units, and efficient communication networks.

In the 1970s, national interest in improvement of local EMSS spiralled. A wide range of research has been carried out on both the clinical and administrative aspects of EMSS programs.[74,75] The Robert Wood Johnson Foundation gave extensive support through grants for innovative EMSS state programs.[76] General hospitals gave increasing attention to the proper organization and staffing of the emergency services in their outpatient departments, as well as to upgrading the efficiency of intensive care units for patients requiring immediate admission.[77] An American College of Emergency Physicians, founded in 1968, grew rapidly to nearly 10,000 members by 1979, and in that year emergency medicine became formally recognized as a specialty by the American Medical Association.[78]

By 1974, legal regulation of ambulance services was implemented in 26 states. Advanced life support, or EMSS programs, with ambulances staffed by trained paramedical personnel—usually under local fire departments—have been organized in about 400 communities.[79] The particularly difficult problems of EMSS development in rural regions, where highway automobile accidents are often extremely serious, have attracted special attention.[80] Improved outcomes of trauma cases from accidents in rural regions have been demonstrated in Illinois, where a statewide EMSS program has been particularly well developed.[81]

There are many more aspects to overall emergency care systems, but this may be enough to indicate the wide range of activities they encompass, of which hospital outpatient care is only one component. In Chapter 4, the spiralling volume of hospital outpatient emergency services, particularly since 1950, has been discussed. In spite of mounting recognition of the need for efficient systems for handling truly emergency cases, it will be recalled that most of the escalating utilization rates has been, not for treatment of urgent and critical conditions, but for simple primary care. Study after study has demonstrated that persons of all income (although more frequently the poor) have been seeking help at hospital emergency departments for minor conditions, mainly because of inadequate access to primary care doctors or other resources for simple medical care.[82] Hospitals have made contracts with physicians with increasing frequency to staff their emergency units around the clock. According to the American Hospital Association, such contracts with full-time physicians were made by 16 percent of U.S. hospitals in 1971 and rose to 23 percent of hospitals in 1975.[83] Only in some larger hospitals is there an attempt to screen entering OPD patients and refer them either to appropriate primary care physicians or to emergency care physicians.

Confining our view to emergency service required to deal with truly critical conditions in urgent need of attention, the hospital OPD is surely the major resource in the nation's entire health care system. Even if he or she has a personal physician, the patient who is suddenly struck with a critical symptom or a serious injury is most likely to seek care at the nearest general hospital. Clinics under the several other types of sponsorships play various roles in the provision of emergency services.

Health department clinics with traditional preventive objectives would rarely, if ever, be confronted with emergency cases, but some of the newer public health clinics providing general ambulatory care do get such cases. Since most general clinics are located in poverty districts of cities, they may be the most convenient medical resource in neighborhoods where trauma tends to occur at relatively high rates. In unusual integrated local public health agencies, such as that of Denver, Colorado, where peripheral local ambulatory care centers are linked to a central city hospital under unified direction, the neighborhood facility can serve as the first resource for emergency patients, who may then be promptly transported to the hospital.[84,85]

With regard to emergency prevention, some public health agencies operate poison control centers, from which immediate advice or actual service may be given for treatment of anyone who has accidently or deliberately ingested a poison. Most of these units are located in hospitals, with technical information furnished to them by the federal Food and Drug Administration. In 1975, there were an estimated 654 poison control centers in the nation.[86]

School health clinics, although they are staffed mainly by nurses, are largely devoted to first aid for minor illnesses or injuries. Occasionally school children may have serious accidents, for which the school nurse arranges immediate transportation to a hospital. Also, with respect to accident prevention, instruction of children on safety and environmental hazards is a normal part of the school health curriculum.[87] In university health services, emergency precautions are often taken at major athletic events—including the nearby stationing of ambulances—in case of serious injuries.[88]

Emergency first aid for work injuries is a major function of virtually all in-plant industrial health clinics. Very large plants sometimes maintain quarters and equipment for immediate surgical treatment of serious injuries. In smaller plants, industrial nurses customarily maintain regular relationships with a nearby hospital, to which a seriously injured worker may be promptly sent. Safety education of employees is also among the functions of occupational health programs, although this task may be shared with departments of personnel or general management.[89] Safeguards on machinery and other accident prevention strategies are required by legislation and subject to enforcement, usually by state departments of labor or industry.[90]

Private group practice clinics provide emergency medical care in the same sense as does a private physician. It is likely that they play a greater role in emergency service than the average solo practitioner, if only because of the greater visibility of a medical group structure and the higher likelihood of 24-hour availability of some group clinic physician. Moreover, as observed in

Chapter 7, many small industrial plants in an area may contract with a particular private medical clinic for emergency treatment of injured workers. Similar contracts are being made by hospitals for coverage of their emergency departments; counting both full-time and part-time contractual physicians, this was done by 30 percent of U.S. hospitals in 1975.[91] On the other hand, group practice clinics devoted entirely to primary care have been developed adjacent to general hospitals, specifically to reduce the burden of primary care patients coming to the hospital OPD.[92]

Finally, among the specially sponsored clinics financed by government, any of the ambulatory facilities for federal beneficiaries may be presented with emergency care problems. For obvious reasons, this would apply with special significance to clinics for military personnel; even in times of peace, training maneuvers may result in many injuries or collapse due to general stress.

The locally sponsored health centers supported by federal grants occasionally treat emergency cases from their immediate neighborhoods. In the poverty areas where they are often located, injuries due to accident or violence are relatively frequent, so that the health center can be the closest source of first aid. The earliest neighborhood health centers of the 1960s, it will be recalled, were often built precisely at the site of urban riots where, for many social and economic reasons, rates of crime and violence were exceptionally high. Among other voluntary health agencies, the American Red Cross plays a special role in providing emergency services in communities struck by natural disasters, as well as in its continuing preventive training programs on techniques of first aid.[93]

Thus, in spite of the overriding importance of the hospital outpatient department in providing emergency medical care, it is evident that many other types of clinics contribute to the full spectrum of services. Beyond clinics, of course, are the numerous strategies for communication, transportation, and prevention, required for achieving a comprehensive emergency care system in a community. Supportive of all these activities are training programs and official regulations to assure that proper standards are being followed. The widespread acceptance of the concept of a comprehensive system of emergency care is noteworthy in this field, in contrast to the customary objections to such integration in so many other sectors of American health service.[94] One is reminded of the social spirit attained at times of war, when the nation can rapidly mobilize collective efforts and self-discipline seldom achieved at other times. Perhaps there are implications in the contemporary development of EMSS that may apply to policy formulation in other sectors of American health care.

Organized Home Care

A quite different type of technical service related to ambulatory care is the organized delivery of health services to patients in their own homes. While not constituting a form of clinic, organized home care is intended to serve a some-what corresponding purpose: to provide needed health services outside a hospital ward. Also, like organized out-of-hospital services of other types, home care programs with a common objective may be sponsored by several different types of agencies.

Care of patients in their own homes is, of course, as old as the healing arts, but organized delivery of such care, with various types of skilled personnel furnishing a coordinated range of services, originated only in recent times. The first initiative was taken by a hospital, whose long-term patients required certain services but not necessarily hospitalization. Montefiore Hospital in New York City provided such a combination of services to terminal cancer and other chron-ically ill patients having suitable home conditions, beginning in 1949.[95] For the next decade, organized home care programs were launched mainly by hospitals, sometimes with the collaboration of voluntary visiting nurse associations (VNA).[96] A major rationale in the first years was the capability of home care to provide good quality services at lower costs per case than inpatient hospital care, while also releasing hospital beds for patients with more acute needs.[97]

When federal legislation on health insurance for the aged (Medicare) was enacted in 1965, a great boost was given to the organized home care movement. Medicare paid for services not only in general hospitals and "extended care facilities" (skilled nursing homes), but also, under specified conditions, for defined services rendered to the patient at home by approved "home health agencies." Approval was ordinarily required from the state health department.[98] With this immense increase in financial support, home health agencies and organized home care programs expanded rapidly. Counting only home health agencies approved for participation in the national Medicare program, their numbers increased from 1,275 in 1966, to 2,185 in 1976.[99]

Most of this home care program growth, furthermore, was attributable to establishment of approved programs by agencies other than hospitals. Health departments and voluntary VNAs, in particular, had long been providing certain nursing services to chronically ill homebound patients. Now, by supplementation of those services with the skilled services of rehabilitation personnel, social workers, etc., these local programs could become certified for Medicare reim-bursement. As a result, the great majority of approved home health agencies soon came to be sponsored by community agencies outside hospitals.[100]

Nevertheless, hospital-sponsored home care programs increased from only a handful in 1956—about 30, according to an American Medical Association survey[101]—to 456, or 7.0 percent of all hospitals reporting to the American Hospital Association (AHA) in 1977.[102] An AHA survey in 1972 indicated that the scope of services offered by these hospital-based programs was exceptionally broad, including laboratory services, drugs, nutritional counseling, and medical equipment as well as the more common nursing, physical therapy, and social work services.[103] In spite of this, many hospital-sponsored home care programs have not been approved or sought approval under Medicare. Moreover, just as the early hospital-founded home care programs obtained nursing services from VNAs, today many VNA-sponsored and other types of home care programs acquire certain services (e.g., laboratory tests) from hospitals.

As of 1977, the most numerous home health agencies participating in Medicare were those sponsored by local health departments. In that year there were 2,496 Medicare-approved home health agencies in the nation, and their sponsorships were distributed as follows:[104]

Sponsoring Agency	Percent
Local health department	50
Visiting nurse association	20
Combination of the above	2
Independent voluntary nonprofit agency	12
Hospital	11
Proprietary agency	4
Other	1
All sponsorships	100

Source: Jane Stewart, Home Health Care (St. Louis, Mo.: Mosby Co., 1979), p. 26.

Among the above array of sponsorships, the VNA is a type of voluntary health agency not otherwise concerned with operation of clinics. The independent voluntary nonprofit agencies conducting home care programs are essentially a product of the Medicare law, as are the proprietary (for-profit) agencies. While constituting only a small proportion of the home health agencies, these programs have focused on Medicare patients, and this has led to their carrying relatively large caseloads. Thus, the average hospital-based program might carry at any one time about 50 patients in its home care department, while the independent and specialized home health agencies often carry caseloads of several hundred patients.

Utilization data for all organized home care programs in the nation are not available, but for persons covered under Medicare—probably a high proportion of the total—the experience has been tabulated for 1974.[105] In that year 393,000 Medicare enrollees received services from home health agencies—a rate of 16.5 per 1,000 eligible. The aggregate home health visits that year were 8.1 million, an average of 20.6 visits for each patient served. In the period before Medicare, organized home care was provided largely for low-income patients, not served by a private physician; with the advent of Medicare, patients of all income levels have become recipients of these services. Forty-seven percent of Medicare patients served by home health agencies received fewer than 10 visits during the year, while 2 percent received 100 visits or more. Of the total visits 65 percent were nursing services, 23 percent were home health aide services, and 10 percent were physical therapy services.

Organized home care services are clearly a relatively new mode for delivery of out-of-hospital medical care, even though they are not ambulatory in the usual sense. As the aging of the population continues and people are surviving with their chronic disorders, and as inpatient hospital care continues to be expensive, one may expect organized home care programs to increase in importance. Indeed, data released in 1980 showed Medicare-supported home health agency visits to have risen during 1978 to more than 17 million.[106]

Other Special Technical Services

Beyond emergency services and organized home care, there are several other organized resources for delivery of special ambulatory or out-of-hospital services.

Clinical laboratories, for example, are principally associated with hospitals, health departments, and group practice clinics, as discussed in previous chapters. Out of a total of 13,626 such laboratory units nationally in 1976, however, 3,628 were independent facilities.[107] These constitute resources for organized delivery of certain technical services that might otherwise be provided in individual physicians' offices.

Organized dental clinics have been noted in connection with public health programs, school health services, and other sponsoring agencies. Private group dental practice, however, has not been discussed. Grouping has not been so strong a movement in dentistry as in medicine, but it is growing. An American Academy of Dental Group Practice defines this form of clinic as having "three or more dentists cooperating in the delivery of dental care under a formal arrangement in which facilities, personnel, expenses, income, or any combination of these are shared."[108] By this definition (although somewhat less detailed), a survey by the USPHS identified 715 such clinics in 1970, involving 3,148 dentists (of whom 2,412 were full-time and 736 were part-time).[109] This constituted 3.3 percent of active civilian dentists in the United States at the time.

Kidney dialysis is a sophisticated medical procedure most frequently carried out in hospitals. In 1972, "end-stage renal disease"—for which this costly life-extending procedure is performed—was made a benefit of Medicare, and this led to a great increase in organized dialysis services. By 1977 there were 841 Medicare-approved kidney disease treatment centers in the nation. Of these 655 were in hospitals and 186 were freestanding units.[110] Of the latter, 3 percent were under governmental sponsorship, 24 percent under voluntary nonprofit auspices, and 73 percent were proprietary.

Finally, an innovative and particularly significant type of technical service that has recently been developed for ambulatory patients in the United States is the ambulatory surgical center. Because of the spiralling costs of inpatient hospital care, in the 1960s university hospitals began to experiment with performance of elective surgical operations, under general anaesthesia, in their outpatient departments. (This is not to be confused with minor surgical procedures, often done in the physician's office under local anaesthesia. It involves orthopedic, plastic, urological, or other operations definable as "major surgery" but having a low operative risk and feasible to perform without the patient remaining in the hospital overnight.)[111] In 1970, the Phoenix Surgicenter, the first freestanding and independently owned (i.e., not linked to a hospital) ambulatory surgical facility, was opened in Phoenix, Arizona.[112]

Soon after, a number of other such freestanding surgicenters were established throughout the United States. By 1974 a Society for the Advancement of Free-Standing Ambulatory Surgical Care was founded, representing 57 such units.[113] Nearly all of these are owned and operated by physicians, individually or in partnerships. At the same time, the movement has led many hospitals to increase low risk major surgery as a regular OPD service.[114] The freestanding surgicenters, by various estimates, had increased by 1976 to around 100.[115] As hospital costs continue to soar, the number of these new types of ambulatory care facility will doubtless grow.

This completes our review of the panorama of clinics in the United States, in which they have been analyzed by selected purposes. To classify the great multiplicity of units according to all possible purposes—along the three dimensions of person, disorder, and service—would be a monumental task. This account may serve to illustrate, however, the scope of organizational sponsorships that should be considered, if one wishes to describe clinics with a certain type of purpose. To mention purposes not considered here, one might wish to learn, for example, about clinics for the aged, clinics for cancer, or clinics providing pharmaceutical services; with some effort, such descriptive overviews would also be feasible. This way of considering clinics may be helpful in relation to objectives in national health planning. At the same time, the results tend to underscore the complexities of the entire American health care system.

NOTES

1. American Hospital Association, *Reshaping Ambulatory Programs* (Chicago: AHA, 1973).

2. National Cooperative Services Center for Hospital Management Engineering, *Examination of Case Studies on Ambulatory Care Systems* (Chicago: Hospital Research and Educational Trust, 1975).

3. Blue Cross/Blue Shield of Greater New York, *Organization and Processes of Hospital Based Ambulatory Care* (New York, April 1975).

4. Center for Community Health Systems, *Community Hospitals and the Challenge of Primary Care* (New York: Columbia University, 1975).

5. U.S. Public Health Service, *Promoting the Health of Mothers and Children, Fiscal Year 1973,* DHEW Publication (HSA) 74–5002 (Washington: 1974), p. 26.

6. Butler, Patricia, "An Advocate's Guide to Early and Periodic Screening, Diagnosis and Treatment," *Clearinghouse Review,* May 1976, pp. 1–11.

7. Holahan, John, *Financing Health Care for the Poor: The Medicaid Experience,* Working Paper No. 976–01 (Washington: The Urban Institute, 1974).

8. Lewis, Charles E.; Rashi Fein; and David Mechanic, *A Right to Health: The Problem of Access to Primary Medical Care* (New York: John Wiley & Sons, 1976), pp. 144–164.

9. Mullen, L. R., and A. G. Schneider, "HMOs and the Poor: Another Look at the California Experience," *Health Law Project,* Library Bulletin 323, July 1976.

10. President of the United States, *The Budget for Fiscal Year 1981* (Washington: 1980), p. 252.

11. *National Association of Community Health Centers, Inc.,* booklet (Washington: 1979).

12. U.S. Public Health Service, *Maternal and Child Health Services of State and Local Health Departments—Fiscal Years 1974, 1975, 1976,* DHEW Pub. No. HSA 79–5734 (Washington), p. 45.

13. Ibid., p. 2.

14. U.S. Public Health Service, *Children Who Received Physicians' Services under the Crippled Children's Program, Fiscal Year 1973,* DHEW Pub. No. HSA 77–5731 (Washington: 1977), p. 8.

15. Novick, Lloyd F.; A. Mustalish; and G. Eidsvold, "Converting Child Health Stations to Pediatric Treatment Centers," *Medical Care* 13 (1975): 744–752.

16. U.S. National Center for Health Statistics, *National Health Survey: Physician Visits—Volume and Interval Since Last Visit, United States 1975,* Vital and Health Statistics Series 10, No. 128, (Washington: April 1979), p. 31.

17. Alcohol, Drug Abuse, and Mental Health Administration, Office of Program Planning and Coordination, *The Alcohol, Drug Abuse, and Mental Health National Data Book* (Washington, unpublished report, December 1979), p. 54.

18. Silver, George A., *Child Health—America's Future* (Germantown, Md.: Aspen Systems Corp., 1978).

19. U.S. Public Health Service, *Child Health in America,* DHEW Pub. No. HSA 76–5015, (Washington: 1976).

20. Mott, F. D., and M. I. Roemer, *Rural Health and Medical Care* (New York: McGraw-Hill Book Co., 1948).

21. Roemer, Milton I., *Rural Health Care* (St. Louis, Mo.: C. V. Mosby Co., 1977), p. 77.

22. U.S. Public Health Service, *Maternal and Child Health Services of State and Local Health Departments—Fiscal Years 1974, 1975, 1976,* Table 7.

23. Williams, Pierce, *The Purchase of Medical Care Through Fixed Periodic Payment* (New York: National Bureau of Economic Research, 1932).

24. Somers, Herman M., and Anne R. Somers, *Doctors, Patients, and Health Insurance* (Washington: Brookings Institution, 1961), p. 230.

25. U.S. Public Health Service, *Medical Groups in the United States, 1959,* PHS Pub. No. 1063 (Washington: 1963).

26. Roemer, Milton I., "The Ecology of Group Medical Practice in the United States," *Medical Care* 12 (1974): 627–637.

27. Kane, Robert L., "Problems in Rural Health Care," in *Health Services: The Local Perspective* (New York: Academy of Political Science, 1977), pp. 136–147.

28. Ahearn, Mary C., *Health Care in Rural America,* U.S. Department of Agriculture, Agriculture Information Bulletin No. 428 (Washington: July 1979), p. 12.

29. U.S. National Center of Health Statistics, *The National Inventory of Family Planning Services: 1975 Survey Results,* Public Health Service Pub. No. (PHS) 78–1814 (Washington: April 1978), p. 12.

30. Kane, Robert L., "Problems in Rural Health Care," pp. 142–143.

31. Roemer, Milton I., "Historical Perspective on Rural Health Services in America," in *Rural Health Care,* (St. Louis, Mo.: C. V. Mosby Co., 1976).

32. *Rural Health Communications,* an International publication by the Clearinghouse for Rural Health in conjunction with the American Rural Health Association , (February 17, 1978), p. 3.

33. Bible, Bond L., "National Rural Primary Care Association—An Idea Whose Time Has Come" *National Rural Primary Care Association,* (Waterville, Me.: January 1980), p. 1.

34. Council on Rural Health, American Medical Association, *Health Care Delivery in Rural Areas: Selected Models* (Chicago: AMA, September 1969).

35. American Osteopathic Association, *The Rural Clinic Program* (Kirksville, Mo.: 1978).

36. Bernstein, James D.; F. P. Hege; and L. C. Farran, *Rural Health Centers in the United States* (Cambridge, Mass.: Ballinger Publishing Co., 1979).

37. Plumb, William: October 1979, personal communication.

38. Holland, Charles D., and B. T. Durmaskin, "Progress in the Development of Rural Primary Care Clinics in West Virginia," *Public Health Reports* 94 (1979): 369–371.

39. U.S. Bureau of Community Health Service, *Building a Rural Health System,* DHEW Pub. No. (HSA) 76–15028 (Washington: 1976).

40. American Hospital Association, *Hospital Statistics 1978 Edition* (Chicago: AHA, 1978), p. 196.

41. U.S. Alchohol, Drug Abuse, and Mental Health Administration, *The Alcohol, Drug Abuse, and Mental Health National Data Book* (Washington: January 1980), p. 25.

42. U.S. National Institute of Mental Health, *1979 Directory of Federally Funded Community Mental Health Centers* (Washington: 1979), p. 2.

43. Kahne, M. J., and C. G. Schwartz, "The College as a Psychiatric Workplace," *Psychiatry* 38 (1975): 107–123. See also: Bloom, B. L., "Current Issues in the Provision of Campus Community Mental Health Services," *Journal of the American College Health Association* 18 (1970): 257–264.

44. Goldbeck, Willis B., "Corporate Mental Health Benefits," in Richard H. Egdahl, ed., *Background Papers on Industry's Changing Role in Health Care Delivery* (New York: Springer-Verlag, 1977), p. 100.

45. U.S. Alcohol, Drug Abuse, and Mental Health Administration, *National Data Book,* p. 52.

46. American Hospital Association, *Hospital Statistics 1978 Edition,* p. 195.

47. Commission on the Accreditation of Rehabilitation Facilities, *Standards and Accreditation Program for Rehabilitation Facilities* (Chicago: January 1977).

48. Association of Rehabilitation Centers, *1968 Directory of Rehabilitation Facilities* (Washington: July–August 1968).

49. Kessler, Henry H., "The Employability of the Handicapped" in *Proceedings: Sixth Annual Meeting,* Industrial Hygiene Foundation of America, (Pittsburgh, Pa.: 1942).

50. U.S. Bureau of the Census, *Persons with Work Disability,* Census of the Population 1970, Final Report PC (2) -6C (Washington: 1973), pp. 1–3.

51. U.S. Office of Economic Opportunity, Executive Office of the President, *Need for Subsidized Family Planning Services: United States, Each State and County, 1969* (Washington: 1970), p. 3.

52. U.S. National Center for Health Statistics, *Health Resources Statistics, 1976–77 Edition* (Washington: 1979), p. 387.

53. American Hospital Association, *Hospital Statistics 1978 Edition*, p. 197.

54. Torres, Aida, "Organized Family Planning Services in the United States, 1968–1976," *Family Planning Perspectives* 10 (1978): 83–88.

55. U.S. Department of Health, Education, and Welfare, *Report of the Secretary of Health, Education, and Welfare Submitting Five-Year Plan for Family Planning Services and Population Research Programs* (Washington: October 1971).

56. Zelnik, M., and J. F. Kantner, "The Resolution of Teenage First Pregnancies," *Family Planning Perspectives*, 6 (1974): 74–80.

57. Alan Guttmacher Institute, *Planned Births, the Future of the Family and the Quality of American Life* (June 1977), p. 12.

58. U.S. National Center for Health Statistics, *The National Inventory of Family Planning Services: 1975 Survey Results*, (PHS) 78–1814 (Washington: April 1978), p. 3.

59. U.S. National Center for Health Statistics, *Directory: Family Planning Service Sites, United States* (Washington: November 1977), p. 1.

60. Torres, Aida, "Organized Family Planning Services," p. 87.

61. Ryder, N. B., and C. F. Westoff, "Wanted and Unwanted Fertility in the United States, 1965 and 1970," in U.S. Commission on Population Growth and the American Future, *Demographic and Social Aspects of Population Growth* (Washington: 1972).

62. Ryder, N. B., "Recent Trends and Group Differences in Fertility," in C. F. Westoff, ed., *Toward the End of Growth* (New York: Prentice-Hall, 1973).

63. Roemer, Ruth, "Legalization of Abortion in the United States," in Joy and Howard Osotsky, eds., *The Abortion Experience, Psychological and Medical Impact* (Hagerstown, Md.: Harper & Row, 1973), pp. 280–301.

64. Forrest, Jacqueline D.; C. Tietze; and E. Sullivan, "Abortion in the United States, 1976–1977," *Family Planning Perspectives* 10 (1978): 271–279.

65. Potts, Malcolm; P. Diggory; and J. Peel, *Abortion* (Cambridge, England: Cambridge University Press, 1977), pp. 83–107.

66. Countywide Conference on Emergency Medical Services, *Proceedings: EMS*, Los Angeles, Calif., June 1972.

67. Ibid.

68. Curry, G. J., "Immediate Care and Transport of the Injured: History and Development," in *Immediate Care and Transport of the Injured* (C. J. Curry, editor) (Springfield, Ill.: C. C. Thomas, 1965), p. 9.

69. U.S. National Center of Health Statistics, "Ambulance Services" in *Health Resources Statistics 1976–77 Edition* (Washington: 1979), pp. 353–354.

70. Dunlap and Associates, Final Report: *Economics of Highway Emergency Ambulance Service*, 2 vols. (Washington: July 1968).

71. Mehren, E. W., "Ambulance Association of America," in G. J. Curry, ed., *Immediate Care and Transport of the Injured* (Springfield, Ill.: C. C. Thomas, 1965), p. 10.

72. National Academy of Sciences, National Research Council, *Roles and Resources of Federal Agencies in Support of Comprehensive Emergency Medical Services* (Washington: March 1972).

73. Sadler, Alfred.; B. L. Sadler; and S. R. Webb, *Emergency Medical Care: The Neglected Public Service* (Cambridge, Mass.: Ballinger Co., 1977), pp. 11–14.

74. Willemain, Thomas R., and R. C. Larson, eds., *Emergency Medical Systems Analysis* (Lexington, Mass.: Lexington Books, 1977).

75. U.S. National Center for Health Services Research, *Emergency Medical Services Systems Research Project Abstracts, 1979,* DHHS Pub. No. (PHS) 80–3271 (Washington: 1980).

76. Robert Wood Johnson Foundation, "Emergency Medical Services," *Special Report,* No. 2, 1977.

77. American Hospital Association, *Emergency Services: The Hospital Emergency Department in an Emergency Care System,* (Chicago, Ill.: AHA, 1972).

78. American College of Emergency Physicians, "Emergency Medicine Becomes a Formally Recognized Specialty," *News of Emergency Medicine,* news release, March 16, 1979.

79. U.S. National Center for Health Statistics, "Ambulance Services," p. 353.

80. Waller, Julian A., "Rural Emergency Care—Problems and Prospects," *American Journal of Public Health* 63 (1973): 631–634.

81. Mullner, Ross, and J. Goldberg, "An Evaluation of the Illinois Trauma System," *Medical Care* 63 (1978): 140–151.

82. U.S. Health Care Facilities Service, *Selected References on Hospital Outpatient and Emergency Activities,* HEW Pub. No. (HSM) 73–4024 (Washington: 1973).

83. American Hospital Association, "Ambulatory Care Survey Shows Gain in E.D. Contract Physicians," *Hospitals,* JAHA, March 16, 1977, pp. 177–180.

84. Cowen, D. L., "Community Health—A Local Government Responsibility," *American Journal of Public Health,* 61 (1971): 2005–2009.

85. Shonick, William, and W. Price, "Reorganizations of Health Agencies by Local Government in American Urban Centers: What Do They Portend for 'Public Health'?" *MMFQ/Health and Society,* Spring 1977, pp. 233–271.

86. U.S. National Center for Health Statistics, "Poison Control Centers," in *Health Resources Statistics 1976–77 Edition* (Washington: 1979), pp. 429–431.

87. Punke, H. H., "Safety and Early Childhood Education," *Journal of School Health,* 41 (1971): 146–153.

88. Garrick, J. G., "Prevention of Sports Injuries," *Postgraduate Medicine* 51 (1972): 125–129.

89. Howe, H. F., "Preventing Occupational Health and Safety Hazards in Small Employee Groups," *American Journal of Public Health* 61 (1971): 1581–1852.

90. Guenther, G. C., "Williams-Steiger Occupational Safety and Health Act," *Journal of Occupational Medicine* 13 (1971): 317–321.

91. American Hospital Association, "Ambulatory Care Survey Shows Gain in E.D. Contract Physicians."

92. Ullman, Ralph; J. A. Block; N. C. Boatright; and W. C. Stratmann, "Impact of a Primary Care Group Practice on Emergency Room Utilization at a Community Hospital," *Medical Care* 16 (1978): 723–729.

93. National Academy of Sciences, National Research Council, *Accidental Death and Disability: The Neglected Disease of Modern Society* (Chicago: American Medical Association, Commission on Emergency Medical Services, January 1970).

94. Hanlon, John J., "Emergency Medical Care as a Comprehensive System," *Health Services Reports* 88 (1973): 579–587.

95. Bluestone, E. M., "The Principles and Practice of Home Care," *Journal of the American Medical Association* 155 (1954): 1379.

96. Littauer, David; I. J. Flance; and A. F. Wessen, *Home Care,* American Hospital Association, Hospital Monograph Series No. 9 (Chicago: 1961).

97. Rogatz, Peter, et. al., *Organized Home Medical Care in New York City* (Cambridge, Mass.: Harvard University Press, 1956).

98. Ryder, C., and B. Frank, "Coordinated Home Care Programs in Community Health Agencies— A Decade of Progress," *American Journal of Public Health* 57 (1967): 261.

99. U.S. National Center for Health Statistics, "Home Health Services" in *Health Resources Statistics 1976–77 Edition* (Washington: 1979), pp. 393–397.

100. Van Dyke, Frank, and V. Brown, "Organized Home Care: An Alternative to Institutions," *Inquiry* 9 (1972): 3–16.

101. American Medical Association, "Organized 'Home Care Programs' in the United States," *Journal of the American Medical Association* 164 (1957): 298.

102. American Hospital Association, *Hospital Statistics 1978 Edition*, p. 198.

103. Richter, Lorraine, and A. Gonnerman, "Home Health Services and Hospitals," *Hospitals, JAHA*, May 16, 1974.

104. Stewart, Jane, *Home Health Care* (St. Louis, Mo.: Mosby Co., 1979), p. 26.

105. U.S. Social Security Administration, *Health Insurance Statistics: Medicare—Utilization of Home Health Services, 1974*, HEW Pub. No. (SSA) 78–11702 (Washington: November 1977).

106. U.S. Health Care Financing Administration, *Health Care Financing Notes—Medicare: Use of Home Health Services, 1978*, HCFA Pub. No. 03025 (Washington: June 1980).

107. U.S. Public Health Service, *Clinical and Public Health Laboratory Survey, 1977* (Atlanta: Center for Disease Control, 1977).

108. American Academy of Dental Group Practice, *Accreditation Program for Dental Group Practice* (Madison, Wis.: 1976).

109. U.S. Public Health Service, Division of Dental Health, *Group Dental Practice in the United States, 1971*, DHEW Pub. No. (NIH) 72–189 (Washington: 1972).

110. U.S. Public Health Service and U.S. Social Security Administration, *End-Stage Renal Disease Information System: Directory of Medicare-Approved ESRD Suppliers* (Washington: 1977).

111. O'Donovan, Thomas R., *Ambulatory Surgical Centers: Development and Management* (Germantown, Md.: Aspen Systems Corp., 1976).

112. Reed, Wallace A., and J. L. Ford, "The Surgicenter: An Ambulatory Surgical Facility," *Clinical Obstetrics and Gynecology* 17 (1974): 213.

113. "New Centers for One-Day Surgery," *Medical World News*, 16, no. 2, January 27, 1975, pp. 65–66.

114. Kennedy, Harriet Page, "Could Ambulatory Surgery Save $1.6 Billion a Year?" *Medical Tribune*, January 24, 1979, p. 17.

115. Irwin, Theodore, "We Need More Same-Day Surgical Centers," *Today's Health* 54 (1976): 10–11.

Chapter 12
Clinics of Health Maintenance Organizations

Although this book is focused on the organized *delivery* of ambulatory health services, rather than their organized *financing,* there is one important component of the U.S. health care system that involves a combination of both of these social processes and requires discussion. This is the health maintenance organization, or HMO.

INTRODUCTORY DEFINITION

By a very simplified definition, the HMO is an organized system of comprehensive health services, provided to an enrolled population for a fixed prepaid per capita expenditure. These comprehensive services include therapeutic and preventive ambulatory health care. Arrangements for these services usually, but not always, involve clinics. The financial support of these clinics, however, differs from that of most other types of clinics discussed in this volume, because it comes from an insurance fund to which contributions have been made by or on behalf of HMO enrollees. This combination of the clinic pattern with insurance financing creates dynamics quite different from those in other settings; the incentives of the HMO physician are significantly different. This exerts impact on overall expenditures for health care and has important implications for the entire American health care system.

A more detailed explanation of the HMO, as formulated by the federal government in 1971, states that it is an organized system of health care based on four principles. The HMO:

1. accepts responsibility to provide or otherwise assure the delivery of
2. an agreed upon set of comprehensive health maintenance and treatment services for

3. a voluntarily enrolled group of persons in a geographic area, and
4. is financed through a pre-negotiated and fixed periodic payment made by or on behalf of each person or family unit enrolled in the plan.[1]

Although this formulation refers to an "organized system of health care," the absence of any specific reference to clinics or even hospitals is noteworthy. This very breadth and flexibility of the concept, as we shall see, have been a crucial factor in back of the promotion of the idea by the federal government in the 1970s. This was a significant change from previous government policy, and to appreciate the meaning of this policy change, it is necessary to review briefly the historical background of health insurance in America and the origins of the "prepaid group practice movement."

THE DEVELOPMENT OF HEALTH INSURANCE

Organized financing of medical care was first confined to the poor, through mechanisms of public revenues and charity. In the city-states of ancient Greece impoverished freemen were treated by official doctors, supported from tax funds, as were the "worthy poor" in English towns under the Elizabethan Poor Laws.[2] Hospitals in the Middle Ages were supported by the charity of the Christian Church.

With the Industrial Revolution, there arose in Europe a working class that was dependent on wages for survival. If unemployed, the worker and his family would soon become destitute; however even when employed, the worker earned very little. For protection against the economic blow of serious illness, workers organized various forms of local cooperative societies to which they would make periodic contributions. Then, if sickness struck, payments could be made to them in partial compensation for lost wages as well as for the costs of medical care and drugs.[3] By the mid-nineteenth century, such local "sickness funds" were particularly numerous in Germany, and in 1883, that country enacted the first law mandating that low-paid workers *must* belong to a sickness fund. This marked the birth of the concept of "social insurance," or social security.[4] In subsequent decades, the idea spread throughout Europe, and over the years there has been a steady extension of population coverage and the scope of health services insured.

In America, as in Europe, insurance against the risks of sickness started in the nineteenth century in working populations, both for replacement of wages lost and for the costs of medical care. The early need was most prominent in isolated industries—mines, lumber camps, railroad construction sites—where local doctors and hospitals were lacking. To assure that medical care would be available to workers, the company management would deduct small amounts from each month's wages to build up a sickness fund; sometimes employers would also contribute to the fund. From this fund, one or more doctors and other personnel would be salaried, and sometimes a small hospital could be built.[5] In certain large cities, other insurance plans were organized by fraternal lodges composed mainly of European immigrants; these sometimes paid for limited care by a general practitioner on salary. In 1914 there were 179 fraternal lodges in the United States with 7.7 million members; only about one percent of their benefits (worth $97 million), however, went for medical care.[6] In the early twentieth century, some private insurance companies began to sell individual (not group) policies that insured against income loss due to sickness and covered some medical care costs.[7] The aggregate U.S. population covered by all these health insurance programs, however, was small.

Not until the Great Depression in 1929 did the insurance idea become applied in a major way to meet health care costs in America. The main initiative was taken not by workers, but by hospitals, which found themselves in serious debt because of a lack of patients (who could not afford the costs). A mechanism started quietly by individual hospitals in Dallas, Texas; New Orleans, Louisiana; and elsewhere appeared attractive: these hospitals sold low-cost insurance to employee groups to cover future hospitalization costs. In New Jersey, several hospitals joined together to form a nonprofit corporation for marketing such insurance. By 1934, the idea was so widely accepted that it was endorsed by the American Hospital Association (AHA). A set of standards was issued for these hospital insurance plans, and the movement adopted a symbol: the Blue Cross.[8]

In spite of initial opposition to Blue Cross by the medical profession (who termed it "socialized medicine"), by 1939 these views changed; in California the state medical association organized a similar nonprofit insurance program to pay doctor bills in hospitalized cases. The "California Physicians' Service" concept soon spread to other states, and in 1946 the American Medical Association (AMA) endorsed it, symbolizing these state plans with the "Blue Shield" emblem.[9] By the end of World War II, millions of people were insured against the medical and institutional costs of hospitalized illness.[10] Both of the "Blue" plans paid the providers directly for the service, rather than reimbursing the patients.

Toward the end of World War II, observing the success and financial feasibility of these nonprofit programs, the commercial insurance industry set out to market similar group insurance for hospital-related health care. Since insurance companies were already selling policies for pensions and other benefits to groups of industrial workers, they made rapid progress in selling this type of health care insurance. Unlike the "Blue" plans, however, insurance companies would indemnify the patient certain fixed amounts for various hospital and medical services, rather than paying providers directly, and if the actual charges were higher, the patient would have to pay the difference.[11] This enabled these carriers to keep insurance premiums relatively stable when hospital and medical charges were rising. Also, insurance companies (unlike the "Blue" plans) engaged in "experience rating"—offering lower premiums to lower risk groups.

For these reasons, the commercially sponsored health insurance plans soon exceeded the Blue plans in enrollment. By 1960, a solid majority of the American population were enrolled in insurance programs that paid for all or most of the costs of hospitalization—the commercial plans insuring the lion's share. The significant weakness of the whole voluntary health insurance movement was its meager coverage for out-of-hospital ambulatory medical care.

From about 1930 to the present, the health insurance plans sponsored by providers, Blue Cross and Blue Shield, and by commercial insurance companies clearly occupied center stage in American efforts to ease the impact of medical care costs. At the same time, though much less conspicuously, there were taking shape several small insurance programs offering a much broader scope of benefits and sponsored mainly by consumer groups. In order to be capable of supporting comprehensive physicians' care—that is, for the outpatient as well as the inpatient—these programs usually furnished medical care through group practice clinics, in which doctors were on salary. Identified as "prepaid group practice plans" or sometimes simply as "group health plans," these programs were the progenitors of the HMO.

PREPAID GROUP PRACTICE INSURANCE PLANS

The early insurance programs associated with isolated industries and fraternal lodges have been noted, but these financial support programs did not evolve into a national movement. The former were essentially an aspect of personnel policy in selected enterprises; the latter were small, unstable, and of limited scope.

Certain organized efforts to establish insurance for comprehensive medical care, however, evolved into a national movement with a social impact greater than might be inferred from the relatively small numbers of persons enrolled. It was perhaps the relationship of these efforts to the consumer cooperative movement that endowed them with a kind of idealistic and missionary spirit that enabled them to resist opposition, survive, and spread.

A prototype of these group health plans was the Cooperative Community Hospital, started at Elk City, Oklahoma in 1929.[12] Through the courageous leadership of one doctor, Michael Shadid, and the staunch support of a few hundred members of the local branch of the National Farmers' Union, funds were raised to build a small hospital. Farmers paid monthly membership premiums entitling them to virtually complete medical and hospital care. Services were rendered by a full-time salaried staff of doctors, nurses, and other personnel based in the hospital. Dr. Shadid was expelled from the local medical society and bitterly attacked; the opposition from Oklahoma's medical profession made frequent reference to Dr. Shadid's "foreign" background (he was an immigrant from Lebanon). The attacks only served to strengthen the determination of the farmers and the small group of idealistic doctors to continue with their Community Health Association, as it was later called. By 1945, the membership had grown to 2,600 families with more than 10,000 members.[13]

Another early program that pioneered the model of prepaid group practice was the Ross-Loos Clinic Plan in Los Angeles, California. The courageous doctors in this story were Dr. Donald Ross, who had moved to southern California from Canada, and Dr. Clifford Loos, a local surgeon; the members were employees of the Los Angeles City Department of Water and Power. In 1929, the doctors formed a group practice clinic and made an agreement with the Department of Water and Power (DWP) to provide complete medical care to those employees who so desired.[14] Since this program was located in a large city, there was no need to construct a new hospital—arrangements were made for access to beds in an existing voluntary nonprofit general hospital. In the first year about 2,000 DWP employees enrolled in the plan, and soon after membership was opened to other employee groups, both public and private. By 1941, enrollment had grown to 77,000 persons, and the salaried staff of physicians, nurses, and other personnel expanded to 265. As in Oklahoma, opposition from the local medical profession was intense. Drs. Ross and Loos and their medical colleagues were expelled from the county medical society, and only after a lengthy controversy were they reinstated. The onset of the Great Depression in late 1929, with economic pressures felt by all physicians, doubtless softened the attitude of the AMA to the concept of prepaid group practice.

A third pioneering program that contributed significantly to the prepaid group practice movement was that of the Group Health Association in Washington, D.C. In 1933, President Franklin Roosevelt's New Deal brought to the nation's capital hundreds of socially oriented new government employees; a group of them soon formed a consumer cooperative for medical care—the Group Health Association (GHA). GHA employed doctors and others on salary, and acquired an ambulatory care facility. Opposition from the local medical society in this instance took the form of denying hospital admitting privileges to GHA physicians. In response, GHA took legal action accusing the District of Columbia Medical Society, as well as the AMA, of violation of the Sherman Anti-Trust Act, claiming that they were obstructing a new form of "trade" in medical services. After a lengthy court battle, GHA won in 1943, and the medical societies were convicted in the federal courts of "criminal conspiracy in restraint of trade."[15]

This legal victory for prepaid group practice was an important milestone in the movement for health care cooperatives and prepaid group practice. In 1946, another crusading organization was founded in Seattle, Washington: the Group

Health Cooperative of Puget Sound.[16] Learning a lesson from the GHA experience in Washington, D.C., the Puget Sound Cooperative proceeded to build its own hospital and clinic facilities. Moreover, after World War II, in rural areas of the western United States, many small group health cooperatives were organized, with only a few hundred members each and loose linkages with private group practice clinics of a few doctors. In 1950, it was estimated that more than 100 of these had sprung up in 21 states.[17] With the general prosperity of the 1950s, however, and the rapid extension of conventional health insurance reviewed earlier, few of these small programs survived.

The crusading spirit that generated consumer-sponsored health insurance programs linked with group practice clinics was bound to become focused in a national association. This first occurred in 1937, when the Cooperative League of the USA established a Bureau of Cooperative Medicine; by 1940 this became a separate entity: the Cooperative Health Federation, which later changed its name to the Group Health Federation of America. Another postwar development, discussed in Chapter 7, was the organization by labor unions of labor health centers, which provided various scopes of organized ambulatory care with insurance support from workers and employers; in 1954 this gave rise to the American Labor Health Association. In 1959 the Group Health Federation of America and the American Labor Health Association united to form the Group Health Association of America (GHAA).[18]

All the consumer-sponsored health insurance plans linked to prepaid group practices that arose between 1929 and 1941 were relatively small, with a few thousand members each. The Ross-Loos Clinic Plan was larger, but it was actually not consumer-sponsored; it was owned and controlled entirely by the doctors, and its members came from selected enterprises, not from a cooperative. In 1942, however, a health insurance program linked to an organization of salaried group practice doctors was established that grew rapidly to a size and national importance out of all proportion to the pioneers in the field. This was the Kaiser Foundation Health Plan in California.[19]

Henry J. Kaiser was an energetic and imaginative industrialist on the West Coast, engaged in production of steel, aluminum, and various types of machines. With U.S. entry into World War II, Kaiser Industries undertook shipbuilding on a massive scale. Almost overnight thousands of workers and their families were attracted to the Kaiser shipyards in northern California. A sudden and extensive need for medical care arose. To meet it, the Kaiser company engaged the services of Dr. Sidney Garfield, a physician who had recently organized general health services for the employees of several construction companies building an aqueduct across the desert of southern California. Dr. Garfield, in the customary tradition of industrial medicine, initially employed physicians on salary to work in clinics built by the corporation. Instead of handling only work-connected conditions, however, they provided general medical care to employees and their families. A nonprofit foundation was also established to build hospitals with capital loans and grants from the corporation. The costs of operation were met by monthly contributions from both workers and management.

At the end of World War II in 1945, thousands of shipyard workers were laid off, but a medical care establishment with numerous general medical clinics, hospitals, and hundreds of salaried doctors and allied personnel was in place. It was decided to open membership to other employment groups. People, many of whom were newcomers to the West Coast with no ties to a family doctor, joined in thousands. By 1950, the Kaiser Foundation Health Plan enrollment had 154,000 members; by 1960, it had 808,000; and by 1970 it surpassed 2.1 million.[20] The limiting factor in membership growth was the speed with which facilities could be constructed and doctors recruited.

As the number of physicians rose in the postwar period, problems developed between them and Dr. Garfield and the Kaiser Corporation; issues concerned not only salaries but also the professional freedom of the physicians. Matters were settled by establishment of three autonomous legal entities, each of which had exclusive contractual relations with the other two. The hospitals and other facilities remained the property of the Kaiser Health Foundation. The health insurance organization, which marketed the whole program, collected the premiums, and disbursed the funds, became the nonprofit Kaiser Health Plan. The physicians formed a business partnership known as the Permanente Medical Group ("Permanente" is the name of a town in northern California). The Medical Group, in turn, engages the nurses and other personnel in the clinics (but not in the hospitals). Each year the Health Plan contracts with the Medical Group to provide its members for negotiated per capita payments with comprehensive physicians' care, and it contracts with the Foundation to operate the hospitals. If a surplus remains in the Health Plan fund at the end of the year (which has usually been the case), it is divided equally as a bonus to the Medical Group and a grant to the Health Foundation. The overall Kaiser-Permanente Medical Care Program has prospered under this tripartite arrangement; it has expanded further in membership, in locations (several outside of California), in scope of services, and in national importance.

In New York City, an important program combining health insurance with group medical practice started in 1947.[21] The major impetus for this came neither from a group of consumers nor an industrial corporation, but from the government of the City of New York, through the initiative of Mayor Fiorello La Guardia. Loans from the Rockefeller Foundation and other philanthropies were crucial in getting started. The Health Insurance Plan of Greater New York, or HIP, was launched to provide comprehensive insured medical care to employees of the city government and other employment groups, as well as to demonstrate the value of prepaid group practice.[22]

The HIP concept differed not only from the various consumer-sponsored prepaid group practice plans of the 1930s but also from the Kaiser program. Established as a nonprofit corporation, HIP stimulated and assisted in the organization of about 30 autonomous private group practice clinics at different locations throughout the large New York metropolitan area. The HIP headquarters marketed membership in the plan among city employees and others and collected the premiums. Each member was free to choose among any of 30 medical group clinics for his or her ambulatory medical care. The medical group clinics would each receive payment from HIP on a monthly per capita basis, according to the number of members selecting that clinic. Professional and technical standards that had to be met by each participating clinic were established and monitored by a "medical control board" composed of representative physicians from the whole network of clinics. Patients needing hospitalization would be admitted to any community hospital with which the physician was affiliated; not until about 1960 did HIP acquire a hospital of its own, and this could serve only a small share of the membership.

The capitation payments made by HIP to each clinic were intended to cover all ambulatory care costs as well as physician services to hospitalized patients. Hospital charges, however, were paid by the New York Blue Cross plan, which each HIP member was obligated to join. In addition, certain special services, such as bedside nursing care at home or complex physical rehabilitation, were provided at HIP's expense through contracts with outside agencies. In its early years, HIP enrollment grew rapidly, and by 1959 it had reached 550,000—about 6 percent of the New York City population. Over the next 20 years, however, the rate of growth slackened, reaching about 770,000 in 1979.

By about 1960, it was obvious that the Kaiser Foundation Health Plan and the Health Insurance Plan of Greater New York were the two giants in a heterogeneous array of health care organizations combining insurance for relatively comprehensive medical care rendered through doctors based in group practice clinics. The combined membership of Kaiser and HIP in 1960 was about 1,360,000. The total number of persons enrolled nationally in prepaid group practice plans, roughly equivalent to the current definition of HMOs, in 1960 is not certain, but in 1964 there were an estimated 150 prepaid group practice plans with about four million persons enrolled.[23]

In 1959 the U.S. federal government became involved with voluntary health insurance through enactment of the Federal Employees Health Benefits Program (FEHBP).[24] This program provided for federal government payment of half of the premium for coverage of any federal employee in a health insurance plan approved by the U.S. Civil Service Commission. In addition to the large "Blue" and commercial health insurance programs, the commission approved prepaid group practice plans in ten geographic areas with such plans and a substantial number of federal employees.[25] This provided a very conspicuous basis for comparison of the experience of thousands of persons in the same communities covered by insurance plans employing contrasting patterns of medical care delivery. In July 1960, there were 558,600 federal employees in the above ten areas, of whom 73,000 (13.1 percent) were enrolled in prepaid group practice plans. Among other things, this permitted the first nationwide analysis of hospital utilization in comparable populations enrolled in conventional health insurance plans and in prepaid group practice plans.

The findings were startling. In 1960–61, federal employees enrolled in the "Blue" and commercial insurance plans were hospitalized at a rate of 670 and 660 days per 1,000 persons per year respectively, compared with 406 days per 1,000 for employees enrolled in the prepaid group practice plans.[26] The same sort of differentials were found for each age group examined separately. The differentials were similar for rates of elective surgical procedures, such as tonsillectomy, hysterectomy, and appendectomy. Since hospitalization is by far the costliest component of medical care in the United States, the implications of these findings were very great. The lower hospital expenditures of prepaid group practice plans were to play a major part in the formulation of federal policy on HMOs a decade later.

One other crucial influence on HMO policy formulation was the organization of the Foundation for Medical Care in San Joaquin County, California in 1954.[27] This is a prosperous northern California county into which the Kaiser Foundation Health Plan was about to make inroads; plans were being drawn for building new clinics in the county. In response, physicians in the local medical society decided that they could match Kaiser's program of comprehensive care through multiple private offices, the challenge was to set up a system for monitoring each physician's work (through review of claims for payment of fees) in order to eliminate overservicing. Evidence of reduction of fee-for-service claims under the San Joaquin model was actually meager, but the concept was attractive, and it spread to other counties in the western states.[28] Perhaps more important in the long run, the medical care foundation demonstrated that health insurance for comprehensive physician and hospital care was feasible through conventional private practices, if local doctors were receptive to the idea.

RISE OF THE HMO STRATEGY

In 1965, Titles XVIII and XIX were added to the Social Security Act, bringing about statutory health insurance for the aged and public assistance medical care for the poor. In spite of the spectacular growth of voluntary health insurance reviewed earlier, the prominent weaknesses in coverage were for the aged and the poor—the very people with higher rates of illness and less money to pay for it. Medicare (Title XVIII) and Medicaid (Title XIX) set out to fill these gaps.[29]

The administrative structure of these programs, particularly Medicare, was highly permissive.[30] While fee-for-service was the prevailing method of paying for physician services, no fee schedules were negotiated or established; instead, physicians were to be paid "usual, customary, and reasonable" (UCR) charges, and hospitals were to be paid "reasonable costs." By not "accepting assignment" from a patient, physicians could require extra payment from the patient beyond the UCR fee. Administrative handling of claims from all health care providers (physicians, hospitals, and others) was done not by the government, but by fiscal intermediaries—essentially Blue Cross, Blue Shield, or commercial insurance companies. These entities carried no risk and simply got reimbursement from the government for all the claims they paid out, plus administrative expenses. Medicare expenditures for the hospital care of the aged, who were 10 percent of the U.S. population, soon constituted about 40 percent of hospital income.[31]

Under these condtions, it was inevitable that expenditures for health services in the United States rose at an annual rate much higher than over the previous decade. As a share of gross national product (GNP), health expenditures rose from 5.8 percent in 1966 (the effective starting date of Medicare) to 7.2 percent in 1970.[32] These spiralling costs created problems not only for federal and state governments (the latter had to finance about half the costs of Medicaid), but for every citizen who had to pay for medical services either directly or through voluntary insurance. Expressions of alarm were heard from all sides; newspapers and magazines referred repeatedly to the nation's facing a "health care crisis."[33] In July 1969, an official statement was issued from the White House, which read: "We face a massive crisis in (health care) and unless action is taken, both administratively and legislatively, to meet that crisis within the next two to three years, we will have a breakdown in our medical care system."[34]

It was in this atmosphere that the federal government sought desperately for some method to reduce medical care costs, even if this meant a modification of traditional patterns long sanctified by the American medical profession. The first clue of the new thinking was an official statement on "Medicare and Medicaid Reforms" issued by the Secretary of Health, Education, and Welfare (HEW) in March 1970. Among other things, the Secretary referred to the need for "drastic changes in our outmoded and fragmented medical care systems"— rather surprising words from a cabinet member in the conservative Nixon administration. After calling for various administrative changes that might yield savings in Medicare and Medicaid programs, the statement continued: "Today we propose an even more fundamental change. We are asking for authority, under the Medicare and Medicaid law, to enter into health maintenance contracts guaranteeing health services for the elderly and the poor at a single fixed annual rate for each person served."[35]

A year later, in February 1971, President Nixon sent to the U.S. Congress a "Message . . . Relative to Building a National Health Strategy." Many subjects were discussed in this document, but especially noteworthy was a section under the heading "Reorganizing the Delivery of Service," which said:

In recent years, a new method for delivering health services has achieved growing respect. This new approach has two essential attributes. It brings together a comprehensive range of medical services in a single organization so that a patient is assured of convenient access to all of them. And it provides needed services for a fixed contract fee which is paid in advance by all subscribers.

Such an organization can have a variety of forms and names and sponsors. One of the strengths of this new concept, in fact, is its great flexibility. The general term which has been applied to all of these units is 'HMO'—'Health Maintenance Organization'.[36]

In October 1971, a unit to promote HMOs was established in HEW.[37] Using funds and general authority already available, the federal government began to stimulate the establishment of local comprehensive prepayment medical care programs, which a few years before had been clearly opposed by the private medical profession and virtually ignored by government at every level. Two years later, in December 1973, the "Health Maintenance Organization Act of 1973" was passed by Congress and became law.[38] This legislation provided federal grants for studies, planning, development, and even initial operating expenses of HMOs. It invalidated numerous state laws that restricted the development of consumer-sponsored health insurance plans. It set up a system of federal approval to ensure that HMOs met certain standards, after which all approved HMOs had to be offered as an option by employers (with fringe benefit programs for their employees) in the local area. Several of the standards for HMO approval in the 1973 law were very demanding, and in the first years very few HMOs became qualified. As a result, amendments were legislated in 1976 to render qualification easier and to increase the extent of federal subsidy.[39]

The sequence of events just reviewed may explain why, in the 1970s, a conservative U.S. federal government should rather suddenly embrace and support a pattern of health care delivery, now labeled the HMO, which a short time before was widely regarded as dangerously unorthodox. Tracing the development backward, the immediate stimulus around 1970 was the spiraling costs of medical care brought on, or surely aggravated, by the Medicare and Medicaid laws enacted in 1965; the largest component in cost escalation was hospitalization. Experience throughout the 1960s, however, particularly under the FEHBP, demonstrated dramatically that hospital utilization rates and costs under comprehensive prepaid group practice plans were substantially lower than under conventional patterns of medical care supported by the dominant health insurance programs. The prepaid group practice programs had been attempting to broadcast their advantages for years, and HIP in New York had conducted meticulous research demonstrating not only lower hospital utilization, but also better health results for its members, including lower perinatal mortality rates.[40]

The GHAA since 1959 had been speaking nationally as the voice of scores of consumer-sponsored comprehensive prepaid health care plans. But not many people listened, least of all the U.S. medical establishment and the government.

The seeds of change began to take root with the alarming rise in medical care costs after 1966. In 1959, the AMA, after years of frontal opposition, softened its attitudes, and even found some merit in comprehensive prepaid medical care plans. That year the "Report of the Commission on Medical Care Plans," chaired by Dr. Leonard Larson, who was also chairman of the AMA Board of Trustees, was accepted by the AMA House of Delegates.[41] Although it took some time for the Larson Report to filter down to local medical societies, that process was accelerated by the medical cost inflationary problem. In January 1969, a conservative Republican administration, under President Richard Nixon, took office. From its viewpoint the central issue in the health field was the cost escalation, and this led to the White House statement of July 1969.

Credit for tying all the pieces together in a form acceptable to a conservative national government is usually given to Dr. Paul Ellwood, a Minnesota Republican physician not previously identified with the movements for either health insurance or group medical practice. It was he who recognized not only the long-demonstrated *economies* of prepayment for comprehensive (in contrast to solely hospital-linked) medical care, but also the *multiplicity* of models by which it might be delivered—including private solo medical practices under medical society-sponsored "foundations."[42,43] Recitation of the economies and quality assets of this health care insurance/delivery combination was virtually confined to research findings on the prepaid group practice model (particularly HIP of New York and the experience under the FEHBP), but this did not seem to be noticed. Pluralistic modes, nongovernmental sponsorships, local initiative— these were the hallmarks of a thoroughly American ideology. It remained only to give the idea a name not stigmatized by previous controversy; the phrase chosen was a happy one—health maintenance organizations, or HMOs.

In the period following February 1971, after a presidential message heralded the HMO as a crucial "new approach" that was important in "building a national health strategy," public discussion of the idea reached a fever pitch. The GHAA rode the crest of the wave. Its 1971 annual meeting featured not only the dedicated crusaders, but notable spokesmen of the nation's medical care establishment—representatives of the AHA, the Association of American Medical Colleges, the commercial insurance industry, the Blue Cross Association, local medical societies, and large corporations.[44] University-sponsored conferences were devoted to HMOs.[45] More than 100 pages of the *Harvard Law Review* one month gave a painstaking analysis of the legal and social issues involved.[46] Congressman William Roy in the U.S. House of Representatives sponsoring HMO legislation published a whole book on the subject.[47] Congressional hearings on the proposed legislation attracted widespread attention.[48] Various medical specialties explored how HMOs would affect their own fields.[49] Notes of caution were struck by the AMA,[50] but rarely in the development of the whole U.S. health care system has an idea been so widely and searchingly discussed as a prelude to national legislative action.

FEDERAL PROMOTION OF HMOs

With official establishment of the Office of Health Maintenance Organizations in the U.S. Public Health Service (PHS), and congressional appropriations for HMO promotional subsidies taking effect in July 1974, the movement entered a new stage. In each of the ten regional offices of the PHS around the nation, officers were stationed to advance the movement under the new law. Guidebooks were issued to assist local organizations in solving the practical problems of developing an HMO.[51-53] In 1974, the prestigious Institute of Medicine of the National Academy of Sciences called for even more forthright leadership by the federal government in HMO promotion, concluding: ''The Committee calls for prompt and vigorous action by the Administration, the Congress, and the states to undertake the further steps to assure that a fair market test of the HMO model of health care delivery can proceed forthwith.''[54]

In the first year or two following passage of the 1973 federal law, however, the development of new HMOs was relatively slow. The stringent standards imposed by the law for a new HMO to become federally qualified, it was argued, discouraged many existing prepaid group practice programs from even applying, let alone serving to stimulate the founding of new HMOs.[55] By the end of the second year of the statutory subsidy program, 409 applications for financial support had been received, but grants for feasibility studies, planning, or initial development had been awarded to only 168 organizations;[56] moreover, by October 1976, only 32 HMOs had become federally qualified.

In January 1977, a new federal administration under the Democratic party took office. Efforts were soon made to inject greater vitality into the HMO program. Administrative changes were made in the federal management of the program in order to accelerate the grant application review process.[57] (Legislative amendments of 1976 to facilitate the operations of the whole program have been noted earlier.) Much of the rapidly rising costs of medical care was being felt by corporate managements in the form of high health insurance premiums paid as employee fringe benefits under conventional health insurance programs, and in light of this, in 1978 and 1979 government appealed directly to corporate leadership to explore the whole HMO alternative.[58]

These modified policies brought results, and in 1978-79, new HMOs were launched, and established ones grew in enrollment more rapidly than in the previous five years.[59] During 1976, national HMO enrollment grew by only 1.7

percent over 1975; in 1977, the growth rate was 5.0 percent over the previous year; and in 1978, it accelerated by 18 percent to 7.5 million persons.[60] The number of HMOs federally qualified had risen from 32 in 1976 to 118 in March 1980.[61] There are many HMO-type organizations in the United States, moreover, that meet the general definition of HMOs but that are not federally qualified. Further, many of both the qualified and nonqualified HMOs have arisen and grown without benefit of federal subsidy. In November 1978, further amendments to the HMO Act reflected increasing congressional confidence in the soundness of the concept and further liberalized the basis of federal subsidy.[62] All in all, the viewpoint was rapidly spreading that HMOs were becoming a significant component of the American health care system. Moreover, many staunch advocates of free private enterprise were expressing the view that because of its competitive influence, the HMO either was already or would soon be inducing modified and more economical performance in the mainstream of U.S. private medical practice.[63,64]

MAJOR CURRENT FEATURES OF HMOs

Differentiation among the various forms of HMOs may be made along several dimensions, but most important from the perspective of this book, is the distinction between HMOs delivering medical services through organized clinics, as distinguished from others that arose initially in the 1950s as medical care foundations representing many private practitioners in an area.[65] In recent years the latter type of HMO has come to be designated as the "individual practice association," or IPA model, of HMO. Since the IPA models of HMO do not constitute clinics (organized ambulatory health service programs), except insofar as some of the individual practices may be small medical groups, they do not, strictly speaking, concern us in this book.

Basic HMO Clinic Models

Federal reports now classify HMOs providing services through clinics as being of two subtypes: (1) the group model, in which medical services are provided by a legally autonomous entity with which the governing body of the HMO *contracts* for provision of services to HMO members; and (2) the staff model in which the physicians and others in the clinic team are directly engaged by the HMO as its staff or employees. Federal HMO reports, moreover, provide information on HMO-type organizations that are currently not federally qualified (whether or not they have even applied for such status), as well as HMOs that are federally qualified. Both qualified and nonqualified types together are often designated simply as "prepaid health plans."

As of June 30, 1979, there were 215 prepaid health plans in the United States with a total enrollment of 8,226,053 persons.[66] Of these, 99, with 69 percent of the total enrollment, were federally qualified. With respect to their mode of health service delivery, 136 of the 215 total plans, with 6,941,781 members (84 percent of the total enrollment) applied a clinic pattern of health care delivery. With regard to clinic organizational status, the distribution was as follows:

Type of HMO Clinic	Number of Prepaid Plans	Enrollment (1979)
Staff (employees)	63	1,295,126
Group (contractual)	73	5,646,655
All Clinic Types	136	6,941,781

Source: USPHS, *National Census of Prepaid Plans 1979* (Washington: DHEW Pub. No. (PHS) 80–50127, 1980), p. 5.

The great majority of HMO enrollment in prepaid plans using clinics is in the group model—81 percent—wherein the medical group has a somewhat autonomous contractual relationship with the governing body of the HMO. The preponderence of this model is doubtless influenced heavily by the membership of the large Kaiser-Permanente Medical Care Program, which uses the group organizational model.

Sponsorship

The earliest pioneers of the HMO concept, it will be recalled, were organizations of consumers—sometimes consumer cooperatives, however other groups and organizations have also had sponsoring roles. The fraternal lodges alluded to earlier constituted some of these groups; health care insurance was only one of their objectives.[67] The medical care programs in isolated industries were financed mainly by wage deductions, even though they were usually set up by employers. Even the important progenitors of the current HMO movement in the 1930s and 1940s, in addition to consumer groups, were private physicians (Ross-Loos), large corporations (Kaiser), and city governments (New York HIP).

Leaving aside the IPA models (sponsored historically by associations of private physicians) sponsorships of prepaid group practice types of HMOs have become even more varied today. Determination of an HMO's sponsorship is made all the more difficult by the increasing tendency for more than one type of entity to become involved in launching a single HMO: for example, a consumer organization and a private medical group, working through a joint contract. Perhaps this explains why federal statistical reports on HMO development do not currently categorize the sponsoring bodies.

A national nongovernmental survey of HMOs and HMO-type programs, conducted in 1973, did inquire about sponsorship.[68] About 100 organizations were identified at the time, and responses were received from 77. These were analyzed in three subsets: (a) those operating before July 1, 1973 outside the state of California, (b) those operating only after July 1, 1973 outside of California, and (c) all HMOs within the state of California. The largest number of HMOs were in the first category: there were 51 in this class. The possible sponsors were divided into nine types, which one can classify as follows:

A. Providers of health care
    1. physician groups
    2. hospitals
    3. medical schools
B. Insurance agencies
    4. Blue Cross/Blue Shield
    5. commercial insurance companies
C. Consumers of health care or their agents
    6. private corporations (as employers)
    7. consumer groups
    8. labor unions
D. None of the above
    9. other

Source: Robert E. Schlenker, J. N. Quale, R. L. Wetherville, et al. *HMOs in 1973—A National Survey* (Minneapolis, Minn.: Interstudy, 1974).

Indicative of the complex arrangements among these nine types of sponsors is the distribution of the 51 HMOs in category (a) according to the number of different sponsors involved in each:

Number of Sponsors	Number of HMOs	Percent of HMOs
1	17	33
2	17	33
3	12	24
4	3	6
5	2	4
Total	51	100

Source: Robert E. Schlenker, J. N. Quale, R. L. Wetherville, et al. *HMOs in 1973—A National Survey* (Minneapolis, Minn.: Interstudy, 1974), pp. 47–60.

Thus, only one-third of the 51 HMOs operating outside California before July 1973 had a single sponsor; and a second third had two sponsors; the balance had three, four, or even five different sponsors.

Aggregating the data from all 77 HMOs responding in this 1973 survey, the distribution of sponsoring entities was as follows:[69]

Physician groups	44
Hospitals	23
Medical schools	5
Blue Cross/Blue Shield	15
Commercial insurance companies	13
Private corporations	13
Consumer groups	15
Labor unions	5
Other	23

Source: Robert E. Schlenker, J. N. Quale, R. L. Wetherville, et al. *HMOs in 1973—A National Survey* (Minneapolis, Minn.: Interstudy, 1974), pp. 47–60.

This adds up to 156 sponsoring bodies for 77 HMOs, an average of two sponsors each. Because of the dispersion of numbers of sponsors for different HMOs shown above, one cannot properly calculate a percentage distribution of HMO sponsorship from these figures. It is evident, however, that in aggregate various providers of health care (particularly physician groups and hospitals) participate in HMO sponsorship more frequently than insurance agencies or even consumers. Yet the most notable fact is the very multiplicity of types of organization that play some part—usually in combination with other bodies—in sponsoring HMOs.

In recent years the initiative being taken by carriers of traditional health insurance in promoting HMOs is noteworthy. In previous decades, as noted earlier in this chapter, the major carriers of health insurances—Blue Cross and Blue Shield plans and commercial companies—were largely dedicated to preservation of the status quo in patterns of health care delivery. They wanted to provide insurance support for conventional services by private doctors and community hospitals. As health care costs escalated in the late 1960s, however, their attitudes manifestly changed: both the "Blue" plans and insurance companies came to realize that they could sponsor money-saving HMOs as well as their customary insurance offerings. As early as 1971, Paul Ellwood could report that, "22 of the 70 Blue Cross Association member plans either have established or are negotiating affiliations with prepaid group practice plans."[70]

Sometimes, as in the development of the Harvard Community Health Plan, a Blue Cross organization served under contract as a marketing agent for the HMO; as its salesmen contacted employment groups to sell Blue Cross membership, they also told potential members about the HMO option. More often, however, these large insurance carriers developed relationships with several existing private group practice clinics, and negotiated links with them along the same lines as did the HIP of New York in the 1940s. Blue Cross of Southern California, for example, began organizing such a network of relationships with private medical clinics in 1974; by 1980, "Health Net," as it was called, had affiliations with 36 well-established private group practice clinics throughout the Los Angeles metropolitan area.[71] By June 1979 Health Net had become federally qualified, had an enrollment of 17,500, and was growing rapidly.

Commercial insurance carriers have played a different role with respect to HMOs. A few large companies have simply purchased certain existing HMOs. Thus, in 1980 the 50-year-old Ross-Loos Clinic Plan in Los Angeles was purchased, along with all its staff and assets, by a large eastern insurance company.[72] The program continues to operate under its original name. Nothing in the HMO legislation prohibits HMOs from operating for profit and paying dividends to stockholders. For some years, moreover, the nation's largest HMO, Kaiser-Permanente, has been expanding beyond its California origins by purchasing previously functioning prepaid group practice plans in other states, such as Ohio and Texas. It would seem that the general trend of American businesses to merge may ultimately apply to HMOs also.

Size and Age of HMOs

As one would expect from the history of the HMO movement, the great majority of HMOs have small enrollments and have been established in recent years, while a few of the older ones have large memberships and account for a high percentage of the total national HMO enrollment. As of June 30, 1979, the enrollment distribution of the HMO or HMO-type plans was as follows:[73]

Plan Enrollment	Percent of Plans (N = 215)	Percent of Members (N = 8,226,053)
Under 25,000	79	17
25,000–99,999	15	15
100,000 & over	6	68
All sizes	100	100

Source: USPHS, *National HMO Census of Prepaid Plans 1979* (Washington: DHEW Pub. No. (PHS) 80–50127, 1980), p. 4.

Thus, 6 percent of the HMOs (14 plans), each with enrollments of 100,000 or more, have over two-thirds of the total national HMO enrollment.

A similar skewed distribution is found with respect to the age of HMOs. As of June 30, 1979, the 23 HMOs (11 percent of the total) that have been operating for ten years or more had 68 percent of the national enrollment, while the 89 percent of HMOs younger than this had only 32 percent of the total enrollment. These relationships, of course, will change, as the younger plans grow in membership.

Resources

A great deal might be said about the resources of HMOs of the group practice model, but perhaps it is enough to state that their range of services offered, staffing, facilities, and administrative arrangements are as varied as their sponsorships. By definition, all HMOs provide physician services, both ambulatory and inpatient, as well as hospitalization. The group practice model plans all provide a broad range of laboratory and x-ray diagnostic examinations also. Beyond this, the range of ''supplemental health services,'' as they are called in the HMO Act, may vary widely, including such services as visual refraction with eyeglasses, dental services, long-term rehabilitation, out-of-hospital prescribed drugs, and others.[74]

The staffing of HMO clinics with physicians and others is also highly variable. To some extent physician-population ratios have been worked out on the basis of the older prepaid group practice plans, such as Kaiser-Permanente and HIP of New York. A governmental guidance manual suggests a schedule of physicians, by specialty, that has been found to be suitable. In terms of full-time equivalents (FTE), an average enrollment of 10,000 persons in a clinic model HMO would require medical staff as follows:[75]

Medical Specialty	Physicians (FTE) per 10,000 members
General practice and internal medicine	4.2
Pediatrics	1.5
Obstetrics and gynecology	0.8
Surgery	0.7
Ophthalmology	0.3
Dermatology	0.3
Radiology	0.3
Ear, nose, and throat	0.2
Orthopedics	0.2
Other	0.8
All physicians	9.3

Source: Health Maintenance Organization Service, *Finance Planning Manual* (Washington: DHEW, c. 1973), p. 13.

In practice, there is naturally much variation around such norms as these, depending not only on the exact population being served and the productivity or work output of particular physicians, but also on the ability of the HMO or its affiliated medical group to recruit physicians of the desired specialties. The implication of such standards is, of course, that HMOs with small memberships require certain types of specialist on only a part-time basis. On the other hand, HMOs organized on the HIP-New York model of multiple private group practices can enjoy great flexibility in staffing; only a proportion of each group clinic's patients need be HMO members, so that superfluous physicians in certain specialties can occupy the balance of their time with private non-HMO patients. Similarly, HMO patients requiring certain specialists not adequately represented in the medical group may be referred elsewhere for service (at the expense of the HMO). As a rough approximation, clinic model HMOs apparently have about one FTE physician per 1,000 members.

Nurses, technicians, and other allied personnel in an HMO clinic are engaged, as a rule, in some proportion to the available physicians. Large HMOs, like Kaiser-Permanente, have found it feasible to use nurse-practitioners to perform various procedures in the clinic team that might otherwise require the time of a doctor. Larger HMOs can achieve efficiencies from greater use of automated laboratory equipment and in provision of other services amenable to economies of scale. Personal preventive services, such as well baby examinations, are ordinarily provided by HMO pediatricians and pediatric nurses, but some preventive services, such as health education or counseling adolescents on behavioral problems, may be furnished entirely by allied personnel.

Hospitalization in all but a few HMOs is provided in community hospitals, in which the participating doctors have appointments. There is usually a tendency to concentrate admissions in one or two hospitals, in which the HMO clinic physicians can acquire reasonable status on the medical staff. This remains an important consideration, in light of the competitive role and interprofessional friction felt by HMO physicians, who are typically a minority on the staff of any community hospital. The major exception is the Kaiser-Permanente HMO, which controls and operates about 25 of its own hospitals. With the managerial efficiencies that such exclusively controlled HMO hospitals can yield, the Kaiser-Permanente program has found that a ratio of only about 1.8 general hospital beds per 1,000 members (compared with more than 4.0 general beds per 1,000 for the U.S. population as a whole) has been quite adequate.[76] (This has many implications for hospital utilization rates, which will be discussed below.) Otherwise, only a half dozen HMOs nationally own and control their own hospitals.

EVALUATION OF HMOs

Few subjects in the field of health care organization have stimulated as much evaluative research as HMOs, comparing their performance, along various dimensions, with conventional patterns of medical care delivery. Many important evaluative studies were done in the 1950s, comparing prepaid group practice programs with private fee-for-service medical practice, and focusing on a few such programs with good record systems, such as HIP of New York and Kaiser-Permanente. Several overall reviews have been published, bringing together the findings of numerous specific empirical investigations.[77-81] More recent studies have attempted to explain more fully some of the principal performance characteristics of HMOs, such as the much lower rates of hospital utilization by their members[82] or the ultimate effects of HMO service on the health of their members.[83]

From the "clinics" perspective of this book, it is not necessary to recount the details of all that has been learned about HMO clinic dynamics in the United States. The highlights of certain features, particularly health care costs under HMOs, the quality of health care they render, and regulatory problems, will, however, be presented.

Costs

The evidence is overwhelming that the total costs of health service for members of HMOs of the group practice model are substantially lower than costs for comparable populations served by conventional private medical care. That was, indeed, the primary reason for promotion of the health maintenance strategy by President Nixon in 1971. This does not mean that the insurance premiums for HMO membership are necessarily lower than for other health insurance programs, since the latter often have a much more restricted range of benefits. It is the aggregate cost of insured services plus private out-of-pocket expenditures for noninsured services (or extra charges) that is appreciably lower under HMOs.

The principal reason for lower costs is the considerably lower rate of hospital utilization (both in admissions and in days per 1,000) among HMO members. The differential has been from 10 to 40 percent in diverse studies. Since hospitalization is the costliest element in the full spectrum of medical services, the savings are considerable. The rate of use of ambulatory services has generally been about the same in HMOs as with conventional insurance, but considering the low use of inpatient care the rate of ambulatory service usage may be regarded as *relatively* higher.

The lower hospital utilization under HMOs cannot be attributed to their attracting a healthier population than other health insurance plans. In fact, although evidence on this point is not all consistent, HMOs appear to attract into membership persons of higher health risk, as reflected by their past history of illness, their ethnic composition, and other attributes.[84] The explanation is almost certainly referrable to the incentives and motivations of physicians (who make the decisions on hospitalization of patients) under HMOs of the group practice model. Thus, unlike the physician in conventional fee-for-service individual medical practice, the HMO group practice physician has no financial incentive to hospitalize patients who could be served on an ambulatory clinic basis. If less money is spent on hospitalization, more is retained in the fixed overall HMO budget to pay the physician and the clinic staff. By contrast, in private solo practice not only is there a fee incentive toward hospitalization, but the case management is promptly strengthened by an array of diagnostic and treatment procedures in the hospital (usually at insurance expense) that are not available in a doctor's office.

In fact, evidence is accumulating that even *without* the financial dynamics of HMOs, group medical practice leads to lower rates of hospitalization than solo practice.[85] In a sense, the group practice clinic is competing with the hospital for earnings from elaborate diagnostic and treatment procedures that are simply not feasible in the solo practice. In Hawaii, for example, the hospitalization rates of insured patients served by private group practices have been found to be about the same as under the prepaid group practice of the Hawaiian Kaiser-Permanente HMO.[86]

Another explanation of the strikingly lower hospitalization rates under group practice HMOs is the constraint of a generally lower supply (bed-to-population ratio) of available hospital beds. In the large Kaiser-Permanente HMO, where we have noted the ratio of general hospital beds to population is less than half the nationwide ratio, this constraint is obvious. Even in the New York HIP prepaid group practice program, where general community hospitals are used, there is evidence that the beds made available to patients of HIP doctors have been restricted.[87] This does not mean that these HMO patients are kept from needed hospital admission and accumulate on waiting lists; rather, it appears that HMO group clinic physicians simply learn to practice medicine comfortably under conditions of a lower hospital bed supply. Indirectly confirming this are the findings on hospital use under the IPA model of HMOs; in the settings of multiple solo practices, in spite of HMO budgetary ceilings, hospitalization rates are almost as high as under ordinary health insurance.[88]

Other factors contributing to the lower costs of group practice model HMOs are their capability of using lower-priced generic drugs and their proved provision of a higher rate of preventive services, such as immunizations and periodic checkups.[89] Prompt access to ambulatory care is also likely to be less expensive, in the long run, than delayed access (from the frequent copayment deterrents under conventional health insurance) with resultant more serious disease requiring hospitalization.[90] On the whole issue of economies of scale in group practice versus solo practice per se, there is continuing debate, but the predominant conclusion of economists is that such economies are usually, if not always, achievable.[91]

Whatever the reasons, the ultimate economies of HMOs are no longer questioned. It has been argued that costs of health care in the U.S. could be greatly reduced if free market impediments could be regulated to a degree that would lead a gradually increasing proportion of the population to join HMOs.[92] The question remains, however, about the quality of care rendered by HMOs— particularly the effect on their health status. Are the economies achieved at the expense of a reduced quality of care and health status in HMO members?

Quality of Health Care

Studies of prepaid group practice models of HMOs over the past 20 years or more indicate that the quality of care provided in group practice HMOs is equal to or better than that offered in conventional private medical practice. For some years, the quality of health services in the United States has been measured according to the conceptualization proposed by Donabedian in 1966, i.e., by "structure, process, and outcome."[93] "Structure" refers to the qualifications of the resource inputs—such as the specialty training of physicians or the adequacy of laboratory facilities. "Process" refers to the attributes of the services provided as judged by expert observers; i.e., do these services correspond to generally accepted standards of good diagnosis and treatment (even proper prevention) of disease? "Outcome" refers to the results of the health service: are the people served healthier under one pattern of care than another? Another indirect outcome measurement might be the level of satisfaction of people with services under a particular program.

By structure indicators, a review of all objective studies of HMOs available leads Harold Luft to conclude:

> In summary, the structural data suggest that the quality of medical care is at least as good in HMOs as it is in the fee-for-service (FFS-private practice) sector . . . Thus . . . the HMO does offer an informational advantage: a randomly chosen HMO physician is likely to be better qualified than a FFS practitioner randomly chosen.[94]

Regarding process measures, the findings of studies vary, depending on the research technique used. In the review of investigations by John Williamson and colleagues, however, 49 studies, applying reliable methods and comparing HMOs with private practice, by process criteria, were identified.[95] Of these, 34 found the care in HMOs to be superior to private care, 11 found them to be about equal, and only 4 found HMO care to be inferior to that provided in conventional private practice.

Most people would consider the ultimate test of quality in any health program to be the outcome of care. In a sense, measurements of structure and process are used because they imply the probability of a certain outcome, and because such measurements are easier to make reliably.[96] The first impressive evidence of superior HMO outcomes came from HIP New York in the 1950s in studies showing lower perinatal mortality in HIP childbirths than in a matched population of childbirths in New York City's general population.[97] Subsequent studies, whether using mortality rates, disability days, recoveries from specific types of disease, or other indices, have been less conclusive. Harold Luft's summary of outcome evaluations is simply: "In general, the data suggest the HMO outcomes are not very different from those of conventional practice."[98] Williamson's review of 15 outcome investigations found 8 of them to show HMO results superior to conventional private practice, 6 of them the same, and only 1 inferior.[99]

More research is necessary to determine whether HMO savings in health care costs are achieved without some sacrifice in the quality of care. This uncertainty remains, even though the empirical studies done have been almost entirely on the prepaid group practice model of HMO and within the larger and longer established such programs, where one would expect quality to be at its best. The only reported outcome study on an IPA model of HMO showed no difference in quality from that in a comparable population served by conventional medical care.[100]

Both the IPA group practice and the HMO models have also had serious problems in many spheres. Not only have some shown evidence of poor quality care, but also of serious misrepresentations to consumers and of fiscal corruption.[101]

Problems and Regulatory Needs

Because of the cost-savings of HMOs, action was taken in California in the early 1970s to promote this pattern of medical care among Medicaid recipients.[102] The expenditures required in the state government to finance medical care for the poor under the Medicaid law were rising rapidly; encouraging enrollment of these public aid beneficiaries in HMO prepaid health plans could potentially reduce state expenditures. In an effort to implement this policy, the state encouraged establishment of dozens of new prepaid health plans (PHPs), and in a few years some 250,000 Medicaid-eligible persons were enrolled.[103] Virtually no standards were set, however, for the structure or operation of these plans or for marketing them to eligible poor persons. As a result, problems rapidly arose.

Contrary to the claims of the PHP salesmen, health services were often not available at the announced clinic site.[104] Patients with serious illnesses requiring much care would find their PHP membership terminated. Some PHP patients were hospitalized in county public hospitals (at general revenue expense), although the premiums paid by the state to the PHP on behalf of indigent beneficiaries were expected to pay for all care, including hospitalization. Fiscal maneuvers, yielding large profits to the PHP owners, were exposed repeatedly.

In a word, free market operation of HMO health programs led to corruption. The modified incentive of the HMO concept—to discourage the overservicing of patients so common in the private fee system—led to extreme underservicing, with exploitation of both poor patients and the state government.

In response, the state of California passed legislation to impose strict regulatory controls on medical staffing, content of services, physical facilities, quality controls, and all aspects of the administrative and fiscal operations of HMOs. As a result, the great majority of these PHPs, which were fundamentally profiteering and corrupt, closed down.[105] Only because of regulation, in other words, were Medicaid beneficiaries in California preserved from the corruption of the HMO idea that was found to occur in the free market.

Other states learned a lesson from California and passed similar regulatory legislation for HMOs.[106] Such legislation constituted a recognition that HMOs, in spite of their merit, were not self-regulatory in a free market. By 1978, special legislation had been enacted in 34 states and U.S. territories that authorized the regulation of HMOs by various branches of state government. The most frequent requirements of these statutes were: nonprofit status, consumer representation on the governing board, specified standards for participating physicians and other health care providers, a mandatory period of "open enrollment" each year to avert biased "selection of risks," and conformity with federal HMO Act requirements on capital funding and financial reserves.

Thus, the rise of health insurance and its combination with organized clinics, first developing into the prepaid group practice pattern and then the HMO movement, has given new importance to the issue of the health care delivery system. An idea that was once identified only with a handful of social crusaders and scorned by the main medical establishment evolved into a program backed with the prestige and financial resources of the federal government. Its value in reducing overall health care expenditures has been established, although its effects on the health of people remain still somewhat unclear. Even if time should prove that the HMO yields definite financial savings without any sacrifice of health care quality, the concept remains subject to abuse and therefore it requires careful regulation.

All HMOs are different; even within the group practice model, there are great variations with size of enrollment, managerial efficiency, and other factors. A painstaking study by the U.S. General Accounting Office, restricted to group practice HMOs, recently concluded:

> "There are significant economies of scale in providing comprehensive prepaid care. If the HMOs studied (20 with enrollments from 1,000 to 37,000) continue to grow, the per unit cost of care will fall. However, sufficient demand and good management are prerequisites for these HMOs to achieve lowest per unit cost."[107]

Like the other clinics reviewed in this volume, the HMO clinic has great potential, but it does not eliminate the need for sound administration and rational planning of the nation's health care system.[108]

NOTES

1. U.S. Department of Health, Education, and Welfare, *Health Maintenance Organizations—The Concept and Structure* (Washington: Health Services and Mental Health Administration, March 1971).

2. Goldmann, Franz, *Public Medical Care: Principles and Problems* (New York: Columbia University Press, 1945).

3. Frankel, Lee K., and M. M. Dawson, *Workingmen's Insurance in Europe* (New York: Russell Sage Foundation, 1911).

4. Sigerist, Henry E., "From Bismarck to Beveridge: Developments and Trends in Social Security Legislation," *Bulletin of the History of Medicine* 8 (1943): 365–388.

5. Williams, Pierce, *The Purchase of Medical Care Through Fixed Periodic Payment* (New York: National Bureau of Economic Research, 1932).

6. Schwartz, Jerome L., "Early History of Prepaid Medical Care Plans," *Bulletin of the History of Medicine* 39 (1965): 450–475.

7. Follman, Joseph F., *Medical Care and Health Insurance* (Homewood, Ill.: Richard D. Irwin, 1963).

8. Goldmann, Franz, *Voluntary Medical Care Insurance* (New York: Columbia University Press, 1948).

9. Somers, Herman M., and Anne R. Somers, *Doctors, Patients, and Health Insurance* (Washington: Brookings Institution, 1961).

10. Health Insurance Institute, *Source Book of Health Insurance Data* (New York: 1975), p. 20.

11. Dickerson, O. D., *Health Insurance* (Homewood, Ill.: Richard D. Irwin, 1963).

12. Shadid, Michael A., *A Doctor for the People* (New York: Vanguard Press, 1939).

13. Shadid, Michael A., *Doctors of Today and Tomorrow* (New York: Cooperative League of USA, 1947), pp. 217–238.

14. Kisch, Arnold I., and Arthur J. Viseltear, *The Ross-Loos Medical Group: A Comprehensive Prepaid Group Practice Establishes Itself in California*, U.S. Public Health Service, Medical Care Administration, Case Study No. 3 (Washington: June 1967).

15. Hansen, Horace C., "Group Health Plans—A Twenty Year Review," *Minnesota Law Review*, March 1958, p. 530.

16. MacColl, William A., *Group Practice and Prepayment of Medical Care* (Washington: Public Affairs Press, 1966).

17. Johnston, Helen L., *Rural Health Cooperatives* (Washington: U.S. Department of Agriculture and U.S. Public Health Service, 1950).

18. W. Palmer Dearing, "The Challenge of Comprehensive Health Care," *American Journal of Public Health* 52 (1962): 2071.

19. de Kruif, Paul, *Kaiser Wakes the Doctors* (New York: Harcourt, Brace and Co., 1943).

20. Somers, Anne R. (editor), *The Kaiser-Permanente Medical Care Program* (New York: Commonwealth Fund, 1971), p. 197.

21. Baehr, George, *Ten Years of Service: 1947–1956* (New York: Health Insurance Plan of Greater New York, 1957).

22. Baehr, George, "Professional Services under Medical Care Insurance," *American Journal of Public Health,* February 1951.

23. Weinerman, E. Richard, "Patients' Perceptions of Group Medical Care: A Review and Analysis of Studies on Choice and Utilization of Prepaid Group Practice Plans," *American Journal of Public Health* 54 (1964): 880–889.

24. Ruddock, Andrew E., "Federal Employees Health Benefits Program: History and Future of the Federal Program—1964," *American Journal of Public Health,* January 1966.

25. Henderson, Marie, "Federal Employees Health Benefits Program: Role of Group Practice Prepayment Plans," *American Journal of Public Health,* January 1966.

26. Perrott, George S., "Federal Employees Health Benefits Program: Utilization of Hospital Services," *American Journal of Public Health,* January 1966.

27. Krantz, Goldie, "The San Joaquin Foundation for Medical Care," *American Journal of Public Health,* January 1961.

28. Sasuly, Richard, and C. E. Hopkins, "A Medical Society-Sponsored Comprehensive Medical Care Plan," *Medical Care* 5 (1967): 234–248.

29. Myers, Robert J., *Medicare* (Bryn Mawr, Pa.: McCahan Foundation, 1970).

30. Feingold, Eugene, *Medicare: Policies and Politics* (San Francisco, Calif.: Chandler Publishing Co., 1966).

31. Somers, Herman M., and Anne R. Somers, *Medicare and the Hospitals: Issues and Prospects* (Washington: Brookings Institution, 1967).

32. Gibson, R. M., and C. R. Fisher, "National Health Expenditures, Fiscal Year 1977," *Social Security Bulletin,* July 1978, pp. 3–20.

33. For example, "U.S. Medical Crisis Soars with Fees," *Los Angeles Times,* April 12, 1970, p. 6.

34. Quoted in: Kissick, William L., "Health-Policy Directions for the 1970's," *New England Journal of Medicine,* 282 (1970): 1343–1354.

35. Finch, Robert H., Secretary of Health, Education, and Welfare, "Statement on Medicare and Medicaid Reforms," Washington, March 25, 1970, unpublished document.

36. *Message from the President of the United States Relative to Building a National Health Strategy,* 92nd Cong., 1st sess., House Document No. 92–49, February 18, 1971.

37. Strumpf, George B.; F. H. Seubold; and M. B. Arrill, "Health Maintenance Organizations, 1971–1977: Issues and Answers," *Journal of Community Health* 4 (1978): 33–54.

38. U.S. Social Security Administration, *Health Maintenance Organization Act of 1973,* Research and Statistics Note (Washington: March 12, 1974).

39. Skolnik, Alfred M., "Health Maintenance Organization Amendments of 1976," *Social Security Bulletin,* April 1977, pp. 48–51.

40. Densen, Paul M.; Eva Balamuth; and Sam Shapiro, *Prepaid Medical Care and Hospital Utilization,* American Hospital Association, Monograph No. 3 (Chicago: AHA, 1958).

41. American Medical Association, *Report of Commission on Medical Care Plans,* Leonard Larson, chairman, *Journal of the American Medical Association, Special Edition,* January 17, 1959.

42. Ellwood, Paul M.; N. N. Anderson; J. E. Billings, et al., "Health Maintenance Strategy," *Medical Care,* 3 (1971): 291–298.

43. Ellwood, Paul M., "Health Maintenance Organizations: Concept and Strategy," *Hospitals, JAHA,* March 16, 1971, pp. 53–56.

44. Group Health Association of America, *Proceedings: XXII Annual Group Health Institute*, Detroit, Mich., May 16–17, 1972 (Washington: 1973).

45. For example, University of Chicago Graduate School of Business, *Health Maintenance Organizations: A Reconfiguration of the Health Services System* (Chicago: Proceedings of the Thirteenth Annual Symposium on Hospital Affairs, May 1971).

46. Greenberg, Ira G., and Michael L. Rodburg, "The Role of Prepaid Group Practice in Relieving the Medical Care Crisis," *Harvard Law Review* 84 (1971): 887–1001.

47. Roy, William R., *The Proposed Health Maintenance Organization Act of 1972* (Washington: Sourcebook Series, 1972).

48. U.S. Congress, Senate, Committee on Labor and Public Welfare, Subcommittee on Health, *Health Maintenance Organization and Resources Development Act of 1972*, Cong., 1972.

49. For example, Gibson, Robert W., "Can Mental Health Be Included in the Health Maintenance Organization?" *American Journal of Psychiatry*, 128 (1972): 33–40.

50. "HMO Caution Urged: AMA asks halt in funding, study of existing plans," *American Medical News*, April 17, 1972, p. 1.

51. U.S. Public Health Service, *Inclusion of Pharmaceutical Services in Health Maintenance and Related Organizations*, DHEW Pub. No. (HSA) 74–13017 (Washington: 1974).

52. Health Maintenance Organization Service, *Financial Planning Manual*, U.S. Department of Health, Education. and Welfare (Washington: c. 1973).

53. U.S. Health Resources Administration, *HMOs—Their Potential Impact on Health Manpower Requirements*, DHEW Pub. No. (HRA) 75–4, (Washington: August 1974).

54. Institute of Medicine, National Academy of Sciences, *Health Maintenance Organizations: Toward a Fair Market Test* (Washington: May 1974), p. 66.

55. Dorsey, Joseph L., "The Health Maintenance Organization Act of 1973 (P.L. 93–222) and Prepaid Group Practice Plans," *Medical Care* 13 (1975): 1–9.

56. Strumpf, George B.; F. H. Seubold; and M. B. Arrill, "Health Maintenance Organizations," p. 35.

57. Roemer, Milton I., "Moving Ahead with HMO Development," unpublished report to the Assistant Secretary for Health, U.S. Department of Health, Education, & Welfare (Washington: August 1, 1977).

58. National Chamber Foundation, *A National Health Care Strategy* (Washington: 1978).

59. Loebs, Stephen F., "Dramatic Rise in National Growth of HMOs," *Hospitals, JAHA*, August 16, 1979, pp. 96–98.

60. Viet, Howard R., "A New Era for HMOs," *Group Practice*, July 1979, p. 6.

61. U.S. Office of Health Maintenance Organizations, "Federally Qualified Health Maintenance Organizations," (Washington (unpublished report), March 1980).

62. U.S., Public Law 95–559, November 1, 1978.

63. Enthoven, Alain C., "Consumer-Choice Health Plan," *New England Journal of Medicine*, 298 (1978): 650–658, 709–720.

64. Christianson, Jon B., and Walter McClure, "Competition in the Delivery of Medical Care," *New England Journal of Medicine*, 301 (1979): 812–818.

65. Egdahl, Richard E., "Foundations for Medical Care," *New England Journal of Medicine*, 288 (1973): 491–498.

66. U.S. Public Health Service, *National HMO Census of Prepaid Plans 1979*, DHEW Pub. No. (PHS) 80–50127 (Washington: 1980), p. 5.

67. Falk, I. S.; C. R. Rorem; and M. D. Ring, *The Costs of Medical Care*, Committee on the Costs of Medical Care, Pub. No. 27 (Chicago: University of Chicago Press, 1933), pp. 463–464.

68. Schlenker, Robert E.; J. N. Quale; R. L. Wetherville; and R. McNeil, Jr., *HMOs in 1973— A National Survey* (Minneapolis, Minn.: InterStudy, 1974).

69. Ibid. pp. 47–60.

70. Ellwood, Paul M., "Health Maintenance Organizations: Concept and Strategy," p. 56.

71. "Health Net: Insurance for your bills. A staff of doctors for your health," *Los Angeles Times,* June 10, 1980.

72. Sing, Bill, "INA (Insurance Company of North America) Health Plan Buys Ross-Loos for $30 Million," *Los Angeles Times,* June 3, 1980.

73. U.S. Public Health Service, *National HMO Census of Prepaid Plans 1979*, p. 4.

74. Birnbaum, Roger W., *Health Maintenance Organizations: A Guide to Planning and Development* (New York: Spectrum Publications, 1976), p. 53.

75. Health Maintenance Organization Service, *Financing Planning Manual,* p. 13.

76. Somers, Anne R., ed., *The Kaiser-Permanente Medical Care Program,* p. 65.

77. Donabedian, Avedis, "An Evaluation of Prepaid Group Practice," *Inquiry* 6 (1969): 3–27.

78. Weinerman, E. Richard, "Patients' Perceptions of Group Medical Care," *American Journal of Public Health* 54 (1964): 880–889.

79. Klarman, Herbert E., "Analysis of the HMO Proposal—Its Assumptions, Implications, and Prospects" in *Health Maintenance Organizations: A Reconfiguration of the Health Services System* (Chicago: University of Chicago School of Business, 1971), pp. 24–38.

80. Roemer, Milton I. and William Shonick, "HMO Performance: The Recent Evidence," *MMFQ/ Health and Society,* 51 (1973): 271–317.

81. Glasgow, John M., "Prepaid Group Practice as a National Health Policy: Problems and Perspectives," *Inquiry* 9 (1972): 3–15.

82. Luft, Harold S., "How Do Health Maintenance Organizations Achieve Their 'Savings'?" *New England Journal of Medicine* 298 (1978): 1336–1343.

83. Williamson, John W.; F. C. Cunningham; and D. L. Ward, "Quality of Health Care in HMOs as Compared to Other Settings—A Literature Review and Policy Analysis" (Washington: DHEW Office of Health Maintenance Organizations, April 1979)(unpublished report).

84. Roemer, Milton, I.; R. W. Hetherington; C. E. Hopkins, et al., *Health Insurance Effects: Services, Expenditures, and Attitudes under Three Types of Plan* (Ann Arbor, Mich.: University of Michigan School of Public Health, 1972), pp. 14–17.

85. Scitovsky, Anne A., and N. McCall, "Use of Hospital Services under Two Prepaid Plans," *Medical Care* 18 (1980): 30–43.

86. Stacey, James, "Hawaii's Prepaid Plan Eyed as U.S. Model," *American Medical News,* January 11, 1980, p. 13.

87. Roemer, Milton I., and Max Shain, *Hospital Utilization under Insurance,* American Hospital Association, Monograph No. 6 (Chicago: 1959).

88. Perrott, G. S., *The Federal Employees Health Benefits Program* (Washington: U.S. Civil Service Commission, 1971).

89. Luft, Harold S., "Why Do HMOs Seem to Provide More Health Maintenance Services?" *Milbank Memorial Fund Quarterly/Health and Society* 56 (1978): 140–168.

90. Roemer, Milton, I.; C. E. Hopkins; L. Carr; et al., "Co-Payments for Ambulatory Care: Penny-wise and Pound-foolish," *Medical Care* 13 (1975): 457–466.

91. Yett, Donald, "Evaluation of Methods of Estimating Physicians' Expenses Relative to Output," *Inquiry* 4 (1967): 3–27.

92. Enthoven, Alain C., "Consumer-Choice Health Plan."

93. Donabedian, Avedis, "Evaluating the Quality of Medical Care," *Milbank Memorial Fund Quarterly* 44 (1966): 166–206.

94. Luft, Harold S., manuscript of a comprehensive book on HMOs, November 1979; book to be published in 1981.

95. Williamson, John W., et al., "Quality of Health Care in HMOs," pp. 33–34.

96. Roemer, Milton I., "Evaluation of Health Service Programs and Levels of Measurement," *HSMHA (Public Health) Health Reports* 86 (1971): 839–848.

97. Shapiro, Sam, "End Result Measurements of Quality of Medical Care," *Milbank Memorial Fund Quarterly* 45 (1967): 7–30.

98. Luft, Harold S., 1979 prepublication manuscript on HMOs.

99. Williamson, John W., et al., "Quality of Health Care in HMOs."

100. Newport, John, and M. I. Roemer, "Comparative Perinatal Mortality under Medical Care Foundations and Other Delivery Models," *Inquiry* 12 (1975): 10–17.

101. Schneider, A. G., and J. B. Stern, "Health Maintenance Organizations and the Poor: Problems and Prospects," *Northwestern University Law Review,* March-April 1975.

102. Brian, Earl, "California's Emerging Prepaid Health Plans," (Sacramento: California Department of Health, 1972) (unpublished report).

103. D'Onofrio, Carol N., and P. D. Mullen, "Consumer Problems with Prepaid Health Plans in California," *Public Health Reports* 92 (1977): 121–134.

104. U.S. Congress, Senate, Committee on Government Operations, Permanent Subcommittee on Investigations, *Hearings on Prepaid Health Plans* 94th Cong., sess., March 13–14, 1975.

105. Roemer, Milton I., "Better Weather Ahead for California's Prepaid Health Plans," *Impact: American Medical News* 19 (1976), pp. 7–8.

106. Aspen Systems Corporation, *Health Maintenance Organization Laws—A National Overview* (Washington: U.S. Office of Health Maintenance Organizations, c. 1978).

107. U.S. General Accounting Office, *Health Maintenance Organizations Can Help Control Health Care Costs* (Washington: Report to the Congress by the Comptroller General of the United States, May 6, 1980).

108. Institute of Medicine, *Health Planning in the United States: Issues in Guideline Development* (Washington: National Academy of Sciences, March 1980).

Chapter 13

Utilization of Clinic Services

The objective of this book is to offer the reader an understanding of organized ambulatory health services (OAHS) in America, and previous chapters have approached this by analyzing the variety and characteristics of clinics providing these services. In this chapter, we will explore the subject from the other side—that of the population using organized ambulatory health services. What can be said about the extent and nature of that utilization?

To examine clinic utilization in its proper perspective, it is important to consider first the dimensions of ambulatory health care as a whole—whether provided by individual practitioners or clinics. Then we will discuss what is known about the proportions of ambulatory care that people received in clinic settings, and trends in these proportions. Third we will offer some estimates of the service output of clinics, as reported in data from the clinics themselves or the basis of inferences about the magnitude of clinic services. Fourth, we will present the findings on usage of organized ambulatory health services, derived from a survey of households in Los Angeles County, California. Finally, some general comments will be offered about clinic utilization in the United States.

AMBULATORY CARE VISITS IN THE UNITED STATES

The most complete and reliable information about the receipt of ambulatory services of physicians in the United States comes from the national Health Interview Survey (HIS) that has been conducted by the U.S. Public Health Service (PHS) since 1957.[1] Interviews, soliciting information on illness experience, medical services received, health expenditures, and other health-related matters, are conducted periodically on a sample of thousands of households throughout the nation. In recent years this has involved some 40,000 households with about 120,000 persons; sophisticated statistical adjustments are made to assure that the final data are representative of the experience of the U.S. population as a whole, excluding those who are in an institution (on the average day of the year) or in military service.[2]

Thus, a recent report of the HIS findings indicates that in 1978, the average civilian person (noninstitutionalized) in the United States had 4.8 visits with a physician during the year.[3] A "physician visit" is defined as a consultation with a physician (including both doctors of medicine and of osteopathy) or an encounter with a nurse or other person acting under a physician's supervision. This contact may take place in the doctor's office, the patient's home (even by telephone), or in any other ambulatory care setting. It does not include contacts that occur while a patient is in a hospital (or other institutional) bed. The civilian noninstitutionalized population of the United States in 1978 was about 213 million and the aggregate number of such ambulatory care visits in 1978 was approximately 1,022,400,000.

Like all averages, the figure of 4.8 visits per person per year is a combination of rates of ambulatory care that vary greatly by age and sex. These breakdowns in 1978 were as follows:

Age (years)	Male	Female	Total
Under 17	4.2	4.0	4.1
17–24	3.0	5.5	4.3
25–44	3.4	5.8	4.7
45–64	4.7	5.9	5.3
65–74	5.5	6.8	6.2
75 and over	6.4	6.4	6.4
All ages	4.0	5.4	4.8

Source: U.S. National Center for Health Statistics, Current Estimates from the Health Interview Survey, United States 1978 (Washington: DHEW Pub. No. (PHS 80–1551, 1979), p. 37.

Thus, considering the sexes separately there are generally higher rates of ambulatory physician contacts by females, but the differential is greatest during the childbearing period of 17 to 44 years of age. Under age 17 and over age 75, the rates are virtually the same. Considering men and women together, there is a steady rise in the rate of physician visits with age: by age 65, the rate becomes 50 percent higher than under age 17. The latter rate of 4.1 contacts, however, conceals a much greater frequency of ambulatory care contacts under age 4 years, and particularly during infancy (under age one year), than from 5 to 17 years.

These global data on ambulatory services may be analyzed along other dimensions that reflect various social features of American society. Thus, the rate of physician visits is generally higher in urban areas than in rural areas. This differentiation is reported as rates within "standard metropolitan statistical areas'' (SMSA) and outside such areas. In the more urbanized areas in 1977 there were 4.9 physician visits per person per year, compared with 4.4 in more rural areas.[4]

Analyzed by family income, the frequency of ambulatory care visits in recent times is remarkably uniform, when compared to the steep differentials that prevailed 50 years ago. The epochal study of the Committee on the Costs of Medical Care, conducted 1928–31, found a steady gradient for the rate of physician contacts per person per year, with increasing affluence. The dollar amounts of annual incomes, of course, differed greatly in this period from today, so that it is most meaningful to consider the relationships, rather than the actual income figures. These relationships for the United States in the years 1928–31 were as follows:[5]

Annual Family Income	Doctor Visits per Person per Year
Lowest (under $1,200)	1.9
Second	2.0
Third	2.3
Fourth	2.7
Fifth	3.6
Highest ($10,000 and over)	4.7

Source: I. S. Falk, M. C. Klem, and N. Sinai, *The Incidence of Illness and the Receipt and Costs of Medical Care among Representative Families,* Committee on the Costs of Medical Care, Pub. No. 26 (Chicago: University of Chicago Press, 1933), p. 110.

This gradient prevailed in spite of the findings of the first National Health Survey, done in 1935–36, that the days of sickness per person per year showed a gradient of rates in the very opposite direction; that is, there was more sickness as one descended the income ladder.[6]

In 1977, however, the HIS findings for the nation as a whole were as follows:

Annual Family Income	Doctor Visits per Person per Year
Lowest (under $5,000)	5.8
Second	4.9
Third	4.7
Fourth	4.7
Highest ($25,000 or more)	4.8

Source: National Center for Health Statistics, *Disability Days, United States—1971* (Washington: DHEW Pub. No. (HRA) 74–1517, June 1974), p. 6.

Although definitions of ''doctor visits'' differed in these two studies, almost 50 years apart, the changed relationship of ambulatory care received to family income level is unmistakable. In 1977, the poorest families actually had more physician contacts per person per year, in appropriate relationship to the higher burden of illness among the poor that still apparently persists. For 1971 (the most recent year for which sickness data have been reported in the National Health Survey by income level), the relationships of sickness to income were as follows:

Annual Family Income	Restricted Activity Days per Person per year
Lowest (under $3,000)	33.7
Second	20.7
Third	15.3
Fourth	12.8
Fifth	11.8
Highest ($15,000 or more)	11.3

Source: U.S. National Center for Health Statistics, *Disability Days—United States—1971* (Washington: DHEW Pub. No. (HRA) 74–1517, June 1974), p. 6.

A likely explanation of this dramatic change in the relationship of ambulatory services to income level over this span of years was the enactment in 1965 of the Medicaid and Medicare laws, which financed medical services for the poor and the aged. Other relevant influences have doubtless been the greater national supply of doctors, urbanization and improved transportation, and higher general levels of education. Also contributory has been the extended availability of ambulatory services in clinics, as will be discussed below.

These relatively crude statistics on physician visits, of course, tell us nothing about the nature of those doctor-patient encounters. In spite of the levelling out of relationships to income level, there is much reason to believe that the quality of ambulatory services is higher for more affluent families. One reflection of this, for example, is the percentage of children (under 15 years of age) who see a pediatrician during the year. The following relationships were reported in 1964:[8]

Annual Family Income	Percentage of Children Seeing a Pediatrician during the Year
Under $2,000	9.6
Second	12.8
Third	21.6
$7,000 and over	29.4

Source: U.S. National Center for Health Statistics, *Medical Care, Health Status, and Family Income* (Washington: PHS Pub. No. 1000, Series 10, No. 9, 1964), p. 29.

The overall trend of ambulatory services received by the American population is noteworthy. When this subject was first studied in 1928–31, the finding was 2.6 physician visits per person per year. The national survey yielding this figure, however, was limited to white families; had it included all racial groups, the overall rate would have probably been lower. When the continuing National Health Survey was launched in the late 1950s, ambulatory doctor visits were defined to include medical advice by telephone; in 1958–59, the rate of visits was reported as 4.7 per person per year, and 4.2 excluding telephone contacts.[9] By 1971, the National Health Survey HIS finding was 4.9, and, as noted earlier, it had approximately leveled off to 4.8 doctor visits per person per year in 1978. The same factors noted above—urbanization, improved transportation, higher educational levels, more doctors and allied personnel—in connection with family income differentials, undoubtedly explain the overall increase in ambulatory services over the past five decades. Probably the higher proportion of aged, among whom chronic illness is more prevalent, has a bearing on the trends, although this must be considered in relation to the sharp decline in communicable diseases among children and the decline of tuberculosis among all age groups.

With respect to overall ambulatory care in the United States, information on the principal diagnoses for which visits were made is available from a separate National Ambulatory Care Survey started in 1973.[10] These data are limited, however, essentially to ambulatory services rendered by doctors in office-based private medical practice (including private group practice) and they do not include services rendered in hospital outpatient clinics or other types of clinics. In spite of this limitation, the findings help to fill out the picture of ambulatory medical care in the nation. Information was gathered from about 2,500 practicing physicians who reported on 60,000 patient visits during a one-week period (these weeks were spread throughout the year, to adjust for the seasonality of illness).

For the calendar year 1975, according to the above survey, patient visits to all "office-based physicians" in the United States numbered 567,600,000.[11] Since there were about 215,000 such office-based physicians in the nation that year, this would mean an average of 2,640 office visits per doctor per year. Each visit was estimated to average about 15 minutes, although it was naturally longer for more serious conditions and shorter for less serious. The distribution of visits, by severity of the case was:

Severity of Case	Percent
Serious or very serious	19
Slightly serious	32
Not serious	49

Source: U.S. National Center for Health Statistics, *The National Ambulatory Care Survey: Background and Methodology* (Washington: DHEW Pub. No. (PHS) 78–184, 1980).

Relating the aggregate visits to the U.S. civilian noninstitutionalized population in 1975, the rate of visits to office-based physicians was 2.7 per person per year. Household interviews found about 4.2 total ambulatory care services per person per year in the late 1970s, if telephone contacts are excluded. Thus, the 2.7 visits to office-based physicians (including group practices) amounted to 64 percent of the total. The remaining 36 percent of doctor visits presumably occurred in clinics or other settings.

Of these visits to office-based physicians, 60 percent were to doctors in solo practice. Therefore, if the 2.7 visits to office-based physicians are adjusted to take account of the 31 percent of such physicians in group practice (as of 1975), the visits to individual practitioners amount to 1.9 per person per year. In relation to 4.2 total ambulatory services (excluding telephone contacts), this amounts to 45.2 percent of patient-physician encounters. The remaining 54.2 percent of physician visits presumably occurred in clinics of some sort, as will be discussed.

With respect to the principal diagnostic categories of the 567.6 million office visits, according to the judgment of the physician, the frequency distribution was as follows:[12]

Principal Diagnosis	Percent
Respiratory system disease	14.1
Circulatory system disease	9.9
Nervous system and sense organ disorder	7.9
Accidents, poisoning, and violence	7.2
Genitourinary system disease	6.6
Musculoskeletal system disease	5.8
Skin and subcutaneous tissue disease	5.0
Symptoms and ill-defined conditions	4.6
Mental disorders	4.4
Endocrine, nutritional, and metabolic diseases	4.3
Infective and parasitic diseases	4.0
Digestive system diseases	3.5
Neoplasms	2.4
Other diagnoses	1.4
Diagnosis "none" or "unknown"	1.1
Examinations without sickness and "special conditions"	17.8
All diagnoses or conditions	100.0

Source: U.S. National Center for Health Statistics; The National Ambulatory Medical Care Survey: 1975 (Washington: DHEW Pub. No. (PHS) 78–1784, 1980), p. 7.

The discrepancy of this frequency distribution of ambulatory visit diagnoses from the nation's leading causes of death is noteworthy. Although diseases of the circulatory system and malignant neoplasms (cancer) account for 56 percent of the deaths in the United States, they caused only 12.3 percent of the visits to office-based physicians. As common experience suggests, respiratory tract conditions are the most frequent cause of visits to a doctor's office.

Still another way of analyzing office visits to doctors has been formulated in the National Ambulatory Care Survey—the "principal reason" as perceived by the patient, rather than the doctor's judgment of the major diagnosis. Along this dimension, the findings of the 1977 survey were as follows:[13]

Principal Reason for Visit	Percent
Symptoms felt by patient	55.9
Diagnostic, screening, and preventive service	18.3
Care of known chronic disease	9.4
Specific treatment (dressing, injection, etc.)	8.5
Injuries	4.4
Administrative reason	1.8
For test results and other	1.7
All reasons	100.0

Source: U.S. National Center for Health Statistics, *The National Ambulatory Medical Care Survey: 1977 Summary* (Washington: DHEW Pub. No. (PHS) 80–1795), p. 19.

Certain characteristics of private medical practice are revealed also by the fact that, among all patient visits in 1977, only 15 percent were by new patients and 85 percent were by former patients—with either an old or a new problem. Moreover, even though the great majority of American private practitioners are specialists, only 5 percent of office visits were by reason of referral from another physician; 95 percent of visits were made directly by the patient without referral. The majority of all patient visits resulted in advising the patient to return to the same doctor. The breakdown of the doctors' disposition of cases in 1977 was:[14]

Doctors' Disposition of Patient Visit	Percent
Return at a specified time	60.8
Return, if needed	22.6
No follow-up planned	11.2
Telephone follow-up planned	3.2
Patient referred to another physician	2.5
Admit to a hospital	2.0
Return to a referring physician	0.8
Other	1.3

Source: U.S. National Center for Health Statistics, *The National Ambulatory Medical Care Survey: 1977 Summary* (Washington: DHEW Pub. No. (PHS) 78–1795), p. 19.

Since a small proportion of patients seen had more than one of the above types of dispositions, the percentages add to slightly over 100 percent.

AMBULATORY CARE BY PLACE OF SERVICE

In the perspective of this book, more important than the characteristics of ambulatory care discussed above is the question: where did the person receive the service? What proportion of the roughly one billion ambulatory care visits to doctors (or persons working under a doctor's supervision) in the United States, in the late 1970s, took place in organized settings—in clinics of some sort? A precise answer to this question is not simple.

The ongoing HIS fortunately reports on "place of visit" of ambulatory services, as indicated by the patient. Thus, in 1975—when the national average was 5.1 physician visits per person per year, rather than 4.8 as found in 1978—there were a total of 1,056,094,000 visits by the civilian noninstitutionalized U.S. population. By place of visit, these were distributed as follows:[15]

Place of Visit	Percent
Doctor's office (solo or group)	68.0
Hospital outpatient department	12.9
Telephone	12.5
Industrial health unit	0.9
Patient's home	0.8
Other places or unknown	5.0
All places	100.0

Source: U.S. National Center for Health Statistics, Physician Visits—Volume and Interval Since Last Visit, United States 1975 (Washington: DHEW Pub. No. (PHS) 79–1556, 1979), p. 31.

Several observations must be made on the above tabulation. First, the 68 percent of visits reported in "doctors' offices" do not distinguish individual offices from group practice clinics. As noted in Chapter 8, in 1975 out of all U.S. physicians (215,400) in "office-based medical practice," 31 percent were in group practice, as defined by the American Medical Association (AMA). The productivity of group practice physicians, moreover, has been found to be greater than that of solo practitioners, as measured by the output of services per doctor per week.[16] Therefore, one may infer that at least and probably more than 31 percent of the doctor's office visits apply to physicians in group practice clinics. (Indeed it may be recalled, from the National Ambulatory Care Survey reported above, that 40 percent of the medical practices surveyed by random selection were "other than solo practice.") Theoretically, the same dichotomy should apply to services by telephone.

Accordingly, one may recast the tabulation offered above in a manner that takes account of group practice clinics as one of the places where ambulatory services are provided both in person and by telephone. This would yield the following:

Probable Place of Visit	Percent
Individual doctor's office*	55.5
Group practice clinics*	25.0
Hospital outpatient departments	12.9
Industrial health units	0.9
Patient's home	0.8
Other places or unknown	5.0
All places	100.0

Source: Author's derivation from data of the National Center for Health Statistics.
* Includes encounters by telephone (about 16 percent of visits).

Another relevant observation about the HIS data on place of visit is that the interviewer's questionnaire asks about anyone in the household who "had seen or talked to a doctor . . . at a clinic, hospital, doctor's office, or some other place."[17] In probing the response, the answer must be put into one of the following seven categories:

1. Doctor's office (group practice or doctors' clinic)
2. Telephone
3. Hospital outpatient clinic
4. Home
5. Hospital emergency room
6. Company or industry clinic
7. Other (specify)

It may be noted that there is no identification of public health or health department clinics, school or college clinics, mental health clinics, private agency clinics, or any of the variety of community health centers or similar freestanding clinic structures discussed in Chapters 9 and 10. Moreover, in the vast majority of households the respondent is most likely to be the housewife or mother of a family—someone who is not as likely to know about visits to organized units, by other family members, as she is to know about visits to a private doctor (for which appointments are normally made in advance). Since the "recall period" for all questions about ambulatory services is only two weeks, the respondent is not likely to overlook or forget visits to a private medical office, for which a fee is normally paid, as readily as visits to a public health, school, or other community clinic, for which fees are usually not charged.

For these reasons, it appears likely that visits to several of the types of clinic reviewed in previous chapters of this book are underreported in the national HIS. Accordingly, it would be reasonable to infer that virtually all of the visits attributed to "other places or unknown" are, in fact, to one or another of these organized settings. On these presumptions, the tabulation above may be aggregated into two main categories, as follows:

Probable Ambulatory Care Site	Percent
Individual doctor's office or patient's home	56.3
Organized clinic	43.7
All sites	100.0

If our presumption on underreporting of clinic visits by household members other than the respondent is correct, it would be reasonable to assume that the proportion of ambulatory services rendered in organized settings is higher than indicated by the surveys cited above.

Further support for this reasoning is suggested by findings of a special substudy, conducted on a one-third sample of the HIS population for 1974. This substudy asked respondents about *all* the different places where members of the household had received *any* ambulatory health care during the previous year.[18] At the time, about 207,334,000 people were in the U.S. noninstitutionalized civilian population, and the sample reported the persons obtaining ambulatory medical services at least once at some ten different places. The distribution, for obvious reasons, differed markedly by family income levels—lower income families making greater use of public clinics and hospital outpatient departments. The findings are shown in Table 13–1. Since many household members obtained services at more than one source during the year, the percentages in Table 13–1 total more than 100 percent. One may note, for example, that although only 0.9 percent of HIS-reported doctor visits occurred in industrial health units, during the year 3.1 percent of persons made some use of such clinics.

With respect to family incomes, it is evident from Table 13–1, that private doctors' offices, as well as group practices, are more likely to be visited by higher income families; this applies also to contacts by telephone. For hospital emergency rooms, the use is more frequent by low-income families, but this gradient is markedly steeper for the use of scheduled hospital clinics. For public health clinics and neighborhood or community health centers, the frequency of use is also markedly higher by the poor. The greater use of industrial health units by higher income persons may reflect higher wage levels in larger enterprises, where such clinics are much better developed.

Similar relationships to family income level are found in the HIS data on ambulatory care utilization, by place of care during the previous two weeks. These data are shown in Table 13–2.[19] Even though these figures combine solo and group practice, it is evident that both of these private sites are more frequently used by higher income groups, as is telephone service, while hospital outpatient departments and the "other and unknown" places are much more frequently used by persons from poorer households.

Table 13–1 Use of Diverse Sources of Ambulatory Medical Care During the Year: Percent of Persons Using Specified Sources, by Family Income, United States, 1974

Source of Care	Annual Family Income				
	Under $5,000	*$5,000 –9,999*	*$10,000 –14,999*	*$15,000 & over*	*All Incomes*
Private doctor's office	54.6	56.2	59.1	62.5	58.2
Group practice	13.0	14.8	17.7	19.7	16.6
Telephone	10.4	14.4	17.9	19.6	16.1
Hospital emergency room	15.9	15.6	14.3	12.5	14.1
Hospital scheduled clinic	13.1	10.0	7.7	7.2	8.9
Industrial clinic	1.7	3.0	3.4	3.9	3.1
Public health clinic	5.0	3.3	2.1	1.4	2.6
Neighborhood health center	2.2	1.1	0.8	0.4	1.0
Patient's home	2.0	1.4	1.1	1.7	1.5
Other	2.7	2.2	2.2	2.9	2.5

Source: U.S. National Center for Health Statistics, *Advancedata—Access to Ambulatory Health Care: United States, 1974* (Washington: No. 17, February 23, 1978), p. 5.

Table 13–2 Physician's Ambulatory Service by Place of Visit: Percentage Distribution by Family Income, United States, 1975

Place of Visit	Annual Family Income						
	Under $3,000	*$3,000 –4,999*	*$5,000 –6,999*	*$7,000 –9,999*	*$10,000 –14,999*	*$15,000 & over*	*All incomes*
Doctor's office (solo or group)	63.0	65.5	66.6	65.9	68.6	70.3	68.0
Hospital outpatient department	17.7	16.3	16.2	15.4	12.5	8.9	12.9
Telephone	8.7	9.6	9.3	12.3	13.5	15.4	12.5
Industrial health unit	0.2	0.5	0.6	0.9	1.3	1.0	0.9
Patient's home	1.0	1.3	1.3	0.6	0.4	0.6	0.8
Other & unknown	9.4	6.9	6.0	4.9	3.7	3.7	5.0
All places	100.0	100.0	100.0	100.0	100.0	100.0	100.0

Source: U.S. National Center for Health statistics, *Physician Visits—Volume and Interval Since Last Visit, United States 1975* (Washington: DHEW Pub. No. (PHS) 79–1556, 1979), p. 31.

Still another way of acquiring insight from the HIS data on ambulatory care is to note trends over time, by place of visit. The percentage distribution for the year July 1963–June 1964 may be compared with that for 1975:[20]

Place of Visit	1963–64	1975
Doctor's office (solo or group)	69.8	68.0
Hospital outpatient department	11.9	12.9
Telephone	10.6	12.5
Industrial health unit	0.6	0.9
Patient's home	5.4	0.8
Other and unknown	1.6	5.0
All places	100.0	100.0

Source: U.S. National Health Survey, *Volume of Physician Visits by Place of Visit and Type of Service* (Washington: PHS Pub. No. 1000, Series 10, No. 18, 1965), p. 24.

Leaving aside the undoubted increase over this decade in the proportion of visits to group practice clinics included under "doctor's office," it is evident that the proportion of visits to organized settings (including "other and unknown") has been increasing. At the same time, the sharp decrease in the relative number of home calls and the increase in medical services by telephone are noteworthy.

Another study with information on trends in the use of clinics over time has been done by the Center for Health Administration Studies at University of Chicago, in cooperation with the federal government.[21] In this study, a national sample of people were asked about their "usual . . . source of regular medical care," and the responses were compared for 1963 and 1970. Over even this short span of years, the percent of responses stating "clinics," according to family income level, were as follows:

Family Income	Clinic as Regular Source of Care	
	1963	1970
High	7	14
Middle	10	17
Low	17	24
All incomes	11	18

Source: Ronald Andersen, R. M. Greeley, J. Kravits, et al., Health Service Use—National Trends and Variations, Center for Health Administration Studies, Univ. of Chicago, and National Center for Health Services Research and Development (Washington: DHEW Pub. No. (HSM) 73–3004, 1972), p. 4.

One more set of data on trends is available from unpublished HIS tabulations furnished by the National Center of Health Statistics. These permit calculations of percentage distributions, as follows:[22]

Source of Ambulatory Visit	1969	1978
Doctor's office (solo or group)	70.0	67.2
Telephone	11.9	11.8
Hospital OPD	10.3	13.6
Industrial health unit	1.2	0.9
Patient's home	2.3	0.8
Other	3.8	5.2
Unknown	0.5	0.5
All places	100.0	100.0

Source: U.S. National Center for Health Statistics, HIS, unpublished data furnished by Ethel Black, February 1980.

These data (except for the small percentages reported for "industrial health units") confirm the findings of other studies noted above. The separation here of "other" from "unknown," moreover, tends to confirm the premise suggested above that the combined rubric of "other and unknown" probably reflects principally clinic sites.

Thus, whatever may be the exact current proportion of ambulatory care services in the United States being provided in clinics, the trend toward their growth seems clear. This trend is particularly striking with respect to clinic services on which explicit data are available, such as hospital OPDs, group practice clinics, and community health centers. On the basis of data reported in previous chapters, the magnitude of current use of diverse clinics may also be estimated.

SOME ESTIMATES OF OVERALL CLINIC UTILIZATION

The data reported above have been derived from household respondents, except for one set of findings limited to information from private medical offices. Further light may be shed on a difficult question by considering reports coming from several diverse sources that *operate* clinics. Although some of these reports are also subject to errors in reporting or problems from nonuniformity of definitions, certain inferences may be drawn from the available data.

Regarding hospital outpatient department services of all types (scheduled clinics, emergency services, and referred services), the American Hospital Association (AHA) reported 263,775,000 visits of all types in 1977. The exact meaning of this figure, however, is not entirely clear. The AHA's annual survey questionnaire states: "An outpatient visit is a visit by a person not lodged in the hospital . . . (counting) each appearance of an outpatient in each unit (of the outpatient department)."[23] Thus a patient coming to either a scheduled clinic or the emergency room, may be referred to one or more other "units" (e.g., the radiology department, an ophthalmology clinic, a physiotherapy department, or the like) during the same visit. If so, the ambulatory care experience may be reported as two or three visits, rather than one. Yet, depending on the record system of the hospital, such discrete counting may or may not be implemented. In any event, this probably explains why the AHA source reports 264 million OPD visits for 1977, while for 1975 the national HIS data yield a figure of only 137 million (that is, 12.9 percent of 1,056,000,000) visits. Moreover, another tabulation of the National Center for Health Statistics based on its "master facility inventory" yields a figure of 236,041,000 for 1973.[24] In light of these discrepancies, it is probably most prudent to regard the midway figure as the most reasonable for purposes of aggregate estimation. (The federal master facility inventory, it should be noted, counts a patient's services at different specialty sessions, after one entry to an OPD, as several "visits.")

Regarding health department clinics, review of the material in Chapter 5 permits estimates for the early 1970s of total visits to well baby clinics (about 5,000,000), venereal disease clinics (about 2,800,000), family planning clinics under these auspices (8,282,000), and crippled children's clinics (770,000). These total 16,852,000, without consideration of health department clinics for tuberculosis, special immunizations of adults, or general primary care. A conservative total estimate would probably be 20 million visits per year.

The services of school and college clinics are difficult to estimate. Based on inferences from data in Chapter 6, one might guess that children visit school nurses at least 40 million times during a recent year. If one assumed that no more than 10 percent of these visits involved service by or under the direct supervision of a physician, one would derive an estimate of 4 million. University and college health services reports would yield a similar estimate of 30 million general encounters, but a higher proportion of these are likely to involve definite medical care; if this proportion is assumed to be 33 percent, the estimate would come to 10 million. In combination (without including secondary schools) the medical visits at educational institutions would amount to about 14 million per year.

Services of in-plant industrial units are likewise very difficult to estimate. In Chapter 7, it was noted that, out of about 60 million workers in the nonagricultural workforce, 21 percent, about 12 million, were at sites served by an industrial nurse. One of the few studies examining utilization of in-plant clinics found it to amount to 40 visits per 1,000 workers per day in 1948; this would amount to the astonishing rate of 9.6 visits per worker per year. If this rate were applied only to the 12 million nonagricultural workers in plants with an industrial nurse, it would lead to an estimate of 115 million. Applying the same ratio as we did to school children, that is, about 10 percent presumed to see a physician or a nurse under such medical direction, would yield an estimate of 11.5 million industrial clinic medical visits. This figure is not very far from one estimated by the National Center for Health Statistics from the HIS in 1978—8,967,000 in-plant clinic visits.[25] In the light of a high probablity of underreporting of workplace visits by HIS household respondents, it would seem reasonable to elevate this figure to about 10 million visits to industrial health units.

Estimates regarding patient visits to private group practice clinics may be made by different approaches. Earlier in this chapter, it was noted that 31 percent of U.S. doctors in office-based practice in 1975 were in medical groups. If services by telephone are excluded, 25.0 percent of the total ambulatory visits reported in the HIS would be to group practice clinics; in 1975, when the total ambulatory doctor visits came to 1,056,094,000, this would yield an estimate of 264,024,000 visits to group practice clinics. In Chapter 8, however, a calculation based on the annual output of group practice doctors (even adjusting for those in part-time group practice) led to an estimate of 375,734,000 patient visits per year.

The latter figure, from a survey by the AMA, however, did not exclude visits to patients in hospital beds. Since hospitalization in short-term general hospitals averages about 1.2 days per person per year, to eliminate visits to hospitalized patients (typically one doctor visit per day), the above figure should be reduced by about 20 percent to reflect ambulatory care only. This would reduce the estimate to 300,587,000 ambulatory visits to group practice clinics, which is much closer to the estimate of 264,024,000 based on the HIS calculation. Selecting a figure midway between these two estimates, based on different methods, would yield a reasonable estimate of 282,305,000 visits to group practice clinics per year.

For the special governmentally financed clinics, utilization data are available on certain categories from official reports; on other categories, only the rough estimates may be offered. Thus, in Chapter 9 information is given on clinics serving designated federal beneficiaries; the problem in several official reports is that no distinction is made between ambulatory services at freestanding clinics and those at hospital OPDs. Nevertheless, one can infer that around 1975 military personnel (and some dependents) were provided about 18 million visits at nonhospital facilities; veterans received about 3 million; Indians (in 1971), 1,352,000; and merchant seamen and associated persons eligible, 800,000. Altogether, one may estimate about 23 million visits per year provided in nonhospital clinics for federal beneficiaries. (This does not include an estimated 700,000 ambulatory clinic services to federal prisoners.)

The numerous and varied federally financed but locally sponsored and operated community health centers are other sources of organized ambulatory services of uncertain quantity that are doubtlessly expanding. Unpublished data from the U.S. Public Health Service indicates about 498,000 visits per year to migrant health and certain other special rural clinics as of 1978; the varied other health centers were estimated to provide 4,216,000 visits.[26] Total visits in this heterogeneous category numbered 4,714,000 in 1978.

The remaining categories of clinics, discussed in both Chapters 9 and 10, are of a bewildering variety. Many are sponsored by voluntary health agencies oriented to special types of person or disease. The free clinics, serving mainly young men and women (usually living apart from their families) of limited income were estimated in the early 1970s to be providing 754,000 ambulatory services a year. Numerous reports have been issued on overall patients (not visits or services) served by public and private clinics in selected fields such as mental health or family planning. In 1975, freestanding psychiatric clinics were estimated to be serving 1,590,000 patients, while family planning clinics served 5,113,000 women. The services provided to many of these patients, however, are included already in the utilization data on hospital OPDs, health department clinics, community health centers, and so on. The problem, therefore, of avoiding double counting is enormous. In the absence of data, one might avoid offering even an estimate for these remaining sources of clinic service. On the other hand, there may be conceptual value—for the sake of future studies that might explore comparison with the 1970s—to offer a conservative estimate. If the aggregate of these diverse clinic services is assumed to be, let us say, 25 percent of the figure estimated earlier for health department clinics, the number for a recent year would be five million. Even if this estimate is far off the mark, its overall impact on clinic statistics would not be great, and considering all the other organized clinic activities discussed in earlier chapters, (about which utilization data are entirely lacking), such an estimate is probably conservative.

In spite of the fact that the above figures are only rough estimates, they permit us to compile a tabulation on the general order of magnitude of diverse clinic services in the United States during a year in the period around 1975. In order to take account of the assumptions about data on school and industrial clinics, under which the vast majority of visits to nurses only (without any physician involvement) have been excluded, it is reasonable to refer to this tabulation as "medical visits." The results appear in Table 13–3.

It is tempting to relate the overall 595,060,000 clinic medical visits to the national volume of ambulatory services of all types. According to the national HIS in 1975, there were 5.1 visits per person per year, in the civilian noninstitutionalized population that then totaled 209,150,000. The figures in Table 13–

Table 13–3 Medical Visits to Organized Clinics During a Year: Estimated Number and Percent of Visits to Clinics, by Type of Sponsorship, United States, about 1975.

Sponsorship	Number	Percent
Private group practices	282,305,000	47.4
Hospital outpatient departments	236,041,000	39.7
Federal beneficiary clinics	23,000,000	3.9
Health department clinics	20,000,000	3.4
School and college health services	14,000,000	2.4
Industrial health units	10,000,000	1.7
Community Health Centers	4,714,000	0.8
All other clinics	5,000,000	0.8
All clinics	595,060,000	100.0

3 include, however, medical visits by military personnel (both in freestanding military clinics and in military hospitals). It would therefore be plausible to add on the military (but not the institutionalized) population—yielding a total population of 210,828,000. At a rate of 5.1 visits per person per year, this would mean 1,075,223,000 doctor visits in all.

This total for physician visits must, however, be adjusted if it is to serve as a denominator to which the aggregate for clinic visits in Table 13–3 is to be related. It must be increased to take account of the excess clinic visits, over the HIS data, incorporated in the numerator. These consist essentially of 18,281,000 additional visits to group practice clinics and 99,041,000 additional visits to hospital OPDs. All together, therefore, an increment of 117,382,000 visits must be added to the denominator to yield a total of 1,192,605 physician visits in all places. Relating the aggregate estimate of 595,060,000 clinic visits to this total yields a proportion of 49.9 percent.

If we calculate the denominator on the basis of 1978 HIS data (when the overall rate of physician visits was 4.8 rather than 5.1 per person per year), then this figure would be 1,022,400,000 visits for the civilian noninstitutionalized population. Adding on military personnel would come to 1,024,078,000. Relating the aggregate estimate of 595,060,000 clinic visits to this modified denominator would yield a proportion of 58.1 percent.

To recapitulate the several estimates: from the National Ambulatory Care Survey, one may infer that 54.2 percent of physician visits in the nation occur in organized clinics; data reported by the clinics themselves yield an equivalent estimate of 49.9 percent, with a denominator of total patient-physician encounters based on 1975 HIS findings, and 58.1 percent if this denominator is based on 1978 findings. A simple averaging of these three figures would suggest that in the 1970s around 54.1 percent of physician visits in the United States occurred in some type of clinic.

It is evident that these are rough calculations. Although an attempt has been made to avoid double counting it may not have been entirely successful. Several of the figures in Table 13–3 are based on reports or estimates of years other than 1975. On the other hand, the HIS findings on total national physician visits of 5.1 per person per year in 1975 and 4.8 in 1978 may both underestimate clinic visits by all household members, for reasons discussed earlier. A crucial statistical problem relates to hospital OPD services. Thus, we have chosen a "middle ground" figure of 236,041,000 for the nation, even though the AHA reported 264,000,000 OPD visits in 1977; moreover, even an official publication of the National Center for Health Statistics lists 272,317,000 hospital OPD visits occurring in the nation one year earlier, in 1976.[27] Likewise, for group practice clinic visits, we have chosen a figure midway between estimates derived from two different types of calculations.

In view of the many statistical difficulties, it is perhaps most prudent to conclude that: around the mid-1970s, *about half* of all medical services provided to ambulatory persons in the United States were given in an organized setting of some type, as distinguished from the pattern of private solo medical practice. On the basis of recent trends, furthermore, the proportion of these services rendered in clinics appears to be rising. It is very likely that in future decades organized clinics will be the predominant source of ambulatory health care for the U.S. population.

UTILIZATION OF CLINIC SERVICES IN LOS ANGELES COUNTY

As for previous services reported in this book, an attempt was made to explore the overall utilization of OAHS in Los Angeles County, California. In 1974, as part of the Los Angeles Metropolitan Area Survey (LAMAS) conducted by the University of California, Los Angeles (UCLA), several questions were posed to sample households on the use of ambulatory medical services.

The LAMAS is conducted periodically by the UCLA Survey Research Center, which selects a representative sample of the county population for interviews. Approximately 1,000 households are visited, and interviews are conducted by carefully trained personnel.[28] In the February 1974 survey, the household respondent was asked when was the last time that each person in the family (respondent, spouse, or child) saw a doctor? Then a card was shown listing 11 types of places where this medical encounter might have taken place, as follows:

1. Doctor's private office (solo practice)
2. Private medical clinic or group practice, including clinics operated by Kaiser, Ross-Loos, etc.
3. Respondent's home
4. Hospital clinic or emergency room
5. Hospital bed
6. Industrial or company clinic
7. Local health department clinic (e.g., a district health center operated by the Los Angeles County Department of Health)
8. School clinic
9. Other government clinic of any type (e.g., a V.A. or military clinic, which is *not* part of a hospital, a County-operated mental health center, etc.)
10. Other private agency clinic of any type (e.g., Planned Parenthood, a Cancer Society or Heart Association clinic, a "free clinic," etc.)
11. Another place

Additional questions were asked in LAMAS about the family's income level and certain other demographic attributes.

In this survey, 1,069 households were interviewed and information was collected on the 1,069 respondents plus 615 spouses and 456 children, for a total of 2,140 persons. With respect to the interval since a physician was last seen anywhere by various family members, the distribution of responses was as follows:

Interval	Percent
Within the past month	38.1
1–3 months	17.6
3–12 months	23.1
12 months or more	20.4
Never	0.8

Source: UCLA Survey Research Center, unpublished data, 1974.

Since doctor visits occurring one year ago or more are likely to be remembered poorly, analysis of the visits by place were limited to those occurring within 12 months. On this basis the findings were as follows:

Place of Visit	Number	Percent
Private doctor's office	1,014	60.7
Group practice	377	22.6
Hospital OPD	124	7.4
Hospital inpatient ward	41	2.5
Patient's home	14	0.8
Health department clinic	26	1.6
Industrial health unit	23	1.4
School health clinic	13	0.8
Other government clinic	34	2.0
Other voluntary clinic	4	0.2
All places	1,670	100.0

Source: UCLA Survey Research Center, unpublished data, 1974.

It will be noted that this Los Angeles County interview schedule did not allow for "telephone service" as a response, but it did include doctor visits to hospital inpatients. In any event, the rough correspondence to findings of the nationwide HIS described earlier in this chapter is noteworthy. Perhaps most interesting is the reporting of a relatively greater proportion of visits to clinics sponsored by health departments, industries, schools, and other agencies. When such clinics were specifically identified in a household interview, these amounted to 6.0 percent of the most recent visits in Los Angeles County in 1974. Also, group practice clinics, when specifically mentioned, were reported as the site of 22.6 percent of the last visits to doctors.

Analysis of the LAMAS data by family income level, also shows a distribution similar to that nationally. Since a breakdown of the responses by income levels yields fairly small numbers in some categories, certain sites of service may be clustered. Thus, we can observe the percentage distributions of places of service among the 502 "affluent" persons (family incomes of $20,000 per year or more) and the 391 "poor" persons (family income of less than $7,000 per year):

Place of Visit	Percent of Persons	
	Affluent	Poor
Private doctor's office	67.7	56.0
Group practice	22.9	20.5
Hospital OPD or inpatient ward	5.2	13.0
Health department or school clinic	0.8	4.6
Industrial clinic	1.2	0.5
Patient's home	1.4	0.8
Other agency	0.8	4.6
All places	100.0	100.0

Source: UCLA Survey Research Center, unpublished data, 1974.

Except for the use of group practices and industrial clinics, organized settings are much more likely to be used by low-income persons, a finding that corresponds again to nationwide findings.

MEANING OF CLINIC UTILIZATION TRENDS

The data reviewed above show that health services provided in clinic settings of various types play a larger role in U.S. ambulatory care today than one might gather from the traditional image of the American health care system. The trends are clearly toward an increasing importance of clinics, relative to the individual private medical practitioner. What is the meaning of these developments?

As discussed in Chapter 1, *most* Americans still regarded a private physician or family doctor as their usual or regular source of medical care, as of 1974. When asked if they had a regular source of medical care, 80.5 percent of respondents in a national sample answered affirmatively; of these, 62.8 percent reported a private doctor as that source.[29] The balance either had no regular source of care or indicated some other source—usually a clinic. Considering the universe of respondents, this means that around 63 percent of 80 percent of people—or roughly 50 percent of the population—regarded themselves as having a regular family doctor. Thus, the overall situation in 1974, with respect to the U.S. population's usual or regular source of medical care, was as follows:

Regular Source of Care	Percent
Private doctor	50.4
Group practice clinic	21.6
Other type of clinic	6.6
No regular source	14.9
Unknown	6.5
All responses	100.0

Source: U.S. Center for Health Statistics, *Advancedata: Access to Ambulatory Health Care: United States, 1974*, pp. 2–4.

There is little doubt that the proportion of persons who regard an individual doctor as their usual source of medical care has been steadily declining. In contrast to the 50.4 percent having such a sense of connection with a private doctor in 1974, a nationwide survey in 1958 had found 81 percent of people to have a family doctor.[30] The now classical study by Earl Koos in "Regionville" (a town in upstate New York) in the early 1950s reported 64 percent of people to have a family doctor, and this declined to 32 percent among low-income groups.[31]

There are doubtless many reasons for the declining dependence on individual physicians and increasing dependence on organized clinics for health care. The reduced availability of general medical practioners is surely one reason that has been recognized for many years.[32] The other side of the coin, of course, has been the steady growth in specialty medicine, due not only to the complexity of medical science and the greater material rewards for specialists, but also to the demands of an increasingly sophisticated population for the best treatment of any disease.[33] At the same time, American patients have become sensitive to the problems of fragmentation in health care—the loss of sensitivity to the patient as a whole human being—long associated with medical and surgical specialization. Over 40 years ago a distinguished professor of medicine could write about the problems in and the importance of treating "the patient as a person."[34]

Medical and political leadership in the United States has become quite aware of the problem—which is usually referred to as a growing "shortage of primary care."[35-37] Major responses have been to increase the professional stature of the general practitioner by creating a formal specialty of family practice, by subsidizing residency training in primary care specialties, and by training physician extenders (physician assistants and nurse practitioners) to provide primary care, particularly to people in urban and rural poverty areas.[38] Another important response has been the multifaceted movement to establish community health centers in innercity slums and in impoverished rural areas.[39]

Implicit in the community health center movement is the capability of these facilities to bring together a team of medical and allied personnel. The hospital outpatient department, and even an emergency room within it, is regarded by the average person as providing a coordinated range of services that are available at any hour. For the more affluent patient, the private group practice clinic has the equivalent comprehensive scope of technical services under one roof.

Thus, the rising use of clinics should be understood not only as a result of the decline of generalists and the impersonality of care by individual specialists. It means also a reasonable response of people to their perception of a need for the structuring of health care delivery in a properly coordinated manner. An insightful study in one eastern city showed the basic rationality of consumers in their choice of a place for obtaining medical care.[40] Considerations of technical quality were combined with psychological factors, convenience, and costs; all in all, the choice of a clinic for care resulted from a reasonable blending of several criteria.

In a word, the early conception of the clinic or the dispensary as a second-class resource for the socially disadvantaged has become gradually replaced by a conception of the clinic as a site for obtaining access to a reasonable combination of medical and allied skills. The evolution is similar to that of the hospital, although occurring a century or so later. At this stage, distinctions are still being made, with eligibility for clinics often being linked to economic level. The scheduled clinic of a hospital OPD or the community health center is to the poor what the private group practice clinic is to the mere affluent. The two images, however, are merging, as one can see in the community mental health center, the well-developed comprehensive industrial health unit, and especially in the clinics of health maintenance organizations (HMOs), which serve people of every social class.

The role of clinics in bringing together the services of many professional disciplines has implications for interpretation of the data on ambulatory care utilization reviewed in this chapter. One visit to a clinic—typically means much more health service than one visit to a solo practitioner. At the group practice clinic, the hospital OPD, the community health center, many clinics of health departments, large factories, universities, military facilities, the patient typically receives more than one unit of service. Small wonder that the count of 264 million "hospital clinic visits" in 1977, derived from AHA, which got its data from hospital clinic records, is almost double the figure derived from the national HIS in 1975, which indicated 137 million visits. Each patient entering the hospital OPD receives services from an average of nearly two specialty units. It is probable that separately definable services amount to more than this, and the same doubtless applies to those who attend group practice clinics, community health centers, and other organized units. By contrast, the visit to a solo practitioner, at which a need for special extra service is detected, may require additional visits to a laboratory, a radiologist or other specialist, a physical therapist, or elsewhere. Most often, as noted in the data on disposition of cases from the national Ambulatory Care Survey, referrals to other physicians are not made (whether or not they are needed) by the solo practitioner; the patient simply receives a narrower range of service.

Thus, insofar as one of the social responses to the shortage of primary care in America has been an expansion of clinics, the effect has meant an enrichment of the content of health care. Just as the hospital has provided a steadily broadened composition of inpatient care (perhaps excessively so) the clinic has had similar meaning for ambulatory care. In private group practices, under fee-for-service remuneration, a tendency toward excessive multiplication of services may also occur. In its worst form, there have been the scandalous "Medicaid mills" in which the indigent patient gets every medical procedure that can yield a government fee.[41] On the other hand, as noted in Chapter 12, many private group practices may give useful services that reduce the ultimate need for hospitalization. Without the economist's "perverse incentive," as found in the fee system, the clinic can mean comprehensive care but not extravagance. As in the HMO or the clinic in any well-administered system of general health service, the clinic may provide not only primary care but much beyond this level.

Thus, our earlier conclusion that the American health care system has reached a point, where about half of the ambulatory services are provided in organized settings, is surely a modest estimate of the situation. If a sound and thorough method of recording the technical content of ambulatory health services were available and implemented—as has been proposed[42]—it is likely that much more than half of the volume of U.S. ambulatory care would be found to be provided within organized settings. The path ahead is probably clear. It should not mean the continued expansion of the volume of OPD emergency room services—episodic, superficial, disconnected—with which neither patients nor doctors are satisfied.[43] With recognition of the underlying impetus to current trends, i.e., the need and demand of people for effective primary care, the growth of clinics should mean greater, not lesser, sensitivity to the wisdom of serving the patient as a person, along with delivery of a full range of technically appropriate services.

NOTES

1. U.S. National Center for Health Statistics, *Health Interview Survey Procedure, 1957–1974,* U.S. Public Health Service, DHEW Pub. No. (HRA) 75–1311 (Washington: April 1975).

2. U.S. National Center for Health Statistics, *Current Estimates from the Health Interview Survey, United States-1978,* DHEW Pub. No. (PHS) 80–1551 (Washington: November 1979), p. 37.

3. Ibid., p. 30.

4. U.S. National Center for Health Statistics, *Health-United States 1979,* DHEW Pub. No. (PHS) 80–1232 (Washington), p. 132.

5. Falk, I. S.; M. C. Klem; and N. Sinai, *The Incidence of Illness and the Receipt and Costs of Medical Care Among Representative Families,* Committee on the Costs of Medical Care Pub. No. 26, (Chicago: University of Chicago Press, 1933), p. 110.

6. Britten, Rollo H.; S. D. Collins; and J. S. Fitzgerald, "The National Health Survey—Some General Findings as to Disease, Accidents, and Impairments in Urban Areas," *Public Health Reports,* 55 (1940): 444–470.

7. U.S. National Center for Health Statistics, *Disability Days, United States-1971,* DHEW Pub. No. (HRA) 74–1517 (Washington: June 1974), p. 6.

8. U.S. National Center for Health Statistics, *Medical Care, Health Status, and Family Income,* Public Health Service Pub. No. 1000, Series 10, No. 9 (Washington: May 1964), p. 29.

9. Axelrod, S. J.; A. Donabedian; and D. W. Gentry, *Medical Care Chart Book, 6th ed.* (Ann Arbor, Mich.: University of Michigan School of Public Health, September 1976), p. 35.

10. U.S. National Center for Health Statistics, *National Ambulatory Care Survey: Background and Methodology,* DHEW Pub. No. (HRA) 74–1335 (Washington: 1974).

11. U.S. National Center for Health Statistics, *The National Ambulatory Medical Care Survey: 1975,* DHEW Pub. No. (PHS) 78–1784 (Washington: January 1980).

12. Ibid., p. 7.

13. U.S. National Center for Health Statistics, *The National Ambulatory Medical Care Survey: 1977 Summary,* DHEW Pub. No. (PHS) 80–1795 (Washington).

14. Ibid., p. 18.

15. U.S. National Center for Health Statistics, *Physician Visits—Volume and Interval Since Last Visit, United States 1975,* DHEW Pub. No. (PHS) 79–1556 (Washington: 1979), p. 31.

16. Graham, F. E., "Group vs. Solo Practice: Arguments and Evidence," *Inquiry,* 9 (1972): 58.

17. U.S. National Center for Health Statistics, *Physician Visits,* p. 52.

18. U.S. National Center for Health Statistics, *Advancedata—Access to Ambulatory Health Care: United States, 1974,* No. 17 (Washington: February 1978), p. 5.

19. U.S. National Center for Health Statistics, *Physician Visits,* p. 31.

20. U.S. National Health Survey, *Volume of Physician Visits by Place of Visit and Type of Service, United States, July 1963–June 1964,* Public Health Service Pub. No. 1000, Series 10, no. 18 (Washington: June 1965), p. 24.

21. Andersen, Ronald; R. M. Greeley; J. Kravits; et al., *Health Service Use—National Trends and Variations,* Center for Health Administration Studies, University of Chicago and National Center for Health Services Research and Development, DHEW Pub. No. (HSM) 73–3004 (Washington: October 1972), p. 4.

22. U.S. National Center for Health Statistics, Health Interview Survey, Washington, 1980; unpublished data furnished by Ethel R. Black.

23. American Hospital Association, *Hospital Statistics 1978 Edition* (Chicago: AHA), p. XXVIII.

24. U.S. National Center for Health Statistics, *The Nation's Use of Health Resources—1976 Edition,* Division of Health Resources Utilization Statistics, DHEW Pub. No. (HRA) 77–1240 (Washington), p. 27.

25. National Center for Health Statistics, Division of Health Interview Statistics, Washington, 1980; unpublished data from the Health Interview Survey.

26. U.S. Public Health Service, Bureau of Community Health Services, Washington: 1980; unpublished data.

27. U.S. National Center for Health Statistics, *Health Resources and Utilization Statistics, 1976,* DHEW Pub. No. (PHS) 79–1245 (Washington), p. 10.

28. UCLA Survey Research Center, "Some Questions and Answers about the UCLA Survey Research Center," *The Surviewer,* February 1973.

29. U.S. National Center for Health Statistics, *Advancedata: Access to Ambulatory Health Care: United States, 1974,* pp. 2–4.

30. Health Information Foundation, "A View of Our Family Physician," *Progress in Health Services,* June 1958.

31. Koos, Earl L., *The Health of Regionville* (New York: Columbia University Press, 1954).

32. White Kerr L., "General Practice in the United States," *Journal of Medical Education* 39 (1964): 333–345.

33. Mechanic, David, "Some Notes on the Future of General Medical Practice in the United States," *Inquiry,* 6 (1969): 17–26.

34. Robinson, G. Canby, *The Patient as a Person* (New York: Commonwealth Fund, 1939).

35. Bergen, Stanley S., "On the Crisis of Access," *Medical Tribune,* November 19, 1975, p. 9.

36. Stevens, Rosemary, *American Medicine and the Public Interest* (New Haven: Yale University Press, 1971).

37. Almy, Thomas P., "Primary Health Care—A Crisis of Expectations," *The Pharos,* January 1975, pp. 8–13.

38. Roemer, Milton I., "Primary Care and Physician Extenders in Affluent Countries," *International Journal of Health Services* 7 (1977): 545–555.

39. Bodenheimer, Thomas S., "Pattern of Ambulatory Care," *Inquiry* 8 (1970): 26–37.

40. Stratmann, William C., "A Study of Consumer Attitudes About Health Care: The Delivery of Ambulatory Services," *Medical Care* 13 (1975): 537–548.

41. Bellin, Lowell E., and F. Kavaler, "Policing Publicly Funded Health Care for Poor Quality, Overutilization and Fraud—The New York City Medicaid Experience," *American Journal of Public Health* 60 (1970): 811–820.

42. Murnaghan, Jane H., ed., *Ambulatory Care Data—Report of the Conference on Medical Care Records,* supplement to *Medical Care,* 11, no. 2, 1973.

43. Weinerman, E. R., "Research into the Organization of Medical Practice," *Milbank Memorial Fund Quarterly,* 44 (1966), part 2: 104–145.

Chapter 14

Organization and Administration of Clinics

Having reviewed the background, variety, current features, and utilization of clinics in America, we will now examine certain aspects of organization and administration that are relevant to an understanding of any social effort to provide organized ambulatory health services (OAHS).

INTRODUCTION

It would not be feasible to analyze and quantify every component of the structure and administrative process involved in all the OAHS activities reviewed in this volume. We have found clinics to be of many sponsorships and with a vast variety of objectives. Some types of clinics have functioned for decades, even centuries; others have emerged only in the last twenty years or so, and still others are even more recent newcomers to the health care scene. In some settings, a given type of clinic may be rigidly set in its ways; in other settings, it may be innovative and continually changing. Clinics of every type may be small or large, and the large ones tend to be more complex in structure and function than the smaller ones.

With such diversity, generalizations are difficult, and yet an account of the full spectrum of administrative variations within each category of clinic would be a gargantuan task. Instead, we shall consider simply the main features that define the nature of a clinic—what it is and what it does. Perhaps this chapter may be regarded as a "manual" for learning about the anatomy and physiology of the organism, the "clinic," with a few specific examples here and there.

This "manual" for clinic analysis will divide the task into nine parts, relevant to all clinics:

1. administrative structure and lines of authority,
2. functions (population served and services provided),

3. means of financial support,
4. staffing,
5. patterns of service delivery,
6. physical facilities, equipment, and supplies,
7. methods of regulating the quality and efficiency of output,
8. techniques of evaluation, and
9. major problems and main trends.

ADMINISTRATIVE STRUCTURE AND AUTHORITY

The principal axis of classification of OAHS entities in this book has been their sponsorship. From this there logically follows much information about administrative structure and lines of authority. Most fundamental is the clinic's place in its environment: its level of sovereignty.[1]

Level of Sovereignty

Insofar as sovereignty is concerned, a clinic may be: (1) completely autonomous, (2) part of a larger entity that is relatively autonomous, (3) one component in a system or network of clinics or other facilities.

Illustrative of the completely autonomous clinic is the private group practice set up by a number of physicians. Aside from regulatory impacts of laws of licensure, zoning ordinances, etc., such a clinic is entirely its own master. The freestanding community health center has somewhat equivalent sovereignty, although dependence on federal grants, of course, imposes various requirements on performance. A local women's clinic or holistic health center, not part of a larger association, enjoys similar autonomy.

Doubtless more common is the clinic that is part of a larger entity—the latter, however, being independent. This would apply to clinics in the majority of voluntary hospitals. The clinic comes under the hospital's overall administration, but the hospital is ordinarily quite autonomous (when the hospital is public and part of a network, such as a Veterans Administration hospital, this would differ). The industrial health unit in an independent firm (i.e., not one factory in a large corporate system) would represent this level. As discussed in Chapter 7, there may even be varying degrees of sovereignty or autonomy in occupational health services, depending on the management level to which the clinic is responsible, i.e., the personnel department, top administration, or another department.

The third level of sovereignty is seen both in public and private sectors. Clinics in the military services, the Indian Health Program of the U.S. Public Health Service (PHS), or in a state Crippled Children's Program operating clinics at numerous sites would illustrate this pattern. Likewise a private but nationwide

Society for Crippled Children and Adults or a national corporation (e.g., General Motors, Inc.) with plants throughout the nation—each having its industrial clinic—would represent this level of sovereignty. Most large organizations, such as these set standards that each local unit is expected to follow. Yet, in American culture, much leeway is usually allowed for local initiative beyond a minimally mandated level. In a school system with scores of elementary and secondary schools, for example, one frequently sees variations in emphasis at different school clinics—one perhaps focusing strongly on problems of child behavior, another on child nutrition, and so on. The prevailing American ideology is to stress freedom of local response to diverse local needs, even in a bureaucratic system.

Nevertheless, the level of sovereignty is bound to affect everything a clinic does. Within each of the three levels described, there are further variations, depending on personalities, the length of tenure in office of various personnel, and the circumstances at a given time and place. At periods of crisis, or some abrupt environmental change, a clinic of any level of sovereignty is bound to exercise greater autonomy.

Governance

Associated with the level of sovereignty is the form of governance over clinic operations. At the top of most organizations, both private and public, sponsoring clinics in the United States, there is usually a board of directors. In some highly autonomous and independent clinics, or even some clinic systems, however, there may be a hierarchical structure that leads to a single individual.

Boards of directors have the merit of not only bringing together many minds for the formulation of policy decisions, but also of spreading responsibility for the results of decisions that may generate problems or sharp hostilities. Methods of assembling boards vary; boards of education governing public school systems are most frequently elected in the United States; boards of health, which govern public health agencies, are usually appointed by an elected official or officials, although sometimes the types of persons to be included may be spelled out by law. Most voluntary hospital boards are self-appointed—starting with the founders of the facility and then self-perpetuating by internal choice of their own successors. In recent years, pressures have mounted in the United States for deliberate inclusion of some ordinary consumers, patient representatives, or nonprofessionals on the boards of directors of public health agencies, community health centers, hospitals, and other organizations serving the general community.[2] The strongly dominant role of "citizen boards" in certain types of clinics is discussed below.

A pyramidal structure of governance leading to one top official—sometimes with advisory bodies—is found in several government agencies sponsoring clinics, such as the Veterans Administration, or the Indian Health Program under the USPHS (headed by the surgeon general), not to mention the active military service branches. These powerful top officials are typically appointed by an elected executive (a president or governor). In an independent group practice clinic, the director may be the founding individual doctor, though in a large group an executive committee is often elected by the member physicians.

Even though major policy decisions are made by the top governing board or executive, American administrative style favors dialogue beforehand with all principal parties, to enable prediction of a decision's ultimate effects and to emphasize democratic processes before a final decision is reached.[3] Delegation of authority and responsibility to echelons below the top is also a hallmark of American administrative style, and can play a large part in avoiding bottlenecks and achieving rapid movement along the procedural paths of any organization.

The legal status of an organization determines, in some cases, its type of governance. Incorporation (with its concomitant limitation of liability and its perpetual life) in virtually all states requires establishment of a board of directors.[4] Status as an association, partnership or sole proprietorship allows other patterns of governance.

Consumer Participation

A special aspect of administrative governance in recent years, as noted earlier, has been the participation of consumers not only in the policy formulation on clinics and health centers, but also in their management. As discussed in Chapter 9, a consumerism movement gained momentum in the 1960s, when many American cities were shaken with riots of minority ghetto populations.[5] In response, representatives of the poor were not only given a voice in the governance of neighborhood health centers, but in time these people were vested with majority control; the top managerial posts were typically given to minority group individuals with leadership qualities and often no prior training; administrative skills would be learned from experience, reading, night courses, and so on.[6,7] Often local volunteers participated in daily operations as receptionists or clerical aides, while at the same time serving as observers and advocates on behalf of the often bewildered patient. Local neighborhood youth were often engaged as outreach workers to spread the message, door-to-door, about the services available at community health centers.

The concept of a stronger consumer voice soon spread beyond the inner city health center environment into the field of mental health, general comprehensive health planning, boards of health, and so on.[8,9] In the 1970s, national legislation in almost every aspect of the health field provided for some degree of consumer input to policymaking.[10] Toward the late 1970s, however, some skepticism developed about the impact of consumers, as long as their participation was mainly at the lower echelons of the health care system;[11] moreover, when a lay person became sufficiently motivated to become employed in a health care program, he or she would become disqualified from playing a consumer role.

Management

The day-to-day process of administration or management of clinics permits countless variations. Prevailing U.S. concepts emphasize maximum involvement of all components of an organization in the decision making process, so that all health workers feel they have a voice in management of the clinic. A science of management has been developed, in which strategies to fulfill the needs of an organization to survive and grow have been combined, at least in theory, with policies that take account of the sensitivities of participating individuals.[12]

In the management of clinics, regardless of the level of sovereignty and the locus of governance, there are several distinct requirements for efficiency. The flow of patients, for example, is important in any health facility or health program, but in large or even medium-sized clinics smooth patient flow is a crucial feature for efficient use of both staff and patient time.[13] The process of supervision and delegation of authority requires consideration both within the walls of a clinic and in the relationships of a clinic to its higher echelons, if it is a part of a larger system. In large teaching hospitals, with complex outpatient departments, there are exceptionally difficult relationships to maintain between specialty subunits of the OPD and corresponding specialty departments for the inpatient wards.[14] Competent management requires a unique combination of administrative skills with sensitivity to patients; proper and rapid flow of activities is necessary, but patients obviously cannot be handled like auto parts on an assembly line. More sophisticated judgment is perhaps required for large clinic management than for the management of a hospital inpatient service, where the time element is not so constantly pressing.[15] Each of the components of clinic organization—financing, personnel, equipment, records, etc.—has its managerial demands, as will be noted below.

As clinics have grown, particularly in hospital OPDs, management engineering strategies, long applied in overall hospital administration, have been directed to improvement of clinic efficiency.[16] Except for private group practice clinics and most HMO clinics, virtually all clinics face the special managerial problem of uncertainty about the number of patients to be handled on any given day, or even in any given hour. Scheduled appointments may be made, but among many low-income people, who face difficulties in transportation and home life, the rate of broken appointments is often high.[17] From the patient's point of view, a special advantage of most clinics, in contrast to the private medical practitioner, is the freedom to come for help at any time. Reconciling the life circumstances of clinic users with the requirements for efficient management presents a special challenge.

FUNCTIONS: PEOPLE SERVED AND SERVICES PROVIDED

Because of the incremental, largely unplanned and piecemeal development of the whole U.S. health care system, most clinics are restricted to persons of specified characteristics—defined demographically, pathologically, or in both ways. Part of the clinic administrative process is therefore the determination of eligibility. In relatively small, self-contained entities, such as a school or factory or military post, this presents no significant problem. In scheduled clinics of hospitals, however, and many health department clinics, a procedure may have to be established for screening new cases for eligibility. In hospitals, financial investigations to determine if the patient was indigent enough to qualify for care were formerly conducted by social workers.[18] For the past two or three decades, this role has been abandoned by these trained personnel and transferred to admission clerks, so that social workers may devote their time to more important aspects of patient care. In community health centers supported by federal grants, eligibility has often been defined on the basis of the patient's place of residence, which must be nearby. In the clinic of an HMO, the patient has to present a proper membership card for access to services.

Almost the only clinics theoretically open to anyone who comes are the emergency room of the general hospital and the private group practice clinic. Even in these, however, access in reality may not be automatic. The receptionist in a group practice typically seeks information about the patient's occupation, insurance coverage, status in a government aid program, or the like; if the case is not urgent and the patient appears to lack financial means, he or she may be turned away. In the emergency units of voluntary hospitals located in a city containing also a public hospital, the practice of "patient dumping" to the municipal or county facility has aroused more than one scandal in the public press.[19,20]

The volume of patients served on the average day by clinics is highly variable. Emergency departments of general hospitals in large cities are typically busy places, particularly in the evening hours or on weekends, when private physicians are least accessible.[21] Preventive clinics of health departments, by contrast, are frequently underutilized, and staffs seek techniques for better marketing of their product.[22] One of the compelling reasons, in fact, why public health leaders have been advocating coordination in the delivery of preventive and therapeutic services has been to increase the ability of the health department to convince people of the value of preventive services.

The scope of services provided at clinics varies from very narrow to very comprehensive, depending largely on historical and social origins. Broadly speaking, one may observe a somewhat cyclical trend. The earliest dispensaries both in Europe and America, as discussed in Chapter 2, were broad in scope, though intended only for the poor. Early clinics for special beneficiaries of government also provided a wide scope of services. As the private medical profession became socially and politically stronger, the newer types of clinics established—in voluntary and public health agencies, schools, and factories— were narrow in scope, focusing on particular types of diseases or injuries, and largely preventive in orientation. The leadership of the sponsoring agencies of these clinics usually wished to avoid controversy that might come from private doctors, who regarded organized clinics as competitive.[23] To retain the good will of physicians, the scope of clinic service became limited not only to the poor, who constituted a burden in the private medical market, but also to defined disorders. When circumstances created an obvious need for serving children or adults of adequate income (as in schools or factories), then the constraint of scope was defined still differently and therapy was separated from prevention or early disease detection. The latter could be provided under organized auspices, but for treatment the child or adult was referred to a private doctor.

In the early 1950s, the cyclical trend of clinic scope moved again toward greater comprehensiveness. In this period, the population's demands for medical services rose sharply for many reasons. Insurance support was growing, family incomes were higher, transportation and urbanization were increasing, medical science—with antibiotics, antihypertensives, surgical advances, etc.—had more to offer, and people were living longer only to get more chronic diseases.[24] Along with this, the costs of medical care rose rapidly. In response, the prepaid group practice idea, reviewed in Chapter 12, gained momentum. The private group practice clinic, long stigmatized as unorthodox, was somewhat grudgingly accepted by traditional medicine. With the 1960s and the rediscovery of poverty, the comprehensive neighborhood health center emerged, not only for public welfare recipients, but for all people living in certain low-income sections.

Private physicians, particularly those whose offices were located in or near poverty districts, were initially hostile to the rebirth of comprehensive ambulatory care centers.[25] But with enactment of Medicare and Medicaid in 1965, two changes occurred. The American Medical Association (AMA), which had vehemently opposed this legislation, lost much of its effectiveness in Washington.[26] Secondly, the payments made to private practitioners by Medicaid and Medicare proved to be a financial bonanza.[27] Doctors were busier than ever with patients whose fees were paid by voluntary insurance, Medicaid, Medicare, and other programs. The perception of competition from a community health center became blurred. By the early 1970s, federal support for all sorts of urban and rural community health centers (as discussed in Chapter 9) and for promotion of HMOs (as discussed in Chapter 12), could be offered, with only half-hearted opposition from the private doctors of the nation.

Along with the new health center movement, health departments began to broaden the scope of their traditional maternal and child health clinics and to establish general primary care clinics, as reported in Chapter 5. The rural health movement, which had proceeded at rather low ebb for many years, took on new vitality. Small towns and villages were encouraged to improve their access to general health services by taking deliberate steps to organize rural health centers or primary care centers.[28,29] Hospitals, recognizing the patterns of use of their emergency rooms by predominantly nonurgent cases, faced the realities and organized general primary care clinics.[30,31]

While the current cyclical movement of the range of services offered by clinics is toward a broadened scope, the narrowly defined clinics of the previous phase have by no means disappeared. Thousands of clinics, as we have found, with restricted objectives—defined by type of person or type of disorder—continue to operate. The content of "comprehensiveness," in fact, is continually being enlarged. Now that general treatment of disease in organized ambulatory care settings has become less controversial, one sees another rediscovery—this time a new recognition of the value of prevention.[32] In the enthusiasm of community groups for comprehensive medical care resources, the federal government reminds everyone of the profound importance of health promotion and disease prevention. Ambulatory care facilities are advised how to incorporate active health education about sound living or life style in their programs.[33]

In a sense, the swing from specialization to greater generalism seen in clinical medical practice, with the rise of family practice as a specialty, is mirrored in the trend of clinic functions. Although specialization continues in both worlds, the social pressures are mounting for strengthened resources for comprehensive health service.

FINANCIAL SUPPORT

Financial support for clinics is traditionally divided into two basic categories: capital and operating. Capital support concerns the costs of construction of a facility or the purchase of major pieces of equipment that function for long periods of time. Support for operations concerns the day-to-day services of the facility and its staff, consumable supplies, utilities (heat, light, water, etc.), and other related expenses.[34] In the overall financing of clinics, as of hospitals, operating costs are much greater in the long run than capital costs. The largest component of operating costs, in turn, is ordinarily the compensation of personnel.

Sources of Economic Support

Economic support for health services as a whole is derived from a variety of sources. Broadly speaking, there are five principal sources of support of health services in general: private individuals or households, charitable donations (including donated labor), industrial management, voluntary insurance, and government revenues.[35] The same five sources of support, either alone or in various combinations, apply to clinics.

Considering health services as a whole, long-term historical trends have been toward a greater share of costs becoming borne by the several social or collective sources, in contrast to individual financing. This has been generally true throughout the world, but the strength of this trend in the United States has not always been appreciated.[36] In the United States a rising overall expenditure for health purposes has gone hand in hand with an enlarging share of that expenditure coming from social (sometimes called third party) sources. In 1929 the U.S. economy put about $3.6 billion into the health sector, which constituted 3.5 percent of gross national product (GNP) at the time. By 1978, the economy put $192.4 billion into the health sector, and this constituted 9.1 percent of GNP.[37] Over this same span of years, however, the proportion of these amounts derived from purely personal sources changed radically. In 1929, direct individual payments accounted for 88.4 percent of the total and all social sources only 11.6 percent; by 1978, these relationships had become completely reversed, so that individual payments accounted for only 32.9 percent of the total, and all social sources combined, 67.1 percent.[38] From the beginning, however, clinics have been predominantly supported from social sources; these financial trends tend to explain in part the economic basis for the steady growth of organized delivery of ambulatory health services through clinics.

Considering U.S. health services as a whole, the percentage distribution of the several sources in 1978 was as follows:

Source	Percent
Personal payments	32.9
Charity and industry	1.3
Voluntary health insurance	27.0
Government revenues	38.7
All sources	100.0

Source: R. M. Gibson, ''National Health Expenditures, 1978,'' *Health Care Financing Review* 1, no. 1 (1979), pp. 1–36.

With respect to clinics as a whole, we do not know the total expenditures, nor their distribution by source, but one can be certain that the mixture of sources is quite different from the above. The proportion of funding derived from personal payments must be lower than in the above listing, and the shares from the other sources, particularly government revenues, must be greater. The proportion of total health spending derived from charitable donations plus industrial management (1.3 percent combined) is small only in relation to the large amounts derived from other sources; this fraction actually amounts to about $2.5 billion, and much of this is probably referrable to the operation of clinics.

The government revenue source of 38.7 percent consists of 11.0 percent from state and local governments and 27.7 percent from the federal government, the vast bulk of which is for the financing of Medicare and Medicaid.

Capital costs for the construction of clinic facilities are probably derived from governmental and other social sources even more than the operating costs. The construction of most of the clinics reviewed in this book has been financed as part of the cost of construction of their parent facilities—hospitals, schools, factories, or the many other structures in which clinics of health departments or the diverse special public and voluntary agencies are located. The clinics of private medical group practices and the freestanding community health centers are the types most frequently constructed with separate capital funds, although these units may be located in quarters rented in a structure designed for other purposes. When capital funds are needed for clinic construction, they may come from government grants, philanthropic donations, public bonds, or private bank loans.

The operating costs of certain types of clinic are derived almost totally from government revenues. This would apply to most clinics of health departments, even though in recent years, faced with funding cutbacks in local government these clinics may levy small charges on nonindigent patients. It would apply to all public school clinics, although not to those in private elementary and secondary schools. In universities, both public and private, special student fees, which amount to a type of health insurance, are often payable annually. Clinics for designated federal beneficiaries are wholly financed from national revenues.

In-plant medical services are ordinarily financed wholly by industrial management. Corporations also usually contribute much larger amounts toward fringe benefits of voluntary insurance for employee general medical care, but these funds are included within the 27 percent of health spending listed above as derived from "voluntary health insurance." The ultimate impact of these costs falls on the whole national population, insofar as they are paid from earnings and also deductible by firms as business expenses for the purpose of income taxes.

The funding of HMO clinics, as evident from Chapter 12, is almost entirely from voluntary insurance contributions. Insofar as government grants or loans have assisted in the initiation of HMOs, these play a small part. The enrollment of Medicaid beneficiaries in certain HMOs also means public revenue support.

The financial support of private group practice clinics is derived mainly from a combination of private payments and voluntary insurance. Medicare payments, however, are doubtless playing an increasing part as group practices increase and become available to the nation's 26 million aged and disabled beneficiaries. In 1977 "supplementary medical insurance" under Medicare paid out $5,767,000,000.[39] Roughly half of this, or $2,883,500,000, may be estimated as attributable to out-of-hospital ambulatory care. With group practice doctors constituting about 31 percent of office-based physicians, this would yield an estimate of $894 million going to group practices from Medicare alone. For the 66,000 doctors in group practice, this would mean average annual gross earnings from Medicare of about $13,500. Rough as this exercise in estimating may be, it reflects perhaps the substantial impact of government support for services even in private group practice clinics.

The many types of federally funded and locally sponsored community health centers, discussed in Chapter 9, are supported principally by federal government grants. It is noteworthy that, while many federal health programs have suffered cutbacks or merely static funding in recent years, the federal budgeting for community health center support has risen. Thus President Carter's budget for the fiscal year 1980–81 called for grants of $353 million for these units, in contrast to $320 million spent in the previous fiscal year.[40] (After 1981, however, this trend will probably be reversed.) These health centers also attempt to collect small fees from their low-income patients, but these absorb only a very small percentage of the costs.

The most complicated financing of clinic services doubtless applies to those of hospital OPDs. The sources of funding differ for the three types of ambulatory services, as reviewed in Chapter 4. Simplest is the support for referred services, which are essentially like the support for private inpatient care, that is, personal payment or reimbursement from voluntary or social insurance. Emergency room services, being rendered to persons of all income levels, are similarly charged for, with payment coming from personal sources, voluntary insurance, Medicare, or Medicaid; when there is no payment, costs are absorbed from other sources of hospital income.

The sources of payment are most diversified for the services of scheduled clinics. Insofar as low-income beneficiaries of Medicaid and/or Medicare are served, these public programs pay the charges. Occasionally voluntary health insurance is available for working people in low-paid employment. Charges are often levied on a sliding scale, so that even very poor patients make small partial payments. The hospital may have a charitable endowment to help support these outpatient services to the poor, or regular grants may come from a United Way campaign for these services. For certain specific clinic sessions, such as family planning or services to crippled children, earmarked grants may be received from state government agencies (which derive their funds largely from federal sources). It is commonplace, nevertheless, for scheduled clinics to be regarded by hospital administration as a deficit department that must compensate for its losses by deriving support from other hospital departments (e.g., radiology or pharmacy) that earn more than their actual cost.[41]

Clinic Accounting

Determination of the precise costs of providing clinic services is a complex task in accounting about which there has been much debate. When conventional accounting methods are used, the costs of a visit at a hospital OPD are usually calculated to be higher than a similar visit to a freestanding clinic or health center.[42] The difference is usually due to the many partial costs of overall hospital operation (including administration, laboratory, laundry, etc.) that are assigned to the OPD—on the basis of space occupied, personnel time involved, and other factors. Yet, those fully accounted costs are seldom payable by the patient, or even by categorical third party support programs, such as Medicaid or private insurance.

Reasonable accounting procedure for the operation of health facilities in general, and clinics in particular, has long been a subject of importance in the administration of hospitals, since effective management depends on a detailed knowledge of the operational points of origin, or cost centers, of all expenditures.[43] The issue has grown as more government programs have evolved, particularly Medicare and Medicaid, requiring payment of "reasonable costs" for the services delivered—these being calculated according to regulations that exclude the cost of activities not strictly linked to the provision of patient care, such as teaching, research, public relations, and so on. To enable hospitals throughout the nation to cope with regulatory requirements, the AHA has issued recommended accounting procedures.[44,45]

Leonard Rosenfeld has described the many difficulties in proper assignment of overall hospital costs to the operation of ambulatory services:

> In developing methods of cost finding for ambulatory facilities, existing practice which emerges primarily from experience in administration of inpatient facilities must be examined with great skepticism. . . . Whereas in the past, for example, floor area has been widely accepted as a method of allocating such costs as housekeeping and plant maintenance and operations to inpatient and outpatient services, these relatively simple formulae may not be acceptable in the future. Not taken into account in this formula are such factors as intensity of utilization of space, the differences in complexity of equipment to be maintained, and the varying degree of use of such utilities as electricity, heat, steam, and the like. Greater justification will be required than ever before concerning allocation of costs of staff time between inpatient and outpatient services.[46]

To enable the numerous freestanding community health centers to calculate correctly their costs in order to yield reasonable reimbursement from third party payers of charges per visit, and also to plan properly for the necessary costs of staffing and operations, the USPHS has issued manuals for reasonable financial planning.[47] It is noteworthy, that such manuals emphasize the need to consider not only the direct cost of furnishing a unit of medical service but also the associated cost of outreach to the surrounding population to market the services, the costs of quality controls of clinic staff performance, and the inherent costs of data collection and fund management themselves.

At the root of many of the deficiencies in ambulatory care delivery at various sites, of course, is the inadequacy of financial support. In schools, industrial firms, military posts, and even hospitals, the operation of clinics is regarded as ancillary to another principal purpose. When funding is restricted, these secondary services are naturally the first to be reduced. The generally better staffed and equipped settings of private group practices and HMOs are doubtless due not only to their more abundant sources of funding, but also to the top priority of ambulatory services in these types of clinic. The primary objective of a group practice clinic is first-class ambulatory service that will be attractive to the patient and possibly reduce the need for costly hospital admission. One can appreciate why one knowledgeable business expert in the field has written: "The only cure for the present problem of ambulatory care financing is comprehensive national health insurance."[48]

CLINIC STAFFING

The crucial importance of adequate clinic personnel and appropriate use of their skills in delivering patient care have been discussed in previous chapters. Here we may take note only of some general issues concerning the staffing of clinics. The very raison d'être of clinics, in contrast to solo medical practice, is to bring together persons with diverse skills to produce a product—ambulatory medical care—with greater efficiency. As pointed out by Michael Davis years ago, a major rationale for the early development of clinics, under both hospital and public health auspices, was the belief in their greater efficiency, by mobilizing personnel of lesser training to carry out functions not really requiring the time or skill of doctors.[49] As we have observed throughout, such rationalization of many health care functions, by delegation of tasks to nurses and others, still remains a hallmark of clinics.

Procedures for appointing personnel to staff clinics vary with their sponsorship. In general, the appointment process in clinics under direct governmental control requires merit system or Civil Service formalities throughout the United States. This would apply to the clinics of health departments, public school systems, public hospitals, and those in the several special programs for government beneficiaries. In spite of the fair and reasonable social objectives of these public personnel systems, it has long been claimed that their rigidity may impair hiring and firing the most appropriate individuals; public hospitals, in particular, have been accused of retaining incompetent personnel because it is so bureaucratically complex to discharge such persons, once they are appointed.[50] This is also one alleged reason why some public hospitals that operate large outpatient clinics have been transferred in recent years to private management firms, which are not bound by Civil Service personnel requirements.[51] Privately operated clinics have great freedom in selection of personnel, although this may permit abuses of nepotism or ethnic bias. Standards of the Joint Commission on Accreditation of Hospitals impose certain criteria for staff appointments in voluntary hospitals.[52]

In some types of clinics, a sharp distinction exists between the formal relationship of physicians to the clinic organization, in comparison with that of all other staff members. Because of their long historic tradition as independent licensed practitioners, doctors are often not willing to accept appointments as employees of an agency, public or private. To cope with these attitudes, physicians are frequently engaged for clinic service in hospitals, health departments, schools, factories, and elsewhere on a contract basis. Thus, they serve as independent contractors rather than as agency employees.[53]

In spite of the autonomous status of physicians in most clinics, there are frequent problems in relationships between them and administrative authorities. The tradition of sovereignty about technical or professional decisions in medicine leads many physicians to be resistant to the bureaucratic requirements of any organizational structure.[54] Clinic administrators, therefore, tend to concentrate their attention on fiscal and organizational matters and on the work of nonmedical personnel, allowing physicians a maximum of freedom in their functions.

In most of the clinics reviewed in this volume, physicians serve on a part-time basis, and the greater share of their time is spent in private practice or in another position. This is true of medical service in most scheduled hospital clinics, except in large teaching hospitals with large numbers of interns and residents; however, even the latter ordinarily spend most of their time on the inpatient wards. It is also true in most health department clinics, school and industrial units, and in specialized clinics for mental disorders, family planning, or crippled children, whether under private or public sponsorship. For these services the doctor is typically paid a fixed stipend per hour or per session.

In many hospital emergency rooms, however, when patients can afford to pay or are covered by some third party payment program, the physician may earn patient fees quite aside from the charges levied by the hospital for all the supportive services. Likewise in private group practices, as discussed in Chapter 8, a great variety of income-sharing arrangements are followed. Most of these assign a portion of each patient's fee to the doctor giving the service (presumably as a financial incentive). In HMOs of the group practice model, straight salaries are most frequent, although their levels vary with qualifications, seniority, and responsibility; there may also be bonuses at the end of the year if the HMO has a net balance due to prudent expenditures on hospitalization and other doctor-prescribed services. Physicians in federal employment staffing clinics ordinarily receive full-time salaries.

By far the greater proportion of clinic staffs are nurses, clerks, technicians, and other allied personnel. As these personnel work with physicians, there tends to develop a relationship of trust and mutual respect, so that in time the physician usually delegates more responsibilities to others, particularly to nurses.[55] Long before the formal movement arose for training physician extenders (nurse practitioners and physician assistants), clinic nurses performed many procedures on the basis of the physician's "standing orders."[56] As we have noted, in schools and industrial plants clinic staffing for much the greatest part of the time is solely by nurses. The same applies to many well baby clinics of health departments, to health posts serving American Indians, and to prison clinics.

With the rise of the nurse practitioner movement, more extensive responsibilities have been assigned to qualified nurses. It is noteworthy that the pioneer demonstrations in this field started at teaching hospital clinics, where a diagnosis had already been established on patients with chronic disorders; the task was to monitor these patients for changes in signs or symptoms that indicated a need for modified therapy.[57] Later, primary care responsibilities were assigned to physician extenders, both in teams and at isolated posts.[58] Primary care demands judgmental competence for initial diagnosis and case management. As noted earlier, it is significant that other industrialized countries, with much larger proportions of generalists in medicine, are quite willing to use ancillary personnel for midwifery, anesthesia, well baby checkups, and many procedural tasks, but have refrained from using them for the subtle decision making functions involved in good primary care.[59]

Still, it has been shown that the nurse stationed in a public school clinic can be trained to offer more effective care for the common ailments of young children.[60] Also, there is presumptive evidence that the services of physician extenders are generally better accepted by patients and less subject to error when they are working in a clinic setting with physicians and others close at hand.[61] Modern refinements of time and motion studies, long used in industry, have demonstrated the savings possible in unit costs of an ambulatory care clinic, by careful analysis of patient care functions, and assignment to the nurse practitioner or other personnel of every task within his or her capabilities.[62,63] Indeed, more than 700 discrete tasks involved in general primary care have been identified in order to facilitate rational task delegation to all sorts of personnel in various types of clinics.[64]

The crucial requirement for proper clinic staffing remains the recruitment and retention of physicians. As Rosenfeld has brought out, the physician, unlike the other clinic personnel, typically has "the option of private practice," and this must be counterbalanced not only by adequate monetary rewards, but by various perquisites (holidays, pensions, etc.), as well as by professional incentives such as paid study leave, opportunities for research and continuing education, and a stimulating professional environment.[65] Indicative of the importance of such incentives has been the experience of the U.S. National Health Service Corps (see Chapter 9) in the retention of physicians at underserved areas of assignment. When these young doctors in the early 1970s were assigned to isolated posts, only 3 percent remained at these sites following their mandatory service period. After 1975, the Corps doctors were sent mainly to organized ambulatory care settings, working in clinic teams of health professionals. As a result, some 50 percent of the Corps doctors have chosen to remain at these sites for more than one year beyond their official tour of duty.[66]

HEALTH CARE DELIVERY PATTERNS

The greatest variations in patterns of health care delivery are probably seen in the flow charts of patient care at the organized clinics of large hospital outpatient departments. Typically, various sessions are scheduled in accordance with the medical and surgical specialties. The new adult patient is usually directed to the general medical clinic, where an initial examination is done. Referrals are then made as necessary to other specialty clinics. All too often, however, there is little coordination among the different specialists serving one patient with multiple problems. This is especially common among the aged. Attempts have been made in some teaching hospital OPDs to establish long-term relationships between the patient and a primary physician, who then becomes responsible for the coordinated and comprehensive care of the patient.[67]

In the 1950s and 1960s, recognition of the need for integrated patient care in an era of enormous specialization was expressed through advocacy of comprehensive medical care.[68] In the 1970s, the same issue became epitomized in defining a new role for family practice or family medicine.[69] The point of entry of all patients theoretically became the family practice clinic, and the physician would maintain contact with the patient following all services from specialists. Unfortunately, this theoretical model often has remained an abstraction, and family practice clinics operate more or less in isolation from the spectrum of OPD specialties.

Well-organized HMO group practice clinics, such as in the Kaiser-Permanente program, make an effort to link every enrollee to a primary physician, who may be an internist, a general practitioner, a family practice specialist, or a pediatrician.[70] Implementation is often difficult, however, because of the waiting time (that may be several weeks) for appointments in nonurgent cases. Rather than accepting such delay, many patients prefer to go directly to a walk-in clinic, where they can see the physician on duty immediately. Thus, continuity of care is sacrificed for the sake of prompt attention. In all group practices, prepaid and conventional, it has been shown, moreover, that the extent of true grouping or professional interchange for coordination of individual patient care can be highly variable; some medical groups unfortunately have constituted little more than a sharing of office quarters and earnings, but not of the delivery of medical care.[71] With more experience, it is hoped that truly collaborative work should evolve.

Under health department sponsorship, well baby clinics have tended to develop a rather uniformly standardized pattern of health care delivery.[72] Typically, the infant or small child is undressed by the mother and weighed by the nurse. The nurse also asks the mother about any problems recognized in the baby's development and behavior. Advice is given on diet, toilet training, hygiene, safe play arrangements, sleep patterns, and so on. Often no physician is seen, unless there is a problem that the nurse identifies as requiring medical attention. Public health clinics for venereal disease or tuberculosis tend to be less standardized, but physicians are always in attendance. Multiphasic screening programs, conducted by health departments, usually follow an assembly line procedure: the patient moves from test to test under the guidance of technical staff. There is no physician in attendance; test results are then mailed to the patient with advice that he or she consult a personal physician about any possible abnormal findings.

In industrial clinics, nurses available usually screen all patients. The nurse's judgment determines whether or not an injured or sick worker should be sent somewhere for immediate medical attention. In very large plants, where physicians may be on duty full-time, such screening by nurses is still the general rule. The same applies in school health clinics. For those occasions when large numbers of school children are to receive physical examinations, the nurse usually tests vision with a Snellen chart, determines the child's weight and height, and takes a brief medical history. The physician then does the physical appraisal which includes principally examination of the throat, the heart, general posture, and the basic indicators of development.[73]

At community health centers, two patterns of patient care have evolved. If the attendance is relatively low, all new patients usually see a general practitioner, with referrals as indicated to specialists. When there is heavy utilization, the medical staff may be divided into teams, each of which consists of an internist or general practitioner, a pediatrician, and a gynecologist-obstetrician. The patient, or preferably the entire family, becomes attached to one of these primary care teams, where most needs can be met; referrals are still made to specialists, but the patient is always supposed to return to the team for continuing care.[74]

Whatever pattern may be designed for primary health care, some type of patient referral becomes necessary sooner or later. Referrals are often necessary to resources outside the clinic where the patient was first seen. In metropolitan areas, the numbers and types of places for obtaining specialized services can be bewildering, so a directory may be essential. Social workers attached to the larger clinics can be invaluable in guiding patients to appropriate resources.[75]

The atomosphere of clinics obviously influences the attitudes of both patients and professionals. Many studies have shown the disagreeable aspects of large, crowded public hospital OPDs.[76,77] Yet on analysis, one invariably finds that in these settings the staff is too small for the patient load, so that waiting periods are long and the time with the doctor is short. The majority of patients come without prior appointments. Since the patients are typically indigent, attitudes toward them are often condescending; and because of the pressure of other waiting patients, examinations may be perfunctory.[78] At the same time, the clinic structure in a group practice, either private fee-for-service or prepaid HMO, can yield a sensitive and agreeable atmosphere for all parties.

Regionalization of health services has long been advocated as a strategy for assuring the appropriate technical level of care for people, wherever they may live.[79] Only in a few special subsystems of health care, such as the Veterans Administration, the Indian Health Service, or certain demonstration programs (e.g., the Rochester Regional Hospital Council in upstate New York), however, has the concept been effectively implemented. The federal Regional Medical Program for Heart Disease, Cancer, and Stroke (RMP), enacted in 1966, financed the spreading of technical ideas from medical schools to peripheral hospitals, but did little to establish the two-way flow of patients and consultation services among hospitals or clinics in a certain area, as theoretically envisaged in the regionalization idea.[80]

The challenge that most clinics face is to organize their pattern of health service delivery so that the patient receives continuity of care. That is, the doctor or other health care provider seeing a patient should be fully informed on what has gone before, so that needless duplication is avoided and the case can be managed effectively in coordination with services from other previous or current providers. When medical services were less complex, continuity was supposedly provided by the family doctor. A good system of records as well as telephone communications, however, can provide continuity, along with the advantages of appropriate specialty services.[81] In clinics, where personnel may change from week to week, an effective system of records becomes all the more essential. As we will see below, this inherent need for communication in most clinics has led to the development of careful record systems that are usually more comprehensive than those found in the average private medical practice.

PHYSICAL FACILITIES, EQUIPMENT, AND SUPPLIES

The physical facilities (floor space and the arrangement of quarters) obviously exert a substantial influence on the functioning of clinics. Broadly speaking, they tend to be most adequate in newer structures, if only because the importance of good quality ambulatory medical care has become increasingly appreciated in recent times.

Thus, hospitals built many years ago made hardly any space provisions for outpatients; as demands for ambulatory care increased, quarters were improvised. The same applies to health departments, the functions of which were initially limited largely to regulation of environmental sanitation and rarely involved operation of clinics. The typical quarters of a county health department before 1945 were converted storage rooms in the basement of the local courthouse.[82] Likewise, old schools and old factories rarely made any provision for health care space.

As the value of organized ambulatory services has become better recognized, clinic facilities have greatly improved. Virtually every modern general hospital makes relatively spacious allowance for clinic examining rooms, waiting areas, rooms for minor surgery and other therapies, staff offices, and so on.[83] Under the Hill-Burton Hospital Construction Program, model architectural plans were widely distributed on arrangements suitable for general hospitals of different sizes.[84] Similar model designs have been published for local health centers, in the sense that that term in the 1940s and 1950s was used to define a structure to house local Health Departments. Hospital architecture has become a specialty, and clear definition of clinic functions is expected to precede the decisions on physical structure.[85] For some years, "rule of thumb" standards were used for clinic space—such as 1,000 square feet per physician or one square foot per patient (not per visit) served per year—but, with experience, standards based on more precise functional analyses have been formulated.[86] Precise room arrangements and space vary with the specialty services, the relative demands for true emergency care, and so on.

Much careful architectural planning has gone also into the design of freestanding community health centers.[87] In contrast to the depressed and dilapidated housing conditions in urban slums, these structures usually stand out as symbols of both scientific service and dignified care for the poor. The same impressive picture of modernity and functionalism applies to many of the newly constructed ambulatory care facilities of HMOs.[88] One senses almost a spirit of defiance against the stigmatized image of the past in these structures; to assert that prepaid group practice is by no means inferior to traditional private medicine, but actually superior to it, the message is conveyed with steel, glass, and stylish ceramic materials. Private group practices, often located in suburban areas where land is relatively abundant, have long been models of architectural innovation. By skillful arrangement of medical offices and several small separated waiting areas, a highly personal atmosphere can be conveyed to counteract effectively the all too common notion of clinics as second-class places for the poor.

Although some social planners scoff at concerns for "bricks and mortar," in contrast to the more basic issues of competent personnel and sound policies, the fact remains that physical structures and layouts can have a great influence on staff morale, patient acceptability, and total program effectiveness. Good facilities include not only examining and waiting rooms but ancillary facilities for laboratory tests, proper storage space for supplies and drugs, record cabinets, the appropriate equipment for medical examinations and ambulatory therapy, and so on. Attractive colors can have an impact on the moods of everyone, and even background music has its value. Furniture should be functional, attractive, and durable. All these things have a price, but there is no reason why such expenditures snould not be made in organized health care settings as readily as they are usually made in the private doctor's office.[90]

Effective physical planning of hospitals and their outpatient departments has challenged the inventiveness of systems engineers for many years. Careful study of the flow of activity in a busy OPD service can usually disclose ways that efficiency can be improved by redesigning space layout, equipment, procedures, or personnel functions.[91] Implementation of clearly desirable changes is often impeded in public facilities because of lack of initial funds, even though one can readily predict future savings from greater efficiency. Attitudes of conservatism and inertia, moreover, can sometimes block technological improvements of ambulatory care facilities as surely as the complexities of a setting.[92]

CONTROLS OF QUALITY AND COSTS

Most of the administrative processes and conditions discussed above have an impact on the quality of care provided by a clinic as well as its costs. Beyond these, there are features within every organized ambulatory care program that have crucial significance for the maintenance of high quality performance. Also, the U.S. health care system includes several requirements that exert external controls on the operation of all clinics. The main features of these two forms of quality and cost control may be briefly considered.

Internal Controls

Within virtually every clinic, there are lines of authority and responsibility intended to assure that various activities are properly carried out. In larger clinics the degree of supervision tends to be more rigorous. Enforcement of standards is also likely to be greater in public clinics than in private clinics. In a private clinic at the most autonomous sovereignty level, e.g., a free clinic, the internal organizational structure is likely to be quite loose; for such settings, external controls (discussed below) are more important.

The framework of authority needed to assure maintenance of defined standards includes three elements: supervision, delegation of responsibility, and feedback. A vast literature of organization research has explored the general workings of this process in private industry and governmental agencies.[93] Much attention has been given to the problem of reconciling the psychological needs of individuals with the requirements for organizational effectiveness, in order to create personal incentives consistent with organizational objectives.[94] In the ambulatory health services, the special issue of achieving teamwork between the traditionally independent physician and other health personnel has been noted above. The worldwide trends toward increasingly complex organizational relationships in the delivery of health services have demanded increasing sophistication about effective strategies in the management process.[95]

Beyond the influences on performance of day-to-day supervision and peer review by colleagues, larger clinics often establish units for the specific purpose of self-evaluation. In the relatively small clinics of most local health departments, public schools, industrial firms, or nonmetropolitan hospitals, this is seldom feasible. But in large OPDs of teaching hospitals, large group practices, major university health service programs, many community health centers, and so on, such quality assurance mechanisms are being increasingly implemented.[96,97] Various methods of such internal self-appraisal are possible, but all of them require some form of consensus among the health personnel in the program, agreement on standards or criteria for evaluation, a reliable system of records (reflecting everything actually done in the process of patient care), and a constructive (rather than punitive) procedure for reporting assessments in ways that will induce improvements.[98]

Accurate and yet nonburdensome medical records are so crucial to quality assessment—both internal and external—that a great deal of effort has been put into the implementation of record systems in ambulatory care programs. Medical records of hospital inpatients have become increasingly standardized, and they have been subject to quality assessment through medical audits of charts since the 1920s.[99] The conditions of ambulatory care, where patients are usually seen only for brief encounters and records are often perfunctory, make objective evaluation more difficult. To tackle this problem, special efforts have been made since the late 1960s to develop record systems specifically suited to the pressures typical in organized ambulatory care settings, yet adequate to permit reasonable quality surveillance.[100,101] This movement has also been fueled by the needs of health services research, which would permit comparative evaluations of the process and outcomes of differing methods of ambulatory care delivery in the pluralistic U.S. health care system.[102]

With respect to quality assurance in community health centers financed by federal grants, special methods of evaluation have been developed, which in turn have led to the incorporation of certain recordkeeping procedures in these facilities.[103] The very process of conducting these assessments in scores of health centers throughout the nation has doubtless contributed to the improvement of internal peer review policies. In the same sense, uniform record systems have been promoted in prepaid health care plans or HMOs, as instruments both for internal quality assurance and for external comparative evaluations.[104]

Mechanisms for the control of costs in organizations generally involve periodic reviews of expenditures in relation to previously established budgets.[105] In clinics, where the utilization rates are often only crudely predictable, it is usually necessary for administrative heads to allow a great deal of leeway in ultimate expenditures.[106] This is easier when the clinic is part of a larger system, in which trade-offs are possible between one component and another. It is also easier, of course, in clinics that earn income from patient fees. Fixed ceilings on expenditures can impair the quality of services toward the end of a fiscal year unless managerial surveillance has controlled expenditures prudently from the start of the year.

A final internal procedure for quality assurance in clinics is the maintenance of clearly visible and convenient channels for expression of grievances by patients.[107] For inpatient hospital care, solicitation of patient comments on the services received has long been commonplace. In ambulatory care settings, however, such procedures are rarely implemented. Newly organized HMOs, which face the challenge of winning over their members to the different and often strange pattern of ambulatory care delivery, often establish an office of consumer relations.[108] The task of this office (usually one person in the small HMO) is not only to be available for complaints, but to issue information bulletins on HMO procedures in order to avert difficulties. Problems identified from patient comments are brought to the attention of the HMO management for possible correction.

External Regulation

When a clinic is part of a larger system, as noted above, its operations are subject to a degree of outside control from the higher echelons of that system. Beyond this, various processes have evolved that are imposing an increasing amount of regulation or control on clinics from different levels of government or from the private sector of society over and above the entity in which the clinic is a part.

First, one must consider personnel licensure laws that govern medical and most other health personnel working in clinics.[109] More direct is the extensive legislation on licensure of hospitals that has been enacted in every state of the nation since the Hill-Burton Act of 1946.[110] Initially, these statutes were relatively modest in their requirements, being concerned mainly with physical facilities, sanitation, safety, and so on; gradually, however, many states have widened the scope of these laws.[111] The chief problem is laxity of enforcement, due to weak inspectional staffs in state government.[112] Insofar as hospitals are subject to state review and approval (usually by the state department of health), this legislation includes the structure and staffing of outpatient departments.

State legislation on public school systems often contains provision for nursing services being available for first aid, but seldom requires school health clinics as such.[113] State labor legislation on factory inspection also may mandate the availability of medical and/or nursing service for first aid, without specifying standards for clinics.[114]

In recent years, a number of states have enacted specific legislation on free-standing clinics, to establish minimum standards of structure and staffing. In California, for example, a statute in 1978 provided for licensure by the State Department of Health Services of various types of community clinic, free clinic, employees' clinic, and certain other ambulatory care facilities not coming under the jurisdiction of other state laws. Exempted are clinics of public health agencies, hospitals, schools, and most private medical groups. Included, however, are "surgical clinics" (or "surgicenters"), "chronic dialysis clinics," "rehabilitation clinics" and certain "multi-specialty clinics" . . . operated by a "nonprofit corporation" (the latter to be licensed "on a trial basis").[115] In 1979, the California State Department of Health Services inspected and licensed about 600 clinics of all types, most of these being community clinics as defined by law. Under this category there were numerous federally funded but locally sponsored nonprofit rural health clinics, clinics for psychiatric care, for drug abuse, and for family planning service; the state has also licensed voluntary clinics for crippled children and for self-care by women's organizations.[116]

A similar statute was enacted in New Jersey in 1976. The regulations under this law illustrate the broad scope of concern of this new type of state government control.[117] The standards were applied initially to facilities providing six types of health services: (1) primary care to adults and children, (2) comprehensive pediatric care, (3) family planning services, (4) prenatal and postpartum care, (5) surgical services, and (6) drug abuse treatment. With respect to ambulatory care facilities for primary care to adults and children, for example, licensure requires such standards as a full-time administrator (if more than 20,000 patient visits per year occur); that various specified diagnostic tests be performed on certain patients (e.g., an electrocardiogram on persons over 40 years of age); that health education and counseling be provided by qualified personnel; that specified emergency equipment (e.g., oxygen inhalation machine) be on hand; that minimum levels of medical, nursing, and other staff be maintained; that medical records be properly kept; and even that appointments shall be offered to patients as well as walk-in arrangements. A federal review of state legislation in this field in 1979 indicated that there were 19 states that had licensure programs for general and/or special outpatient clinics unconnected with hospitals; another 12 states had separate licensure for ambulatory surgery centers.[118]

While most governmental controls on regulation of clinics emanate from the state level, some are an indirect consequence of federal grant programs.[119] Thus, the grants for numerous types of community health center, reviewed in Chapter

9, stipulate that certain minimum standards of physical structure, staffing, services, and administration be followed. The same applies to federally subsidized community mental health centers, group practice clinics in HMOs, and family planning clinics. It applies also to the older public health grant-in-aid programs for maternal and child health services, venereal disease control, and other programs involving various categorical clinics. Another indirect influence on almost all clinics is the federal Food, Drug, and Cosmetic Act, with its many regulations on drugs available for general use.[120] Even at the state level, grants to local voluntary agencies may provide a justification for special forms of regulation not otherwise authorized; this was cogently illustrated by the "ghetto medicine" program in New York City between 1969 and 1977, under which special subsidy of voluntary hospital OPDs serving the poor was the basis for authorizing quality controls over those hospital clinics by the city department of health.[121]

External regulatory impact on clinics comes not only from government. Perhaps the most widely pervasive influence of all in the United States has come from the Joint Commission on Accreditation of Hospitals (JCAH), which represents wholly voluntary professional associations.[122] In its early years, the JCAH showed little interest in promoting standards for hospital OPDs, but later, its standards came to include specifications for emergency services and, on an optional basis, scheduled clinics.[123] In 1973, moreover, the JCAH started plans for a national program of voluntary accreditation of "freestanding ambulatory health care facilities and neighborhood health centers."[124] These would apply to surgicenters, kidney dialysis centers, radiation centers, birth control and abortion clinics, and other nonhospital outpatient facilities. Implementation of this program was delayed, however, because of a jurisdictional dispute with the American Group Practice Association (AGPA), which had been approving private group practice clinics since 1968. In 1976, the problem was resolved by broadening the JCAH sponsorship to include the AGPA as well as other bodies representing clinics.[125]

In 1979, disputes in the field of voluntary accreditation of ambulatory care facilities recurred, and a new organization was formed: the Accreditation Association for Ambulatory Health Care (AAAHC).[126] The AAAHC was formed by joint action action of six bodies exclusively concerned with organized ambulatory health services: the American College Health Association, the Free-Standing Ambulatory Surgical Association, the National Association of Community Health Centers, the Group Health Association of America (GHAA), the Medical Group Management Association, and the American Group Practice Association. The last two of these bodies were previously identified with the organization known as the American Association of Medical Clinics, whose standards had been widely distributed since 1970.[127] Even earlier the GHAA had promulgated standards for prepaid group practice plans, which defined criteria for membership in this association.[128]

Thus, private associations, without any legal sanctions, have served to promote elevation of standards in several types of clinic, both attached to and independent from hospitals. The very initiation of these several standard-setting movements reflects the growing importance of organized ambulatory care programs in the overall U.S. health care system.

EVALUATION OF CLINIC SERVICES

In the previous section we have reviewed strategies applied for the *promotion* of good quality care in clinics, both from within a clinic and from external influences, governmental or private. How does one determine the effectiveness of these strategies, or more generally how does one *evaluate* the services provided by a clinic?

Largely because of the great diversity of patterns for organization and delivery of health services in America and public debate about the relative merits of different patterns, much work has been done to develop instruments for measuring the quality of care. For decades the impact of various public health programs, such as diphtheria immunizations, had been measured by declines in death rates from specific infectious diseases. Evaluation of the quality of programs of general medical care, involving heterogeneous diseases and populations, was much more difficult. Serious methodological studies of this problem began in the 1960s.

Avedis Donabedian did much to clarify the development of evaluative methods by distinguishing three basic sets of criteria: the "structure," the "process," and the "outcome" of programs being studied.[129] Ideally, one might always wish to know the final outcome of a program in terms of the ultimate health status of the population served—rates of mortality, recovery from illness, degrees of residual disability, and so on.[130] In practice, however, such outcome measurements may be difficult to determine, particularly in a form that distinguishes the influence of the health service from many other determinants of health (characteristics of the patients, severity of the disease, environmental circumstances, and so on). There may be good reason, therefore, to prefer evaluation based on "process" measurements; that is, by review of the precise technical services rendered, with judgment of how closely they approximate criteria of good medical care as stipulated by recognized experts.

In 1973, Robert Brook made an exhaustive review of all methods of health service evaluation developed up to that time and also tested different methods applied to one series of 296 patients.[131] He found substantial variations in the evaluations based on application of different methods, particularly as between use of process and outcome criteria, and concluded: "the most valid approach to assessing quality of care, given the present state of the art, is individual case analysis of *both* medical care process and patient outcome."

In the 1970s, greater attention was focused specifically on the problems of evaluating ambulatory care, as distinguished from inpatient care. A review published in 1974 found that all previous studies of ambulatory care—in both organized settings and individual medical practices—were based essentially on process measurements; the reviewer concluded that in ten such studies identified all "seem to agree that the extent to which there is quality of care in an ambulatory setting is correlated with the extent to which the physicians there are performing in accord with generally accepted standards of medical practice."[132] Another literature review of ambulatory care evaluations, published in 1977, reports progress toward measurement of patient outcomes from ambulatory care, but stresses the persistent methodological problems, such as lack of an easily definable "episode of illness in ambulatory care," the "non-uniformity of medical records in different settings," the uncertainty about "the ambulatory patient's adherence to (medical) instructions" compared with hospitalized patients, and so on.[133]

The most recent studies have attempted to evaluate differences in the quality of care provided to patients served in different ambulatory care settings. One study compared the services rendered to 300 chronically ill patients referred from a large hospital OPD to those received in several freestanding community health centers.[134] Conclusions on quality per se could not be drawn, but it was found that when these patients were served at the community health centers, they had a higher rate of visits, a greater rate of laboratory tests, and more drug prescriptions than at the hospital OPD. A study of health outcomes for five disease problems in children, treated in six different ambulatory care settings, was reported in July 1980. The settings were: (1) private physicians in solo practice, (2) private group practices, (3) prepaid group practices, (4) hospital scheduled clinics, (5) hospital emergency room, and (6) separate public clinics for children or families. When adjustments were made for the socioeconomic status and the previous health problems of the children using the diverse settings, important differences in outcome were identified; namely, "children using solo practitioners had generally higher-than-expected illness prevalences, while those using prepaid group (practices) and hospital outpatient departments had uniformly lower-than-expected prevalences."[135]

Another type of evaluation of clinics has been to study their effect on rates of admission to hospitals. An early study at one of the first neighborhood health centers in the nation showed a marked reduction of the rate of hospital admissions in the low-income population served.[136] Similar findings were reported more recently for patients using a separate primary care center, in contrast to those using a traditional medical clinic in the OPD of a busy teaching hospital.[137]

It will be recalled from Chapter 9 that many evaluative studies were made on neighborhood health centers when these facilities were introduced in the 1960s. While process measurements showed services in these clinics to compare favorably with those rendered in private medical practice, their costs per visit were found to be relatively high. Numerous studies have also compared the per unit costs of group practice clinics with such costs of solo practice. While economists differ in their findings, most consider medical grouping to yield economies of scale, whether or not these are passed on to the patient in lower charges. As discussed in Chapter 12, evaluations of HMOs have been abundant but they apply to the comprehensive range of their services, rather than being limited to ambulatory care.

All in all, the growth of clinics has led to expansion of general interest in evaluation of the quality and costs of ambulatory health service. Since the clinic marks a departure from the conventional pattern of private medical practice, there is a widely felt challenge to prove its value. At the same time, the organizational character of clinics makes their performance more readily measurable than is the performance of independent private physicians. The clinic is obviously a more visible place than a private office; whatever deficiencies may apply to its services are clear for many people to see. In hospitals, the work of private practitioners is subject to a great deal of peer review, and one may hope that equivalent assessments of quality will eventually be made on the work done in private medical offices compared with that done in clinics.

MAJOR PROBLEMS AND TRENDS

The advantages of the organization of resources to produce ambulatory services through clinics are clear enough, but for each advantage there is a corresponding problem in administration. Each benefit, or potential benefit, has its price. Clinics permit services of certain types to be planned and offered in some reasonable relationship to social needs. But planning cannot always be effectively done. Many obstacles—financial or political or traditional—can obstruct the rational planning of clinics.

Clinics can bring together and coordinate a wide range of personnel and equipment and render comprehensive services. But this requires administrative understanding and skill, which are not easily acquired. Difficulties may and often do arise in interpersonal relationships within organizations. The time periods required for different processes in a clinic's program may vary, so that bottlenecks may obstruct the smooth flow of services. Administration requires the exercise of authority and the delegation of tasks, which may not be effectively carried out by the several persons concerned. Achieving teamwork is an art for which not everyone has the talent.

Clinics may be capable of using money more efficiently than individuals, but the money must be available. For most clinics, financial support requires decisions at some higher level on the expenditure of funds derived in some collective way. Competing objectives, however, may restrict the allocations much below the level needed. The resultant inadequacy of resources nearly always means delivery of inadequate services.

Efficient use of clinic resources requires a reasonable flow of persons or patients, but many difficulties may obstruct this flow. Patients needing the services may not be aware of them; marketing or outreach may be lacking. Transportation may be deficient. Precisely because the clinic centralizes several services in one place, patients may have to travel greater distances to benefit from the comprehensive care. In recognition of insufficient utilization rates, certain clinics may be open only a few hours a week, and this creates problems for everyone needing service at other times.

Many clinics in America have developed to meet very specialized needs. High quality services may therefore be assembled for the particular problem, but several health problems may exist in the same individual. From the patient's perspective, therefore, clinic services may be fragmented. To complicate this, clinics may be restricted in the types of person eligible to use them.

Insofar as clinics successfully coordinate many skilled services in one place, they should be more convenient for patients. But the resultant size of clinics can create problems; unless very skillful management divides a large system into many smaller parts, the size of the larger clinics can lead to impersonality. The assembly line in industry is not a process suitable to human beings with their variations and sensitivities.

Clinics can apply systems of uniform records, with appropriate storage and retrieval, so that continuity can be maintained in patient care, even if doctors or other health personnel may change. But operation of good record systems is not easy; it requires special skill and resources. If a record process breaks down, patient care can suffer.

The combination of several health personnel in a clinic permits ongoing peer review that can help to maintain the quality of performance, but this is not automatic. Teamwork requires both diligence and diplomacy. If poor quality work is detected, its correction requires deliberate but prudent intervention.

Many clinics permit the theoretical integration of preventive and treatment services in dealing with the same patient. But social tradition and even law may obstruct such integration. Inability to offer an obviously necessary corrective therapy for a detected disorder may mean that the patient will fail to get the proper treatment entirely or only at a higher cost.

Most clinics need physicians and can establish conditions for their more effective work; however, being part of a pluralistic health care system, clinics cannot always recruit the doctors required. The lucrative opportunities of private medical practice may mean that only less experienced or less competent doctors accept clinic assignments. Sometimes idealism motivates a physician to work in certain clinics, but this trait is not always plentiful enough to yield the numbers of doctors needed.

Although the physical plants of clinics can be made attractive and efficient, the use of old and improvised quarters may be dictated by the organizational circumstances in which clinics originate. Rather than waiting for the accumulation of capital funds required for constructing ideal facilities, clinics may adjust to whatever is available. The handicaps in mood and behavior created by poor physical quarters may not always be self-evident.

One could recite further potential advantages of clinics and the problems they face in reality. Yet the overall growth of organized patterns for delivery of ambulatory services surely indicates that their advantages exceed their disadvantages. With experience in the operation of clinics and with increasing appreciation of their benefits, the problems are being overcome. The stigma of the clinic as a place of care for the second-class citizen is gradually being replaced by a recognition that it is an effective setting for provision of modern scientific and also humanistic health service. On a world level, the issue has been formulated as the need of all persons for access to effective and efficient resources for primary health care.[138] The clearly increasing collectivization of funding for health care creates pressures to assure that the money be wisely spent. The pattern of general ambulatory service organization, toward which these trends seem to be moving, will be explored in Chapter 15.

NOTES

1. Sheldon, Alan; Frank Baker; and Curtis P. McLaughlin, eds., *Systems and Medical Care* (Boston: The MIT Press, 1970).

2. Douglass, C. W., "Representation Patterns in Community Health Decision-making," *Journal of Health and Social Behavior,* March 14, 1973.

3. Barnard, Chester, *Functions of the Executive* (Cambridge, Mass.: Harvard University Press, 1938).

4. Southwick, Arthur F., and George F. Siedel, *The Law of Hospital and Health Care Administration* (Ann Arbor, Mich.: Health Administration Press, 1978), pp. 31–87.

5. Blauner, Robert, "Internal Colonialism and Ghetto Revolt," *Social Problems,* Spring 1969.

6. Notkin, Herbert, and Marilyn S. Notkin, "Community Participation in Health Services: A Review Article," *Medical Care Review* 27 (1970): 1178–1201.

7. Parker, Alberta W., "The Consumer as Policy-Maker—Issues of Training," *American Journal of Public Health* 60 (1970): 2139–2153.

8. Hersch, C., "Social History, Mental Health, and Community Control," *American Psychologist* 27 (1972): 749–754.

9. Glogow, Eli, "Community Participation and Sharing in Control of Public Health Services," *Health Services Reports* 88 (1973): 442–448.

10. Milio, Nancy, "Dimensions of Consumer Participation and National Health Legislation," *American Journal of Public Health* 64 (1974): 357–363.

11. Paap, Warren R., "Consumer-Based Boards of Health Centers: Structural Problems in Achieving Effective Control," *American Journal of Public Health* 68 (1978): 578–582.

12. Simon, H. A., *The New Science of Management* (New York: Harper, 1960).

13. Reuter, L. F., "Programming Ambulatory Care Facilities and Manpower," *Medical Care* 12 (1974): 173–184.

14. Hudson, James I., and Marcel D. Infeld, "Ambulatory Care Reorganization in Teaching Hospitals," *Journal of Ambulatory Care Management*, 3, no. 1 (1980): 31–50.

15. Goldsmith, Seth B., *Ambulatory Care* (Germantown, Md.: Aspen Systems Corp., 1977).

16. National Cooperative Services Center for Hospital Management Engineering, *Examination of Case Studies on Ambulatory Care Systems* (Richmond, Va.: November 1975).

17. Go, Howard T., and Arthur Becker, "Reducing Broken Appointments in a Primary Care Clinic," *Journal of Ambulatory Care Management*, 2, no. 2 (1979): 23–30.

18. See, for example, "Financial Investigations" in MacEachern, Malcolm T., *Hospital Organization and Management* (3rd ed.) (Berwyn, Ill.: Physician's Record Co., 1957), p. 698.

19. de Vise, P., "Cook County Hospital: Bulwark of Chicago's Apartheid Health System," *The New Physician* 20 (1971): 394 ff.

20. Roemer, Milton I., " 'Patient-dumping' and Other Voluntary Agency Contributions to Public Agency Problems," *Medical Care* 11 (1973): 30–39.

21. University of Chicago, Graduate Program in Hospital Administration, *Organization for Ambulatory Care: A Critical Appraisal* (Chicago: 1977).

22. Cooper, Philip D.; R. B. Maxwell; and W. J. Kehoe, "Entry Strategies for Marketing in Ambulatory and Other Health Delivery Systems," *Journal of Ambulatory Care Management* 2, no. 2 (1979): 47–54.

23. Rosen, George, "The Impact of the Hospital on the Physician, the Patient and the Community," *Hospital Administration* 9 (1964): 15–33.

24. Roemer, Milton I., "Changing Patterns of Health Service: Their Dependence on a Changing World," *The Annals of the American Academy of Political and Social Science* 346 (1963): 44–56.

25. Madison, Donald L., "Organized Health Care and the Poor," *Medical Care Review*, August 1969.

26. Harris, Richard, *A Sacred Trust* (New York: Penguin Books, 1969).

27. Harmer, Ruth, *American Medical Avarice* (New York: Abelard-Schuman, 1975), p. 237.

28. Brown, Douglas, et al., *Prescription for Primary Health Care: A Community Guidebook* (Ithaca, N.Y.: Cornell University, Primary Care Development Project, 1976).

29. Bernstein, James D.; F. P. Hege; C. C. Farrah, *Rural Health Centers in the United States* (Cambridge, Mass.: Ballinger Pub. Co., 1979).

30. Bryant, John H., et al., *Community Hospitals and Primary Care* (Cambridge, Mass.: Ballinger Pub. Co., 1976).

31. Block, James, et al., "Hospital Sponsored Primary Care: The Community Hospital Program," *Journal of Ambulatory Care Management* 3, no. 1 (1980): 1–13.

32. U.S. Public Health Service, *Healthy People: The Surgeon General's Report on Health Promotion and Disease Prevention*, DHEW (PHS) Pub. No. 79–55071 (Washington: 1979).

33. U.S. Public Health Service, *A Guide to Health Education in Ambulatory Care Settings*, DHEW Pub. No. (HSA) 78–5501 (Washington: May 1978).

34. Mitchell, W. E., and I. Walter, *State and Local Finance* (New York: Ronald Press, 1970).

35. World Health Organization, *Financing of Health Services*, WHO Technical Report Series 625 (Geneva, Switzerland: 1978), pp. 35–37.

36. Harris, Seymour E., *The Economics of American Medicine* (New York: Macmillan Co., 1964).

37. Gibson, R. M., "National Health Expenditures, 1978," *Health Care Financing Review* 1, no. 1 (1979): 1–36.

38. Ibid.

39. U.S. Health Care Financing Administration, *Medicare: 1977 (Reimbursement by State and County)*, HCFA Pub. No. 03001 (Washington: December 1978).

40. American Public Health Association, "Revised Budget Spells Health Cutbacks," *The Nation's Health*, May 1980, p. 8.

41. Berman, R., and T. Moloney, "Where Does the Real Fiscal Control of the Outpatient Department Lie?" *Hospitals, JAHA* 51, no. 10 (1977): 99–100.

42. Gold, Marsha, "Hospital-based versus Free-standing Primary Care Costs," *Journal of Ambulatory Care Management* 2, no. 1 (1979): 1–20.

43. Leroy, Martin T., *Hospital Accounting Principles and Practice* (Chicago: Physicians Record Co., 1958).

44. American Hospital Association, *Uniform Chart of Accounts and Definitions for Hospitals*, (Chicago: AHA, 1965).

45. American Hospital Association, *Statement on the Financial Requirements of Health Care Institutions and Services* (Chicago: AHA, 1969).

46. Rosenfeld, Leonard, *Ambulatory Care: Planning and Organization*, National Technical Information Service, PB 204–925 (Washington: February 1971), p. V–15.

47. U.S. Public Health Service, *Financial Planning in Ambulatory Health Programs*, DHEW Pub. No. (HSM) 73–3027 (Washington: July 1973).

48. Berarducci, Arthur A., "Toward Economic Self-Sufficiency" in *Hospitals*, special issue on "Ambulatory Care: The Center of the System," March 1, 1975, pp. 63–65.

49. Davis, Michael M., *Clinics, Hospitals and Health Centers* (New York: Harper & Bros., 1927).

50. Gerdes, John W., "Anticipated Directions for the Future of Public General Hospitals," *American Journal of Public Health* 59 (1969): 680–688.

51. Roemer, Ruth, and William Shonick, *Private Management of California County Hospitals* (Berkeley, Calif.: University of California, Institute of Governmental Studies, 1980), p. 8.

52. Joint Commission on Accreditation of Hospitals, *Accreditation Manual for Hospitals* (Chicago: JCAH, 1970).

53. Roemer, Milton I., "Contractual Physicians in General Hospitals: A National Survey," *American Journal of Public Health* 52 (1962): 1453–1464.

54. Goss, Mary E., "Influence and Authority Among Physicians in an Outpatient Clinic," *American Sociological Review* 26 (1961): 39–51.

55. Connelly, John P., et al., "The Physician and the Nurse: Their Inter-professional Work in Office and Hospital Ambulatory Settings," *New England Journal of Medicine* 280 (1969): 645–649.

56. Bullough, Vern L., and Bonnie Bullough, *The Emergence of Modern Nursing*, (New York: Macmillan Co., 1969).

57. Lewis, Charles E., and Barbara A. Resnick, "Nurse Clinics and Progressive Ambulatory Care," *New England Journal of Medicine* 277 (1967): 1236–1241.

58. Baker, A. S., "Primary Care by the Nurse," *New England Journal of Medicine* 290 (1974): 282–283.

59. Roemer, Milton I., "Primary Care and Physician Extenders in Affluent Countries," *International Journal of Health Services* 7 (1977): 545–555.

60. Silver, Henry, "The School Nurse Practitioner Program: A New and Expanded Role for the School Nurse," *Journal of the American Medical Association* 216 (1971): 1532.

61. Lawrence, D., "Physician Assistants and Nurse Practitioners: Their Impact on Health Care, Access, Cost, and Quality," *Health and Medical Care Service Review* 1 (1978): 2.

62. Golladay, F. L., et al., "Allied Health Manpower Strategies: Estimates of the Potential Gains from Efficient Task Delegation," *Medical Care* 11 (1973): 457–469.

63. Haynes, M. A., and G. Wolde-Tsadik, *Task Delegation in Ambulatory Care Settings: A Methodological Approach* (Los Angeles: Charles R. Drew Postgraduate Medical School, December 1975).

64. Golden, Archie S., *An Inventory for Primary Health Care Practice* (Cambridge, Mass.: Ballinger Pub. Co., 1977).

65. Rosenfeld, Leonard S., *Ambulatory Care,* pp. VII–53–65.

66. Harris, Patricia R., Secretary of Health, Education, and Welfare, *1978 Annual Report on the National Health Service Corps* (Washington (processed): August 1979).

67. Snoke, P. S., and E. R. Weinerman, "Yale Studies in Ambulatory Care: III Comprehensive Care Programs in Medical Centers," *Journal of Medical Education* 40 (1965): 625–657.

68. Reader, George G., and Mary E. W. Goss (editors), *Comprehensive Medical Care and Teaching* (Ithaca, N.Y.: Cornell University Press, 1967).

69. Lewis, Charles E., "Family Practice: The Primary Care Specialty" in Lewis, C. E., R. Fein, and D. Mechanic, editors. *A Right to Health—The Problem of Access to Primary Medical Care* (New York: John Wiley & Sons, 1976), pp. 76–91.

70. Weiner, Herman, "Organization and Responsibilities" in Somers, Anne R., ed. *The Kaiser-Permanente Medical Care Program* (New York: Commonwealth Fund, 1971), pp. 91–96.

71. Weinerman, E. Richard, "An Appraisal of Medical Care in Group Health Centers," *American Journal of Public Health* 46 (1956): 300–309.

72. Wallace, Helen M., *Health Services for Mothers and Children* (Philadelphia: W. B. Saunders Co., 1962), pp. 8–19.

73. Nader, Philip, ed., *Options for School Health* (Germantown, Md.: Aspen Systems Corp., 1978).

74. Anderson, Elizabeth J., et al., *The Neighborhood Health Center Program—Its Growth and Problems: An Introduction* (Washington: National Association of Neighborhood Health Centers, 1976).

75. Cauffman, Joy G., et al., "Health Information and Referral Services Within Los Angeles County," *American Journal of Public Health* 63 (1973): 872–877.

76. Deeping, E., "Next Please! Experience of the OPD," *The Hospital* 65 (1969): 349–350. October 1969.

77. Strauss, A. L., "Medical Organizations, Medical Care, and Lower-Income Groups, *Social Science and Medicine* 3 (1969): 143.

78. Dutton, Diana B., "Patterns of Ambulatory Health Care in Five Different Delivery Systems," *Medical Care* 17 (1979): 221–243.

79. Saward, Ernest W., ed., *The Regionalization of Personal Health Services,* (rev. ed.) (New York: Prodist, 1976).

80. Bodenheimer, T. S., "Regional Medical Programs: No Road to Regionalization," *Medical Care Review* 26 (1969): 1125.

81. Starfield, Barbara; D. Simburg; S. Horn, et al., "Continuity and Coordination: Their Achievement and Utility," *Medical Care* 14 (1976): 625.

82. Mountin, Joseph W., "The Housing of Health Departments," *Public Health Reports* 57 (1942): 781–789.

83. Burgun, J. A., "Matching Design to Function at the Outpatient Department," *Hospitals, JAHA,* February 1, 1966, p. 58.

84. U.S. Public Health Service, Health Care Facilities Service, *Hospital Outpatient and Emergency Activities—Functional Programming Guidelines,* HEW Pub. No. (HSM) 73-4002 (Washington: December 1972), p. 00.

85. Wheeler, E. T., *Hospital Design and Function* (New York: McGraw-Hill, 1964).

86. Rosenfeld, Leonard S., *Ambulatory Care,* pp. VIII-10-18.

87. U.S. Office of Economic Opportunity, *Guidelines for the Development of Space Allocations for Neighborhood Health Centers* (Washington: April 1970).

88. U.S. Bureau of Community Health Services, *The Health Maintenance Organization Facility Development Handbook* (Washington: DHEW, 1974).

89. U.S. Department of Housing and Urban Development, *Group Practice Facilities: A HUD Handbook* (Washington: 1973).

90. Neutra, Raymond; D. Neutra; and R. Neutra, "The Architect's Role in Encouraging Wider Use of Outpatient Facilities," *Hospitals, JAHA,* September 16, 1969, pp. 53–57.

91. Flagle, Charles D., "Operations Research in a Hospital" in Charles D. Flagle, ed., *Operations Research and Systems Engineering* (Baltimore, Md.: Johns Hopkins Press, 1960), pp. 763–785.

92. Murray, Raymond H., "Technology in Ambulatory Health Care: Problems and Predictions," *The Pharos of Alpha Omega Alpha* 34 (1971): 13–19.

93. March, James G., and H. A. Simon, *Organizations* (New York: Wiley & Sons, 1958).

94. Argyris, C., *Integrating the Individual and the Organization* (New York: Wiley & Sons, 1964).

95. World Health Organization, *Modern Management Methods and the Organization of Health Services,* WHO Public Health Papers No. 55 (Geneva, Switzerland: 1974).

96. U.S. Department of Health, Education, and Welfare, *Quality Assurance of Medical Care,* proceedings of conference at St. Louis, Mo., 23–24 January 1973 (Washington: 1973).

97. Joint Committee on Quality Assurance, "Quality Assurance (Peer Review) of Ambulatory Child Health Care," *Medical Care,* October 1974.

98. Michnich, Marie, et al., *Ambulatory Care Evaluation: A Primer for Quality Review* (Los Angeles: University of California, School of Public Health, 1976).

99. Lembcke, Paul A., "Evolution of the Medical Audit," *Journal of the American Medical Association* 199 (1967): 543–550.

100. U.S. Public Health Service, *An Ambulatory Service Data System* (Washington: Division of Health Care Services, May 1969) (unpublished report).

101. Murnaghan, Jane H., ed., *Ambulatory Care Data: Report of the Conference on Ambulatory Medical Care Records,* supplement to *Medical Care* 11, no. 2 (1973).

102. Lewis, Charles E., "The State of the Art of Quality Assessment—1973," *Medical Care* 12 (1974): 799–806.

103. Albert Einstein College of Medicine, Department of Community Health, *Ambulatory Health Care Services Review Manual,* National Technical Information Service (PB-226 783) (Washington: December 1973).

104. U.S. National Center for Health Services Research & Development, *Guidelines for Producing Uniform Data for Health Care Plans,* DHEW Pub. No. (HSM) 73-3005 (Washington, July 1972).

105. Kissick, W. L., "Planning, Programming, and Budgeting in the Health Field," *Medical Care* 5 (1967): 201.

106. American Hospital Association, *Budgeting Procedures for Hospitals* (Chicago: AHA, 1961).

107. Lebow, J. L., "Consumer Assessments of the Quality of Medical Care," *Medical Care* 12 (1974): 328–337.

108. Gumbiner, Robert, *HMO: Putting It All Together* (St. Louis, Mo.: 1975), pp. 114–123.

109. Forgotson, Edward H.; Ruth Roemer; and Roger W. Newman, "Legal Regulation of Health Personnel in the United States," in *Report of the National Advisory Commission on Health Manpower*, 2 vols., (Washington: November 1976), 2: 279–541.

110. Taylor, Keith O., and Donna M. Donald, *A Comparative Study of Hospital Licensure Regulations* (Berkeley, Calif.: University of California, School of Public Health, 1957).

111. Fry, Hilary, *The Operation of State Hospital Planning and Licensing Programs*, American Hospital Association, Hospital Monograph Series No. 15 (Chicago: 1965).

112. Worthington, William, and L. H. Silver, "Regulation of Quality of Care in Hospitals: The Need for Change," *Law and Contemporary Problems (Health Care—Part I)* 35 (1970): 305–333.

113. Eisner, Victor, and L. B. Callan, *Dimensions of School Health* (Springfield, Ill.: Charles C. Thomas, 1974).

114. For example, see State of California Administrative Code, Title 8, Industrial Relations, Chapter 4, Division of Industrial Safety, Sec. 3400, "Medical Services and First Aid" (Sacramento: 1979).

115. California Business and Professions Code, Sec. 1241; California Health and Safety Code, Sec. 437.10, AB 1781, "Clinic Licensure" (Sacramento: 1978).

116. Marcus, Debbie, California State Department of Health Services, Licensing and Certification Division, June 1977: personal communication.

117. State of New Jersey, *Standards for Licensure of Ambulatory Care Facilities* (Trenton, N.J.: May 1976) (unpublished document).

118. U.S. Health Resources Adminstration, *Health Planning Information Series—Characteristics of State Health Facility Licensing Pratices: A Comparative Review* (Washington: HRA, 1980), unpublished report, pp. 46–50.

119. Rice, James A., "Federal Regulation in the Ambulatory Health Care Sector," *University of Toledo Law Review* 6 (1975): 822–836.

120. Anderson, Odin; J. Young; and W. Jansen, "The Government and the Consumer: Evolution of Food and Drug Laws," *Journal of Public Law* 13 (1964): 189.

121. Jonas, Steven, *Quality Control of Ambulatory Care: A Task for Health Departments* (New York: Springer Pub. Co., 1977).

122. American Hospital Association, *Hospital Accreditation References* (Chicago: AHA, 1965).

123. Joint Commission on Accreditation of Hospitals, *Accreditation Manual for Hospitals* (Chicago: JCAH, 1970).

124. "JCAH Sets Guidelines for Free-standing Facilities," *American Medical News*, 3 September 1973.

125. "Ambulatory Care Facility Accrediting Agency Opens," *American Medical News*, 23 February 1976.

126. "Ambulatory Care Groups Form Accreditation Body," *American Medical News*, 22 June 1979.

127. American Association of Medical Clinics, *Accreditation Program of the American Association of Medical Clinics* (Alexandria, Va.: AAMC, 1970).

128. Group Health Association of America, "Revised Working Standards for Group Health Plans," *Group Health & Welfare News*, special supplement, May 1964.

129. Donabedian, A., "Evaluating the Quality of Medical Care," *Milbank Memorial Fund Quarterly*, 44, Part 2 (1966): 166–206.

130. Roemer, Milton I., "Evaluation of Health Service Programs and Levels of Measurement," *HSMHA Health Reports* 86 (1971): 839–848.

131. Brook, Robert H., *Quality of Care Assessment: A Comparison of Five Methods of Peer Review,* U.S. National Center for Health Services Research & Development, DHEW Pub. No. HRA-74–3100 (Washington: July 1973).

132. Shortridge, Mary Helen, "Quality of Medical Care in an Outpatient Setting," *Medical Care* 12 (1974): 283–300.

133. Christoffel, Tom, and Martha Loewenthal, "Evaluating the Quality of Ambulatory Health Care: A Review of Emerging Methods," *Medical Care* 15 (1977): 877–897.

134. Goodrich, Thelma Jean, and G. A. Gorry, "The Process of Ambulatory Care: A Comparison of the Hospital and the Community Health Center," *American Journal of Public Health* 70 (1980): 251–255.

135. Dutton, Diana B., and Ralph S. Silber, "Children's Health Outcomes in Six Different Ambulatory Care Delivery Systems," *Medical Care* 18 (1980): 693–714.

136. Bellin, S. S.; H. J. Geiger; and C. D. Gibson, "Impact of Ambulatory-Health-Care Services on the Demand for Hospital Beds," *New England Journal of Medicine* 280 (1969): 808–812.

137. "Study Says Primary Care Clinics Cut Admissions, Length of Stay," *Health Care Week,* July 24, 1978.

138. World Health Organization, *The Declaration of Alma Ata* (Geneva, Switzerland: 1979).

Chapter 15

Future Models of
Ambulatory Care

The background, the structure, and the functions of America's heterogeneous organized ambulatory health services (OAHS) have now been described. In this chapter, we shall look ahead and consider how the whole complicated situation might be improved, so that a more efficient and effective general health care system might be attained.

First we shall try to summarize the major issues emerging from the analysis of diverse clinics in the nation. Secondly, a brief glimpse will be taken of major experiences and trends of other nations with respect to clinics and health centers in the modern world. Third, the fundamental importance of sound economic support for clinic services will be explored. Fourth, we will consider the need for a mechanism of coordination of all clinic services and why we believe that this responsibility could be most appropriately assigned to public health agencies. Fifth, we will explore how each of the current types of clinic activity might function in coordinated health service areas. Finally, we shall try to envisage the place of clinics in an improved national health care system in the United States.

MAJOR CURRENT ISSUES OF AMBULATORY CARE

In the previous pages, we have found how—among the major sectors of health services—ambulatory care has been the one most recently subject to systematic organization and planning. Perhaps by its inherent nature, the initial search of a sick person for help seemed to warrant a one-to-one relationship—consultation with a neighbor, a friend, eventually someone deemed to be skillful in healing, later a formally trained doctor of medicine. Only as problems came to be perceived in carrying out this simple process, were social actions considered necessary to bring together patient and healer.

When medical care became a commodity for which a price was to be paid, poverty became an obvious obstacle to needed service. From this perceived need there emerged first the dispensary, then the hospital outpatient department, then various programs of financial support for purchase of health service from private providers, then a whole array of special clinics or health centers organized and financed specifically to serve the poor. Actions were taken both by government and by voluntary bodies; some clinics were focused on certain diseases or certain types of poor people, while others offered general primary care.

The rise of the public health movement—organized social action to prevent disease due to an unsanitary environment and to limit the spread of communicable disease—gave rise to other clinics. Although the objective of these clinics was initially preventive, the concept of prevention gradually widened, so that ambulatory services were also organized for the *treatment* of infectious diseases such as tuberculosis and syphilis. Babies and pregnant women were served in order to reduce infant and maternal mortality. Gradually an even broader concept of prevention was implemented through clinics that facilitated early detection of chronic (even noncommunicable) diseases. Early attention was given to mental disorders, too, in an effort to avert a later need for hospitalization.

Still other clinics emerged from the circumstances of life at congregate places, such as schools and factories. The basic environment of schools, where one child with an infection could spread the disease to others, created a need for deliberate intervention with organized health service. At the workplace, especially as industry became increasingly mechanized, the hazards of accidents (and enactment of social compensation laws) underscored the need for first aid services. As organized health services took shape both in schools and in industry, their potential for a wider range of functions became evident. The school provided a locale for early detection of physical and mental defects that might impair the child's general development and his ability to learn. The factory provided a locale for detecting impairments that might handicap the worker from doing certain jobs or might aggravate the risk of accidents. Colleges and universities created other obvious needs for organized health care because so many students, young adults, were separated from the health protection of their families.

Another stimulus came from the private practice of medicine itself. Specialization in medical science and the multiplication of nursing and allied health disciplines subdivided the science and art of medical care. To offer the patient the full range of needed skills required a team of personnel. The patient could assemble this team by travelling from place to place, but why should not the members of the team be assembled in one location? Hence the private group practice clinic concept arose. In later years, the idea was modified (largely for the convenience of doctors rather than patients) to yield single specialty groups, but even these achieved a certain level of coordination.

Still more forms of organized clinic for delivery of ambulatory care were stimulated by other social developments. The need for efficient and effective health care in military establishments was recognized from ancient times. Similar requirements were appreciated for other special population groups—military veterans, merchant seamen, American Indians, and prisoners. Certain diseases of great social impact—because of their severity and chronicity—could not be left to management in a purely private, individualistic medical market. Special government agencies were organized accordingly to deal with mental disorders and severe physical handicaps, and clinics were an obviously practical solution to many of their problems. Almost every serious disease generated a voluntary group of people to combat it, and disease-specific voluntary agencies gave rise to scores of additional clinics.

The United States was almost unique among the world's industrialized nations in its failure to enact a system for general social financing of health service, and problems persisted for the poor and the near-poor. Many of the financial problems of the voluntary health insurance movement, which grew rapidly after 1940, were corrected by enactment in 1965 of Medicare and Medicaid. These fiscal support programs paid for health care in the medical mainstream of private doctors and voluntary hospitals. Yet access to needed care remained deficient in urban slums and rural areas; unmet social needs were dramatized by riots of minority racial groups. In response came the neighborhood health centers of the U.S. Office of Economic Opportunity (OEO) in 1964. The idea caught on, and over the next 15 years the Congress appropriated special funding of additional clinics for rural people, for youth, for families, for agricultural migrants, for the people of Appalachia, and for community health centers of all sizes and shapes. Private doctors, who objected at first, eventually found themselves too busy with private paying patients as well as beneficiaries of Medicaid and Medicare, to mount their customary opposition to these competitive modes of health care delivery.

The complexity of OAHS, as well as the increasingly elaborate technology of American medicine, gave rise to further reactions. Let us have our own nonbureaucratic, nonregulated free clinics, said the alienated youth of the 1960s. Likewise, the women's liberation movement brought forth the feminist women's clinics, while the back-to-nature enthusiasts of a previous era gave rise to holistic health centers. The spiralling costs of hospitalization stimulated other forms of organized out-of-hospital service: organized home care, surgicenters, and other forms of less costly institutionalization. The importance of split second timing, rapid transportation, and properly staffed and equipped clinics—efficiently linked together—provoked a nationwide movement for emergency medical service systems.

Each of these several streams of development of clinics had its reasons for arising, and each stream flowed its own course, quite unrelated to the others.

Meanwhile, private individual and medical practices continued side-by-side. The traditional American image of the personal doctor and the private patient in an individual medical office was still regarded as the norm; yet by 1980, that tradition had come to apply to no more than half of the patient-doctor ambulatory encounters in the United States during a year. This was quite aside from all the inpatient service rendered in the highly organized and bureaucratic settings of some 7,000 general and special hospitals. It was also aside from all the organized activities involved in environmental sanitation, mass health education, public and nonpublic regulation of health resources and their performance, organized health care financing, and all the other processes that constitute a nation's health care system.

Just within the sector of clinics, however, the problems and issues are many. On the most elementary level is the utter complexity and incoordination of the services and facilities sketched above. Each of the special clinic types ordinarily copes with its own problems in its own way, quite unaware that coordinated efforts might be helpful to all parties. What are some of the other major problems and issues beyond this?

Most pervasive, with the probable exception of group practices (private or prepaid), are the uncertainties of financing. Almost all other types of clinics, with an occasional exception for a specific facility, e.g., the outpatient department of a well-endowed voluntary hospital or the student health service of a prestigious private university, tend to be chronically short of funds. In clinics linked to an institution with primary objectives outside the health field, the dynamics are obvious; public schools are for education, factories are for production and profits, prisons are for punishment or correction, and so on; health care is secondary to these objectives, and if funds become short its priority is bound to be low.

Even where health protection is the avowed primary objective, social priorities for economic support of clinics may not be high. The many clinics of hospitals, health departments, community health centers, or voluntary health agencies are oriented largely to the poor. These are a marginal segment of society. They are often psychologically alienated and do not vote in elections. Unless some visible crisis occurs, such as a violent ghetto riot, they may be largely disregarded by the local and the national power structure.[1] Hence, the clinics that serve their health needs may be kept open, but little more. Whether articulated or not, there is a moralistic undertone that the poor are, in some degree, to blame for their poverty and that they cannot therefore expect to be served in elegant surroundings.

The ideological and political explanations are subtle and complex, but the net result is evident everywhere. In modern capitalist and free enterprise societies, the public sector, compared to the private, is starved.[2] As welfare states in Western Europe and elsewhere have been maturing, this has been slowly changing, and at a slower pace redistributional justice has also come to be accepted in the United States. In the main, however, frugality is still the watchword in publicly supported health programs, whether for clinics or for public hospitals.[3] The same applies to clinics supported by charitable contributions, particularly when they deal with long-term mental or physical disorders, the treatment of which is inherently expensive.

Many other problems are indirectly related to inadequate financing, but also have separate roots of their own. Public health clinics, for example, are sometimes criticized for being staffed by incompetent personnel, particularly the physicians. The same has been said of school medical officers, the salaried doctors in community health centers, or those in occupational medical programs. Evidence for these beliefs is seldom offered, but there can be no question about the generally lower economic rewards and lower social status associated with most salaried positions in American medical culture.[4] The notion is widely held that the most competent doctors go into private medical practice; only those who cannot survive in the free competitive market take a salaried post. These views may not apply to salaried positions in medical schools or famous group practice clinics, like the Mayo Clinic , but they nonetheless handicap the recruitment of physicians and other personnel for many organized clinic programs.

Even when clinics are well-funded, well-staffed, and well-equipped, they still may bear the stigma, inherited from their past, as second-class places for the poor. This has been true of many of the community health centers established through federal subsidies in the 1960s and 1970s; in spite of excellent resources and appropriate locations in low-income neighborhoods, their rates of utilization have been relatively low. Persons eligible for Medicaid support, with entitlement to consult private physicians, have generally preferred the latter. Thus, the community health centers have been used mainly for the "near poor" or the non-Medicaid needy people who could not afford to pay private doctor fees.

These preferences were quantified in a study of 18,384 Medicaid-eligible persons who made at least one visit to the Watts Health Center in fiscal year 1968–69. In this low-income, predominantly black, neighborhood of Los Angeles, there were 43,300 people eligible to use the Watts Health Center (WHC).[5] Of this population, 26,300 were estimated to be eligible for Medicaid, yet 7,916 persons, or 30.1 of Medicaid beneficiaries, did not use WHC services at all during the year. Moreover, only 3.8 percent of the users made the WHC their exclusive source of care; 96.2 percent consulted private health care providers as well. In the fiscal year studied, Medicaid payments on behalf of the 18,384 WHC users amounted to $4,368,951, but only 10.3 percent of this money was paid to the Watts Health Center, while 89.7 percent went for fees to private health care practitioners and hospitals.

From the viewpoint of private business enterprise, many clinics may be regarded as doing a poor job of marketing.[6] Even the use of outreach workers has evidently not been effective in attracting patients. This problem is even greater with respect to many health department clinics, where services offered are purely preventive. In the absence of a definite symptom, many people lack the motivation to seek immunizations, health counseling, or medical examinations that might reveal some unrecognized disorder. Health education by public health agencies, schools, and voluntary health agencies attempts to influence the behavior of people toward personal preventive objectives, but these efforts have had limited success.[7]

The fact that each of the several categories of clinics functions separately impairs their relationship with each other and with other major sectors of the health care system. Probably most serious is the weak linkage between many clinics and hospitals. Furthermore, within hospitals maintaining large outpatient departments, including scheduled clinics, there may be strained relationships between the OPD and the inpatient ward staffs of the same specialty. Poor linkages between clinics of other agencies and hospitals create even more serious problems. For example, a woman followed in a health department prenatal clinic may have pregnancy problems that are not well communicated to the hospital where she will deliver her infant. The injured child seen by a school nurse or the injured worker given first aid by an industrial nurse may arrive at a hospital emergency room with no more than a fragmentary note soliciting help.

Of course, some clinics attempt to establish good communications with selected nearby hospitals, rehabilitation facilities, or individual practitioners, but everything depends on the initiative of particular clinic personnel. All too often, however, clinics behave as part of the administrative entity to which they belong and not as part of a system with primary, secondary, and tertiary care components. (Health maintenance organization (HMO) clinics are the exception to this criticism, of which more will be said below.)

In spite of the difficulties of clinics, as we have found in the previous chapters, their importance and the general recognition of their value have been gradually increasing.[8] Their technological advantages are slowly being found to outweigh the humanistic handicaps associated with their past image and with the deficiencies of their financial support. Especially important in this transformation of social attitudes has been the growth of private group practice clinics, along with clinic type HMOs, both of which are clearly visible outgrowths of the dominant private medical culture. The ascending importance of organized clinics and health centers in other nations, particularly where general health care financing has been largely collectivized, may add perspective to an understanding of the movement toward organization of ambulatory health services in the United States.

ORGANIZED AMBULATORY CARE IN OTHER COUNTRIES

In Chapter 2 we reviewed the rise of the early dispensaries in Europe and the emergence of the ambulatory care health center in developing countries. We noted the epochal Dawson Report of 1920, which recommended organized health centers as the standard model for delivering ambulatory services, both preventive and therapeutic, to the entire British population. Although this report was not implemented at the time in Great Britain, a very similar concept became the central principle of the health care system of the Soviet Union, the world's first socialist nation, born after the Russian Revolution of 1917.

In the years since then, the health center concept has spread and been implemented throughout the world. In the socialist countries, now constituting about one-third of the world's population, organized health centers have become almost the exclusive mode for delivery of ambulatory care, integrating personal preventive and treatment services. In virtually all the developing countries of Asia, Africa, and Latin America, health centers have also become the dominant means for provision of modern ambulatory health services, not only by ministries of health but also by "social security" and other agencies serving various segments of the population. In the industrialized and capitalist countries of Western Europe and elsewhere (e.g., Japan and Australia) health centers, while not yet predominant, have been rapidly rising in importance.[9] The major highlights about the delivery of ambulatory health care in these three broad groups of countries may be of interest. (It should be evident that within each grouping, there are numerous variations.)

Socialist Countries

Soon after the Russian Revolution of 1917, the ruling political party declared that health service should be a government responsibility, freely accessible to all without charge.[10] This would be done by greatly expanding the training of doctors and allied health workers, all of whom would be engaged as civil servants. Prevention and treatment would be integrated, with emphasis on prevention. Ambulatory services would be provided by teams of salaried doctors, nurses, and other personnel, working at health centers, often called "polyclinics," conveniently located throughout cities and rural areas.

This ideal plan was not implemented overnight. The years following World War I and the Revolution, were turbulent, and the first "Five-Year Plan"—the subsequent hallmark of socialist economic and social development—did not get under way until 1928. The major efforts of the early years were directed to a massive increase in the output of medical personnel, construction of health centers and hospitals, building up a chemical industry to produce drugs (among other products), and establishing a governmental framework for administration of the whole system.[11]

The pattern of ambulatory care delivery that emerged varies between cities and rural areas, and is by no means identical everywhere in the USSR. Its essential features, however, are as follows:[12] for each local area of 10,000 to 50,000 people (varying with population density) there is an ambulatory care center. The basic team for primary care consists of an internist or general practitioner, a pediatrician, an obstetrician-gynecologist, a dentist, nurses, and numerous allied personnel. Because this primary care team is composed of several specialists working together, the facility is often called a "polyclinic," rather than health center. Each basic primary care team serves a population of about 4,000 persons in the adjacent area; thus, a polyclinic serving a district with 40,000 population would have ten teams. To back up these primary care teams, there are secondary level specialists, such as ophthalmologists, neurologists, and orthopedic surgeons at hospitals or, in metropolitan areas, at "specialized polyclinics." Patients are referred to these secondary facilities as necessary; however, simple laboratory tests or procedures can be performed at the primary care unit.

No charges are levied for any service at the polyclinic or hospital. For certain prescribed drugs, which are purchasable in governmental pharmacies, there are small charges, but these are waived for pensioners, military veterans, persons with serious chronic disorders, and so on. At larger factories or mines, there are also polyclinics that may be used by the workers, in addition to their neighborhood polyclinic. Persons with chronic diseases or at special risk of disease for any reason are summoned back for periodic examinations and care—a process known as "dispensarization." Much attention is given to health education, immunizations, and environmental hygiene. Every new medical graduate must spend three years at a rural post, after which he or she (most Soviet physicians are women) is free to go wherever there is a position open. Private practice has never been prohibited in the USSR, and a little of it exists, but one can appreciate that the number of patients willing to pay private fees is very small when extensive services are available free of charge.

Much more could be said about OAHS in the USSR, and numerous published accounts are available.[13,14] Suffice it to say that the essential framework of the Soviet health care system has been emulated in other countries of Eastern Europe that became socialist in political structure after World War II.[15] Variations naturally are found, in accordance with certain national traditions. In Poland, for example, where a very strong tradition of independence characterized the peasantry, the rural people were not fully covered by the national system until 1972, some 25 years after the birth of the Polish People's Republic.[16] In Czechoslovakia, the medical schools have remained within the universities and under the general supervision of the ministry of education, although in the Soviet Union the schools of medicine, as well as all other programs for training health personnel, are integrated with the health services under the unified ministry of health.

The People's Republic of China, established in 1949, emulated the Soviet model for its first dozen years or so; then in 1962, China departed sharply from the Soviet-led group of nations. Its health care system moved away from a centralized hierarchical framework and put its major stress on "local self-reliance."[17] Ambulatory care remained organized, but the most local units were much smaller. The vast rural population was organized into "communes" for collective agricultural production; these had from 20,000 to 50,000 people. In most communes, there is a health center for ambulatory care, but also with a few beds; the staff includes at least one modern physician. The basic primary care unit, however, is a health post at a more peripheral level—in a "production brigade" of about 1,500 people. Here, the local clinic is staffed mainly by the "barefoot doctor," a peasant who has been trained for only a few months to give preventive services (including family planning) and treat common ailments. Difficult cases are referred to the commune health center or a county hospital (several communes compose a county).

In the health centers, in addition to one modern or "western-type" physician, there are usually doctors of traditional Chinese medicine, nursing assistants, sanitarians, and others. One of the important precepts by which China differs from the USSR is its effort to combine or integrate the delivery of traditional and western medicine. Another difference is that, at the most local level of the production brigade, the health care is not a responsibility of the ministry of health, but rather of the commune.[18] Thus, the cost of operating the barefoot doctor's clinic is borne by the commune (out of its earnings from the sale of agricultural products), and small fees are also payable by the local people who come for care.

Still another model has been implemented in Cuba, which underwent this political and economic transformation to socialism after 1959. In spite of its predominantly rural and agricultural character, the Cuban health care system became modeled not on China's system but on that of the Soviet Union. Thus, there is a definite hierarchical framework starting at the level of the local health area of 20,000 to 40,000 people served by a polyclinic.[19] For several years the next level was the health region, of which there were 39, but in the early 1970s this was changed to a smaller unit—the municipality. Above the 169 municipalities, there are 8 health provinces; these, in turn, are directed by the ministry of health in the capital, Havana. Cuba has been able to train relatively large numbers of doctors to staff its polyclinics and hospitals, along essentially the same lines as the USSR. No charges are made for polyclinic or hospital services.

Developing Countries

The many developing countries are much more variable than the world's socialist countries, but they have in common their relatively small degree of industrialization, their economic dependence on agriculture or natural extractive production (mining or petroleum), and the prevailing poverty and low levels of literacy of their populations. One can distinguish the most severely "underdeveloped countries'' of sub-Sahara Africa and parts of Asia, where the gross national product (GNP) per capita is typically under $500 per year, from the more transitional "developing countries" of Latin America and the Middle East, with GNPs per capita of $500 to about $2,000 per year.[20]

In both these types of "less developed countries" (LDC), the organized health center and more peripheral health posts or health stations play a substantial role in the delivery of ambulatory health care. In the more severely underdeveloped countries of Africa and Asia, collective economic support of health services is weak, so that most of the money spent for health purposes comes from private households. Thus in Ghana, a former British colony (Gold Coast) of western Africa, the World Bank estimates 4.0 percent of GNP to be devoted to health purposes; of this, however, 73 percent is derived from personal household expenditures and only 27 percent comes from all government sources.[21] In Thailand, with a per capita GNP of $420, the relationships are similar; this monarchy in Southeast Asia, never a colony, spent in 1977 about 4.16 percent of its GNP on health purposes. Of this amount, however, 65 percent came from private household expenditures, 33 percent from government, and only the trifling remainder from voluntary agencies or foreign aid.[22] These large private sector proportions, illustrated by countries such as Ghana and Thailand, reflect not only the substantial expenditures of the small upper class for private medical care, but also the numerous small expenditures of the masses of poor people on self-medication, traditional healers, and even care by private doctors.

Insofar as the governments of these poorest LDCs, however, provide modern ambulatory health services, it is through various clinics—rural and urban health centers and rural health posts. The staffs of these ambulatory care centers are principally made up of middle-level health personnel—health officers, medical assistants, village health workers, and other auxiliaries. The handful of trained physicians located outside the main cities are either in government hospitals or in private practice. Government health facilities for both ambulatory and inpatient care may even require small fees from all but the most destitute patients. The planning of all these countries, nevertheless, calls for gradual extension of national population coverage with a regionalized network of health centers—very simple at the rural periphery, with increasingly specialized and better-trained staff as one moves toward the larger towns and provincial capitals. The model laid out in India in 1946 (in the Bhore Commission Report) and again in 1962 (in the Mudaliar Report) is being adopted, at least in theory, in most of these LDCs.[23,24] In practice, of course, plans often remain only partially fulfilled.

The more transitional LDCs might be illustrated by Lebanon and Egypt in the Middle East or by Mexico and Peru in Latin America. In all these countries, while a substantial private sector persists, major steps have been taken by government to extend ambulatory health services through a network of organized health centers throughout the country. Thus, in Lebanon (GNP of $1,070 in 1978), there are scores of primary care centers (health centers and dispensaries) offering general preventive and treatment services to the rural population.[25] In addition, in the main cities where a certain amount of industry has developed, a small program of medical care under social security financing has been started for industrial workers and government employees. Social security funds are not used to pay private medical fees, however, but to support special clinics staffed with salaried doctors for serving insured persons.

In Latin American countries, the patterns of organized ambulatory care are similar, although somewhat more highly developed. Thus, in Mexico (with per capita GNP of $1,120), the Ministry of Health and Social Assistance operates hundreds of health centers staffed with both doctors and auxiliary personnel to serve the rural population.[26] The Mexican Institute of Social Security, which started in 1942 in the national capital, has gradually extended its population coverage through an impressive network of health centers and hospitals, staffed with salaried doctors and allied personnel. In addition, there are similar organized health care facilities for government employees, petroleum workers, and railroad workers. Altogether, about one-third of the Mexican population was eligible in 1980 for the relatively well-developed health services of the overall social security system.[27]

It is noteworthy that these somewhat more prosperous LDCs of Latin America and the Middle East, in launching social insurance programs for the sections of their population with regular wages or salaries (typically a minority), have not felt obligated to emulate the European patterns of simply reimbursing private practitioners. The market for private practice earnings has been so small and the social insurance device has been so effective in raising funds, that many physicians are pleased to accept employment (usually two-to-four hours per day) in organized facilities for both ambulatory and hospital care. This pattern has been adopted throughout these developing countries because of its greater economies and because it is more amenable to planning and regulation than the pattern of private medical practice.[28]

In a word, the health problems of the developing countries of the world have been stimulating increasing efforts to provide health services along organized lines. The burden of preventable infectious disease, as well as all types of disease and injury for which effective treatment is known but not applied, are still enormous.[29] But through international health activities, knowledge—both bio-medical and organizational—is being rapidly spread to all countries. The faulty strategies of the era of imperialism, when European technologies were mechanically transplanted to the colonies without regard to the real needs of their populations, are being replaced by far more democratic and objective concepts of technology transfer—that is, the transmission of scientific knowledge, but with recognition that its mode of application must be determined by the people of each country.[30] Accordingly, it is not surprising that ambulatory health services of all types in the developing countries are becoming increasingly organized, both in their economic support and in their pattern of delivery.[31]

Industrialized Countries

The variability in social structure, including the health services, is probably greater among the 30 or 40 predominantly industralized and capitalist countries of the world than among the socialist or developing countries. In this grouping, one may conceive of a spectrum of health care systems, ranging from the most individualistic and entrepreneurial, represented by the United States and perhaps Australia and South Africa, to the most socially oriented (while still not socialist), represented by countries such as Sweden and Great Britain. In between, there are the many other welfare states of Western Europe, Canada, Japan, New Zealand, and perhaps Israel.

In almost all of these countries, there are systems of national health care financing that make medical services economically accessible to virtually the entire national populations.[32] The exceptions are the three most individualistic countries: South Africa, Australia, and the United States. In these countries voluntary health insurance is still the major mechanism for financing medical care for the self-supporting population, while various general revenue-financed programs provide care (with limitations) for the poor. Associated with the national health care financing systems, there has been a gradual extension of organized clinics or health centers to furnish ambulatory services more economically and effectively.

Thus, in France, where national health insurance is the financing mechanism and where medical individualism is quite strong, there has still been a growth of health centers, in which physicians work on salaries. Preventive services are provided at these facilities through financial support from local government, while treatment commands fees from the social insurance program.[33] In Belgium, health centers restrict their functions to prevention (mainly maternal and child health services), but many local health insurance societies have organized polyclinics with an array of specialists working together.[34] These specialists are paid fees by the health insurance program; however, unlike specialists in purely private practice, they cannot demand supplementary personal payments from the patients.

Group medical practice of private physicians has also been growing slowly in Western Europe. Unlike the U.S. pattern, however, most European medical groups consist entirely of general practitioners, among whom there is some quasi-specialization, such as in disorders of children, gynecological problems, or skin diseases.[35] In West Germany, these are designated as communal practices, and about 300 of them were estimated to be functioning in 1970. In

Canada, group practice has been growing as rapidly, or perhaps more rapidly, than in the United States, mainly along multispecialty lines. More than one-third of Canadian medical groups, however, consist only of general practitioners.[36]

Of particular interest in Canada has been a deliberate national government policy, promoted also by many of the provincial governments, to encourage the establishment of community health centers. Unlike the U.S. usage of this term, these Canadian health centers are intended to serve anyone who chooses to come to them, not solely the poor. The objective is to bring together general practitioners and some specialists, along with nurses and other personnel, to provide fairly comprehensive ambulatory care. Local groups of citizens are encouraged to take the leadership in organization of these units. The costs would be met by the national insurance program for physicians' care.[37,38] These facilities have been organized with special enthusiasm in the province of Quebec, where certain citizen groups have looked upon the projects as a rallying point for general political activity.

In Sweden, health insurance on a voluntary basis and operated through local societies has existed since the nineteenth century. In 1931, it was made mandatory for certain occupational groups, and in 1962, population coverage became universal. Hospitalization for the total population, however, was long financed mainly from general revenues, with only small charges to the insurance funds. In the overall Swedish health care system, hospital service traditionally got the greatest emphasis and absorbed the lion's share of expenditures. In reaction to this, government policy changed in the 1960s to encourage development of health centers for ambulatory medical care; these would function as satellites of the hospitals and be staffed mainly by general practitioners with ancillary staff.[39] Because of the strength of Swedish local governments, which must take the initiative for health center construction, progress has been relatively slow. But the planning calls for eventual coverage of the entire country with health centers, in place of private medical offices.

In New Zealand, where universal health insurance has been in effect since 1939, there has also been a rising wave of interest in health centers as a setting for improved general medical practice. There has long been a sharp distinction in this small country between specialists, who are salaried and hospital-based, and general practitioners, who have typically practiced from private individual quarters in the community. In order to strengthen their position, the general practitioners have actually favored the establishment of health centers in which they could rent space and be assisted by nurses, social workers, and others.[40] Accordingly, the New Zealand Regional Hospital Boards have been authorized to construct these facilities entirely for primary ambulatory care.

Among the industrialized welfare states, perhaps the most significant trend toward widespread use of health centers for primary care of the general population is seen in Great Britain. Unlike nearly all the other (nonsocialist) national health care systems, the British National Health Service (NHS) is financed mainly from general revenues, rather than from social insurance collections. The original planning of the NHS called for a network of local ambulatory care facilities, along the lines of the 1920 Dawson Report; in the political debate that ushered in the NHS in 1948, however, this feature was dropped.[41] The British general practitioners had opposed health centers as the setting for their practices, for fear that they would lead eventually to employment by the government and loss of their independence. In the 1960s, however, attitudes changed. To ease the pressures on their professional lives, general practitioners had gradually been joining together in small partnerships of two, three, or four. By 1966, it was estimated that only 25 percent of them remained in completely solo practice.[42]

In the 1950s, after the wartime destruction, the British government began building new towns to reduce the congestion in London and other large cities. In these freshly planned communities, health centers were also built—usually providing space for a few general practitioners, district nurses, social workers, laboratory technicians, and clerks. There was no lack of applications from practitioners to occupy these quarters, for which they paid rent; they remained in private practice, with their "capitation" lists, as before. By 1968, there were 93 such health centers operated by local and public authorities.[43] By 1971, some 475 health centers were in operation or under construction in Britain, with quarters to accommodate 2,600 practitioners.[44] These facilities housed from 1 to 22 doctors each, with an average of 5.5.

Thus, in all the major types of country throughout the world, one can see movements for increased organization of the delivery of ambulatory health services. The objective everywhere is to arrange for provision of a comprehensive range of health care skills that isolated medical practitioners cannot offer. Through teams of personnel of various types, it is expected that services of better quality can be provided in an efficient manner.

It is important to recognize that almost everywhere organized ambulatory care centers are intended to serve their total surrounding populations, not exclusively the poor or other selected groups. Even when, as in Latin America, there are health centers limited to insured persons, other such facilities ordinarily serve the noninsured population. This broad scope of eligibility is associated with the basic coverage of populations by systems of national health insurance or other forms of economic support giving universal entitlement to health care. In many impoverished developing countries, where governmental financial support is weak, charges may be collected for health center service from those who can afford to pay. But patients are not turned away on the grounds of being too affluent. This connection between systems of financing and patterns of delivering health service is fundamental. If we are to envisage greater efficiency and effectiveness in the organized provision of ambulatory care in America, therefore, it is essential to consider the basic mechanisms by which the services should be financed. In the next section this matter will be discussed.

EFFECTIVE NATIONAL FINANCING OF HEALTH SERVICE

The diversity of sources and mechanisms for financing ambulatory services in the United States is evident from all preceding chapters. Difficulties in the economic support of various types of clinics were summarized in Chapter 14, particularly with respect to clinics dependent on government revenues. In Chapter 12 we observed the advantages enjoyed by clinics receiving stable support from health insurance contributions under the HMO model. Any planning for a future model of efficient and effective delivery of ambulatory services must inevitably start with provision for a sound system of financing.

The heterogeneous and complicated pluralism of current American financing of health care has obviously resulted from our national history. The social and political forces that have led to national health insurance or national health service systems in so many other countries have obviously not prevailed in the United States. Yet this country has not been devoid of social efforts to achieve a national program for financing comprehensive medical care. Before considering the main features of a desirable future system of health care financing, we may review briefly the highlights of past efforts and achievements and note some of the major legislative proposals that have been before the nation in recent times.

The initial support of a network of hospitals for merchant mariners, launched as far back as 1798, was through mandatory deductions from the seamen's wages. In later years, this was changed to financial support by a tax on shipowners, and still later to support from general federal revenues.[45] The concept of mandatory or social insurance to finance medical care, in any event, did not spread to other occupational groups.

In 1910, following the example of Europe, the first action was taken by a state government, New York, to require employers to have insurance for protecting workers against the costs of industrial accidents, through compensation both for wage loss and for the provision of medical care.[46] After some contention in the courts, the principle of worker's compensation was extended to all 50 states. Even though many inadequacies still exist, the coverage and benefits of these laws have gradually been widened. In 1915, a few years after the first workmen's compensation act, efforts began toward broadening the principle to apply insurance to all types of injuries or illnesses in workers. Bills were introduced in a dozen states between 1915 and 1920, but none passed.[47]

The 1920s were a conservative period in America but, with the Depression of the 1930s, the issue of national health insurance was raised again. It was considered for inclusion in the Social Security Act of 1935, but ruled out by President Franklin Roosevelt for fear it might jeopardize passage of the whole law; instead Titles V and VI on grants to the states for public health activities were included.[48] In July 1939, Senator Wagner, sponsor of the Social Security Act, set out to fill the gap by introducing the first national health insurance bill. It would have provided grants to the states to assist them in developing state health insurance programs for workers, along the lines of the 1915–20 proposals. A few months later, however, World War II broke out, and social legislation of this sort was put aside to pursue the war effort.[49]

In the midst of World War II, postwar planning was launched in several fields, including national health insurance. The first bill was introduced again by Senator Wagner and others, but this time it called for a single nationwide mandatory health insurance system.[50] The bill went through a series of modifications and was the subject of repeated congressional hearings over the next decade. It generated a storm of opposition from the medical profession, the commercial insurance industry, and others, although it was supported by organized labor. One positive effect was clear, however; this legislative threat served as a strong stimulus to the growth of voluntary health insurance, including both the "Blue" plans and those of commercial insurance companies.[51]

The major gaps in voluntary health insurance coverage were the aged and the poor, leading—again after extended controversy—to enactment of Medicare and Medicaid in 1965.[52] Only five years later, spiralling medical and hospital costs (due in part to the open-ended fiscal arrangements of Medicare itself) led to introduction in Congress once again of national health insurance (NHI) bills. In 1970, Senator Edward Kennedy proposed an NHI program more sweeping than any earlier proposals. It would have covered the entire U.S. population for very comprehensive services, with no cost-sharing by patients, and 50 percent input from general revenues.[53]

The sense of need for social action was so great that over the next five years at least 20 further NHI bills were introduced in Congress.[54] Every viewpoint in the political spectrum was represented, including that of the American Medical Association, which had for years opposed any legislation in this field. Some proposals clung to the voluntary insurance principle, but encouraged enrollment through subsidies to low-income families. Other proposals mandated enrollment in existing private health insurance programs. Still others would have established a national social insurance system—some with limited benefits and others (particularly the Kennedy "Health Security" bill) with comprehensive benefits. At every session of Congress, modified versions of each of the bills were usually offered. In 1974, Congressman Dellums introduced a proposal for establishing a "national health service," which would be financed entirely from general revenues, cover the total population for complete health care, and have government take over all health facilities and employ all doctors and other personnel as salaried civil servants.[55]

When a new federal administration took office in January 1977, the NHI debate entered still another stage. Certain new approaches to national health care financing were put forward, several of them embodying incentives for people to enroll in HMOs. President Carter, after some delay, proposed an NHI approach that would unify the administration of Medicare and Medicaid (with greater cost-containment features) and mandate the enrollment of virtually all other people in private insurance plans with comprehensive benefits, but allowing substantial out-of-pocket deductibles (up to $2,500 per policyholder per year).[56] Protection against catastrophic health care costs also was embodied in other bills.

As of late 1980, no final action had been taken on any NHI proposal. National health expenditures continued to rise both absolutely and relative to the nation's GNP. There was a widespread belief that the national economy could not afford an NHI program, since it would increase the federal budget. Strangely, the basic dynamics of social financing of health services—that is, to substitute public for private expenditures and to render those expenditures more subject to prudent regulatory controls—seemed to be poorly understood.[57] Few seemed to appreciate that U.S. overall expenditures for health care, in the absence of general NHI, were higher—both in dollars and as a percentage of GNP—than those of other comparable countries having broad programs of NHI or national health service systems in place.[58]

Thus, more than 40 years of NHI debate left America with a great deal of voluntary health insurance—particularly for hospital-related-care—plus Medicare and Medicaid. The last decade of the NHI debate, from 1970 to 1980, did, however, seem to attain consensus on certain points. With many variations in the contours of coverage, benefits, and administrative policy, a point has been reached where the country's major political parties agree that: (a) some federal legislative action is necessary to assure greater social financing of health services, (b) adequate population coverage requires some degree of compulsory enrollment, (c) regarding health services, certain governmental standards will be necessary to assure a minimum scope, and (d) some combination of regulation and/or incentives will be necessary to control the costs and quality of health care. Beyond these broad principles, one may infer that the majority view favors financing through some process of earmarked insurance (rather than using general revenues), and also that the existent structure of private health insurance programs that have developed over the last 50 years should play a part in the administration of any NHI system. With the changed federal administration in 1981, however, the prospects of specific NHI legislation grew dimmer.

This is not the place to debate the advantages and disadvantages of the many approaches to improved national financing of health services. With respect to a goal of more efficient and effective delivery of ambulatory health services, one may simply conclude that a firm, nationwide mechanism for adequate economic support of those services will be necessary.

COORDINATION OF AMBULATORY CARE: A TASK FOR PUBLIC HEALTH

Adequate nationwide financing of ambulatory health care is necessary, but it is not sufficient to assure a sound future structure for these services in the United States. It is also necessary that there be a rational administrative structure that can assure effective delivery of ambulatory health services.

Earlier in this chapter, we summarized the problems resulting from the complicated pluralism of the numerous unrelated clinics, as well as the other components, of the U.S. health care system. How can the great and diverse resources for ambulatory care reviewed in this volume, be best mobilized? Diversity and independence have their value, which should not be sacrificed for the sake of a tidy but bureaucratic organization chart.[59] But diversity need not yield an organizational jungle, with waste, inefficiency, inequities, and countless other problems. Health care in general, and ambulatory services in particular, are too important to leave to the vagaries of a wildly free market with its abundantly demonstrated human and economic ill effects. Reasonable planning and coordination are essential if national health care resources are to be most effectively allocated and used. What process or what agency in the U.S. health care system could do this best?

In our view, this role should be played by the agency of government, at all levels in the United States political structure, historically established to protect the public health. In the light of the very modest role played by public health agencies in the U.S. health care system over the last 30 years or so, this recommendation may seem surprising. The reasons for it, however, are based on historical, technical, and sociopolitical considerations.

Public Health Development

Since the early nineteenth century in the United States, the major responsibilities for protection of the health of the population—insofar as social actions were possible and necessary—have been assigned to the branch of government that gradually evolved into the health department.[60] The first such steps were taken at the level of cities or towns, when boards of health were established to cope with epidemics and to enforce regulations for maintaining a sanitary environment. When the need for similar functions was recognized at a broader geographic level, state health departments were established—the first in Massachusetts in 1869. In 1879 a National Board of Health was established, but it had a short life of only four years; the political structure of the young nation was still too diffuse and decentralized.[61] Not until 1912, did the United States Public Health Service (USPHS) take shape, evolving from the largest and longest established health agency in the federal government, the Marine Hospital Service. As we have observed in Chapter 5, at the local level preventive functions in tuberculosis and venereal disease control, child health protection, and other fields—started by voluntary agencies—were continually being transferred to local health departments; such transfers were intended to assure program stability.

Even in these early years of the current century, certain health functions had been assigned to other branches of state or national governments. The first Food and Drugs Act, e.g., was assigned to the federal Department of Agriculture. Factory inspection to protect the health and safety of workers was naturally made a function of state departments of labor or industry; similarly, workmen's compensation laws, concerned with work-related injuries, became the responsibility of special state government commissions. The Children's Bureau was established in 1912 for protection of the general welfare of children; since prevention of child labor was a prominent problem, this Bureau was logically placed in the federal Department of Labor. Child and maternal health programs came later, and their management was delegated to the Children's Bureau in the Labor Department.[62] When a network of federal hospitals was launched for military veterans after World War I, Congress planned to delegate their management to the USPHS, but the latter agency (unfortunately, in our view) chose to decline this broadened role.

With the Depression starting in 1929, the Social Security Act of 1935, and the entire New Deal period from 1932 to 1945, health activities in the national government took a major turn toward consolidation. The Social Security Act, particularly Title VI, assigned large new responsibilities to the USPHS—grants-in-aid to the states for a steadily widening range of public health activities, and establishment of national health research laboratories (later the National Institutes of Health). These grants, in turn, greatly strengthened state and local health departments. In 1939, the Federal Security Agency was formed, bringing together the Public Health Service, the Social Security Administration, the Food and Drug Administration, and other agencies concerned with health and welfare; the Children's Bureau was transferred to the Federal Security Agency in 1946.[63] In 1953, the FSA was converted into the Department of Health, Education, and Welfare (HEW), which acquired still further health-related functions, such as those of the Office of Vocational Rehabilitation.

At the state and local government levels, somewhat similar consolidations of authority were taking place, particularly in the two decades after World War II 1945–1965.[64] In several state governments, departments of health were brought together with other departments responsible for social welfare and sometimes mental hospitals. In several large cities and counties, health departments were joined with agencies responsible for public hospitals.[65]

The administrative policies implemented in the major health legislation enacted after World War II reflected the high importance attached in this period to public health agencies.[66] Thus, the Hospital Survey and Construction (Hill-Burton) Act of 1946 launched the first national government program not only for subsidizing the construction of needed hospitals (both public and voluntary nonprofit) but also for statewide planning of the location, size, and functions of these facilities. Responsibility for administering the Hill-Burton Act was assigned to the USPHS at the national level, and to the state health departments of almost every state. The National Mental Health Act of 1946, promoting organized ambulatory mental health care on a large scale for the first time, followed similar administrative policies. Even the various national health insurance bills of the 1943–1952 period, while not enacted, assigned administrative responsibility to "the Surgeon General of the U.S. Public Health Service."

In 1954, the Indian Health Service was transferred from the Department of the Interior to the USPHS. The 1956 law establishing a continuing National Health Survey assigned this task not to the Census Bureau of the Department of Commerce but to the USPHS. Also in 1956, a National Library of Medicine was established under the USPHS. When government made its first cautious entry into the proud field of medical and allied professional education—initially with the Health Research Facilities Act of 1956 and then more directly with the Health Professions Educational Assistance Act of 1963—once again the top responsibilities were assigned to the USPHS.

All these authorities vested in the USPHS did not necessarily create equivalent responsibilities for public health agencies at the state and local levels. Universities with professional schools already existed and were training health personnel, so that the federal government dealt directly with them. But where an intermediate-level agency was needed, as in the hospital construction, mental health, or certain other (e.g., chronic disease control) programs, the usual selection was the state health department. This state public health agency, in turn, related customarily to its constituent local health departments. Thus, up to about 1960, as we have noted in Chapter 5 and at other places in this volume, the scope and status of public health agencies at all political levels were increasing.

Decline of Public Health Responsibilities

A turning point came with the enactment in 1965 of Titles XVIII and XIX of the Social Security Act—Medicare and Medicaid. These two medical care programs involved government expenditures—mainly federal but partly state (50 percent of Medicaid)—so great as to dwarf all other organized health programs in the nation. Thus, in 1970 for example, the total expenditures for activities of public health agencies at all three government levels aggregated to about $1.78 billion. In that year the expenditures for Medicare and Medicaid alone amounted to $12,362,000,000 or about seven times as much.[67] Yet the major responsibilities for these giant public programs were not assigned to the

USPHS nor to state or local health departments. Federal management of these large funds were made a responsibility of two other parts of HEW (the Social Security Administration and the Social and Rehabilitation Service), later combined into the Health Care Financing Administration. At the state level, the administration of Medicare (involving payment of millions of medical and hospital claims) was delegated to nongovernmental fiscal intermediaries—essentially private health insurance plans; administration of Medicaid was assigned principally to state departments of social welfare. Certain responsibilities on certification of health care providers for participation in Medicare were assigned to state health departments, but for the most important of these functions (approval of hospitals), the nongovernmental Joint Commission on Accreditation of Hospitals was soon substituted.

After Medicare and Medicaid, the tide of authorization of significant responsibilities in the field of organized health services turned clearly away from the public health agencies. The U.S. OEO law was passed in 1964, and its establishment of neighborhood health centers in poverty areas began the next year. OEO was not even within HEW, and it had no link to the national public health structure. Moreover, various political considerations led to emphasis on the assumption of responsibilities by community groups; in effect, local health departments played virtually no part in the development of neighborhood health centers.[68] Even when the subsequent community health center movement (see Chapter 9) was transferred to the supervision of the USPHS at the federal level, health departments could play hardly any local role.

The Regional Medical Program for Heart Disease, Cancer, and Stroke (RMP) was enacted in late 1965 to complement the large fiscal investments for Medicare and Medicaid with efforts to improve the *quality* of medical care; the strategy would be to spread knowledge from centers of medical science (primarily medical schools) to peripheral facilities and programs in a region.[69] Federal responsibility for RMP was, indeed, assigned to the USPHS, but the law was written so as virtually to assure that the funds would be channeled to medical schools, hospitals, and similar entities. By 1972, the nation was blanketed with 56 RMPs, of which 33 were directed by universities, 19 by new or existing corporate bodies, and 4 by medical societies.[70] Once again, an innovative and robust health program was launched throughout the nation, without involving a single state or local health department.

In 1966, the first U.S. law on Comprehensive Health Planning (CHP) was enacted. Since about 1960, voluntary agencies for planning hospital construction (beyond the constraints applicable to facilities getting Hill-Burton grants) had been appearing in many metropolitan areas, but the CHP law granted funds to every state for establishment of state and local (called "area-wide") health planning agencies. The scope of these agencies was presumably comprehensive; their aim, in the language of the law, was "to support the marshalling of all health resources—national, state, and local—to assure comprehensive health services of high quality for every person . . .''[71] As with RMP, federal responsibility for the CHP law was assigned to the USPHS, and State Health Planning Agencies were designated by the governors of 56 states and territories; of these the state health departments were assigned this responsibility in only 26 jurisdictions.[72] More important were the 198 local or area-wide CHP agencies established; of these, as of 1972, 150 were new private nonprofit entities, 45 were special quasi-governmental district councils, and only 3 were units of local government (not necessarily health departments). In practice, the state and local CHP agencies devoted their principal attention to hospital planning, even though their scope theoretically extended beyond this to include all public health and other organized services.[73] Yet at the local level, health departments played almost no part (except perhaps for membership of the local health officer on the CHP agency board) in this whole planning process.

The last straw in the by-passing of public health agencies came with the enactment of the National Health Planning and Resources Development Act of 1974. This legislation replaced both the RMP and CHP laws with a nationwide planning program of much broader scope and authority.[74] Under it, top administration is again vested in the USPHS, but in the jurisdictions of 57 states and territories there are State Health Planning and Development Agencies (SHPDA) appointed by the governor. Of these about 30 have been placed within state health departments. At the all-important local level, the United States has been blanketed with local Health Systems Agencies (HSA), numbering 203 in 1979; of these, 178 were private nonprofit agencies, and only 25 were even part of local government (not necessarily linked to the local health department).[75] The language of the federal law made it difficult, indeed, for local health departments to play this crucial planning role.

Thus, after gradual expansion in their scope of responsibilities until about 1960–65, the *relative* importance of public health agencies in the United States began to decline. The word "relative" is to be emphasized, because health departments have not actually become weaker; as we have seen in Chapter 5, the populations they serve and the volume of services they provide have been steadily increasing. The trend, however, has been for the assignment of *new* responsibilities, involving social organization, financing, delivery, and planning of personal health services (not to mention environmental health protection, which we have not discussed), to be made to other governmental and voluntary agencies. Thus, the overall organization of health services in America has steadily been growing, but health departments, particularly at the local level, have played very little part in that growth process.

The previous paragraphs have shown this by-passing of public health agencies within the sphere of legislation and government. But in the nongovernmental sector of health service the role of public health agencies has been even less significant. Relevant to the general organization of U.S. health services, one may take note of such robust movements as: health insurance (both voluntary and statutory), hospitals (their internal structure and their environmental relationships), health manpower training and regulation, group practice (private and prepaid), and the whole movement for surveillance of the quality of health care. The development of the clinics analyzed throughout this book (except those in Chapter 5) has also been largely independent of the public health movement.

This relative decline of the public health movement has been attributed, among other things, to a failure of public health professionals to recognize the belief of Americans ". . . that diffusion of responsibilities to the many would better serve our democracy than centralization of authority in the hands of a few."[76] One may interpret the developments in another way, however. There has, in fact, clearly been an increasing centralization of power in the American health care system. The public sector, as we have seen, has steadily enlarged, while the private sector has declined. Individualism in health care—both its financing and delivery—has been steadily replaced by social or collective action of all sorts.

But in reaction to these inexorable trends, which are seen in virtually all countries of the world, the private establishment in American medicine has fought successfully to weaken government's impact by a strategy of dispersion and fragmentation. In this establishment, one must include not only private physicians, but also the voluntary hospitals that they typically dominate, the pharmaceutical companies with which they are allied, and even the medical schools that tend to share their viewpoints. All these components of the health care system tended to view the extending power of government with alarm, fearing that it would diminish the independence of private sector medicine. If these trends could not be stopped, at least their impact could be weakened.

Conservative opposition to this gradual replacement of rugged individualism in health service with an increasingly organized health care system was mirrored in the halls of the U.S. Congress. The strategy of opposition may not have been so crude and deliberate as the military policy of "divide and conquer," but its effects were the same. No single agency—particularly at the state and local levels—would be permitted to become too powerful. Insofar as authority was to be delegated below the national level, it would go mainly to medical schools, voluntary hospitals, private insurance carriers, or wholly new nongovernmental bodies—*not* to the public health agencies. The failure of public health professionals, if any, has not been to serve as advocates for excessive centralization. Rather, it has been their failure to acquire the role of the *decentralized* agency for local management of the several health-related programs for which national governmental legislation was already being enacted. Most serious have been the difficulties stemming from the assignment of responsibilities for local health planning to essentially independent voluntary local bodies. On a world scale, there is no function more central to the public health agencies than comprehensive health planning.

One may identify several reasons for the fainthearted posture of most American public health professionals in recent decades. State and local boards of health have traditionally been dominated by private physicians and related provider interests.[77] The status and salaries of public health officials have been kept low, so that the field has not attracted many strong personalities. The fighters and idealists brought forward by the vibrant years of the New Deal have been largely replaced by a generation of "officeholders." Their mission has been not so much to tackle unmet social needs as to keep programs on an even keel; this usually means avoiding controversy. Such a posture is natural enough to the local health officer entering the field after retirement from private medical practice. His or her kinship is closer to former colleagues in the medical society than to the common people. The 1960s and 1970s produced in America many young activists, eager to bring about social reform, but few of them entered public health work. This, like other parts of government, was seen as representing the status quo, and social change, it was believed, demanded action in the community. Public health was regarded as a task for managers, not for fighters against the establishment. Such attitudes and values had been commonplace in the public health movement during the early years of the twentieth century; they were cogently reflected in the history of the American Public Health Association.[78]

A Broader Vision

In the period 1930–1950, a fresh and inspired posture was adopted by public health. This was an era of social reform, and the viewpoint was perhaps best epitomized by the public health leader, Dr. Joseph W. Mountin (1891–1952).[79] It was a viewpoint recognizing the need to enlarge the role of public health agencies at every level—national, state, and local—to protect the health of the population. Thus, the health department's concern must be for the provision of needed medical care as well as for prevention; it must be for chronic and mental disorders as well as for communicable diseases; it must be for planning of hospitals as well as planning of water supplies; it must be for the national distribution of private physicians to serve the sick as well as the distribution of public health nurses to help keep babies well.

Mountin was not alone; he articulated the views of many. In 1944, under Mountin's leadership, the American Public Health Association spoke up in favor of a "national health program." Its recommended scope went far beyond traditional public health, to include comprehensive medical care for everyone. For administration of this broad program, the 1944 statement declared:

> A single responsible agency is a fundamental requisite to effective administration at all levels—federal, state, and local. The public health agencies—federal, state, and local—should carry major responsibilities in administering the health services of the future. Because of administrative experience, and accustomed responsibility for a public trust, they are uniquely fitted among public agencies to assume larger responsibilities and to discharge their duties to the public with integrity and skill.[80]

To those who questioned whether public health agencies were capable of carrying such broad responsibilities, Mountin, along with other leaders such as C. E-A. Winslow (of Yale's Department of Public Health) or Martha Eliot (of the U.S. Children's Bureau), responded that, with assignment of greater duties, their capabilities would expand.

This had been the experience when, during World War II, administration of the Emergency Maternity and Infant Care (EMIC) program, which involved nationwide provision of obstetrical and pediatric services to the wives and infants of military men, was assigned to state health departments.[81] It was also the experience with the Hospital Survey and Construction Act program after 1946, the National Mental Health Act at the same time, and the operation of the Indian Health Service after 1954. All these programs meant new functions for public health agencies—functions that they assimilated and performed well.

As we have seen, however, after about 1960 new and important tasks in health service administration were assigned to other agencies. The organization of the U.S. health sector continued to increase, even at an accelerated pace, but under auspices other than health departments. The resultant dispersal of authority added further complexities to the already pluralistic American health care system. The difficulties and incoordination of health program management, regulation, and especially planning have meant not only higher administrative costs. More important, they have led to the enormous problems in the overall costs of and access to health services that the nation faces today. More rational structuring of the U.S. health care system is clearly necessary if its future functioning is to be coordinated, effective, and efficient.

This can be achieved if our national network of local, state, and federal public health agencies is consciously strengthened to play the role for which they were legally established.[82] Given broader responsibilities, public health agencies will attract the personnel and develop the competence necessary. Their role of filling the gaps left in personal health care, due to the inadequacies of the private sector, will be broadened to one of planning and monitoring the entire health care delivery system—both its public and private sectors. Development of such a role for public health agencies would, of course, require fundamental changes in health legislation and health policy. These could not be made overnight, but would be quite feasible over a period of years. The value of such arrangements for the coordinated provision of ambulatory health services would be particularly great. More than the other components of health service (hospitalization and environmental protection), ambulatory care delivery is woefully fragmented.

COORDINATED AMBULATORY CARE IN HEALTH REGIONS

If public health agencies gradually attained the administrative role envisaged above, they would become responsible for planning and overseeing all personal health care in every region of the nation. Our focus here is on the implications of such a structure for the ambulatory services. What could be expected in a future U.S. model for coordinated delivery of ambulatory health care?

The fundamental long-term prerequisite of sound economic support of health services for everyone has been discussed earlier. Even if national health insurance legislation, with total population coverage, should be enacted, however, it is not likely to pay for every aspect of personal health service. On-the-job health care for industrial workers, for example, would still probably depend on support from industry, and health services for school children would doubtless remain the financial responsibility of educational authorities. We may realistically assume, therefore, that any future model of ambulatory care in the United States will depend on financial support from multiple sources. Accepting this, the delivery of services could still be planned and coordinated by public health agencies in every region of the nation.

Delineation of the territory of the United States into health regions has already been substantially achieved under the provisions of the National Health Planning and Resources Development Act of 1974.[83] Slightly over 200 Health Service Areas have been mapped out; each of these constitutes, in effect, a health region. In such a region, there are expected to be resources for essentially comprehensive health services for every resident—nearby or by referral within the region. Since the U.S. national population is 220 million, the average population per Health Service Area is about 1.1 million, but the range of actual populations is, of course, wide—from about 100,000 to more than 7,000,000. At present, a Health Systems Agency (HSA) is responsible for health planning in its region; as noted earlier the great majority of HSAs are voluntary nonprofit entities.

In the model recommended here, one would expect HSAs to evolve into publicly accountable governmental public health agencies. Many features of current HSA structure should be retained—particularly their supervision by a board composed of representatives of health care providers and consumers, the latter being a majority. Board members might be subject to election (as is now common for local boards of education) or to appointment by elected officials. Since most HSAs now usually include jurisdictions encompassing several counties and municipalities, certain legal adjustments would probably be required, but there is no reason that these could not be made. All sorts of multijurisdictional districts have long been functioning in the United States for special purposes, such as water supply systems or hospital construction and operation. We may speak of these, in the current context, as "public health regions" (PHR).

In each PHR, clinics for organized delivery of ambulatory health services, as described in previous chapters, may be assumed to exist. At the same time, there would be thousands of individual practitioners of medicine and related health disciplines. On the basis of trends reviewed in earlier chapters, however, one could reasonably expect that the extent of purely private, solo medical practice would gradually decline; the majority of individual doctors and other health care providers would become affiliated in time with group practice clinics, hospital outpatient departments, or other health care settings. Eventually, one may expect that all or nearly all personal health services would be provided by one or another of a spectrum of clinics and health centers conveniently accessible to the population.

With some system for universal financing of personal health care in effect, a crucial change would occur in the eligibility of people to seek service at the various clinics: the criterion of poverty or indigency, now so important in access to various clinics, would disappear. Eligibility to use a particular clinic might, indeed, depend on other factors, such as membership in a certain HMO or some other local health insurance plan; attendance at a school clinic might require being a student in the school, or attendance at an emergency clinic might require the patient to have a truly urgent condition. Any eligibility criteria, in other words, would be definable—on the basis of the technical capabilities of the clinic—but *not* on the basis of socioeconomic status.

The PHR agency would have the task of mapping out the existing clinic resources in its region, in relation to the distribution of the regional population. One would expect that general hospitals would provide a kind of skeletal framework, around which the clinics in each region—or in each geographic subdivision of a region—would function. Clinics need not be administratively supervised by hospitals to serve as peripheral "satellites" to them. One would hope that each person would develop the custom of obtaining primary health care at a nearby clinic or health center. For specialized service beyond the capacity of the primary care unit, referral could usually be made to the hospital OPD.

For general primary health care, each region would eventually be blanketed with clinics of various origins. Most would probably be derived from private group practices. Others would evolve from the diverse community health centers, under numerous sponsorships, that have arisen since the 1960s. Some would be the outgrowth of branch clinics that had been established by hospitals. Some might develop from ambulatory facilities established originally for federal beneficiaries, such as American Indians, but extended henceforth to serve other people as well.

The future role of clinics focusing on specialized health problems would allow various options. Clinics devoted to mental disorders, for example, might continue to play this role; the same could apply to special clinics for crippled children or for the followup of patients with tuberculosis. Specialized modalities for certain disorders might still be justified in the most coordinated network of clinics. This could apply whether the clinic had been established and sponsored originally by a voluntary or a public agency. On the other hand, certain clinics, evolving in the past to adjust for deficiencies in the private medical system, might not have a future role. This would apply, for example, to well baby or prenatal clinics conducted traditionally by health departments. Such clinics are not attended today by affluent families because pediatric or obstetrical care is normally obtained from private physicians. In the future model of ambulatory services outlined here, everyone would have similar access to equivalent private care from a clinic of his or her choice. Administration of the whole regional system by a public health agency, moreover, should assure incorporation of preventive concepts into the health services provided at *every* clinic; whatever weaknesses may have characterized health departments in the past, their preventive orientation is surely a major strength that one may expect in PHR agency policy.[84]

Clinics at schools and workplaces should undoubtedly continue, in order to care for the special problems of children or workers. In all likelihood, they should be expanded to achieve coverage according to certain minimal standards. Small industrial plants could be served by cooperative or joint health units covering employees of several plants in an area. Financial support for these services would still be expected from schools and enterprises, but the standards of their staffing and operation would be monitored by the PHR agency. Such a policy would be intended to assure a reasonable quality of services. Occupational health services, for example, should not suffer erosion due to being a lesser priority than production and profits. (Obviously, new legislation would be required to implement such policies.)

The PHR agency, in a word, should be responsible for arranging the accessibility to ambulatory health services of all the people in its area. Financial support for the services would come theoretically from a National Health Insurance (NHI) program, supplemented by support from certain other sources, such as schools, industrial firms or, indeed, prisons. Whether or not other sources of financing could be expected—such as voluntary health agencies or local government—would depend on the scope of the NHI legislation. If NHI benefits are not comprehensive—for example, excluding mental disorders or alcoholism—separate local support for such services should surely be encouraged. If entitlement is not universal then other financial arrangements would be necessary to assure health services for noncovered people. The PHR agency's precise functions would depend on the nature of the mechanism for financing health care that evolves in the United States.

CLINICS IN A NATIONAL HEALTH CARE SYSTEM

Although this book has focused on clinics, it is obvious that ambulatory health services, whether organized or not, are not the totality of a health care system. In the sphere of prevention, there are large tasks of environmental protection and of general health education; in the sphere of treatment, there are the crucial services of hospitals. For the overall achievement of health, moreover, society must be concerned with far more than the delivery of health care. Every aspect of life and the world around us has its bearing on individual and community health.[85]

Yet, of the many components of health care systems, the services to ambulatory persons are probably the most diverse and administratively complex. They have originated from a variety of historical backgrounds and have taken shape in a multitude of forms. Because of their heterogeneity they have been difficult to organize effectively and efficiently in relation to the needs of people.

The birth and development of the hospital, as an organized process for the care of the bed patient, were linked to social objectives of merciful care for the poor. The social stigma associated with these origins has virtually disappeared, although it lingers in the wards of large public hospitals still oriented to the poor. The clinic had a similar but later origin, and the stigma persists much more strongly; a high proportion of clinics remain oriented largely to the poor. Like hospital development over the last century, however, the clinic is now rapidly evolving into a structure whose purpose is not charity but efficiency in mobilizing human and technological resources. In the health care systems of virtually all countries, clinics are playing an expanding role. In an ideal health care system for America, the clinic would be the crucial mechanism for unifying the application of the science with the art of medicine, both for the promotion of health and the prompt treatment of the sick.[86]

It is easy enough to sketch the outlines of an ideal health care system, but how do we get from here to there? Trends in the United States suggest steady movement toward greater organization of health services due to pressures coming from many sources. There is the advance of technology that demands organization to acquire its benefits. There are the spiralling costs that demand organization to avoid waste. There are the impacts of mass education and democracy that demand organization for the achievement of equity in the distribution of health services.

At the same time, there are counterpressures in reaction to these trends. As in past eras there are those who decry the mechanization of health care and call for return to an individualistic past.[87] There are those who blame current health care problems, particularly cost escalations, on excessive regulation; the recommended solution is a return to free trade and competition.[88] There are even those who assail the concept of health care as a right and urge its candid recognition as a market commodity.[89]

But the forces for social change are strong. The collectivization of health care financing is proceeding in America, as elsewhere in the world. If only to help assure that socially derived health monies are prudently spent, organization and coordination are increasingly demanded.[90] Reasonable regulation and control are essential. As a seasoned professor of medicine has said, "The exercise of control (in the health field) is full of risk, but the failure to control is infinitely riskier."[91] The story of clinics is only one chapter in the saga of the social organization and control of health services in the United States. It is surely not the last chapter, but in the current era it may shed some light on the dynamics of the entire American health care system.

NOTES

1. Mills, C. Wright, *The Power Elite* (New York: Oxford University Press, 1957).

2. Galbraith, Kenneth, *The New Industrial State* (Boston: Houghton Mifflin, 1967).

3. Commission on Public-General Hospitals, *The Future of the Public-General Hospital* (Chicago: Hospital Research and Educational Trust, 1978).

4. Back, Kurt W., et al., "Public Health as a Career of Medicine: Secondary Choice within a Profession," *American Sociological Review* 23 (1958): 533–541.

5. Gartside, Foline; C. E. Hopkins; and M. I. Roemer, *Medicaid Services in California under Different Organizational Modes* (Los Angeles: University of California, School of Public Health, December 1973), pp. 138–169.

6. Neal, Helen (editor), *Better Communications for Better Health* (New York: National Health Council and Columbia University Press, 1962).

7. Rosenstock, Irwin, et al., "Why People Fail to Seek Poliomyelitis Vaccination," *Public Health Reports* 74 (1959): 98–104.

8. Roemer, Milton I., "From Poor Beginnings, the Growth of Primary Care," *Hospitals, JAHA* March 1, 1975, pp. 38–43.

9. Roemer, Milton I., "Organized Ambulatory Health Service in International Perspective," *International Journal of Health Services* 1 (1971): 18–27.

10. Sigerist, Henry E., *Socialized Medicine in the Soviet Union* (New York: W. W. Norton & Co., 1938).

11. Field, Mark G., *Soviet Socialized Medicine* (New York: The Free Press, 1967).

12. Lidor, I. P.; A. M. Stochik; and G. F. Tserkorny, *Soviet Public Health and the Organization of Primary Health Care for the Population of the USSR* (Moscow: Mir Publishers, 1978).

13. Hyde, G., *The Soviet Health Service: A Historical and Comparative Study* (London: Lawrence and Wishart, 1974).

14. Popov, G. A., *Principles of Health Planning in the USSR* (Geneva, Switzerland: World Health Organization, Public Health Paper No. 43, 1971).

15. Weinerman, E. R., *Social Medicine in Eastern Europe* (Cambridge, Mass.: Harvard University Press, 1969).

16. Roemer, Milton I., and Ruth Roemer, *Health Manpower in the Socialist Health Care System of Poland*, U.S. Health Resources Administration DHEW Pub. HRA 77–85 (Washington: 1977), p. 4.

17. Sidel, Victor W., and Ruth Sidel, *Serve the People—Observations on Medicine in the People's Republic of China* (New York: Josiah Macy, Jr. Foundation, 1973).

18. Quinn, Joseph R., ed., *Medicine and Public Health in the People's Republic of China*, Department of Health, Education, and Welfare, Fogarty International Center (Washington: 1972).

19. Roemer, Milton I., "Health Development and Political Policy: The Lesson of Cuba," *Journal of Health Politics, Policy, and Law*, 4 (1980): 570–580.

20. World Bank, *Health Sector Paper* (Washington: 1980), pp. 67–70.

21. Ibid., p. 85.

22. Roemer, Milton I., *Analysis of a National Health Care System: The Case of Thailand* (New Delhi: World Health Organization, South East Asia Regional Office, 1981).

23. India, Health Survey and Development Committee (Hon. Justice Bhore, Chairman), *Report* (Delhi, India: Manager of Publications, 1946).

24. Takulia, H. S., et al., *The Health Center Doctor in India* (Baltimore: Johns Hopkins Press, 1967).

25. U.S. Department of Health, Education, & Welfare, Office of International Health, *Syncrisis: The Dynamics of Health—Syria* (Washington: 1978).

26. Roemer, Milton I., *Medical Care in Latin America* (Washington: Pan American Union, 1964), pp. 125–168.

27. Lopez-Bermudez, Antonio, national public health consultant, Mexico City: July 1980, personal communication.

28. Roemer, Milton I., *The Organisation of Medical Care under Social Security: A Study Based on the Experience of Eight Countries* (Geneva, Switzerland: International Labour Office, 1969), pp. 181–226.

29. Bryant, John, *Health and the Developing World* (Ithaca, N.Y.: Cornell University Press, 1969).

30. Basch, Paul E., *International Health* (New York: Oxford University Press, 1978).

31. Roemer, Milton I., *Comparative National Policies on Health Care* (New York: Marcel Dekker Co., 1977).

32. U.S. Social Security Administration, *Social Security Programs Throughout the World, 1979*, SSA Pub. No. 78–11805 (Washington: May 1980).

33. Roemer, Milton I., *Evaluation of Community Health Centres*, World Health Organization, Public Health Paper No. 48 (Geneva, Switzerland: 1972), pp. 18–19.

34. Roemer, Ruth, and Milton I. Roemer, *Health Manpower Policies in the Belgian Health Care System*, Health Resources Administration, DHEW Pub. HRA 77–38 (Washington: 1977).

35. Canadian Association of Medical Clinics and Medical Group Management Association of Canada, *New Horizons in Health Care: Proceedings, First International Congress of Group Medicine* (Winnipeg, Manitoba: Wallingford Press, 1970).

36. Roemer, Ruth, and M. I. Roemer, *Health Manpower Policy under National Health Insurance—The Canadian Experience*, Health Resources Administration, DHEW Pub. HRA 77–37 (Washington: September 1977).

37. Conference of Health Ministers, Community Health Centre Project, *The Community Health Centre in Canada*, 3 vols. (Ottawa: Information Canada, 1972).

38. Canadian Department of National Health and Welfare, Directorate of Community Health, *Community Health Centres in Canada* (Ottawa: March 1974).

39. Lindgren, S. A., "Sweden," in I. Douglas-Wilson and Gordon McLachlan, eds., *Health Service Prospects: An International Survey* (London: The Lancet and The Nuffield Provincial Hospitals Trust, 1973), pp. 99–123.

40. Dixon, C. W., "New Zealand," in John Z. Bowers and Elizabeth Purcell, eds., *National Health Services: Their Impact on Medical Education and Their Role in Prevention* (New York: Josiah Macy, Jr. Foundation, 1973), pp. 81–91.

41. Lindsey, Almont, *Socialized Medicine in England and Wales: The National Health Service 1948–1961* (Chapel Hill: University of North Carolina Press, 1962).

42. Medical Practitioners Union, *Design for Family Doctoring* (London: Medical World, 1967).

43. Curwen, M., and B. Brookes, "Health Centres: Facts and Figures," *The Lancet* 2 (1969): 945–948.

44. Forsyth, Gordon, "United Kingdom" in *Health Service Prospects: An International Survey*, pp. 1–35.

45. Straus, Robert, *Medical Care for Seamen: The Origin of Public Medical Service in the United States* (New Haven: Yale University Press, 1950).

46. Somers, H. M., and A. R. Somers, *Workmen's Compensation: Prevention, Insurance, and Rehabilitation of Occupational Disability* (New York: Wiley & Sons, 1954).

47. Millis, Harry A., and R. E. Montgomery, *Labor's Risks and Social Insurance* (New York: McGraw-Hill, 1938).

48. Schottland, Charles E., *The Social Security Program of the United States* (New York: Appleton-Century-Crofts, 1963).

49. Harris, Richard, *A Sacred Trust* (New York: New American Library, 1966).

50. Falk, I. S., "Health Services, Medical Care Insurance, and Social Security," in *The Annals of the American Academy of Political & Social Science* (Medical Care for Americans) 273 (1951): 114–121.

51. Somers, Herman M., and Anne R. Somers, *Doctors, Patients, and Health Insurance*, (Washington: Brookings Institution, 1961).

52. Feingold, Eugene, *Medicare: Policies and Politics* (San Francisco, Calif.: Chandler Publishing Co., 1966).

53. Committee for National Health Insurance, *Health Security Program* (Washington: July 1970).

54. U.S. Congress, House of Representatives, Subcommittee on Health of the Committee on Ways and Means, *National Health Insurance Resource Book*, rev. ed. (Washington: August 1976).

55. Dellums, R., "Health Rights and Community Services," *Congressional Record* vol. 120, no. 158, 17 October 1974.

56. U.S. Senate Committee on Finance, *Background Material on Health Insurance—Descriptions of Bills Pending in Committee and the Administration Proposal* (Washington: Committee Print CP 96–17, 14 June 1979).

57. Roemer, Milton I., "National Health Insurance as an Agent for Containing Health-Care Costs," *Bulletin of the New York Academy of Medicine* 54 (1978): 102–112.

58. Roemer, Milton I., "The Foreign Experience in Health Service Policy" in Arthur Levin, ed., *Regulating Health Care: The Struggle for Control* (New York: Academy of Political Science, 1980), pp. 206–223.

59. Churchman, C. West, *The Systems Approach* (New York: Dell Publishing Co., 1968).

60. Ravenel, M. P., *A Half Century of Public Health* (New York: American Public Health Association, 1921).

61. Rosen, George, *A History of Public Health* (New York: MD Publications, 1958), pp. 248–250.

62. Mustard, Harry S., *Government in Public Health* (New York: Commonwealth Fund, 1945).

63. Wilson, Florence A., and Duncan Neuhauser, *Health Services in the United States* (Cambridge, Mass.: Ballinger Publishing Co., 1974), pp. 104–107.

64. Hanlon, John J., *Public Health Administration and Practice*, 6th ed. (St. Louis, Mo.: C. V. Mosby Co., 1974), pp. 292–308.

65. Shonick, William, "Mergers of Public Health Departments with Public Hospitals in Urban Areas: Findings of Twelve Field Studies," *Medical Care* (supplement) 18, no. 8 (August 1980).

66. U.S. Public Health Service, *Health in America: 1776–1976*, DHEW Pub. No. HRA 76–616 (Washington: 1976).

67. McMillan, Alma W., and A. K. Bixby, "Social Welfare Expenditures, Fiscal Year 1978," *Social Security Bulletin,* May 1980, p. 13.

68. Feingold, Eugene, "A Political Scientist's View of the Neighborhood Health Center as a New Social Institution," *Medical Care,* 8 (1970): 108–115.

69. Marston, Robert Q., and Karl Yordy, "A Nation Starts a Program: Regional Medical Programs, 1965–1966," *Journal of Medical Education* 42 (1967): 17–27.

70. U.S. Health Services and Mental Health Administration, *Regional Medical Programs—Fact Book,* DHEW Pub. No. HSM 73–7001 (Washington: November 1972), p. 10.

71. Shonick, William, *Elements of Planning for Area-wide Personal Health Services,* (St. Louis, Mo.: C. V. Mosby Co., 1976), pp. 159–160.

72. U.S. Health Services and Mental Health Administration, *Directory of State and Areawide Comprehensive Health Planning Agencies under Section 314 of the Public Health Services Act,* DHEW Pub. No. HSM 73–14,000 (Washington: July 1972), p. vii.

73. Jacobs, Arthur R., and R. B. Froh, "Significance of Public Law 89–749—Comprehensive Health Planning," *New England Journal of Medicine* 279 (1968): 1314–1318.

74. Klarman, Herbert E., "National Policies and Local Planning for Health Services," *Milbank Memorial Fund Quarterly* 54 (1976): 1–28.

75. Institute of Medicine, *Health Planning in the United States: Issues in Guideline Development* (Washington: National Academy of Sciences, 1980), p. 26.

76. Rogers, David E., "A Private Sector View of Public Health Today," *American Journal of Public Health* 64 (1974): 529–533.

77. Gossert, D. J., and C. A. Miller, "State Boards of Health, Their Members and Commitments," *American Journal of Public Health* 63 (1973): 486.

78. Roemer, Milton I., "The American Public Health Association as a Force for Change in Medical Care," *Medical Care* 11 (1973): 338–351.

79. Joseph W. Mountin Memorial Committee, *Selected Papers of Joseph W. Mountin, M.D.,* (Washington: the Committee, 1956).

80. American Public Health Association, "Medical Care in a National Health Program," *American Journal of Public Health* 34 (1944): 1252–1256.

81. Sinai, Nathan, and O. W. Anderson, *EMIC (Emergency Maternity and Infant Care),* (Ann Arbor, Mich.: University of Michigan School of Public Health, 1948).

82. Grad, Frank P., *Public Health Law Manual* (Washington: American Public Health Association, 1975).

83. Institute of Medicine, *Health Planning in the United States: Issues in Guideline Development*.

84. Miller, C. Arden, et al., "Role of Local Health Departments in Delivery of Medical Care," *American Journal of Public Health,* publication pending.

85. U.S. Public Health Service, *Healthy People: The Surgeon General's Report on Health Promotion and Disease Prevention,* DHEW Pub. No. 79–55071 (Washington: 1979).

86. Roemer, Milton I., "An Ideal Health Care System for America," in A. L. Strauss, ed., *Where Medicine Fails* (New Brunswick, N.J.: Trans-Action Books, 1973), pp. 77–93.

87. Halberstam, Michael J., "Liberal Thought, Radical Theory and Medical Practice," *New England Journal of Medicine* 284 (1971): 1180–1185.

88. McClure, Walter, "On Broadening the Definition of and Removing Regulatory Barriers to a Competitive Health Care System," *Journal of Health Politics, Policy, and Law* 3 (1978): 303–327.

89. Sade, Robert M., "Medical Care as a Right: A Refutation," *New England Journal of Medicine* 285 (1971): 1288–1292.

90. Roemer, Milton I., "From Health Insurance to Health Care Systems—An International View," in *Social Medicine: The Advance of Organized Health Services in America* (New York: Springer Publishing Co., 1978), pp. 530–543.

91. Murray, Raymond H., "Technology in Ambulatory Health Care: Problems and Predictions," *The Pharos of Alpha Omega Alpha* 34 (1971): 13–19.

Index

About the Author

MILTON I. ROEMER has been Professor in the School of Public Health at the University of California, Los Angeles since 1962. He taught previously at the Cornell University Institute of Hospital Administration (1957-61) and at Yale Medical School (1949-51). Dr. Roemer earned the M.D. degree in 1940 and holds also master's degrees in sociology and in public health.

Dr. Roemer has served at all levels of health administration—as a County Health Officer in West Virginia, a state and provincial health official in New Jersey and Saskatchewan, Canada, a commissioned officer of the U.S. Public Health Service in Washington, and a Section Chief of the World Health Organization headquarters in Geneva, Switzerland. He is a Diplomate of the American Board of Preventive Medicine (1949); he was an elected councillor of the American Public Health Association for nearly a decade and Chairman of its Medical Care Section in 1956-57. In 1972 he was elected President of the California Academy of Preventive Medicine and in 1974 was elected to the Institute of Medicine of the National Academy of Sciences.

As a consultant to international agencies, Dr. Roemer has studied health care organization in 51 countries on all the continents. He is the author of 25 books and over 300 articles on the social aspects of medicine. In 1977, he was the recipient of the American Public Health Association International Award for Excellence in Promoting and Protecting the Health of People.